W9-DAU-578

A DICTIONARY OF SHAKESPEARE'S SEXUAL PUNS AND THEIR SIGNIFICANCE

A DICTIONARY OF SHAKESPEARE'S SEXUAL PUNS AND THEIR SIGNIFICANCE

Frankie Rubinstein

Second Edition

MACMILLAN

First edition 1984
Second edition 1989

Published by
THE MACMILLAN PRESS LTD
Houndmills, Basingstoke, Hampshire RG21 2XS
and London
Companies and representatives
throughout the world

Printed in Hong Kong

British Library Cataloguing in Publication Data
Rubinstein, Frankie
A dictionary of Shakespeare's sexual
puns and their significance.—2nd edn
1. Drama in English. Shakespeare, William,
1564–1616. Puns. Special subjects, Sex
relations—Encyclopaedias
I. Title
822.3′3
ISBN 0–333–48865–2 (hc)
ISBN 0–333–48866–0 (pbk)

Contents

Acknowledgements

I thank my mother, a beautiful and wise woman, who gave me two fathers: the first, a sensitive amateur artist, who viewed life through a moral prism; the second, a Rabelaisian man, a bold and brilliant teacher, who showed me there was no conflict between their two visions. I wish, also, to express my gratitude to the staff of the Macmillan Press – in particular, T. M. Farmiloe and Julia Steward, for their understanding and counsel in the making of this book; Valery Rose, for her patience and skill in shepherding the typescript through the editorial process; and Graham Eyre, a copy-editing genius, for his faithfulness to detail, sensitivity to the nuances of language and kind concern for the needs of both book and author.

Bryn Mawr, Pennsylvania F. R.

Preface to the Second Edition

The new words in the Supplement deal more extensively with the Sonnets and include more references to similar puns that were made by Shakespeare's contemporaries, as well as by the classical writers with whose works he was familiar. The puns are discussed in their contexts to stress the point that they are intrinsic, not accessory, to Shakespeare's thought processes and (un)consciously influence the choice of subsequent words – so that it is no surprise that a scene in which Caesar's AMBITION is described in venal and anal terms should conclude with Antony's boast that the fleeing conspirators 'Belike . . . had some notice of the people,/How I moved them'. He moved them emotionally, to violence and arson, yes, but the unthinking, fickle populace (see WEEPING) are regarded as prostitutes and asses, and Antony MOVEd them (caused the bowels to act). Similarly, in *MWW*, when Pistol terrifies Ford with the implication that he will soon be a CURTAL dog, emasculated through cuckoldry, we are readied and on track for the more subtle jest when Pistol himself is called one of Falstaff's 'discarded' (CARD/cod: scrotum) or un-manned 'men', 'out of service', a standard pun on copular service. I have tried to indicate such threads with suggestions that the reader 'see' related words.

In addition to the new puns, the Supplement contains amplifications and corrections of old entries; and, for the convenience of scholars and theatre-goers, all the puns have been incorporated into one complete, revised Index.

I acknowledge with appreciation the encouragement of Robert Y. Zachary; and the unfailing assistance of Frances Arnold, the sponsoring editor, who has been most understanding from the inception of the Dictionary. And I count myself fortunate to have had, once again, the benefit of the editorial expertise of Valery Rose and Graham Eyre.

F. R.

To Alvin Zachary Rubinstein

Introduction

About anyone so great as Shakespeare it is probable that we can never be right; and if we can never be right, it is better that we should from time to time change our way of being wrong.

T. S. Eliot

After generations of annotated volumes of Shakespeare, untold numbers of glossaries and analytical works, countless performances of the plays in virtually every major language of the world, we may still find significant meanings and insights into the human condition not seen, ignored, lost – these simply because of their sexual or bawdy content. The blinders of mores, taboos, censorship, fear of censorship, biases, blockages and the like have been perpetuated by scholars, directors and audiences of Shakespeare's plays.

However, we are witnessing a virtual explosion in free expression on sexual subjects – in criticism, theatre, cinema and television, and thus in audience and reader sophistication. This is a happy time to write on Shakespeare's sexual puns and their significance.

This dictionary is intended as a contribution to the understanding and enjoyment of Shakespeare. It is not a study of 'bawdy' if by that word one means pointless obscenity or, as Eric Partridge did in his classic *Shakespeare's Bawdy*, 'such terms as fall "within the meaning of the Act" '. I do not minimise the contribution of him on whose shoulders we stand in suggesting that a sophisticated reader of our decade might guess at much in that glossary and realise that 'ability', 'abstinence', 'abuse', 'accost', 'achieve', 'action' and 'adulterate', for example, mean in certain contexts sexual ability, sexual abuse, sexual action, and the like.

One purpose of this dictionary is to identify the hundreds upon hundreds of still unnoted puns and to indicate their enrichment of the plays; to extend *the* Act of Partridge to cover *those many* acts usually ignored in textual footnotes – the erotic practices of heterosexuals and homosexuals (including lesbians), perverts, castrates, and the impotent; to illustrate that the scatological puns appeared usually in a context that was also sexually bawdy, and that the ethnic puns were as sexually snide then as now. In short, to show that Shakespeare, who we say understood and wrote of the human heart in all its facets, its frailty as well as its nobility, did exactly that.

A second purpose is to reawaken us to the value of reading and hearing Shakespeare word by word, giving full weight to each one and asking why the line was so and not otherwise. We must *visualise* each thing, each action, each modifier; staging, props and gesture cannot do it for us. For example, a TAPER[1] should evoke more than merely the intellectual concept of something that gives light. It is a wax candle. It has a particular shape; and it burns, so is subject to all the puns that have been made on that word: ardently with love, torturingly with venereal disease. And it tapers, meaning it shoots up like a spire or it diminishes in width and thickness and gradually decreases in activity and power. Once we start *seeing* like this, the bawdy, the beauty, and the brilliance of lines such as the following can be understood: 'And tapers burn so bright and every thing/In readiness for Hymenaeus stand' (*TA*, I.i.324). Or 'O, let me clip ye/In arms as sound as when I woo'd, in heart/As merry as when our nuptial day was done,/And tapers burn'd to bedward!' (*Cor*, I.vi.32). Heeding each word, we shall not miss the eroticism in burning tapers. Asking why every *thing*, why *stand*, why *bedward*, we will see the complementary bawdy implications (even without being told by Partridge, Colman *et al.* that these words are frequent sexual puns on the 'penis', 'phallic erection', and 'bed of love-making'. And, though Hymenaeus is Latin for a wedding and for the god of marriage (represented as a young man carrying a *torch* and a veil), we shall realise that every thing is standing and tapers are burning for hymen, the virginal membrane, as well as for Hymen, the god.

Were we an Elizabethan audience and truly word-conscious, we should realise that Marcius's 'taper' demands our attention since it was anticipated by Cominius's 'tabor', and that 'arms' encompasses both the affection and the military calling of the two speakers. We should know that MERRY often meant bawdy or wanton (as in *H5*, I.ii.271–2) and should recognise the merry/marry (K; as in *RJ*, IV.i.89) and 'nuptial' wordplay. We should also hear the pun on woo'd/wood (as in *1H6*, V.iii.77–90 – woo'd/would/wood), with the latter's potential for burning and its alternate meanings of passionate and enraged. Then we should see what Shakespeare intended: a whole sentence ablaze with sexual and military ardour.

Elizabethan scholars agree that we labour at a disadvantage because words were 'used in a way to which, without some training, we are no longer accustomed to respond'.[2] The Elizabethan audience was 'far more educated by ear and memory than we are, quicker in the uptake', says A. L. Rowse.[3] They were up to date on the 'latest jokes with words' and were 'so well trained in the art of listening that they could hear a complicated joke on hour and whore', says Marchette Chute.[4] This dictionary is intended to be a tool that can heighten our awareness of Shakespeare's words, their Elizabethan meanings, their connotations – and their consequent puns.

One way of determining whether Shakespeare intended a pun is to see if meaning is enhanced, and it is by the bulk of those I have selected. They act as signposts that Shakespeare stopped here and so should we. They alert us to larger metaphors or themes we might otherwise overlook and may be compared with biblical wordplay, which is based on the belief that names were keys to the nature and essence of a being or thing: 'God Yahweh formed man from clods in the soil and blew into his nostrils the breath of life' (Gen 2:7) – *'ādām* means 'man' and *'ᵃdāmā* means 'soil'.[5] Hence original man, Adam, made of clay.

When lines seem trite, self-evident, repetitive, or even lacking in sense, it may be that a pun carries the meaning. Samuel Johnson's criticism should be reversed – 'Reason, propriety, and truth' were not sacrificed by the Shakespearean 'quibble' but emerge from it. A simple example can be found in *VA*, 867–9, in which love-sick Venus 'hears no tidings of her love:/She hearkens for his hounds and for his horn:/Anon she hears them chant it lustily'. If to you the horn is only a musical instrument, the lines will be understood on one level only. But, if you see a second meaning of horn, i.e. the penis, or, as Partridge says, 'especially *penis erectus*', then you not only have a bawdy pun but also have given proper weight to the implication of 'lustily'. And for him who is rereading the poem – and it is only the rereader who can know the richness of Shakespeare's punning – the sensual impact of the line might be enhanced by his anticipating the later scene with another kind of horn – a tusk – and Adonis's death when 'the loving swine/Sheath'd unaware the tusk in his soft groin' (1115). The motif of Adonis's 'having a coital relationship with the hunted boar' has been pointed out;[6] his death being a kind of parallel to the sexual experience he had tried to avoid with Venus: 'I know not love . . . nor will not know it,/Unless it be a boar, and then I chase it' (409).

Though a pun need not be repeated in order to be valid, when it is we feel confirmed in our judgement. Recurring word-clusters may also provide substantiation of intent. In *VA*, 867–9, the movement from *hears* to *hearken* and back to *hears* is the repetition in variation that is so often the sign of a pun. It directs our attention to 'hearken', derived from 'hark', i.e. to listen to and go in quest of – both of which Venus is doing; but its significance lies in its repeating the earlier ear–hearken–hears cluster, used by Venus when she urged Adonis to hunt, not the boar, but 'Wat', the hare: 'poor Wat . . . Stands on his hinder legs with listening ear,/To hearken . . . Anon their loud alarums he doth hear' (697). Adonis pursuing the hare, symbol of lust and dedicated to Venus – this is the hunt Venus would have preferred, a reversal of their situation, and Adonis pursuing her. She is identified with Wat: personified, he 'Stands on his hinder legs'; he, too, *hearkens*, and he, too, hears the hounds anon; briers scratch his legs as bushes twine about hers. Cf. *AYL*, IV.iii.18: 'Her love is not the hare that I do hunt'.

The hare, also called a 'bawd' (*OED* 1592) or prostitute (P), is Shakespeare's punning perception of Venus. Adonis had described her as one that 'lends embracements unto every stranger./You do it for increase: O strange excuse,/When reason is the bawd to lust's abuse!' (790). Venus's hearkening for Adonis's 'horn' is one more punning element in the total picture of venereal excitement, meant to remind us that there are actually two simultaneous chases, Adonis's of the boar and Venus's of Adonis – and both are venery, i.e. the pursuit of beasts of game and/or the pursuit of sexual pleasure.

Of course, some puns are fun in and for themselves, of which the following from *Romeo and Juliet* is typical. 'By my [or "this"] count' is used twice in the play (the only two occurrences of the phrase in Shakespeare) and each time it means not only 'by my [this] reckoning' but also 'by my [this] cunt'.[7] First, Juliet's mother says, 'ladies of esteem,/Are made already mothers: by my count,/I was your mother much upon these years/That you are now a maid' (I.iii.71).

Since Shakespeare's puns tend to grow out of one another, to dispose themselves not around a focal point but as in a helix, a simple pun often alerts us to the more subtle one. That function is performed here by the obvious pun depending for its humour on the contrast between the woman who was *made* and her who is a *maid*, 'making', as Partridge illustrates, meaning 'effectual copulation'; and it is by her 'count' that Lady Capulet was made a mother. In Juliet's repetition of her mother's pun, 'O, by this count I shall be much in years/Ere I again behold my Romeo!' (III.v.46), there is supportive sexual innuendo in the pun on YEARS/arse and the introductory 'O'. As Shakespeare says in *MWW*, IV.i.53, in a pun on *fuck*: 'What is the focative case, William? – O, – vocativo, O.' Both 'O' and 'case' are puns on the pudenda (K; P).

Some of these puns may seem outrageous: Shakespeare's wit, like his genius, is unbridled. Ultimately each reader must decide for himself what meaning is pertinent, what irrelevant: whether what he is reading is a word with one simple clear-cut meaning, or a pun that functions coherently and consistently on two – or more – levels, or an ambiguity whose value lies in its connotations and overtones, indeed, in suggesting a word that may not even have been expressed.[8] As Hilda R. Hulme says, 'To "prove" the existence of an indecent joke which the dramatic context seems strongly to suggest is not always easy.'[9] A ROSE is a rose is a rose – but it is also a maidenhead, a pudendum, and a whore; it depends on where it is and whose it is.

Often, to make sense of difficult transitional or comic scenes and asides, we may find puns are our most helpful guide – and through them we may discern the continuity of important themes. For this reason alone, abridgement of the plays should be resisted. Let us look at several puns in one line of the comic interchange between certain Commoners and the tribunes that opens the play *Julius Caesar*. We shall focus on the cluster around the word ALL, which can mean any part of the pubic–anal area: the penis, a hole-boring tool, like the awl; the arse; the vulva, a (w)hole – i.e. all the 'holy [*sic*] reasons' for which the Clown in *AW*, I.iii.33, is marrying. To Shakespeare 'All is whole' (V.iii.37); and 'whole' means a *hole*, i.e. pudendum, rectum. (See P, s.vv. Whole, Hole, Holy.)

'Truly, sir, all that I live by is with the awl: I meddle with no tradesman's matters, nor women's matters, but with awl. I am, indeed, sir, a surgeon to old shoes.' This cobbler disclaims meddling (sexual intimacy) with the matters of the tradesman (brothel-keeper or bawd) or with women's matters (feminine pudenda; sexual intercourse). (For these puns see P; C.) Yet the all/awl does have *something* to do with these matters for, first, he did not need to mention them, and, second, he makes an exception to his disclaimer using 'but' and 'with awl', the latter punning on with his awl, withal or nevertheless, and a third pun meaning that, though he does not meddle, i.e. does not use his awl or sexual tool in such matters, still he does something *with all* the matters. The exception he makes is that with his awl he mends 'old shoes'. Since in his mind this activity has relevance to and yet must be distinguished from the first part of his sentence, we shall, for the time being, take old shoes to mean shoes of those in the trade, of tradesmen's (whores and pimps – P) shoes. For further clarification, see MATTER; OLD.

Or he may be a cobbler not by trade but only in the sense of that word's meaning a bungler, a botcher (*OED*; *Tim*, IV.iii.285). This is the meaning taken by the Tribune, for, though the Commoner has answered the question as to his trade with 'I am but, as you would say, a cobbler', Marullus, unsatisfied, persists, 'But what *trade* art thou? Answer me *directly*' (italics added). Finally the Commoner redescribes himself as 'indeed, sir, a surgeon to old shoes'.

Since Shakespeare, like his contemporaries,[10] used 'surgeon' and 'surgery' to allude to treatment of venereal disease (*Per*, IV.vi.29; see P), we see it is not shoes as such that the cobbler mends. He had also called himself a 'mender of bad soles' – as cobbler, the bad soles of shoes; but, as surgeon, the bad soles, bottoms or arses of whores – diseased and needing a surgeon. Marullus heard this bawdy implication, for he called the Commoner a 'naughty knave' – 'naughty' meaning obscene, bawdy; a 'naughty house', a brothel (*MM*, II.i.77); and a 'naughty man', a whoremonger (P; F&H; C). A similar pun on the SOLE as the arse is made in *The Two Gentlemen of Verona*, II.iii.19, when Launce, after deliberation, decides the shoe 'with the hole in it' must be his mother (not his father) – 'the worser sole'. (See WORSE for puns on *whores*.)

The Commoner continues, 'when they are in great danger, I recover them', meaning he resoles the 'old shoes'. But 'great danger' certainly implies more than a hole in a shoe, and in conjunction with 'recover' suggests serious sickness, in this context, venereal disease.[11] Recovering refers to the cure this 'surgeon' effects and, since 'cover' means, and puns on, mount coitally (*OED*; P), *re*cover indicates that they will be well and able to work, to fornicate and procure (to pander, as in *MM*, III.ii.57). Cf. *recouvrer*, to recover, to procure (Cot).

So, though the cobbler meddles with no tradesman's or women's MATTERS, yet all he lives by is with the *awl* – yes, by recovering or curing the *all*, the (w)hole, or the diseased penis, vulva and arse(hole).

This metaphor continues in his boast, 'As proper men as ever trod upon neat's leather have gone upon my handiwork.' HANDIWORK is used three times by Shakespeare and the other two times it is explicitly 'God's handiwork' or the human body and is related to the act of creation. So not only do proper men walk upon his leather shoes, but they also tread and go, both of which mean copulate (P), *upon* the bodies of his cured whores. And the LEATHER or skin, a common pun on pudendum and whore,[12] is 'neat', a quibble on cow-hide and on clean or free from contagious disease (*OED* 1611; *1H4*, II.iv.502: 'wherein neat and cleanly').

These are not idle bawdy puns; they are Shakespeare's commentary on the conspirators. The citizens are 'Kind souls'; Caesar was a 'good soul'; and Brutus, the 'Soul of Rome', 'will make sick men whole', though some are 'whole that we must make sick'. So Brutus, too, is a cobbler, dealing in soles, holes and mendings: his 'unkindest cut of *all*' and 'the *hole* you made in Caesar's heart' (italics added) are sad echoes of the cobbler with his hole-boring awl. Brutus's dagger, his manhood, and his deed of murder stand condemned by the association. And unfortunately, in the assassination aftermath, Brutus, like the cobbler, proves a botcher who bungles. He who had said, 'Let us be sacrificers, but not butchers' winds up one of the 'butchers', as Antony labelled the conspiracy. 'So are they *all*, *all* honourable men –' (italics added).

Brutus was the surgeon who hoped to cure the ills of Rome by ridding it of Caesar, who, he said, 'hath the falling sickness'. It cannot be accidental that Shakespeare chose this sickness, this phrase that reflects the disease-ridden 'falling trade' – as prostitution was known – that the cobbler tried to mend. Nor is it accidental that 'Cassius' sounds like *casus*, from L *cadere*, to fall; and 'Casca', It *cascare*, to fall. Cassius's refutation tars them all: 'No, Caesar hath it not; but you and I/And honest Casca, we have the falling sickness.' To understand this as meaning epilepsy just because Plutarch mentions Caesar's 'falling sickness' is to ignore a powerful symbol. Shakespeare could have said 'epilepsy' directly, as he does in two other plays (in *Othello* even saying, 'My lord is fallen into an epilepsy' – IV.i.51) but he was aiming for the more important symbolic identification of epilepsy and syphilis – both known as the 'foul disease' (*OED*)[13] – the latter typifying corruption, decay, and perhaps 'Caesar's ambition', as in *2H6*, I.ii.18: 'the canker of ambitious thoughts'. (See WORM, *RJ*, for puns on the chancre of syphilis.)

The big question Shakespeare tackles in this metaphor of mending with an awl that makes holes as it sews, of mending with a dagger that made holes in Caesar's body as the conspirators did, is the moral one of men mending by murder. Is this final solution properly only God's? The first line in Act I, 'Is this a holiday?' (holy day),[14] starts the wordplay – holy/hole/whole, all – that contains this ultimate question. Shakespeare frequently makes the point that one recovers what is lost ('That so he might recover what was lost' – *1H6*, II.v.32). Hence the cobbler spoke of recovering those *soles* in great danger, the lost *souls*. ('We have here recovered the most dangerous piece of lechery' – *Ado*, III.iii.180.) But this may properly be the job of religion and its servants. Hence Brutus wished to think of the conspirators as 'sacrificers' and not 'butchers'. The question, of course, is, which were they?

It is genius, and it is all lost when the puns are lost.

Shakespeare's plays contain references to perversions such as incest, planning to rape a woman on the pillow of her husband's murdered body, killing children and serving them cooked to their unwitting mother. The literary London of his time was characterised by 'a kind of horrified fear of sex coupled with a fascinated interest in its abnormalities'.[15] The theatres were in Southwark, the centre for brothels, bear- and bull-baiting; clients of the one passed the clients of the other. There was a Molly-house or male brothel in Hoxton. In these houses 'doubtless in true bordel tradition there would be . . . all the equipments needed by sadists and masochists, with the necessary female (or if need be, male) partners'.[16] Although the Tudor Acts prescribing death were in force, there were known homosexuals in the court circles and among writers, including Francis Bacon and Christopher Marlowe. Only 150 years later, Tobias Smollett wrote of homosexual prostitution and of hermaphroditic waiting-women; reason tells us these were not inventions of his century. Philip Henslowe and Edward Alleyn, who financed the Globe, of which Shakespeare was part-owner, operated brothels. Alleyn's wife was carted away from one of which she was proprietress. When old Lord Hunsdon, the Queen's Lord Chamberlain, died, the Queen appointed his son George Carey, 'Widely reputed to be a sodomite as well as suffering from syphilis', whom satirist John Marston lampooned: 'at Hoxton now, his monstrous love he feasts: for there he keeps a bawdy-house of beasts'.[17] The prevailing horrors and the relatively futile treatment of the pox may account for the high incidence of punning on it in the plays.

Juvenal, Vergil, Ovid, Greek and Roman playwrights whom Shakespeare read and drew on, wrote of and punned on farting, defecation, dildoes and pederasty. So did Shakespeare's contemporaries. Even theoretically it is difficult to believe with Partridge that this man – the greatest and truest mirror of far more than his own time – 'disdained' scatology; alluded to homosexuality 'very seldom and most cursorily', and never to lesbianism, 'an extremely rare deviation in Shakespearean England'; and of the 'nine terms' that 'may be presumed to allude' to masturbation, 'none alludes to a woman's self-pollution'.[18] But we need not rely on theorising; we have the puns.

It is not for me to explain why others have ignored or minimised Shakespeare's handling of these subjects. Perhaps it was discretion, 'The better part of valour', as Falstaff puts it (*1H4*, v.iv.121) in a hardly valorous moment when he saves his life by counterfeiting death and then as another manifestation of valour proceeds to stab a man he knows to be already dead. But, unlike Hotspur, Shakespeare has refused to die.

The higher incidence of sexual, including homosexual,[19] references in my definitions and consequent interpretations of the plays has, for me, no bearing on Shakespeare's sexuality: male writers have created great fictional women, women have created male characters, and homosexuals have created both – to say nothing of not having to be a murderer to create a Macbeth. But I think it a mistake to overlook the playing of women's roles by boys under eighteen – even more to the point, their delivery of women's lines – with all the ambiguities that can stem therefrom. In a different context, Harold C. Goddard speaks of the 'nature of human imagination, which has scarcely altered in a thousand years',[20] and we know the reaction of a modern audience to a 'drag' theatrical troupe or to the well-known androgynous actors or the singers of the pop world. The Elizabethan audience was oblivious to neither the sex nor the age of the players (Cleopatra: 'and I shall see/Some squeaking Cleopatra boy my greatness/I' the posture of a whore' – *AC*, v.ii.220; Rosalind: 'If I were a woman I would kiss as many of you as had beards' – *AYL*, Epil.). The restriction of women's roles to very young males because even a shaven face and relatively lower voice would have dispelled theatrical 'illusion' raises the question whether the essential maleness was ever completely forgotten. Troupes of child actors commanded the highest admission fees; A. L. Rowse quotes a protest against the performances of the 'Children of her Majesty's Chapel, "the lascivious writhing of their tender limbs, and gorgeous apparel" and *other uses* to which they were put' (italics added).[21] One must wonder at the Jacobeans' 'strange pleasure in watching violent and sexually perverse dramas . . . performed by children'[22] – even written for them, like George Chapman's *Gentleman Usher* (1605), a bawdy satirical play acted by actors aged eight to ten.

If we accept this awareness, many puns become clear. In *The Tempest*, Miranda declares her love to Ferdinand: 'that dare not offer/What I desire to give, and much less take/What I shall die to want. But this is trifling;/And all the more it seeks to hide itself,/The bigger bulk it shows' (III.i.77). The involved wordplay – contrasting 'offer' and 'give' with 'take' and 'want'; 'less' and 'trifling' with 'more' and 'bulk' – is the usual indication that there is more than meets the eye. BULK meant the body of a living creature, a projecting part, and to swell, meanings on which Shakespeare elsewhere puns. Here we have an image strongly suggestive of a phallic erection that cannot be hidden, a situation familiar to us from other plays ('love is like a great natural, that runs lolling up and down to hide his bauble in a hole' – *RJ*, II.iv.96). Reconciling this image to a woman's speaking of the nature of her love becomes easier when we realise that 'she' is a 'he'. Perhaps Miranda is glancing at that which on Ferdinand is showing 'bigger bulk', and Shakespeare is posing, as William Empson would say, a deliberate ambiguity for the enriched pun and the delight of the audience.

Or let us take something critics have called an anomaly, the association of one of Shakespeare's least attractive characters, Cloten in *Cymbeline*, with one of his loveliest lyrics (II.iii.22–30). It is a lovely lyric, on one level; but we are supposed to hear all the levels of Shakespeare's meaning, and when we do there are fewer anomalies and fewer things to explain away.

Here I merely want to point out that in the last couplet there is at least the possibility of a pun, since it is being sung not to a woman but to a boy playing the role (though he is off stage): 'With everything that pretty is,/My lady sweet, arise:/Arise, arise.' What I am suggesting is that 'arise' sung several times to a male could bring to mind a phallic erection, especially if he is to arise with every pretty 'thing', euphemism for the sexual organ (for use as penis, see P; C; F&H), and especially in the bawdy context of Cloten's having requested the musicians to 'penetrate her with your fingering, so: we'll try with tongue too'. The adaptation I am proposing is that her thing is really his thing and therefore her desired arising assumes a particular coloration. Colman says 'try with tongue' could allude to cunnilingus; however, could it not equally suggest what he recognises as 'the nearest homosexual equivalent' in a similar use of tongue in *TGV*, II.iii.52–5?

That 'arise' was intended as a bawdy pun is bolstered by other sexual innuendo in the same line, namely the use of PRETTY (ME 'prati') as a pun on *prat*, the buttocks (*OED*; P). This was a not uncommon word-association in Shakespeare's circle and times: Edward Alleyn wrote a letter for his apprentice, John Pyk, and jocularly signed it 'your petty, pretty, prattling, parleying pig'. Alleyn either deliberately punned on John Pyk/pig/Gk *pyge* (the rump) or else merely used current slang that had incorporated the pun: 'What prate ye, praty pyggsney.'[23] In *MND*, III.i.173, Titania orders her elves to light night-tapers 'at the fiery glow-worm's eyes,/To have my love to bed and to arise'. The close succession of her 'love' (whom we know to be Bottom), 'bed' and 'arise' indicates her anticipation of the sexual erection; again it is an ass/arse or prat (Bottom wearing his ass's head) that is to arise.[24]

Arising only secondarily refers to the 'lady', to Imogen. The emphasis is on Cloten's *erection*, for it is, after all, the development of his character the scene intends to further. Even in the lyric sung to her, it was 'Phoebus 'gin arise' – a quibble on Phoebus, the sun, and Cloten, the son. This emphasis starts in the first line of the scene, when Cloten is called 'the most coldest that ever turned up ace'.[25] Here, in an ace/ass pun (K; noted in the Cambridge University Press edition of *Cymbeline*), it is again an ass (arse) that arises, that Cloten turns *up*. Concentration on Cloten's erection, expressed through the word 'up', continues in his saying 'I am glad I was up so late; for that's the reason I was up so early'. And by the end of the scene he has made his decision to 'be revenged', which later becomes his plan for rape.

Most of Shakespeare's sexual puns have been interpreted in the light of male–female intercourse and with a too-heavy emphasis on female, at the expense of male, genitals. (Partridge claims there are fewer 'penis-terms' than 'pudendum muliebre'.) I propose that we remain open to the possibility that the context may ask us to employ analogous images. Not all concavities are vaginas; there are also anuses in Shakespeare's world. Not all globes are breasts or wombs; there are testicles. And the arse or prat or any punning synonym may not only mean the woman's buttocks and vaginal orifice, but apply equally to the man's buttocks and anal orifice, or for that matter to the woman's anus.

For example, Partridge confines Shakespeare's bawdy use of the word RING to the vulva; but, looking at Shakespeare's use of the word, we find that pun is too restrictive. Here is just part of the raw material from which he may have fashioned his alternate pun: L*anus*, meaning ring; and the shape of the rounded anus itself.

In *Twelfth Night* our first introduction to a ring occurs in 'Run after that same peevish messenger,/The county's man: he left this ring behind him' (I.v.319). There is the same confusion about the ring, whether it is a man's or woman's (the Duke's or Olivia's) as there is about the messenger who 'left' it: Viola, a girl, passing herself off to the Duke as Cesario, 'an eunuch', whom Olivia believes to be a boy and is enchanted by. The confusion is capsulated in the paradox the 'county's man': 'county' or 'count' (pun in *cunt* – see p. xi) when joined to 'man' yields exactly what we have, a girl–boy, Viola–Cesario, a eunuch. And this girl–boy has left a ring BEHIND.

The play's bisexual tensions[26] emerge from the revealing quibble in 'left' and 'peevish' – left, i.e. not right; and peevish, i.e. perverse (Shakespearean use – *OED*) or deviating from right. Shakespeare is determined that we see the messenger as peevish: Malvolio repeats it in his lie (II.ii.14) that has elicited much critical commentary. If we keep in mind Olivia's instant infatuation, her inability to distinguish between girl and boy, between sister and brother, we shall see the deviation or perverseness at which Shakespeare is hinting. This glimmer of lesbianism, noted also by Colman – 'She loves me, sure . . . I am the man', says Viola (II.ii.23) – is reflected in the glance at male homosexuality in the immediately following scene, when Antonio expresses (i.48) sentiments for Sebastian (Viola's twin brother) corresponding to those of Olivia for Viola: 'I do adore thee so/That danger shall seem sport [copulation – P; F&H; C]'. Sebastian had said that *both* he and his sister were 'left behind' – like the ring. The repetition of this pun is a further link between the two scenes and the sexual ambivalence they contain.[27]

We learn exactly what the ring is when the priest, speaking of the marriage of Olivia to Sebastian, says it was 'Confirm'd by . . . joinder of your hands,/Attested by . . . close of lips,/Strengthen'd by interchangement of your rings' (V.i.160). You may think these are merely wedding rings, but if you are impressed by the parallelism of the three participial phrases, each containing a parallel prepositional phrase, then you will see that, preserving the parallel, 'rings' is the third in a list of body-parts; and, that being the case, the mutual 'interchangement'[28] must imply *both* male and female genitals or that ring both sexes share in common, the anus and by transference the arse, that bawdy anatomic catch-all.

In *1H4*, III.iii, the ring is again a pun on the anus. Falstaff claims his pocket was picked of a ring while he slept 'behind the arras'. Of the eleven times Shakespeare uses ARRAS, eight of them are 'behind the arras', and suggest an arras/arse pun. The Prince allegedly said, 'that ring was copper'. Falstaff threatens to cudgel him 'if he said my ring was copper'. And the Prince repeats 'I say 'tis copper'. Now this is either tedious nonsense, or it has a point, presumably a funny one. And funny it is – when we see the bawdy underpinnings. Copper is L*aes*, *aeris*; and 'made of copper' is L *aenus*. So the purpose of having Falstaff sleep BEHIND the arras was to introduce in that preliminary pun the COPPER,[29] i.e. venereal, ring – the ass/*aes* or arse/*aeris*, ring; the ring that was made of copper or the anus/*aenus*. Falstaff eventually backs out of the argument with 'as thou art but man, I dare; but as thou art prince . . .', a verbose construction explained by its effusion of ass/arse puns: as/ass; ART, L *ars*; but/butt.

The bawdy reduction of Falstaff's ring to his arse, as the only possible thing in his pocket that could have been picked[30] (it turns out there never was a ring) is supported in similar rank bawdiness and vilification of the Hostess: 'Setting thy womanhood aside, thou art a beast to say otherwise' – 'What beast! why, an otter' – 'An otter, sir John! why an otter?' – 'Why, she's neither fish nor flesh; a man knows not where to have her.' Footnotes say 'where to have her' means what to make of her, though 'where' is not what and 'have' means not make but possess, and specifically possess carnally (P) – and she is to set her womanhood aside. And why does Shakespeare choose an otter, the only time he uses this word, which he even emphasises with the pun in *other*wise?[31] Because the Hostess and Falstaff have something in common: his was a *seal*-ring and she is an *otter*, another aquatic mammal 'often taken as the type of an amphibious creature'. And both are being twitted about their arses (see OTHER). 'Amphibious' means of ambiguous or double nature; hence Ben Jonson named 'a land and sea Captain' Thomas Otter; Charles Cotton said the 'Hermaphrodite' is 'amphibious'; and Henry Fielding humorously described transvestite clothing as 'amphibious'. Colman also sees these lines as a reference to anal intercourse, though he comes to it by a different route, pointing out that 'neither fish nor flesh' implies 'neither male nor female'.

The sterility of the usual footnotes for a modern reader can, unfortunately, be too easily illustrated, their uselessness often in direct proportion to their erudition. Rowse called it making Shakespeare dull with 'mountains of commentary'.[32] Lear's disgust for the 'face between her forks' of a simpering dame certainly meant the genital 'face'; the *OED* uses this line as illustration of the fork of the human body. So it seems a little like dragging a red herring across the trail to define forks as 'ornaments for holding up the hair' and not to hint at a sexual quibble. Another example is the dry glossing of an incredible tour-de-force of 35 lines all centring on ass puns, starting with 'Judas I am', the jest being laid wide open by the concluding 'For the ass to the Jude . . . Jud-as, away!' (*LLL*, v.ii.599). Yet footnotes treat all the in-between comic references to faces literally, ignoring the frequent Shakespearean pun on the FACE as the buttocks. Cf. *les fesses*, buttocks (Cot); and *fesse*, popular slang for prostitute (F&H, s.v. Barrack-hack).

Holofernes, a farcical schoolmaster, acting Judas Maccabaeus in an entertainment, is baited by his audience who claim 'thou hast no face', to which he retorts, 'What is this?' Elizabethans would have known the jest, so his question may have been accompanied by a flowery gesture encompassing both of his 'faces'. His audience answers him with a list of quibbles on various faces. One that desperately needs an explanation if it is to be witty is 'The face of an old Roman coin, scarce seen.' I suggest this is the ancient Roman copper as or *asse* (Cot); 'This new brasen Asse . . . stamped with a two-faced Janus' (*OED* 1601); subject of a pun in Plautus, *Asinaria*, 590: 'To whop those asses if they happen to start braying in the wallet here.' And, of course, of the two human faces, the ass/arse is the one 'scarce seen'. See OLD for puns on whores.

Calling Holofernes 'Monsieur' (v.i.47) reminds us we are in France and are speaking French, in which *fesses* are buttocks. When told the entertainment would be shown 'in the *posteriors* of this day' (94), Holofernes finds 'the word is well *culled*, *chose* . . . I do *ass*ure you, sir, I do *ass*ure' (italics added). Cul (*OED*) and *cul* (Cot) mean arse; Fr *chose* is the pudendum (P, s.v. Culled; F&H). How many clues do we need to know what face he has and what he is?

Another face, 'A cittern head', is glossed by W. J. Rolfe, learned editor of Shakespeare's plays (and by others following his lead) as the head of a cittern or guitar, often grotesquely carved. Yet he undoubtedly knew a cittern head meant a dunce, in other words, an ass: as John Marston wrote in the Prologue to *The Sourge of Villanie*, 'Shall brainlesse cyterne heads, each jobernole. . . .' He probably also knew the cittern was a pun on a whore. In Farmer & Henley, under 'Barber's music', we read that barbers provided citterns for waiting customers: in *The Honest Whore II* by Dekker (v.ii), Matheo speaks of a barber's citterne for every serving-man to play upon. In *The Silent Woman* by Ben Jonson (III.v), Morose says of his wife, whom his barber had recommended, 'I have married his cittern that is common to all men' ('common' applies to a prostitute – *OED*; P). This is the humour underlying Holofernes's saying, 'You have *put* me *out* of countenance' and 'you have *out*-faced them all' (italics added). He is punning on 'put' as to put coitally (*OED*; P) and on *fesse* and OUT (*hors* – Cot) as whores and on *fesso* (a woman's 'quaint or water-box', i.e. cunt – F). His audience – 'as he is an ass' – has described him in terms of the ultimate degradation, a whore's ass.

It was probably Rolfe's feeling that an educated audience would see the puns or that it was poor taste or inexpedient to footnote them. Shakespeare's witty bawdry was often intended for sophisticated audiences in the court, the house of some nobleman, or the Inns of Court. We are frequently told, as if by way of apology, that the ribaldry was for the 'groundlings'. Yet Chute makes the point that Elizabethan audiences have been misrepresented and that the groundlings, the young apprentices sent up to London to learn a trade, 'belonged as a class to one of the most privileged and intelligent groups in London'.[33]

One could go on and on to show how the modern non-specialist reader, even a well educated one, is left in total ignorance of the fun. It is such gaps as these that this dictionary seeks to fill.

Puns have many levels of meaning. Vulgar punning on the subject of fucking and buggering, name-calling such as 'whoreson' (son-of-a-bitch), is sometimes intended literally; more frequently it is figurative speech. It means no more than – and yet as much as – such language today. It is man's way of expressing the strength of an emotion, his anger or fear in the face of an antagonistic, destructive force, larger than he is, perhaps; a feeling for which the language of reason may seem inadequate. To the extent that we believe that the corpus of Shakespeare's work mirrors life, we should expect to find all kinds of sexuality, both as symbol and as substance, appearing across the stage he has set for us.

The emphasis in this dictionary is on literary interpretation, not phonetics or etymology. Any such information offered is tentative and meant to be suggestive only. It may or may not have been related to the formation of these puns, which must, ultimately, stand or fall on their own merit, on their contribution to understanding and enjoying the plays.

I do not minimise the threat some of the puns pose and can understand reluctance to open the Pandora's box. They may require radical reinterpretations, expose a seamier side to lines of lovely poetry, or upset cherished images of favourite characters. However, they are invaluable indicators of larger dramatic issues, reveal the complexity of many characters who might otherwise prove one-sided or banal, often rescue lines from meaninglessness, and provide intellectual stimulus and delight. The balance-sheet is in their favour.

Finally, whether the puns are deliberate or unconscious is a question sometimes raised by those who feel that, if they are not deliberate, then they may safely – and happily – be ignored. It is asked more often by Americans than by English. To look at a British newspaper is to see why: I have chosen, at random, the *Guardian*, 2 July 1981 – and here are some of the headlines. Pick your field. Politics? 'Blasted nuisance' (effect of nuclear weapons on communications systems). Business? 'How an industry took a pasting' (monopoly rules applied to roadside-poster marketing-company). Sports? 'Hitchhiker thumbs nose at challengers' (the *Hitchhiker* won the sailing race). Movies? 'A wizard knight club' (review of film *Excalibur*). Science? 'Keeping bats out of hell' (on their declining population, fewer roosting-places, and insect food being done away with).

These are Shakespeare's heirs who may not have his genius, but they have his will! And, if the puns were unconscious, does it really matter? If they come from his depths and speak to ours, perhaps that is the very source of their power over us, as potent as his conscious craft.

NOTES

Abbreviations are explained in the list on pp. xxi–xxiii; for publication details of modern works first cited in abbreviated form, see the Bibliography, pp. 353–7.

1. Words in small capitals are developed in the Dictionary.
2. L. C. Knights, *Explorations* (New York: New York University Press, 1964) p. 18.
3. A. L. Rowse, *William Shakespeare: A Biography* (New York: Harper & Row, 1963) p. 68.
4. Chute, pp. 102–3.

5. *The Anchor Bible: Genesis*, ed. and trs. E. A. Speiser (New York: Doubleday, 1964) pp. 14, 16.
6. C, p.159; Keach, pp. 79–81.
7. F&H, s.v. Shap, the female pudendum. Count: 'a woman's shappe', *con*. See also Burford, *'Orrible Synne*, p. 230; C, p. 182, for a possible account/cunt pun in Son 136. *H5* Folio sp. 'count', pun on *con* (III.iv.47–53). See K, s.v. GOWN/con, for the pun in 'count'.
8. Empson, *Seven Types of Ambiguity*. I am deeply indebted to this study on ambiguities, which Mr Empson defines as 'any verbal nuance, however slight, which gives room for alternative reaction to the same piece of language'.
9. Hulme, p. 114.
10. John Marston, *The Dutch Courtesan*; 'house surgeon Mary Faugh' (II.ii) is the 'Bawd' (I.ii); see BARBER.
11. In many clusters, recovery and danger are associated with the plague (VD), disease and lechery: 'He is so plaguy proud that the death tokens of it/Cry "No recovery"' (*TrC*, II.iii.188); 'be cured of this diseased opinion . . . 'tis most dangerous' (*WT*, I.ii.298); 'dangerous piece of lechery' (*Ado*, III.iii.179).
12. Leather: 14th–20th c., skin; 16th–20th c., female pudendum (P2). Leather: mutton, i.e. prostitute (F&H, s.v. Stretch). L *scortum*: hide; harlot.
13. See *OED*, s.v. Foul: 'The f. disease or evil: (a) epilepsy, (b) syphilis.' Shakespeare spoke of the 'foul disease' in *Ham*, IV.i.21, and *KL*, I.i.167, the 'evil', 'The mere despair of surgery', in *Mac*, IV.iii.146 – and I think it a fair assumption he knew these terms were applicable to both epilepsy and syphilis. See P and C for bawdy puns on 'fall'. Dekker and Middleton, *The Honest Whore I*, II.i.30: 'down and arise, or the falling trade'.
14. Kökeritz notes the holiday/holy day pun in *KJ*, III.i.81.
15. Chute, p. 200.
16. Burford, *Queen of the Bawds*, p. 73.
17. Ibid., p. 56.
18. P, pp. 8, 13, 25. Colman, however, points out the force of 'Shakespeare's references to chamber-pots, close-stools or flatulence'. He also notes 'lightning-flickers of lesbianism' that 'play round the two young women in their private conversations' in *Twelfth Night* (pp. 4, 86). For literature on the lesbian theme in the 16th–17th c., see West, pp. 178–9. Cf. Jonson, *The Underwood*, xlix, 'An Epigram on the Court Pucelle': 'What though with tribade [Lesbian] lust she force a muse'.
19. We use the term 'homosexual' to cover engaging in homosexual practices the one time under discussion, some time, or all the time; understanding that in literature, as in life, homosexuality does not exclude affairs or marriage with women or the having of children by them.
20. Goddard, vol. I, p. 8.
21. These are the same 'children' who 'are most tyrannically clapped for't' in *Ham*, II.ii.354. This quibble of Rosencrantz on 'clap' (coit – P; gonorrhoea – *OED*) dovetails with the sentiments of the City Fathers. Dryden in *MacFlecknoe* speaks of the 'Nursery' (the theatre in which young actors were trained) as the place 'Where unfledged Actors learn to laugh and cry,/Where infant Punks [whores] their tender Voices try'. And Jonson in *The Devil is an Ass*, II.iii, tells of a 'very pretty fellow', an 'ingenious youth' who was brought to parties 'Drest like a lawyer's wife' and would 'talk bawdy' so that 'It would have burst your buttons' (in the 16th c. these commonly referred to those on the codpiece; see BUTTONS).
22. *The London Theatre Guide, 1596–1642*, ed. Christopher Edwards (London: Burlington Press, 1979) p. 38.
23. Chute, p. 217; F&H, s.v. Pigsney (Skelton 1529).
24. *A Midsummer Night's Dream*, New Variorum edn, ed. Furness, quotes scholars who wonder that Shakespeare, usually so observant, could make such an error as to speak of lighting tapers at the glow-worm's eyes, when, they say, everyone knows the fire is in the glow-worm's tail. Whenever a Shakespearean error is mentioned, one should suspect the possibility of an overlooked pun: by 'eyes' Shakespeare *meant* the tail (i.e. posterior) and

was making one of his frequent puns on eyes (arse), which – in this disputed line – leads right into the pun on Titania's desire to have her love a*rise*. See EYES.

25. This line is one of several (Cloten was also called a 'capon') that permit speculation that Cloten was bisexual. In a review of the 1979 Stratford production of *Cymbeline*, the actor of Cloten was described as having assayed 'the epicene' (*Observer*, 22 Apr 1979). In 'turned up ace', 'turn' is copulate (P; F&H).
26. A Stratford production of *Twelfth Night* was praised by reviewer Robert Cushman for successfully conveying these tensions in an atmosphere that is 'in Auden's phrase a bit whiffy': 'the most believable boy–girl since . . .'; and 'an Orsino . . . as apt to fondle a page as a mistress, who at the close addresses himself to the wrong twin'.
27. The pun on BEHIND is strengthened by the rapid succession of arse puns in the one sentence: Sebastian was left 'behind' and would have so 'ended' had he not been taken from the 'breach' (common breach/breech pun) of the sea by Antonio.
28. Guilt by association links interchangement to sexual intercourse: 'joinder . . . close . . . interchangement'. CLOSE = the sexual embrace, as in 'and 'twere dark, you'ld close sooner' (*TrC*, III.ii.51). To JOIN (L *copula*) = copulate.
29. 'Venereal' means of or ptg to COPPER, formerly called Venus by chemists. In alchemy Venus is the metal copper, which was anciently used for mirrors, a mirror still being the astrological sign for the planet Venus.
30. Picking pockets – mentioned six times in this scene – is not merely picking them of money but quibbles on sexual digging or piercing: 'this house is turned bawdy-house; they pick pockets'.
31. K, p. 109. 'Th' was pronounced 't' as in the goat/Goth pun, *TA*, II.iii.110 and death/debt pun in *1H4*, I.iii.185.
32. Interview on the Dick Cavett television show, 1 Dec 1978.
33. Chute, p. 39. Ann Jennalie Cook, *The Privileged Playgoers of Shakespeare's London* (Princeton, NJ: Princeton University Press, 1981), makes an even stronger case for a 'privileged' clientele, saying plebeians were much less frequently in the audience, and in much smaller numbers, than has been assumed.

Guide to the Use of the Dictionary

1. When a word is printed in small capitals, that word is defined and analysed under its alphabetical listing in this dictionary.

2. Any meaning assigned to an English word can be found in the *Oxford English Dictionary* and was current in Shakespeare's time unless otherwise noted. Words were used as puns or colloquially, however, often long before the entry; for example, Kökeritz says that '*Madam* is monosyllabic . . . like modern *ma'am*, recorded from the 17th century (*OED*) but certainly much older.' Also 'cock' is a 'Penis (vulgar) 1730' in the *OED*, though as early as the 15th c. it was a euphemism for the penis (TWR, s.v. Cok).

3. Similarly, puns on foreign words always assume the usage of Shakespeare's time, as established from such sources as the dictionaries of Cotgrave and Florio. Where there are difficulties in establishing contemporary usage, this is noted.

4. Puns established by Eric Partridge in *Shakespeare's Bawdy* or E. A. M. Colman in *The Dramatic Use of Bawdy in Shakespeare* are taken as 'givens' and cited, except when they were found wanting.

5. Unless this dictionary says no date is given (n.d.), a pun cited from Farmer & Henley was used either earlier than Shakespeare or contemporaneously.

6. Puns used so frequently that they appear in the footnotes of almost any text or that can be verified in the dictionaries are referred to as 'common' puns.

7. Similar puns by other writers are quoted. This does not suggest that either artist directly derived his pun from the other, but that similar bawdy metaphors, fancies or conceits may arise spontaneously and/or circulate freely in the creative atmosphere.

8. Quotations from the text of Shakespeare are from the Globe Edition, *Complete Works of William Shakespeare*, ed. W. G. Clark and W. A. Wright. The line-numbering is in agreement with this edition; with G. L. Kittredge, *The Complete Works of Shakespeare* (as used by Helge Kökeritz in *Shakespeare's Pronunciation*); and with the listings in Bartlett's *Concordance to Shakespeare* and in A. Schmidt's *Shakespeare-Lexicon.* Line-references indicate the line in which the particular word or phrase under discussion appears. Where there is no such reference point, *quoted* (as distinct from *cited*) passages are identified by the number of their first line.

9. Biblical quotations in the dictionary are from the Authorised Version of 1611.

Abbreviations

SHAKESPEARE'S PLAYS AND POEMS

AC	*Antony and Cleopatra*	*Mac*	*Macbeth*
Ado	*Much Ado about Nothing*	*MM*	*Measure for Measure*
AW	*All's Well that Ends Well*	*MND*	*Midsummer Night's Dream*
AYL	*As You Like It*	*MV*	*The Merchant of Venice*
CE	*The Comedy of Errors*	*MWW*	*The Merry Wives of Windsor*
Cor	*Coriolanus*	*Oth*	*Othello*
Cym	*Cymbeline*	*PP*	*The Passionate Pilgrim*
Ham	*Hamlet*	*Per*	*Pericles*
1H4	*Henry IV, Part 1*	*R2*	*Richard II*
2H4	*Henry IV, Part 2*	*R3*	*Richard III*
H5	*Henry V*	*RJ*	*Romeo and Juliet*
1H6	*Henry VI, Part 1*	Son(s)	Sonnet(s)
2H6	*Henry VI, Part 2*	*TA*	*Titus Andronicus*
3H6	*Henry VI, Part 3*	*Tem*	*The Tempest*
H8	*Henry VIII*	*TGV*	*The Two Gentlemen of Verona*
JC	*Julius Caesar*	*Tim*	*Timon of Athens*
KJ	*King John*	*TN*	*Twelfth Night*
KL	*King Lear*	*TrC*	*Troilus and Cressida*
LC	*A Lover's Complaint*	*TSh*	*The Taming of the Shrew*
LLL	*Love's Labour's Lost*	*VA*	*Venus and Adonis*
Luc	*The Rape of Lucrece*	*WT*	*The Winter's Tale*

OTHER KEY SOURCES

AV	Authorised Version of the Bible (1611).
B	E. Cobham Brewer, *Dictionary of Phrase and Fable*, new rev. edn.
B2	E. Cobham Brewer, *The Reader's Handbook.*
C	E. A. M. Colman, *The Dramatic Use of Bawdy in Shakespeare.*
CD	*The Century Dictionary.*
Cham	*Chambers Twentieth Century Dictionary.*
Cot	Randle Cotgrave, *A Dictionarie of the French and English Tongues.*
Dict. Cant. Crew	B. E., Gent., *A New Dictionary of the Terms Ancient and Modern of the Canting Crew . . . .*
F	Giovanni Florio, *A Worlde of Words, or Dictionarie in Italian and English.*
F&H	J. S. Farmer and W. E. Henley, *Slang and its Analogues.*
G	Frances Grose, *Dictionary of the Vulgar Tongue.*
K	Helge Kökeritz, *Shakespeare's Pronunciation.*
OED	*Oxford English Dictionary.*
P	Eric Partridge, *Shakespeare's Bawdy.*

P2	Eric Partridge, *A Dictionary of Slang and Unconventional English.*
TWR	Thomas W. Ross, *Chaucer's Bawdy.*
W	*Webster's New International Dictionary*, 2nd edn, unabridged.

See also Bibliography.

OTHER ABBREVIATIONS

A few very common Latin abbreviations (e.g., i.e., etc.) are excluded from this list, as are titles, county and American state abbreviations. 'Mistress' is abbreviated 'Mrs' only when it refers to married women.

abl.	ablative
adj.	adjective
adv.	adverb
alt.	alternative
anat.	anatomy
Anon.	Anonymous
arch.	archaic
biol.	biology
Bk	Book
bot.	botany
c.	century, canto, circa
cf.	*confer* (compare)
ch.	chapter
Cor.	Corinthians
Dan.	Daniel
dat.	dative
def.	definition
Deut.	Deuteronomy
dial.	dialect
dim.	diminutive
Du	Dutch
E.	of Ephesus
eccl.	ecclesiastical
ed.	editor, edited by
edn	edition
Eliz.	Elizabethan
Eph.	Ephesians
Epil.	Epilogue
equiv.	equivalent
esp.	especial(ly)
euph.	euphemism
fig.	figurative(ly)
Fig.	Figure
Fr	French
freq.	frequent(ly)
Ger	German
Gk	Greek
gram.	grammar
her.	heraldry
hort.	horticulture
ibid.	*ibidem* (in the same place)
imp.	imperative
incl.	including
Ir	Irish
Isa.	Isaiah
It	Italian
Jer.	Jeremiah
Jgs	Judges
Kgs	Kings
L	Latin
l.	line (pl. ll.)
Lam.	Lamentations
Lev.	Leviticus
lit.	literal(ly), literature
LL	Late Latin
ME	Middle English
med.	medical
MFr	Middle French
MHG	Middle High German
MLG	Middle Low German
mod.	modern
mus.	music
N.	Northern
naut.	nautical
n.d.	no date
no.	number
Num.	Numbers
obs.	obsolete
occ.	occasionally
OE	Old English
OFr	Old French
OHG	Old High German
orig.	original(ly)
p.	page (pl. pp.)
para.	paragraph
partic.	particularly
perh.	perhaps
Pet.	Peter
pers.	person
pfx	prefix

pl.	plural
pop.	popular
Port	Portuguese
prob.	probably
Prol.	Prologue
pron.	pronounced
Prov.	Proverbs
Ps.	Psalm
Pt	Part
ptg	pertaining
q.v.	*quod vide* (which see)
ref.	reference
rev.	revised
Rev.	Revelation
Rom.	Romans
S.	of Syracuse
Sam.	Samuel
Sc	Scottish
sfx	suffix
sg.	singular
Sh	Shakespeare(an)
sl.	slang
Song Sol.	Song of Solomon
Sp	Spanish
sp.	spelling
specif.	specifically
st.	stanza
s.v.	*sub voce* (under the word) (pl. s.vv.)
syn.	synonym
theol.	theology
trad.	tradition(ally)
transf.	transference
trs.	translation (pl. trs), translated (by), translator
Univ.	University
usu.	usual(ly)
var.	variant
VD	venereal disease
vol.	volume
vv.	verses
W.	Western

A

Abhor Whore (K). Abhorson: a whore's son (C; P).

Oth, IV.ii.163: 'I cannot say "whore":/ It doth abhor me now I speak the word'. See WORD/ whored.

MM, II.ii.29: 'There is a vice that most I do abhor,/ And most desire should meet the blow of justice' – the vice of fornication.

MM, II.iv.183: 'Before his sister should her body stoop/ To such abhorr'd pollution'. STOOP: to fornication. Pollution: seminal emission apart from coition (*OED*; TWR, s.v. Polucion); sexual defilement (P).

See WORSE, *Cym.*

Abomination, abominable Sodomy, bestiality. The 'abhomynable synne': committing homosexual acts (TWR). 'And there were also sodomites in the land: and they did according to all the abominations . . .' (1 Kgs 14:24); 'If a man also lie with mankind as he lieth with a woman, both of them have committed an abomination' (Lev 20:13). Deloney, *Jack of Newbury*, ch. 1: 'the bellwether of her flock fancying one of the ewes . . . and seeing Gratis the shepherd abusing her in abominable sort (subverting the law of nature)' ran against and killed him. Jonson, *Bartholomew Fair*, IV.iv: actors 'are an abomination: for the male among you putteth on the apparel of the female, and the female of the male'.

MM, III.ii.25: 'From their abominable and beastly touches' you drink and eat, the Duke tells the bawd, Pompey Bum (the posteriors – F&H), whose 'bum is the greatest thing about' him (ABOUT/ a butt). From a-*bum*-inable, BEASTLY (sodomitical) touches (copulations – C; P) he earns a living; 'in the beastliest sense' he is Pompey the Great.

2H6, IV.vii.44. After calling the Dauphin 'Monsieur Basimecu' (Fr *baisez ma cul*, kiss my arse), Cade similarly insinuates that Lord Say, whose very name, 'say', means SILK (effeminate), is a sodomite (see BUCKRAM). Say is 'filth' who 'traitorously corrupted the youth', using 'abominable words' unfit for Christian ear.

AC, III.vi.94: 'adulterous Antony, most large/ In his abominations, turns you off;/ And gives his potent regiment to a trull,/That noises it against us'. Antony's bisexuality was well known: 'he loved women – yes, and boys were all right, too; [he] . . . took his fun where he found it' – Ernest Mason, *Tiberius* (New York: Ballantine, 1960) p. 18. 'Large' means generous with one's body and licentious (*Ado*, II.iii.206). Antony turns (in the bed – C; P) off his wife and gives his potent regiment (genitals – P) to a TRULL (slut) given to anal sex (*trulla*, slut; *trullo*, anus, fart – F), who NOISES it (farts). This may be part of Cleopatra's 'infinite variety' (see VARIETY, buggery) that 'custom' (sexual usage – C; P) could not 'stale' (dull, whore).

See HOMO.

About A bout: a sexual bout (C; P); a round at any kind of exercise. *Aboutir*: confine in the end (Cot). *A bout*: the end of anything (Cot). Pun on the buttocks.

MM, III.ii.215. Mistress Overdone says Lucio maligns her in calling her bawd: 'he goes about to abuse me!' He goes *to* the *end* to ABUSE (misuse sexually).

KJ, I.i.170. The Bastard jests on his illegitimacy: 'Something about, a little from the right,/ In at the window, or else o'er the hatch . . . have is have, however men do catch.' Something, perh. some *thing* (the sex-organ – C; P), went about, lit. a roundabout way, a LITTLE

(L *-culus*; pun on *culus*, arse) from the RIGHT (L *rectum*), in at the window or O'ER/whore the hatch, floodgate or sluice, however men to CATCH (fornicate, impregnate).

2H4, III.ii.246. Mouldy (MOULD, coit) says that, if they draft him, 'my old dame will be undone now for one to do her husbandry and her drudgery' – undone husbandry, hers and the farm's. In the same vein he adds, 'she has nobody to do anything about her when I am gone'. A bout: 1601, the going and returning of the plough. No one will plough (P) the land or her; no one will 'do' (coit – C; P) ANY (ass) thing (pudendum – C; P). So Falstaff leaves him home for 'service' (coition – C; P).

2H4, III.ii.302. For his army Falstaff takes Wart, who 'shall charge you and discharge you with the motion of a pewterer's hammer, come off and on swifter than he that gibbets on the brewer's bucket'. Load and unload his gun, yes, but 'charge' means sexually (C; P) and 'discharge' is ejaculate semen (C; P). A 'caliver' (handgun with ref. to the *size* of the *bore*) is put 'into Wart's hand'; and Shallow says, 'He is not his craft's master: he doth not do it right.' Not master of his CRAFT (L *ars*/arse); told to 'manage me your caliver', he doesn't do it 'right' or *ritto* (right, stiff-standing – F). He reminds Shallow of a 'little quiver fellow, and a' would manage you his piece thus; and a' would about and about, and come you in and come you in'.

A *bout* is the head of an arrow (Cot). And Wart (small protruberance) reminds Shallow of someone with a little QUIVER (case) for arrows or (Cot) *flèches*/flesh, a little codpiece; and he would manage him (touch, handle, for sexual satisfaction – P) his little PIECE (penis) in a sexually ineffective manner – about and about and come you in and come you in – and achieve nothing (like the inadequate phallic erection of Adonis, who also could not 'manage': 'mounted for the hot encounter:/All is imaginary . . . He will not manage her, although he mount her;/That worse than Tantalus' is her annoy' – *VA*, 598). In this context, can one really say that this is only how Wart managed the caliver put into his hand and how the other fellow managed his 'quiver' and 'piece'?

See VIRTUE, *WT*; BRAINS, *Ham*; ABUSE, *MM*; SMILE, *Cor*; INDEED, *MWW*.

Absolute Of an ass/arse (hole). From OFr *assolu*, MFr *absolut.* Lute (L *lutum*, mud, a filthy fellow): mud. Cf. *TSh*, II.i.147, which puns on 'lute' (mud, clay solder – *OED*) and soldier/solder: Kate will 'prove a soldier [Folio, souldier]:/Iron may hold with her, but never lutes'.

Oth, II.i.193. The scene that concludes with Iago's decision to 'Make the Moor love me . . . For making him . . . an ass' starts the metaphor in Othello's greeting Desdemona, 'O my fair warrior!' and again, 'O my soul's joy! . . . My soul hath her content so absolute' – he cannot speak 'enough [ENOUGH, Fr *assez*] of this content'. (1) These two warriors (he is a 'soldier' – 36) CONTENT/contend, in amorous struggle (C; P); (2) Othello's SOUL/SOLE (bottom, arse) has its content, i.e. that which it contains, *ab-* (of) *soul-* (arse) *lute*. This self-appraisal is repeated in Emilia's calling him 'As ignorant as dirt': IGNORANT (lewd) arse-dirt (V.ii.164).

Roderigo, we next learn, is another of the 'base' men (217) with a 'soul' (223) who also loves Desdemona. And so does Iago, 'Not out of absolute lust' or lust of the ass, but as revenge because the 'Moor/Hath leap'd into my seat' (leap: copulate – C; P). Presumably he means Emilia's seat, but there is an ambiguity in 'my' seat, reinforced by two other of his phrases: (1) 'gnaw *my* inwards [INWARDS, lit. bowels]'; (2) 'content *my* soul' (italics added). Having been buggered (fig.), he shall bugger Othello.

Mac, I.iv.14. In a previous scene Duncan spoke of lost faith in one who shall no more 'deceive' him (L *fallo*). Now he says, 'There's no art/To find the mind's construction in the face:/He was a gentleman on whom I built/An absolute trust.'

Duncan's was the *absolute* trust of an ass or arse, who lacked real arse or force – as he says, the ART (L *ars*) to understand men. Cawdor was deceitful (L *fallax*, *-acis*) – had the phallus or penis, was potent and ambitious for power. And Duncan had failed to recognize this construction (erection) in Cawdor's FACE (buttocks) and MIND (arse). By contrast, the helpless Duncan built (erected) an absolute (asinine) trust on him. Macbeth then enters and Duncan greets him as 'worthiest cousin', failing again to recognise deceit. To *cozen* is to deceive (*R3*, IV.iv.222: 'Cousins, indeed; and by their uncle cozen'd').

AC, IV.xiv.117. Diomedes addresses Antony as 'Most absolute lord' toward the end of a scene in which Antony has seen himself as a degraded 'body' that could not hold its 'shape' (SHAPE, sexual organs), and has said, 'there is left us/ Ourselves to end ourselves. . . . [Cleopatra] has robb'd me of my sword.' All that is left him is to end (be an ass/ arse): Cleopatra has taken his sword (penis – C; P), symbol of manhood. He sees disgrace 'behind' him, refers twice to his 'baseness' (base or bottom), and then ineffectually tries to kill himself and must ask the guards to 'make an end/ Of what I have begun' – make an *end* of the job he had begun, of making an arse of himself.

H5, III.vii.27. In the puns on the Dauphin's openly bestial passion for his horse, his 'mistress' (see BEAST), is one contrasting his 'Pegasus' (PEGASUS, bestial lover) with 'any that treads but on four pasterns', or is, in his French language, *assolé*: 'settled (as a horse &c.) upon all his feet' (Cot). He would not 'change' his horse for any arse-hole. It is a 'most absolute and excellent horse' and 'enforces homage'. Absolute, being absolute in degree, cannot, of course, be compared; but MOST (*fin* – Cot) stresses its rump. His horse is EXCELLENT (lewd, partic. of the buttocks) and enforces HOMAGE (sodomy).

See COURTIER, *MWW*.

Abuse Use: copulate (C; P); abuse: adultery (P). It is also incest, prostitution, masturbation and sodomy. *Bougironné*: 'Buggered, abused by a Sodomite'; *lanterné*: 'abused, buggared' (Cot). 1 Cor 6:9: 'fornicators, nor idolaters, nor adulterers, nor effeminate, nor abusers of themselves with mankind'.

Per, I.i.126: 'As with foul incest to abuse your soul . . . By your untimely claspings with your child'. Abuse of the SOUL/ SOLE (bottom or arse).

MM, II.i.43. Pompey Bum, a 'parcel-bawd', and FROTH (q.v. for masturbatory puns), his customer, do 'nothing but use their abuses in common houses [brothels – C]'. See ABOMINATION.

Ham, II.ii.632. Hamlet fears the ghost is a 'devil' with 'power/ To assume a pleasing shape' – with POWER (potency of the arse; cunted) to *ass*ume a pleasing (erotically – C; P) SHAPE (genitals – *OED*). This DEVIL (bisexual) 'As he is very potent with such spirits,/ Abuses me to damn me'.

Hamlet, self-styled 'whore', 'drab' and 'ass' fears being abused (buggered) by the *potent* devil, fears being damned, made the *dam* of the devil (DAMN/ dam – K): in *CE*, IV.iii.54, the Courtezan is 'the devil's dam . . . thereof comes that the wenches say "God damn me"'. Hamlet suspects the devil is author of his thoughts, which are, after all, political heresy: cf. 'buggery' ('abominable heresy' and 'sodomy' – *OED*). See SPIRIT, RESOLVE.

TN, V.i.20. The Clown's foes tell him he is 'an ass', but his friends 'make an ass of' him, so 'by my friends I am abused'. His friends make an *ass* of him, abuse, bugger him; for them, he is 'the worse [WORSE/ whores]'.

Access Sexual entry.

TGV, III.i.109. The Duke pretends to admire a lady who is 'kept severely from resort of men,/ That no man hath access by day to her'. To the advice 'then, I would resort to her by night' he answers, 'Ay, but the doors be lock'd'. The sexual nature of the access is implicit in (1) both men's use of RESORT, a brothel (resorter: a brothel frequenter); (2) the locked DOORS (vulva) that bar the access.

Ham, II.i.110. Since Ophelia has just described the disarray in Hamlet's clothing on his visit to her closet, 'as you did command,/ I . . . denied/ His access to me' may be a sexual quibble. Especially since she equates her denying access with her father's command that had been to 'lock herself from his resort' (ii.143).

MM, II.iv.18. Angelo's servant tells him Isabella is at the door: 'One Isabel, a sister, desires access to you.' Angelo answers, 'Teach her the way. (*Exit Servant.*) O heavens!' Consumed by lust, he misinterprets *desires* access to mean the willingness of this virgin to submit to him sexually. And the servant's identification of her as a SISTER (she is both Claudio's sister and a novice to the sisterhood), he chooses to hear as meaning a whore (1550). Teach her the way: to coit – P.

Mac, I.v.45. Lady Macbeth calls on spirits to 'unsex' her, to 'Stop up the access and passage to remorse,/That no compunctious visitings of nature/Shake my fell purpose' – stop up the *access* to remorse, the vaginal PASSAGE. She wants no COMPUNCTIOUS (q.v.) visitings (L *com* + *punctum*, prick), no prick (penis – *OED*; P), no visits of NATURE (semen – *OED*) to SHAKE (in coitus; make impotent) her PURPOSE (buttocks). She rejects woman's role and attributes (*R3*, II.vii.211: 'gentle, kind, effeminate remorse').

This speech will echo tragically (1) in Macbeth's finding he has 'no spur/To prick the sides of my intent' (I.vii.25) – no SPUR (prick – *OED*) with which to prick or urge on his INTENT (sexual probing). All he has is 'Vaulting' (leaping coitally – C; P) ambition that 'falls on the other [side]'. Macbeth will fall on the *derrière* (Fr, the backside) – or on his arse. (2) It will echo also in Macbeth's despair at his 'barren sceptre' (III.i.62), the barren SCEPTRE (phallus) that leaves him childless and probably impotent.

His inability to ride the horse (common metaphor for to achieve with a woman) anticipates the personal and political disaster to come.

Accommodate Fornicate. *Accommoder une femme*: to use a woman (Cot). Easement: accommodation, entertainment (*OED*); sexual intercourse (TWR, s.v. Esement). Accommodation houses: brothels (F&H n.d.); a commode: 1700s, a bawd.

TrC, V.ii.194: 'a commodious drab [whore]'.

2H4, III.ii.72. Bardolph (who had been a-whoring with Falstaff – II.iv.290) reacts to an inquiry about Falstaff's 'wife', 'Sir, pardon; a soldier is better accommodated than with a wife.' Shallow: 'Accommodated! it comes of "accommodo": very good; a good phrase.' Bardolph insists it is not a phrase, he knows 'not the phrase' and will 'maintain the word with my sword to be a soldier-like word'.

Both men are right: (1) 'accommodated' is a good phrase because it puns on FRAYS, 16th c. for brawls and deflowers; (2) 'accommodated' is a WORD/is whored. In *MWW*, II.i.13, Falstaff will not say 'pity me; 'tis not a soldier-like phrase; but I say, love me' – not 'pity' but *love* and *accommodate* pass muster for being soldier-like (Sh's only two uses of this phrase – or word).

Oth, I.iii.239: 'I crave fit disposition for my wife . . . with such accommodation and besort/As levels with her breeding.' Newly married Othello craves accommodation fit (apt for love-making – C; P) for Desdemona's breeding – ostensibly her good upbringing, but a pun on pun on producing offspring. His use of 'accommodation' is innocent but it anticipates his future attack on his wife as a 'whore' and their home as a brothel where he pays 'money' to Desdemona's servant Emilia, whom he treats like the bawd.

Achitophel A pimp. See COUNSELLOR; SMOOTH, *2H4*.

Acorn (1) Conical head of the penis. Glans (L *glans*, acorn): 1650, the glans penis; and an acorn. *Balane*: an acorn; and the top of a man's yard, i.e. penis (Cot).

(2) Testicle. A nut: the glans penis (*OED*). Jove's nut: the acorn (*W*; *CD*). See NUT (testicle).

Cym, II.v.16. Posthumus envisions Iachimo's seduction of his wife: 'Like all a full-acorn'd boar, a German one,/Cried "O!" and mounted'. The blatant sexuality of the metaphor includes puns on (1) GERMAN/germen, a seed-vessel (*OED*) or semen (P); (2) the 'O' or pudendum (P); (3) mount – in coitus (*OED*; P). The usual gloss of a well-fed boar, full of the traditional food of the swine, mast or acorns, is hardly adequate to Posthumus's feelings about this well-hung seducer, this full-acorn'd *boar* – a prototype of lust (C), as in *VA*.

AYL, III.ii.248:

Celia. . . . take a taste of my finding him. . . . I found him under a tree, like a dropped acorn.
Rosalind. It may well be called Jove's tree, when it drops forth such fruit.

The acorn is God's fruit (reproductive seed and its envelope), in this case the nut or acorn. Celia puns on taking a taste (enjoying carnally – F&H; P); on a TASTE, i.e. a *test* (of God's forbidden fruit); and on the testes.

Both girls say the fruit *dropped*, Orlando's emotional and physical dejection ('the weakest kind of fruit/ Drops earliest' – *MV*, IV.i.116). Also, drop occurs freq. in clusters with stones (testicles), as in the bawdy 'The fall of every Phrygian stone will cost/ A drop of blood' (BLOOD, *TrC*). Orlando, too, says his fruit drops or HANGS (q.v.).

As Celia says, 'He was furnished like a hunter' (259) – FURNISHED (sexually equipped) for venery (hunting; sexual intercourse).

Acquaint(ance) See QUAINT.

(Ad)venture Copulate. Venture: prostitute (C). Middleton, *Michaelmas Term*, I.i: 'how looks thy little venturing cousin?' – 'like a lute that has all the strings broke; nobody will meddle with her' – 'there are doctors . . . will string her again, and make her sound as sweet' as ever: *A Chaste Maid in Cheapside*, IV.i: 'O venturous baggage!'

RJ, II.ii.84. Romeo says love 'lent me counsel' – LENT (yielded sexually) COUNSEL (a bawd's advice) – and, were Juliet on a far-away 'shore' (SHORE, brothel), he would still 'adventure for such merchandise' (i.e. that which is bought and sold). See DOVE, ANCIENT.

Per, I.i.22. With 'inflamed desire' for Antiochus's daughter, Pericles swears 'To taste the fruit of yon celestial tree,/ Or die in the adventure'. Tasting fruit was an Elizabethan concept for copulation (Marston, *The Insatiable Countess*, III: 'I'll lead the way to Venus's paradise, where thou shalt taste that fruit that made man wise'). Pericles will adventure, will TASTE (try sexually) the fruit from the celestial tree – an allusion to the eating of the fruit of the tree in paradise, and the introduction of mortality; hence he'll 'die in the adventure'.

2H6, II.i.101: 'thou lovedst plums well, that wouldst venture so'. As in *Per* above, a man ventured for fruit; he ventured the PLUM tree (q.v.), legs and pudendum.

H8, II.iii.25. An old courtesan would 'venture maidenhead for't [the crown]' and predicts that Anne, too, would 'venture an emballing' to get 'little England'.

See SHEEP, *MV*; TOMBOY.

Advocate Procurer, bawd. Attorneys' signs in the Netherlands read: 'Advocaat en Procureur, Mr –'. 'Procurator' and 'procureur' mean advocate but pun on 'procurer'. *Un advocatière*, Rabelais: 'ponce', pimp (F&H). This pun unites three scenes in *WT*.

II.ii.39. Paulina offers to be the Queen's 'advocate' and take her infant to its father, the King, who believes his queen an 'adulteress' and the baby a 'bastard'. 'Advocate' is sadly prophetic, for her greeting, 'I come/ From your good queen' elicits (iii.58) his sarcastic 'Good queen!' – GOOD (whore-like) QUEEN/ quean (harlot). Paulina refutes the implication: 'Good queen, my lord,/ Good queen; I say good queen'. But the King maintains the sexual guilt of both women by calling Paulina, the advocate, a 'most intelligencing bawd!'

IV.iv.766, 768. The above scene is linked to this comic one by two more bawdy puns on 'advocate', as a shepherd is off to speak to a different king but about the same infant, now grown into lovely Perdita.

> *Autolycus.* What advocate hast thou to him?
> *Shepherd.* I know not, an't like you.

Through a quibble on an't/ aunt, 'advocate' is equated with *aunt*: I know not aunt like you, says the shepherd to Autolycus, who had (iii.11) used 'aunts' to mean procuresses (*OED*; P). By l.827 Autolycus offers to 'tender [TENDER, offer sexually] your persons to his presence' in return for 'gold', i.e. be their aunt. He joins the list of those who are advocate (bawd) for Perdita.

> *Clown.* Advocate's the court-word for a pheasant: say you have none.

Shepherd. None, sir; I have no pheasant, cock nor hen.

'Courtesan' meant a prostitute, a courtier, and court language (of Italy): 1549, 'do speak the courtisane'. The Clown explains that Autolycus, who called himself 'courtier cap-a-pe', is a COURTIER (pimp), and when he says 'advocate' he uses court language, the court-word for what they, the rustics, mean by 'pheasant'. Like the quail (P), guinea-hen (P) and partridge (F&H), the pheasant too (F&H n.d.) – used only this once by Sh – means a bawd or courtesan. No *pheasant* may pun on no *faisans* (pheasants – Cot), no *feasance*, a legal term – court-word or advocate.

v.i.221. We come full circle with this last use of 'advocate'. Perdita's lover asks her father, the King, to win over his father to their marriage, to 'Step forth mine advocate'. But the King – believing himself a widower and not recognising his long-lost daughter – is smitten with her beauty and says if he were advocate he would 'beg your precious mistress' for himself. 'To beg (an advocate)' is to 'solicit' (*OED*): if advocate, the King would beg or solicit (pimp – P) for himself. And now it is the turn of the original 'advocate', Paulina, whom he had once accused of being a bawd, to reprimand *him* for his salaciousness and say his 'eye hath too much youth in't'.

Oth, III.iv.123. When Cassio asks Desdemona to be the 'means' to 'ransom me into his [Othello's] love again', she answers, 'My advocation is not now in tune'. 'Ransom' (price paid for redemption) reinforces the metaphor of Desdemona as MEANS (bawd), whom Cassio pays for her advocation or procuring of Othello's love.

As in *WT* above, advocate and solicitor (i.e. advocate and immoral importuner – P; *OED*) overlap. Desdemona speaks of her advocation and says 'thy solicitor shall rather die/Than give thy cause away' (iii.27) – portent of her very fate. Before he kills Desdemona, 'the strumpet', Othello tells her, 'If you bethink yourself of any crime/Unreconciled as yet to heaven and grace,/*Solicit* for it straight' (v.ii.28; italics added).

Affection Sexual desire, with emphasis on the buttocks. The seat of the affections and the affections themselves were the 'reins': (1) the loins; (2) the kidneys. *MV*, IV.i.50: 'Cannot contain their urine; for affection'. Affection meant an abnormality, a disease (*LLL*, II.i.230: 'infected', 'affected'): see EVIL, *Cor.*

Ham, I.iii.34: 'keep you in the rear of your affection'.

AYL, IV.i.212: 'my affection hath an unknown bottom', protests Ganymede, accused of misusing her sex in her 'love-prate' (PRAT(E), buttocks). See MISUSE.

TN, II.v.29, Malvolio: 'Maria once told me she [Olivia] did affect me: and I have heard herself come thus near, that, should she fancy, it should be one of my complexion.' Had Olivia come near/neer (the kidney), had she affected him (this 'affectioned ass' – see CON), did she FANCY (amorous inclination) one of his 'complexion' or COLOUR/It *culare* (arse), then she did affect, desire, an ass/arse.

Tem, III.i.75: 'Fair encounter/Of two most rare affections! Heavens rain grace/On that which breeds between 'em!' In this encounter (love-match – P) of two MOST (Fr *fin(e)*; pun on buttocks) RARE (dial. form of *rear*) affections (these two young asses he affectionately mocks), Prospero asks the heavens to rain on what breeds, yet wants the reins applied till marriage, for if Miranda's virginity be broken, 'No sweet *as*persion shall the heavens let fall/To make this contract [CONTRACT: sexual union] grow' (IV.i.18; italics added).

See FAST, *Cym*; CREATURE, *H8*.

Age(d) A whore; venereally diseased. An age/ague pun, with ref. to the sweating stage of the ague, *sweating* being a sign of lechery as well as a sign of VD and one of its treatments (C; P). Jonson, *Bartholomew Fair*, II.v: 'how she drips! she's able to give a man the sweating Sicknesse, with looking on her!'. Covent Garden or Drury Lane ague was syphilis, 17th c. In *R2*, II.i.72, the sick and 'aged Gaunt' is told he presumes on 'an ague's privilege' – pun on 'privilege of age' (*Ado*, v.i.60).

2H4, I.ii.111, Falstaff: 'I heard say your lordship was sick . . . Your lordship, though not clean past your youth, hath yet some smack of age in you, some relish of the saltness of time'. Being 'not clean' past his youth cannot mean the number of his years – in which the Chief Justice is far past his youth – but refers to 'not clean' as not chaste and not cured of contagious disease (*curer*, to clean, to recover – Cot: 'thus I cured him; and this way will I . . . wash your liver as clean as a sound sheep's heart' – *AYL*, III.ii.442; 'fornication, adultery, and all uncleanliness' – *MM*, II.i.82). His lordship is sick, has some smack (a sexual innuendo – P) of the whore, some relish of the saltness, i.e. lechery, of time. 'Smack' and 'relish' are Fr *gout* and pun on GOUT (a venereal symptom). That his smack of *age*, the whore, is VD, is the smack (1570, kiss) of the whore, is reaffirmed when Falstaff says the King, too, is sick and 'fallen into this same whoreson apoplexy', a 'whoreson tingling'.

Cor, III.i.177. Coriolanus and friends throw off a tribune who has attacked him: 'Hence, old goat!'; 'Aged sir, hands off'; 'Hence, rotten thing! or I shall shake thy bones/ Out of thy garments.' 'Aged sir' and 'old goat' pun on *age* and Gk *aigos* (a goat, prototype of lechery – C; P). 'Aged' and OLD both pertain to the whore and her disease: the 'aged sir' is and has a rotten thing – a rotten (infected with VD – C; P) thing (penis – P). And it will be easy for Coriolanus to shake his aged bones, ague'd with the bone-ache (VD – C; P). The ague is any fit of shaking (*OED*), and to SHAKE (1450, a fever sign) is also a symbol of loose living.

These puns convey a central theme, Coriolanus's contempt for the people, 'The common file – a plague!' (I.vi.43); and for their tribunes, 'The tongues o' the common mouth' (III.i.22). The people are common (whore-like – C; P) – with the whores' plague (L *lues*) diseases, their lues or syphilis.

Tem, IV.i.260:

Prospero. Go charge my goblins that they grind their joints
With dry convulsions, shorten up their sinews
With aged cramps, and more pinch-spotted make them
Than pard or cat o' mountain.
Ariel. Hark, they roar!

What might seem a list of unrelated non-bawdy afflictions is really a list of venereal symptoms – fulfilment of Prospero's threat in 1.192: 'I will plague them all,/ Even to roaring.' And already they roar from his plague, the lues or VD. First, 'grind' (F&H; *macinio* – F) and 'charge' (C; P) mean assail sexually; charge (with gonorrhea – C; as in *2H4*, II.iv.58) their JOINTS (sex-acts; penises). Second, SHORTEN/*scortare* (F), connotes the shortened or impotent, diseased penis suffered if one associates with whores (L *scortari*). Third, 'aged cramps' rewords 'old cramps' – Prospero's curse of I.ii.369, also linked to bone-aches (VD – C; P): 'I'll rack thee with old cramps,/ Fill all thy bones with aches!' Fourth, convulsions are violent shaking, like the ague, and pun on age that also shakes ('shakes for age' – *TA*, I.i.188). And these convulsions are DRY (impotent and syphilitic). Last, they shall be pinch-spotted ('the pox pinches' – *2H4*, II.ii.258) with spots of the PARD/ lepered (q.v.) and CAT O'MOUNTAIN (whore). Not age's innocent cramps, but ague'd bone-ache, syphilitic cramps, were Prospero's charge.

All/Awl (1) Penis: the awl is a hole-boring tool. Dekker, *The Shoemaker's Holiday*, I.i: 'if you take her husband away from her a-night, you undo her . . . for he's as good a workman at a prick and an awl as any is in our trade' – 'O let him stay, else I shall be undone.'

(2) Vulva: a hole/ whole (TWR; P) or all – a 'hole' being the vulva (C; P).

Mac, III.ii.4. A sexual metaphor for the political reality. Lady Macbeth: 'Nought's had, all's spent,/ Where our desire is got without content.' 'Nought' and *naught* (Elizabethans did not consistently distinguish) pun on the sex-act (F&H; C; P), as in *R3*, I.i.97. The naughty (i.e. wicked) murder is done. Coitus has been had (carnally possessed – C; P), is over with; the all or penis is spent (depleted of semen – F&H; C; P), can do no more. Political and sexual desire have been got without CONTENT: (1) satisfaction; (2) that which is contained ('zeal strives to content, and the contents/ Dies in the zeal' – *LLL*, V.ii.518). Nothing is in her womb. Sexual intercourse between the Macbeths has been fruitless and probably ceased: a tragic outcome of her having called on the spirits to 'unsex me' (COMPUNCTIOUS). This sentence restates her husband's anguish (III.i.61) that, unlike Banquo, he is not 'father to a line of kings' but has a 'fruitless crown' and 'barren sceptre' (a spent SCEPTRE, penis – or awl). Desire without content is an interesting reversal of *contenter ses désirs* (to copulate – F&H, s.v. Ride, n.d.).

H8, II.iii.67. Amidst lewd jests on whether Anne will VENTURE (prostitute – C) a maidenhead to be a queen, the Lord Chamberlain enters and offers her the title of Marchioness. Anne: 'I do not know / What kind of my obedience I should tender; / More than my all is nothing'. The pun on 'all' as a whole / hole is repeated in 'nothing' (C; 'O' – P). She need not worry; nothing more than her 'all' is expected: it is the KIND (sexual organs; sex – *OED*) she is expected to TENDER for the title. Paying in kind meant, then as now, in goods instead of money. Cf. *MV*, I.iii.86: 'woolly breeders . . . doing of the deed of kind'. (NOTHING / NOTING, copulating.)

R3, II.iv.52. Queen Elizabeth, worried over the King's death and the vacant throne, says, 'Ay me, I see the downfall of our house. . . . Insulting tyranny begins to jet / Upon the innocent and aweless throne. . . . I see, as in a map, the end of all.' The all / awl or penis pun clarifies the old puzzle over this use of 'aweless', used one other time, in *KJ*, I.i.266, where it means without awe or (as Onions says) fearless. That definition, however, not working here, it is hypothesised that 'aweless' means that the throne does not inspire awe, though Onions adds that this meaning is 'rare, in sense not freq. in Eliz. period'.

But 'aweless' as a pun on awl-less tells us exactly what the throne lacks: a man, an awl, a penis, symbol of potency and power. The Queen sees the downfall, the phallic exhaustion, of her house (HOUSE / hose, penis) – the end of *all* – as opposed to the tyranny that begins to JET (1600, a protruding part; sexual spasm – P2), that has the phallus and power. (See all–awe–withal quibble in *H5*, I.ii.216–25, again apropos of a king's 'powers'.)

And so the throne gets Richard III, last of the Plantagenets, Richard who opened the play with a long description of his physical (phallic?) inadequacies (see Index), but who is long on 'tyranny' (v.ii.2; iii.168) into which went his energies.

Son 31. Concluding 'And thou, all they, hast all the all of me', this sonnet uses 'all' seven times in much the same way that Sons 134–6 use the notorious 'will' to mean sexual desire and the genitals (C; P).

JC. For quibbles on the all and awl, see Introduction, pp. xi–xiii.

Altar The arse. L *aras*, *aris*: altar, as in *amicus usque ad aras*, a friend even to the altar (of sacrifice); or *pro aris et focis*, for altars and firesides.

VA, 103, Venus: 'I have been woo'd . . . by the stern and direful god of war. . . . Over my altars hath he hung his lance, / His batter'd shield, his uncontrolled crest, / And for my sake hath learn'd to sport and dance, / To toy, to wanton, dally'.

Her boast opens with two arse puns: (1) the STERN or buttocks; (2) the god of WAR / whore, Mars or *Ares*. Over her altars, her arse, he hath poised his martial gear, his genitals: (1) his penis or lance (P); (2) his scrotum, the shield – a pun on shield (Gk *sakos*) and bag (*sakkos*); a 'bag' being the scrotum (P) or the 'bagge of the genitras' (*TWR*). His shield is explicitly BATTERED from coition. His 'uncontrolled crest': a quibble on the cresting action of the genitals, the crest of the martial helmet, and the crest or tuft on the head of a *cock*.

All this he does for Venus's SAKE / *sakkos*, her bag (to 'bag', 14th–17th c., meant to beget, conceive – F&H: 'Well, Venus shortly bagged, and ere long was Cupid bred'). For the sake of Venus, the god of war (Mars or Ares) hung his gear over her alt*ars*, her arse, and learned to sport, dance, toy, wanton, and dally – each one of which is a pun on to copulate (TWR; C; P). Though he has only one lance, one shield and one crest, they were hung over her alt*ars* (pl.). Cf. Lyly, *Endymion*, I.iii:

Tophas. Learned? I am all Mars and Ars.
Samias. Nay, you are all mass and ass.

1H4, IV.i.116. Vernon describes the virility of Harry and his comrades, 'All furnish'd, all in arms' – all FURNISHED (sexually endowed), ALL in ARMS (both words punning on the penis) –

'all plumed [PLUMES, penises] . . . Glittering in golden coats [COATS/ cods – K] . . . full of spirit [SPIRIT: ardour; semen] . . . Wanton as youthful goats, wild as young bulls'; Harry himself, 'cuisses on his thighs, gallantly arm'd' did 'Rise' and 'vaulted' (verbs of phallic erection and copulation – F&H; P) with 'ease [EASE, ass/ arse] into his seat', witching the world with his 'horsemanship' (coital skill – P). See ANGEL for the rest of the metaphor.

This is the enraging erotic picture that sets Hotspur so 'on fire' that he must destroy it, convert the glittering and golden image into one that is 'hot and bleeding' (red was a conventional epithet of gold – *OED*): 'Let them come . . . like sacrifices in their trim,/ And to the fire-ey'd maid of smoky war/ All hot and bleeding will we offer them: /The mailed Mars shall on his altar sit/ Up to the ears in blood.' Let them come in their *trim* (F&H; P): (1) their plumes and coats; (2) to possess sexually or deflower. 'Trim' evokes the blood of deflowering – these young men are sacrificed to the *maid* of war and the *mailed* Mars, bloody sacrifices to the alt*ars* of both (for the loss of 'l', see K, p. 312: childe/ chide; wilde/ wide).

No longer is Harry the 'feather'd Mercury' who rose and vaulted; gone is the metaphor of potency, of the FEATHER (penis). Each element of the conceit is debased: no longer fleet Mercury, but the mailed Mars who *sits*, and no longer at ease in his seat, but on his altar (arse) up to his EARS/ arse in blood (Mars was the heraldic name for the tincture gules or red, 1572). 'Harry to Harry, shall, hot horse to horse' – HORSE/arse.

Alter (1) Copulate. Lit. change, substitute one thing for another; obs. exchange.

(2) Assume alternate sexual role. 'Alter' is to vary. L *alter*: the other, opposite. Dekker and Middleton, *The Honest Whore I*, IV.iii: 'Y'are changde, y'are altred' – 'Changde sir, why true . . . maisters serve their prentiss: Ladies their Servingmen, men turn to women' – 'And women turne to men.' Pun on one sex serving (*OED*; P) and turning to (P) another for copulation. *Positions* are altered (who serves whom); a sex-change is undergone.

TN, II.v.172. A forged letter says Olivia 'would alter service with thee': (1) Malvolio would be her lord, she his servant; (2) they would have *altar* service, would marry; (3) they would 'alter' or exchange *service* (coitally – *OED*; TWR; P).

MWW, II.i.52. Mrs Ford could 'be knighted' if she were to 'go to hell' for an 'eternal moment' – so ludicrous a phrase we must suspect punning. Mrs Page: 'What? thou liest! Sir Alice Ford! These knights will hack; and so thou shouldst not alter the article of thy gentry.' 'Sir', though dial. for women, here stresses the pun on 'be knighted' and *benighted*, i.e. involved in moral darkness ('go to hell'). Hack: prostitute, bawd (F&H; W; *OED*); and fornicate (P, s.v. Hick). This is what the knight Sir John would do, offering his sexual services solely to get at her husband's purse, and what he would have her do. She would alter or change (1606, exchange of merchandise) for his the article (joint connecting two parts of the body) of her GENTRY/ gender.

The puns on adultery are clear. Is the nature of the copulation also clear? Both Falstaff and her husband anticipate that the encounter will be sexually bestial: (1) Falstaff identifies himself and Mrs Ford with the bull Jove and Europa (v.v); (2) Mr Ford calls his wife, himself and/ or Falstaff a MONSTER (homosexual; see SHARE, SHOW); (3) he ends the scene planning to pimp for Falstaff and his wife: 'if she be otherwise, 'tis labour well bestowed'. If she is honest, good; but if she be OTHER (L *alter*), an ass/ arse, it will have been labour or lechery (*besongner*, to labour or lecher with – Cot; TWR) WELL (whore-like) BESTOWED (like a beast). Cf. Jonson's use of 'change' for sexual bestiality in *Volpone*, III.vi: 'My eunuch sing . . . Whilst we, in changed shapes, act Ovid's tales,/ Thou, like Europa now, and I like Jove . . . and, for a change,/ To one of our most artful courtezans . . . I will meet thee in as many shapes' (SHAPE, sex-organs, male and female – *OED*).

This leads to the only unexplored phrase, 'thou liest!' and its possible pun on LIE (bugger). Was her friend's warning not to *alter* her gentry or gender a warning not to go to hell for buggery as well as adultery? 'Buggery' also meant heresy (*OED*), for which the trad. punishment was burning ('Transparent heretics, be burnt for liars' – *RJ*, I.ii.96). Is this the reason for Mrs Ford's oxymoron, her ETERNAL (lit. infernal, damned) *moment* in 'hell'? Mrs Ford's next line was 'We burn daylight' – see BURN DAYLIGHT (wanton revelling).

This scene, which begins with Mrs Ford's asking Mrs Page for 'counsel' (COUNSEL, to play the whore, bawd), ends with Mrs Page's suggestion they 'consult' (counsel) together.

MV, IV.i.242, Shylock: 'There is no power in the tongue of man / To alter me: I stay here on my bond.' But the bond (L *copula*) is denied him and he *is* altered (is, on that score, screwed or buggered, fig. castrated). He loses *copula* / copula (sexual union), manhood, just as he had earlier lost the flower of his sexual union, Jessica, and with her (II.viii.20) his 'Two stones' or testicles (JEWEL), a 'sealed bag' (SEAL, scrotum).

Gratiano says (IV.i.366) Shylock does not have left 'the value of a cord' with which to 'hang' himself – does not have left rope (cord for hanging – *OED*) or ROPE (the penis). He cannot 'stay' a man, for a stay meant a rope and a prop; and, as Shylock says (375), 'You take my house when you do take the prop / That doth sustain my house; you take my life / When you do take the means whereby I live.' They take his HOUSE (penis), his LIFE (penis), his prop or penis (Middleton, *A Chaste Maid in Cheapside*, III.ii: a cuckold praises his wife's lover who 'with a prop upholds my wife and me' – with his prop regularly *upholds* her pregnant belly and generously *supports* them all).

They alter or emasculate Shylock. Gratiano, who was even willing that his wife die, or, as he put it (291), go to 'heaven' so that she might entreat 'some power to change this currish Jew' (change: make a sex alteration; cf. Jonson, above), says render him 'A halter gratis' – a h*alter*, like the puns in Arden / harden, ear / hear, etc. (K).

See TIGER, *Cor*.

An/Anne An ass. Fr *âne*: an ass; also a dunce. Though spelled *asne* (Cot), it was pronounced *âne*, the 's' sound having started to disappear from pronunciation as early as the 11th c., as in so many French words; see E. Bourciez, *Précis de phonetique française* (Paris: Klincksieck, 1958) pp. 155–9.

MWW, I.iv.133–7, Mistress Quickly: 'You shall have An fool's-head of your own. No, I know Anne's mind for that: never a woman in Windsor knows more of Anne's mind than I.' See An / Anne (K) for relevance to a fool's head. But there are other puns based on the French doctor's language. Dr CAIUS (himself an ass) will not 'have' *Anne* Page – Mistress Quickly twice says she know's Anne's MIND (ass / arse). Instead he will have *An* fool's head, the head of an *âne* or ass (like Bottom's in *MND*). He will have an fool's head of his OWN, his ane or ain (Sc); cf. Bottom's 'you see *an ass*-head of your *own* – *MND*, III.i.120; italics added.

Caius says he will marry Anne Page (*un page*: a serving-boy – Cot) and he does: 'By gar . . . I ha' married un garçon, a boy' (V.v.220).

See ANNUAL, *H8*; ANY; BEHIND, *Ado*; YEAR, *Ado*.

Ancient Bawd, whore. *Ancien*: stale (Cot); and a 'stale' is a whore (*OED*; P). 'Ancient' means hoary (hoar / whore – P; K). Dekker, *The Honest Whore II*, IV.iii: Mrs Horseleech is 'A woman of a good house, and an ancient, shee's a Bawde'; *The Guls Hornbook*, Proem: Dekker invokes Sylvanus, identified with satyrs and distinguished for lasciviousness, 'venerable father of antient (and therefore hoary) customs'.

RJ, II.iv.150. In a series of ribald puns at the Nurse's expense, Mercutio hails her as 'A bawd, a bawd, a bawd! So ho!' and launches into obscene verse on 'something stale and hoar' and 'an old hare hoar'. A bawd (1592) was a hare; and 'So ho', a hunting-cry, reinforces their identity here. His mockery culminates in 'Farewell, ancient lady' – reestablishing her as the bawd, the stale (*ancien*), and the hare / hoar / whore.

III.v.235: 'Ancient damnation! . . . Go, counsellor', says Juliet to the Nurse, who had already once played the bawd (fig.) in irresponsibly promoting the forbidden intercourse of Juliet and Romeo, and is now with equal alacrity counselling not only an immoral but an illegal liaison with Paris. The implication of bawd in *ancient* damnation is repeated in COUNSELLOR (bawd).

IV.i.111. Juliet will be entombed in 'that same ancient vault' and 'a vault, an ancient receptacle' (iii.39). L *cella* is a vault, a receptacle and a brothel. Hence the ancient vault and ancient receptacle are brothels (for ancients), a metaphor Romeo develops in imagining that in 'This vault' Juliet is kept as 'paramour' by 'amorous' Death, the pimp (see INTEND).

These *double entendres* in 'ancient' etc. do not mean that the Nurse is lit. a bawd or Juliet a whore; but they do reflect the way Juliet is bandied about as a sexual pawn by all the adults. And perhaps Sh was not in total disagreement with his source, Brooke's *Tragicall Historye of Romeus and Juliet* (1562): 'this tragical matter written, to describe . . . a couple of unfortunate lovers, thralling themselves to unhonest desire . . . attempting all adventures of peril for th'attaining of their wished lust . . . abusing the honourable name of lawful marriage to cloak the shame of stolen contracts' ('To the Reader'). See LADYBIRD.

Oth, I.i.33. In Dekker's *The Honest Whore II*, V.ii, a whore tells her bawd to walk faster: 'are not you, bawd, a whore's ancient, and must not I follow my colours?' This pun may go a long way toward answering what is for many the enigma of Iago, Othello's 'ancient', an ensign, bearer of the colours. Iago pretends to pander for Roderigo, to be the 'means' (MEANS, a pander) to his 'desires' for Desdemona (II.i), whom he will 'enjoy' if he 'put money in [his] purse' (I.iii) – to which purse Iago has 'the strings' (II.i.).

With the characteristic significance of first speeches, Iago's concludes, 'Abhor me' (the same ABHOR/whore pun that Desdemona makes). His second speech, in which he says, 'I know my price' (his *mark*et price or whore's fee – C; P) concludes, 'And I – God bless the mark! – his Moorship's ancient.' This elicits Roderigo's 'By heaven, I rather would have been his hangman.' There are several parallels: one calls on God, the other on heaven. Roderigo would rather have been Othello's hangman, Fr *pendeur*, than have been his ancient, his *pander* or whore (see PAINT for other pander/*pendeur* puns).

'God bless the mark' was a parenthetic expression of irony or scorn, used to avert evil (*MV*, II.ii.25). It is a singularly pertinent phrase for Iago, since 'mark' (which he uses seven times) is another meaning of ensign (L *insigne*, a distinctive mark). Iago is asking God's blessing for himself and expressing contempt in 'his Moorship's ancient', a quibble on Othello the *Moor* and *moor* or anchor ship.

Why does he replace the conventional 'his worship' with this strange compound of 'Moor' and 'ship', meant to be heard as such, like the pun in 'what news with your mastership?' – 'With my master's ship?' (*TGV*, III.i.281)? Because our attention is meant to be drawn to Iago's role as his Moor's ship (L *navis*) or *knave*. Sh frequently puns on SHIP and 'knave' (whore). The only other military ancient in Sh is another 'knave', one who openly calls himself 'old' and 'bawd' (two aspects of ancient): 'Aunchient Pistol! you scurvy, lousy knave, God pless you!' (*H5*, V.i.19, 89–91). And God is asked to bless him, too. (See SWAGGERER, pimp – as Pistol is called in *2H4*.)

And the Moor's knave is ancient ('his Moorship's ancient'). Iago defines his relationship with Othello: 'I follow him to serve my turn upon him. . . . You shall mark/Many a duteous and knee-crooking knave,/That . . . Wears out his time, much like his master's ass . . . and when he's old, cashier'd' (I.i.42). 'Serve one's turn' is satisfy sexually (C; P – *TA*, II.i.95; *LLL*, I.i.300) and Iago serves his turn upon Othello. A 'turn' is a sexual bout (P; *Oth*, IV.i.264); it is also a stratagem or trick. And, though he contrasts himself with knee-crooking knaves, it is a common Sh device for a character inadvertently to describe himself in delineating others. Iago's wife says a 'knave' tricked Othello: 'The Moor's abused [ABUSE, sexual misuse] by some most villanous knave' (IV.ii.139); Iago calls his own schemes 'knavery' (I.iii.400).

He is the knave who wore out (coitally – C; P) his time like his master's ass, cashier'd, laid aside, passed over for the lieutenancy (I.i.9–32) in favour of Cassio: his jealousy emerges in 'the knave is handsome, young' – the sexual jealousy of the older (ancient) discarded knave. He calls Cassio ignorant of battle as a SPINSTER (whore), whereas he, Iago, fought 'at Rhodes, at Cyprus and on other grounds Christian and heathen'. At *Rhodes*: with *roads* (prostitutes – C; P)? at *Cyprus*, licentious island of Aphrodite: with *Cyprians* (prostitutes – *OED*)?

His name is his character: *Santiago*, Sp war-whoop on engaging with Moors or other infidels. Santiago is St James, St Jaques (*AW*, III.v.98). Iago, James, Jaques (Sp a braggart, smooth combing of the hair; also a pimp – Rosensweig). Iago is Jack, the figure that strikes the bells ('Jack o' the clock' – *R2*, V.v.60). See FIX for more on this metaphor. He wears out his time much like his master's ass: *he* is the Jack (lit. knave, male ass), the knee-crooking knave: he kneels and swears (III.iii.479) 'I am your own for ever' – Othello's OWN (ass). (Knave–jack puns: *RJ*, II.iv.160–1; IV.v.147.)

Had Iago been Othello's ancient, his ass, in more ways than one – his military whore, his pander? And, if so, would not this give new, strong reason for Iago's intense, obsessive jealousy of Desdemona and every male in the play?

Angel Catamite, male paramour. Ingle, enghle (Jonson), ningle (F&H): prob. *inghel*, *enghel*, angel. *Cinedo*: ingle, 'buggring' boy (F).

'Angel' and 'Fallen angel': homosexual (Rodgers). Gen 19:1–7: 'there came two angels to Sodom' and Lot begged 'the men of Sodom' to do no wickedness to them, offering his 'daughters' instead. Certain revisionists, making a case that the Bible is not against sodomy, say 'know them [the angels]' meant only get acquainted; a futile exercise since in a similar story, Jgs 19:22–5, the phrase has unquestionable sexual intent. In the 17th c. some thought angels made love though 'there be neither lust nor difference of sex amongst them' (1659 – Broadbent, p. 147). This idea accords with Plato's views on homosexual or 'heavenly' love (see HEAVENLY, *TGV*).

1H4, III.iii.40. Pun on ingle: (1) a fire; (2) a catamite (*OED*). Bardolph's 'face' reminds Falstaff of 'hell-fire', a 'ball of wildfire', a 'bonfire-light'. Falstaff could 'swear by thy face . . . "By this fire, that's God's angel" '. And he does swear/*suer* (sweat – Cot) 'By this fire', by this ingle, by the FACE (arse) of Bardolph – that is, 'God's angel' in hell-fire. That would be the *fallen* angel Lucifer (see DEVIL, reputedly hermaphroditic, bisexual, who 'pricked down' Bardolph – *2H4*, II.iv.359).

MND, III.i.132. When *Bottom* 'will sing' (coit – P), he chooses the song of a turd. He sings of the 'ousel cock' (blackbird, *Turdus merula*) and 'throstle' (song thrush, *Turdus musicus*). His song awakens Titania: 'What angel wakes me . . . ?' (See THROSTLE.)

Cym, III.vi.43. Imogen, in boy's clothes, is called 'a fairy'; 'By Jupiter, an angel . . . No elder than a boy!' By Jupiter (L equiv. of Zeus, elder lover of GANYMEDE/catamite), Imogen looks like an angel and a BOY (catamite, L corruption of Ganymede). In IV.ii Belarius says he 'must be our house*wife*' (italics added; see HOUSEWIFE, whore) and the enamoured Arvirasus exclaims, 'How angel-like he sings!' How LIKE (Gk *homoios*, *homo-*) an angel he sings (lures sexually – C; P). See WAG.

MWW, II.ii.73, Mistress Quickly: 'I had myself twenty angels given me this morning; but I defy all angels . . . they could never get her so much as sip on a cup with the proudest of them all'. Gold angels are offered by ingles 'smelling so sweetly, all musk'; but Mrs Ford won't sip a CUP (sign of GANYMEDE, cup-bearer and boy lover of Zeus) with these effeminates. These angels are the 'lisping hawthorn-buds, that come like women in men's apparel' (III.iii.79).

1H4, III.iii.200:

Prince. O, my sweet beef, I must still be good angel to thee: the money is paid back again.
Falstaff. O, I do not like that paying back; 'tis a double labour.

In *MWW* above, Falstaff compared himself to Zeus, 'Jove [who] wast a bull' and makes 'a man a beast [BEAST, sodomite]'. Here again he is sweet *beef* (see PACIFY for sexual implications) to his 'sweet wag', Hal (I.ii.18, 26, 50). WAG: effeminate boy. *Zanzeri*: 'Ganimeds . . . Nigles [ingles], Wanton boies. Also knavish wags'; *zanzerare*: to ingle boys or wantonly play with them against nature (F). In *2H4*, I.ii.186, Falstaff is 'ill angel' (ILL, L and It *male*) to Hal, who is here the good angel and gold angel (gold coin). Hal is the angel/ingle who PAID/Gk *paid* (a homosexual boy), *back* again. Falstaff complains of DOUBLE (homosexual) labour, lechery (*besongner*, to labour, to do or lecher with – Cot; TWR).

IV.i.108. See ALTAR for the beginning of the metaphor in which Hal, like 'an angel dropp'd down from the clouds,/To turn and wind a fiery Pegasus/And witch the world with noble horsemanship' – puns on the gold coin orig. called an angel–noble, then either half separately. This *noble* Prince, this *angel*, dropped down to turn (C; P) and WIND ('turn her and wind her' – 16th c. for coit) a fiery (sexually ardent – C; P; ingle: fire) or ingle-like PEGASUS (gelding, eunuch), as if to WITCH (a bisexual, a castrater), to screw or bugger the whole world with his noble 'horsemanship' (sexual prowess – P) – symbol for his military vigour. See *H5*, III.vii.58, where 'horsemanship' is again tied to Pegasus and sexuality.

Ham, III.iii.69. Claudius's speech that starts 'my offence is rank, it smells to heaven' uses anal metaphors to convey the unnaturalness of what he goes on to call 'A brother's murder' – what the Ghost had called 'Murder most foul . . . But this most foul, strange and unnatural'. Claudius: 'Help, angels! Make assay! Bow, stubborn knees'. For his foul, rank-smelling murder of one of rank; for his rank (in sexual heat) OFFENCE (coitus, with esp. ref. to the buttocks); for the STRANGE and UNNATURAL (both meaning sexually deviant) fig. buggery of his brother and for the literal offence of fornication with his brother's wife – Claudius calls on angels to help him make *ass*ay, and to bow or bend (Gk *ankylos*; L *angulus*) his knees.

R3, IV.i.69. Anne married Richard when he had scarce washed the blood 'from his hands/ Which issued from my other angel husband'. 'Other angel' is a deliberate ambiguity: (1) her first one, an angel in character and/ or in heaven; (2) Richard the CROOKED (L *angulus*) or impotent, another (sort of) angel husband: 'never yet one hour in his bed/ Have I enjoy'd the golden dew of sleep,/ But have been waked by his timorous dreams'. Anne had called him a bugger (UNNATURAL) who dreamt on nought 'but butcheries' (but/ butt BUTCHERY, buggery). In his bed she lacks the golden DEW/ It *due* (two, testes) of SLEEP (sexual intimacy) with her impotent husband, who she fears 'will . . . shortly' (pun on his SHORT will, i.e. penis – C; P) get rid of her. Yes, she has 'been waked' and will be waked (the vigil by a dead person, as in 'wakes and wassails' – *LLL*, V.ii.318) or killed by Richard's dreams (of another marriage); for, in the next scene twice Richard says, 'Anne . . . is sick and like to die' – Anne, whom he had wooed, saying, 'Your beauty, which did haunt me in my sleep/ To undertake the death of all the world'.

See ALTAR, *1H4*; PERFECT, *TGV*.

Anger, angry Phallic erection; pregnant. *Engain*: anger; *engainer*: to sheathe, to put up into the sheath (L *vagina*, sheath for the sword) – Cot. *Enger*: to extend itself, make grow, fill with increase; *s'ingerer*: to thrust in (Cot). Anger: 16th c., inflamed state of any part of the body. Dryden, Song from *An Evening's Love*: 'Anger rouzes love to fight/ And his only bayt is,/ 'Tis the spurre to dull delight,/ And is but an eager bite,/ When desire at height is' (*Penguin Book of Restoration Verse*, p. 158). Anger *rouses* love; it is the 'spurre' (prick – *OED*).

Oth, V.i.11. Since Act I Iago has angered Roderigo in both senses: exasperated him and aroused him sexually with 'thou shalt enjoy her [Desdemona]'. 'I have rubb'd this young quat almost to the sense,/ And he grows angry . . . Every way makes my *gain*' (italics added). This follows a quick-fire succession of puns in which he twice tells Roderigo to 'stand' (erect phallus – C; P), wear his 'good rapier bare, and put it home' (*engain* it) – rapier, penis symbol; put, place coitally (P); HOME, vulva – and 'fix [FIX, coit] most firm thy resolution [RESOLUTION: coition; testicles]'. Roderigo, in turn, fears to 'miscarry in't', lacks devotion 'to the deed [coitus – P]' and yet concludes, 'Forth, my sword'.

A 'quat' is a pustule or 'small boil'; it was 'Applied contemptuously to a (young) person' (*OED*). Since (1) 'rub' means caress manually, specif. masturbate (F&H; P); and (2) 'sense' pertains to sensual pleasure (*OED*; P), it is clear which of Roderigo's parts Iago has aroused to a state of inflamed ardour so that it 'grows [*enger*] angry'. The puns perfectly convey the sexual irritation and anxieties of the two. See STRAIGHT.

MND, II.i.112: 'the spring, the summer,/ The childing autumn, angry winter, change/ Their wonted liveries, and the mazed world,/ By their increase, now knows not which is which.' The world cannot distinguish the four seasons since all are procreative, each *engers*, has increase, i.e. progeny. Winter – normally barren – is *angry* winter and, like *childing* autumn, it is curiously fertile (summer buds on winter's icy crown). This pun on 'angry winter' helps solve the old question of whether Sh intended autumn to be chiding or childing. Both: 'childing' was intended to convey creation *and* scolding, just as angry does. Cf. the same quibble in *Oth*, IV.ii.114: 'I am a child to chiding.'

Nature's anger (its turmoil and its sexuality) simply mirrors the 'wrath' and the sexual edginess of its fairy rulers, Oberon and Titania, she having 'forsworn his bed' and each accusing the other of extramarital affairs, i.e. sexual activity in the wrong place and time, like that of the seasons, which is aping theirs. Their quarrel over a 'changeling' child is likewise mirrored in the 'change' of the seasons' usual 'liveries' – a pun on the distinctive uniform or seasonal dress, and on deliveries or births. (See SUDDEN, *AYL*, for the phrase 'wrath of love'.)

H8, I.i.133: 'to climb steep hills/ Requires slow pace at first; anger is like/ A full-hot horse, who being allow'd his way,/ Self-mettle tires him'. To *climb* the hill, i.e. mount the lover (P; hillocks are posteriors – P) requires at first a slow pace (tempo or gait of intercourse – P). Anger/*enger* (to extend) or sexual readiness is like the full-hot HORSE (phallus – TWR; coition – F&H) – the suffused penis, which if uncontrolled will expend its mettle (its ardour or semen – P) on itself, will tire and fail to climb the hill, i.e. achieve intromission (perhaps a metaphor of premature ejaculation). Buckingham is also warned to 'allay, the fire of political passion' lest he 'singe' himself (141; SINGE, emasculate).

See STING, *2H6*.

Annal See ANNUAL, ANNAL.

Anne. See AN / ANNE.

Annual, annal Anal; of the ass. A year, L *annus*.

H8, II.iii.64. An old court courtesan, identified only as 'Old Lady' (L *anus*), talks to ANNE, whose name also puns on the ass (*âne*) – an animal Sh associates with bearing burdens and with the human ass/ arse. She asks what burden Anne's 'limbs' and 'back' would be willing to bear to become a queen. An entering Chamberlain wants to share the 'secret' (allusive to sexual secrets – C; P) of their conference. He mentions that 'high note's' taken of Anne's 'many virtues'. 'Note' means notice and puns on Gk *notos*, the back, Anne's back that the Old Lady had suggested could prostitute itself. (Cf. similar pun in Griffith's saying the Queen is being made an ass of, being 'call'd back'; and the Queen's reply 'What need you note it?' – II.iv.128.) 'High note's' evokes musical NOTES or pricks, specif. prick-song (*RJ*, II.iv.21), which is played *above* (*high* notes) PLAIN song. The King offers Anne a TITLE (his ass/ arse and prick) and 'annual support' – *support* meaning to bear, and *annual* support to bear his arse and eventually his ring, L *anus*. This is what the Old Lady had anticipated in asking if Anne had 'limbs/ To bear that load of title' (LOAD, semen) or if her 'back' was too weak to 'vouchsafe this burthen' and to 'get a boy' (the son Henry wanted). After the Chamberlain leaves she jeers, 'I know your back will bear a duchess . . . Are you not stronger than you were?' See PINCH.

Cor, V.vi.114, Coriolanus: 'Measureless liar . . . Boy! O slave! . . . give this cur the lie . . . thrust the lie unto him'; 'Boy! false hound! If you have writ your annals true'. Aufidius had called Coriolanus BOY (catamite). But it is he who is *measureless* – without measure (penis – P); he who is the cur and hound (DOG, sodomite), the SLAVE (sodomite) to have the lie *thrust unto* him (sexual thrust of the penis – C; P), the LIAR (It *bugiardo* / buggered), and should write his annals TRUE (Fr *trou*, the anus). See RARE.

See INCH, *Tem*.

Answer (1) A coital thrust; a prick. Lit. return hit in fencing (*TN*, III.iv.305: 'I had a pass . . . he gives me the stuck in . . . and on the answer').

(2) *Ansare*: pant, gasp; long or desire till one be out of breath (F).

AW, II.ii.14. The Clown's 'answer will serve all men', 'fits all buttocks', and is an 'answer of most monstrous size'. See SIZE (Fr *taille* / tail).

Son 50. How 'heavy' do I journey away, says a reluctant lover, on his 'beast'; 'The bloody spur cannot provoke him on/ That sometimes anger thrusts into his hide;/ Which heavily he answers with a groan,/ More sharp to me than spurring to his side'. With ANGER (sexual desire) the lover thrusts a bloody SPUR (prick) into hi*s* (*h*)*ide* (HIDE and SIDE: loin, womb, buttock). The BEAST answers with his GROAN / groin – his GROAN (cry on sexual penetration – P) that reminds the lover of 'my joy behind [BEHIND, rump]'. Cf. a similar conceit in Chaucer's 'Tale of Sir

Thopas', 43–126: as he 'priketh' on his horse (Chaucer uses some variation of 'prick' nine times in 83 lines), Sir Thopas fell 'in love-longynge' and 'pryked' his steed until 'His sydes were al blood'.

Man and beast are paralleled: horse *answers heavily* his *heavy* rider with a groan (*ansare*). But, on the return journey (Son 51), 'Then should I spur. . . . Then can no horse with my desire keep pace' – then horse can not answer lover's pace (sexual gait, and desire – P).

H5, iv.i.200: 'I do not *desire* he should answer for me; and yet I determine to fight *lustily* for him' (italics added) – the freq. metaphorical mix of sexual and military prowess.

See CROOKED, *3H6*; STIR, *Tim*.

Any Buttocks. *Âne* (Rabelais, *asne*): ass. *Aines*: groin, of man or woman; *ains*: but (Cot). See AN/ANNE.

AW, II.ii.17: 'fits all buttocks . . . or any buttock'.

Cym, I.iv.65. Speaking of women, the Frenchman, to whom *con* is a woman's cunt (Cot), says, ' 'twas a contention . . . contradiction . . . country mistresses . . . constant-qualified and less attemptable than any the rarest of our ladies in France'. Each man claims his own mistress is more chaste than any/*âne* other ass or rear in France – any the rarest (RARE/ rear) of French ladies.

Tem, II.ii.136, Trin*culo*: 'O Stephano, hast any more of this?' – to which Steph*ano* replies, 'The whole butt, man.' The butt: a cask of wine and a buttock. Whole: hole or pudendum (K; P); hole or anus (TWR). 'Holland': hole-land, anal area (P).

Both men are asses; note the revealing suffixes of their names: (1) *ano*, fundament or bum (F); (2) *culo*, fundament, arse or tail (F). 'Trin*culo*, if you trouble him *any* more in's *tale*' (III.ii.55; italics added).

MWW, II.ii.249. The disguised Ford encourages Falstaff to woo his wife: 'lay an amiable siege . . . win her to consent to you: if any man may, you may as soon as any' – lay (for sex – C; P) his siege (arse – *OED*) to win her CONSENT/ cunt. He may *as* soon *as* any (said twice). Falstaff: 'you prescribe . . . very preposterously'. VERY PREPOSTEROUSly (of the posteriors), indeed: Falstaff is to make an ass of himself; screw her; and, fig. bugger Ford.

See CON, *TN*; ABOUT, *2H4*; SWINGE, *2H4*.

Appear See PEAR/PAIR.

Applause A flatus. A clap is any explosive sound. *Claquer*: to clap (Cot). *Cloque*: a fart (Leitner).

TrC, I.iii.163. Achilles is full of his own 'airy fame' – an inflated opinion, hot air or flatus that Ulysses parodies in describing Achilles, who 'lies' in his tent: 'with him Patroclus/ Upon a lazy bed . . . Breaks scurril jests . . . and when he speaks,/ 'Tis like a chime a-mending . . . from the tongue of roaring Typhon. . . . At this fusty stuff/ The large Achilles, on his press'd bed lolling,/ From his deep chest laughs out a large applause'.

Large (obscene, licentious) Achilles, lazy and LOLLing (in dubious sexual activity), LIES (buggers), on his twice-mentioned bed that is press'd (as in coitus – TWR; P), with Patroclus, his 'masculine whore' (v.i.20). Like the Greeks, Sh links pederasty with farting, for the puns on the flatus follow immediately. He puns on *peder*asty / Gk *pordos* (a fart) and L *petere*, to break wind. Patroclus speaks like a chime (*cloque* – Cot) or fart (*cloque* – Leitner). His voice is a-mending, i.e. it is broken: it *breaks* JESTS (farts). Fr *casse*: breaks, of the voice; *cas*: buttocks. The voice of this masculine whore breaks (and mends) scurril (*mendeux* – Cot) jests (scurril/ SQUIRREL, a whore). Patroclus's VOICE/ vice is buggery: his voice mends – L *mendax*, *-acis*, lying – it lies, like him on the bed, and buggers.

At Patroclus's fusty (evil-smelling) stuff, the large Achilles laughs. In the context of a 'roaring Typhon' (ROAR, fart) or whirl*wind*, a typhoon from the sea, 'large' (applause) suggests its nautical meaning of 'with a large wind' – the WIND (flatus), the laugh or loffe (obs.) of Achilles, who emits *loffe* (farts – F) luff (to windward) – a large windy applause for Patroclus from Achilles's *deep* chest. 'Deep' (i.e. the sea) continues the nautical metaphor; it also means having dimension downward: Achilles's applause comes from his downward, lower chest (*casse*); his *cas* or buttocks; caisson or chest for explosives.

Nestor mocks the 'broad Achilles' (BROAD: a looseness of the bowels; effeminate), and Ulysses ends the scene with a plan 'that will physic the great Myrmidon/Who broils in loud applause' (379) – physic and empty him of his gas, the broiling or turmoil in his bowels.

Apples Testicles.

TN, v.i.230. Antonio looks at Sebastian and Cesario: 'How have you made division of yourself?/An apple, cleft in two, is not more twin/Than these two creatures.' An apple, cleft in TWO (testes) is not more TWIN (testes) or *didimos* (Gk, testicle; twin).

See SKIN, *1H4*; HANG(ING), *LLL*; MALICE.

Approach Enter sexually. 'Abroach' is pierce a butt (wine-cask; buttocks). 'Broach' may be applied to a woman as to a cask (P): see BUSINESS, *AC*.

RJ, I.i.111:

Montague. Who set this ancient quarrel new *abroach*? . . .
Benvolio. Here were the servants of your adversary,
And yours, close fighting ere I did *approach*:
I drew to part them. . . . [Italics added]

Tybalt had jested that Benvolio's sword (penis – C; P) was 'drawn' among the 'hinds' (servants, specif. their behinds). Drawn: (1) draw liquor out of a broached butt, as in III.i.9; and (2) expose a sword or penis (C; P).

Benvolio has merely reworded Tybalt's bawdry in saying he *approached* and *drew* to part (PART, buttocks division) the servants (hinds and butts) in their CLOSE (sexually intimate) fighting. Both men describe the swords as approaching and broaching (goosing) butts.

Tim, II.ii.106, Fool: 'When men come to borrow of your masters [usurers], they approach sadly . . . but they enter my mistress' house [a brothel] merrily'. They sadly approach the one, and merrily enter (or broach) the other, both house and mistress. Cf. *MM*, III.ii.7: 'of two usuries, the merriest [prostitution]' was put down.

IV.iii.216, Apemantus: 'Thou gavest thine ears like tapsters that bid welcome/To knaves and all approachers.' The TAPSTER (pimp) gives a welcome ear to all approachers of his casks, as he gives his EARS/arses (of his whores) to the welcome knaves or abroachers of those other *butts* he sells.

2H4. Two similar sentences in two different scenes illustrate how subtly Sh's puns sustain a theme.

IV.ii.14. John reproaches York for 'Turning the word to sword' (the broaching sword as in *RJ* above): 'Would he abuse the countenance of the king,/Alack, what mischiefs might he set *abroach*', this man who is 'The very *opener* and intelligencer' (italics added). York would ABUSE (bugger) the COUNTENANCE/continence (count/cunt – C; K) of the King.

V.v.8, Falstaff: 'I will leer upon him [the King] as 'a comes by; and do but mark the countenance that he will give me.' But the King forbids the 'Approach' (65) of Falstaff, one of my 'misleaders'. Thus the *approach*ing Falstaff is identified with men such as York who *abroach* mischiefs – the mis*chiefs* such as York and the mis*leaders* such as Falstaff, who abuse their chief and leader, the King.

York would bugger the King politically – with his sword (penis – C; P); and Falstaff, too, would prick him – mislead him sexually (TUTOR). The puns focus on abroaching the butt: do *but*/butt *mark* – the butt aimed at in archery (the mark often has a prick upon it: 'Let the mark have a prick in't' – *LLL*, IV.i.133); mark: sexual target improperly limited to the *female* pudendum (C; P).

Hal forbids the future approach/abroach of Falstaff.

See SWINE, *KJ*.

Arm Penis. Weever, *Faunus and Melliflora*, 993: 'He would have sealed with the cheefest armes of his desire, the waxe that Venus warmes.'

TSh, I.i.5: 'And by my father's love and leave am arm'd/ With his good will'. Lucentio is armed with a will (penis – C; P) as GOOD as his father's.

R2, I.iii.1: 'is Harry Hereford arm'd?' – 'Yea, at all points; and longs to enter in.' Virility conveys military strength. Harry is armed at all *points*: (1) those that hold up the breeches; (2) the head or glans of the penis, exposed in erection, *long*ing to enter in (C; P).

See ENGINE, *TrC*; WITCH, *R3*; SICK, *TrC*.

Arras Arse. Of the eleven times Sh uses 'arras', eight are accounted for by the phrase 'behind the arras' (BEHIND, buttocks). Shirley, *The Lady of Pleasure*, I.ii:

Celestina. What hangings have we here!
Steward. They are arras, madam.
Celestina. Impudence! I know't.

(pun on arras/ arse/ ours).

1H4, II.iv.577. Falstaff is 'Fast asleep behind the arras, and snorting like a horse.' L *flatus*: a snorting, a flatus or fart – like that of a HORSE ('orse/ arse). Aristophanes, *The Knights*, 103–21: 'How loudly the Paphlagonian farts and snores!'

Ado, I.iii.63: 'I whipt me behind the arras'.

See LOBBY, *Ham.*

Art L *ars*, 16th c. pun on 'arse'. Dekker, *The Guls Hornbook*, ch. 2: brewers of 'purgations', 'Physicke', practise '*Ars Homocidiorum*, an Art'. Nashe, *Anatomie of Absurditie*: some 'never tasted of anything save the excrements of Artes'.

MWW, II.ii.244: 'use your art of wooing; win her to consent to you'. Use his art (*ars*) to win her CONSENT (a CON, pudendum pun).

Mac, IV.iii.143: 'The great assay of art.'

See ENOUGH, *MND*; EXCELLENT, *H8*; TRANSFORMATION, *CE*; ABSOLUTE, *Mac*; CONTRARY, *MWW*; KEEN, *MND*.

Ass Sh never used 'arse'; like his contemporaries, he used 'ass' to pun on the ass that gets beaten with a stick and the arse that gets thumped sexually, the ass that bears a burden and the arse that bears or carries in intercourse (P). Cf. K, p. 142, for the beare/ bare and wrong/ rung (rounded stick, penis) puns in *2H4* II.i.40: 'unless a woman should be made an ass and a beast, to beare every knave's wrong'. Ass: vulgar, dial. sp. and pron. of 'arse' (*OED* 1860).

KL, I.iv.177, Fool: 'after [you] cut the egg i' the middle, and eat up the meat, the two crowns of the egg [are left]. When thou clovest thy crown i' the middle, and gavest away both parts, thou borest thy ass on thy back o'er the dirt: thou hadst little wit in thy bald crown, when thou gavest thy golden one away . . . thou gavest them the rod, and put'st down thine own breeches'.

A ref. to Aesop's fable, but let us not ignore the Fool's fable – of egg and crown, both cut i' the middle, leaving Lear bare (destitute), with a bare ass/ arse. He put down his breeches, the garment over his breech (lit. buttocks – 'both parts'). Lear *bore* his ass and *bared* his arse. The past tense of 'bear' was 'bare'; 'bore' was not general till after 1600 (*OED*). Cf. a similar cluster of puns in *Ham*, IV.v.164: 'bore him barefaced on the bier;/ Hey non nonny, nonny, hey nonny': (1) bare FACED (arsed); (2) NONNY, It *nanni*, name for tame asses (i.e. Polonius).

The Fool moralises that Lear was an ass or fool when he gave his daughters his gold crown: (1) the coin – his wealth; (2) the sovereign's crown – his authority. He was left with a 'bald' crown: (1) his head; (2) his CROWN (lit. rounded summit of an elevation; pun on buttocks: *cul-pele*, 'bauld-arst, bare taild, pild-breecht' – Cot). Lear was bald (ME 'bare'; 'ballard', bald-headed) and balled, minus the ball (*OED*: golden orb that goes with the sceptre – *H5*, IV.i.279) and his own balls: he was 'a shealed peascod' (219), a *cod* without *pease*, an empty *codpiece* (see TRAIN for his emasculation). He gave away the golden crown and then gave the

rod (verge: penis, rod, sceptre – *OED*). He put down his breeches and his breech: he bared *the ass on his back* over dirt (excrement – *OED*).
See AN; WEIGHT; YEAR.

Assail(ant) (1) Assail sexually (P). (2) *Asseler*: go to stool, evacuate anally (Cot).
3H6, I.i.65:

King Henry. My lords, look where the sturdy rebel sits,
Even in the chair of state: belike he means,
Back'd by the power of Warwick . . .
To aspire unto the crown. . . .
Clifford. . . . He durst not sit there. . . .
Let us assail the family of York.

Anal puns denigrate the *sturdy* (only here in Sh; prob. a pun on this *turdy* rebel, who *sits* in a 'chair of state' or a stool (*OED*; *W*; see STATE), which also means a seat for evacuating the bowels. There he is *back*ed and *as*pires. Clifford responds that he durst not *sit*, that they will *ass*ail him, will *asseler* or go to stool and evacuate the turd, remove him from the royal seat.
RJ, I.i.219. Rosaline 'will not stay the siege of loving terms,/ Nor bide the encounter of assailing eyes,/ Nor ope her lap to saint-seducing gold'. Romeo failed to assail her sexually: she won't OPEN her lap (sexual parts – TWR; P) or bide his encounter (sexual – P). Benvolio turns this reluctant praise of her chastity into scatological mockery. Triggered by Romeo's use of SIEGE (privy, rectum, excrement – *OED*; P) and 'assailing', he says he'll show who 'passed that passing fair' (PASS: discharge excrement).
Cym, II.iii.44. Cloten, established 'ass' (I.ii.39; II.i.58) who (3) 'turned up ace' (ace/ass – K), says if he could win Cymbeline's 'stern daughter' (STERN/ buttocks), he'd have 'gold enough' (GOLD, excrement; ENOUGH, It *assai*, mus.): 'I have assailed her with music but [/ butt]'.
See STIR, *AYL*.

Assembly Coitus, a sexual union. L *coetus*, *coitus*: union, assembly, meeting. See MEETING.
CE, V.i.60. The Abbess hopes Adriana 'reprehended' her husband for his sexual transgressions: 'Haply, in private.' Adriana: 'And in assemblies too.' REPREHEND: L *reprehendere*, to reprove and also to seize, hold fast. Adriana holds her husband fast in PRIVATE/ the privates (genitals – P), perhaps a masturbatory image; and she holds him in assemblies, or in coitus, too.
AYL, III.iii.50, Touchstone: 'here we have no temple but the wood, no assembly but horn-beasts'. Seeming to speak of a simple ceremony, a small assembly of witnesses – mostly animals – he is really punning on the inevitability of cuckoldry, a theme his speech develops: (1) there is no temple or forehead without (obs. meaning of 'but') the wood – of the cuckold's horns (*TA*, II.iii.62: 'Thy temples should be planted presently/ With horns'); (2) there is no assembly, no coitus, but (except) that of horned beasts – of cuckolded men (*Oth*, IV.i.63: 'A horned man's a monster and a beast'). See MEET.
Ado, IV.ii.57: 'Claudio did mean . . . to disgrace Hero before the whole assembly, and not marry her'. This is a slight variation of III.iii.172, when Claudio 'swore he would meet her . . . before the whole congregation . . . and send her home again without a husband', at which time the plan was termed a 'most dangerous piece of lechery'. And so it would have been – to MEET her, whore her, not marry her. In both versions, 'congregation', 'assembly' and 'meet' allude to Hero's alleged premarital coitus; and each is given a visual boost in being described as the *whole* assembly and the *whole* congregation, since 'whole' is *the* hole or vulva (P).

Away Often appears with and reinforces other puns on whore and fornication. To 'away' is, in mod. sl., to go fuck yourself. A 'way' is a coital way and compares to a 'road' (prostitute – P): see WARRANT.
MWW, I.iii.91. Falstaff sends his page on a pimp's errand (SHORE) that Nym and Pistol had

refused: 'Rogues, hence, avaunt! vanish like hailstones, go: Trudge, plod away o' the hoof; seek shelter, pack!' – TRUDGE and PACK, like pimp and whore; plod, i.e. labour, away o' the hoof (foot of animals of the HORSE/ whores kind). Cf. Dekker, *The Shoemaker's Holiday*, III.i: Eyre calls his wife a 'powder-beef-quean' (whore): 'Away, rubbish! vanish, melt like [Falstaff's "hailstones"] kitchen-stuff'. He even sends for beer from the 'Boar's Head', Falstaff's haunt.

2H4, II.ii.91: 'Away, you whoreson upright rabbit, away!' Bardolph's epithets flow from talk of a 'red lattice' (RED LATTICE: brothel, tavern) and getting a 'maidenhead'. Go fuck yourself, you whoreson, upright (standing act of coition – F&H n.d.) rabbit (known for rapid breeding: rabbit-warren, a brothel – *OED*). Go upright: directive to servants sent for liquor (F&H). Upright man: 'Chiefest' of gang of beggar thieves who gets 'first tast' of the virgins (Dekker, *The Bel-man of London*, p. 103).

See HORSE, *KL*; OUT, *AW*; MEANS, *CE*; GRACIOUS, *TGV*.

B

Bad 1. ME 'badde', OE *baeddel*: hermaphrodite. A 'badling': till 1600, a womanish man. These meanings dropped out as 'bad' came to mean evil. L *male mas* (bad, ill man): unmanly, effeminate.

TrC, v.iv.15, Thersites: 'that mongrel cur. Ajax, against that dog of as bad a kind, Achilles' (with his male lover Patroclus). They are both of the same KIND, lit. sex, gender. For Ajax's sexual impotence, see DOG (sodomite) and GOUT.

AW, v.iii.202. Diana's evaluation of Parolles, 'So bad an instrument [penis – P]: his name's Parolles', is confirmed by Lafeu: 'I saw the man today, if man he be.'

2. Bawd (P).

See CREATURE, *WT*; WORSE, *Per*; FIE, *TGV*.

Bandit, banish Anus, excrement, a whore; treat like excrement. Perhaps a pun on the sound of 'shit' and *usciti*, 'men banished or outlawed'; *uscito*, 'gone forth', 'beene taken for the . . . ordure of any beast'; *uscita*, 'a gap or opening; Also whatsoever goeth out' (F). *Banditi*: outlaws; *banditore*: banisher (F). Hebrew *tsa'ah* meant both 'going out' and 'excrement'.

Tim, III.v.98: 'Banish me! . . . banish usury' – pun on usury/*uscire*, 'to goe forth' (F). Usury: prostitution (C; P). *See* WOUND: the banished Alcibiades retaliates that the Senators are usurers, buggers.

IV.iii.400. 'Banditti' seek the gold, some 'ort of his remainder', from the cave of the 'melancholy' (MELANCHOLY, a bowel disorder) Timon. It is 'noised' (NOISE, fart) he hid it, so they make '*ass*ay' (italics added). Timon says the earth feeds on 'general [GENERAL, a whore's] excrement', so why shouldn't they; and he gives them his GOLD (excrement).

See PERFECTION, *TGV*; GRIEF, *RJ*; TUTOR, *2H4*; CRAFTY, *Cym*.

Bank 1. The arse. *Banc*: a seat (Cot).

1H4, III.i.65: 'thrice from the *banks* of Wye/And sandy-*bottom*'d Severn have I sent him/*Boot*less home and weather-beaten *back*' (italics added). Thus Glendower describes how he made an impotent arse of Henry: less his BOOTS (buttocks, coitus) a WEATHER/wether or castrated male. He then does the same to Hotspur (TWO HOURS) in their anticipated division of the land. To his son-in-law he *ass*ignes certain parts (Mortimer says the river is 'gelding' his share); to himself 'all the *fertile* land'; and to Hotspur 'the remnant' (RAG, *TSH*: a remnant, castrate). Hotspur says the division does 'rob me of so rich a *bottom*'. See RIGHT.

2. Moral decay. Bank: the table of a dealer in money. The Bank: the brothel-quarter of London, home of the SISTERS of the Bank, or Bankside Ladies. Jonson, 'An Execration upon Vulcan': 'the Winchesterian Goose [whore] Bred on the Banck . . . When Venus there maintain'd the Misterie'.

MV, v.i.54: 'How sweet the moonlight sleeps upon this bank!' says Lorenzo of Portia's place at Belmont. 'Sit, Jessica. Look how the floor of heaven/Is thick inlaid with patines of bright gold'; but 'this muddy vesture of decay' keeps us from hearing the soul's harmony. Thus Act v takes us back to I.i when Bassanio spoke of Portia's '*gold*en fleece/Which makes her *seat* of Belmont' (170; italics added) the seat (*banc*) or bank he aimed to marry 'to get clear of all the debts I owe' (134). These puns plus those in ll. 1–20 on SUCH (L *sic*/sick), and the admission of muddy (smutty, bawdy – P) decay, suggest Sh was less than enchanted with the moral atmosphere at Belmont. They support the interpretation of an idle, dissatisfied society: 'Gold is the symbol of this world of pleasure' and 'money' is the base on which it rests (Goddard, pp. 83 and 113). See RIPE.

See SLEEP, *TrC*; WITCHCRAFT, *Oth* and *CE*.

Barbarian, Barbarous Of buttocks; of excrement. Gk *borboros*: mud, mire, bog (BOG, QUAGMIRE: buttocks). Borborygm: 1719, rumbling in the bowels (*OED*).

LLL, v.i.86:

Holofernes. O, I smell false Latin; dunghill for unguem.
Armado. Arts-man, preambulate, we will be singuled from the barbarous.

The cluster 'smell', 'dunghill', ARTS/ arse and 'barbarous' leads to jests on 'the *posterior* of the day' (italics added) and how it pleases his grace to 'with his royal finger, thus, dally with my excrement, with my mustachio' (see INWARD).

TA, II.iii.78. Bassanius tells 'abominable' (ABOMINABLE, sodomitical) Tamora that she 'wander'd hither to an obscure plot,/ Accompanied but with a barbarous Moor' because of her 'foul desire'. Sh links 'foul' to the anus and excretion ('foul and muddy'; 'foul indigested lump'; 'foul ends'; and 'foul bogs'). Tamora's foul desires can be satisfied with but/ butt a barbarous moor (a bog), miry buttocks. See TAME.

H5, I.ii.271. Henry says the Dauphin sent TENNIS-BALLS (testicles) in recollection of Henry's 'wilder days' when 'We never valued this poor seat of England;/ And . . . living hence, did give ourself/ to barbarous license'.

He lived HENCE (whoring) with *his* seat, his POOR/ L *puer* (a boy) seat that participated in wildness, perhaps in a BOY's (catamite's) barbarous licence.

See TURK, *Oth*; HENCE, *H5*; SLAVE, *TrC*; THRASH, *Trc*.

Barber Whore. Barber's chair: prostitute (F&H). *Barbiera*: she-barber, strumpet (F). The barber treated VD. Marston, *The Dutch Courtesan*, I.ii: 'my right precious pandress, supportress of barber-surgeons'. Jonson, *The Silent Woman*, III.v: 'barbers cure botches and burnes'; carted bawds employ his 'bason'. See Introduction, p. xii.

AW, II.ii.17: 'It is like a barber's chair that fits all buttocks'.

MND, IV.i.25, Bottom: 'I must to the barber's monsieur; for methinks I am marvellous hairy about the face; and I am such a tender ass, if my hair do but tickle me, I must scratch.' *Bottom* is a TENDER *ass*, hairy ABOUT (Fr *à bout*, at the end) the FACE (arse/ ass), for he is wearing an ass's head. *Barbiglione*: hairs or roughness about the pubes (F). He tells 'Cavalery' (CAVALIER, a pimp) Cobweb he must to a barber – for if his hair does but/ butt tickle (excite sexually – F&H; masturbate – P; F, s.v. *fricciare*), he needs scratching (manual caressing – C; P). Cf. Durfey, *Madam Fickle*, III.i, for a pun on 'cobwebs' as (1) worn-out threads in a man's 'breeches' and (2) his *cobs* or testicles (*W*; *CD*): 'Peace be to the ancient cobwebs betwixt the seams'. The masturbatory conceit develops in Bottom's request for DRY (L *assus*) OATS (testicles), a 'handful or two of dried peas,' and a 'bottle of hay': a *manipule* is a grip or fistful, a bottle (Cot). Bottom wants a bottle, a *manipule* of hay or oats, wants to be manipulated, masturbated – for which end he had asked Mustardseed to lend a 'neaf', fist, grip, *manipule*. See CAVALIER. Bottom may have piles (C), then associated with VD (THREE-PILE), and therefore must to the barber–surgeon for the itch.

See WILLOW, *Oth*.

Batter(y) Assail sexually. *Bateur*: a beater, swinger, thresher (Cot). Swinge: beat and copulate (F&H). *La grange est près des bateurs* (the barn stands near the threshers): used of 'a Nunnerie thats neere unto a Fryerie' (Cot). Dekker and Massinger, *The Virgin Martyr*, IV.i: 'make her thy whore . . . imagine thou assulst a towne. . . . Come, and unseene, be witnesse to this battry.' *Foutoir*: battering-ram; *foutre*: to lecher (Cot).

Luc, 1171. Lucrece describes her rape as 'Her mansion batter'd by the enemy'. Marston,

Pigmalion's Image, ix: 'his eye discended so farre down Love's pavillion: / Where . . . Venus hath her chiefest mantion'.

H5, III.iii.7. Henry says once he begins his 'battery' on Harfleur, he won't leave till the 'flesh'd soldier' has mowed down like grass their 'virgins'. Flesh: achieve coitus (C; P).

See ALTAR, *VA*; FRANCE, *1H6*.

Beast(ly), bestial A eunuch; one given to bestiality (unnatural connection with an animal; buggery). Wycherley, *The Country Wife*, v.iv: women ask the 'eunuch', 'tell me, beast, when you were a man', why he preferred whores. 'As rancke bougers with mankind, and with beasts, as the Saracens are' (1555): in law, sodomy sometimes included bestiality. 'To serve his beastly lust, he will lead a bowgard's life' (*OED*, s.v. Bugger, 1587). Marston, *The Scourge of Villanie*, satyre vii: 'such lewd viciousness . . . Sodome beastlines'. Jonson, *Bartholomew Fair*, IV.iv: a man refuses 'a silken gown, a velvet petticoat', saying 'Keep it for your companions in beastliness'.

MWW, v.v.10. Falstaff, wearing a stag's horns, hopes to seduce Mrs Ford, his 'doe with the black scut', and Mrs Page: 'Divide me like a bribe buck'. He compares himself to Jove, who wooed Europa in the form of a bull (*bestia*, a bull's pizzle, a man's penis – F): 'O Jove, a beastly fault! And then another fault in the semblance of a fowl [wooing Leda in the form of a SWAN] . . . a foul fault! When gods have hot backs, what shall poor men do?' (FAULT, buttocks).

R3, III.v.81: 'hateful luxury, / And bestial appetite in change of lust'. Edward's luxury (lechery) was HATEFUL (Fr *haineux* / of the anus); a bestial appetite in lust (the 'beastly lust' of a bugger, above). See SERVANT.

H5, III.vii.22. The Dauphin calls his horse 'le cheval volant, the Pegasus' (see PEGASUS for this pun on Fr *volant*, a capon), 'a beast for Perseus', whose 'dull elements . . . appear [(AP)PEAR/*a pair*, mate] . . . only in patient stillness while his rider mounts him'. 'My horse is my mistress' (47) says the Dauphin, and when he mounts (coitally – C; P) this gelding, it stands in PATIENT stillness (role of the female or passive male). These are 'allusions to bestiality' (C, s.v. Horse).

See CREATURE, *CE* and *TA*; ILL, *RJ*; ABOMINABLE, *MM*.

Beat Cudgel sexually. Beet: kindle a fire, arouse amorously. *The Court of Love*, 323: 'stiren folk to love and beten fire / On Venus awter'.

RJ, I.iv.28: 'Prick love for pricking, and you beat love down'.

AW, II.iii.269. Lafeu has again called Parolles a whore and an effeminate. Parolles: 'I'll beat him . . . if I can meet him . . . an he were double and double a lord. . . . I'll beat him, an if I could but meet him again.' Beat and MEET (fuck) him in a DOUBLE (homosexual) meeting (L *coitus*). When Lafeu re-enters, Parolles approaches: 'I most unfeignedly beseech your lordship' – a quibble on 'feign' and *foigne* (be offended at; also, as *feindre*, feign – Cot) and *foin* (copulate – C; P). (See OFFENCE.)

Lafeu: 'thou art a general offence, and every man should beat thee: I think thou wast created for men to breathe themselves upon thee'. He is a GENERAL (whore-like) OFFENCE (a whore's arse). *Effoncer*: to beat the bottom (as of a vessel – Cot); and every man should beat his arse, screw this whore, who is 'not worth another word [*parolle* – Cot]'. Parolles is a WORD / whored.

Lafeu hammers mercilessly: he was created for men to breathe upon (earlier Lafeu had punned on BREATHE / breed, q.v.). L *flatus*: a breath, a fart – Parolles ('beaten in Italy' – ITALY, home of buggery), meant to be buggered, farted upon.

A significant word in Parolles's history is DRUM (q.v.). In their final exchange (v.iii.322) Lafeu says, 'Good Tom Drum, lend me a handkercher. . . . wait on me home, I'll make sport with thee'. Good Tom Drum (a thing to be beaten), LEND (fuck) him; wait on him HOME (where one comes sexually) and they will make sport (sex-play – C; P), Tom Drum's Entertainment: a 'very clumsy sort of horse-play' (B). Jonson, *Every Man in his Humour*, III.i: 'compare him to . . . a drum for every one may play upon him' – 'a child's whistle were far the fitter'.

See FLUTE, *AC*; ENOUGH, *Tem*; OLD LADY, *MWW*

Be-gar, by-gar Like BEGGAR, a pun on *bugger*. See PEASANT, *MWW*; COWARD, *MWW*; AN, *MWW*.

Beggar Whore, sometimes a bugger; arse. *Belistre*: beggar, rogue; *belistresse*, quean (whore), woman beggar; *belistrerie*: begging, a lewd, filthy act; *herre*: beggar; *herry*, arse (Cot). Beaumont and Fletcher: 'Beggars must be no choosers' (W). A don of Oxford, Maurice Bowra, a bisexual, told by his friends that he could not marry a particularly plain creature, replied, 'buggers can't be choosers' – *Maurice Bowra*: *A Celebration*, ed. H. Lloyd-Jones (London: Duckworth, 1974) p. 150. In a letter on university affairs, he made the same pun, calling one man a 'back-stabber', another 'the Queen-maker' – and (playing on John Gay's *Beggar's Opera*) the controversy 'The Bugger's Opera' (p. 62).

TrC, III.iii.143. Achilles asks 'am I poor' (74; POOR: homosexual, stinking). He says men 'pass'd by me/As misers do by beggars'. They PASS by (emit a fart). Earlier (see APPLAUSE) the Greeks had mocked the idle buggery (and farting) of Achilles and his lover Patroclus, the 'airy fame' (I.iii.144) of this arse (*herry*: silent 'h'), this beggar (*herre*); such is the 'breath fame blows' (244), a flatus, L *flatus*: a breath, blowing.

Cor, III.ii.117. Coriolanus is ready to sell himself in the 'market-place' in order to gain public office: 'possess me/Some harlot's spirit! my throat of war be turn'd . . . into a pipe/Small as an eunuch . . . a beggar's tongue/Make motion through my lips, and my arm'd knees . . . bend like him/That hath received an alms'. He describes the role of the harlot (*cortegiana* – F), the eunuch (*cortegiano* – F) or male harlot with his small pipe (penis – C; P), his tewel or tuwel (chimney-pipe for smoke; and Chaucer's pun on the anus – TWR); his bent position (Ger *gebogen*, adj.: bent, vaulted, fornicate); and his beggar's TONGUE making motion (sexual movement – P) in his throat of WAR/whore. See KINDLY for the prostitution of his tongue.

TN, III.i.62. The Clown begs Viola for coins and calls himself a 'Pandarus': 'begging but a beggar: Cressida was a beggar'. In Eliz. lit. the name Cressida stood for 'whore' just as her uncle's stood for 'pander'. Among Sh's women beggars are the whores in *Tim*, IV.iii.273 and *H8*, II.iii.83; Margaret (TRULL and perh. sodomite); Cleopatra ('whore' who played at sexual role-changing; see Index), who asked if Caesar would 'have a queen [QUEEN/quean, whore] his beggar'; Jaquenetta (DAMSEL) and Cressida (WARD), who were taken sexually from the rear.

The scene is an elaborate conceit on who is the bigger 'beggar' (bugger and arse): the Clown, Viola, Orsino or Olivia: (1) a husband is a 'bigger . . . fool' (40) than the Clown, whom Viola calls 'Olivia's fool' (36); (2) Viola–Cesario, who comes to 'solicit' (beg alms, pander – *OED*) 'On his [Orsino's] behalf' (116), is the girl–boy who must fend off Olivia's 'love' and concludes it is she who is Olivia's 'fool' (156).

MM, III.ii.130. The Duke denies being 'inclined that way' (sodomitically: see ITALY). Lucio: 'your beggar of fifty . . . his use was to put a ducat in her clack-dish; the Duke had crotchets in him'. 'Use' is sexual habit (P); 'clack-dish', pudendum (C; P). But clack (tongue – F&H) and clack-box (mouth) may intend a sexual variation: the Duke put ducats (obs. duckets), little dukes, in her clack-dish. Lucio: 'I was an inward of his' (INWARD/innards, bowel; pun on buggery) and 'I know the cause of his withdrawing': drawing (L *duco*, duct), pun on duke/ducat and draw (expose the penis – C; P). On hearing this and that he had CROTCHETS (sexual deviants) in him, the disguised Duke concludes that '*back-wounding* calumny . . . strikes [rapes – C; P]' all (197; italics added).

R3, I.ii.42. Richard tells those 'that bear the corse' to set it down: 'by Saint Paul, I'll make a corse of him that disobeys' – by St PAUL (a centre for whores) he'll make a corse/COURSE (whore) of the (pall) bearer who disobeys.

1st Gentleman. My lord, stand back. . . .
Richard. Unmanner'd dog! stand thou when I command:
Advance thy halberd higher than my breast,
Or, by Saint Paul, I'll strike thee to my foot
And spurn upon thee, beggar, for thy boldness.

Richard resents (1) being called 'lord' ('crooked, deformed' person – F&H), a pun on Gk *lordos*, bent backward (see Cor above for pun on 'bent', fornicate); (2) being told to STAND BACK, another slur on his back, with implications of buggery; (3) the suggestive low positioning of the halberd (a 5–7 foot long-handled weapon) pointed at his BREAST (arse; lit. bulging part of anything – *W*). Therefore he calls the man an UMANNNER'D (unmanly) DOG (sodomite), who may stand (C; P) with erect penis (halberd) only at Richard's command. By St PAUL'S, he will strike (rape – C; P) him to his foot. Perhaps self-consciousness about his own sexual problem precipitates his attack: his FOOT (fuck – C; P) is a small penis, it is not a yard (penis – *OED*). Cf. *LLL*, v.ii.676: the effeminate Armado 'Loves her by the foot' – 'He may not by the yard.' Richard will SPURN (fuck) this beggar/bugger.

See COURTIER, *H8*; PEACH, *MM*; PEASANT, *TSh*; BUTCHER, *Cor*; SERVANT, *2H4*; NAPLES; *3H6*; LEAN, *MV*; SCRUBBED.

Behind The buttocks. Weever, *Epigrammes*, The Third Weeke, v, with ref. to the man in the moon: 'If please him pisse, then he doth send us raine'; vi: 'From whence doth come this root-uprising wind?/From the moons man, when he doth blow behind'.

CE, III.i.76: 'A man may break a word with you, sir, and words are but wind,/ Ay, and break it in your face, so he break it not behind.' Dromio E's jest on the wind that breaks behind (a flatus) is stressed by its being but/butt wind, and by the response it elicits: 'It seems thou want'st *break*ing: out upon thee, *hind*!' (italics added).

Ado, III.v.41. To show God's predicament in trying to be even-handed, Dogberry says, 'an two men ride of a horse, one must ride behind'. This is true in a double sense: one would be behind the other; and one would be on the rump or behind (of the horse). Sh begins and ends this quip with a pun: AN/Fr *âne* (ass) for the first word, and *behind* for the last. Also, one is 'ane' (Sc and obs.), so it may truly be said that the *one* behind is the ass (*âne*). Cf. *donner d'une*: to make a fool of (Cot).

However, the punning is probably not all that innocent, for 'two to ride upon one asse, or horse' and 'to do, any way, like an asse' is *baudiner* and connotes *baudoüiner*: 'to doe, leacher, or ingender, like an Asse' (Cot).

See HORSE, *Ado*; HEART, *MND*; Introduction, p. xv, *TN*; LOBBY, *Ham*; LOVE, *TSh*.

Bestow Engage in sexual bestiality or sodomy, an 'unnatural form of sexual intercourse, esp. that of one male with another' (*OED*); which sometimes, in law, includes bestiality (*W*). *CE*, II.ii.80: 'bestows on beasts'.

AYL, IV.iii.87. Orlando has been participating in mock (?) love-making with Ganymede, who he thinks is a boy, but a loose one, perhaps a homosexual or young eunuch: 'The boy is fair,/Of female favour, and bestows himself/Like a ripe sister' – he is of female favour (the sexual parts and the giving of them – P) and bestows himself like a RIPE (sexually wanton) SISTER (q.v.) or whore.

2H4, II.ii.186. Poins and Hal plan to observe Falstaff in action with Doll, 'some road', 'as common as the way between Saint Alban's and London' ('road', 'way' and 'common' mean a whore – C; P). 'How might we see Falstaff bestow himself tonight in his true colours, and not ourselves be seen?' asks Hal. TRUE/*trou* (anus – Cot) and COLOUR/*culare* (arse-gut – F) used together suggest entry from the rear esp. since the Prince goes on to compare Falstaff's wooing to that of Jove, who seduced Europa in the guise of a bull, an act of sexual bestiality. Falstaff will bestow himself like a BEAST: 'From a God to a bull? a heavy declension! it was Jove's case.' A pun on grammatical declension of cases and on the low hanging of a bull's and Jove's heavy genitals: his case (P)/*cas* (Cot). This identification of Falstaff and Jove started when Falstaff signed a letter to Hal 'Sir John with all Europe [Europa]' (146), and Hal spoke of him as the 'town bull' (172).

See SHARE, *MWW*; ALTER, *MWW*.

Bite 1. To coit, lit. pierce (see O'ER, *TrC*); to whore or *buy it* (see OUT, *AW*; MATTER, *AC*). Bite: woman's privities; biter: 'wench whose **** is ready to bite her a–se; a lascivious, rampant wench' (G). Cunt-beten: an impotent man (TWR, s.v. Queynt). *Potage de la bite*: semen; *prendre du potage de la bite*: fornicate (Cot).

Ado, IV.i.172. Hero is 'guiltless here / Under some biting error' – accusation of adultery.

MM, I.iii.19. The city has 'most [MOST, buttocks] biting laws' – arse-biting laws, against fornication; but it failed 'To use . . . the rod'.

2. Bugger. *OED*, s.v. Bugger, 1704: 'Beaus, Biters, Pathics, B—rs and Cits'. Beaus: fops. Pathics: passive male homosexuals; b—rs: buggers; Cits of COCKNEYS: effeminate males.

H5, v.i.43. Fluellen makes Pistol 'eat' (use up coitally – P) and 'bite' his leek, and threatens, 'I have another leek in my pocket, which you shall eat'. He twice mentions the 'sauce' (SAUCE: semen; clap or pox) for the LEEK (testicle) and calls Pistol a 'scurvy', 'scauld' knave (venereally infected – P; *OED*). The erotic scene, evoking penilingus, concludes, 'All Hell shall stir for this': STIR: arouse sexually (C; P), specif. buggery (*bouger*, stir – Cot).

1H4, II.i.20. 'ne'er a king christen could be better bit than I have been since the first cock', says a carrier who enters bearing a 'lantern' (*lanterné*, buggered – Cot) which he refuses to lend Gadshill so the latter can see his 'gelding' (eunuch), saying he knows 'a trick [sexual ploy – C; P] worth two [TWO, testes] of that'. He has been bitten by 'fleas' (L *pulices*) since the first cock (L *pullus*, an endearment). PUNY: fleas, bed-bugs, buggers. Being bitten by FLEAS was a common 16th c. bawdy conceit. Perh. he was bitten by a cock (penis – F&H; P) as well as fleas, by a *pullus* as well as *pulices*; for the Second Carrier says, 'this is the most villanous house in all London road for fleas: I am stung like a tench', and 'this house is turned upside down'. He, too, has been bitten and stung (STING, a prick). He, too, has been buggered: the HOUSE (brothel–inn) is villainous (given to vile, depraved, criminal acts; *vilain bougre*, lewd archaism – Robert Burton, p. 201); is the worst in the road (whore – C; P); is turned (sexually performed – C; P) *up*side *down* (lit. def. of PREPOSTEROUS, the posteriors, buggery) – is arsy-versy.

The little scene has three sections, each introduced by a new character and each repeating the story of those who 'prey on . . . ride up and down on' others' (BOOT). Gadshill tells the Chamberlain 'Go to; "homo" is a common name to all men. Bid the ostler bring my gelding out of the stable . . . you muddy knave'. Go to: go to it (C; P) or screw (*Oth*, IV.ii: told to 'go to', Roderigo cries, 'go to! I cannot go to, man' – i.e. get sexual entry to Desdemona). Again a 'gelding' (eunuch) and Sh's only HOMO (q.v.), a *common* name, pun on (1) common noun, i.e. of gender, indeterminately either masculine or feminine; (2) of a whore (*OED*; P). This common noun, 'Homo', refers to Gadshill and his 'cock-sure' cohorts, as he calls them – his cock-SURE / sewer whores – and a MUDDY (shitty) knave. Are they the cocks, the *pullus*es or *pulices*, that bit the carriers? They *are* the cock-sure thieves who, he says, will 'steal' (bite: 17th c., swindle) from the travellers. Neither carrier will LEND (buttocks; coit) a lantern (refusing to be *lanterné* again?). Cf. Rabelais, Bk II, ch. 31 (1654 trs.): 'lantern-carrying hag [old whore]'. *Zanzeare*: be bitten by gnats (*zanzere*); *zanzeri*, ingles; *zanzerare*, to sodomise (F). In *2H4*, v.i, these men 'will backbite' and are 'backbitten . . . for they have marvellous foul linen'. Cf. BUCKRAM.

Tem, II.ii.10. Prospero's spirits 'pinch' (PINCH: prick, screw, and make impotent) Caliban and frighten him with 'urchin shows', with show of pricks (urchins: deformed brats, hedgehogs; and SHOWS (Fr *monstre* / MONSTERS, homosexuals): 'they [are] set upon me . . . And after bite me, then like hedgehogs which / Lie tumbling in my barefoot way and mount / Their pricks at my footfall'.

Puns on copulation – and buggery – come fast and furiously: (1) spirits are *set upon* him (incite to coitus – C; P); (2) they *after* bite or screw him behind; (3) like HEDGEHOGS (buggers), they LIE (*bugiare* – F) buggering and *tumbling* (coiting – C; P); (4) and they *mount* (coitally – P) their *pricks* (penises – *OED*; P) at his bare*foot* *foot*fall (FOOT, coit – C; P; also bugger); (5) he is 'wound with adders . . . with cloven tongues' – is WOUND (pricked, fucked), with their STINGS (pricks), ME term for adders' tongues. See PINCH: Prospero directs his urchins to render Caliban impotent; and this they do when they prick him. Prick (farriery, 1591): to pierce and wound a horse's foot, lame him – as Caliban is wound with adder's pricks and made LAME (impotent).

Blister Syphilitic sore. Shirley, *The Lady of Pleasure*, II.ii: Scentlove, a 'scout of Venus' wild fowl' who takes the 'first fruits' of a woman in exchange for introducing her to a wealthy lord, is called 'blister-maker of the town'.

Ham, III.iv.44: 'takes off the rose/From the fair forehead of an innocent love/And sets a blister there'. The ROSE (chastity) is replaced by the *red* blister of (1) the brand on the whore's forehead; (2) the burning (syphilis – *OED*).

Tem, I.ii.324: 'a south-west blow on ye/And blister you all o'er!' Caliban hopes Ariel and Prospero blister all O'ER/whore-like, from a blow (L *plaga*), a whore's blow (coital thrust – C; P), a burning (syphilitic – *OED*) plague. See PINCH.

RJ, I.iv.75: 'O'er ladies' lips, who straight on kisses dream,/Which oft the angry Mab with blisters plagues'. The same QUEEN/quean Mab who comes 'tickling' (masturbating, fucking – F&H; P) a 'parson's nose' (rump – P) with a 'tail' also 'gallops' (like a HORSE/whore) O'ER/whore-like ladies' LIPS (vaginal, too), dreaming of kisses (coitus – P), which she plagues with blisters if their breaths are 'tainted' (depraved, rotten) with 'sweetmeats' (penis – F&H n.d.; meat: genitals – F&H). Cf. Webster, *The White Devil*, III.ii. 'Shall I expound whore to you? . . . They [whores] are first,/Sweetmeats which rot the eater'.

Blood Sexual emissions (sexual passion – P). See FROTH for 16th c. synonyms for semen, incl. MILK and blood, esp. 'heated' blood. Marlowe's 'thrice-decocted blood' or seminal fluid (F&H, s.v. Cream). Liquids resembling blood, such as plant sap, wine ('blood of grapes' – Gen 49:11).

Tim, IV.iii.432, Timon: 'Go, suck the subtle blood o' the grape,/Till the high fever seethe your blood to froth,/And so 'scape hanging'. – suck the SUBTLE blood of the grape, the WINE (semen) from the sutler, who supplies liquors and also the services of a whore, the sucking of whose 'blood' leads to disease; 'scape hanging by dying of syphilis.

IV.iii.539: 'And may diseases lick up their false bloods!' May the lecher's disease lick (*lecher* – Cot) up, consume their blood-semen and leave them sterile – Timon's unvarying curse (ll. 82–7; 140–60).

H5, II.iii.59. Pistol and his 'Voke-fellows in arms' are off to France, 'like horse-leeches . . . To suck, to suck, the very blood to suck!' Boy: 'And that's but unwholesome food, they say.' Like HORSE/whores' leeches, they will suck whores' blood: like *leeches* they will *lecher* (lick, lap up – Cot), i.e. suck.

TrC, IV.v.224: 'There they stand yet, and modestly I think,/The fall of every Phrygian stone will cost/A drop of Grecian blood.' Hector is thinking MODESTLY (of pudenda): the Trojans still stand (with erectile potency – C; P), and Hector threatens, for every PHRYGIAN (frigging or masturbating) stone (testicle) they lose, the Greeks, too, will drop some blood and semen. A threat of death and, possibly, the not uncommon practice of castrating the enemy (cf. *1H4*, I.i.44).

Oth, V.i.36, Othello: 'Thy bed, lust-stain'd, shall with lust's blood be spotted'. Othello intends the bed of this 'strumpet' Desdemona, which he believes is stained with the semen of lust, to be spotted with her life's blood. He may have planned to stab Desdemona, though he stifles her at the last moment. It is possible that 'I would not have thee linger in thy pain:/So, so' means not more stifling, but that he then uses the weapon he *had brought with him* and which is taken from him by Montano (ii.239). This image of blood-stained sheets would complete the request of Desdemona (IV.ii.105) that Emilia 'Lay on my bed my wedding sheets' (those sheets spotted with virginal blood), and Emilia's saying (iii.22) that she laid 'those sheets you bade me'.

I.iii.339. Told by Iago to 'go to bed, and sleep' (305), the sexually frustrated Roderigo responds, 'I will incontinently drown myself' – which, in the context of going to bed and in his use of 'will' (the penis – C; P), suggests the incontinence of a wet-dream or of masturbation (DELICATE). Iago: 'It is merely a lust of the blood and a permission of the will. Come, be a man. Drown thyself!' Iago dismisses love as the *permission* or letting of the will (to let: allow fluid to escape, shed blood), letting semen flow from the will or penis, a remedy for lust, like medical blood-letting.

Blood is freq. linked to generating: 'the issue of your loins . . . blood of your begetting' (*Cym*, v.v.331); 'disclaim all my paternal care . . . and property of blood' (*KL*, I.i.116); 'out of my blood/ He [God]'ll breed revengement [Henry's son]' (*1H4*, III.ii.6).

See SPIRIT, *WT*.

Blunt Impotent, castrated. To make dull or blunt is to rebate: her., to diminish by removal of a projection; cut short, esp. the arm of a cross. 'Mourned' or 'blunted' (morné), of a lion rampant: without teeth or claws. Marston, *Antonio and Mellida*, v.i: 'Lady, my wit hath spurs, if it were dispos'd to ride you' – 'Your wit's spurs . . . dull, blunt, they will not draw blood . . . . [There is not] any wrong they can do to ladies.' His SPUR (prick) is impotent to deflower a lady.

CE, II.i.93. The jealous and rejected Adriana says, if 'barren my wit' it is because 'Unkindness blunts it'. She – her WIT (genitals) – is barren and blunt because of her husband's neglect, his UNKINDNESS (physical unnaturalness).

IV.ii.21. Adriana says her husband 'is deformed, crooked, old and sere,/ Ill-faced, worse-bodied, shapeless everywhere;/ Vicious, ungentle, foolish, blunt, unkind,/ Stigmatical in making, worse in mind.' She derides him for being physically deformed, small of penis or castrated: (1) everywhere shape*less* (SHAPE, genitals); (2) blunt – a projection removed or an arm cut short; (3) CROOKED (impotent); (4) UNKIND (unnatural). In making (copulation – P) he is STIGMATIC, characterised by sexual deformity.

This immediately retracted attack on his masculinity encapsulates her misery at being supplanted by the Courtezan: he is WORSE/ whores bodied, has WORSE in mind and is stigmatical, i.e. branded, the penal branding of whores.

MM, I.iv.60. 'This is the *point*' (italics added), says Lucio. Angelo's 'blood/ Is very snow-broth; one who never feels/ The wanton stings and motions of the sense,/ But doth rebate and blunt his natural edge' – BLOOD or semen like snow; no wanton STINGS (pricks, penis) or motions (sexual desires – C; P). Angelo's natural edge (NATURE, generative organs), like the edge of a sword, is blunt or rebated, diminished, impotent.

TSh, III.ii.13. The scene opens: 'this is the 'pointed day'. The bridegroom, who did ''point the day of marriage', does not appear. There is no point (penis – C; P) for Kate, who says, 'No shame [SHAME, genitals] but mine', and who calls Petruchio a fool, 'Hiding his bitter jests in blunt behaviour'. Bitter or biting (to BITE, copulate) jests hidden in blunt, impotent behaviour: like their wedding-night.

See CUP, *2H6*; STERN, *2H6*.

Board 1. Coit (P).

2. Arse/ ass. Board: *asse* (F), *ais* (Cot). 'Bourd' (obs. form of 'board') meant a JEST (arse/ ass).

TN, I.iii.60. Sir Andrew desires 'acquaintance' (ACQUAINTANCE, carnal knowledge) of Maria or 'Mary Accost'.

Sir Toby. You mistake, knight: 'accost' is front her, board her, woo her, assail her.
Sir Andrew. By my troth, I would not undertake her in this company. Is that the meaning of 'accost'?

Sir Andrew MISTAKES (takes the wrong way, sexually), hears 'mistake' as *must take*. Perhaps misled by 'board' and ASSAIL (sexually, with stress on the *ass*), he says he would not in company UNDERTAKE (the sex-act, with ref. to position) Maria.

TSh, I.ii.95. Hortensio: 'Petruchio . . . I will continue [what] I broach'd in jest', i.e. that Petruchio marry Kate. 'Continue' (CON, cunt; cf. CONTINUAL) sets the tone for what Hortensio broached (stuck into, coitally – C; P) in jest or bourd and what Petruchio will board in JEST (the rear end), for he 'will board her, though she chide as loud/ As thunder when the clouds in autumn crack'. He will marry and board Kate – make an 'ass' of her (III.ii.234) – though she chide as loud as THUNDER (a flatus) when clouds crack (*pet*: 'A fart . . . or cracke' – Cot). And in autumn and *in autem* (the church – *W*; thieves' cant – F&H), at the wedding, he kisses her 'with such a clamorous smack/That at the parting all the church did echo' (180). The ECHO (a flatus) repeats the sound of the parting (see PART, 2) of their LIPS (anus).

MV, I.iii.22. Shylock questions the financial solvency of Antonio, whether he is 'sufficient' (Fr *assez*) – in other words, whether his argosies (what he had called his 'bottom' – i.42) will come in:

Shylock. . . . *But* ships are *but* boards, sailors *but* men. . . . [Still, he will take the bond.]
Bassanio. Be *ass*ured you may.
Shylock. I will be *ass*ured . . . and, that I may be *ass*ured. . . .

(Italics added.) Antonio's 'means are in supposition' (18). (Cf. *CE*, III.ii.50: 'supposition' and 'sink' pun on *sub-position*, on the bottom). Antonio's means (mean/men – K) and sailors that are but/butt men may sink to the *bottom*. And if his ships, which are but/butt boards (arses), fail to come in, the ass/arse that is forfeit, the pound of flesh, is his own (see DEAR).

See CUP, *2H6*; INFINITE, *AW*; TIGER, *TN*.

Bob Of women, to fuck ('he with young Kate had been bobbing' – Broadbent, p. 79); of men, to bugger, emasculate. Lit. curtail ('bobtail tyke' – KL, III.vi.73). Bobtail: a lewd woman; impotent man or eunuch (F&H, s.v. Old).

R3, V.iii.334. Richard tells his army, 'Remember whom you are to cope withal', an army led by 'a paltry fellow . . . A milk-sop'; 'let men conquer us,/And not these bastard Bretons; whom our fathers/Have in their own land beaten, bobb'd, and thump'd,/And . . . left them the heirs of shame./Shall these . . . lie with our wives?'

The sexual thrust of the speech, English virility (they will cope, i.e. screw, the French – C; P) and lack of French manhood, typified by their leader, suggests that the French were not only beaten militarily but also BEATEN, sexually cudgelled. They were bobbed, emasculated, buggered, left without balls or valour. A previous generation of English (our fathers) had bobb'd (jumped up and down; made a fool of) both the wives and their husbands; had thump'd ('jump her and thump her' – *WT* IV.iv.196) or slept with French wives and daughters and left them the heirs of shame, left them with children, with these current Bretons: the heirs of SHAME/Fr *chemer* (decrease, abate), the abated, cut short, bobbed, emasculated bastard Breton heirs.

Bog(gler) Bog: buttocks (P). L *lustrum*: a bog; a brothel (Cicero). Etherege, *The Man of Mode*, I.i: the 'Orange-Woman' is 'an overgrown jade' who covers her 'baldness' (a VD symptom), a 'resty bawd'; and they bid her farewell with, 'Farewell, bog –'.

CE, III.ii.121:

Antipholus S. In what part of her body stands Ireland?
Dromio S. Marry, sir, in her buttocks: I found it out by the bogs.

H5, III.vii.61: 'they that ride so and ride not warily, fall into foul bogs'. See STRAIT STROSSERS for the buggery inherent in this pun.

AC, III.xiii.110. Antony says he found Cleopatra 'a morsel cold upon/Dead Caesar's trencher', though she undoubtedly also has 'hotter hours' (HOURS/whores): 'You have been a boggler ever'. The 'boggler' is the hawk that does not keep to one quarry but turns to and fro (Henn, p. 119), as Cleopatra does from lover to lover. The gods 'seel our eyes' (another image from falconry) and in 'our own filth drop our clear judgements' – in filth of our OWN, arse or bog. Cf. HAGGARD, *TN*.

See QUAGMIRE.

Boils Symptom of VD, linked to whores. 'Boil' means stew, which, in turn, meant a prostitute or brothel.

Cor, I.iv.31: 'Boils and plagues/Plaster you o'er, that you may be abhorr'd . . . and one infect another . . . You souls of geese'. Every phrase reviles the soldiers as infected whores: (1) plague (L *lues*) or lues, a spreading disease, esp. syphilis; (2) plaster, as in 'The harlot's cheek, beautied with plastering art' – *Ham*, III.i.51; (3) O'ER and ABHOR/ whore; (4) geese/ *gueuse* (a harlot – Cot). Likewise, a goose is a prostitute (P), and a Winchester goose is a syphilitic lesion or one thus infected (F&H; P).

MM, V.i.320. The Duke observes 'corruption boil and bubble/ Till it o'er-run the stew'. Boils or disease of the O'ER/ whore in the stew.

KL, II.iv.226. Lear calls Goneril/ gonorrheal (see LAME) 'a disease that's in my flesh . . . a boil,/ A plague-sore, an embossed carbuncle,/ In my corrupted blood'. 'Boil' is companioned with (1) a disease in the flesh (body of a prostitute – P); (2) corrupted (i.e. infected) blood; (3) a plague-sore; (4) a carbuncle (which Sh combined with bubo, syphilitic lesion, to form 'bubukle' in *H5*, III.vi.108) that is embossed. Cf. *AYL*, II.vii.67: the 'embossed sores . . . thou with license of free foot hast caught' – caught with licence of FOOT/ Fr *foutre* (fucking) with a free (sexually loose – C; P) foot – like that of Goneril. Gonorrhea was a worry of the 16th c.: Marston, in *The Dutch Courtesan*, II.ii, calls it 'Venom de Gonory'.

Bolt/boult 1. Penis. A 'pintle' meant both a penis and a bolt. Cf. Chaucer, 'The Shipman's Tale', 316: Sir John held 'hire in his armes bolt upright'. The usual gloss is that this means flat on her back, but one cannot help wondering about that upright (obs., lying at full length) bolt.

MND, II.i.165. That which is called Cupid's 'butt-shaft' in *LLL* and *RJ* (butt, the posterior, the prick in archery; shaft, a slender rod; an arrow) is here called Cupid's 'love-shaft' or the 'bolt of Cupid'. When the bolt 'fell upon a little western flower,/ Before milk-white [that flower turned] purple with love's wound'. This is a description of defloration (WEST, the buttocks area), and Puck will use as an aphrodisiac the juice of this flower that turned purple or bled from love's WOUND (a prick – *OED*), the 'bolt of Cupid'.

TrC, Prol. 18. The following puns are admittedly highly conjectural; but the introduction to *TrC*, perhaps the most openly seamy of Sh's plays, with direct and frequent mention of male homosexuality, cannot be read as if it is an architectural and geographical treatise: 'massy staples/ And corresponsive and fulfilling bolts,/ Sperr up the sons of Troy'.

Staples are loops, bent rods for passing into a wall, the passive receptor into which the fulfilling bolt is shot, to sperr up (bolt up) the Trojans. This use of 'sperr' (the only time in Sh), if a correct emendation to the Folios, which say 'Stirre up', would seem to pun on SPUR (penis), literally a device 'for pricking' (*OED*); and on the metal spur or gaff fastened to the leg of a gamecock for fighting purposes. As 'Stir up' (C; P) or arouse sexually (STIR, bugger) – and 'stir up' is a freq. phrase of Sh's – it might also pun on stirrup, a U-shaped clamp, repeating the image of the staples.

Virgil calls the Trojans 'scarcely men' (*Aeneid*), and a Trojan is a 'person of dissolute life' (*OED*). Sh would have known that *Iliades* (Ovid) meant Ganymede, the young male in a homosexual relationship. Is this the implication behind the 'massy staples' (a 'masse stapler' is a rogue disguised as a woman – F&H n.d.)? The description of the Trojans follows upon that of the 'sixty and nine' Greeks (how old is this expression for orogenitalism? – Rodgers) who 'Put forth toward Phrygia'. To 'put' is (1500s) to introduce the male to the female for breeding; 'put forth', to extend the hand; and PHRYGIAN is masturbation or sexual bestiality. 'The theme of the vicious, effeminate Greek constantly recurs in Roman literature' (Horace, p. 273).

'Now expectation, tickling skittish spirits,/ On one and other side, Trojan and Greek': 'tickle' is copulate, masturbate (F&H; P), *fricciare* (tickle, masturbate; prick forward – F) – i.e. masturbation of their SPIRITS (penises), and tickling of the OTHER (arse) side.

The *expectation* on *one and other side* is repeated in IV.v.146: 'There is *expectance* here from *both* the *sides*,/ What further you will do' – 'We'll *answer* it [ANSWER, a coital thrust];/ The issue is *embracement*'. And, again (l. 155): 'signify this *loving* interview/ To the *expecters* of our Trojan part;/ *Desire* them home. Give me thy hand'. (Italics added.)

BOTH SIDES is a pun on ambisexuality (and deceit): the Greeks expect the Trojan PART (genitals; division in the buttocks); *desire* them HOME (orgastically), so give a HAND (phallus –

K), in masturbation. Is all this not relevant to the sperring up or stirring up of the sons of Troy? (See RIGEL for other puns in these lines.)

2. To bolt is to copulate. *Beluter*: to boult, to swive, i.e. copulate (Cot). Boult, a pimp in *Per* (see CAVALIER), is appropriately named.

TrC, I.i.18. Impatient for Cressida, Troilus is told by Pandarus that he must 'tarry the bolting.' 'tarry the grinding [carnal copulation – C; F&H)' and 'tarry the leavening' or rising (phallicly).

3. 'Bolt' also means ejaculate hastily, blurt out; and, of root-crops ('root' is penis – C; P), to run to seed immaturely without the usual thickening of the root. Both definitions suggest premature ejaculation. Nashe, *Strange News*: 'dribbed [shot wide or short of the mark] forth another fooles bolt'.

H5, III.vii.132: 'A fool's bolt is soon shot.' Shoot: point the male generative organ (P).

AYL, V.iv.67. Touch*stone* is 'very swift' 'According to the fool's bolt, sir, and such dulcet diseases'. The usual gloss is that the fool's bolt is a blunt-headed arrow (in itself suggesting ineffectual penetration); however, the condition is a disease and DULCET (testicles – *OED*), a disease of the *stone* (testicle; 'lascivious, lustful' – *OED*), a disease of lechery, connoting impotence from syphilis; it is SUCH (*tale* – F) a disease of the tale (arse, penis – K; P).

See SCANTY, *KL*.

Boot Coition; the buttocks. Cf. butt: to strike against; a thick end; buttocks. *Bout*: the end or extremity; *bouter*, to thrust forward (Cot). Bouts: sexual exercise (P).

1H4, II.i.91: 'not pray to her [the commonwealth], but prey on her, for they ride up and down on her and make her their boots'. The commonwealth is, in mod. sl., being screwed, in a metaphor in which the woman (her) is their boots – and is not only their prey, or booty as usually glossed, but specifically the very body, butt(ocks), they ride (copulate – P) UP AND DOWN on. Her being the butt is reinforced by the question 'will she hold out water in a foul way?' – for a butt is, in the leather trade, a hide of *sole*-leather (for boots, waterproof one hopes), and she is 'liquored' (greased). COMMONWEALTH is a combination of *common* (whore – P); and *wealth* (booty). See K, on body/beauty/booty.

TrC, IV.v.40:

Cressida. The kiss you take is better than you give;
  Therefore, no kiss.
Menelaus. I'll give you boot, I'll give you three for one.

'Kiss' is a euphemism for coition (P), as Menelaus knows when he offers boot, or something given to equalise an exchange – his three for one. 'To play three to one though sure to lose' and 'to engage three to one' meant amorous congress (G; F&H, s.v. Greens). Menelaus offers his butt, his THREE (complement of genitalia) for her one (Sc ane), her ass (Fr *âne*) or butt. He offers boot or profit (pun on sexual satisfaction – P).

Botcher/butcher Fornicator; bugger. Flesh-monger: 16th c., butcher, pander, fornicator. Botchour: obs. sp. of 'butcher'. The butcher's prick was a common item and as commonly punned on. Dekker and Massinger, *The Virgin Martyr*, II.i: 'Bawdy Priapus, the first schoolmaster that taught butchers to stick pricks in flesh, and make it swell, thou know'st, was the only ningle [ningle, ingle: a buggering boy – F&H; male paramour in a 'bad sense' – *CD*] that I cared for under the moon.' Durfey, 'Tom Tinker', in *Wit and Mirth*: 'I met with a Butcher a killing a Calf,/I then stepp'd up to him and cryed out half:/At his first denial I fell very sick,/And he said it was all for a touch of his——'.

1H4, I.i.13, King: 'Did lately meet in the intestine shock/And furious close of civil butchery' – did meet/meat (K) in butchery; did MEET (coit) in intestine shock (internal; in the bowel), in the CLOSE (intimacy, lechery) of butchery/buggery. In *2H4*, III.i.107, Henry again speaks of 'inward wars' – INWARD (intestine, intimate) WARS/whores who deceived him.

Like Henry's previous image of the soil that daubed her lips 'with her own children's blood', this metaphor of buggery, repeated in the 'ill-sheathed knife' – the sheath (L *vagina*) was, instead, ILL (L *male*), homosexual – is meant to convey the unnatural opposition of 'acquaintance, kindred and allies' in this war. See MISUSE for 'people butchered' and sexually misused.

Cor, I.ix.88. Coriolanus feels 'bound to beg/ Of my lord general' that he give freedom to a poor man (L *puer*, an unmarried man, boy) at whose house Coriolanus 'sometime lay . . . . he used me kindly'. He lay (for the sex-act – C; P) and was used (coitally – C; P) KINDLY (sexually) by the POOR (pederast).

The GENERAL (whore-like) answers, 'O, well begg'd! / Were he the butcher of my son, he should/ Be free as is the wind.' If 'butcher' means only slaughterer and is not a pun on 'bugger', the General's charity is hardly paternal and completely bewildering. See BEGGER/ bugger.

AW, IV.iii.211. Parolles says Dumain had been a 'botcher's prentice in Paris, from whence he was whipped for getting the shrieve's fool with child'. Though only prentice, he was already a botcher, bungler, as well as a botchour/ butcher (pricker, fornicator), for he bungled in impregnating not just *a* fool, but the sheriff's – for which he was WHIPPED (in Paris, where *fouet* means whip and *fouettage* whipping, castration). For spreading such gossip, Parolles is to be 'whipped through the army' – the *arme* or weapon (Cot), i.e. penis (C; P). *He* is to be castrated, says Bertram; and he was (KNOT; SHAME; BOTH-SIDES).

R2, I.ii.3, Gaunt:

the part I had in Woodstock's blood
Doth more solicit me than your exclaims,
To stir against the butchers of his life!
But since correction lieth in those hands
Which made the fault that we cannot correct,
Put we our quarrel to the will of heaven:
Who, when they see the hours ripe on earth
Will rain hot vengeance on offenders' heads.

His brother was buggered as well as murdered, or Gaunt is using buggery metaphorically for the crime's vileness. The claims of his blood relationship rouse him more than the *ex*claims of his brother's wife. But he refuses to take an eye for an eye, to STIR (bugger) the butchers of his brother, as she solicits. Solicit or entice to prostitution reinforces the pun in the action she is urging, the stirring or vengeful screwing of the murderers. She answers, 'Finds brotherhood in thee no sharper spur [SPUR, penis]?' and says in acting so he is 'Teaching stern [STERN, the buttocks] murder how to butcher thee'.

Since he cannot correct (make *right*, L *rectum*) the FAULT (a breach/ breech), he chooses to leave the offenders – the RIPE (sexually rotten) HOURS/ whores – to heaven for correction (OFFENCE, sexual crimes, specif. relating to the buttocks). And when those hands – the hands of God – see these butchers or buggering whores, they will rain hot vengeance on the heads of these sodomites, just as the Lord rained brimstone and fire on Sodom and Gomorrah (Gen 19:24).

See BUNG-HOLE, *H5*; SHIP-BOY, *KJ*; UNNATURAL, *R3* (another ref. to the rain of Sodom).

Both-sides Ambisexual; lechery.

AW, IV.iii.251 and 267. Bertram says Parolles is a 'Damnable both-sides rogue!' He is a traitor and an ambisexual – damned by the Bible and by law. DAMN: dam, a woman; to be damned, treated like one.

Bertram adds, 'I could endure any thing before but a cat, and now he's cat to me.' (1) Cat: 16th c., a whore; here perhaps a catamite. If so, Parolles is a catamite and *chattemite* (dissembler – Cot) – a both-sides rogue. (2) Repetition and slightly awkward wording indicate a pun: he is *cat to me*, like appendec*tomy*, sounds like *cat-tome* – L *tome*, cut – esp. since two scenes later (see SAFFRON) Parolles is 'snipt'. Bertram calls Parolles a eunuch, a castrated whore.

Ham, II.ii.370. On the controversy over 'children' who act, Rosencrantz tells Hamlet,

''Faith, there has been much to do [lechery – P; *besongner*, "to doe, or leacher with" – Cot] on both sides'. The Lord Mayor and City Fathers of London regularly used to protest against the child actors and the 'other uses to which they were put'. See Introduction, p. xiv and note 21, for quotes from Sh's contemporaries on their sexual exploitation. Etherege, *The Man of Mode*, II.ii: Dorimant, based on the bisexual libertine John Wilmot, 'talked to the vizards [VISARDS, prostitutes – *OED*] i' the pit' and went 'behind the scenes and fawned upon those little insignificant creatures, the players'. Chute, p. 231, says child actors appealed to the 'more cultured and wealthy clientele' – intriguing preference for a serious theatre-goer. And the children in *this* play, each acting a pretence – Ophelia, Laertes, Hamlet (see BRAINS), even Rosencrantz and Guildenstern ('the indifferent children of the earth' – II.ii.231) – they also are victims of (others') lechery. And in the end, as Horatio says, 'They bleed on both sides' (V.ii.315).

TrC, III.iii.266: 'He's grown a very land-fish, languageless, a monster. A plague of opinion! a man may wear it on both sides, like a leather jerkin.'

Ajax is a MONSTER (hermaphrodite, homosexual, thing of contraries), a land-fish. A plague on such OPINION (penis, or 'doxy': 1530, a prostitute) – on such a LEATHER (L *scortum*, leather; a prostitute) jerkin – that a man may wear (coitally – C; P) on both sides.

See BOLT, *TrC*.

Boult See BOLT.

Bowels The arse; also, like BOWLS, balls or testicles.

KJ, II.i.210: 'The cannons have their bowels full of wrath' – full bowels which expel wrath. But the cannons' balls are also full of wrath: 'He reputes me a cannon; and the bullet [obs. for cannonball], that's he' – *LLL*, III.i.65.

1H4, V.iii.36: 'God keep lead out of me! I need no more weight than mine own bowels.' Falstaff needs no more WEIGHT (L *as* / ass) than his own bowels. Maybe he also puns on lead (balls) or plumbs, lead weights – and his own balls, PLUMS or testicles (P). Cf. *H5*, I.ii.282: 'turn'd his balls to gun-stones' (stones are testicles and units of weight).

See CAMEL, *TrC*.

Bowl(er) Testicle (ball); pelvis; sex-play. Lit. a round mass that can be rolled in games; a basin (L *pelvis*). Love-making was freq. described in metaphors taken from the game of bowls, as in Webster, *The White Devil*, I.ii: the Duke is 'like an earnest bowler / He very passionately leans that way / He should have his bowl run'; 'Faith his *cheek* . . . would fain / *Jump* with my *mistress*' (italicised words are bowling-terms).

LLL, IV.i.140:

Costard. She's too hard for you at pricks, sir; challenge her to bowl.
Boyet. I fear too much rubbing. . . .

At *pricks* (archery) she is *too hard* for him. And *Boy*et (little BOY) also fears *to bowl* (two balls); he fears *too* much *rubbing*, a bowling-term for one ball's grazing another, and a pun on a fricative caress, masturbation (F&H; C; P).

AC, III.xiii.184, Antony: 'Come, / Let's have one other gaudy night . . . fill our bowls once more. . . . Come on, my queen; / There's sap in't yet. The next time I do fight / I'll make death love me'. Their bowls (his balls and her pelvis) will be filled. There's still sap: (1) life and hope; (2) wine in their bowls; (3) the kind of SAP (semen) that will fill their pelvises and make death love him (a little death: orgasm – P).

See DEWLAP, *MND*; QUICK, *MWW*.

Boy 1. Passive homosexual. 'In many contexts, and almost invariably in poetry, the passive partner is called *pais*, "boy" (plural *paides*)' (Dover, p. 16). Lucretius, Bk IV, 'Concerning the Nature of Love', trs. Dryden: 'Whether some beauteous Boy's alluring face, / Or lovelyer Maid with unresisted Grace' (*Signet Classic Poets of the 17th c.*, vol. II, p. 196). Wilmot, 'Upon his Drinking a Bowl': 'Then add Two lovely Boys;/Their Limbs in Amorous folds intwine.' Donne, Satire iv, 'The Court': 'Who loves whores, who boys, and who goats'. Boy: to play a woman's part (*OED*) – 'Some squeaking Cleopatra boy my greatness' (*AC*, v.ii.220). Also used for those at the other end of the spectrum, as in Wycherley, *The Country Wife*, I.i: 'Who do you call shadows of men?' – 'Half-men' – 'What, boys?' – 'Ay, your old boys, old *beaux garçons*, who, like superannuated stallions, are suffered to run, feed, and whinny with the mares . . . though they can do nothing else.'

Cym, v.v.105: 'The boy disdains me,/He leaves me, scorns me. Briefly die their joys/That place them on the truth of girls and boys.' Lucius means the girl–boy Imogen–Fidele (see CATTLE).

LLL, I.ii.186. Cupid's 'disgrace is to be called boy; but his glory is to subdue [SUBDUE, seduce – *OED*] men'.

IV.iii.169. Biron mocks his friends' loves: 'And Nestor play at push-pin with the boys'. 'Push-pin', a child's game, also meant copulation (F&H). Did Nestor play at push-pin with the *boyaux* (bowels – Cot) or *beaux* (Wycherley above)? Jonson, *Volpone*, III.vii: 'Think me . . . impotent . . . That I had Nestor's hernia'. See SLAVE, *Cor* for a similar pun.

Ado, v.i.91: 'Boys, apes, braggarts, Jacks, milksops!' – who ape or pretend to be men. Milksop: effeminate man, as in 'To wedden a Milksope or coward ape' (Chaucer, in *OED*). Jack: term of contempt (F&H); Sp *jaque*: braggart, smooth combed hair; Sp sl., pimp (Rosensweig). They are 'fashion-monging boys,/That lie and cog' (94) – that mong or sell FASHION (Fr *taille*), and COG (deceive like a pimp, an effeminate).

2. *Boye:* hangman, executioner (Cot). Hangman: Fr *pendeur*, pun on *pander* (PAINT, *MWW*). How well HANGED (between the legs) a man is reflects his masculinity.

Ado, III.ii.11. Cupid is a 'little hangman' or pander.

TGV, IV.iv.60. Launce was to deliver Proteus's dog to Silvia, but that 'squirrel was stolen . . . by the hangman boys in the market-place' so Launce gave her his own dog, 'as big as ten of yours'. So much for Proteus's 'gift' (GIFT) and 'present' (PRESENT), two puns on the genitals.

At Silvia's his dog (1) 'steals her capon's leg' (10); (2) offends by 'pissing', first in the 'company of three or four gentlemanlike dogs, under the duke's table' and then by heaving a 'leg' on Silvia herself. Capons or castrates are on, under and around the table: a duke is a Doge/DOG (eunuch); and his 'gentlemanlike dogs' are a reflection on his companions. 'Gentleman' (jocular and contemptuous – *OED*) is for Sh always opprobrious. Goddard (vol. II, p. 46) says that in Parolles, Shakespeare's wrath against the 'gentleman' culminates: 'In Proteus and Valentine he paints various shades'.

As in the past Launce had saved the dog from being 'executed', he again saves him from the gentlemen who would have 'hanged' him, from the duke who said, 'Hang him up' – from the *boyes*. This recital angers Proteus: 'stay'st thou to vex [VEX, fart on] me here?'

Launce's calling Proteus's dog a SQUIRREL (whore) that was STOLEN (made a stale or whore) by hangman boys, parodies his master, 'Sir Proteus' (I.i.70), and that other gentleman of Verona, his friend 'Sir Valentine', who, with the other hangman boys, are venal SQUIRES (pimps). They and the other boys are squirely (see SQUIRREL for John Lyly's pun on squirrilite/scurrility).

See BUDGE, *TSh*; PEASANT, *MWW*; CROOKED, *3H6*; SLAVE, *Cor*, *TGV*; CATTLE; ANNUAL, *Cor*.

Brag Pun on the codpiece (*braguette* – Cot) and its contents; on *braguerie*, wanton tricking, lascivious pranking (codpieces were 'often conspicuous' – *OED*; court jesters wore particularly noticeable ones). Sp *braga*: breeches; *bragudara*: crotch; *bragazas*: man easily ruled or henpecked; *da bragado*: of depraved sentiments; energetic, firm. Sp sl. *bragado*: 'Heavy hung', virile (Rosensweig).

See COMPASS, *MWW*; (Ac)QUAINT, *MV*; SPANIARD, *2H4*.

Brains 1. Excrement: *bran*, *bren*(Cot). Fr *breneux*, *-euse*: soiled with excrement.

Ham, II.ii.376:

Guildenstern. O, there has been much throwing about of brains.
Hamlet. Do the boys carry it away?
Rosencrantz. Ay, that they do, my lord: Hercules and his load too.

To gloss this only as HERCULES carrying the world on his shoulders (and the boys competing with the Globe company, which had a sign of him in this posture) ignores the context, the controversy over child actors (see BOTH-SIDES), the throwing about of brains, i.e. the crap being said on the subject (both off *and* on stage – 374), and the boys carrying it (the brains) away, as well as HERCULES and his LOAD (excrement) from the Augean stables (see RARE, *MND*).

Hamlet expresses guilt (617) over failing to fatten the kites with his uncle's 'offal'; and in the same speech calls himself 'an ass . . . a whore . . . a very drab,/ A scullion! Fie upon't! foh! About my brain!' Kites and offal refer right back to the child actors, 'little eyasses' (also hawks), their load and those brains. The little eyas Hamlet, who shares their problem of 'succession' (368), also must get rid of crap: he is (1) an ass; (2) a VERY (It *assai*) drab or whore; (3) a drab colour, a brownish YELLOW (excrement) – a shit; (4) a SCULLION (whore), q.v., who disposes of scullery offal. This leads into the next series of puns on 'brain': (1) FIE (shit) upon it; (2) foh, used for foul smells (*Oth*, III.ii.232: 'Foh! one may smell . . . most rank,/ Foul'); (3) ABOUT/*à bout* (Fr, at the end or butt) my brain (see FANCY for anal puns on Yorick's 'skull').

Poor Hamlet, who had said (I.ii.152) his uncle was '*but* no more like my father/ Than I to Hercules' (italics added), has the Herculean labour of cleaning the stables: 'Something is rotten in the state of Denmark' (I.iv.90) – the STATE, chair of state or stool (throne, privy, and excrement – *OED*), of Denmark. Fie upon it, about, says Hamlet, meaning his uncle's offal and his own brain or turd. (Marston, *Antonio's Revenge*, V.ii: 'Thou art another Hercules to us/ In ridding huge pollution from our state.')

See FAN, *1H4*; QUAGMIRE.

2. Testes. Skull and head (fig. the brains): L *testa*; *teste* (Cot). *Teste*: part in the brain so-called because of resemblance to a man's stones (F). Brain/ barren is a common pun: in *TrC*, I.iii.327, we have 'brain as barren'; and in Shirley's *Lady of Pleasure*, I.i, Aretina is adulterous because her husband, and all country men, have 'brains,/ And barren heads standing as much in want/ Of ploughing [copulation – F&H; P] as their ground'.

TN, I.v.92: Malvolio calls the Clown 'a barren rascal: I saw him put down the other day with an ordinary fool that has no more brain than a stone'. The Clown is a barren-brained RASCAL (castrate – G), without testicles, i.e. stones. He was put down (sexually – C; P) with a fool that had no more brain than a stone (has brain); and/ or no more brain than (he had) a stone.

Cym, IV.ii.113. Guiderius mocks Cloten as a 'fool, an empty purse;/ There was no money in't: not Hercules/ Could have knock'd out his brains, for he had none'. 'Purse' meant a scrotum (*OED*; P); 'no money in the purse' meant impotent (F&H). Cloten is a fool – an impotent one: no money in the purse, no brains. See PHRYGIAN, *MWW*, for another empty (impotent) purse.

TA, V.iii.133. Marcus says, if his family had done wrong, they would 'headlong cast us down,/ And on the ragged stones beat forth our brains,/ And make a mutual closure of our house'. The Andronici family (Gk *andro-*, male) would end themselves by casting themselves, HEADS (*teste*) down and beating out their brains on the stones; or by casting down their testicles (testes), beating out their stones – RAGged (castrated) scrotums, proof of inability to perpetuate their family. They would cast us (L *castus*, chaste) *down*. See the DETESTED (de*tested*) Andronici.

See DOG, *MWW*.

Breast Buttocks, stern. Perh. influenced by sterna (Gk *sternon*, breast), breast-bone; *ars*, breast of a horse (Cot). Both areas are two mounds. Bosom: sexual parts (P).

LLL, IV.iii.173. Biron taunts his love-sick friends, 'Where lies thy grief . . . where lies thy pain? . . . all about the breast:/ A caudle, ho!' Always cynical Biron refers less to heart-ache than pain in the tail (arse – K; P). Caudle, a traditional drink for the sick and new mothers, puns on *caudal*, like or near the tail. Where lies their GRIEF (bowel-pains; colic), he mocks, knowing well the bowels were believed to be the seat of the tender emotions. (In *2H6*, IV.vii.95, when Lord Say, accused of a corrupting effeminacy, of coming 'behind [BEHIND] folks', admits his 'cheeks [CHEEKS, buttocks] are pale' and 'Long sitting' has made him 'full of sickness [SICKNESS: effeminacy; pregnancy]', Cade wishes him a 'hempen caudle' – pun on *caudle*, the drink, and *caudal*, the tail-like rope's end to hang him.)

TN, II.iii.20:

Sir Toby. Welcome, ass. Now let's have a catch.
Sir Andrew. By my troth, the fool has an excellent breast. I had rather than forty shillings that I had such a leg, and so sweet a breath to sing, as the fool has . . . thou wast in very gracious fooling last night. . . . I sent thee sixpence for thy leman: hadst it?

'Ass' and CATCH (a man's prick) trigger Andrew's response that by his TROTH/trot (bawd) the Clown has an EXCELLENT (lewd, esp. of the arse) breast and leg and was in GRACIOUS (sexually well-endowed) fooling (folly: sexual wildness – P) last night, when Andrew sent him SIXPENCE (a trot's fee), for a leman or lover. The Clown's EXCELLENT breast resolves itself into a tail: *such a* leg and *so* (both *tale* – F) sweet a breath. Andrew wants SUCH (a tail) a leg and breath (length and breadth?) with which to sing (take someone sexually – C; P), to sing the CATCH (prick-song). In the last night he mentions a similar conversation took place, but then it was Andrew whose legs and thighs were praised, and the gracious fooling was quite bawdy (see EXCELLENT).

See TURK, *Oth*.

Breath(e) Breed. Gen 2:7: 'the Lord God formed man . . . and breathed into his nostrils the breath of life'. Langland, *Piers the Ploughman*, Bk XI: some birds conceive at their beaks through the act of breathing. The editor says 'This curious idea is derived from Aristotle, *Hist. of Animals*, Bk vi. c.ii Sect. 9.' Sh uses this idea in 'The Phoenix and the Turtle', 17: 'And thou treble-dated crow,/That thy sable gender mak'st/With the breath thou giv'st and tak'st'.

AW, II.i.76. Lafeu tells the King his FISTULA (impotence) can be cured: 'I have seen a medicine/That's able to breathe life into a stone,/Quicken a rock'. He knows a medicine that can *breathe* life into the King's impotent rocks and stones (testicles) so that they will be able to *breed* life.

1H6, v.iv.127: 'To ease your country . . . and suffer you to breathe in fruitful peace'. Fruitful is more often associated with breeding than with breathing. 'Country' puns on the 'cunt' (C; P) that will be EASED (provided sexual intercourse) when men breathe and breed in fruitful PEACE (genitals) and a truce is signed.

2H6, III.ii.398: 'To have thee with thy lips to stop my mouth;/So shouldst thou either turn my flying soul,/Or I should breathe it so into thy body,/And then it lived in sweet Elysium'. The vivid physical image in the first half of the sentence indicates that the second half is not purely ethereal and that breathing *into* her *body* is the act of coition during which Suffolk's soul enters into what Sh calls Elysium and his contemporary Robert Herrick called the 'postern gate to the Elysian fields' (F&H, s.v. Monosyllable), the vulva. He wants 'to die . . . like a pleasant slumber in thy lap' (389) – die (the sexual orgasm – C; P), in her lap (pudendum – TWR; P); and requests that she let him 'stay, befall what may befall!' – *fall* in death as in post-coital detumescence (C; P).

An old folk belief was that the form taken by the soul as it escaped through the mouth was that of a mouse (*W*; B) – Suffolk's 'flying soul' or *Fledermaus* (Ger, flying mouse, bat). 'The word for mouse is often transferred to the musk sac, the scrotum, vulva, and other bodily parts' (*W*, s.v. Musk). Mouse: to womanise (C; P); 16th c., the mouth; the penis (F&H n.d.). See EXERCISE, *Oth*, for breaths that 'embraced'.

Per, II.iii.101: 'Here is a lady which wants breathing too:/And I have heard you knights of Tyre/Are excellent in making ladies trip'. Thaisa wants the rapid breathing attendant upon dancing; but her father equates breathing with a trip (sexual misstep – C; P), in which, he says,

Pericles EXCELS (lit. raises high; pun on to do so sexually). Thaisa will be raised high during figures of the dance and after her breathing/breeding, in pregnancy. This foreshadows her trip (voyage) with Pericles, in which it seems she again wants (lacks) breathing, presumably dies in delivering a child, awakes and 'a warmth/Breathes out of her' (III.ii.94).

1H4, IV.i.11. Hotspur and Douglas exalt themselves to godhood. Hotspur swears 'By God' and asks 'approve me, lord' of this 'approved Scot' (I.i.54, ironically then his foe). And this 'Lord Douglas' (as Hotspur calls him, V.ii.33) says, 'Thou art the king of honour:/No *man* so potent *breathes upon the ground*/But I will beard him' ('the Lord God formed *man* of the dust *of the ground and breathed*' life into him – Gen 2:7). (Italics added.) PROVE: be virile.

Douglas's middle clause ambiguously swings both ways: back to Hotspur, this king (epithet for God) more potent than man who breathes and breeds; and ahead to the foe he will beard. This idolatry will be punished: by calling Hotspur *king of honour*, Douglas unconsciously prophesies his downfall, for 'In the multitude of people is the king's honour, but in the want of people is the destruction of the prince' (Prov 4:28). And a want of people (their desertions before and on the field) is Hotspur's ruin. As Prince Hal had promised *his father*, the anointed King, 'this same child [not "king"] of honour . . . Hotspur, this all-praised knight . . . For every honour sitting on his helm/Would they were multitudes . . . he shall render every glory up,/Yea, even the slightest worship. . . . This in the name of God, I promise here' (III.ii.139).

See MODEST, *AC*.

Bridle Prepare the HORSE/whores for riding (fornication – C; P). Bridal: nuptial, a bride being a spouse of either sex.

See KNOT, *AW*; SUBJECT, *CE*; FIE, *TSh*.

Broad(er) Obscene, effeminate. Broad awake: 'physiologically allusive to sexual intercourse' (P). *Brodier*: arse, tail (Cot). 'Broad arse', Gk *euryproktos*: a term of derision as in Aristophanes, *The Clouds*, 1083–104: 'What's the matter with being a broad-arse?' – 'Is there anything worse than that?' This condition resulted from having a radish forced up the anus by an offended husband (Dover, p. 140). In *Thesmophoriazusae*, the effeminate Agathon is accused of having been a male prostitute, 'And you, you *katapugon* ["male who submits to anal penetration"], are wide-arsed – not just in words, but in submissiveness!' (Dover, pp. 141, 113). Cf. *langage brode* : 'a loose, laskie squattering, scurvie; also, an effeminate, language or speech' (Cot) – the equiv. of today's 'verbal diarrhoea'.

TrC, I.iii.190. Ajax is compared to the 'broad Achilles'. Both men are elsewhere called 'ass' and 'effeminate' (see Index).

See STIR, *Tim*; STAND BACK; FAN, *TrC*; CHEVERIL, *RJ*.

Brook (1) Enjoy carnally. Lit. to enjoy.
(2) Pimp. Broke (obs. form of 'brook'); a pimp.
MATTER, *MWW*; SPREAD, *Ham*.

Buckram Effeminate, impotent; fit for buggery. Buckram: ME 'bougeren'; Fr *bougran*; Ger *buggerom*. Puns on *bougrin*: buggering, fit for buggery (Cot).

2H6, IV.vii.28, Cade: 'Ah, thou say, thou serge, nay, thou buckram lord . . . [who gave up] Normandy unto Mounsieur Basimecu, the dauphin of France'. Lord *Say* (a cloth, formerly partly of silk – *OED*) is serge (L *sericus*, silk fabric) and buckram, a fine material artificially stiffened, hence a false appearance of strength. Say is SILKEN (effeminate – *OED*); he looks like but is not a man; he is a bugger who gave up NORMANDY (q.v.) to the Dauphin, Monsieur Basimecu (*baisez mon cul*, kiss my backside – P). See ABOMINABLE and SILK for his sodomy.

1H4, II.iv.213–43. Ostensibly describing a theft by men who, it is said five times, wore buckram, Gadshill *et al*. describe their rout in terms of their having been buggered. As Falstaff and crew were 'sharing' (SHARE, copulate; the pubes – *OED*) among themselves, 'some six or seven fresh men set upon us'. The men FRESH (with sexual prowess) or freshmen (Eliz. term for first-year men at Oxford and Cambridge; Ger. equiv. *Fuchs*, a term that, if known to Sh, would have connoted *fucks) set upon* them (set on, incite to coitus – P). They 'unbound the rest, and then come in the other': unbound the REST (support for a fire-arm; an erect penis) and then *come in* (coitus – C; P) the OTHER (arse). Falstaff says that 'came all a-front and mainly thrust at me', who 'took all their seven points [erect penises – C; P] in my target, thus'. The target or *mark* in archery was the *butt*, in the centre of which the prick was placed; this pun is repeated when Hal says he not only hears him but does 'mark' him, too. Then, 'Their points being broken –', 'Down fell their hose', inserts *Poins* (who had actually been one of the masked points). He sarcastically converts Falstaff's meaning (points of their swords) to the points that hold up a man's hose (16th c., breeches) and his HOSE (penis) – the point (penis – C; P; the 'prick' on a dial – *OED*).

Falstaff continues, 'three . . . came at my back and let drive at me'. THREE (penis and testes) let drive (*let rive*, split, tear apart) at his *back*. The 'eleven buckram men grown out of the two' (242; ELEVEN: with penis erect; *grown* out of the TWO, the testes) were 'in buckram' (218), pun on *bougrin*: 'fit for buggerie; whence; *Chausses à la bougrine*', straight venetian hose without codpiece (Cot). So, when these fell down, down and out fell the HOSE, penis (see STRAIT STROSSERS).

Broken points is a recurrent 16th c. jest: in Dekker's *The Shoemaker's Holiday*, v.ii, 'Lusty Firk [fuck – C; P]' was talking of 'laced mutton' (prostitutes) and saying he would have 'lammed', beaten and made lamb (mutton) of, some men he was fighting: 'O heart, my codpiece-point is ready to fly in pieces every time I think upon Mistress Rose.'

These puns demonstrating the bisexual humour of the Boar's Head crew are summed up by Hal: 'These lies [LIE, bugger/It *bugiare*, lie] are like their father that begets them; gross [obscene] . . . open [OPEN, sexually available] . . . thou whoreson, obscene, greasy tallow-catch [CATCH: penis, fornicator]'. See BITE for puns on buggery in the scene antecedent to the robbery; CATERPILLAR for the original scene; and DEXTERITY and SAME for Hal's further mockery of the event.

Wycherley, *The Country Wife*, Epil., gives his view of the scene: 'Next, you Falstaffs of fifty, who beset/Your buckram maidenheads, which your friends get;/And whilst to them, you of achievements boast,/They share the booty, and laugh at your cost./In fine, you essenc't [perfumed] boys, both old and young. . . .' See BOY, Wycherley.

Budge(r) Bugger: a sodomite (TWR, s.v. Bouger); *bugerare* (to bugger – F).

RJ, III.i.58: Mercutio 'will not budge for no man's pleasure'. Pleasure is sexual (P), as when Peter 'saw no man use you [Nurse] at his pleasure' (II.iv.164). See CONSORT, ZOUNDS, for details.

JC, IV.iii.44. Brutus will not be exploited, screwed, by Cassius: 'fret till your proud heart break;/Go show your slaves . . . make your bondmen tremble. Must I budge? . . . must I stand and crouch/Under your testy humour? . . . You shall digest the venom of your spleen'. Let Cassius fret, i.e. rub (masturbate – F&H); *fregare*, rub up and down, frig (F); make the Cynick friction. Let his bondmen or SLAVES tremble (with ecstasy: 'a hand that kings/Have lipp'd, and trembled kissing' – *AC*, II.v.30). Brutus will not budge/bugger for Cassio; not stand (erect penis – C; P) and CROUCH/crotch under (in intercourse) when Cassius's testy humour desires. The pun on testy/teste (testicle) is reinforced by SPLEEN (male generative organ and its secretion). Cassius must digest (eat, i.e. fret) his own spleen. See CAIUS for his screwing himself in this scene.

TSh, Induction, i.14. Sly, the tinker (a bodger, botcher, or beggar) is dead drunk. He tells the hostess, who threatens to call a borough, 'Go by, Jeronimy; go to thy cold bed, and warm thee'; 'I'll answer him by law: I'll not budge an inch, boy; let him come, and kindly.' 'Go by, Jeronimy', Sh's only ref. to St Jerome, may be a pun on go *bougirroner* (bugger – Cot). Sly puns on 'kindly', i.e. lawful holding of a lease of land. He is entitled to the land he lies on and will not budge an inch or an INCH (see for later use as small arse). The Hostess (whom he calls BOY, catamite) may choose to be buggered by a borough (arch. and Sc burgher); she may let him come (have a sexual spasm – P), and KINDLY (sexually) – she may *kindle* herself ('warm thee') in her cold bed. But Sly will ANSWER him (a coital hit; lit. return thrust in fencing), not be buggered but 'Screw him!'

A Lord then sees the drunken Sly, whom he calls a 'monstrous beast' (MONSTER and BEAST, homosexual and bugger) and a 'swine' (SWINE, bugger). He tells his attendants to take Sly to a room in his home, hung 'round [ROUND, homosexual] with . . . wanton pictures', bring in a page dressed 'like a lady', who will woo him with 'kind embracements' and call him 'husband'; 'do it kindly . . . it will be . . . excellent,/ If it be husbanded with modesty' – KINDLY (sexually), EXCELLENT (lewd) husbanding. The Lord is familiar with the ambisexual abilities of his 'boy' (to BOY: play a woman's part – P; *OED*); 'I know the boy will well usurp the grace,/ Voice, gait and action of a gentlewoman' – GRACE (genitals), VOICE/VICE (pudendum, closed thighs – P), GATE/GAIT (arse or vulva) and action, sex-act (C; P). He anticipates with *long*ing ('I long to hear him call the drunkard husband'), the sexual excitement of a voyeur, the way his men will have to 'stay themselves from laughter/ When they do homage to this simple peasant'. They must not give way to LAUGHTER (fornication) over the HOMAGE (homosexual activity) given this PEASANT (hind). They must not let 'over-merry [MERRY, lusty] spleen [SPLEEN, producer of both merriment and semen] . . . *grow* into extremes' (italics added).

A scene in the 'bedchamber' shows Sly's attempts to get 'madam wife' to 'undress you and come now to bed'. The strolling players hired by the Lord to entertain Sly and his 'wife' with the *TSh* then arrive. The First Folio does not separate the Induction from the play; this must have thematic implications. In the Royal Shakespeare Company's production, London, April 1979, one actor played both Sly and Petruchio. This 'pleasing stuff' as Sly calls *TSh* (for eroticism of 'please' and 'stuff', see P) is set in 'fruitful Lombardy' (LOMBARDY: 'The sin of Buggery brought to London by the Lombards' – ÓED, s.v. Bugger, 1617).

See FOOT, *1H4*; STAND BACK, *1H6*; CONSORT, *RJ*; SLAVE, *Cor*.

Buggery Buggery is abominable heresy: sodomy (*OED*). However, just as in today's speech to be fucked or screwed means to be rendered impotent, ruined; and to fuck means to destroy or betray, so to be buggered also meant to be figuratively emasculated, unmanned, rendered powerless. Buggery is a frequent Sh metaphor for betrayal or murder, especially within families or nations, for a politically heretical or an unnatural act.

'Vulgar idiom in many languages uses "buggered" or "fucked" in the sense "defeated", "worsted", and some Attic vases are pictorial treatments of this notion' (Dover, p. 105). Dover gives an example in which the Italian *inculato* (*culo*, arse) was applied to a defeated football team. It is the buggered and not the buggerer who is considered tarnished.

And it is in this light that the puns on buggery are often to be understood, as in BEGGAR, BUTCHER, LIAR, CROOKED, etc. The amount of actual sodomy in the plays cannot be measured by references to it, any more than the amount of fucking or screwing can be measured by the frequency of these words in 20th c. speech. As Mrs Page says in *MWW*, IV.ii.108: 'We do not act that often jest and laugh'.

It ought be mentioned, for the understanding of the puns, that buggery (sodomy) is not exclusively male. In Greek vase-painting, penetration is commonly portrayed from the rear and 'in some cases there can be no room for doubt that it is the woman's anus, not her vagina, which is being penetrated' (Dover, p. 100). Rowse, p. 100: 'the figure "shows the woman hath a mind to the quent, but seems she is or will be a harlot. And because . . . she useth sodomy." ' Thomas Shadwell, 'The Medal of John Bays': 'Calls himself whoremaster and sodomite,/ Commends Reeves' arse and says she buggers well' (*Signet Classic Poets of the 17th c.*, vol. II, p. 389). Wycherley, *The Country Wife*, IV.iii:

Horner [lover]. . . . but I'll get into her the back way.
Jasper [husband]. Wife! He is coming into you the back way.
Lady. Let him come, and welcome, which way he will.

Other quotations from Sh's contemporaries are in this dictionary. We need, of course, be aware – as Sh's audience was – that the lines of 'women' were delivered by boys.

Bulk Buttocks. Lit. body, belly; greater part. Bulk up: cause to swell. A bulker (arch.) is a strumpet (who sleeps on bulkheads), as in Durfey, *Madam Fickle*, v.i: 'this damn'd bulking quean [whore]'. John Oldham, 'The Streets of London': 'my Foot/Shall march about your Buttocks: whence d'ye come,/From what Bulk-ridden Strumpet reeking home?' (*Penguin Book of Restoration Verse*, p. 247).

WT, II.i.20, 2nd Lady: 'She is spread of late/Into a goodly bulk; good time encounter her!' Superficially, Hermione's goodly bulk is mere recognition of her pregnancy. But the language reflects the gossip: (1) SPREAD (open to coitus); (2) encounter (the sex-act – P). A few lines later her husband, like the 2nd Lady, uses GOOD (adulterous) twice: 'she is a goodly lady' and 'she's goodly', but you must add, 'She's an adulteress.' Bulk is, then, part of the allegation that Hermione is a strumpet; that, as her husband says, not he but her lover 'Has made thee swell thus'.

2H4, III.ii.277. Falstaff does not judge by 'the limb, the thewes, the stature, *bulk* and *big ass*emblance of a man!' (italics added).

See STRAIGHT, *Oth*; SHED, *TrC*; Introduction, p. xiv, *Tem*.

Bung(hole), bungle Anus. *Cul de cheval*, lit. horse's anus: ugly fish resembling man's 'bung-hole' (Cot).

2H4, II.iv.138, Doll: 'Away, you cut-purse rascal! you filthy bung, away! by this wine, I'll thrust my knife in your mouldy chaps'. The usual gloss of 'bung' as mere reiteration of cut-purse overlooks the wine Doll swears by, with its connotations of wine-cask and bung (stopper and hole); and her next image of thrusting a knife into Pistol's MOULDY (venereally diseased) chaps (open fissures), his *chiappe* (buttocks – F) – puns that explain his being a *filthy* bung(hole), and, since *chapon* is a capon (Cot), that dovetail with his being a CUT (gelding – *OED*) purse (scrotum – *OED*; P) (castrate) – epithets more fitting the whore who had just called Pistol 'base', the bottom or cul (anus – *OED*) of anything. In ll.43, 58, Doll twice calls Falstaff 'muddy' (MUDDY, shitty). Does 'the old boar feed in the old frank', Hal had asked (ii.159). He does, and Doll calls him (iv.241,235) 'boar-pig [Gk *pyg*, rump]' and 'whoreson chops [i.e. chaps – *OED*; *chiappe*, buttocks]'. See SAUCE.

Ham, v.i.227: 'To what base uses we may return . . . trace the noble dust of Alexander . . . find it stopping a bung-hole'. This pun on Alexander, who was 'buried' and returned to 'stop a beer-barrel' (a bier or burial-barrel), as in life he stopped a different kind of bung-hole (his pederasty was famed, his lover Hephaestion likening them to Achilles and Patroclus), is repeated: Hamlet says Caesar, also turned to clay, stopped 'a hole to keep the wind [WIND, flatus] away' and 'a wall to expel the winter's flaw!' – Caesar's 'base' use is to patch a hole in a WALL (buttocks), to expel the flaw or crack (*pet*: fart, crack – Cot). See CURIOUS for Horatio's appropriate reply.

H5, II.ii.115. Henry calls three traitors 'monsters' (MONSTERS, buggers). Scroop, who 'knew'st the very bottom of my soul' (VERY, the arse; bottom; SOUL, the arse), was 'wrought upon . . . preposterously' (PREPOSTEROUSly: of the buttocks; of buggery) by a devil who 'got the voice [VOICE/VICE] in hell for excellence [EXCELLENCE: L *ex* + *cellere*, to raise high; pun on lewdness and sodomy]'. Scroop is told to rise, 'stand up', while other tempters, notably serpents, are condemned to crawl: 'All other devils that suggest by treasons/Do botch and bungle up damnation/With patches, colours . . . But he that temper'd thee bade thee stand up . . . He might return to vasty Tartar back/And tell the legions 'I can never win/A soul so easy as that Englishman's!' *Bungle* with *patches* and COLOURS/(It *culare*, arse) has a ring too like *stopping* up a *bunghole* (*Ham* above) not to be making the same pun (see TARTAR).

The DEVIL (bisexual) that *temper*'d (1593, to corrupt or pervert) and seduced Scroop (who, in turn, buggered Henry) might *return back* – redundancy to stress the area of the body discussed. He well might tell the OTHER (arse) devils who BOTCH (bugger) that he can never win a SOUL (arse) so EASY/Fr *aisé*/ass as that English/ingle-ish-man's (K): an ingle, a catamite.

Henry's passionate renunciation culminates in likening Scroop's 'revolt' to 'Another fall of man', also brought about by a devil, the 'same demon that hath gull'd thee [Scroop] thus'. The SAME (homosexual) demon who GULLed (buggered) Scroop also made a 'gull' (buggered man) of Malvolio (*TN*), and he, too, came from TARTAR. Cf. *Shakespeare Quarterly*, vol. 32, no. 2 (Summer 1981) p. 230, review of *Henry V*: 'effeminate portrayal of Scroop . . . in his final scene, delivered his lines with a simpering lisp'.

Burn daylight Revel wantonly; usu. glossed as 'waste time'. Cf. Plautus, *The Twin Menaechmi*, 150–60: at the courtesan's the men 'comburamus diem' – (1) burn up day; (2) consume in revelling (*Cassell's Latin Dictionary*).

RJ, I.iv.43:

Mercutio. . . . Come, we burn daylight, ho!
Romeo. Nay, that's not so.
Mercutio. I mean, sir, in delay
We waste our lights in vain. . . .
Take our good meaning. . . .

Since Mercutio is impelled to say, take my *good* meaning, it seems likely it is this other that Romeo heard; esp. since in *Cor*, II.i.234, Sh links Phoebus, sun-god of daylight, to wanton revelling: 'wanton spoil/ Of Phoebus' burning kisses' – wanton spoil (sexual violation – P) of burning (with ardour and with VD – *OED*; C; P).

See ALTER, *MWW*.

Business Coitus (F&H; P). Jonson, *The Devil is an Ass*, V.i: a man reports the theft of a whore's 'shoes . . . And garters I had given her for the business'.

AC, I.ii.178. Antony says 'The business' Fulvia broached needs him. Enobarbus: 'And the business you have broached here cannot be without you; especially that of Cleopatra's, which wholly depends on your abode' – the broaching (coitus – P) wholly/hole (pudendum – P) of Cleopatra's business. See STEEL.

See KEY, *MM*; RIPE, *MV*; CONSORT, *CE*.

Butcher See BOTCHER/BUTCHER.

Buttons On the codpiece or breeches. Anon., 'One Writeing against his Prick': 'doe not dare/ To Peepe or take the aire/ But through a Button hole, but pine and dye/ Confin'd within the Codpiece Monestry' (*Penguin Book of Restoration Verse*, p. 184).

MWW, III.ii.71. The Host praises Fenton as a lover: 'he capers, he dances . . . he will carry't, he will carry't; 'tis in his buttons, he will carry't'.

The manly Fenton can CAPER and DANCE (fornicate), unlike the effeminate *Slender* ('slight ones will not carry it', *AW*, IV.i.42), who probably cannot 'carry it' (see UNMANNERLY) to a wife. '. . . 'tis in his buttons' is probably an equiv. of ' 'tis in his breeches' (*KJ*, III.i.201: 'Your breeches best may carry them'). Marston, *Antonio and Mellida*, V.ii: 'he that hath the best parts of – I'll prick him down for my husband' – 'when she is pricking down the good parts of her servants [remember me]. As I am a true knight, I grow stiff; I shall carry it.'

See SILK, *RJ*.

C

Cackle (1) Voice of a male effeminate, a castrate. Lit. sound of a hen or capon. Thomas Heyrick, 'The Battle between the Cock and Capon': Chanticleer is defeated by a 'Castrate' who 'would have Crow'd, to show the Victory:/ But barr'd by former wrongs [a housewife's "bloody Knife"] that faculty,/ He Cackled something out' (*Penguin Book of Restoration Verse*, p. 272).

(2) Voice of a whore. Lit. sound of a goose. (Winchester) goose (C; P), green goose (F&H), *gueuse* (Cot): a whore.

(3) Voice of a cuckold, cokil (*OED*; TWR). L *cuculus*, cuckoo: bird of cuckoldry (C; P). *Cuculare*: to play the cuckoo, to hood (F).

(4) Voice of a hypocrite, one who wears a HOOD (L *cucullus*).

KL, II.ii.89: 'Goose, if I had you upon Sarum plain,/ I'ld drive ye cackling home to Camelot'. According to some authorities, the Camelot of Arthurian romance was Winchester (*W*; B). On Sarum PLAIN (Biblical cities of the plain: land of sodomites) Kent would peddle this (Winchester) goose (prostitute – F&H; P), this *gueuse* (whore – Cot), this cackling male whore, home to Camelot. Puns on (1) Fr *gueuse*, a small article made of camlet cloth; also, of little value; (2) Fr *Camelot*, pedlar (*W*). See CAMEL (fornicator).

MV, v.i.105. Portia's talk of 'sounds' is part of a thematic pun on her own VOICE/VICE, her duplicity and sexuality (K); it is tied to a pun on season/ seisin (confiscate – K; possession – *Cham*) – both puns running through Acts I–V. Portia says the nightingale would go unheeded were it to 'sing . . . When every goose is cackling' for 'things by season season'd are/ To their right praise'. Lorenzo recognises 'the voice,/ Or I am much deceived, of Portia', who says, 'He knows me as the blind man knows the cuckoo,/ By the bad voice.' She has the bad, caco- (Gk *kakos*), voice; does she have its bad vice, destruction of its foster-parents (WIND, *1H4*); does she destroy a father (our Father, theol.)? And is she, like it, a cuckold?

SEASON–season'd ties her speech (1) to the court she has just left, where 'seasons' and 'season'd' are used; and (2) to Bassanio's 'In law, what plea so tainted and corrupt/ But, being season'd with a gracious voice,/ Obscures the show of evil . . . no vice so simple but assumes/ Some mark of virtue' (III.ii.76). Shylock's was the plea of law but hardly the gracious voice obscuring evil, vice assuming virtue, not the voice that seasoned (confiscated – K). That voice was either (1) Portia's, the voice of 'mercy', i.e. grace, God's grace, defending Antonio, who called himself (IV.i.114) a 'tainted wether [eunuch]' – wether/WEATHER, lit. seasons (is his, then, the plea so tainted and corrupt?); or (2) the Duke's ('your grace'), who read the letter from Bellario – belle aria, a song for a single voice (when no other goose is cackling) – asking for 'gracious' acceptance of Portia, whom he names 'Balthasar' (and whom Shylock calls 'Daniel'). Dan 1:7: 'the prince of the eunuchs . . . gave unto Daniel the name of Belteshazar'. Balthasar–Portia, come 'in my [Bellario's] stead', to be his voice, his substitute, lit. a vice. But a VICE (K) is also a screw (*Ado*, v.ii.21). Who screwed and/ or was screwed by whom in court? Who season'd (season: copulate with – *OED*; SCREW) or screwed? Who confiscated, took seisin or possession: Antonio, or Portia, who said Antonio 'Shall *seize one* half his [Shylock's] goods' (IV.i.353; italics added), and the state the other half? Portia, who says that Shylock's 'life lies in the mercy/ Of the duke only, 'gainst all other voice' – 'gainst the mercy and the voice of God, a voice not heard when every goose (Ger and Du *gans*; *ganza* – F; 'The geese . . . be called Ganzae' – *OED*, s.v. Ganza, 1601; Butler, *Hudibras*, Pt II, c.iii.781: 'ganzas') is cackling '*gainst* it, for *gains*. 'Down therefore and *beg mercy* of the Duke', she says; '*Beg . . . leave to hang* thyself' Gratiano says in the next line (cry *cockles*, be hanged – B; G), for 'Thou has not left the value of a *cord*' (italics added)? Or is it Antonio, who said Shylock must become a Christian and 're*cord* a gift . . . of all he dies possess'd' to Lorenzo and Jessica (italics added)? 'My deeds upon my head', Shylock had said. And they 'send the deed after' him, 'give him this deed' – the deed (copulation – TWR; C; P) or screwing pursues him: 'This deed will be well welcome to Lorenzo' says Portia – to Lorenzo whom Antonio calls the 'gentleman [Gentile/gentle: *MV*, II.vi.51 – K]/That lately stole [STOLE, made a stale or whore of] his daughter'.

This is an intricately woven web of puns, difficult to untangle, flattering to none, but crucial to understanding the play. A 'substitute' shines brightly only when the 'king' is not by, says Portia (V.i.94), who substituted not only for Bellario but also for *the* king, i.e. God; and, according to some critics, a lamentable job in dealing out mercy was done by this substitute or vice, this bad voice, in portioning grace (ME, the favour of God and God himself).

In her male dress, Portia has a *bad* voice (BAD: hermaphroditic – *OED*; effeminate – *W*); the SHOW (Fr *monstre*/MONSTER, hermaphrodite, cuckold) of EVIL (L *male*), obscured by a gracious voice: GRACIOUS (sexually well-endowed) with all GRACES (genitals), and 'furnished' with Bellario's 'opinion' (IV.i.157) – FURNISHED (sexually) with his OPINION (penis). And another girl–boy, Jessica (she, too, has an 'opinion' – III.v.76, 907), wishes to be 'obscured' and is – in what her husband calls 'the lovely garnish of a boy' (II.vi.45)! Masculine women, effeminate men – capons who cackle.

Portia compares Lorenzo to a blind man hearing a cuckoo (cuckold). In *Ado*, II.i.205, Claudio is called 'blind man' by Benedick, who thinks him a cuckold; in Chaucer's 'The Merchant's Tale', the 'cokewald' January is blind. Lorenzo jests that Launcelot has cuckolded him (*cucuglio*: cuckoo; hood – F). Obscured women and blind men. Blind means lacking in moral perception, L *caecus* (from *caecare*, make blind, make obscure). It means a deceit, and a bandage or hood for the eyes, esp. in games (like 'hoodman blind' in *Ham*, III.iv.77).

Portia had left Lorenzo and Jessica 'In place of Lord Bassanio and myself' – the couples are mirror images (two daughters who deceived fathers to acquire husbands who were lured by their money: see Index). *Lord* Bassanio, whom in her idolatry she calls her 'king' and 'governor' (Ps 22:28: 'the kingdom is the Lord's: and he is the governor'), to him Portia commits her 'gentle' spirit (III.ii.165). Jessica, too, was 'a gentle, and no Jew' (II.vi.51, Folio sp.).

Antonio meant Shylock when he said, 'The devil can cite Scripture for his purpose . . . O what a goodly outside falsehood hath!' (I.iii.99). But whom did Sh mean, for others, too, quoted Scripture in the courtroom *and* wore false hoods (*bourlet*: 'the Hood worne by . . . Lawyers' – Cot). Gratiano had said that at Belmont he would act a part, not be bold of 'voice' but 'put on a sober habit . . . Wear prayer books in my pocket . . . while grace is saying, hood mine eyes' (II.ii.199). Bassanio inadvertently describes this hypocrite not only as he is while grace is said at Portia's table, but also as he is when it is said in the courtroom, 'In religion,/What damned error, but some sober brow/Will bless it and approve it with a text' (III.ii.77) – the sober habit and sober brow of Gratiano who swore 'by my hood' Jessica was no Jew. Belmont and Venice, world of hoodwinked and hoodwinkers.

These puns anticipate the finale, the RINGS (genitals) the men gave away; the alleged cuckolding; the unavoidable underplay of buggery, since the girls disguised as boys are, of course, really boys. Is it not worthy of attention that, the trial over, Portia and Nerissa 'away tonight' – but Bassanio lacks a sense of urgency or haste and sends Gratiano after the learned doctor, both to give him his ring and to invite him to Antonio's, and he tells Antonio that not until 'the morning early will we both/Fly toward Belmont: *come*, Antonio' (IV.i.456; italics added). Thus he projects an all-male overnight party, though he had promised Portia 'till I *come* again,/No bed shall e'er be guilty of my stay,/No rest be interposer 'twixt us twain' (III.ii.327; italics added). Come (sexually – C; P) to Antonio: no REST (support for erect penis) interposes betwixt *these* TWAIN (homosexual love).

'Cackle' – Sh's ultimate jest at the expense of the Belmont lovers, the husbands of whom Shylock says, 'These be the Christian husbands' (IV.i.295): Bassanio would 'sacrifice' his wife to deliver Antonio (286); Gratiano, too, would wish his 'wife . . . in heaven' to entreat the powers to 'change' Shylock (see ALTER, *MV*, emasculate). Cackle: sound made not by the cock who crows but by the capon who can't. These morally blind people are also sexually blind, i.e. (hort.) without buds or eyes, without a terminal flower. They are sterile.

Caius An ass/arse (Fr *cas*). Genitals (case – K; P).

MWW. K says, 'Caius is merely a fanciful Latin respelling of *Keys*', but also notes (p. 178) that 'key' 'had two pronunciations' and rhymes with 'may', 'survey' as with 'be', 'thee'.

(1) 'Master Doctor Caius, the renowned French physician [*mire*]' is an ass/arse. Mire: to defecate on; dirt (P): see ANNE, CONTRARY, DRY, ELDER, PHYSICIAN. (2) A 'case' was a condition, esp. a physical one. (3) The 'case' or genitals is a concern of physicians. (4) Caius is 'Master Caius, that calls himself doctor of *physic*' (italics added), a word that in play after play means to dose or purge the bowels. (5) The scene in his house opens, 'I pray thee, go to the casement, and see if you can see my master, Master Doctor Caius, coming' (*case*ment and Caius, in line with 'see' and 'see', 'master' and 'Master'). (6) His own first speech is, 'Pray you, go and vetch me in my closet un boitier vert, a box, a green-a box; do intend vat I speak? a green-a box.' This French-speaking Dr Caius calls repeatedly for his box or *casse* (Cot) and for his *boîtier* or surgeon's case of instruments, and for the simples he would not for the world 'leave behind [BEHIND, rump]'. (7) 'I pray' and 'Pray you' pun on PRAY/*après* (behind). (8) Dr Caius, the *cas* or arse, the behind or *derrière*, says, 'If *dere* be one or two, I shall make-a the turd' (italics added). The arse will make-a the turd: a piece of dung, a contemptible person.

I find no similar function served by the pronunciation 'keys'.

JC, IV.iii.6: 'You wrong'd yourself to write in such a case.' Brutus says *Caius Cas*sius did *wrong* to *write* in a *case* involving bribes; esp. since Caius has 'an itching palm' and kept 'rascal counters from his friends'. Merchants' cash or counters: *casse* (F). Again the pun signifies asinine behaviour, for just as in *MWW* Dr Caius is called ELDER (ass), so Cassius, who called himself an 'older' soldier, a few lines later modifies it to 'elder'. Cassius did WRONG (a penis – K), did prick or screw himself in the eyes of Brutus, who refuses to be buggered by him: see BUDGE.

Camel Outstanding for its *hump*, 'Once a fashionable word for copulation' (G). Dekker, *The Shoemaker's Holiday*, V.V: 'six and fifty-year old, yet I can cry hump!' with 'this old wench'. Sh uses camel for a fornicator, adulterer or bugger, perh. because the hump is on the back or because, as beast of burden, it carries on its back.

Ham, III.ii.394:

Hamlet. Do you see yonder cloud that's almost in shape of a camel?
Polonius. By the mass, and 'tis like a camel, indeed.

By the mass, it is like a camel INDEED/in the deed (P) of intercourse, humping. After comparing it to two more 'backed' creatures, Hamlet says, 'They fool me to the top of my bent' – to the top (mounting sexually – *OED*; P) of his bent (Ger *gebogen*, bent, fornicate) back or hump: they screw him.

TrC, I.ii.271. The Greeks are 'Asses, fools, dolts!' And Achilles, whose love for young Patroclus is under constant attack, is 'a drayman, a porter, a very camel'. All carry on their backs: asses, a VERY camel and a PORTER (pimp and pederast). See WARD.

II.i.59. Like Achilles (see BAD), Ajax is an 'ass' and a 'thing of no bowels' (BOWELS, balls); and he is told 'do, camel; do, do'. 'Do' is fornicate (P); 'to doe or leacher with' (*besongner* – Cot). See SLAVE, TAME for Ajax's pederasty.

R2, V.V.16. Richard says he is a CREATURE encompassing a female brain and a male soul, a combination of the sexes who will people a 'little world'. ' "Come, little ones", and then again,/ "It is as hard to come as for a camel/To thread the postern of a small needle's eye." ' He distorts Mark 10:24–5: 'Children . . . it is easier for a camel to go through the eye of a needle', confusing camels (L *cameli*) with camel-eye.

So much successive bawdiness is never coincidental: (1) it is a *little* world with *little* ones and a *small* eye. LITTLE puns on -cule, -culus (diminutive suffix) and cul(e), L *culus*, buttocks, anus; (2) it is as hard (a phallic erection – C; P) to come (have a sexual spasm (C; P) as for the camel or pederast to thread the POSTERN (back door; arse) – the small needle's eye, *cul d'un esguille* (Cot); the EYE (anus). In *TrC* (above), Ajax, told to 'do camel', was not man enough to 'stop the eye of Helen's needle' (II.i.87).

See MULE, *Cor*; CACKLE, *KL*.

Caper (1) Cavort lecherously. L *caper*: goat, prototype of lechery (C; P). Linked often to a kind of all-male buffoonery, or to effeminate males.

(2) Sp *Capar*: to castrate. Chapman, *All Fools*, II.i: 'I am no husband of my qualities', says Valerio, as '*He untrusses and capers*.' His qualities are that same 'quality' in the Grecian youths to which Troilus feared Cressida would succumb, the 'gifts of nature [NATURE, genitals], / *Flowing* and *swelling* o'er' (*TrC*, IV.iv.78; italics added). Valerio's friends *see* them: 'See what a caper there was!' and 'See again!' and 'O that his father saw these qualities' (his father who believed him TAME, lit. cut, passionless). Etherege, *The Man of Mode*, II.ii: the hero mocks an ex-mistress for taking on Sir Fopling Flutter, a 'cock-fool', 'a senseless caper'.

2H6, III.i.365: 'I have seen / Him caper *upright* like a wild Morisco' (italics added).

R3, I.i.12: 'He capers nimbly in a lady's chamber / To the lascivious pleasing of a lute'.

MV, I.ii.66. Portia mocks Monsieur Le Bon, FRENCH lord: 'God made him . . . therefore let him pass for a man . . . he is every man in no man; if a throstle sing, he falls straight a capering . . . if I should marry him, I should marry twenty husbands.' If a THROSTLE (a dainty fellow or turd) sing (copulate – C; P), he falls (for coitus – C; P) STRAIGHT (L *rectum*) like an ass a-capering. He can only pass for a man, is no man, and would be TWENTY (q.v., *MV*) i.e. a SCORE (a cut, a gelding) of husbands. (Caper: a term of contempt, as in 'capering Monsieur from France' – Johnson's *Dictionary*.)

1H4, III.ii.63. Henry compares Hal to the effeminate ex-king Richard: 'The skipping king, he ambled up and down [UP AND DOWN, whore-like] . . . Mingled with capering fools . . . profaned with their scorns . . . gave his countenance . . . [to] stand the push / Of every beardless vain comparative'. He MINGLED (fornicated – C; P; esp. homosexually) and, profaned by their SCORN / scoring (coiting), stood their PUSH (phallic thrust); he, skipping, they, capering and beardless ('A yoong beardlesse Ganymede whom he loved' – *OED*, s.v. Ganymede, 1603; 'thou thin-bearded hermaphrodite' – Dekker, *Satiromastix*, I.ii).

See BUTTONS, *MWW*; EXCELLENT, *TN*.

Capocchia Foreskin or prepuce. This word is glossed as 'simpleton' (*capocchio*: a loggerhead – F); but since Sh chose to use capocchi*a* (foreskin – F), we should explore the possibility that that is what he intended. White notes that *capocchio* means a silly person but 'capocchia, something quite different'.

TrC, IV.ii.33. Pandarus mocks Cressida and Troilus after their first night together and asks, 'how go maidenheads?' He wants her to mouth what he brought her 'to do' (three times), i.e. the act of sex (P). 'Alas, poor wretch! ah, poor capocchia! hast not slept tonight? would he not, a naughty man, let it sleep?' Cressida turns to Troilus: 'Did not I tell you? Would he were knock'd i' the head!'

The 'simpleton' interpretation assumes Pandarus is still addressing Cressida. However, he had started out with 'maidenheads' (pl.), so is he not now turning to Troilus's share in the proceedings and addressing 'it', the poor capocchi*a* that the naughty man had not let rest? Cressida's angrily wishing Pandarus 'were knock'd i' the head!' reinforces the pun on prepuce, since KNOCKED is 16th c. for screwed (F&H), and the 'head' is the maidenhead and the prepuce (C; P). In addition, it is the capocchi*a*, the head of a nail, that would get knocked.

Captain Epithet for a pander, braggart, ass. Fr *captain*: swaggerer, bully, braggart. 'Captain Arthur Severus O'Toole, a notorious braggart and pimp of the period . . . [is] one instance of decayed Army officers turning highwaymen, tobacco merchants, and panders. O'Toole may have served as the model for Rowley's Irish pimp, Captain Albo' in Middleton and Rowley's *A Fair Quarrel* of 1617 (from programme notes for a National Theatre performance, London, summer 1980). Ex-captain turned pimp is a stock character of the period. Jonson: (1) in *The Alchemist*, v.v, 'the Captain Pandar'; and (2) in *Bartholomew Fair*, Captain Whit, the bawd.

2H6, IV.i.107. Suffolk derides 'this villain here,/ Being captain of a pinnace': (1) captain of a man-of-war's tender; (2) pimp for a whore ('punk, pinnace and bawd' – Jonson, *Bartholomew Fair*, II.i). See CUP, LOBBY.

AW, IV.iii.367: 'Captain I'll be no more;/ But I will eat and drink, and sleep as soft/ As captain shall: simply the thing I am/ Shall make me live . . . for it will come to pass/ That every braggart shall be found an ass.' Captain Parolles had played pimp for Bertram while in the army. (*Tim*, III.v.49: 'the ass more captain than the lion'.)

2H4, II.iv.151–9. Doll Tearsheet blisters Pistol: 'Captain! . . for what? for tearing a poor whore's ruff [pudendum – P] in a bawdy house? He a captain! hang him, rogue! . . . A captain! God's light, these villains will make the word as odious as the word "occupy"; which was an excellent good word before it was ill sorted: therefore captains had need look to't.' Doll is right that 'captain' had been lowered in status along the same lines as 'occupy', which, meaning to take possession of or fill up a space, also meant to coit (P). Swift, *Gulliver's Travels*, Pt III, 'Voyage to Blubbdubdrib': 'the pox' was brought 'into a noble house' by interruption of lineages by 'gamesters . . . captains, and pick-pockets'.

Carack/crack 1. Female pudendum; prostitute (F&H, s.v. Crack; P). See LAND, *Oth*.
2. A flatus. *Pet*: a fart, a crack (Cot). See SPAIN, *CE*.

Card, discard Cod, scrotum; whore. Castrate.

TA, vi.100: 'That codding spirit had they from their mother,/ As sure a card as ever won the set'. Tamora's sons, the rapists, got their codding, i.e. lecherous, spirit from a SURE/ sewer (whore) card (a queen) – Tamora, QUEEN/ quean of the Goths (goat/ Goth: symbol of lechery – K).

KJ, v.ii.105. 'I am too high-born' to yield, says Lewis, who swears 'by the honour of my marriage-bed' to fight. 'Have I not here the best cards for the game,/ To win this easy match . . . shall I now give o'er the yielded set?' The best cods for the game (sex-play – C; P) and the EASY (sexual intercourse) match (love-bout – C; P) are his set (two matching things – *OED*), his TWO/ TOO testicles, born/ borne high. But (137) John's 'hand [HAND, penis]' wins.

KL, III.iv.74: 'discarded fathers' is another metaphor for the castration of Lear by his daughters: thrown out and also dis-codded, impotent (RAG; TRAIN).

See PACK, *AC*; PRIVATE, *TN*; TRUMPET, *KJ*.

Cast Eject waste, like a bird that is given stones to help it cast. Excrement of an earthworm (*W*).

MM, III.i.93. Comparing Angelo to a 'falcon', Isabella says, 'His filth within being cast, he would appear/ A pond as deep as hell'.

Cym, v.v.222: 'cast mire [defecate, urinate – P] upon me'.

AYL, III.ii.376: 'I will not cast away my physic but on those that are sick'.

See PHYSICIAN, *H8*; LAND, *Mac*; POOP, *AC*; EVIL, *AYL*; MOVE, *TGV*.

Cat o' mountain Whore. 'Cat' meant whore; Fr *catau* (pron. cat-ō): slut. Mountain/ mounting: mount the female in breeding (K). Jonson, *Bartholomew Fair*, IV.iii: a 'ramping Jade' and a 'Bawd' engage in name-calling, in 'Cat-a-mountain vapours!' Thomas Nashe, *Have With You to Saffron Walden*: 'Pol-cat and Muske-cat? there wants but a Cat a mountaine' – 'polecat' and 'musk-cat' mean prostitute (*OED*).

See RED LATTICE, *MWW*; AGE, *Tem*.

Catch (1) Male prick: *caiche* (penis – Cot), equiv. of It *catzo*.

(2) Female pudendum, 17th c.: 'Adam caught Eve by the fur-below [pubic hair],/ And that's the oldest catch I know' (F&H, s.v. Fur-below).

(3) Fornicate; impregnate.

3H6, III.ii.23. Gloucester watches his brother try to seduce Lady Grey: 'An if what pleases him shall pleasure you./Fight closer, or, good faith, you'll catch a blow [coital thrust, pregnancy – C; P].'

TSh, II.i.205:

Katherina. Asses are made to bear . . . .
Petruchio. Women are made to bear . . . .
Katherina. No such jade as you, if me you mean.
Petruchio. . . . I will not burden thee
. . . but young and light –
Katherina Too light for such a swain as you to catch . . . .

Quibbles on (1) asses/arses and jades (worn-out horses, 'surfeit-exhausted' males – P); (2) 'mean' as middle term of a syllogism; (3) 'light' as wanton and as too frail to bear in intercourse (the burden of the male) and in pregnancy; (4) 'burden' as a song refrain, and 'mean' as a tenor voice; (5) a 'catch', a round, song for several voices, that repeats the previous words for comic effect, as they are doing. Petruchio will never catch her, make her bear in coitus or be round in pregnancy. Kate will never be the burden or undersong for him to sing mean, tenor, or prick-song above – to catch.

See PEACE, *TN*; BREAST, *TN*; NUTS, *TrC*; ABOUT, *KJ*.

Caterpillar Pederast, as in 'I found a cursed catalogue of these veneriall caterpillars who were suppressed with the monasteries in England, in the time of king Henry the eight, with the number of trugs which each of them kept in those daies' (F&H, s.v. Trug, a young boy used sexually).

R2, II.iii.166. Bolingbroke goes after 'The caterpillars of the commonwealth,/Which I have sworn to weed and pluck away', meaning Bushy and Bagot, Richard's lovers (III.i.2–15). Puns on (1) taking caterpillars off flowers; (2) plucking (deflowering – P; F&H) the deflowerers, the caterpillars of the COMMONWEALTH (whores), who, like weeds, also deflower and destroy.

III.iv.47. The gardeners use similar metaphors with similar overtones in describing the garden with 'knots disorder'd . . . Swarming with caterpillars' and the need to 'Cut off the heads of too fast growing sprays,/That look too lofty in our commonwealth' – 'The noisome weeds, which . . . suck . . . fertility from wholesome flowers'. These are 'The weeds . . . That seem'd in eating him [Richard] to hold him up . . . I mean the Earl of Wiltshire, Bushy, Green.' Remove the potency, cut off the HEADS the *teste* (heads – F)/testes, of those who eat (coitally consume – C; P) Richard. See SHED, *TrC*, for the same image.

1H4, II.ii.86, Falstaff: 'Strike; down with them; cut the villains' throats . . . whoreson caterpillars . . . down with them; fleece them' – strike (coit, rape – C; P); DOWN (coitally), (said twice). *Down* with the whoreson *cater*pillar: Gk *kata*, down; cat (16th c.), whore. Throat-cutting is castration (CUT, *MWW*). Fleece (i.e. hair) or remove the down of the caterpillar/Fr *chatepelose*, hairy cat. Like 'pluck' (*R2* above), 'fleece' means rob, victimise. It may also connote castrate, for immediately after Falstaff's 'fleece them' the travellers say, 'O we are undone, both we and ours forever!' In *R2* above, the KNOTS (flower-beds) or testicles were 'disordered'; here, likewise, the men's knots are untied, UNDONE: they shall have no 'ours' or posterity, no 'forever' – their hair/heir (K) is removed. Note in *R2* the Gardener cut off the *too* fast-growing sprays that were *too* lofty (the TWO testes); he wanted everything 'even in our government' (even, flat, smooth, docked). (The metaphor is the common equation of loss of money with loss of potency and power.)

Cattle/chattel Whores. Human beings, in contempt (*OED*; F&H): 'concubines, and cattell of that sort' (John Evelyn, in *OED*). Cf. Chaucer, 'The Shipman's Tale', 272, 316: Sir John borrowed 'An hundred frankes . . . For certein beestes ['stock or cattle' – *OED*, s.v. Beasts] that I moste beye'. In return, the lender's wife 'accorded with daun John/That for thise hundred frankes he sholde al nyght/ Have hire in his armes bolt upright'. Marston, *The Dutch Courtesan*, I.i: a man 'consorted with his movable chattel, his instrument of fornication, the bawd Mistress Mary Faugh'. Middleton, *Four Fine Gallants*, I.ii: told he is 'never without moveables!', the bawd-gallant says, 'Ay . . . the goodly virginities that have been cut up in my house'.

AYL, III.ii.85, Touchstone: it is a 'sin . . . to get your living by the copulation of cattle; to be bawd to a bell-wether'.

435, Rosalind: 'He was to imagine me his love, his mistress . . . for every passion something and for no passion truly any thing, as boys and women are for the most part cattle of this colour'. Women and BOYS (catamites) – like Rosalind, who poses as the boy GANYMEDE, from which 'catamite' derives – are, like cattle, promiscuous in passion.

See FIELD, *TSh*, CLOSE, *H5*.

Cavalier A ladies' man, a man for the whores; lit. a horseman (HORSE/ whores) and a woman's escort. *Chiavellare*: to grope at a woman's privities (F). It *cavallo*: mackerel; a mackerel (obs., a pimp).

Per, IV.vi.12. Marina refused all the brothel customers and Boult (*chiavello*, a boult – F), the pimp, says, 'I must ravish her, or she'll disfurnish us of all our cavaliers'.

H5, III, Prol., 24. The ship holds a 'due [DUE/ It *due*, two, testes] course [COURSE, sexual encounter] to Harfleur', full of 'cull'd . . . cavaliers' (culls: testes – F&H; cul: rump – *OED*). The next scene opens with Henry's exhortation 'Once more unto the breach [/ breech: buttocks – TWR]'. A freq. mix of military and sexual metaphors for male courage (and foolishness).

MND, IV.i.25. Nick (slit or breach – K) Bottom has an itch that sounds like bleeding piles (BARBER). Cobwebs were put on cuts to stop the bleeding, and Bottom asks someone 'to help Cavalery Cobweb to scratch [caress manually – C; P]' – *chiavellare*, grope at the privities. See BARBER.

Centaur/centre Symbol of sexual bestiality, half-man, half-horse (see NORMAN; SEMIRAMIS). The vulva: 'centrique part' (Donne, in F&H, s.v. Monosyllable). Cotton, 'Forbidden Fruit': the lover's 'bliss' is 'something lower than the wast,/ And in your Garden's Centre plact' (*Penguin Book of Restoration Verse*, p. 176). Marston, *The Dutch Courtesan*, I.i: the 'deadly sin' of 'Lust' is similarly placed, being 'one of the middle sins' ('myddel': erotic area – TWR; P).

KL, IV.vi.126. To Lear, woman is like a 'soiled horse'; 'Down from the waist they are Centaurs' – sexually bestial centres, HORSES/ whores' arses.

RJ, II.i.2. Romeo tells himself, 'Turn back, dull earth, and find thy centre out'; and then (II.ii.3), as astronomy would have it, he finds that around which the dull earth orbits, its 'centre' – for 'Juliet is the sun'.

See WITCHCRAFT, *CE*; EPHESUS, *CE*.

Chattel See CATTLE (whores).

Cheeks Buttocks. Dekker and Webster, *Northward Hoe*, II.i: 'If I catch master pricklouse ramping so high again. . . . I'll make him know how to kiss your blind cheeks sooner.' A logical comparison in the long list of interchangeable features of face and genital area: nose, TONGUE, EYES, EARS. See TWR, p. 185, for reproduction of 'a grotesque with a second face for genitals'.

MND, IV.i.2, Titania (to Bottom, with his ass's head): 'While I thy amiable cheeks do coy . . . And kiss thy fair large ears, my gentle joy'. She does coy (OFr *coi*, *coit*) or caress his cheeks; and she does kiss (coit – P) his EARS/ arse. A review of the Peter Brook production of *MND* (*Newsweek*, Oct 1975) observed, 'When Titania coos over Bottom's "amiable cheeks", it's his behind she's addressing; and when the drugged Queen and the transformed rustic awaken, their positions are as clear as an erotic drawing by Ingres.' See SLIP for Bottom's 'cowslip [cow-dung] cheeks'. *Coy*: 'Sinke [cesspool]; or, as Fosse coye [latrine]' (Cot).

Tim, IV.iii.115, Timon: 'let not the virgin's cheek/ Make soft thy trenchant sword'. Soft:

weak, effeminate, unmanly, as in 'grows soft and effeminate' (Bacon, in *OED*). Don't, says Timon, be deterred from rape and murder because it is a virgin's cheek; don't let your sword (penis) therefore be softened or ineffective. Cf. STEEL, *RJ*.

LLL, IV.iii.109: 'Air, quoth he, thy cheeks may blow;/ Air, would I might triumph so!' Dumain wishes he, too, could blow (make a coital thrust – C; P) her cheeks (see VELVET for the rest of this speech). Since Sh intends these odes as mockery of the men, perh. the cheeks blow with a flatus (L *flatus*, a blowing) – the men's hot air. Blowing in *triumph* puns on blowing in a trump or trumpet (trump: a corruption of 'triumph', as in take with a trump at cards). When a TRUMPET (pun on the arse) blows, the sound it makes is called 'bray', the same word used for the sound of an ass.

See FANCY, *AYL*.

Cheer 1. Defecation. *Chier*: to shit (Cot). 2. Flesh, the human body (*chair* – Cot). Jonson, *Bartholomew Fair*, V.iv: 'Mashter . . . helpe a very sicke Lady, here, to a chayre, to shit in.' See cheer/chair (K), as in *Mac*, V.iii.20. 'Cheer' means fare, welcome, entertainment.

TSh, Induction, ii. The Page, disguised as a woman and accompanied by attendants, enters.

Page. How fares my noble lord?
Sly. Marry, I fare well; for here is cheer enough. Where is my wife?

A transition through *marry* to *fare*, *cheer*, and a *wife*. Sly sees he will fare well ENOUGH (Fr *assez*/of the ass) – but which particular 'cheer' is his?

Tim, III.vi.56. Timon invites is sycophantic followers to a banquet consisting of the contents of his chamber-pots. As the 'covered dishes' arrive, one lord says, 'Royal cheer, I warrant you.' And so it is, royal, i.e. real, *chier* or shit, which he then throws into their faces. See SPUR; and GOLD for a similar performance.

TA, V.iii.28. Titus prepares a banquet made of the ground bodies (*chair*) of Tamora's sons. It is 'stern and bloody' and contains 'hateful liquors'. It is made of their buttocks (STERN and bloody) and the HATEFUL (Fr *haineux*/anus) liquors from the anus and bowels. Lickerish and liquorish: lecherous; of a cook, skilful. He greets them, 'welcome, all: although the cheer be poor,/ 'Twill fill your stomachs'. Welcome is cheer, and the cheer – or fare – that Tamora eats is POOR/L *puer* (a boy), her boys. After she eats, he tells her the cheer that filled her stomach was the 'flesh [*chair*] that she herself hath bred': (1) the brede (i.e. roast meat) and (2) what filled her stomach in pregnancy, when she bred. (Her POOR boys, now 'stern and bloody', were probably sodomites: see Index.)

See RAISE, *1H6*.

3. Love. Fr *cherer*: to cheer; *cherir*: to love.

CE, III.ii.26. 'Comfort my sister, cheer her, call her wife;/ 'Tis holy sport'. She is urging Antipholus not merely to raise his wife's spirits, but also to make physical love to her whom he has neglected: 'comfort' is solace amorously (P); 'sport' is amorous activity (C; P), especially when it is *holy* (of the hole or vulva – F&H; P).

See MILK, *AC*.

Cherry Maidenhead; vulva. Cherry-pit: child's game of rolling pits into a small hole; sometimes with less innocent meaning, as in Herrick, 'Cherry-pit': 'Julia and I . . . playing for sport at Cherry-pit . . . I got the pit [PIT, female pudendum – F&H], and she the stone [testicle].'

MND, V.i.192, Thisby: 'My cherry lips [LIPS, labia pudendi] have often kiss'd thy stones'.

TN, III.iv.129. When Toby tells Malvolio ''tis not for gravity to play at cherry-pit with Satan', it is not that gravity or old age should not play a child's game (as usu. annotated), which Malvolio is *not* doing; but that he should not play, as he *is* doing, at lechery and thoughts of love-making, such as 'sleeping' with Olivia and her cherry PIT (female pudendum), her 'C's, her U's and her T's . . . her great P's. . . .' (II.v.50–100), or CUT (pudendum – C; K).

See SHARE, *MND*; WITCH, *CE*.

Cheveril Penis, vagina. Lit. kid leather; fig. flexible.

R.J., II.iv. 87, Mercutio: 'O, here's a wit of cheveril, that stretches from an inch narrow to an ell broad!' Romeo's WIT (penis) stretches – the INCH (penis) STRETCHES (coitally) to a BROAD, obscene ell: (1) a measure; (2) an L (with the provocative right-angled extension).

H8, II.iii.32. An old court whore tells Anne there are gifts 'the capacity/Of your soft cheveril conscience would receive,/If you might please to stretch it' – 'Nay, good troth' – 'Yes, troth, and troth; you would not be a queen?' Were Anne to STRETCH (coitally) her cheveril *con*science (cunt – P) and TROT(H) (trot: play the whore – C; P), she could become Henry's QUEEN/quean (whore).

Chin Penis. The lively interest Sh's heroines show in chins is not a fetish: (1) chin (Gk *genys*) and birth (L *genus*) pun, as in 'new-born chins' (*Tem*, II.i.249); (2) pun on 'mental' (of the mentum or chin), *mentola* (privities – F) and *mentule* (a man's yard or penis – Cot). Marston, *The Dutch Courtesan*, IV.iii: 'Softer than . . . an old man's *mentula*'.

Tem, IV.i.183. (1) Varlets 'prick'd their ears'; (2) 'pricking goss and thorns . . . enter'd their frail shins. . . . I left them/I' the filthy-mantled pool . . . dancing up to the chins that the foul lake/O'erstunk their feet.' A physical feat difficult to visualise unless the chins are penises, as suggested by all the 'pricking'. Note the pun in filthy-*mantled* and their filthy *mentules*. See SHIN (penis).

AYL, III.ii.223. Rosalind is wildly impatient to know who writes the love-verses she found hanging on a tree: 'Is he of God's making? What manner of man? Is . . . his chin worth a beard?' Told he has but a little beard, she says, 'Why, God will send more . . . let me stay the growth of his beard, if thou delay me not the knowledge of his chin.'

To gloss this as Rosalind will wait patiently for the beard, but please hurry with the man's name, is to ignore what she says. Her emphasis is on manliness: what MANNER (in the sex-act – *OED*) of *man*. Is he of 'God's making' or a tailor's? (Two for whom Sh had most contempt, Osric and Parolles, were made by tailors. In *AW*, II.v.18, Lafeu asks who is Parolles's 'tailor', for 'there can be no kernel in this light nut; the soul of this man is in his clothes' – no seed in the nut, no testicle in the scrotum-pouch and codpiece he wears.) And 20 lines later Celia puns on Orlando's ACORN (glans penis; testicle).

So it is 'knowledge' (lit. sexual intimacy) *of his chin* (mental) that Rosalind wants: *mentule* knowledge. In the context of his being a man of God's making (God is mentioned twice) and that which she wants knowledge of hanging on a tree, we are reminded of the APPLE (testicle) and Adam and Eve and carnal knowledge, 'knowledge of his chin'.

H5, III.iv.37. Having just mistaken 'neck' for 'nick' (vulva – F&H; K), Katherine, the French princess, asks what 'le menton' is. Alice: 'de chin'. *De* means 'of' so her answer is 'of the chin' or mental, and a pun on *mentule*, penis. The bawdry is compounded when Katherine calls it 'De sin', since 'sin' (arch.) meant fornication.

MV, II.ii.100. When the partially blind Gobbo tells his son Launcelot 'thou hast got more hair on thy chin than Dobbin my fill-horse has on his tail', the juxtaposition of chin and tail (penis – K; P) is part of the general bawdiness intended to focus attention on this important comic scene that evokes the biblical story of Isaac, another father with dim sight who was also deceived by hairy skin (alluded to in I.iii.74). Like Jacob, Launcelot, too, asks for his father's blessing (90): the heir (K; P) is as deceptive as the hair – indeed, so are all the heirs in the play. A few scenes later Jessica deceives her father and elopes, stealing a 'casket'; and in Act III Portia sidesteps the letter of her father's will and clues Bassanio on which 'casket' to choose; after which he talks of the deceptive beards on men's 'chins' and deceptive 'golden locks' on women (Lock: the pudendum – P; and hair: an Eliz. pun on pubic hair – C; P). In *MV* male and female hairs and heirs all deceive. And just as the biblical Jacob and Launcelot Gobbo had received blessings through deceit, so Bassanio receives 'a blessing in his lady' Portia, through deceit (III.v.80).

Cholera Like COLOUR/*culare* (the arse-gut – F).

See PURGATION, *Ham*; FIST, *Per*.

Chronicle Anal: of an ass/arse. *Annales*: 'annales, annuall Chronicles; yearely relations' (Cot). Rabelais, Bk I, ch 19 (the same pun is made in three trs): 'they gave him the chronic – er, colic' (Putnam); 'they might have begot a chronicle [play on "colic" – Nock and Wilson] in the bowels of his braine' (Urquhart and Le Motteux, 1693); 'their chime produced a colicle – I mean a chronicle – a diarrhoea, no! – a diary! – in the bowels of his head' (Le Clercq).

Cor, V.iii.145. Coriolanus's mother, wife, and child appeal to him not to attack Rome, not to let them see 'The son, the husband and the father *tearing* / His country's bowels out' (102). Volumnia says, 'The *end* of war's uncertain, but if he conquers Rome he will be dogged with '*chronicle* thus writ: "The man was noble, / But with his last attempt he *wiped it out*. . . ." ' (See *KL*, IV.vi.136, for anal wiping: 'let me kiss that hand!' – 'Let me wipe it first; it smells of mortality.') She speaks of his trying 'To tear with thunder [THUNDER, a flatus] the wide cheeks [CHEEKS, buttocks] o' the air', and of his 'sulphur' (see DISCHARGE, the flatus and its sulphurous odour). She wins him over to his ultimate destruction: 'I'll *back* with you', he says. (Italics added.)

TrC, II.iii.166. Agamemnon mocks Ajax/*a jakes* (latrine – K; P): 'his own glass, his own trumpet, his own chronicle' – his OWN (arse) GLASS (penis); his own TRUMPET (arse and flatus); his own chronicle.

See GIDDY, *H5*.

Clip(per) Clip: embrace (*OED*; P). Also clip or CUT, i.e. castrate.

H5, IV.i.246: 'it is no English treason to cut French crowns, and tomorrow the king himself will be a clipper'. Pun on clipping coins (coin / quoin: penis – K; Fr *coion* or *couillon*: testicle) and clipping CROWNS, lit. coins, pun on testicles. Henry will be a clipper of French crowns or balls, revenge for those TENNIS-BALLS the French had sent in mockery of him. In a speech filled with sexual puns (most of them in this dictionary), he speaks of his 'hard condition, / Twin-born with greatness . . . the sceptre and the ball, / The sword, the mace, the crown imperial . . . thrice-gorgeous ceremony . . . laid in bed majestical'.

The *hard* condition of the TWIN- (testicle) born SCEPTRE (penis) and ball; sword and mace (staff, club – common penis symbols); the *thrice*-gorgeous (penis and testes, as in THREE) ceremony *laid* in bed: these are metaphors for Henry's potency and the clipping or embracing (the screwing), the emasculation he will deal the French. See TWIN for his 'hard condition'.

See TRAITOR, *LLL*.

Close To lecher. *Frotter leur lard ensemble*: to close, to lecher (Cot). Massinger, *A New Way to Pay Old Debts*, III.ii: 'Virgin me no virgins! I must have you lose that name . . . therefore, when he kisses you, kiss close' – 'this is the strumpet's fashion, sir'. Middleton and Dekker, *The Roaring Girl*, V.i: 'some Italian pander there would tell all the close tricks of courtesans' (see PAINT, *Cym*).

TrC, III.ii.48: 'and 'twere dark, you'ld close sooner . . . rub on, and kiss the mistress', says Pandarus, urging aggression on Troilus.

TA, IV.ii.118. The black hue of Tamora's baby reveals it is her lover, a Moor, who is its father: 'treacherous hue, that will betray . . . close enacts . . . of the heart!'

H5, II.iii.65: 'Let housewifery appear: keep close, I thee command.' Pistol's advice to his wife, usually interpreted as caution, has *double entendres* more fitting his character. He commands like the bully (pimp – F&H) that he is. While at war, he wants the tavern kept open (*aperire*, to open – F): HOUSEWIFERY (whoring) is to APPEAR (fornicate). White speaks of the 'double meaning of Pistol's speech', pointing out that the corresponding Quarto passage 'keep fast thy buggle boe' is bawdy ('The courtesans of Venice which shall tumble and keep their bugle-bows for thee, dear uncle' – Shirley, *The Gentlemen of Venice*, I.i). In the Quarto, 'keep fast' does not mean fastened; in fact, FAST means quick (Pistol's wife, the former Mistress Quickly), living fast and dissolute. Likewise, in the Folio, 'keep close' does not mean closed, but that Mistress Quickly is to KEEP (bawd) the housewives (HOUSEWIFE, whore) of their tavern frotting *leur lard ensemble* – close and lecherous. Samuel Johnson, also sceptical of this speech, says, 'Go clear thy crystals' does not mean dry your eyes, but go wash the drinking-glasses –

Johnson on Shakespeare, ed. Arthur Sherbo (New Haven, Conn., and London: Yale Univ. Press, 1968) vol. II, p. 543.

This interpretation is corroborated in Pistol's advice, 'Look to my chattels and my movables: / Let senses rule; the word is "Pitch and Pay" ': (1) CHATTELS and *movables* were whores; (2) *senses* gratify lusts of the flesh (*OED*), as in Middleton, *A Mad World, My Masters*, I.ii: a 'Courtesan' uses 'all the arguments that sense can frame'; (3) PITCH is an infectious whore. And as such Pistol's wife died, of syphilis, which news elicited his 'Doth Fortune play the huswife with me now?' – ironic reflection of his last words to her.

See BOTCHER, *1H4*; DEVIL, *2H4*.

Cloth Whore. Fem. pudendum. Lyly, *Mother Bombie*, I.iii: if his daughter won't marry the man he chooses, she shall not marry at all; 'shee shall prick on a clout till her fingers ake'. That's the only cloth that shall get pricked. Anon, *The Woman Taken in Adultery* (a medieval miracle play), 147: 'Come forth, thou whore and stinking bitch-clout!'

Ado, III.iv.20: 'By my troth' – speaking as a TROT(H), bawd – Margaret says the Duchess has a wedding GOWN (cunt) that is 'but a night-gown in respect of yours; cloth o' gold, and cuts'. In respect (in coitus – C; P), compared with Hero's it is a whore's gown, meant only for night; a cloth of GOLD (the pudendum of a whore) and CUTS (cunts – K). See GOWN.

Cym, II.iii.128: Cloten calls Posthumus a 'squire's cloth'. A SQUIRE is a pimp and his cloth (LL *pannellus*) is his whore, a panel, parnel or pernel (loose woman, effeminate man, priest's concubine – Hulme, pp. 105–6). Imogen *exactly* rewords the epithet and calls Cloten Posthumus's 'meanest garment' (MEAN, a pimp), which Cloten repeats in fury four times.

Penil: the groin (Cot). See *AYL*, III.iii.90: 'panel'.

See (AC)QUAINT, *AYL*; PAINT, *TrC*.

Coat Scrotum. Cf. coat/cod (K) in *MWW*, I.i.15–27 (accompanied by the pun on luces/louse – crablice in the codpiece).

TN, IV.i.33:

Sir Toby. Hold, sir, or I'll throw your dagger o'er the house.
Clown. . . . I would not be in some of your coats for two pence.

A dagger is an obelisk or the *second* foot*note*: NOTE, testicle (see RE, second note on the musical scale, for a similar pun). It is also a short, pointed weapon which Toby will throw over the HOUSE/HOSE (penis) – a castration threat. Not for *two* pence – not for two *pens* (penises – P) – would the Clown be in their cods or codpieces.

STRIPE, *WT*; SILK, *2H6*; DOUBLE, *MND*; ALTAR, *1H4*.

Cockney A mother's darling who becomes an effeminate man (F&H), a milksop (*OED*). A cock-ay or cock's egg, an absurdity: a small, malformed egg (*OED*). Lyly, *Euphues*: 'I made thee a wanton, and thou hast made me a foole; I brought thee up like a cockney, and thou hast handled me like a cockescombe.' 'I bring up like a cocknaye, je mignotte' (Palsgrave, in *CD*) – *mignoter*, make a wanton of (Cot).

TN, IV.i.15. Clown mistakes Sebastian for his twin sister, Viola–Cesario: 'Vent my folly! I am afraid this great lubber, the world, will prove a cockney. I prithee now, ungird thy strangeness and tell me what I shall vent to my lady.' Two insults: (1) ungird his message, which the Clown will vent (anus, bodily discharge – *OED*); (2) ungird his STRANGENESS (effeminacy), his girdle that secures his garments, and reveal through the vent (slit in a garment) his little, malformed cock's egg or testicle. Then this LUBBER (an effeminate) would prove to be a cockney, girl–boy, for she lacks that which PROVES (testes). The Clown is almost right, even so, for Sebastian does love Antonio homosexually (see Index).

Cog To gull, esp. sexually; typical of a whore, pimp, effeminate male. *Fregare*: 'to frig [masturbate – F&H] . . . to cogge . . . or gull' (F). *Coglionare*: to play with one's stones; to cog, deceive (F). *Coger*: to fuck (Rosensweig).

MWW, III.iii.76, Falstaff: 'I cannot cog . . . like a many of these lisping hawthorn-buds, that come like women in men's apparel'.

See PAUL'S, *R3*; BOY, *Ado*.

Collier See COLOUR.

Colour / choler / collier (1) Arse (cul – *OED*). *Culare*: arse-gut (F). *Culier*: of the arse (Cot).
(2) To embrace (*colere*, to coll, embrace, honour – F).
(3) Having large testicles, Fr *couillard*.
TN, I.v.6:

Clown. Let her hang me: he that is well hanged in this world needs to fear no colours.
Maria. Make that good.
Clown. He shall see none to fear.

A man who is 'well hanged (betweene the legs)' is a *couillatris* (Cot); being *couillard*, having large testicles, he shall see none (testicles or colours) to fear. See HANG.

1H6, IV.ii.37. The General of Bourdeaux salutes Talbot with 'the latest glory of thy praise / That I, thy enemy, due thee withal . . . These eyes, that see thee now well coloured, / Shall see thee wither'd, bloody, pale and dead'. He acknowledges Talbot's DUE (his two testes), his being well coloured or *couillard* – symbol of strength; but he warns that Talbot will soon be a different kind of colour, pale (*palier*, to colour – Cot) with blood, WITHERED (impotent) and dead.

III.iii.31. 'Your honours shall perceive how I will work / To bring this matter to the wished end.' Their honours (*colere*) will see her bring the MATTER (faecal) to the *end* (*culare*). 'There goes the Talbot, with his colours spread.' Is he *the* Talbot only because she is *La* Pucelle, or is she calling him tail-butt? The Talbot with his colours or flags flying and his colour or arse and tail SPREAD (for sexual service) and cocky. This metaphor began when she said (6), 'Let frantic Talbot triumph for a while / And like a peacock sweep along his tail' – spread his colours.

RJ, I.i. This is the masterpiece of colour / choler / collier puns. Gregory and Sampson, two asses if there ever were any, start the play with 'we'll not carry coals', meaning submit, but introducing the basic pun on coals / *culs* (arses – Cot; like 'cule' – *W*), culls (testes – F&H) and *couilles* (penises and, less properly, testes, also a coward – Cot).

'No, for then we should be colliers' or coal workers. But *collier* is (Cot) a dog- or horse-collar (Jonson, *Every Man out of his Humour*: 'Here comes one that will carry coals, ergo will hold my dog'). This leads right to the puns on 'choler', anger; and on *chaleur*, amorous heat (of a bitch – Cot): 'I mean, an we be in choler, we'll draw' – (1) they will draw or pull as a dog in a collar does; (2) they will draw swords in choler; (3) they will draw (expose the sexual organ – C; P) in *chaleur*. Sampson says, 'A dog of that house shall move me to stand' (MOVE, sexually, to a *stand* or erect penis – P). And soon his 'naked weapon is out'.

And on goes the jolly scene with the drawing of a 'tool' (penis – P) and the cutting off of 'heads of the maids' or 'their maidenheads' – a physiologically inaccurate description for deflowering (even Gregory and Sampson question it). However, a maid also meant a virginal man (*OED*; Chaucer); and his HEAD (prepuce or testes), his maidenhead (P), could be cut off. The pun continues with the word 'back': 'I will back thee' – 'How! turn thy back and run?' *Couler*: to run (Cot); Fr *culer*: to go backwards. Even Sampson's biting his thumb, making the fig of Spain (*H5*, III.vi.62), symbolised extracting figs with one's teeth from the fundament of a mule (F&H; C).

These puns are repeated as each succeeding group enters on stage: Benvolio is 'drawn among these heartless hinds' (servants and hind ends). Capulet has his sword (penis – P) and 'crutch' (alt. sp. for 'crotch'). The servants' choler becomes the Prince's 'rage' (lust; sexual activity – TWR; P), and he calls everyone, 'you men, you beasts [BEAST, sodomite]'.

In short, I.i comments on the tragically asinine behaviour of them all; or on what the Prol. calls the 'fatal loins of these two foes' and the 'parents' rage,/ Which, but their children's end,/ Nought could remove'.

See PRESENTS, *AYL*; PURPOSE, *TN*.

Commit Copulate (adulterously – C; P). Middleton, *Women Beware Women*, II.ii: 'His weight is deadly who commits with strumpets'.

See IGNORANT, *Oth*; OFFENCE, *MWW*; WOUND, *Tim*; PAY, *TGV*.

Commonwealth Whores. Brothel (district). Common: occ. the commonwealth (*OED*). Commoner: whore (P); common: available as a whore (C; P).

See BOOTS, *1H4*; WORM, *1H6*; CATERPILLAR, *R2*; SILK, *2H6*; RUFFIAN, *2H6*; TUTOR, *LLL*.

Compass (1) Penis and thighs. Lit. two equal straight legs connected by a movable joint, or a magnetised needle on a point. (2) To encompass, in coitus.

Donne, 'A Valediction Forbidding Mourning': 'As stiffe twin compasses . . . And though it in the center sit,/ Yet when the other far doth rome,/ It leanes . . . And growes erect as that comes home.'

MWW, III.iii.212. Though Falstaff had said he would be seducing Mrs Ford at that very hour, Ford 'cannot find him: may be the knave bragged of that he could not compass' – BRAGGED/*braguerie* (lascivious bravery – Cot).

Oth, II.i.244. Iago says Cassio dissimulates 'for the better compassing of his salt and most hidden loose affection'. Pun on the compass as an instrument of the salt (i.e. the sailor) and on the penis as the instrument of his salt and loose – amorous and licentious (C; P; F&H) – affection, that is so far hidden (in his codpiece?) but, anyway, needing better hiding (HIDE, L *scrotum*: hide; a prostitute; skin), better compassing – in Desdemona.

TGV, II.iv.214, Proteus: 'If I can check my erring love, I will:/ If not, to compass her I'll use my skill.' If his compass can check his (and its) error – his having strayed in direction from Julia to Sylvia – good; if not, he will try to compass Sylvia, using his SKILL (arse).

IV.ii.92:

Sylvia. What's your will?
Proteus. That I may compass yours.

The *will* is both penis and vulva (C; P).

CE, IV.i.111: Dromio E. says the kitchen wench claimed him for husband, but 'She is too big . . . for me to compass.'

Compunctious Sexual pricking or copulation, L *com* + *punctum*, prick.

Mac, I.v.46. Lady Macbeth, anticipating the murder of Duncan, calls on spirits to 'unsex' her. She rejects all aspects of woman's sexuality: 'make thick my blood' – stop the menstrual flow; 'take my milk for gall'; and 'Stop up the access and passage to remorse,/ That no compunctious visitings of nature/ Shake my fell purpose'. ACCESS is sexual entry. And the passage to remorse is the PASSAGE of the prick, to coitus: a 'prick' (fig.), stinging compunction, remorse (*OED*).

To unsex her, she needs '*murdering* ministers' (italics added), because 'remorse' derives from L *mordere*, to bite; and there shall be neither remorse nor BITE (coitus) for her – no *mordere*, only murder. No visits of NATURE (semen, menses, genitals – *OED*) or human KINDNESS (sexuality); she has just dismissed Macbeth's 'nature' as too full of the 'milk of human kindness'. She wants her milk taken from her, and Macbeth's, too (MILK, semen). No compunction or pricking shall SHAKE (screw) her *fell* purpose – (1) her savage, destructive purpose; (2) her fell or skin PURPOSE (end; pudendum).

Murder replaces sex. Her wish is granted, for a few scenes later Macbeth discovers he has 'no spur/ To prick the side of my intent' (vii.25) – no SPUR with which to prick her SIDE (arch., the female seat of generation or birth); no prick for his INTENT (coitus) or for her PURPOSE. The irony of her wish is that the tragedy of Macbeth's life is having no child, no heir to the throne which he has purchased at such a cost: 'For Banquo's issue have I filed my mind' (III.i.65). See ALL, *Mac.*

Con (1) *Con* (Cot), con (K), coun (P): cunt. L *cunnus*: pudendum, prostitute.

(2) Penis: like many words given only feminine meanings, 'con' is also applicable to the male, esp. if he is being mocked or is effeminate. L *contus*: a long rod, spear, or pike. L *cuneus*: a wedge. 'Creamstick': wedge, penis (F&H). Ger *Bletzer*: creamstick, from *Bletz*, wedge.

(3) The arse.

TN, I.v.186. Cesario–Viola, girl–boy, says her speech is 'well penned, I have taken great pains to con it'. Penned–con is the same pun on penis–cunt as in penance–confessor (P). She took great PAINS/penis to con it.

II.iii.161. 'Cons' is plunked down amidst a host of ass/arse puns made at the expense of Malvolio, who is told 'Go shake your ears': (1) an ass's large ears; and (2) EARS/arse. Maria: 'The *devil* a puritan that he is, or *any thing con*stantly *but* . . . *an* affectioned *ass*, that *cons* state' (italics added). DEVILS are bisexuals; and Malvolio is not any thing constantly; ANY and AN pun on the ass (Fr *âne*); *thing* (C; P) and *constant* are the genitals; and AFFECTION is desire for an ass. Malvolio cons (studies, knows) STATE (the arse): he knows so well how to make an ass of himself.

MND, I.ii.102: 'here are your parts . . . con them by tomorrow night', says Peter (the prick – F&H) Quince (1575, 'coyn(e)'; pun on coin/quoin or penis – K; Fr *coion*, testicle), quibbling on his own name. The actors who are to con their PARTS (genitals – *OED*; P) are (1) Nick (in the breech – F&H; K) Bottom (the ass); (2) Snout (*groin* – Cot); (3) FLUTE (arse, penis). Bottom responds that they will 'rehearse [/rears?] most obscenely. . . . Take pains'. Take PAINS/penis is alluded to in V.i.81, where it is (as in *TN* above) linked to 'con': 'Extremely stretch'd and conn'd with cruel pain'. Cf. STRETCH (coitally): 'so far as my coin would stretch' (*1H4*, I.ii.62).

Conclusion The end or buttocks. Coitus (TWR).

MM, V.i.95: 'the vile *conclusion* I now *begin*' (italics added) to tell is that she 'did yield' sexually.

See CROWN, *MWW*; SCANTY, *KL*; LAME, *Oth*; EXERCISE, *Oth*; MODEST, *AC*; HEART, *Ado*.

Confines In the arse. From L *con* + *finis* (the end, bounds). Perhaps the pun is intensified by the prefix CON (cunt).

See SCUM, *2H4*; ROUND, *AYL*.

Conger/conjure(r) (1) Sexual congress (C; P), L *congres*.

(2) Jests on the penial suggestiveness of L *congrus*, conger or eel (penis – C; P), are as old as Aristophanes' *Lysistrata.* Lysistrata wants (20–36) to discuss 'a big thing' and Cleonice asks '(*taking this in a different sense; with great interest*) And is it thick too?' When the big thing turns out to be a plan 'To exterminate the Boeotians to a man!' Cleonice, undeviating in her interest, asks, 'But surely you would spare the eels', a Boeotian speciality. Cf. *KL*, II.iv.123: a 'cockney . . . put 'em [eels] i' the paste alive . . . knapped 'em o' the coxcombs with a stick, and cried "Down, wantons, down!" '

2H4, II.iv.59. Falstaff calls the sex-act coming 'off the breach with his pike bent bravely', and Doll says, 'Hang yourself, you muddy conger'. Pun on the conger (penis) and the pike, fish with a long, slender snout, and the pike, weapon and penis (C; P). Is Falstaff's MUDDY (shitty) because he comes off the breach, pun on *breech* or buttocks? Some eels live in muddy swamps or BOGS (buttocks and whores – like Doll). The homosexual Gaveston (Marlowe, *Edward*, II.i.4.) is called 'that vile torpedo [L *torpedo*, electric eel]'.

RJ, II.i.26. Mercutio wants to 'raise a spirit in his mistress' circle . . . letting it there stand/Till she had laid it and conjured it down. . . . I conjure only but to raise up him.' (Durfey (?),

'The Bee-hive': 'My mistress' and 'her cunny' can 'pleasing spirits raise, and also lay them down again' – *Signet Classic Poets of the 17th c.*, vol. II, p. 427; see SPIRIT.)

WT, II.ii.400. Polixenes, suspected of sexual congress with his friend's wife, asks Camillo why his friend is so cold: 'I conjure thee, by all the parts of man/ Which honour does acknowledge'. A fitting conjuration: by all the PARTS – ME euphemism for the private parts.

See SINGE, *CE*.

Conjunction, conjunctive Copulate. Copulative conjunction (gram., 1530). Anon.: *The Merry Devil of Edmonton* (1601–8), v.ii: 'A marriage . . . ?' – 'A conjunction copulative; a gallant match'. Chapman, *The Widow's Tears*; v.i: Cynthia is seen kissing a soldier, 'She that lately/ Was at such a height of interjection/ Stoop now to such a base conjunction!'

KJ, II.i.468. Elinor's hope that 'this conjunction . . . this match' is a KNOT (coitus) to 'tie' John's '*ass*urance to the crown' was hasty (italics added).

III.i.227: 'the conjunction of our inward souls/ Married . . . coupled and link'd' – Philip and John were joined like INWARD (intestine) SOULS (bottoms, arses), like links (sausage or PUDDING) or stuffed intestines – two stuffed bowels or arses. See SERVANT, *2H4*.

Oth, I.iii.374: 'Let us be conjunctive in our revenge . . . if thou canst cuckold him, thou dost thyself a pleasure, me a sport.' Iago and Roderigo will act, not merely together, but in a revenge that will be for them both a *pleasure* and a *sport* (the sex act – P), and ruin Othello's marriage.

Conjure See CONGER/CONJURE(R).

Consent Suggests the CON (cunt).

MM, II.iv.161. Angelo tells Isabella to yield 'up thy body to my will [penis – C; P]' and 'Fit [for sexual intercourse – TWR; P] thy consent to my sharp appetite'.

See VERY, *AYL*; ANY, *MWW*.

Consort Coit; a bedfellow.

MND, III.ii.387. Puck tells his 'fairy lord' the damned spirits 'to their wormy beds are gone . . . And must for aye consort with black-brow'd night'. Oberon: 'But we are spirits of another sort:/ I with the Morning's love have oft made sport'. In WORMY (syphilitic) beds, DAMNed (with a dam or woman) spirits *con*sort (CON) or mate with black-browed night for *aye* – the brow over the eye, but which EYE? He is a spirit of another *sort* (con-sort) and his 'I' made sport (played sexually – F; P) OFT (behind) with Morning. Women are traditionally night (Cynthia, moon, sister of Apollo, sun) and men are day: 'why is the good of man with evil mixed?/ Never were days yet call'd two/ But one night went betwixt' (Thomas Campion, 'Kind are her Answers', in *Signet Classic Poets of the 16th c.*, vol. II, p. 82).

RJ, III.i.49

Tybalt. Mercutio, thou consort'st with Romeo, –
Mercutio. Consort! what, dost thou make us minstrels? . . . here's my fiddlestick; here's that shall make you dance. 'Zounds, consort!

Mercutio angrily concludes, 'I will not budge for no man's pleasure, I'.

A consort is a group of musicians, hence the fiddlestick. But it is more like bawdy Mercutio to have gone one step further, punning on 'consort' (and DANCE) as copulate, his fiddlestick as his penis, and exploding that he does not consort with Romeo or BUDGE/ bugger for any man's pleasure (sexual – C; P). See 'ZOUNDS.

CE, I.ii.28, Merchant: 'I'll meet with you upon the mart/ And afterward consort you till bed-time:/ My present business calls me from you now'. A *mart* being where one bargains for women (P), the merchant will *meet* Antonio (meat, flesh of a whore – P; MEET, coit), will join him in whoring until bed-time. Even now he's off for PRESENT (genitals) BUSINESS (sexual intercourse).

See WITCHES, *R3*; PERFECT, *TGV*.

Content(ion) Sexual satisfaction. 'O not so fast! my ravished mistress cries . . . Together let us march into content' (Broadbent, p. 74). Contention: 1579, dispute, contentation (the act of satisfying). Contend: amorous struggle (C; P).

TrC, IV.v.205:

Nestor. . . . Let an old man embrace thee;
And, worthy warrior, welcome to our tents. . . .
Hector. Let me embrace thee, good old chronicle . . . .
. . . I am glad to clasp thee.
Nestor. I would my arms could match thee in contention,
As they contend with thee in courtesy.

(1) Greek and Trojan, soon to con*tend* in military arms, are now con*tent*ing in arms that clasp (sexual embrace – C; P), as Hector embraces Nestor, GOOD old CHRONICLE (arse).

(2) Hector, the Trojan, is welcome to Greek tents. Tents are also probes for wounds and a pun on sexual probes, as in Hector's earlier speech (II.ii.16): 'the tent that searches/To the *bottom* of the *worst*' – in which he deals with whether to return the whore (the WORST/whores) Helen to her husband. (Italics added.)

MV, III.ii.246. (Homo-) eroticism emerges from the concentration of sexual puns as Portia watches Bassanio read Antonio's letter: 'some shrewd *con*tents in yon *same* paper . . . steals the colour from Bassanio's cheek . . . turn so much the *con*stitution/Of any *con*stant man. What, worse and worse! . . . I am *half* yourself,/And I must freely *have* the *half* of anything/That this *same* paper brings you' (italics added). She notes the CON (cunt) or constitution of the constant MAN (*homo*), from whose CHEEKS (buttocks) the COLOUR/Fr *chaleur* (amorous heat) STEALS (stales, makes a whore). Bassanio is not so constant now: he turns (sexually – C; P); he is WORSE/whores and worse. SAME (Gk *homos*, *homo-*) or OE *sam* (half; cognate with 'semi-') is stressed by its unnecessary use the first time and by the repetition of 'same paper' two lines later. The contents are shrewd, lit. depraved and bad (BAD: ME, a hermaphrodite, effeminate man), and she must *have* the HALF (short-hand for homosexual). Bassanio then tells her 'Here is a letter, lady;/The paper as the body of my friend'. Antonio's paper and body (genitals – P) – both are the SAME (homo-).

See ALL, *Mac*; MATTER, *LLL*.

Continual, continuance, continuantly Continence and the cunt.

MM, III.i.249: 'This forenamed maid hath yet in her the continuance of her first affection'. Mariana has the continence of a maid – her cunt yet faithful to Angelo.

2H4, II.i.28. The hostess wishes to arrest Falstaff who 'comes continuantly to Pie-corner – saving your manhoods – to buy a saddle'. Corner (P) and saddle (F&H), both puns on cunt, point up the additional humour in *con*tinuantly, malapropism for 'continuously'. The glossing of Pie-corner as an area famous for eating-places has particular relevance if the saddle refers to that cut of meat known as saddle of *mutton* (common sl. for prostitute – P).

See FRESH, *Per*; CONTRARY, *1H6*; FAST, *Cym*; DOOR, *MV*; COURSE, *MM*.

Contract A sexual union and pun on the cunt. Lit. a betrothal, a marriage, a bringing together of the parts of something.

See ENLARGEMENT, *Cym*; FAST, *MM*; OFFENCE, *MWW*.

Contrary Cunt, like constable (P), confessor (P) and others in this dictionary starting with CON. Anus, the analogous place in sodomy; and penis, perh. as the contrary, opposed place, or through a pun on L *contus*, long rod or pole.

1H6, v.v.64: 'what is wedlock *forced* but a hell . . . continual strife? Whereas the contrary bringeth bliss'. Poor Henry is, 'through *force*' of Suffolk's report, '*ass*ur'd' and asks Suffolk to 'procure' (pimp – P) – for the (politically) forced wedlock – Margaret, between whom and

Suffolk the seeds for her adultery and CONTINUAL (cunt) strife (amorous contention – P) are already sown. (Italics added.)

WT, I.ii.372. Polixenes: 'I met him/ With customary compliments' (custom: sex and prostitution – *OED*; P). But the King, who believes his wife and Polixenes are adulterers by whom her unborn child was conceived, did 'Not speak': 'The king hath on him such a *count*enance/ As he had lost some province and a region/ Loved as he loves himself . . . Wafting his eyes to the *con*trary and falling/ A lip of much *con*tempt . . . leaves me to *con*sider what is *breeding*' (italics added). Wafted his eyes to the contrary: (1) turned them aside; (2) directed them to Polixenes's contrary that he believes guilty of the breeding. To hang the lip is *faire le groin* (Cot); and that is the reaction ('falling/ A lip') of the King, who acts as if he had lost the loved REGION (Fr *contrée*) of his wife's groin – and perhaps of Polixenes's (see Index for their relationship).

MWW, II.i.217. A tale of two men: (1) 'Doctor Caius, the renowned French physician', whose name CAIUS puns on Fr *cas* (buttocks), and whose title puns on Fr *mire* (physician) and 'mire' (urinate, defecate – P); (2) Sir Hugh, whose name is also open to anal puns: hue, COLOUR/ Fr *culier* (of the arse).

Shallow: 'My merry host hath had the measuring of their weapons; and, I think, hath appointed them contrary places'. *Measure* and *weapon*: penis (P); but the humour in this scene is largely excretal. The Host's idea of 'sport' includes keeping the antagonists far apart and assigning them contrary places – for the one, an outhouse, and, for the other, a dung-depot outside town. *Place* and *case*: both (F&H n.d.) place of ease, water-closet or loo (*lieu*: a place – Cot). PLACE: pudendum and anus.

iii.33, 60. The Host calls Caius (1) a 'Castalion-King-Urinal', pun on his casting urine (for disease: *Mac*, v.iii.50) and his being there at the urinal; and (2) 'Mounseur Mockwater' – moun*seur* or *sewer* Mockwater/ *make water*, urinate (C). Dr Caius replies, 'Me tank you for dat' – tank, a storage-place for water.

III.i. Sir Hugh, appointed to the contrary place, awaits the 'doctor of physic' at 'Frogmore': *more*, obs. sp. of 'moor', a wasteland or morass, soft wet ground with insufficient drainage – like a dung-depot. (Smollett, *Humphrey Clinker*, p. 289, greatly influenced by Sh, also exploits the anal humour in 'Frogmore': after a 'glyster' was administered they 'found Frogmore enthroned on an easing-chair under the pressure of a double evacuation'.) His name being Hugh/ hue (COLOUR), he is 'full of chollors' and full of *culare* (arse-gut – F). He is ready for 'the ork' – work, but also a large *butt* or cask (*CD* 1638) – of knocking the 'urinals' of his opponent, a 'reverend gentleman'. Hugh, too, is a reverend or parson; and their titles may very well pun on *Sir-reverence* (a turd – F&H; P), esp. since the Host, on bringing them together, calls them 'Boys of art [ART, L *ars* / arse]' whom he had directed (L *di-rectus-um*) to these wrong *places*. By III.iii the reconciled Evans and Caius are off hawking with friends: Evans will 'make two' and Caius will 'make-a the turd [i.e. excrement; contemptible fellow]'.

See WIND, *1H4*.

Cool Rump or cul(e). Allay sexual ardour (P). See FAN, *AC*; OFFICE, *AC*; LEND, *VA*.

Copatain hat Sign of buggery: a high crowned, conical hat, like a *chappeau fait à l'Albanoise* (Cot). Rabelais, Bk III, ch.25 (1693 trs.): 'Go . . . thou frantick Ass, to the Devil, and be bugger'd, filthy Bordachio that thou art, by some Albanian, for a Steeple-crown'd Hat.' Albanians shared the reputation of Bulgarians for being heretics and sodomites. Bugger (from L *Bulgarus*, Bulgarian): heresy, sodomy (*OED*). Rabelais, *Pantagruelian Prognostication*, ch.5 (1694 trs.): 'bardachios . . . he-whores and sodomites'.

TSh, v.i.70. Visiting his son, Vincentio finds he is being impersonated by a 'pedant' in whom he recognises licentiousness: 'O fine villain! A silken doublet! a velvet hose! a scarlet cloak! and a copatain hat!'; and the role of his son is being played by a servant whose father, Vincentio says, 'is a sailmaker in Bergamo' (which, some eds note, with question, is not a port). But *Berga*, *bergajo* and *carajo* are synonyms for a man's 'prick' (F&H); and Sp *caraja* is a sail. The sails (obs. form of 'sales') this man makes are whores – beastly, filthy (*sale* – Cot) whores. Cf.

Dekker and Middleton, *The Honest Whore I*, I.vi: 'shee's some sale curtizan'. *Saillir*: to leap, as the male on the female (Cot).

A FINE (arse) villain! wearing SILKEN (effeminate) and VELVET (vulva; venereally diseased) DOUBLET and HOSE (testicles and penis; codpiece): DOUBLE, code-word for homosexuality. And a SCARLET (effeminate male whore) cloak and copatain hat! (For similar cluster, see TAFFETA, *LLL*.)

Vincentio correctly appraises the (pederastic) pedant, who had earlier (IV.iv.5) said he and Baptista once 'were ldogers at the Pegasus' – 'I warrant you': LODGERS (whore-mongers), I WARRANT (expletive that puns on *warren* or brothel), at the PEGASUS (symbol of licentiousness and sodomy). See MISTAKE.

Copper 1. Venereal: of sexual intercourse or lust; ptg to copper, called Venus by chemists (Robert Boyle, 17th c. British chemist: 'Blue vitriol, how venereal' – *CD*, s.v. Venereal) and by alchemists. Chaucer, 'The Canon Yeoman's Tale', 276: 'Jupiter is tin / And Venus coper'. The best Roman copper, Cyprian copper, came from Cyprus, birthplace of Aphrodite. Cyprian: one from Cyprus; a strumpet; lascivious.

MM, IV.iii.14. 'Master Copper-spur' was an habitué of Mistress Overdone's brothel, his SPUR (penis) dedicated to Aphrodite.

LLL, IV.iii.386. Biron tells the Lords planning to seduce the French ladies, 'Allons! allons! Sow'd cockle reap'd no corn . . . . our copper buys no better treasure [woman's body – P].' Cyprian 'copper' to buy an Aphrodite, who was born of sea-foam and floated ashore on a seashell: *The Birth of Venus*, 15th c. painting by Botticelli, depicted Aphrodite standing in a huge cockle-shell.

2. Gk *kopros* is excrement. Aristophanes, *The Ecclesiazusae*, 1299–338: a man personifies his need to defecate by saying that Mr 'Kopreios' (trs. as Mr O'Shit) is knocking on his door. Constantine V (8th c.) was surnamed Copronymus, because he soiled the baptismal font (B).

1H4, III.iii.98: 'I have heard the prince tell him, I know not how oft, that that ring was copper!' He told him OFT (pun on *aft*, behind and the posteriors) that Falstaff – who had no metal ring in his pocket, as we learn – had only a copper RING, L *anus*. See Introduction, p. xv and RING for details.

Corinthian Licentious, brazen; from Corinth, ancient Greek city known for dissipation. The famed Corinthian brass, L *Corinthium aes*, would seem to indicate an equivoque in the DRAWERS' (q.v. for buggery) calling Hal 'a Corinthian, a lad of mettle, a good boy' (*1H4*, II.iv.13). He is a Corinthian, a lad of metal and mettle (semen – F&H; P): his is Corinthian *aes* / ass. He is a GOOD boy, an apt fornicator.

Aristophanes, *Clouds*, 707–29: lying with Socrates, Strepsiades complains of the 'bugs' or 'bugbears' (Corinthians were Athenians' bitterest enemies): 'Here are these cursed Corinthians [pun on *koris*, bug] advancing upon me from all corners of the couch . . . biting me . . . gnawing at my side . . . drinking all my blood . . . yanking off my balls . . . digging into my arse . . . killing me!' (PUNY: one of Hal's DRAWERS is likened to a bedbug).

Counsel(lor) A procurer; to pimp. 2 Sam 16.21: Ahithophel, David's 'counsellor', when asked to 'Give counsel', told Absalom, 'Go in unto thy father's concubines . . . and all Israel shall hear that thou art abhorred of thy father.' In *2H4*, I.ii.41, Falstaff damns 'A whoreson Achitophel!' Shirley, *The Lady of Pleasure*, V.i: a reformed Aretina turns away the procuress, saying, 'I'll visit you at home. (*Aside*) – But not to practise / What she expects: my counsel may recover her' – the counsellor will be counselled.

MM, I.ii.109. Mistress Overdone, a 'bawd', is told by her servant Pompey that she has nothing to fear if her 'house' or brothel is 'pulled down', for 'good counsellors lack no clients; though you change your place, you need not change your trade'. 'Trade' (prostitution – C; P) means buy and sell: coun(t)-sellors or sellers of coun(t), cunt (K; P).

Ham. Hamlet calls Polonius (II.ii.174) a 'fishmonger' (procurer – P) and (III.iv.213) 'this counsellor'. Monger or seller of *fish* (women, prostitutes – C; P).

Oth, III.iii. In l.100 Othello says Cassio 'went between' him and Desdemona; and in l.111 he says, 'I told thee he was of my counsel/In my whole course of wooing'. Go-between: pander (C; P). See COURSE (a turn in the bed) for another pun on 'counsel'.

TA, II.iii.24. During a storm, the love-making of Dido and her prince was abetted by a 'counsel-keeping cave'. The cave (L *fornix*: an arched vault; a brothel) performed like a brothel for counsel KEEPing – maintaining a woman for bed-service.

2H4, II.iv.290. While Falstaff was with his 'whore' Doll, Bardolph was 'lisping' to his 'counsel-keeper', the Hostess or bawd.

Countenance Doublet of continence, sexual restraint (*OED*). Count/cunt (C; K).

1H4, I.ii.33: 'chaste mistress the moon, under whose countenance'.

Ham, I.iii.113. Ophelia protests that Hamlet importuned her with love in 'honourable fashion', gave 'countenance to his speech'.

See APPROACH, *2H4*.

Course A run in the bed. *Corser*: to embrace or lay hold of by the body (Cot). *Coureuse*: a notorious whore. Etherege, *She Would If She Could*, I.i: 'some civil officer of the game or other would have . . . given him notice where he might have had a course or two in the afternoon'. The *game* meant was prostitution (F&H).

Oth, IV.ii.93. As if leaving a brothel, Othello shouts at Desdemona's maid, 'We have done our course; there's money for your pains: I pray you, turn the key and keep our counsel.' Doorkeepers were bawds (*Per*, IV.vi.125) and to turn the KEY was their function. See COUNSEL.

MM, II.i.196. Unable to establish the guilt of the apprehended Pompey (bawd) and Froth (customer), the constable is advised, 'because he hath some offences in him that thou wouldst discover if thou couldst let him continue in his courses till thou knowest what they are' – *cont*inue in his courses till his OFFENCES (fornications) become manifest.

See CAVALIER, *HS*; PITCH, *LLL*.

Court (1) To coit. *Court* is short (Cot); and, like SHORT, puns on fornicate. Jonson, Chapman and Marston, *Eastward Ho*, I.ii: Gertrude, who needs no 'Modesty!' now she is about to be married, is ready for 'strong play' 'With arm or leg or any other member, if it be a Court sport'. (See SHORT for Jonson's pun on short sport.)

(2) A cart/court pun (K). Prostitutes were removed in carts (C).

Oth, IV.iii.57: 'If I court moe women, you'll couch with moe men'. Her 'false love' is paralleling 'court' and 'couch' (to coit – P) – tit for tat.

AYL, III.ii.19. Touchstone says that a shepherd's life 'in respect it is not in the court, it is tedious'. Life is, by definition, if not *court* (SHORT, lecherous), then long and tedious.

H8, V.iv.35: 'or have we some strange Indian with the great tool come to court, the women so besiege us? Bless me, what a fry of fornication is at door?' The Indian with his great tool (penis – C; P) is come (1) to the courtyard and (2) to court or fornicate. The sexual licence in the courtyard, among those waiting for this christening, is such 'that this one christening will beget a thousand'.

TSh, I.i.55. Baptista gives the suitors 'Leave . . . to court her [Kate] at your pleasure [sexual – P]'. Gremio: 'To cart her rather.'

IV.ii.27. Bianca seems to engage in rather strenuous love-making, since on observing her (1) Hortensio says, 'See, how they kiss [coit – TWR; P] and court!' and concludes that she is a 'haggard' (HAGGARD, strumpet); and (2) Tranio says, 'see, how beastly [BEASTLY, with sexual bestiality] she doth court him!'

Courtesy In the 16th c. one meaning was a bow, made by bending the knees and lowering the body. Pun on stooping for defecation or for copulation. Note: puns on these two functions overlap, as in Jonson, *The Devil is an Ass*, V.i: Ambler says his friends thought him 'Too chaste' so 'To gi' my body a little evacuation –' – 'Well, and you went to a whore?' interrupts his friend.

III.i: 'But groan, and ha' your courtesies come from you/Like a hard stool, and stink?' Thomas Middleton, *Women Beware Women*, III.i: 'French curtsy' is the French disease, syphilis.
RJ, II.iv.55, 58:

Romeo. . . . my business was great; and in such a case as mine a man may strain courtesy.
Mercutio. That's as much as to say, such a case as yours constrains a man to bow in the hams.
Romeo. Meaning, to court'sy.

(1) Romeo's BUSINESS (coitus) was great. (2) 'Strain' and 'constrain' pun on straining at stool (1500s). See a similar conceit, in Anon., 'On Melting down the Plate: Or, the Piss-Pot's Farewel, 1697': 'To thee [the Piss-Pot] they cringe, and with a straining Face,/They cure their Grief, by opening of their Case [genitals – K; P; Fr *cas*, buttocks]' (*Penguin Book of Restoration Verse*, p. 349).

For the scatology of the immediately preceding lines, see SLOP; for the bawdry, see PINK. See SPAIN, *JC*; DISDAIN, *Ado*; CONTENTION, *TrC*.

Courtier Courtesan or pimp. Courtesan: 16th c., one attached to the court. *Courtisan(e)*: courtier; less properly, strumpet (Cot). *Cortegiana*: strumpet; *cortegiano*: courtier; eunuch (F). See RARELY, *TN*: Viola, 'eunuch' (I.ii.56) and go-between (trad. pander's job) for the Duke and Olivia, is called a 'courtier' by the jealous Sir Andrew.

Cym, III.iv.126. Imogen, learning her husband believed her a strumpet, said a 'Roman courtezan' must have maligned her. That courtesan was actually the courtier Iachimo, who had boasted that an 'accomplished courtier' (I.iv.101) could seduce her.

MWW, III.ii.8: 'now I see you'll be a courtier', says Mrs Page to Robin, who had already been so tarred when he (1) agreed to deliver Falstaff's love-letters, the job of 'Sir Pandarus' (pander) turned down by Pistol and Nym; (2) had been told to 'Sail like my pinnace' by Falstaff. A pinnace is a ship, but also a bawd or prostitute: 'punk, pinnace and bawd' (Jonson, *Bartholomew Fair*, I.i).

III.iii.66. Thinking Mrs Ford has given him a sexual invitation, Falstaff tells her she would 'make an absolute courtier; and the firm fixture of thy foot would give an excellent motion to thy gait'. Believing her a loose woman, he dares call her ABSOLUTE *courtier* and refer to her FOOT (fucking – C; P); and her GAIT/GATE (C; P) or vulva. To all of this she replies, 'Believe me, there's no such thing in me.' *Thing* being a euphemism for the male or female sex-organ (C; P), her response is a delightful *double entendre*.

H8, II.iii.83, Old Lady: 'I have been begging sixteen years in court,/And yet a courtier beggarly . . . and you . . . A very fresh fish here . . . have your mouth fill'd up/Before you open it.' The OLD LADY (L*anus*) is still a poor BEGGARly/buggerly whore; while Anne Bullen, a fresh fish (prostitute – P), has her mouth filled without asking.

Covetousness Lust. Covetous: occ. used for 'covetise', i.e. desire or lust. Rom 7:7: 'for I had not known lust, except the law had said, Thou shalt not covet'.
AYL, III.v.92:

Phebe. Thou hast my love: is not that neighbourly?
Silvius. I would have you.
Phebe. Why, that were covetousness.

Silvius wishes to have (possess carnally – C; P) Phebe – a sentiment she labels as covetousness or physical lust: 'thou shalt not covet thy neighbour's house, thou shalt not covet thy neighbour's wife . . . nor his ox, nor his ass, nor any thing that is thy neighbour's' (Deut 5:21) – a scriptural line that is suggested again in *TSh*, III.ii.232, when Petruchio calls Kate 'my house,/My household stuff . . . my ox, my ass, my any thing'.

See PINCH, *2H4*; STEWARD, *Tim*.

Coward Impotent; effeminate; male whore. Capon: a eunuch; Fr *capon*, coward(ly). Thomas Heyrick, 'The Battle between the Cock and Capon': the housewife 'With bloody Knife did rob him ["Castrate"] of the prize,/ Where *Love* is plac'd, and some say, *Courage* lies' (*Penguin Book of Restoration Verse*, p. 272). Greene, *Friar Bacon and Friar Bungay*, I.viii: Edward loved Lacy 'more/ Than Alexander his Hephaestion', but now that they are rivals for a woman he calls him, 'Base coward . . . too effeminate/ To be corrival'. Montaigne, Bk I, ch. 15: 'cowards', said a lawgiver, 'for three dayes together, clad in women's attire . . . should be made to sit in the market-place'. On transmigration, Plato says in the *Timaeus*, 'Of the men who came into the world, those who were cowards or led unrighteous lives may with reason be supposed to have changed into the nature of women in the second generation.'

MWW, III.i.85: 'By gar, you are de coward, de Jack dog, John ape.' If a word is known by the company it keeps, we note *Ado*, v.i.91: 'Boys, apes, braggarts, Jacks, milksops!' Milksop: effeminate man, as in 'Wedden a Milksope or a coward ape' (Chaucer, in *OED*). (See DOG; BE-GAR.)

2H6, III.ii.307, Queen to Suffolk (like Greene's Lacy, above, he, too, wooed for his king): 'Fie, coward woman and soft-hearted wretch! Hast thou not spirit to curse thine enemy?' No word is wasted: FIE (shit!); coward woman; *soft*-HEART (penis) with no SPIRIT (semen), to CURSE (prick) the enemy.

1H4, I.ii.205: 'I know them to be as true-bred cowards as ever turned back'. In Weever, *Faunus and Melliflora*, 531, it is *women* who are 'true-bred cowards . . . A servile sex'. Falstaff's companions are as TRUE/ *trou* (anus – Cot) bred *as*/ ass ever turned *back*, either in fear or for sexual entry. True-bred: 1596, thoroughbred (of horses); therefore Jonson described whores (HORSE/ whores) as 'true-bred' (see GREEN).

See INFINITE, *AW*.

Crack See CARACK/ CRACK.

Craft(y) The arse or PRAT (buttocks – F&H); arse-like. L *ars*: craft. OE *praet(t)*: craft, trick; *praettig*: crafty.

Cym, II.i.57: 'That such a crafty devil as is his mother/ Should yield the world this ass! a woman that/ Bears all down with her brain; and this her son . . . a wooer/ More hateful than the foul expulsion is/ Of thy dear husband'. A lord compares Cloten's birth to the expulsion of a turd. He came from the anus, not the vagina (see STIGMATIC, *3H6*, for Richard's comparable birth). His mother was a DEVIL, a crafty ass, from which came the young ass Cloten ('and from his [the devil's] backside flew/ A rout of rascals, a rude, ribald crew' – Broadbent, p. 87). She bore in birth, as in defecation, all down with her BRAIN/ Fr *bran* (excrement). He, Imogen's wooer, is an expulsion more HATEFUL (Fr *haineux*), more *anus*-like, than even the foul expulsion (1) of her husband from the country, or (2) of her husband's bowel movement. The Lord concludes praising her 'banish'd' husband: BANISHed, treated like shit (see INCH).

See ABOUT, *2H4*; WITCHCRAFT (L *ars magica*).

Creature Harlot, sometimes a practitioner of sodomy or bestiality. Marston, *The Dutch Courtesan*, I.i: Freevill goes to the 'brothel' to 'see my creature'. Creature of sale: prostitute (P). Thomas Heywood, *A Woman Killed with Kindness*, I.ii: in a short bawdy scene in which the names of dances are puns on coitus – for instance, 'Rogero' (F&H), 'Cushion-dance' (F&H, s.v. Sheets) and 'Sellenger's Round' (F&H, s.v. Sallinger's) – Jack *Slime*, a country fellow, says he can do the 'horse-trick' in dancing as well as the 'serving-men', for 'we have been brought up with serving creatures, – ay, and God's creatures, too: for we have been brought up to serve sheep, oxen, horse, hogs, and such like'. To serve is (*OED*), of a male animal, to cover the female, esp. of stallions (his *horse-trick*). This open bawdry on the country sexual practices of sodomy and bestiality, of serving *such-like* (L *tale*), establishes the 16th c. context of 'creatures'.

R2, v.iii.17: Hal 'would unto the stews,/ And from the common'st creature pluck a glove'. A 'stew' is a brothel; 'common', of a whore (*OED*; P).

H8, III.ii.36, Wolsey: 'My king is tangled in affection to/A creature of the queen's, Lady Anne Bullen'.

Oth, IV.i.96. Iago calls Bianca a 'housewife that by selling her desires . . . it is a creature/That dotes on Cassio'.

III.iii.422. Iago describes a time when he and Cassio, sleeping together, Cassio would throw his leg over Iago's THIGH, 'gripe and wring my hand,/Cry "O sweet creature!" and then kiss me hard'.

TA, II.iii.182, Lavinia: 'no womanhood? Ah, beastly creature! The blot and enemy to our general name!' A blot even to the GENERAL (whore's) name, lacking womanhood (see TRULL, sodomite), she is a BEASTLY (sexually bestial) creature who mates with animals (see SEMIRAMIS).

CE, III.ii.88. The kitchen wench is 'a very beastly creature', a 'very reverent body; ay, such a one as a man may not speak of without he say "Sir-reverence" [excrement – P; F&H]' or an apology said on seeing (or excreting) it. VERY (used twice by Dromio) puns on arse and privy; and BEASTLY sums up the anally erotic creature she is (see SPAIN).

WT, II.i.83. Leontes calls his wife 'adulteress' and 'creature of thy place [PLACE: pudendum; anus]'. She is a 'bed-swerver, even as bad as those/That vulgars give bold'st titles'. She SWERVES (in adultery; in sodomy) in *bed* like a BAD (effeminate) fellow (*OED*). You do 'but mistake' (*butt* MISTAKE) she tells him. MISTAKE (adulterous, anal intercourse; take: coit – C; P) is used four times; and he (EASE) claims her *back* door was open. Leontes may be suggesting a mirror-image of the nature of his own love for POLIXENES: 'You have mistook, my lady, Polixenes for Leontes' (see SPIRIT; CONTRARY).

(Note that Wolsey in *H8*, Iago in *Oth* and Leontes in *WT*, who are themselves probably participants in pederastic relationships – perhaps a metaphor intended to indicate they are buggers of mankind – when accusing a woman of adultery, call her a 'creature'.)

See CAMEL, *R2*.

Crook-back, crooked Impotent, castrated, buggered, cuckolded. Lit. bent at the end like a hook, crook; deviating from rectitude. CROTCHET: a musical note with a crook, not a whole NOTE (penis, testicle); pun on half-men, Fr *croché*, hooked, crooked. 'Bent' is sl. for a homosexual, as in the contemporary play *Bent*, by Martin Sherman.

R2, II.i.133: 'Join with the present sickness that I have;/And thy unkindness be like crooked age,/To crop at once a too wither'd flower', Gaunt tells the effeminate and ineffectual ruler, Richard, who is UNKIND, lit. physically unnatural. Richard, like Gaunt's AGE (q.v.) and 'ague' (116) or syphilis, will crop or cut off Gaunt's flower (the reproductive organs and their envelope), his already TOO (two testes) withered flower or scrotum. Gaunt is the WITHERED (*abbourgri*, withered and crooked – Cot), buggered, uncle, whose son Henry, product of his flower (and author of the metaphor: see SWEET), is banished and now to be cut off from his inheritance, rendered politically impotent by Richard, who will JOIN (copulate) Gaunt's PRESENT (genital) sickness, join in the screwing or destruction of Gaunt, who earlier (TAPER) had used a metaphor of sexual impotence as heralding his death.

AYL, III.ii.86: 'to be bawd to a bell-wether [castrate], and to betray a she-lamb of a twelvemonth to a crooked-pated, old, cuckoldly ram' is a sin. Since rams' horns are naturally crooked, this would seem to lack the slur implicit in both OLD (whored) and 'cuckoldly', but the *crooked* horns of this wether mean he is a cuckold (*cocue*: 'made a Cuckold, or crooked' – Cot).

3H6, II.ii.96. Replying to Richard's 'Are you there, butcher?', Clifford says, 'Ay, crook-back, here I stand to answer thee,/Or any he the proudest of thy sort.' Called a BUTCHER (bugger), Clifford retaliates in kind. He stands (has an erect penis – C; P) ready to ANSWER (return hit in fencing; a coital thrust) the crook or bent back (as in coitus) of ANY/Fr *âne* (ass) of the proudest (pride: sexual heat – *OED*; P) of Richard's *sort*: cf. 'A *sort* of naughty persons, *lewdly bent*' (*2H6*, II,i.167; italics added). Cf. BEGGAR, *Cor* and *R3*, for puns on Ger *gebogen* (beat, fornicate).

In *2H6*, V.i.158 (see STIGMATICAL), Clifford also called Richard 'crooked', sexually distorted. Richard has the *dos d'asne* (back of an ass; 'Ridgill-backed' – Cot). A RIDGEL is a eunuch; and if he, Clifford, is a bugger, then Richard will be the buggered – by Clifford's ANSWER (like the one in *AW*, II.ii.17, that 'fits all buttocks').

3H6, I.iv.75, Margaret: 'where are your mess of sons to *back* you now?/The wanton Edward, and the lusty George?/And . . . crook-*back* prodigy, Dicky your boy' (italics added). The others are wanton and lusty; only for Richard does she use a dim.: Dicky, the BOY (catamite); the crook-back *prodigy*, lit. monster (MONSTER: hermaphrodite; homosexual).

Historical evidence fails to establish Richard was a hunchback, and these puns on deformity suggest that the cross he bore, the hump on his back, was that of a 'boy', a RIDGEL ('a Rigil with one Stone' – *OED* 1678) or male whose genitals are improperly developed or with only one testicle, it being believed the other remained in his back (ridge), undescended. In that sense, Richard was rigged (humped or crook-backed – *CD*). 'Gibbous' (L *gibber*) is hunchbacked; and 'gibbed' is gelded. Richard is a 'bunch-back'd toad' (*R3*, I.iii.246; IV.iv.81) – the bunch on the back of a toad, a *tailless* amphibian Sh links to the gib or castrated cat (*Ham*, III.iv.190: 'paddock [toad] . . . gib').

In III.ii.148 Richard says it is impossible he can 'make my heaven in a lady's lap'; it is 'more unlikely/Than to accomplish twenty golden crowns. . . . O monstrous fault [to think of love]. . . . I'll make my heaven to dream upon the crown'. His FAULT (arse) or imperfection is MONSTROUS (unnatural, malformed) genitals. To find heaven in a lady's lap (pudendum – C; P), to accomplish TWENTY, a score-ing, a coitus, of CROWNS (genitals; surmountings) – is unlikely. He must find heaven in the other golden crown: the 'golden rigol' (*2H4*, IV.v.36). This is the goal of this poor RIGOL or *Rigel* (Ger dial.), barrow hog, castrated before maturity. Richard is the barrow hog (his crest, a 'boar'), who says (*R3*, I.i) he is 'curtailed' (tail cut off, castrated) and his 'delight to pass away the time' is to 'spy my shadow in the sun/And descant on mine own deformity' – the RIDGEL–RIGOL likes to mock himself (*se rigoler* – Cot); it is his solace to sport in the sun with wanton felicity (*se rigoler au soleil* – Cot). He rigoles, i.e. indulges himself wantonly (*OED*, s.v. Rigole – obs., rare), and mocks the deformed sexual organs and ridgel's back he sees in his SHADOW (a half-man). Richard has the *dos d'asne*, the 'Ridgill-backed', highest in the middle, sharpening toward the top, back of an ass (Cot). He descants (1501, sings prick-song; see PLAIN for puns on descant) on his OWN (his ass/arse) deformity, that of his own prick.

In III.ii.170 he wants his 'mis-shaped trunk [to be] . . . impaled with a glorious crown', but he is 'like one lost in a thorny wood,/That rends the thorns and is rent with the thorns' – Richard the crouch-back (hunchback). Crouch: from Fr *crochir*, to become crooked; 'Cross, in its early senses' (*OED*) – Sh's metaphor of Richard bearing his cross on his back (John 19:5, 17: 'the crown of thorns' and 'he bearing his cross').

See CROUCH for puns on the *crotch*, *crutch*, the fork of the human body – symbol of Richard's misery, the crotch of Richard with the undescended testicle, remaining in his back; Richard, the RIDGEL/RIGOL, aiming for the golden rigol or crown.

See BLUNT, *CE*.

Crotchet (1) a sexual embrace. Nashe, *The Choice of Valentines*: Nashe and his mistress kept 'crotchet-time,/And every stroke in order like a chime'.

(2) Of sexual inadequacy or deviation. A crotchet is a perverse fancy or conceit; the diminutive of 'crotch' (fork of the human body – *OED*); and a note that is half the length of a minim (*OED*), its *short* length indicated by a hook or crook. Musical *NOTE*s were 'pricks' (*OED*) and the subject of much bawdry. Rabelais, Bk *V*, ch. 27 (1694 trs.), lists friars and also 'Fryar-minors . . . who are Semibreves of Bulls . . . Minim Fryars . . . Crotchet Fryars [*crochet*: a musical quaver – Cot]' and other 'Diminutives' called Semiquavers. The Crotchet friars were '*crochetés* or crooked, both in the claws they stretched out as they begged, and in their morals' (Le Clercq trs.).

See CROOKED; NOTHING, *Ado*; RE, *RJ*; BEGGAR, *MM*.

Crouch The crotch or crutch, fork of the human body. 'Crouch' and 'crutch' are variations, as in the Crouched-friars or Crutched-friars, so-called from the sign of the cross they wore. (Crutch: var. of 'crouch', cross.)

Tim, v.iv.9. '*Enter Alcibiades with his Powers*': 'the time is flush,/ When crouching marrow in the bearer strong' cries no more to tyranny. The marrow (semen – P), the virility of the *crotch*, called the 'marrows of our youth' in IV.i (like the 'manly marrow' or semen in *AW*, II.iii.298), that had once *crouched* in fear is now, like the time, flush (a rush of fluid); and the bearer is strong.

Alcibiades now has the powers, the potency; and the day of the 'licentious' senators with their 'pursy insolence' – the insolence of the wealthy (1602, the 'purse-proud'), the insolence of *their* purse (scrotum – *OED*; P) – that day is gone. Now 'wrong/ Shall sit and pant in your great chairs of ease,/ And pursy insolence shall break his wind/ With fear and horrid flight'. In the chair of EASE ('stool of ease' – *OED*; see CHEER, Jonson) the pursy (short-winded) puckered mouth (of the anus), shall break his WIND or emit a flatus in fear and HORRID/ whored flight. (See WOUND.)

JC, IV.iii.46. Here, also in a conflict of power, Brutus rebels against Cassius: 'must I stand and crouch/ Under your testy humour?' Must he be the crotch under the testy (irritable or cross, i.e. crouch) humour of Cassius? See BUDGE for the implied passive homosexual role in this crouching. In *Tim* (above) and *JC* there is a parallel in the testy [/ teste] humour' and the 'pursy [purse] insolence', in which 'testy' and 'pursy' are the testes and purse, the scrotum, i.e. the balls or sign of strength, arrogance.

Crown (1) Genitals. A crown is a circle (*KJ*, v.i.2: 'The circle of my glory'); and 'cercal' means ptg to tail (pudendum, penis, rump – C; P).

(2) Mount coitally; lit. surmount something with.

3H6, I.i.195. Henry disinherits his son by an 'unmanly deed' (185): 'I here entail/ The crown to thee and to thine heirs for ever'. The Queen rebels, 'Thou hast . . . given unto the house of York such head . . . To entail him and his heirs unto the crown' (232).

'Entail the crown' (said twice) is transfer not just the crown but also the power symbolised by this circle/ cercal or tail, the penis. The house of York was given HEAD (Fr *teste*/ testicles), male potency, given heirs; *unto the house* of York (L *penes*, in the house of) was given penis, crown, potency and power.

AC, IV.xii.27, Antony: Cleopatra's 'bosom was my crownet, my chief end'. Bosom (C; P): sexual parts; clinch amorously. Cleopatra was his chief end: *chef*, the end of a place, time, business (Cot). Cleopatra: his end in two ways, his sexual partner and a participant in his end or defeat at the hands of Caesar.

IV.xv.63. Antony's last words to Cleopatra are 'my spirit is going; I can no more'. The orgasm is often called a little death: dying in her arms he experiences an orgasm, his SPIRIT (semen) is going. Cleopatra: 'The crown o' the earth doth melt. My lord!/ O, wither'd is the garland of the war,/ The soldier's pole is fall'n; young boys and girls/ Are level now with men.'

Antony's crown doth melt (experience an orgasm – P). WITHERED (fig. buggered or screwed) by this 'strumpet' and her flight at sea is (1) the garland (royal crown) of war, the Roman military corona of Antony the Roman hero; (2) the garland of the WAR/ whore. The *crown o' the earth* melts; the fallen pole completes the picture of defeat and detumescence: a pole/ poll pun (K) on the fallen head, i.e. crown. Now all is level, flat. Quite a contrast to an earlier scene (III.vi.66) when crowns and kings were being raised: 'He hath given his empire/ *Up* to a *whore*; who now are *levying*/ The *kings o' the earth* for war' (italics added). (See MILK: the metaphor continues.)

MWW, III.v.138: 'the conclusion shall be crowned with your enjoying her. . . . You shall have her . . . you shall cuckold Ford.' Brook's enjoyment (sexual – P) will be his having (possessing carnally – C; P), his crowning or sur*mounting* of Mrs Ford's CONCLUSION (coitus – TWR). There is also a pun on *coronet* (crown) and the *cornet* or little horn that will be placed on Ford's head, thus making him a cornute or cuckold; as Ford says, 'I'll be horn mad'.

Crust(y) Veneral scab. *Croust*: crust, scab; *crousteleré*: full of pocks (Cot).

TrC, v.i.5. Thersites had mocked (II.i.6), 'how if he had boils?' and 'those boils did run . . . were not that a botchy core?' Running BOILS (venereal symptom) with a core (med., central part of boils). Then Thersites is himself called a 'core of envy' and a 'crusty batch of nature', a pun on 'core' and Gk *kora*, a crust of bread; on 'botch' and 'batch' (a quantity of bread); and on Thersites, the crusty batch or 'botch in the Groyne, or yard' (Cot, s.v. *clapoir*), a veneral lesion in NATURE (generative organs).

Ham, I.v.72. Hamlet's father was with 'a most instant tetter bark'd about,/ Most lazar-like, with a vile and loathsome crust'. Rabelais, *Pantagruelian Prognostication*, ch. 5 (1694 trs.): 'claps . . . buboes or running nags, pock-royals, botches . . . tetters, scabs'. L *teter*: foul; and the elder Hamlet's tetter suggests the 'foul disease' (syphilis – *OED*); *vermocane*: 'running tetter, frenche poxe', or VD (F). It was lazar-like (LEPROSY, historically often confused with syphilis, both treated in lazar hospitals) and he died of a 'leperous distilment . . . That swift as quicksilver' coursed through his body. That distilment is MERCURY (quicksilver), trad. medicine for treatment of VD. There is the supportive detail that 'thy uncle stole' upon Hamlet: Mercury, Roman god of theft. This hypothesis dovetails with his earlier statement that the 'foul crimes done in my days of nature/Are burnt and purged away'. Scalding and purging were cures for VD (SCOUR).

In his days of nature (of sexuality – see *TrC* above), he committed foul crimes that resulted in the foul disease of syphilis, characterised by burning (*OED*; P). Hence he was burnt here as well as in hell. In this context his loathsome crust is another symptom. In his own words, this king 'Cut off even in the blossoms of my sin' is not the paragon Hamlet describes (III.iv.50–60), ironically calling him 'A station like the herald Mercury'.

He was *cut off* in the blossom (of his sin), nipped in the blossom or castrated ('Nip not the . . . blossoms of your love' – *LLL*, v.ii.812): It *scortare*, to SHORTEN, curtail; pun on L *scortari*, associate with harlots – is this his sin? Cut off even (docked smack smooth: castrated – F&H, 'old' but n.d.) – even and SMOOTH, *Ham* (q.v.).

Thus Sh develops a metaphor for impotence, for what is 'rotten in the state of Denmark' – rotten (venereally infected – C; P), in the royal state or royal seat of Denmark, the STATE (the throne; the arse and its stool or excrement). '. . . thou prunest a rotten tree,/That cannot so much as a blossom yield' (*AYL*, II.iii.63). See BRAINS for details.

Cunning Arse, rear end, a fine ass. *Fin*, *finesse*: cunning; *la fin*: the end (Cot). L *ars*: craft, cunning (Vergil). Cunny: cunt (F&H).

1H4, II.iv.503: 'wherein cunning, but in craft' – three puns on the arse of Falstaff, who is Hal's butt and an ass, a 'stuffed cloak-bag of guts [bowels]' (498).

TSh, Induction, i.92: 'your *cunning can ass*ist me much' (italics added: can/CON, cunt).

Oth, v.ii.11: 'Thou cunning'st [cunning assed?] pattern' – MOST (*fin* – Cot) cunning.

AW, v.iii.217: '*in fine*, Her *infin*ite cunning' seduced him (italics added). See RATE.

Cym, v.v.205. Iachimo tells Cymbeline how he tried to seduce Imogen and convinced her husband that he had 'Your daughter's chastity . . . her bracelet, – / O cunning, how I got it!' The ambiguous reference for *it*: all circular objects evoking the vulva: her chastity, bracelet, O (pudendum – P) cunning. See RING.

TSh, II.i.413. Tranio's use of 'crafty' (406) alerts us to his pun in saying, 'fathers commonly/ Do get their children; but in this case . . . A child shall get a sire, if I fail not of my cunning'. In this not common 'case' (pudendum – K; P), with the help of a servant's cunning, a child shall get (beget) his sire.

See SKILL, *LLL*.

Cup To serve a cup (of wine) is symbolic of pederasty. To be his cup-bearer, the enamoured Zeus, in the guise of an eagle, transported to heaven GANYMEDE (corrupt form 'catamite', young male in a pederastic relationship). Jonson, *Sejanus*, I.i: 'An eunuch Drusus loves' – 'Ay, and his cupbearer.'

2H4, v.iii.56. Shallow is with his 'beggars all' (BEGGARS/buggers), with his Davy whom Falstaff called 'your serving-man' (SERVING-MAN, lover) and 'your husband'. They sing, 'Do nothing but eat, and make good cheer,/ And praise God for the merry year;/ When flesh is cheap and females dear,/ And lusty lads roam here and there/ So merrily'. The humour is anal: (1) eat and make good CHEER/ Fr *chier* (shit); (2) eat (coitally – C; P) and make GOOD CHEER (fornication); (3) praise God for the MERRY (wanton) YEAR (arse) when flesh (fornication – P) is cheap; and (4) females *deer*, i.e. *hinds* (DEAR/ deer, a stock pun) and lusty lads roam MERRILY (wantonly).

Shallow tells Davy, 'Give Master Bardolph some wine'; Davy offers 'A cup of wine, sir?' and Silence sings, 'Fill the cup . . . I'll pledge you a mile to the *bottom*' (italics added). Shallow *ass*ures Bardolph that Davy, the Ganymede, will 'stick by thee, I can assure thee'; Bardolph, 'And I'll stick by him' (STICK, fornicate).

2H6, IV.i.56. Suffolk calls the CAPTAIN (pimp) a lover turned betrayer. He berates this 'jaded groom' (jade: worn-out stallion; surfeit exhausted man – P; GROOM, male whore) who had 'waited at my cup,/ Fed from my trencher, kneel'd down at the board [BOARD, Fr *asse*] . . . in our voiding lobby hast thou stood/ And duly waited for my coming forth.' The Captain is a parasite (lit. one who eats at another's table) who fed from Suffolk's trencher (like the 'serving-boy . . . at Caius' trencher, when for hire he prostituted his abused body' – Jonson, *Sejanus*) and *waited at* his *cup*, i.e. was Ganymede to Suffolk's Zeus.

Suffolk thinks of himself as Zeus: (1) 'Jove sometime went disguised, and why not I' (48); (2) he can't be hurt by this captain of a 'pinnace' (whore – *OED*; see COURTIER, *MWW*) because 'Drones suck not eagles' blood' (109). Suffolk is the eagle Zeus and his BLOOD (semen) cannot be sucked by this Ganymede, this drone and parasite. A drone is a bagpipe; and 'bagpipe', 'suckster', 'cock-sucker', 'cunnilinge' are cross-referenced in F&H as a practice too obscene to define; but under 'gamaruche' they are defined as cunnilingus (by analogy, penilingus).

At the voiding LOBBY (latrine), he had *waited* (17th c., mark of a pimp: in John Ford's *The Broken Heart*, II.ii, an 'old bawdship', also called 'waiter', sat 'i' th' presence-lobby'; see GROOM, *H8*); he had waited *duly* ('wages duly paid' – *H8*, IV.ii.150). In their mutual vilification, the Captain says, 'let my words stab him as he hath me' (stab coitally – C; P), and Suffolk replies, 'Base slave, thy words are blunt and so art thou' (more puns on 'duly': Gk *doulos*, slave; Fr *douillet*, an effeminate person – Cot), The CAPTAIN (pimp) is a base (bottom) SLAVE (pathic), whose WORDS (whores) are as soft, effeminate, dull, BLUNT (impotent) as he, unable to stab Suffolk, who had once stabbed him.

AC, IV.ii.21, Antony: 'Well, my good fellows, wait on me tonight:/ Scant not my cups; and make as much of me/ As . . . Haply you shall not see me more; or if,/ A mangled shadow. Perchance tomorrow/ You'll serve another master.' GOOD fellows (fornicators), *scant* not, make *much* of him who may tomorrow be a mangled SHADOW or half-man, a bisexual, seeking his other half to become whole. See TRANSFORM (assume opposite sexual role) for the rest of this speech, in which he asks one or two servitors to take care of his cups (play Ganymede). Tomorrow they may serve (coitally – *OED*; P) another master. SCANT *not* his cups may allude to the Lex Scantinia, Roman law against homosexuality, that he hopes they will *not* observe. Antony had said (III.iv.6) Caesar 'Spoke scantly of me'; and, indeed, Mecaenas had spoken with Caesar about 'adulterous' Antony 'most large/ In his abominations' (vi.94). Spoke *scantly*, lent 'most narrow measure', yet called him *most large*, MOST (buttocks) large, i.e. obscene, in his ABOMINATIONS (sodomy).

See ANGEL, *MWW*.

Cupid Pander (match-arranger).

MWW, II.ii.141: 'This punk [strumpet, pimp] is one of Cupid's carriers'.

Ado, I.i.186: 'Cupid is a good hare-finder', mocks Benedick. Though 'blind' (256) he found Claudio a good 'heir' to wed (297), Hero – later rejected as a hare (a 'bawd' – *OED*; a prostitute – P), a 'stale' (IV.i.66). Hare/ heir (K).

LLL, III.i.182: 'Dan Cupid . . . Dread prince of plackets, king of codpieces' (see GERMAN).

See BOY, *LLL*; PROVIDE, *TrC*; HANG, *Ado*.

Curious(ly) To be too curious and to shit are both *chiasser* (Cot). *Chiasse*: dregs (Cot).

TrC, III.ii.70, Troilus: 'What too curious dreg espies my sweet lady . . .?'
Ham, V.i.227. Hamlet speculates on man's end:

Hamlet. Why may not imagination trace the noble dust of Alexander, till he find it stopping a bung-hole [BUNG-HOLE, anus]?
Horatio. 'Twere to consider too curiously, to consider so [L *tale*].

AW, I.ii.20, King: 'Frank nature, rather curious than in haste,/ Hath well composed thee. Thy father's moral parts/ Mayst thou inherit too!' NATURE (generative or excretory organs and processes) was curious and *composed* him of compost, i.e. manure, from her FRANK, a pig-sty. His mother had hoped he would succeed his father 'In manners as in shape!' (i.70). But the paralleling puns reveal that Bertram's manhood was of a dubious nature:

King. PARTS (genitals); composed/ compost (manure);
Mother. SHAPE (genitals), to compose; MANNERS/ manures.

Curse, curst 1. A penis. Pun on horn (penis – P), and Gk *keras* (horn). Sometimes the pun includes SPIRIT, Gk *keres*, and GRACE, Gk *charis*.

Ado, II.i.21. If Beatrice is too curst, has too much spirit or *keres*, God will not send her a *keras*, a horn, i.e. a penis or man: 'for it is said, "God sends a curst cow short horns;" but to a cow too curst he sends none' – 'So, by being too curst, God will send you no horns' (and none of his grace, *charis*). Beatrice concurs happily: 'Just, if he send me no husband'. If no husband, no horns of cuckoldry ('an old cuckold, with horns on his head' – 46). And for that 'blessing' or favour or grace from God, that *charis*, she is on her knees every morning. As for a husband with a beard, she prefers to 'lie in the woollen' – another pun, on the kersey, a coarse woollen cloth (mentioned in *LLL*, *MM*, *TSh*), that a curst woman of her spirit (*keres*) prefers to the horn of a husband and the horn of cuckoldry.

2. To prick or screw the enemy. See SPIRIT, *2H6*; COWARD, *2H6*.

Cushion Deriving from Fr and L words for the thigh, it means the fleshy part of the rump (1710, of horse, pig, etc.), and it, too, is sat on. *Cullot*: cushion; *culot*, a little arse, young boy (Cot). Broadside Ballads (1685): 'He pitch'd on a subject was hard by the rump,/ And . . . all the night long he her cushion did thump' (F&H, s.v. Pulpit). Like a bolster (to coit – P), it gets stuffed (in coitus – C; P). Cf. Swift, *Polite Conversation*: 'Poor Miss, she's sick as a cushion, she wants nothing but stuffing.' Finally, a cod means the scrotum; a cushion or pillow.

Cym, IV.ii.212. A group of anal puns contradicts the unrealistic, and unwarranted, picture of perfection many assign Imogen. When Guiderius said (57) that 'grief and patience' were as two vines mingled in the SICK (effeminate male) Imogen–Fidele, his brother answered, 'let the stinking elder, grief, untwine'. Stinking reinforces the pun on ELDER (the arse), which is in apposition to GRIEF (bowel-pain), like its twin MELANCHOLY (bowel-disorder). Believing Fidele dead, Belarius says (203), 'O *melancholy*!/ Who ever yet could *sound* thy *bottom*? find/ The *ooze*. . . . Thou diedst, a *most rare* boy, of *melancholy*' (italics added). This girl–boy, a MOST (the buttocks) RARE/ rear young boy (*culot*) is presumably dead of an UNSOUND (a sick) bottom, an unhealthy MELANCHOLY ('ooze'), lying with 'right cheek/ Reposing on a cushion' – the RIGHT (L *rectum*) CHEEK (buttock) on the cushion or *cullot*, on the little arse of the young boy, *culot*.

If associating Imogen with the arse seems unduly harsh, remember this is the very scene in which she throws herself on the decapitated body of the hated Cloten (often called an 'ass'), believing him her husband merely because he is in her husband's clothes. Where is the vaunted sensibility of this woman who, fondling the loathed body, says (309) 'I know the shape of's leg; this is his hand;/ His foot Mercurial; his Martial thigh;/ The brawns of Hercules'. Which brawns? Brawn is the fleshy part, esp. of the hind leg, like thigh or cushion. The progression of her fondling is reminiscent of Mercutio's conjuring by Rosaline's 'foot . . . leg . . . quivering thigh / And the demesnes that there adjacent lie' (*RJ*, II.i.19). These seem to be the same brawns as in Wilmot's *Sodom*, II: 'A Turkish arse I love with all my heart . . . the brawny muscles of its side / Tickling the nerves'; and in Butler's *Hudibras*, Pt I, c.i. 280: 'The brawny part of Porter's Bum' – the *coussinet de la fesse* (fleshy muscle of the buttock – Cot); a *coussin(et)*, cushion, to sit on. See GIDDY, *H5* for another pun on 'ooze and bottom'.

See SHARE, *MND*; TRUNK, *TA*.

Cut (1) Cunt (C; K). Middleton, *A Chaste Maid in Cheapside*, II.i: 'Can any woman have a greater cut?' Anon., *The Woman Taken in Adultery* (medieval miracle play), 152: 'quean . . . sloven . . . slut! / We shall thee teach . . . A little better to keep thy cut'.

(2) Castrate (*OED*). A gelding, as in Fletcher and Sh, *The Two Noble Kinsmen*, III.iv: 'He's buy me a white cut forth for to ride'.

AC, I.ii.173: 'If there were no more women but Fulvia, then had you indeed a cut, and the case [pudendum – C; P] to be lamented.'

TN, II.iii.203. Sir Toby reassures Sir Andrew, 'if thou hast her not i' the end, call me cut'. Call him a cunt and a eunuch.

MWW, I.iv.118, Caius: 'I will cut his troat . . . [and teach a] jack-a-nape priest to meddle or make. . . . By gar, I will cut all his two stones, by gar, he shall not have a stone to throw at his dog.' (1) He will cut two stones (testicles – *OED*) of his rival for Anne's hand; (2) the throat he will cut is the neck (nape of the jack-a-nape or fop – F&H), but also the *troat* or rutting bellow of the buck; hence (3) he will not be able to *meddle* or *make* (copulate – C; P). Many of the throats cut in Sh's plays are troats.

II.iii.66. Same threat, different conceit: 'Scurvy jack-dog priest! by gar, me vill cut his ears [EARS, testes].' Both threats contain the element of DOG (sodomite, eunuch).

WT, II.iv.627. Autolycus, pickpocket and cut-purse: ' 'twas nothing to geld a codpiece of a purse'; 'I picked and cut most of their festival purses . . . I had not left a purse alive in the whole army.' He robbed but also gulled, made impotent fools of them – took their alive purses (scrotum – *OED*), gelded the codpiece (frequently alludes to the penis itself – G; as in HOUSE, *KL*). Plautus, *Epidicus*, 183, 505–10 has a similar situation: 'exenterem marsupium', trs. eviscerate, gut, disembowel the purse.

See SHAME, *KJ*; BUNG, *2H4*; EXCELLENT, *TN*; CLOTH, *Ado*.

D

Dainty 1. A strumpet. Middleton, *A Trick to Catch the Old One*, v.i: 'Daintily abused! you've put a junt upon me; – a common strumpet.' Wycherley, *The Country Wife*, I.i: a jealous country man is advised to keep his wife in the city, where 'we have such a variety of dainties . . . we are seldom hungry'.

TSh, II.i.190: 'super-dainty Kate,/ For dainties are all Kates'. Kate: old name for a whore (P) – cf. Kate Keepdown, *MM*; Kate, *Tem*, II.ii. Cates: dainties.

H8, I.iv.94, Henry: 'By heaven, she is a dainty one. Sweetheart,/ I were unmannerly to take you out,/ And not to kiss you.' Less concern with manners than with projecting virility: he were UNMANNERLY (unmanly) to take out and not kiss (coit – P) this dainty one, this *sweet* heart, this 'sweet partner' (SWEET, sexually intimate). 'Partners' is next used (v.iii,v) for the baptism of his child, conceived before marriage by the 'dainty one'.

1H6, v.iii.38. Each scorns the other's SHAPE (genitals); then York tells the HAG (masculine woman), Pucelle (lit. slut): 'No shape but his [the Dauphin/ 'Dolphin'] can please your dainty eye' – her slut's EYE (vagina, anus), as in I.iv.107.

2. Effeminate; lascivious. Stone: a testicle, 'lascivious' (*OED*). *Daintiers*: a deer's stones or doucets (Cot). Used freq. with SWEETS/*suites* (boars' testes – Cot). Spenser, *The Faerie Queene*, Bk III, c.xii, st.7: [Ganymede] 'Whom Jove did love . . . Or that same daintie lad . . . so deare/ To great Alcides'. Testicles symbolise the like mates (TWIN) in homosexual love.

Cym, III.iv.167. Imogen is told 'forget to be a woman', 'change' into a boy's clothes, forget her 'dainty trims, wherein/ You made great Juno angry'. Pisanio means her woman's clothes; but 'trim' is castrate (dial., *W*) and copulate (C; P), and it is dainty trims, such as Ganymede whom her husband loved, that really angered Juno.

LLL, IV.i.146. Costard jests of Armado's effeminacy: 'O, a most dainty man!/ To see him walk before a lady and to bear her fan! . . . . and how most sweetly a' will swear!' Dainty and sweetly (Fr *doucettement*): dainties and doucets (stones). He bears her fan and he bares a FAN ('fanny') like hers, this MOST (Fr *fin*) buttocky, dainty man.

TrC, V.viii.20. It is a bitter denunciation of Achilles that he strikes (rapes – C; P) – 'Strike, fellows, strike' – the 'unarm'd' Hector, whom he had expressed 'a woman's longing' to see in his tent 'unarm'd' (see SICK). 'My half-supped sword, that frankly would have fed,/ Pleased with this dainty bait, thus goes to bed.' After his sword (penis – C; P) that would have fed FRANKly (licentiously) as in a pig-sty (Gk *pyge*, buttocks), is pleased (sated sexually – C; P) with its dainty bait, it gets sheathed.

Damn To dam, make a woman of; to whore or fuck. Dam/ damn (K).

MV, III.i.34. Jessica eloped with Lorenzo; she left 'the dam' and 'is damned for it'.

1H4, II.iv.123: 'that damned brawn [Falstaff] shall play Dame Mortimer his wife'.

See PROMISE, *Mac*; OIL, *MWW*; ABUSE, *Ham*; BOTH-SIDES, *AW*; DELICATE, *Oth*.

Damsel Young woman, 'sometimes slightingly' (*OED*). Also a hot iron for warming a bed: *OED* says cf. 1 Kgs 1:1–4, in which a 'young virgin' was to lie in David's bosom 'that my lord the king may get heat'.

1H6, III.ii.56:

Talbot. Damsel, I'll have a bout with you again,
Or else let Talbot perish with this shame.
Pucelle. Are ye so hot, sir? yet, Pucelle, hold thy peace . . . .

'Pucelle', like 'damsel', means both maid and slut. Talbot has no doubts which she is: he will *again* have a bout (sexual encounter – C; P) with her. She asks him whether he is so *hot* (sexually eager – C; P) that the damsel should heat his bed. She will *yet* (his 'again') hold her peace and his PEACE (genitals; see *TN*, *TGV*).

LLL, I.i.292:

King. [You were] taken with a wench.
Costard. I was taken with none, sir: I was taken with a damsel.
King. Well, it was proclaimed 'damsel'.
Costard. This was no damsel, neither, sir; she was a virgin.
King. It is so varied too; for it was proclaimed 'virgin'.

They have difficulty in distinguishing 'damsel' from 'wench' (a free girl) and 'virgin', since it means both. 'Varied' (VARY, in buggery) may be the key: it seems to verify Armado's saying that the sex act in which Costard was taken was PREPOSTEROUS (of the posterior; buggery). In this way, Jaquenetta can be a wench or damsel who would 'serve my [Costard's] turn' (in bed – P) and, technically, still be a virgin. Robert Burton, p. 652: 'the vice is customary to this day; sodomy is (in a manner of speaking) the Diana of the Romans [goddess of chastity] . . . even in the married state, where an opposite part is used from that which is lawful'. Cressida seems to have used this practice also (WARD, *TrC*).

Dance Fornicate ('daunce' – TWR). Dekker and Middleton, *The Honest Whore I*, III.ii: a reformed whore reviles her ex-bawd who 'guard'st the dore/ Whilst couples go to dauncing'. *Danser*: to dance, leap (Cot). Leap: coit (C; P). Cf. *R2*, II.iv.12: 'ruffians [pimps – *OED*] dance and leap'. *De la panse vient la danse*: 'when the bellie is full, the breech would be figging' (Cot).

LLL, II.i.114: 'Did not I dance with you in Brabant once?' Biron's first words to Rosaline are obviously significant since she repeats them verbatim. We can conjecture the kind of dancing they were doing in Brabant (Belgium), because in *CE*, III.ii.142, when asked 'Where stood Belgia, the Netherlands', Dromios answers, 'I did not look so low' (Netherlands: the low countries; pudenda and adjacent area – C; P). This previous dance may explain Biron's cynicism about love (GERMAN). At the end of the play Biron says, 'I will wish thee never more to dance,/ Nor never more in Russian habit wait' – no more lechery for her or for him (RUSSIAN, lecherous).

AW, II.i.33. Bertram, forbidden to go to the wars, must stay in court 'and no sword worn/ But one to dance with!' – no sword except a military sword worn ornamentally at dances, and also the other sword (the penis – C; P) that one dances with.

Ado, V.iv.120, Benedick: 'let's have a dance ere we are married, that we may lighten our own hearts and our wives' heels'. But Leonato, father and uncle of the brides-to-be, having lived through one cancelled wedding when his daughter was called a whore, says, 'We'll have dancing afterward' – not *ere* they are married. He will not permit the men to lighten their OWN HEARTS (both words pun on the arse) or their wives' heels, a phrase that suggests 'lift one's heels' (lie down for intercourse – F&H n.d.)

See CONSORT, *RJ*.

Dancing school Whore-house. Nashe, *The Choice of Valentines*: an angry lover can visit his mistress only in the 'house of venerie', where she does 'in this dancing school abide'. *Danser*: to dance, to leap (Cot). The 'dancing-schools' of *H5*, III.v.32, are the 'leaping houses' of *1H4*, I.ii.9. To the Dauphin's 'Our madams mock at us, and plainly say/ Our mettle [semen – P] is bred out and they will give/ Their bodies to the lust of English youth', Bourbon replies, 'They

bid us to the English dancing-schools' – to learn how to leap (upon the female in copulation – *OED*) like the lusty English youth.
See GRACE, *H5*.

Dark(ly), darkness Old Roman brothels were in vaults, sewers. Brothel, vault: L *fornix*, stem of 'fornication'. Plautus, *Epidicus*, 470–80: a Captain who thought he had bought one girl had another shoved off (*trudis*) on him: 'quasi tu mihi tenebras [*tenebrae*: dark place, underworld] trudis?'

Per, IV.vi.32: 'do the deed of darkness [the sex-act – P]' in the brothel.

MM, IV.iii.164: 'the old fantastical duke of dark corners' would not punish fornication. V.i.279: 'I will go darkly to work with her' – 'That's the way; for women are light at midnight.'

AYL, III.ii.421: 'Love' is 'madness' and 'deserves as well a dark house and a whip as madmen do . . . the whippers are in love too. Yet I profess curing it by counsel' – COUNSEL (whoring) cures love: it deserves the dark HOUSE (brothel) and WHIP (of sexual sadism).
See EPHESUS, *CE*; KNOT, *Oth*.

Dart (1) Penis (TWR; P). Love-dart or *spiculum amoris*: a kind of penis in gastropods; dart-sac: appendage of female reproductive organs, containing the dart (any seeming confusion in def. arises from certain gastropods being hermaphrodites, or starting life a male and ending it as female.

(2) Dartos: contractile tissue under skin of scrotum.

(3) Dart (OFr *dars*): pun on *d'art*, *d'ars* (L *ars*, art), of the arse.

MM, I.iii.2, Duke: 'Believe not that the dribbling dart of love/Can pierce a complete bosom'.

AC, III.i.1: 'Now d*art*ing *Par*thia, *art* thou struck' (italics added). The Parthians (L *Arsaciis*), famed for discharging missiles *backward*, toward their horses' rumps, while in flight, are now struck (screwed – F&H, s.v. Strike; P). 'The ne'er-yet-beaten horse of Parthia/We have jaded out o' the field' (33). They have beaten the HORSE/whores and the HORSE/arse of darting Parthia (and 'Parthian darts' – IV.xiv.70). They have made jades (worn-out horses and whores – P) of them.

H8, I.i.112. A sexual metaphor expresses relative degrees of power: Norfolk describes the 'private difference' – difference in the privates (genitals – C; P) of Buckingham and the Cardinal. He warns the Duke of the Cardinal's 'potency': his 'sword [phallus – C; P]/Hath a sharp edge [sexual desire – P]: it's long . . . It reaches far, and where 'twill not extend,/Thither he darts it . . . Lo, where comes that rock/That I advise your shunning.' The Cardinal not only has a long phallus but is a *rock* of the church, a stone (testicle, 'lascivious' – *OED*): he has a lewd, politically potent dart. (See his MALICE, testicles.)
See SKILL, *LLL*.

Dear Dear/deer would not have been such a 'stock' pun (K), had Sh not seen bawdy possibilities in the female deer or hind and the male deer or hart (HEART, arse) and 'pricket' (*LLL*, IV.ii). Chaucer, *The Legend of Good Women*, 1191: 'The herde of hertes founden is anon/With "Hay! go bet! pryke thow!"' *2H4*, II.iii.12: 'my heart's dear Harry'. *CE*, III.ii.62: 'my dear heart's dearer heart'. *RJ*, I.i.73: 'heartless hinds'. *AYL*, III.ii.107: 'If a hart do lack a hind,/Let him seek out Rosalind.'

MV. The pun is relevant to the love between Bassanio and Antonio:

'Some dear friend dead' (III.ii.248);
'I have engaged myself to a dear friend' (264);
'The dearest friend to me, the kindest [KIND, sex] man' (295);
'Since you are dear bought, I will love you dear' (315, Portia to Bassanio);
'How dear a lover of my lord your husband' (IV.7);
'a bosom [clinch amorously – C; sexual parts – P] lover' (17);

'The pound of flesh . . . Is dearly bought' (IV.i.100) – Shylock, like Portia above, bought flesh, 'Nearest the merchant's *heart*' (italics added).

See castration theme: BOARD, SLAVE, WEATHER.

See INTEND, *RJ*; PURPOSE, *MWW*; LEND, *AW*; OFFENCE, *KJ*; MIND, *Cym*; CUP, *2H4*; SPURN, *TA*; TENDER, *RJ*.

Debt Sexual intercourse. The Bible stipulates that the debt husbands and wives owe one another is that of intercourse: St Jerome translates 1 Cor 7:3 as 'Uxori uir debitum reddat: similiter autem et uxor uire' – the man should pay his wife her debt and *vice versa* (TWR, s.v. Dette). Chaucer, 'The Wife of Bath's Prologue', 130: why did God set it down 'That man shal yeelde to his wyf hir dette? / Now wherwith sholde he make his payment, / If he ne used his sely instrument?'

TrC, II.ii.175: 'Nature craves / All dues to be rendered to their owners: now, / What nearer debt in all humanity / Than wife is to the husband?'

III.ii.58:

Troilus. You have bereft me of all words, lady.
Pandarus. Words pay no debts, give her deeds . . . .

Pandarus urges Troilus to act. Deeds: coital acts; payment of debts (C; P).

Cym, I.ii.13. Two lords engage in double talk, mocking Cloten's cowardice and lack of masculinity:

2nd Lord. His steel was in debt; it went o' the backside the town.
Cloten. The villain would not stand me.
2nd Lord. No; but he fled forward still, toward your face.

The stranger's steel was in debt, L *aes alienum* (lit. another's money), pun on in another's ass/arse, in Cloten's – the 'ass', as the Lord calls him (39). The other man did not stand (have a penial erection – P), or *actually* stand Cloten. But he fled forward still – or fled forward, steel toward Cloten's FACE (arse) as if with his STEEL (penis) he were goosing or buggering Cloten, the one who was really fleeing or running away; the stranger's steel was in debt. (Steel / still – K: 'still locked in steel' – *TrC*, IV.v.195). See Index for Cloten's bisexuality.

Deformed A castrate; fig. impotent, effeminate. *Difformé*: misshapen, out of fashion (Cot).

R3, I.i.20. Richard is 'Deform'd, unfinish'd . . . scarce half made up . . . unfashionable'. Unfinished and *half*-made up precisely describe not the hunch-back but the RIDGEL or male with no or only one testicle ('Worse than a rigil with one stone' – *OED* 1678). He is unfashionable (*difformé*) and deformed. See LAME (impotent) for l.22; and SHAPE.

Ado, III.iii.131: 'But seest thou not what a deformed thief this fashion is?' FASHION or *rigle* (Cot) is a RIDGEL–RIGEL; FASHION (Fr *taille*, a fashion, a cutting) is a CUT (a gelding – *OED*) – a cut-tail.

133: 'I know that Deformed . . . a' goes up and down like a gentleman'. He parades UP AND DOWN like a pimp and a *gentleman*, a word that Sh uses for opprobrium (Goddard, vol. II, p. 46) for effeminates and those who prostitute themselves, such as Rosencrantz and Guildenstern, Osric, Sir Andrew Aguecheek and Parolles. Beatrice would swear that every 'fair-faced . . . gentleman should be her sister' (I.62). To wander UP AND DOWN or *pedigare* may also pun on *pedicare*, to bugger (F).

182: 'And one Deformed is one of them: I know him; a' wears a lock'; and V.i.317: 'Deformed . . . wears a key in his ear and a lock hanging by it'. In the 17th c. a lock or lovelock was a falling curl over one ear 'in fashion with comly pages, youthes, and lewd effeminate, ruffianly persons' (Prynne 1633, in F&H). (A ruffian was a pimp – *OED*.) Ear-lock: 'ear lockes . . . badges of infamy, effeminacy, vanity' (*CD*).

These scenes parody the play's effeminate lovers: (1) Claudio, who will '*lock* up all the gates of love' (IV.i.106: see GATE) and who is asked (II.i.88) 'in what *key* shall a man [MAN, *homo*] take you [sexually – P]' and who is called 'Lord Lackbeard' (V.i.195); (2) Benedick, of the 'fine little one ['wit': WIT, penis]' and 'double [DOUBLE, bisexual] tongue . . . two tongues' (V.i.170), 'virtues' (VIRTUES, virility) Beatrice reputedly did 'transshape' (TRANSFORM: assign alternate sex role or SHAPE, genitals – *OED*). Italics added. See FASHION, PARROT.

Delicate Voluptuous, wanton. 'Delicacye': wantonness (TWR). Chaucer, 'The Monk's Tale': Nero burned Rome 'for his delicasie'; 'The Merchant's Tale', an old lecher marries a young girl, anticipating a life 'so delicat'.

Mac, I.vi.10: Banquo observes Macbeth's castle, where the 'martlet' has 'made his pendent bed and procreant cradle: / Where they most breed and haunt I have observed, / The air is delicate'. The 'luxurious' (see SUDDEN), i.e. lecherous, Macbeth lives here; yet, how ironic, for indoors all is 'fruitless' and 'barren' – and soon there will be 'Lamentings heard i' the air' for the 'New hatch'd' events.

Other birds were known for the same lewd delicacy; in Chaucer's *The Parliament of Fowls* the popinjay is 'ful of delicasye' and Pliny calls the PARROT lecherous (TWR, p. 74).

Oth, I.iii.360. Iago mocks, 'Drown thyself! . . . If thou wilt needs damn thyself, do it a more delicate way than drowning.' If Roderigo must DAMN / dam himself – (1) if he so needs a dam or woman; (2) if he must damn himself (as a suicide would: the drowned Ophelia can have no 'Christian burial' – *Ham*, V.i) – then he should do it the voluptuous way: *die* in orgasm (C; P), in another forbidden activity (see BLOOD, *Oth*; PAY, *H5*).

See DILDO, *WT*; VARIETY, *AC*; THRONG, *Ado*.

Despair Sh freq. mocks the cause or nature of a despair by labelling it 'black', 'muddy' or 'foul', i.e. shitty and evil-smelling. *Scitare* (pron. shitare): to despair, fall into a depression (F; see MELANCHOLY). Cf. dejection: 1605, excrement.

2H6, III.iii.23. The King at deathbed of the Cardinal: 'O thou eternal Mover of the heavens . . . beat away the . . . fiend / That lays strong siege unto this wretch's soul / And from his bosom purge this black despair.' One kind of Mover is called upon to beat away another MOVER (of the bowels), the Devil who lays SIEGE (bowels, an evacuation – *OED*) or excrement on this wretched man's SOUL (arse) and will claim him for the vile and shitty crimes that Beaufort is incoherently reviewing. From his bosom (interior, lap – P) purge (empty the bowels) the black despair. But Beaufort dies, giving no sign to Henry, who had asked for one, that the eternal Mover had heard. 'The abode . . . of churchmen in Satan's rectum is an idea that persisted long after Chaucer' (TWR, p. 82; Ross reproduces a 16th c. woodcut attributed to Lucas Cranach the Elder and showing the 'Pope and cardinals in the Devil's arse').

R3, II.ii.36: 'Oh, who shall hinder me . . . ? I'll join with black despair against my soul' (hinder: posterior).

R2, II.ii.67: 'Who shall hinder me? I will despair', says the Queen, whose 'inward soul' (11, 28) – INWARD (bowel) SOUL (arse) – trembles, and in labour delivers a monstrous prodigy (see SOUL), in an old conceit that the arse and not the womb delivers evil men, such as Cloten (CRAFTY, *Cym*) and Richard (STIGMATIC, *3H6*).

Cor, III.iii.121, Coriolanus: 'curs! whose breath I hate / As reek o' the rotten fens . . . As the dead carcasses . . . That do corrupt my air' – let their enemies' 'plumes / Fan [FAN: buttocks, flatus; see *TrC*] you into despair!' and they be won 'without blows!' No blows but the L *flatus*. 'I turn my back', he says; 'the beast / With many heads *butts* me away' (IV.i.3; italics added).

See MUDDY, *CE*; INCH, *Cym*.

Detested Emasculated, de*testes*d (testes removed). Impotent, effeminate. Marlowe, *Edward II*: Gaveston, the King's lover, 'detested as he is', is a 'monster of men' and 'a slave' (MONSTER and SLAVE: 16th c. puns on sodomites and eunuchs).

KL, II.iv.220: the effeminate Oswald is a 'detested groom'.

TA, II.iii.94: 'These two have 'ticed me hither to this place: / A barren detested vale . . . Here never shines the sun; here nothing breeds' – a *barren de-tested* vale (hollow between two elevations) where *nothing breeds* and there is no *sun*. With this metaphor for the barren groin and the destruction of heirs, Tamora, also called SEMIRAMIS (the castrater), starts her revenge against Titus, responsible for the death of her 'first-born' *son*.

III.i.248:

Messenger. . . . Here are the heads of thy [Titus's] two noble sons . . . .
Marcus. These miseries are more than may be borne. . . .
But sorrow flouted at is double death.
Lucius. Ah, that this sight should make so deep a wound,
And yet detested life not shrink thereat!

The TWO HEADS (*teste* – F) of the two sons, the DOUBLE (testicles) death and deep wound, the testes or life-force of the Andronicus family, is being destroyed – no more may be born(e) – though the detested LIFE did not shrink. The castration image continues in two uses of 'slumber' (253–5): SLUMBER and SLEEP, be rendered impotent. See BRAINS for a similar pun on the end of their house.

TGV, V.iv.39, Silvia: 'I do detest false perjured Proteus' – pun on perjure or bear false WITNESS (L *testis falsus*) and the false *testis* or testicle of Proteus who swore love to her, thus perjuring all former 'oaths' (OATHS / OATS, testes) to Julia with his *testis falsus*, lit. false witness or testicle. For more on his de-tested sexuality, see PERFECT; PEASANT.

See UNNATURAL, *KL*; SMOOTH, *Tim*.

Devil A hermaphrodite or bisexual who had intercourse with man, woman and child. In medieval cathedrals and paintings devils are portrayed with exaggerated sex-organs, lewd tongues and phallic tails. In the great age of witchcraft, 1550–1650, it was believed that 'children of three and four had intercourse with the devil', who 'could assume either sex', and were 'bisexual'. They also enjoyed intercourse with witches. See Allen C. Kore and Edward Peters, *Witchcraft in Europe, 1100–1700* (Philadelphia: Univ. of Pennsylvania Press, 1972). A scrat: a hermaphrodite; a devil; scratch. Old Scratch: the devil. Jonson, *Volpone*, IV.ii: jealous of her husband's companion, whom she takes to be a girl disguised as a man, or a male homosexual whore, the wife accuses her husband of being 'patron, or St George, / To a lewd harlot, a base fricatrice, / A female devil, in a male outside'. The same man was earlier vilified as a 'land-syren here, / Your Sporus, your hermaphrodite' (Sporus, the youth whom Nero castrated and married).

Anal imagery is associated with the devil. Webster, *The White Devil*, III.ii: 'the devil imitates a cannon; wheresoever he comes to do mischief, he comes with his backside towards you'. Cf. Erik H. Erikson, *Young Man Luther, A Study in Psychoanalysis and History* (New York: W. W. Norton, 1962). Luther thought the devil expressed scorn by exposing his rear parts; and a few days before his death he saw the devil outside his window, exposing his naked posteriors (p. 59). Sh's pun link the devil to man's arse: see CRAFTY, *Cym*; CON, *TN*; DESPAIR, *2H6*.

2H4, II.i.19. The Hostess warns Snare to beware of Falstaff, who 'cares not what mischief he does, if his weapon be out: he will foin like any devil; he will spare neither man, woman, nor child'. This recognised pun on foining in fencing and in copulation, the *weapon* being the sword and penis (C; P), is the only instance Partridge accepts as an unequivocal statement of homosexual intercourse. Fang replies, 'If I can close with him, I care not for his thrust . . . an a' come but within my vice'. If Fang (lit. a grip) can CLOSE (in sexual intimacy), can get Falstaff within his VICE (another grip, a screw, and a pun on fornication), he won't worry about Falstaff's thrust (coitally – C; P).

II.iv.362, Falstaff: 'The fiend hath *pricked down* Bardolph . . . his face is Lucifer's *privy*-kitchen . . . . For the boy, there is a good angel about him; but the devil outbids him too' (italics added).

Bardolph's face is the devil's kitchen, where he eats; but his FACE (buttocks) is the devil's privy, where he evacuates. And he gets *pricked* DOWN (for fornication) by the bisexual devil.

As for the BOY (catamite), the devil outbids Falstaff (the GOOD ANGEL: sodomite) ABOUT/ Fr *au bout*, at the end of him, too.

TrC, I.ii.228. Pandarus says Hector has 'hacks' (hack and hackster: fornication; a whore – F&H) from everyone: 'Swords! any thing, he cares not; an the devil come to him, it's all one'. Hector is indiscriminate sexually: swords (penises – C; P) or ANY (Fr *âne*, ass) thing (penis, pudendum, buttocks – C; P). It's all one (Sc 'ain' and 'ane'), all *âne* or ass/ arse to him: let the devil come.

See ABUSE, *Ham*; BUNG, *H5*.

Dew See DUE.

Dewlap The two lips of the vulva. *Landie*: the 'deaw-lap in a womans Privities' or the 'great wings within the lips of a womans Privities' (Cot). By extension, the two testes, two laps (or folds) of flesh. See TWO(FOLD), testes; 'lappe': male folds (TWR).

MND, II.i.50. In between boasting that, disguised as a 'filly', he beguiled a horse by 'Neighing' (NEIGH, fornicate) and that, disguised as a chamber-pot, he slipped from the 'bum' of a defecating old 'aunt' (bawd – C; P) who cried out 'tailor' (see SLIP) is this other exploit of the 'merry' (MERRY, sexually wanton) Puck, which logic dictates ought also be bawdier than merely spilling ale on her lap: 'sometimes lurk I in a gossip's bowl,/ In very likeness of a roasted crab,/ And . . . against her lips I bob/ And on her wither'd dewlap pour the ale'. The crab may be a crab-apple, but APPLE is a testicle; Cancer, the crab, is the sign of the zodiac that governs genitals (TWR); and woman has other LIPS (*labia pudendi*) that Puck – disguised as a testicle – can bob (i.e. delude, as he did the stallion): her dewlap (vulva: lap – C; P) or *ailes* ('sides of a womans privities' – Cot). Puck lurks in her BOWL or pelvis (L *pelvis*, basin; Gk *pellis*, bowl), where he bobs up and down against her lips (*ailes*) making even this wither'd gossip ale-moist with sexual excitement.

IV.i.126. In this scene all the characters of the play appear, the mismated like Titania and Bottom, and all the 'pairs of faithful lovers' (*sic*) to be wedded. Theseus (Duke of Athens) gives orders for his hounds: 'Uncouple in the western valley; let them go.' 'Couple' means copulate; and WEST is the rear end or arse. This directive is probably intended to parallel that of Oberon (King of the fairies), who had also just given orders for the 'release' or uncoupling of Titania and Bottom, an ass/ arse.

In early morning, as Theseus and his wife go 'up to the mountain's top' (*up*; *mountain*/ mounting, copulating – K; P; *top*, copulate – C; P), this ardent lover – whose impatience for the 'nuptial hour' and 'sealing-day' (SEALS, testes) had opened the play – boasts to his betrothed of his hounds' virility as if it reflected on his own: 'bred out of the Spartan kind . . . and their heads are hung/ With ears that sweep away the morning dew . . . dew-lapp'd like Thessalian bulls'. Twice *Theseus* says 'my hounds', and when he compares them to the bulls of *Thess*aly, it is himself he is comparing. *Limiei* (mine, such as mine – F) sounds like *limier* (bloodhound – Cot); and Spartan hounds are bloodhounds or limmers – Theseus is thinking of his own limbs. His hounds are like bulls (C; P) powerful and (if men) habitual copulators. Their HEADS (*teste* – F) or testes are hung (HANG), the EARS (OE sp of 'arse') with testicles so large they sweep away the morning dew (DEW/ It *due* or two testes). The dewlaps (L *palear*, dewlap of an ox) are the two (*due*/ dew) laps of flesh, the testicles. As he concludes this speech, he spies the four sleeping lovers, whom he awakens with 'Begin these wood-birds but to couple now?' – ending as he had begun, on the coupling note. As all the lovers walk off sharing their 'dreams', it only remains for Bottom to make the final commentary that 'man is but an ass, if he go about to expound this dream'.

Tem, III.iii.45: 'mountaineers/ Dew-lapp'd like bulls, whose throats had hanging at 'em/ Wallets of flesh?' Men with testicles like bulls, wallets of flesh or purses (scrota – *OED*; P) hanging at their throats/ troats (rutting bellows: see CUT, *MWW*) – men 'Whose heads [*testes* – Cot] stood [with erect penis – P] in their breasts [fig. the seat of the affections]'.

Dexterity, dexteriously Ptg to the arse. Right: dexter, straight (L *rectum*).

Ham, I.ii.157: 'O, most wicked speed, to post/ With such dexterity to incestuous sheets!' Hamlet's mother posted, i.e. with speed, with wicked 'speed' (sexual potency – C; P) and with dexterity, i.e. with skill and with her behind (L *post*), to and in incestuous sheets.

1H4, II.iv.286. Dexterity is not an attribute one expects of Falstaff, but in the context of buggery (BUCKRAM) Hal says, 'Falstaff, you carried your guts away as nimbly, with as quick dexterity, and roared for mercy and still run and roared as ever I heard bull-calf'. (*2H4*, III.ii.187, Falstaff: 'prick me Bullcalf till he roar again'; – 'What, dost thou roar before thou art pricked?')

Falstaff carried his guts (bowels) as nimbly with *as* quick dexterity – and the comparison is never finished. But, as a pun on as/ ass, the sentence is complete: ass-nimbly with ass-quick dexterity. ME 'nimble', 'nimel': quick at seizing. Cf. Marston, *The Dutch Courtesan*, II.i: 'a puncke . . . smooth thigh, and the nimble Divell in her buttocke'.

This cluster intensifies the picture of Falstaff, cozened ass, in his fear, running (loose in the bowels) and ROARING (farting). See ROAR for others that 'ran' and 'roared'; FART.

TN, I.v.66:

Clown. . . . give me leave to prove you a fool.
Olivia. Can you do it?
Clown. Dexteriously, good madonna.

The Clown, being a 'fool' and an 'ass' (II.iii.15–18), will dexterously prove Olivia is a fool or ass (words Sh interchanges). See MADONNA (a foolish or mad woman; even an ass) for a significant flashback to this scene.

See OLD LADY, *MWW*.

Dice, paradise Genitals. *Tales*: dice (Cot); the game termed 'Cockall' (*OED*, 1586). Tales: penis; female pudendum (K; P).

LLL, IV.iii.143. The King accuses his lords of being willing to break their oath of celibacy 'for paradise' – for a *pair-o'-dice* or tails. See TROTH; PAIR.

AC, II.iii.33. A soothsayer tells Antony that 'at any game' with Caesar he is sure to lose; and Antony says, 'He hath spoken true: the very dice obey him . . . he speeds;/ His cocks do win the battle . . . and his quails ever/ Beat mine . . . . And though I make this marriage for my peace,/ I' the east my pleasure lies.'

Multiple puns on the 'game' of *battle*dore and shuttle*cock*; the 'game' that is hunted, the quail. But basically the 'game' is whoring (C; P) and the 'dice' are *tales*, as is evident from the puns in the 'cocks' and the 'quails' (prostitutes – *OED*; P). In this marriage for his PEACE, to save his PIECE or tail/ tale, he also loses to Caesar. The Soothsayer told a true tale; and Antony acknowledges that Caesar speeds (arrives sexually; is sexually potent – C; P) better than he. See YARE for the continuation of this metaphor when the two men fight, apropos of which Canidius says, 'This speed of Caesar's/ Carries beyond belief' (III.vii.75).

Dildo An artificial phallus. They were made of wax, horn, leather, glass. Thomas Nashe, *The Choice of Valentines*: Mistris Francis, not being satisfied by men, says, 'My little dildo shall supply their kind.' Marston, *The Scourge of Villanie*, Satyre iii: 'How then shall his smug wench . . . quench/ Her sanguine heate? . . . Shee hath her Monkey, & her instrument/ Smooth fram'd at Vitrio'. Marston adds, do not grieve for her lover, who redresses his 'Priape' with 'his Ganimede,/ His perfum'd she-goat, smooth kembd' – matching her bestiality with his own.

WT, IV.iv.195. Autolycus sells dildos: 'He hath songs for man or woman, of all sizes; no milliner can so fit his customers with gloves: he has the prettiest love songs for maids; so without bawdry, which is strange; with such delicate burthens of dildos and fadings: "jump her, and thump her" '.

These are no ordinary songs that he sells (sing: coit – P), in which case men and women of *all sizes* (SIZE, Fr *taille*/ the tail or genitals) would be an irrelevancy. His songs are fits (1500s, songs); no milliner can so fit his customers (prostitutes – *OED*; male frequenters of brothels –

P) as Autolycus can *fit* his (in sexual intercourse, orgasm – TWR; P). Burden is a frequent Sh pun on the weight of the man in intercourse (*RJ*, II.v.78), but these little man-substitutes or dildos are practically weightless, delicate; and they are DELICATE (voluptuous and wanton) burthens. Sh alludes to the selling of dildos by mountebanks, though not by name: see PIN, *WT*; WITCHCRAFT, *Oth*.

Direction An erection, phallic. Sh shows his hand in *MWW*, III.v.41. Falstaff, who has been interrupted in the midst of his ardour and thrown into a ford, is told the perpetrators 'mistook their erection' – that is, the direction they had been given. 'So did I mine, to build upon a foolish woman's promise', he replies. In the following, a final 'd' in a preceding word enables the 'd' in 'direction' to be silent.

Oth, I.iii.300: 'Come, Desdemona; I have but an hour/ Of love, of worldly matters and direction,/ To spend with thee.' Othello has but one hour to spend (to expend semen – F&H; C; P) with Desdemona for (1) love; (2) worldly matters (to 'world' means to populate, to bring a child into the world (*OED*); and MATTERS is sexual concerns); (3) and (d)irection. Notice that 'love' and 'worldly matters' are preceded by 'of' (Fr *de* or *d'*) – Othello has one hour *of* love; *of* worldly matters; and *d'*irection, of erection.

Ham, II.i.66. Polonius asks Reynaldo to say his son was seen in a house of sale, a brothel – as bait to get at the truth of his son's actual sexual misdemeanours: 'By indirections find directions out'. By his invented stories he will find erections out – a quibble on find out or discover; and on find the penis OUT, exposed and whoring.

TSh, IV.iii.117. In the midst of the bawdry on GOWN (cunt – C; P; K), CUT (cunt – C), 'stuff' (semen, whores, coit – C; P), 'yard' (16th c. for 'penis'), and the indecency in 'take up my mistress' gown for thy master's use', the tailor says, 'the gown is made/ Just as my master had direction'!

R3, V.iii.16. Military and sexual terminology frequently overlap to convey power and potency: 'Up with my tent . . . Call for some men of sound direction.' There are two parallel directives: up with the tent, and get men of sound (free from VD – C; P) erection. The same pun is made in ll.290, 302: 'Call *up* Lord Stanley, bid him bring his *power*'; 'A *good direction*, warlike sovereign' (italics added).

Discard See CARD, DISCARD.

Discharge Fart. *Descharger* (Cot), to purge, evacuate. Rabelais, Bk III, ch. 5 (1693 trs.): When paying a debt, the debtor discharges a fart in the creditor's face. Pantagruel fears those who 'shall level the Shot towards my Nose; all the back-cracking Fellows of the World, in discharging of their Postern Petardes, use commonly to say, *Voilà pour les quitters*; that is, For the quit [*quitté*, discharged]'. Sh makes the same pun in *Cym*, V.iv.173, when the gaoler tells Posthumus 'you shall now be *quit* . . . you have no true *debtor* and *creditor* but it; of what's past, is, and to come, the *discharge*' (italics added). This speech had been triggered off by Posthumus's remark that 'the dish pays the shot', idiomatic for pay a debt; but also an allusion to farting, since the tail-*shot* (*pet* – Cot) or the bum-*shot* (Rabelais) is a syn. for the 'discharge' of 'back-cracking fellows' (Rabelais). Posthumus, who had been called 'well cooked' and 'Over-roasted', is the dish who now pays the shot to life and, being quit of his debt, makes the discharge in the face of his creditor, life.

This bawdry sets in perspective the previous 90 lines of bombastic verse about and by Jupiter, the 'thunder-master' (30) – THUNDER being a fart. As Jupiter appears, he '*throws a thunder-bolt*'; 'He came in thunder; his celestial breath [L *flatus*]/ Was sulphurous to smell'.

Disdain Stoop for defecation or fornication. L *dis*: in two ways. 'Dain' means disdain; stink(ing); obs. sp. of 'deign' or condescend, lower oneself. Distain: sexually pollute (P).

CE, III.i.121: 'I'll knock elsewhere, to see if they'll disdain me', says Antipholus E., whose wife has locked him out of his house and who is now off to KNOCK (fornicate) at the Courtezan's

– off to see if she'll disdain him: (1) lower herself literally for coitus; or (2) fig. shit on him as his wife had.

Ado, I.i.119. At their first encounter Benedick calls Beatrice Lady Disdain and marvels she still lives. Beatrice: 'Is it possible disdain should die while she hath such meet food to feed it as Signior Benedick? Courtesy itself must convert to disdain, if you come in her presence.' Beatrice says with such 'meet food' – such meat as he – disdain or defecation flourishes. The bow of courtesy turns into the COURTESY (a stooping for defecation), to eliminate him from her presence. She also mocks him as meet or suitable food, food for MEET (coitus): he is meat (a whore – C; P; meet/meat – K). His coming (an orgasm – C; P) *in* her PRESENCE (genitals) would be a lowering of herself (fig. and lit.), and would stink. Otway, *Venice Preserved*, III.ii: the courtesan says, 'play your tricks over as fast as you can, that you may come to stinking [orgasm] the sooner, and be turned out of doors as you deserve'.

See RAISE, *AW*.

Disperse Render impotent: *dis* (privative) + *purse* (scrotum – *OED*; P).

R3, IV.iv.513. Told 'Buckingham's army is dispersed and scatter'd', Richard rewards the messenger, 'There is my purse'. In contrast to the impotent Buckingham, he has a purse, money, potency.

R2, II.iii.27. Percy's uncle 'hath forsook the court,/ Broken his staff of office and dispersed/ The household of the king'. Loss of power and wealth are symbolised by a broken staff (penis) and spent purse (scrotum).

2H6, V.i.45: 'I do dismiss my powers./ Soldiers . . . disperse yourselves . . . You shall have pay'. (1) York gives up his powers and they, too, disperse and relinquish strength; (2) York will dis-purse: pay them.

See GIDDY, *TA*.

Distinction Pun on 'stink': 'distinct breath' (*TrC*, IV.iv.47) and 'stinking breath' (*JC*, I.ii.248). Breath: L *flatus*.

Cym, IV.ii.248, Belarius: 'bury him as a prince' for 'though mean and mighty, rotting /Together, have one dust, yet reverence . . . doth make distinction' – the Sir-reverence (excrement, turd – F&H; P) of both rich and poor makes the same stink, but the reverence paid the *sir*, the 'mighty', makes the distinction that merits a better burial.

See FAN, *TrC*; FLEW, *TrC*.

Distress Physical discomfort from prolonged phallic erection. From L *distringere*, stretch out.

Per, II.v.46. Pericles denies he had seduced Thaisa, though he desires her: 'A stranger and distressed gentleman,/ That never aim'd so high to love your daughter'. Though a stranger (pun on *distringere*) and distressed/*and a stressed* (stressed, i.e. stretched out – *OED*) gentleman, never did his 'actions yet commence/ A deed might gain her love or your displeasure'. Action and deed: the sex-act (P) – and he never aimed so *high*.

AYL, II.vii.91. The lords Orlando bursts in on call him a 'cock' and ask if he is 'thus bolden'd, man, by thy distress'. Man (be sexually man to a woman – P), L *vir*, stem of *vir*ility, adds to the erectile image. Orlando's hunger, his distress, *has* boldened him (bold: lit. strong; big; of grain, well-filled): his sword is drawn and he apparently also has a visible erection (symbol for his ferocity), for he answers that 'the thorny point/ Of bare distress hath ta'en from me the show/ Of smooth civility'. His physical desires – symbolised by the distressed or stretched out thorny point (thorn: penis – P; point: head of penis – C; P) – take away from him the show or pretence of SMOOTH (impotent, effeminate) civility.

Ditch Birthplace of whores, in two senses: the mother's vulva they leave and the ditch they fall into (L *scrobis*, a ditch; the vulva. See SCRUBBED). *Fossa*: a ditch, grave, pit; woman's vulva (F).

Mac, IV.i.31: 'Ditch-deliver'd by a drab'.

Tim, IV.iii.166: 'be whores still' and 'ditches grave you all!'

AC, V.ii.57. Cleopatra chooses not to be shown 'to the shouting varletry/ Of censuring Rome', but 'Rather a ditch in Egypt/ Be gentle grave unto me! rather on Nilus' mud/ Lay me stark naked, and let the water-flies/ Blow me into abhorring!'

Rather than be shown to the VARLETry (harlotry) of Rome, while a boy imitates her 'I' the posture of a whore' (221), she prefers they *lay* her *naked* in a *ditch* (the whore's posture or position) in Egypt, where insects will *blow* her (lit. lay eggs in) into ABHORring/ whoring. Let insects *deposit their eggs* in her mud, her ditch (and vulva), rather than that the Romans do likewise. For 17th c. use of 'posture' as an indecent pose, see Wycherley, *The Country Wife*, I.i: 'I have brought over not so much as a bawdy picture, new postures' ('indecent illustrations to Aretino's erotic poems' – *Three Restoration Comedies*, p. 155).

IV.vi.38. What a comment on Enobarbus, therefore, that having forsaken Antony, he says, 'I will go seek/ Some ditch wherein to die'.

See SHIN, *Tim.*

Dog Eunuch; sodomite. Dog is not man's best friend in Sh's lexicon, where he is 'vile', 'inhuman' and a 'whoreson'. He is also often curtailed, docked (ME, 'to deprive of some part' – *OED*), like the bobtail (a eunuch, an impotent man – F&H n.d.; a contemptible fellow – *OED* 1619). A curtal dog marked its owner as unfit to course. Deut 23:17, 18: 'There shall be no whore of the daughters of Israel, nor a sodomite of the sons of Israel. Thou shalt not bring the hire of a whore, or the price of a dog, into the house of the Lord . . . both these are abomination unto the Lord thy God.' See PARD, Weever.

MWW, III.v.8. Falstaff had been made such a fool of by the women he had hoped to seduce that he says, 'if I be served such another trick, I'll have my brains ta'en out and buttered, and give them to a dog for a new-year's gift.' If he is served (in copulation – *OED*; P) another trick (sexual swindle – P), he'll give a dog a GIFT (genitals) for new YEAR/ arse. (1) Falstaff, who feels the fool, will give his brains away to a dog who can make better use of them than he has; (2) Falstaff, the sexually frustrated, will have his BRAINS (testes) removed and given to a dog who needs them (echo of an earlier pun on cutting out a man's 'two stones', i.e. testicles, and throwing them at his dog: see CUT). Therefore, Falstaff rejects Bardolph's offer of a brew 'With eggs, sir?' – 'I'll no pullet-sperm in my brewage.'

He will give them for a new year's gift because it is on that day that the Roman Catholic, Eastern Orthodox and Anglican churches hold the Feast of the Circumcision, commemorating the circumcision of Jesus. Also, in the Middle Ages, especially in France, the Feast of Fools was held at Circumcision (*La Circoncision*: New Year's Day – Cot). And Sh, if not Falstaff, probably knew that circumcision symbolised rejection of the sins of the flesh and spiritual purification (Rom 2:25–9).

Circumcision (cut round, short or off) was identified (1) with castration, because both involved cutting the penis (Rabelais calls circumcised Jews 'clip-yards [yard: penis], raskals [RASCAL, a castrate], bob-tails'; (2) with the barbarian, alien, such as 'a turban'd Turk . . . the circumcised dog' (*Oth*, V.ii.355), and the 'currish Jew' (*MV*, IV.i.294).

In the following, 'dog' appears in conjunction with some other sign that the man is a castrate or sodomite.

Tim, V.i.118: 'Out, rascal dogs!' – OUT (a whore), RASCAL (castrate, impotent).

TrC, II.i.8, 39. Slow-witted Ajax is no match for voluble, witty Thersites in their exchange, but he manages to make his point that Thersites is a 'Dog!' and a 'Mistress Thersites'.

V.iv.15, Thersites: 'that mongrel cur, Ajax, against that dog of as bad a kind, Achilles'. A BAD (an effeminate – *W*; *OED*) KIND (sex or gender – *OED*).

R3, I.ii.39: 'Unmanner'd dog . . . [I'll] spurn upon thee, beggar'. He will SPURN (screw) upon the UN-MANNER'D (unmanly) dog; the BEGGAR/ bugger or sodomite.

Tim, I.i.280: 'Away, unpeacable dog, or I'll spurn thee hence.' He tells this eunuch, this dog that has no PEACE/PIECE (genitals – C; P), to bugger off or he will SPURN (fuck) him.

See LIE, *Tem*; VOICE, *Cor.*

Door Women's lips, esp. the *labia pudendi*, lips or folds on either side of the vulva. L *valvae*: folding doors. ('And lips, O you,/The doors of breath' – *RJ*, v.iii.113.) Oldham, 'Upon the Author of a Play Call'd *Sodom*': 'thy Mouth a *Cunt* . . . gag it up, and make't for ever dumb . . . As they a *Door* shut up, and mark'd beware,/That tells infection and the *Plague* is there'.

CE, III.i.120. Antipholus E's wife has locked him out: 'I know a wench . . . . Since mine own doors refuse to entertain me,/I'll knock elsewhere'. KNOCK: 16th c., coit; knocking-house: brothel (F&H). His wife's doors refusing to entertain him (provide sexual hospitality – C; P), he will knock elsewhere.

AC, II.i.13. Pompey does not fear Antony's power, for he 'In Egypt sits at dinner, and will make/No wars without doors'. Since wars *are* made without doors or out of doors, we understand (1) Pompey says Antony will, at most, talk war, for he can make no wars without some gold or money (Fr *d'or*; 'I will make fast the doors, and gild [Fr *dorer*] myself' – *MV*, II.vi.49); (2) Pompey mocks Antony, who makes only indoor WARS (sexual combat): the field Antony fights in is the 'field of feasts' where 'sleep and feeding' – allusive to both sets of lips or doors – will dull him. A feeder is a fornicator, in amorous feeding (P): 'feasts of love' – *LC*, 181.

In the following, 'door' and GATE (vulva – P), used together, reinforce one another.

MV, I.ii.147: 'Whiles we shut the gates upon one wooer, another knocks at the door', says Portia, her name a pun on gate and door, L *porta*. Bassanio needs Antonio's money to woo her because he had been showing 'a more swelling port/Than my faint means would grant continuance' (CONTINUANCE, cunt). The 'Jasons come' because they are not 'ignorant of her worth' (financial and personal): 'her sunny locks/Hang on her temples like a golden fleece'. 'Locks' reinforces the pun on Portia as a door – with locks: with *d'or* (golden) locks, locks of golden hair, her 'golden fleece', quibble on her fortune and hair (pubic – F&H, s.v. Fleece).

While Portia shuts the gates upon one wooer, lit. and fig., for he may never again '*speak* to lady afterward/In way of marriage' (no more doors or *lips* for him; italics added), another *knocks* at the door – or, more grossly, at Portia's nock (posteriors; female pudendum – F&H) or door, hoping for (sexual) admittance and her *d'or* (fortune). Cf. Anon., 'One Writeing against his Prick': 'Did shee not clap her leggs about my back/Her Port hole open?' (*Penguin Book of Restoration Verse*, p. 184).

TN, I,iv.16. The Duke sends Cesario to woo Olivia for him: 'address thy gait unto her;/Be not denied access, stand at her doors . . . there thy fixed foot shall grow/Till thou have audience'. The metaphoric expression of the Duke's ardour is prophetic of the backfiring of his plan, for Cesario–Viola does address her GAIT/GATE or vulva to Olivia, who falls in love with this messenger and does not deny him ACCESS (sexual entry) but encourages him to stand (phallic erection – C; P) at *her* doors or vulva, she, too, hoping his FIXED FOOT (punning on two common Fr words for 'fuck') would *grow*.

Double(t), doubly 1. Homosexual love is a union with one's double: see TWIN. Didymous (Gk *didimos*, a twin; a testicle): double, paired. Used for bisexuality.

MND, III.ii.209. See SHARE, *MND*, for full discussion of Helena's speech to Hermia on the feminine love they had shared:

> So we grew together,
> Like to a double cherry, seeming parted,
> But yet an union in partition;
> Two lovely berries moulded on one stem;
> So, with two seeming bodies, but one heart;
> Two of the first, like coats in heraldry,
> Due but to one and crowned with one crest.

These two young women, the double CHERRY, are actually two young boys (actors), as the audience is aware; and the double cherry with its union in partition is the two testes in one scrotum, the *love*ly berries on one stem, like coats (COATS/cods, i.e. testes – K) – with one stem or penis, crowned with one crest (tuft of feathers, comb of a cock). TWO (repeated three times) and DUE/It *due* (two) both pun on the testicles.

See FAST, *Cym*; PLUME, *Oth*; BEAT, *AW*; PERNICIOUS, *R2*.

2. Doublet and hose: testicles and penis. Doublet: a precious stone of two pieces joyned (E. Coles, *English Dictionary*, 1706). (Stone: a testicle – *OED*.)

AYL, II.iv.7, Rosalind–Ganymede: 'I could find in my heart to disgrace my man's apparel and to cry like a woman; but I must comfort the weaker vessel, as doublet and hose ought to show itself courageous to petticoat: therefore courage, good Aliena!'

Masculine doublet (testes) and HOSE (penis) must comfort (caress sexually – P) and show courage to petticoat (1600, female sex) or placket (female pudendum – F&H; P).

III.ii.206. To Celia's '. . . out of all hooping!', Rosalind–Ganymede responds, 'dost thou think, though I am caparisoned like a man, I have a doublet and hose in my disposition?' Celia is teasing, but Ganymede *is* out of all hooping, stiff-upper-lip and steel or whalebone that formed the hoop petticoat (1548; see FOREST). Having no STEEL (penis) and bone (masculine courage), Ganymede can find no comfort (see above), cannot 'hoop . . . with thy embraces' (cf. *WT*, IV.iii.450) or with 'hoops of steel' (as in *Ham*, I.iii.63).

Dove Whore, Whorr, whoore: coo as a dove. *Gemere*: to whoore or cry as turtle-doves (F). Venus's chariot was drawn by turtle-doves. Jonson, *Bartholomew Fair*: the Justice calls Ursula ('punk, pinnace, and bawd' of I.i) 'Aunt' (bawd) and asks her tapster to bring him what 'thy dove drinketh'.

Tem, IV.i.93: 'her deity . . . and her son/Dove-drawn with her . . . thought . . . to have done/Some wanton charm upon this man and maid'. CUPID (pander) tried to corrupt Ferdinand and Miranda, who had sworn pre-marital celibacy. Anon., *The Merry Devil of Edmonton*, I.iii: 'Cupid wanton as his mother's dove'.

1H6, II.ii.30: 'I scared the Dauphin and his trull . . . a pair of loving turtle-doves' was intended as derision. The TRULL (whore) is Pucelle (syn. for 'slut').

TrC, III.i.140: 'He eats nothing but doves, love, and that breeds hot blood, and hot blood begets hot thoughts, and hot thoughts beget hot deeds, and hot deeds is love.' Doves: an aphrodisiac (C).

Ham, IV.v.167. Ophelia's song, 'hey non nonny, nonny, hey nonny . . . Fare you well, my dove!' is, like her other snatches, bawdy (NONNY; DOWN; STEWARD). It echoes Hamlet's 'farewell' in III.i.142: 'Get thee to a nunnery, go: farewell. . . . To a nunnery, go, and quickly [QUICKLY: name of Sh's bawd] too. Farewell.' In her mad childlike talk, 'nunnery' becomes 'nonny'. She is the nun ('non') told to go to the nunnery (brothel – *OED*): 'Fare you well [WELL: whore; brothel], my dove!'

RJ, I.v.50. Romeo's first reaction to Juliet is 'So shows a snowy dove trooping with crows.' One wonders if this is pure praise: this dove troops with crows; and there was a proverb 'A whoore is like a Crow' – the more she washes the blacker she is; the more she excuses, the more she betrays herself (Cot, s.v. *corneille*). We remember Juliet's making excuses for what Romeo heard her say (II.ii.85–111) on her balcony, immediately following his line that he 'would venture [VENTURE, whore] for such merchandise'. John 2:16: 'And said unto them that sold doves, Take these things hence; make not my Father's house an house of merchandise.'

'Troops' is another tainted word: in *2H6*, I.iii.80, Humphrey's wife, 'base-born callet [whore]' swept through the court with 'troops of ladies', her 'minions'. See ANCIENT for the 16th c. view of Romeo and Juliet, as opposed to a romanticised 20th c. one: contemporaries were inclined to see this disobedient daughter as the dove who whoores or cries.

I.iii.33. ' "Shake" quoth the dove-house: 'twas no need, I trow,/To bid me trudge.' There was never any need to bid this nurse TRUDGE (play the bawd). Juliet told Romeo she'd send for news 'By one that I'll procure to come to thee' – 'procurer' meant a bawd. SHAKE: copulate and whore (F&H); a 'shaker' is short for shaker or fan-tail pigeon (*OED*). (See Mercutio's jests about the FAN-tail of the Nurse, whom he calls 'bawd'.)

Per, IV, Gower 32: 'This Philoten contends in skill/With absolute Marina: so/With the dove of Paphos might the crow/Vie feathers white' (see proverb in *RJ* above). Paphos, ancient home of the famous temple to Aphrodite; hence 'Paphian', ptg to love 'esp. to unlawful sexual indulgence' (*OED*).

Philoten (Gk *philo*, love) contends (struggles amorously – C; P) in SKILL (L *ars* / arse) with Marina, the dove of Paphos, who vailed to 'Dian' with a 'constant pen' (28), provocative combination of CON (cunt) and pen / penis (C; P). Dian is not the goddess of chastity: Marina's mother is 'at Ephesus, / Unto Diana there a votaress' (4), and this is the Diana of Ephesus (v.i.241), goddess of fertility (hence Marina is to be killed by the 'pregnant' instrument of Philoten's mother – 44).

This act finds Marina in a brothel in Mytilene, anciently the chief city of Lesbos, home of Sappho, Lesbian lyric poetess, whom the Greeks named 'the Tenth Muse' (recall Philo*ten*). In Act v, Marina (henceforth always accompanied by 'a young Lady') 'sings like one immortal' and 'dances / As goddess-like to her admired lays' (a description that evokes Sappho).

Down Of a whore, i.e. a cat (F&H). Gk *kat*(*a*), the pfx cat(a)-: down. *Kate* Keep*down*: whore in *MM*. Dekker and Middleton, *The Honest Whore I*, II.1: Bellafronte, the whore, moans 'Down, downe, downe, downe, I fall downe, and arise I never shall' and is advised to leave the 'down and arise, or the falling trade'. Freq. used in refrains, it is more than merely a nonsense syllable: see LAME, Dekker.

TSh, v.ii.35. Petruchio wagers, 'my Kate does put her down'. His Kate (name common to whores for centuries – P; F&H) will show it is the widow who can be put down – for intercourse. Her husband's answer, 'That's my office', quibbles on chastising her and putting her down for OFFICE (copulation). A put (L *pute*): a whore (*CD*). Putage, putery: harlotry. A putour: fornicator (TWR; *OED*).

MWW, I.iv.44. Mistress Quickly, arranger of marriages and adulterous affairs, appropriately sings, 'And down, down, adown-a, &c.' *Con*: 'A womans &c. [cunt]' (Cot).

Ham, IV.v.170. Mad Ophelia with her bawdy songs: 'You must sing a-down a-down, / An you call him a-down-a.' See STEWARD.

JC, v.iv.9. Sh was not able to resist 'O young and noble Cato, art thou down?'

See CATERPILLAR, *1H4*; CONGER, *KL*; EASE, *H8*; ELEVEN, *Per*.

Drawers Lit. TAPSTERS (pimps who draw a head of FROTH on beer and on a masturbated penis). Those who draw (expose the penis – P). Catamites (F&H, s.v. Ganymede: a 'sodomist', a 'pot-boy' – loosely, a drawer of spirits).

1H4, II.iv. First word of the scene is 'Ned' (an ass – F&H; G): 'Ned . . . come out of that fat room, and lend me thy hand to laugh a little'. *Un fat* is an 'asse, a gull' (Cot). Is the FAT room a vat-room or another arse pun? What kind of fat / vat, vessel for liquids, did it contain? 'Fat' meant fertilise the soil: was Ned, the ass, in the privy? He was not with Hal and the 'loggerheads' among the 'hogsheads'. Hal asks 'Ned' Poins to LEND (1550, buttocks; coit) a HAND (for masturbation) so he can LAUGH (Fr *rire* / rear, lift to an erect position) a LITTLE (-cule; pun on *cul(e)*, rump). They will make a gull of Francis, the little drawer (*fregare*: to masturbate, gull – F).

Hal 'sounded the very base-string of humility. . . . I am sworn brother to a leash of drawers; and can call them all by their christian names, as Tom, Dick, and Francis'. He SOUNDded, i.e. probed, the *bottom* of the VERY (mus., It *assai*) *base* string: he is brother to a leash, i.e. a loose string, a loose (wanton – P) string of drawers. Leash (lit. any three things) is here the three drawers – and maybe the proverbial THREE things in men's drawers (undergarments).

Poins: 'what cunning match have you made with this jest of the drawer' – pun on this JEST (Fr *rieur*, a laugher) or *rear* of the drawer, and this *chest* of drawers. A chest is *casse* (Cot); the privities are *cas* and case (K; P). What CUNNING (*fin* – Cot) match (sexual bout – P) has Hal made with Francis, who calls Hal 'Corinthian' (CORINTHIAN, licentious) and whom Hal calls 'puny drawer' (PUNY, lit. bed*bug*, pun on *bugger*) or puny ass / arse. Francis is an 'under-skinker' (Florio–Torriano, *Vocabolario*, 1659: *mescitore*, 'skinker or filler of wine . . . a Ganimede' – F&H, s.v. Ganymede) at whose expense they will LAUGH (fornicate). The scene is a series of puns on arses and buggery; on 'brown bastard'; on 'sugar' (*sucre*; *faire le sucré*, frig, masturbate – Cot) given 'to sweeten which name of Ned [an ass]'; on Hal's asking the 'puny drawer to *what end* he gave me the sugar . . . that his tale [penis, rump -P] to me' (italics added); on 'anon (said seven times), ME 'onan' – pun on Fr *ânon*, young ass, and on *Onan* (Gen 38:9; onanism: masturbation). See TABLE.

Drum Buttocks. Drummers: testicles. *Caisse*: a drum (Cot); *cas*: genitals (Cot), Fr sl. for buttocks. 'Toute': the arse as in an abbot 'turnith up hir white toute,/ And betith the taburs [drums, i.e. buttocks] with is [his] hond' (TWR).

Ado, II.iii.14: 'I have known when there was no music with him but the drum and the fife; and now had he rather hear the tabor and the pipe.' Once it was military music for Claudio (the fife was used chiefly to accompany a military drum), but now he is in love he wants the virile instruments, tabor (pun on TAPER, penis: *Cor*, I.vi.25, 32, 'tabor' and 'tapers') and pipe (penis – C; P). 'Bagge-pipe': penis and scrotum (TWR) – two little drummers and the piper (see HEINOUS, *1H4*). (This may hint at a switch in Claudio's pattern of love-making – from buttocks to penis: see HEARER.)

KL, IV.ii.55: 'Milk-liver'd man! That bear'st a cheek for blows. . . . Where's thy drum?' Goneril mocks her husband's 'manhood' (68) by juxtaposing a drum and his CHEEKS (buttocks) that he bears/bares(?) for *blows*: (1) for beatings and for farting (L *flatus*, a blowing); and (2) for coital thrusts (C; P).

AW, III.vi.37–49:

1st Lord. . . . let him fetch his drum . . . when your lordship sees the bottom. . . .
2nd Lord. . . . hinder not the honour of his design. . . .

1st Lord. A pox on't, let it go; 'tis but a drum.
Parolles. 'But a drum'! is't 'but a drum'?

'Drum', 'bottom', 'hinder', and three repetitions of 'but a drum' (but/butt) are all part of the conceit of making an ass/arse (a *cas*) of Parolles and his drum (*caisse*): 'We'll make you some sport with the fox ere we *case* him' (italics added). See OFFENCE for the rest of their plot; and BEAT for the final pun on his drum.

KJ, V.ii.168: 'Indeed, your drums, being beaten, will cry out;/ And so shall you, being beaten' – beaten on *his* drum.

Dry (1) Barren, castrated. *Sec*: dry, sapless (Cot); *secco*: barren of wit (F); L *secco*: cut off, castrate. Isa 56:3–51: 'neither let the eunuch say, Behold I am a dry tree, For . . . unto the eunuchs that keep my sabbaths . . . I will give them an everlasting name, that shall not be cut off.' A dry hand was an Eliz. sign of impotence (HAND, *Ado*).

(2) Ptg to sodomy. Wilmot, *Sodom*, IV: 'What tho the letchery be dry, 'tis smart;/ Turkish arse I love with all my heart'. Boccaccio, p. 302: 'goes off in his vice in wooden shoes through the dry, while I'm trying to carry someone else in a ship through the rain'. Aldington (ed.) says the first is sodomy, the second is heterosexual coitus. A 'dry bob' is copulation without emission (F&H; G).

(3) Syphilitic. Lev. 13:30: 'If a man or woman have a plague . . . a dry scall, even a leprosy [LEPROSY, syphilis]'. Dekker and Middleton, *The Honest Whore I*, II.i: 'of all filthy dry-fisted knights, I cannot abide he should touch me' – 'Why, wench, is he scabbed?'

TrC, II.iii.80: 'Now, the dry serpigo [syphilis – P] on the subject!'

MWW, I.ii.4. Evans is looking for Mistress Quickly because he wants her 'to solicit' (1593, play the bawd): 'Go your ways, and ask of Doctor Caius' house which is the way . . . there dwells one Mistress Quickly, which is in the manner of his nurse, or his dry nurse, or . . . his washer, and his wringer.' Bawd of the Henry plays and go-between here, too, she is in the MANNER (the sex act – *OED*) and in the MANNER/ manure, his dry (L *assus*), his ass's nurse. She is like Moll Faugh, bawd in Marston, *The Dutch Courtesan*, III.ii: 'Cheaters and bawds go together like washing and wringing.' Laundresses were reputed prostitutes (Webster, *The*

White Devil, IV.i.92). A wringer: a griping in the intestines. Dekker and Middleton, *The Honest Whore I*, III.ii: a bawd is called 'the lechers French disease; for thou dry-suckst him'. In this 14-line scene introducing Caius, the stress on manner, ways and which way suggests which way or manner of coitus (see STRANGE).

In Act III Dr CAIUS (buttocks) emerges as a full-blown ass/arse. Scene i starts with Evans's asking 'which way' Simple looked (Fr *miré*) for the French doctor of 'physic', the 'physician' (Fr *mire*) – PHYSICIAN (arse) and mire (to defecate – P). The question relates (1) back to I.ii and 'which is the way' and 'which . . . manner'; and (2) ahead to V.v, where Caius has ignominiously 'married un garçon, a boy'.

Mac, I.iii.18. A 'rump-fed [freq. glossed fat rump; however, "feed" is graze amorously – C; P] ronyon [strumpet – *MWW*, IV.ii.195]' refuses to share the 'chestnuts in her lap' with a witch. Ronyon (TWR) or runnion (*OED*): the male organ, plus those NUTS (testicles) in her lap, suggests a sexual offence and perhaps deviation. The witch will punish her through her husband: 'like a rat without a tail', she will sail in a sieve and 'drain him dry as hay'. She in a *sieve* will *drain* him dry. (See OATS and BARBER, *MND*, for dry testicles.) Then she displays a 'pilot's thumb,/Wreck'd as homeward he did come'. She is minus a tail (sex-organs – C; P) and he minus a thumb – two castration images. At that moment, Macbeth 'doth come' – he, too, homeward bound and similarly to be wrecked by WITCHES (castraters): Lady Macbeth had called on spirits to 'unsex' her (COMPUNCTIOUS) and Macbeth will be dry, impotent, and childless.

TN, I.iii.80:

> *Sir Andrew*. . . . I am not such an ass but I can keep my hand dry.
> But what's your jest?
> *Maria*. A dry jest, sir.
> *Sir Andrew*. Are you full of them?
> *Maria*. Ay, sir, I have them at my fingers' ends: marry, now I let go your hand, I am barren.

The impotent Andrew of the dry hand is not such an *ass but* he can keep his hand dry (L *assus*), at an unspecified activity. (A still current joke: at a urinal, Harvard reprimands Yale for not washing his hands. Yale: 'At Yale, we don't piss on our hands.'). Maria has dry JESTS (arses) at her fingers' ends (INWARD: 'dunghill, at the fingers' ends'). Jonson said, 'Claw a churl by the culls, and he'll shite in your fist' (F&H, s.v. Culls). See YELLOW and MELANCHOLY.

Due Testicles: *due*, two (F). Middleton, *A Mad World, My Masters*, IV.iv, puns on 'due' as what is owed and as two: 'The guilt *hangs double* . . . *both* I challenge,/And therefore of *due* vengeance it appear'd . . . to whom *both* sins inher'd. What know the lecher when he clips his whore/Whether it be the devil his *parts* adore?' (italics added). Testicles were symbols of lasciviousness. Stone: a testicle; uncastrated; 1602, 'lascivious, lustful' (*OED*).

'Adieu', 'dew', 'due', 'too' and 'two' all pun on the *due*, two (testicles).

Adieu: HANGING, *MWW*; RESOLVE, *Ham*.

Dew: ANGEL, *R3*; RESOLUTION, *Ham*; DEWLAP.

Due: COLOUR, *1H6*; NOTE, *TrC*; TRIBUTE, *2H4*; PAID, *1H4*; DOUBLE, *MND*; RESOLVE, *KL*.

Too: SHORT, *AC*; HORSE, *Ado*; CROOKED, *R2*; TWIN, *H5*; CATERPILLAR, *1H4*, *R2*; RESOLUTION, *Ham*; CARD, *KJ*.

Two: DETESTED, *TA*; DOUBLE, *MND*; RAG, *Oth*, V.i; RESOLUTION, *Ham*.

Dulcet Testicles. *Doucet*: dulcet (Cot). Dulcet: '2.?=DOUCET 3 [a deer's testicles]' (*OED*). Middleton, *The Coxcomb*, II.ii: 'coole your Codpiece, Rogue' – 'What stallion Rogues are these, to wear such dowsetts [doucets], the very cotton may commit adultery'. The dulcet is sweetbread (*CD*), a word related to OE *swēota*, scrotum; Du *zwezerik*, sweetbread, earlier testicles (W). Sir Thomas Overbury, *A Wife* (1613): 'For an inward bruise, Lambstones and sweet-breads are his onely Sperma Ceti' (*OED*). Dowsetts: testicles (F&H, s.v. Cods).

See BOLT, *AYL*; ROUND, *TSh*.

E

Ear Plant part that contains seed.

(1) Testicles. Rabelais, Bk III, ch. 31, says that men whose parotid arteries (behind the ears) are cut are impotent for generation. The French Variorum edn says the reader can guess which ears are meant.

(2) L *vagina*: a vagina; an ear of grain.

(3) Arse; OE *ears*. The wheatear bird is so called in allusion to its white *eeres*, *ers*, arse (*OED*). L *auris*: ear. To plead to deaf ears: 'narrare fabellam surdo assello' (Horace).

(4) To ear: to copulate (C; P), as in *AW*, I.iii.47. Take a stone up in the ear: play the whore (F&H 1704).

3H6, v.i.108: 'Warwick, wilt thou leave the town and fight? Or shall we beat the stones about thine ears?' Stones are testicles.

Cym, II.i.15:

Cloten. . . . not for any standers-by to curtail his oaths, ha?
Lord. . . . (*Aside*) nor crop the ears of them.

The scoffing lord, who a few lines later calls Cloten 'cock and capon too [TOO, testes; his a capon's, castrated]' turns Cloten's jest on curtailing oaths into a castration slur on curtailing (docking a dog's tail, hence mutilating a person in any way) his OATHS (testicles), cropping the ears of his oats ('th' was freq. 't' in puns: Goth/goat; wit/with – K), cropping his seed.

R3, IV.iv.327. Richard tells Elizabeth to prepare her daughter for marriage: 'Make bold her bashful years with your experience;/Prepare her ears to hear a wooer's tale . . . acquaint the princess/With . . . marriage joys'. ACQUAINT her: give carnal knowledge to her. Embolden her YEARS (rear end) and prepare her ears for his tale/tail (rear end – K; P).

See YEAR, *CE*.

Early The rear or behind. 'Rare' and 'rear' and 'rearly' (Fletcher and Sh, *The Two Noble Kinsmen*, IV.i) mean early.

Cym, II.iii.38. The epicene Cloten, who (1) 'turned up ace [/ass – K]' and is an 'ass' (Index), 'was *up* so early' and '*ass*ailed' Cymbeline's '*stern* [STERN, buttocks] daughter' (italics added).

Ease, easy, easily (1) Sexual intercourse (TWR, s.vv. Ese, Esement). Weever, *Faunus and Melliflora*: the amorous nymphs, failing to seduce Fauna with tales of ravished women, 'to bedward . . . them drest/To take their rest, yet tooke no ease in rest' (342); Love's 'play is paine, but yet a paine with ease . . . [whose] fire doth grieve and please' (621).

(2) Relieve through evacuation ('ese' – TWR). Excrement ('esement' – TWR). A privy: a stool of ease (*OED*), *aysement* (Cot). Ease (*aise* – Cot). Ger *Esel*: ass.

2H6, III.i.135: 'mightier crimes are laid unto your charge,/Whereof you cannot easily purge yourself'. Gloucester's inability to purge himself of a charge is compared to the difficulty a constipated arse has in purging itself (evacuation of the bowels) of its charge, i.e. load or burden. A pun on easement of the bowels and Gloucester's easement (legal term for privilege of using something not one's own), his having appropriated the Crown's money while he was 'protector' – his 'mightier crimes' that he cannot purge. See OCCASION for the beginning of the metaphor.

WT, II.i.53. Leontes asks about the escape of Polixenes, whom he believes guilty of adultery with his wife: 'How came the posterns/So easily open?' Pl. posterns because the question means not just the back gate but a more primary resentment, the easy adulterous opening of his wife's *back* door or POSTERN: fundament (buttocks, anus); vulva (F&H).

TSh, V.ii.179. Kate advises wives, 'place your hands below your husband's foot:/In token of which duty . . . My hand is ready; may it do him ease'. Her HAND, in TOKEN (the genitals) of marital duty, is ready to do him ease, in coitus or masturbation: below his FOOT (copulation – C; P; small penis).

H8, I.iv.17:

Sands. I would I were ['confessor'];
  They should find easy penance.
Lovell. Faith, how easy?
Sands. As easy as a down-bed would afford it.

*Con*fession and *pen*ance (sexual compliance – C; P) would be *as* easy. A bed of DOWN (prostitution) would *afford easy payment*. Juxtaposition of con (cunt) and pen (penis – P).

See GOLD, *JC*; PORTER, *MWW*.

Echo A flatus.

Mac, V.iii.53. Macbeth tells the doctor, 'Throw physic to the dogs' – yet, if he could 'purge' Scotland to 'health,/I would applaud thee to the very echo,/That should applaud again . . . what purgative drug/Would scour these English hence? Hear'st thou of them?'

Physic (the practice of medicine and a carthartic or purge) starts the metaphor of emptying Scotland of the English. As purging of the bowels is accompanied by the fart, so the emptying or scouring (SCOUR meant evacuate the bowels; of cattle, diarrhoea) of his land would be accompanied by his APPLAUSE (a flatus) and its echo: applaud *again*. Macbeth asks whether the doctor *hears* of the English, whom he would so noisily expel.

RJ, II.ii.161, Juliet: 'Bondage is hoarse . . . Else would I tear the cave where Echo lies,/And make her airy tongue more hoarse than mine'. (1) Juliet would tear Echo's cave (*valcava*: a hollow cave, used by Boccaccio for 'a womans quaint [cunt]' – F). See would *tear* out and use Echo's TONGUE (clitoris) as the clapper (tongue – F&H) of a bell, to recall Romeo. (2) *Abrocare*: to become hoarse, to fart (F) – another of Sh's gibes at the airy, insubstantial quality of this 'too sudden' love (see MELANCHOLY).

See THRONE, *TN*; BOARD, *TSh*.

Elder, eldest Ass/arse-related. Fr *aisne*: eldest; *asne*: ass, fool; see AN for the silent 's' in OFr. The elderberry was used as a mild laxative (*W*), a diuretic (*CD*). Lyly, *Alexander and Campaspe*, Epil.: 'Laurel for a garland, or elder for a disgrace'.

Cym, IV.ii.60: 'let the stinking elder, grief, untwine' – the stinking arse, in apposition to GRIEF (bowel pain), q.v.

MWW, II.iii.30, Host: 'What says my Aesculapius? . . . my heart of elder?' He jests that the French PHYSICIAN (Fr *mire*/mire, turd), Dr CAIUS/Fr *cas* (buttocks), is a fool and ass: an Aescul- (rump – *OED*) apius – a HEART (arse) of elder.

TN, I.v.121:

Olivia. . . . you see, sir, how your fooling grows old, and people dislike it.
Clown. Thou has spoke for us, madonna, as if thy eldest son should be a fool . . . for, – here he comes, – one of thy kin has a most weak pia mater.

Her eldest son is a fool; 'here he comes' is an ambiguous ref. back to son and ahead to Toby, who 'speaks nothing but madman' ('mad' meant foolish). He is a fool or ass because he has a most weak pia mater, weak brains; and, as her son, he has a *pia mater* (L, pious mother),

Olivia, whom the Clown had just called that most pious of all pious mothers, 'madonna' (see MADONNA, a crucial pun in the play).

LLL, v.ii.609. In an extended conceit on the ass/arse (introduction, p. XVI), Holofernes is mocked for his portrayal of 'Jud-as', an 'ass' – 'For the latter end of his name.' 'Judas was hanged on an elder' – on the *latter end* of Jud-as, his name.

See ANGEL, *Cym*.

Eleven Erotic rising of the penis, and comfort of fornication. Leaven is a raising agent. Fr *levain* and L *levamen*: a raising (in sense of alleviation, comfort – *OED*). Levament: 1623, 'the comfort which one hath of his wife'. *MM*, I.ii.45: 'Madam Mitigation comes!' – the bawd Mistress Overdone who both raises and relieves.

Per, IV.ii.16:

Bawd. . . . 'tis not our bringing up of poor bastards, – as, I think, I have brought up some eleven –
Boult. Ay, to eleven; and brought them down again.

The Bawd *brings up* bastards. She brought up some to (the age of) eleven; brought them up to *leaven* the customers, for which purpose she 'brought them down again' – DOWN (in bed) again and *a gain*. Kate Keepdown is a whore whose bawd 'kept' her child (*MM*, III.ii.215), probably for the same exploitation, to *keep* her *down*.

TN, III.ii.37. Toby advises Andrew to duel with his rival and 'hurt him in eleven places'! In disposing of a male rival, it is not the *number* of hurts that counts, but the *places*, esp. the crucial eleven places. He continues, 'my niece shall take note [NOTE, genitals] of it'.

WT, IV.iii.33. Autolycus sings of his life of thieving and fornication: he is now 'out of service', out of the Prince's service and copular *service* (*OED*; P). Then the Clown starts an equally long soliloquy with ' 'leven wether tods' – his wether (castrated sheep) who cannot 'leven or leaven any more than Autolycus now can. He concludes by asking why his sister wants 'rice' (its only use in Sh), possibly a pun on *rise* and leaven. Cf. BOLT 2, *TrC* ('leaven': rise phallicly).

Enfranchise Leap upon (coitally – C; P). *Franchir*: to free, to leap upon (Cot).

TGV, III.i.151. Valentine's love-letter says, " Silvia, this night I will enfranchise thee." 'Tis so; and here's the ladder for the purpose.' Valentine plans to enfranchise her: free her from her father and leap on her. But her father discovers not only the *letter* but also the *ladder*, the means of ascent, of rising – intended for her PURPOSE (pudendum) – hidden under Valentine's cloak. It was 'quaintly made of cords . . . with a pair of anchoring hooks' (117) – a metaphor evocative of the cunt/QUAINT, testes (a PAIR) and penis (cord or ROPE).

Engine(er) Penis; fornicator. *Engeancer*: to breed; *engeance*, the seed of (Cot). Sir John Denham, 'Natura Naturata': 'Nature . . . With Love enflaming our desires,/ Finds Engines fit to quench those fires' (*Penguin Book of Restoration Verse*, p. 39). Fletcher, *The Wild Goose Chase*, III.i: the rake Mirabel has 'a trick to blow up maidenheads'. It is 'a speedy trick, please you to try it;/ My engine will despatch you instantly'.

TrC, II.iii.8: 'Then there's Achilles, a rare engineer! If Troy be not taken till these two [he and Ajax] undermine it, the walls will stand till they fall of themselves.' Thersites asks the gods to take 'that little little less than little wit from them that they have! which short-armed ignorance itself knows is so abundant scarce . . . the vengeance on the whole camp . . . the bone-ache!' (V)engeance on, fuck, the whole camp – let bone-ache (syphilis – C; P) rot them. Achilles – whose 'masculine whore' (v.i.20) Patroclus enters as Thersites ends his 'execrations' against lechery – is a RARE/rear engineer (of rears) who undermines WALLS (buttocks or breeches), but not the walls of Troy. In them he makes no *brèche* (breach in a wall – Cot).

An *engine* is an instrument of warfare, mother wit, and a tool (*OED*). Thersites wants even their little WIT (penis) destroyed by VD. As for short-armed IGNORANCE (lewdness – *OED*), since Sh is punning on 'short' (brachy-) and 'armed' (brachi-) and *breech*, it is likely he also intended a pun on man's short ARM (penis), as he did in WITCH, *R3*. In the context of war and (military) arms, we hear the same pun that underlay the American World War II phrase, 'short-arm inspection', by which was meant an inspection, not of the men's rifles, but of their *short* arms (for VD). Achilles' engine (wit and penis) is LITTLE (-cule); he's an arse (cule).

AW, III.v.20: 'promises, enticements, oaths, tokens, and all these engines of lust . . . many a maid hath been seduced by them'. Maids are *enginé* (beguiled – Cot) by the *engigneur* (deceiver) – seduced by his promises (the tongue, 'that delightful engine' – *TA*, III.i.82), OATHS (testes), TOKENS (genitals), all the engines of lust.

Enlargement Phallic, then in pregnancy. Lit. to make large; set free. Nashe, *The Unfortunate Traveller*, p. 253: 'Diamente, Castaldo's the magnifico's wife, after my enlargement proved to be with child' – after his release from gaol and his other enlargement.

1H4, III.i.31: 'Diseased nature' erupts; earth 'Is with a kind of colic pinch'd and vex'd / By the imprisoning of unruly wind / Within her womb; which, for enlargement striving, / Shakes. . . . At your birth / Our grandam earth, having this distemperature, / In passion shook.'

Hotspur deflates Glendower's pretensions of an unusual birth at which the earth shook. He says earth was VEXed or farted; it got rid of the WIND (flatus) from the colic (ptg to the bowels) that strove for enlargement. Just as his mother did SHAKE (coitally), so grandam earth's womb shook in passion (in *passing* the wind?), in delivery of wind (Glendower's hot air about an unusual birth). So, in mod. sl., two mothers, simultaneously, delivered a bag of hot air.

Cym, II.iii.125. Cloten says Imogen can have no CONTRACT (marriage; sexual union) with Posthumus: meaner parties may have 'brats and beggary, in self-figured knot; / Yet you are curb'd from that enlargement by' the crown. She may not KNOT (loop coitally – P) and be enlarged by brats.

3H6, IV.vi.5. Being set free, Henry asks the lieutenant, 'At our enlargement what are thy due fees? . . . I'll well requite thy kindness, / For that it made my imprisonment a pleasure; / Ay, such pleasure as incaged birds / Conceive when . . . They quite forget their loss of liberty.'

So many puns on the sex-act make one question the nature of *our* enlargement. He does not use a royal 'we' elsewhere, but says 'I', 'me' and 'my', consistently, leading one to hear the enlargement as mutual: his pleasure (sexual intimacies and spasm – P; F&H) in prison; the DUE (testes, symbol of homosexual love) fees (sexual reward – C; P) for the lieutenant, whom he will WELL (fornicate; penis) requite and QUITE (arch. for repay and quit) / coit in return for the man's KINDNESS (sexual favour); the pun on 'I'll well' and ILL (homosexual) WELL (fornication); and the almost gratuitous use of 'conceive'.

See JAPHET.

Enough (1) Indication the speaker, the one addressed or the subject is an ass: *assez*, enough (Cot). It *assai* (lit. enough); mus., very.

(2) Assay: attempt amorously (P).

H5, III.iv.65. The French princess, mistaking certain English words to mean the genitals, concludes, 'C'est assez [/ asses]'. See EXCELLENT.

Cor, II.i.74:

Menenius. . . . I find the ass in compound with the major part of your syllables. . . .
Brutus. Come, sir, come, we know you well enough.
Menenius. You know neither me, yourselves, nor anything.

Having been called 'ass' with a major PART (split in the buttocks), Brutus retorts they know him one, too; know him well *enough*. But Menenius says they know (perhaps carnally – *OED*; P) neither him, themselves, nor ANY / Fr *âne* (ass) thing – they don't (in mod. sl.) know their arse from a hole in the ground. Like arses 'pinched with the colic' (spasm in the bowels) they sit 'roaring for a chamber-pot' (ROAR, fart). They 'are a pair [PAIR, homosexual] of strange [STRANGE, pederastic] ones'; and he converses 'with the buttock of the night' (56).

MND, III.i.152. 'Thou *art as* wise as thou *art* beautiful' (italics added) are Titania's first words to *Bottom*, who has an 'ass-head'. ART: L *ars* / the arse.

Bottom: 'Not so, neither: but if I had wit enough to get out of this wood, I have enough to serve mine own turn.' He is not *as wise* but has *enough wit* (parallel phrases) to *serve his* OWN (ass / arse) *turn* (fulfil sexual needs – C; P) – enough, *assez*, to assay. Not – neither (like know-no-neither in *Cor* above) may be a pun on NEITHER / NETHER (buttocks).

Tem, III.ii.93. Caliban says, 'Beat him enough; after a little time I'll beat him too.' Beat him enough: beat this ass Trin*culo* on his ass / arse (see ANY) or his cul(e). Perhaps assay him sexually (BEAT, cudgel sexually). See LIE for indications that Caliban, Trinculo, and Stephano are three buggers.

See KEEN, *MND*; LIBYA, *TrC*; VERY, *AYL*.

Entire Sexually potent. Lit. not castrated; a stallion as opposed to a gelding.

Cor, I.iv.55: 'Thou art left, Marcius: / A carbuncle entire, as big as thou art, / Were not so rich a jewel.' His military *strength* is like a JEWEL (testicle), a precious stone (stone: 'Not castrated, entire' – *OED*), richer than an *entire* carbuncle, a precious stone of red colour, in that *his* entirety consists of *two* stones, i.e. testes.

TSh, IV.ii.23: 'I have often heard / Of your entire affection to Bianca; / And since my eyes are witness of her lightness'. To eliminate Hortensio from the competition, Tranio tells him that in flirting with a third lover Bianca offends their virility: the *entire* affection of the one, and the other's EYES (testicles) that are WITNESS (L *testis*: a witness; a testicle).

See UNNATURAL, *KL*.

Ephesian, Ephesus Boon companion (*OED*) and roisterer (*W*) but used less generously by Sh, who means the Ephesians whom the apostle Paul warned to beware the 'sleight [1596, jugglery] of men', not to fall back into 'lasciviousness' and 'lusts' but to 'put on the new man' (Eph 4).

CE. Ephesus, setting for this bawdy play, much resembles Epidamnus, scene of Plautus's *The Twin Menaechmi*, one of the sources of *CE*: there live the worst devotees of sensual pleasure (*voluptarii*) and drunkards (*potatores maxumi*); flatterers, tricksters (*sycophantae et palpatores*); harlots (*meretrices mulieres*). All who come get damned or damaged (*damno devortitur*). In Ephesus too there live 'jugglers . . . Dark-working sorcerers that change the mind, / Soul-killing witches that deform the body . . . prating mountebanks And many such-like liberties of sin. . . . I'll to the Centaur' (I.ii.98).

Jugglers are fornicators (C; P). DARK (whorehouse) working (fornicating – C; P; TWR, s.v. Werke) SORCERERS ('Ribalds, Buggerers, Sorcerers', 1651), whores and buggers that change the MIND (arse). WITCHES are bawds and hermaphrodites that deform, usually castrate, the body (SINGE, *CE*). In this context, prating mountebanks suggests those who mount (coitally – *OED*; P) BANKS (seats) or PRATS (buttocks), and many SUCH-LIKE L *sic*; *tale* – F) sick liberties of sin. He will to the CENTAUR (symbol of sexual bestiality).

IV.iii. Unaware he is being mistaken for his dissolute twin, Antipholus S. describes Ephesus as a place of wanton sexuality where all act as if he were a 'well-acquainted friend' – ACQUAINTED (carnally) with them WELL, as a whore: they tender him money, thank him for KINDNESSES (sexual favours – F&H), offer him 'commodities' (genitals – P) for sale. Why, a 'tailor' (C; P) bought 'silks' (SILK, sign of effeminacy) for him and 'took measure [penis – P] of my body'. To conclude, 'Lapland sorcerers inhabit here' (SORCERERS, whores and buggers: see WITCHES, *CE*). Dromio then asks, 'What, have you got the picture of Old Adam new apparelled?' Has he become the *Old* Adam (unregenerate human nature – *OED*) *new* apparelled? Has he, as the apostle Paul said, 'put on the new man'?

MWW, IV.v.19. In Falstaff's chamber, 'painted about with the story of the Prodigal', is, says Simple, 'an old woman, a fat woman'. Host: 'a fat woman! the knight may be robbed. . . . Sir John . . . art thou there? it is thine host, thine Ephesian, calls.' He insists the fat woman descend and leave his 'honourable' chambers. An OLD WOMAN (L *anus*) is an ass; and a FAT woman is no better (*un fat*, an ass; foppish – Cot). She and Falstaff are one and the same: the knight who 'may be robbed' was indeed *robed* in the 'gown' (GOWN, cunt) of a fat woman (IV.ii.77). These are jests on Nestorianism, the doctrine that the two natures of Christ, divine and human, are not united in one person, a doctrine condemned by the Robber Synod or Council of Ephesus (hence Falstaff may be 'robbed'). This was a live issue in the 16th c., when many Nestorians joined the Roman Catholic Church.

These are puns on (1) the Host of the Inn, the 'Ephesian' – and the Host or bread that is another manifestation of the body of Christ (as the fat woman is another manifestation of Falstaff; cf. Eph 4:4: 'There is one body, and one Spirit'); (2) Simple, who will wait till she who has 'gone up . . . come down' and the Host's insistence, 'Let her descend, bully, let her descend' (Eph 4:10: 'He that descended is the same also that ascended'); (3) Falstaff's room, decorated with the story of the Prodigal (Luke 15: 11–32), who 'wasted his substance with riotous living' and lived 'with harlots' – and Falstaff, accused of harlotry with a fat woman; Falstaff who was not about 'waste' but 'thrift. Briefly I do mean to make love to Ford's wife' (I.iii.471). He puns on thrift and husbandry (with someone else's wife): 'Well-husbanded. Shaks' (*OED*, s.v. Thrift); 'thrift and good husbandry' (*OED*, 1600); 'willing to fall to thrift [they] prove good husbands' (Spenser, in *CD*).

See FRANK, *2H4*.

Errands Run errands: pimp.

MM, III.ii.37: 'the deputy cannot abide a whoremaster: if he be a whoremonger, and comes before him, he were as good go a mile on his errand'.

MWW, III.iv.113. Mistress Quickly 'must of another errand to Sir John Falstaff from my two mistresses' – whom he wishes to make *his* two mistresses.

IV.ii.182. Ford forbids his house to 'a quean. . . . She comes of errands, does she?'

JC, IV.i.13. Lepidus, third member of the triumvirate, whom Antony refers to as an 'ass' and a pimp (GOLD), is 'Meet to be sent on errands': MEAT (the penis)/MEET (coitus).

See GRAZE, *JC*.

Eternal Infernal, damned (*OED*; *W*). Used sometimes with ref. to forbidden, homosexual, love.

Oth, IV.ii.130: 'some eternal villain' is Iago, the 'damned villain' and 'hellish villain' of V.ii.316, 368. See Index for his feelings for Othello.

WT, I.ii.65. Polixenes describes his boyhood 'love' (24) for Leontes: 'Two lads that thought there was no more behind/But such a day tomorrow as to-day,/And to be boy eternal' – to be eternal BOY (Ganymede), young homosexuals. See HEAVEN.

See ALTER, *MWW*.

Evil (1) Effeminate. *Male*: evil, bad, sickness (F). L *male*: ill, excessively; *male mas* (lit. sick man): effeminate, unmanly.

(2) Cack: dung, void excrement. L *caco*: void or defile with excrement; dung. Gk *kakos*, *kako-*: evil, bad.

(3) The cock or penis (F&H; TWR, s.v. Cok).

MM, II.ii.172. 'Modesty' attracts Angelo, not 'woman's lightness' (the 'strumpet' of l.184): 'Having waste ground enough,/Shall we desire to raze the sanctuary/And pitch our evils there? O' fie, fie, fie!' FIE: shit! Why pitch evil or cack on a sanctuary, on Lavinia, the 'saint' (180)? *Having waste ground* ENOUGH (Fr *assez*/asses) connotes the laystall, 'whereon all the dung, and filth of a towne is layed' (Cot, s.v. *voirie*). Laystall, used by Sh's contemporaries (cf. *OED*: Jonson, Drayton, Spenser), makes a nice contrast between 'lay' (unsanctified – *OED*) and 'sanctuary': why 'Corrupt' Lavinia when there are whores on whom to PITCH (whore)?

II.iv.6, Angelo: 'Heaven in my mouth . . . And in my heart the strong and swelling evil/Of my conception'. His prayers are 'empty words', for in his HEART (arse) is (1) sexual desire, the *strong* and *swelling* evil or cock of 'conception'; (2) evil or cack, shit or deceit.

v.i.501. Having deflowered Mariana, Angelo is forced to marry her. Duke: 'your evil quits you well: / Look that you love your wife'. His evil (cock) QUITS / coits him well now, not ill.

Cor, I.i.183. Marcius says that to speak well of the citizens is 'Beneath abhorring [ABHORring / whoring] . . . your affections are / A sick man's appetite, who desires most that / Which would increase his evil'. Their AFFECTIONS (sexual desires, with stress on the buttocks) are those of a sick man, a *male mas*, an effeminate, who desires MOST (*fin* – Cot) the buttocks. To satisfy their appetite they eat what increases their evil, their output of cack. Sh's puns on the cockchafer, who lays his eggs in and eats dung, are a metaphor for male homosexuality: see GIDDY; GREEN SICKNESS.

AYL, III.ii.370. Orlando asks what 'evils' Ganymede's uncle 'laid to the charge [sexual behaviour – C; P] of women'. Rosalind – GANYMEDE (a catamite) answers that the FAULTS (gaps: pudendum and buttocks) 'were all like one another as half-pence are, every one fault seeming monstrous till his fellow-fault came to match it'. LIKE (Gk *homos*, *homo-*) and MONSTROUS connote homosexual; her answer reflects Plato's theory of Lesbianism (see ROUND), of the search for a like, matching HALF to mate with. Half-pence may be HALF-*pens* (penis – C; P). For the sexual ambivalence of her speech, see GENERAL; GIDDY.

She continues that she 'will not cast away my physic but on those that are sick [*male*]'. If she could meet the 'fancy-monger' (FANCY, pederastic), this Ganymede would give him 'good counsel' – not evil, not as a catamite, like now. She would cast away her boy's disguise; CAST (evacuate bowels) away her physic, this shitty disguise, and be wholly a girl. See STIR for the origin of this metaphor of Rosalind's *male* (sick and evil) and male role, her being defiled (*caco*) with cack.

II.vii.67. The Duke addresses Jaques on 'all the embossed sores and headed evils / That thou with license of free foot has caught [and would] . . . disgorge into the general world'. Jaques would disgorge into the GENERAL (whore-like) world his HEADED (with prepuce – C; P; with testes) evil or cock, with its embossed (raised, with a head) syphilitic sores, caught with free, licentious FOOT (fucking – C; P). The evils (Gk *kaka*), the cack would be disgorged by Jaques / a *jakes* (latrine – K; C; P). Thus the Duke reduces Jaques's soliloquy (see HOUR) to its lowest common denominator.

Exceed(ingly) Be virile, full of seed or semen. Lit. extend out. Gen 16:10: 'I will multiply thy seed exceedingly'; 1 Sam 20:41–2: 'and they kissed one another, and wept with one another, until David exceeded. And Jonathan said . . . The Lord be between me and thee, and between my seed and thy seed for ever.'

Cym, v.ii.9. Iachimo's guilt 'Takes off my manhood. . . . If that thy gentry, Britain, go before / This lout as he exceeds our lords, the odds / Is that we scarce are men and you are gods.' Iachimo doubts his own manhood since he was subdued by a 'drudge of nature's [NATURE, sex]'. If Britain's GENTRY (men of *breeding*) go before (exceed, extend farther out phallicly than) this lout, as much as he exceeds (has more strength, virility, seed than) the French, then the French are scarce men and the British are gods.

Relevant to the hypothesis (see Index) that Iachimo is sexually attracted to Posthumus is his saying that this 'carl' (the unrecognised, disguised Posthumus) has 'subdued' (SUBDUE, seduce) him in his own 'profession' (whoring – C; P).

Oth, II.iii.372, Roderigo: 'My money is almost spent; I have been tonight exceedingly well cudgelled . . . the issue will be, I shall have so much experience for my pains'. His money is spent (spend: discharge semen – C; P); he was *exceed*-ingly cudgelled by Cassio, not only beaten but screwed out of his seed: 'no money in the purse' is to be impotent (F&H, s.v. Purse, scrotum), and he has failed to achieve Desdemona. He expects no seminal issue in that direction; the only issue of his PAINS / penis will be experience.

Tim, I.i.290: 'no gift to him / But breeds the giver a return exceeding / All use of quittance'. The GIFT (of sex) given Timon by his sycophantic followers, all of whom prostitute themselves for his favours (see WORD), breeds them in return much more than they give, breeds beyond the seeds expended, exceeding all usual quittance, i.e. repayment – and a pun on QUIT / coit ('use',

too, means sexual use – C; P). Since return exceeding usual repayment is usury (prostitution – C; P), the sordid, self-seeking relationships are defined.
See HEART, *Ado* MERRY, *Cym.*

Excellent Lewd, with ref. to the buttocks and pederasty. From L *cellere*, to raise high (a meaning open to erotic puns), it puns on 'sellary', a lewd person. Jonson, *Sejanus*, IV.v: 'Ravished hence, dealt away / Unto his spintries, sellaries, and slaves [male whores]'.

H8, IV.ii.62. Behind Griffith's description of Wolsey is Sh's ironic comment that he rose high through lewdness and is a political and religious prostitute: 'humble stock . . . Lofty . . . raised . . . [his college] So excellent in art, and still so rising'. Excellent in ART (L*ars* / arse). See TWIN.

WT, IV.iv.434. Polixenes calls Perdita a 'fresh piece / Of excellent witchcraft, who of force must know / The royal fool thou copest with'. She is a FRESH (sexually shameless) PIECE (C; P) of excellent WITHCRAFT (L *ars magica* / arse magic), who knew she coped (copulated – C; P) with royalty.

H5, III.iv.64. When Katherine masters 'corruptible' words, such as 'de nick [vulva], de sin [CHIN, penis], de foot [FOOT, fuck], de coun [cunt]', Alice comments, 'Excellent, madame', and Katherine agrees, 'C'est assez pour une fois' – excellent and *ass*ez (ENOUGH).

TN, III.i.95, Viola: 'Most excellent accomplished lady, the heavens rain odours on you!' She jealously puns on Olivia's arse (which has Orsino's love) and on her being an ass (for rejecting him): Olivia is the MOST (Fr *fin*: the end; excellent) excellent lady. May odours rain on her: *odours* from the *rein* (Fr loin), arse-odours (see RARE).

TrC, I.iii.164. Achilles's male lover entertains him and 'At this fusty stuff' (evil smelling, rank), Achilles 'Cries, "Excellent!" ' and 'still cries "Excellent!" ' See APPLAUSE and LOLL for the puns on farting and pederasty in this speech.

LLL, I.ii.78, 179. Samson (see PORTER, for his carrying on his back) is a lover of 'excellent strength' and Armado does 'excel' Samson in his 'rapier'; yet he fears that Cupid's 'butt-shaft' is 'too much odds for a Spaniard's rapier'. Cupid, whose glory is to SUBDUE (seduce) men (186), will shaft this SPANIARD in the butt.

TN, I.iii.151. Sir Toby and Sir Andrew, in their cups, talk bawdily of each other's 'virtues' (VIRTUE, male prowess): with Andrew's 'gifts' (GIFTS, genitals), Toby says, he 'would not so much as make water but in a sink-a-pace' (scatological pun). He continues, 'legs and thighs. Let me see thee caper: ha! higher: ha, ha! excellent!' The *high* (excellent) hilarity suggests Andrew's capering is lewd, like that of a *caper* (L, he-goat, symbol of lechery). Perhaps it also reveals lack of masculinity: Sp *cabrón* (like *caprone* – F), he-goat and cuckold; in gutter Sp, a castrated goat and cuckold (Rosensweig, p. 37). Sp *capar* is to castrate, and Andrew had earlier answered 'What is thy *excellence* in a galliard, knight?' (127) with 'Faith, I can *cut* a *caper*' (italics added). To Toby's 'And I can cut the mutton [a whore – F&H; P] to't', Andrew came back with his ability in the 'back-trick'. (This is not a known technical term and 'may be unconscious indecency' – Arden edn.) Both men can CUT (a cunt – K; a castrate – *OED*) and one is excellent in the *galli*ard (Galli were self-castrated priests and male prostitutes: see YELLOW for their other relevance to the play). Andrew is, in short, an excellent sellary. See CAPER for a similar scene by a contemporary of Sh, in which the capering involves letting down the breeches. See BREAST.

Exercise Sexual activity. Jonson, *Volpone*, IV.ii: 'This woman . . . is a whore. Of most hot exercise, more than a partrich'. Shirley, *The Lady of Pleasure*, II.i: '[If your blood] desire of any female / Delight . . . Any of her chambermaids to practise on' – 'I know not how I may be for that exercise.'

Oth, II.i.269. Iago describes the 'Lechery' of Cassio and Desdemona, her paddling 'with the palm of his hand': 'They met so near with their lips that their breaths embraced together . . . when these mutualities so marshal the way, hard at hand comes the master and main exercise, the incorporate conclusion.'

Hard at hand, usu. glossed as immediately, but also meaning *hard* at HAND (phallus – K), at masturbation, comes the main ('La main, de hand' – *H5*, III.iv.12) exercise, the CONCLUSION (coitus) incorporate, i.e. united in one body (one of the few sentences abridged by Rolfe, scholarly editor of the 1930s, who meets most of Sh's bawdy head-on).

Cor, IV.iv.14: 'O world, thy slippery turns! Friends . . . Whose hours, whose beds, whose meal, and exercise,/ Are still together, who twin, as 'twere, in love/ Unseparable' yet become foes. Coriolanus turns away from Athens to do Aufidius's 'country service' (country: cunt; service: coitus – *OED*; P). Metaphoric description of a TWIN (homosexual) love: friends who shared HOURS/ whores; bed and exercise; SLIPPERY (epicene) turns (sexual embraces – C; P).

TrC, IV.iv.80. A jealous Troilus tells Cressida, 'The Grecian youths are . . loving, well composed with gifts of nature,/ Flowing and swelling o'er with arts and exercise.' It is the exercise of the GIFTS of NATURE (semen – *OED*), flowing and swelling over with virility that Troilus fears.

See PINCH, *Tem*.

Eyes Human orifices: pudendum (P); anus (the 'nether ye' of Alisoun's rectum – TWR); penis; nipples. Eyeballs or testes. Eight eyes: 'I will knock out two of your eight eyes; a common Billingsgate threat from one fish nymph to another: every woman, according to the naturalists of that society, having eight eyes; viz. two seeing eyes, two bub-eyes, a bell-eye, two pope's eyes, and a ***-eye' (G).

1H6, I.i.49: 'When at their mothers' moist eyes babes shall suck' – the moist 'bub-eyes' above, the bubbies (breasts – F&H), 17th c. term still current. Bub: a drink (F&H).

MM, I.ii.113. Pity will be given Mistress Overdone, bawd: 'you that have worn your eyes almost out in the service' – worn out her arse in service (coitus – P; whoring – C).

LLL, V.ii.421. Biron and the 'lords' are 'infected'; 'They have the plague, and caught it of your eyes . . . the Lord's tokens on you do I see.' TOKENS: (1) pox-spots; (2) genitals – those 'eyes' from which one catches plague, pox (syphilis – P).

H5, V.ii.14. Queen Isabel to Henry, former enemy now marrying her daughter: 'So happy be the issue . . . Of this good day and of this gracious meeting,/ As we are now glad to behold your eyes;/ Your eyes, which hitherto have borne in them/ Against the French . . . The fatal balls of murdering basilisks' but now have changed to eyes of love. His eyes had earlier *borne* the fatal *balls* of basilisks that kill with a glance (like the equally *murdering balls* of the 'eye' of the 'cannon' – III.i.11). But in the context of the issue (heirs) of this GRACIOUS (sexually well-endowed) MEETING (coitus), Henry's *eyes* now bear in them life-giving *balls* (testicles). An ironic echo of the insulting TENNIS-BALLS the Dauphin had sent him!

Ado, V.ii.105, Benedick: 'I will live in thy heart, die in thy lap and be buried in thy eyes' – die (experience an orgasm – C; P) in her lap (vulva – TWR; P), her eyes where he buries himself. Sh freq. calls the womb a burying-place as in *R3*, IV.iv.423: 'in your daughter's womb I bury them . . . in that nest of spicery they shall breed'.

See DAINTY, *1H6*; CAMEL, *R2*; PHYSICIAN, *H8*; FACE, *LLL*; WARD, *LLL*.

F

Face (1) Buttocks, pudendum. Fesse(s): buttock(s) (Cot). *Fesso*: any 'chinke or broken hole. Also a womans privy chinke, quaint or water box' (F). TWR, p. 195, Fig. 10, pictures a 'grotesque with a second face for genitals . . . applauding a nude woman'.

(2) Faeces, faecal waste. Jonson, *Sejanus*, I.i: 'I do not ask you of their urines,/Whose smelts most violet? . . . Or who makes the hardest faces on her stool [seat for bowel evacuation]?' See MUD (Weever); SOUL, *Cor*; STIR, *AYL*; JOINT STOOL.

KL, IV.vi.121. Lear tells of a dame 'Whose face between her forks presages snow' and who 'goes to't/With a more riotous appetite' than a 'soiled horse'. Forks: the human crotch (*OED*). To't is perhaps a toute (arse – TWR); as it is in SMILE, *Cor*.

H5, II.i.87. Falstaff is dying and his boy requests, 'Good Bardolph, put thy face between his sheets, and do the office of a warming-pan.' 'Between the sheets' (F&H; P) and 'do one's OFFICE' (P) mean copulation (*Oth*, I.iii.394: 'it is thought abroad, that 'twixt my sheets/He hath done my office'). The boy's request is inescapably indecent even with the usual gloss of a red-faced besotted Bardolph poking his face between the sheets in lieu of a warming-pan! But a warming-pan is a bed-fellow, albeit usu. a female; a wench (F&H: Ray, *Proverbs*, 1672). A 'put' is a silly fellow or a harlot; and 'to put' means to coit (F&H; P; putage: harlotry – W; putanism: lewdness). It is more likely a bawdy suggestion of the Boy's that Bardolph put his face (butt) between the sheets and perform the sexual OFFICE of the warming-pan for the dying Falstaff – Bardolph's face that Falstaff called 'Lucifer's *privy* kitchen' (italics added) in *2H4*, II.iv.360.

LLL, III.i.199: 'A wightly wanton with a velvet brow,/With two pitch-balls stuck in her face for eyes;/Ay, and, by heaven, one that will do the deed/Though Argus were her eunuch and her guard'. The *one eye* that will do the deed of sex is the vagina (P). Argus: monster of one hundred eyes. The three-eyed monster has two in her face and the one that will 'do the deed'. If, however, Biron means the VELVET (vulva) brow of the wanton, with two EYES (orifices) in her genital 'face', one of which is her vagina, then I suggest the other unflatteringly described pitch-ball refers to the 'blind eye' or anus (F&H). Sh's use of 'pitch' lends credence to this view: 'stinking pitch', 'pitch me i' the mire', 'loved not the savour of . . . pitch' (*Tem*, I.ii; II.ii). See PITCH (It *pegola*: pitch or an infectious whore).

2H4, I.ii.26. Falstaff mocks Prince Hal's 'face-royal' that a 'barber shall never earn sixpence out of'. The usual rather unfunny gloss that this puns on Hal's *kingly* face and the profile on the coin called a *royal* lacks point: the first half is flattering, while Falstaff means to be damaging, and the whole is not typical of his more robust humour. More likely 'face-royal' puns on court face and *courtes-fesses* (one who is 'pin-buttockt' or has small buttocks – Cot); and the profile, HALF-FACED (half-arsed) on the coin. Falstaff mocks Hal's virility: no BARBER (strumpet) will ever earn a SIXPENCE (standard fee) out of his unmanly 'face'. Cf. *AW*, II.ii.4–18, where 'court' – bandied back and forth five times – leads to bawdiness on the 'barber's chair' (prostitute – F&H) that fits all buttocks, including the 'pin-buttock' (the *courtes-fesses*).

See FAN, *RJ*; FLEW, *H8*; Introduction p.xvi.

Fact Copulation. An evil deed or crime, now obs. except in the phrase 'after (or before) the fact'.

2H6, II.i.173: 'naughty persons, lewdly bent . . . Dealing with witches and with conjurors:/Whom we have apprehended in the fact'. Arch. equiv. of 'in the act' (John 8:4: 'this woman was taken in adultery, in the very act'). Since the 'ringleader' of those who were lewdly bent was Gloucester's wife, he was told, ' 'Tis like, my lord, you will not keep your hour' – his wife, the HOUR/whore, apprehended in the fact; a prediction that comes true with her banishment. In biblical use, fornication meant forsaking God for idols, idolatry; and it is this religious heresy, her connection with witches, of which Eleanor is convicted. (See PITCH.)

TA, IV.i.39: 'there was more than one/Confederate in the fact'. In the six other refs to it, Lavinia's rape is called the 'deed' (coition – P).

Fan Buttocks. *Fin*: end (Cot). Fin: obs. for fine, the end. Fielding, *Shamela*, Dedication: Miss Fanny and the Fan and Pepper-Box lodgings pun on the female pudendum, venereally infected (see PEPPER, *MWW*). 'Lucinda's fan, with a looking-glass in it' – *Signet Classic Poets of the 17th c.*, vol. II, p. 253: '*fan* probably also pudendum' with 'implications for the mirror [GLASS, hymen]'.

RJ, II.iv.112:

Nurse. My fan, Peter.
Mercutio. Good Peter, to hide her face; for her fan's the fairer face.

Hardly an innocent juxtaposition of fan and FACE/Fr *fesse* (buttock) when Murcutio has been doing nothing but punning bawdily at everyone's expense and on all the genitals: pumps (F&H), baubles (C; P), tales (C; P), pricks (C; P) and gear (F&H; C).

1H4, II.iii.25, Hotspur: 'I could brain him [a "cowardly hind"] with his lady's fan'. COWARDly (effeminate) *hind* parallels *lady's fan*: (1) hit the *hind* with her *fan*; (2) *brain* him with *bran*, *bren* (a turd – Cot) from her fan (Fr *breneux*, soiled with excrement); (3) give this 'lack-brain' – as he is called – this 'rascal' (RASCAL, castrate) some BRAINS (testes, balls or spirit), of which even his lady's fan has more than he.

TrC, I.iii.27. The fan is connected with its flatus: 'But, in the wind and tempest of her frown,/Distinction, with a broad and powerful fan'. *But* in the WIND (a flatus); DISTINCT/stink with a BROAD/*brodier* (arse – Cot) and POWER-(the arse)ful fan.

AC, I.i.9. Antony's HEART (arse) is 'become the bellows and the fan/To cool a gipsy's lust'. He is lit. and fig. Cleopatra's ass, her bellows (bum – F&H) or *soufflet*, pop. Fr sl. for buttocks. *Souffler*: to blow breath, to hiss behind (Cot). (WHISTLE develops this metaphor.)

II.ii.208. Other 'divers-colour'd fans' besides Antony's 'cool' (COOL/cul, rump) Cleopatra: see VARIETY.

See STERN, *H5*.

Fancy (1) Amorous inclination. Shirley, *Lady of Pleasure*, III.ii: the bawd has 'pretty pictures to provoke the fancy'.

(2) Associated with homosexuality. Spenser, *The Faerie Queene*, Bk XII, c.vii, st. 5: 'The first was Fancy, like a lovely boy,/Of rare aspect, and beautie without peare;/Matchable either to that ympe of Troy,/Whom Jove did love, and chose his cup to bear [Ganymede],/Or that same daintie lad . . . so deare/To great Alcides'.

AYL, III.v.29. Silvius tells the scornful Phebe, 'If ever, – as that ever may be near –,/You meet in some fresh cheek the power of fancy,/Then shall you know' love's wounds. As he predicts, the cheek (CHEEKS, buttocks) is very near – in space as well as time – for GANYMEDE (like Spenser's Fancy) steps forth and Phebe falls in love with her–him in whose cheek is the POWER (buttocks) of fancy.

Ham, V.i.204: 'Alas, poor Yorick! I knew him, Horatio: a fellow of infinite jest, of most excellent fancy: he hath borne me on his back a thousand times; and now, how abhorred in my imagination it is! my gorge rises at it. Here hung those lips that I have kissed I know not how oft.'

It is not the skull, which Hamlet handles comfortably and continues to hold and address ironically, that is ABHORRED/whored to him; but his memories of Yorick, the 'whoreson' mad fellow. Yet the only memory he shares with Horatio (and the audience), the only explanation for his feelings, is that Yorick had borne him on his *back* (Yorick, the King's jester, like Mistress Quickly who had 'borne, and borne, and borne' – *2H4*, II.i.36), and that Yorick was a man of fancy (imagination – *OED*). This is what is abhorred in Hamlet's own imagination. Yorick's fancy was EXCELLENT (lewd, pederastic; L *ex-cellere*: to rise high; pun on 'sellary', a male whore – Jonson, *Sejanus*, IV.v) and Hamlet's gorge rises in remembrance.

Hamlet's 'I knew him, *Hor*atio' (italics added) introduces the possibility that he knew this 'whoreson' in the biblical sense, carnally. Yorick was a man of INFINITE (in-*fin*-ite, in the end) JEST (Fr *rire*/rear). His fancy was MOST (Fr *fin*, the end, the most) EXCELLENT.

It was the fancy and *fin* of him who had borne Hamlet on his back and whose LIPS Hamlet had OFT/aft (behind) kissed (euphemism for coitus – P; also said of one ball touching another when both are in motion, in billiards and other games, as in *Cym*, II.i.2). See FINE for antecedents of this pun; and BRAINS for Hamlet's self-disgust and calling himself a SCULLION (whore), anticipating this 'skull'.

It seems that a youthful erotic episode is now abhorred to him, and he expresses revulsion for *poor* Yorick (POOR, homosexual love; and *puir*, to stink – Cot). 'And smelt so? pah!' he says as he puts down Yorick's skull and proceeds to talk of the dust of Alexander that stopped up a BUNG-HOLE, a man's anus.

See PARTICULAR, *H8*; AFFECTION, *TN*; STERN, *H5*; VARIETY, *AC*.

Fantasy Sexual desire. Lit. take a fancy to (FANCY, once a short form). 'Doon his fantasye': to have intercourse (TWR; P). Byron, *Don Juan*, c.i, st.116: 'O Plato! Plato! you have paved the way/With your confounded fantasies to more/Immoral conduct, by the fancied sway/Your system feigns . . . you're a bore,/A charlatan, a coxcomb, and have been,/At best, no better than a go-between.'

MND, II.i.258. Oberon fills Titania with 'hateful fantasies' (HATEFUL, of the anus), and she falls in love with Bottom, 'an ass' (III.ii.34).

Oth, III.iii.299. Emilia gives Iago Desdemona's handkerchief: 'what he will do with it *Heaven knows, not I*;/*I nothing* but to please his fantasy' (italics added); 'I have a thing for you.' Iago: 'A thing for me? it is a common thing –'. Emilia, whose 'wayward' husband has more love for Othello than for her (HEAVEN knows that, too), is subjected by him to a pun on the thing (vulva – C; P) she has for him being a common (a whore's – *OED*; C; P) thing (see HEAVENLY or homosexual love as distinct from common or heterosexual). This foreshadows his calling her 'Villanous whore!' (V.ii.229) and trying to stab her (as Othello called his wife a 'whore' of 'villanous' secrets and killed her). The handkerchief is for Iago's twofold 'fantasy': (1) to prove Desdemona an adulteress, guilty of NOTHING (copulating), the same nothing with which Emilia vainly tries to please (sexually – C; P) the fantasy of her husband; (2) to regain Othello's love for himself.

MWW, V.v.97: 'Fie on sinful fantasy! Fie on lust and luxury!' The equation of fantasy with lust and luxury (lechery) was anticipated when the Parson told the fairies to 'Raise up the organs ["organs of increase" or womb – P] of her fantasy' (55).

RJ, I.iv.98. Mercutio calls dreams 'children of an idle brain,/Begot of nothing but vain fantasy'. Fairies are parents of dreams; and a strumpet, QUEEN Mab, is the 'fairies' midwife' who 'gallops night by night/Through lovers' brains [BRAINS, testicles]'. They are children of the IDLE (sexually wanton) brain; begot of NOTHING (copulation), but with nothing (genitals – C; P) except in fantasy.

Fart Sh does not use this word, but he puns on the flatus and on the anus as a 'wind-instrument' (*Oth*, III.i.10 – C; P), a common conceit in the 16th c., as in Montaigne, Bk I, ch. 20: 'one, who could at all times command his posterior, to let as many scapes as he would . . . who could let tunable and organized ones'.

He also makes the association with buggery, as did the Greeks. See Aristophanes, *The Knights*, 630–90: 'No sooner had I ended this prayer than a pederast farted on my right'. Puns on the fart continue in the rest of that speech, in the 'vigorous push with my arse', 'winded the matter', 'the blow'. On this subject Dover says (p. 142), 'The anatomy of the anus is altered by habitual buggery, and there are modern jokes which imply (rightly or wrongly) that the sound of farts is affected by these changes.'

The flatus was also considered an expression of pleasurable emotion or excitation, as in Aristophanes, *Peace*, 318 and 336: 'We cannot help giving vent to our joy'; 'I fart for joy'. See TWR, s.v. Fart, in which Ross says, 'Few casual readers of the most famous of all Middle English lyrics "Sumer is icumen in" really understand its eighth line: "bucke uerteth" means that the buck farts to display his ebulient joy over the coming of summer.'

And, finally, the *flatus* (Vergil) was a sign of arrogance, haughtiness, contempt (VEX, *KL*); a sign of pretention, emptiness, vanity (APPLAUSE).

See ROAR, SCAPE.

Fashion(able) (1) To tail: 1562, to fashion, cut. Fr *taille*: fashion, cutting. Puns on the tail (*OED*) and tale (C; P), the rump. See GOWN, *Ado*, *TSh*.

(2) L *fascinum*, *fascinus*: penis; an enchantment by the evil eye and the counter charm, the most popular being a phallus, worn by ancient Roman children. See GIFT, *Ham*; PROPERTY, *Oth*; LAME, *R3*.

(3) Taillé: fashioned, gelded or spayed (Cot). A CUT is a fashion, 1579; a gelding (*OED*).

Ado, III.iii.150, Conrade: 'But art not thou thyself giddy with the fashion too, that thou hast shifted out of thy tale into telling me of the fashion?' (1) He shifted out of telling the tale of the allegedly guilty tale (rump) of Hero, into talking of the other *taille*, 'fashion' (used 10 times in 25 lines). Fashion is a 'deformed thief' (it STEALS, makes stales or whores of people, as he pretended to do of Hero). The Watch knows 'that Deformed [see DEFORMED: Fr *difformé*, out of fashion] . . . a' goes up and down like a gentleman [UP AND DOWN, like a pimp]'. (2) He 'shifted', i.e. played a trick on, Hero ('I will so fashion the matter' – II.ii.47: he so tailored the MATTER, harlotry, that Hero appeared a whore). Conrade suggests that Borachio is GIDDY (lecherous) for his part in the shift, his contribution to what the Watch calls 'lechery'. See UTTER.

The unifying pun is the *taille* or cut (as in *2H4* below). Fashion is a CUT, a eunuch. To 'tail' means to remove the tail or stalk from, as well as to fashion. The men in this play suffer from debility, effeminacy (see DEFORMED). Antonio calls them fashion-monging boys (see BOYS, catamites), who monger or sell their fashions or rumps: there is (I.iii.52) the 'exquisite Claudio'; and (II.i.12) 'half Signior Benedick's tongue in Count John's mouth' (count: cunt; see Introduction, p.xi). As Beatrice says (IV.i.308), she wishes she 'were a man' to set things right, for 'manhood is melted into courtesies . . . and men are only turned into tongue, and trim ones too' – trimmed, cut TONGUES (penises): eunuchs (see WHIPPED).

2H4, III.ii.340, Falstaff: 'I do see the bottom of Justice Shallow' – he sees (*voir* – Cot) the *bottom* of this shallow JUSTICE (*voirie*: justice; a dung-heap – Cot). 'Let time shape, and there an end' – let it fashion, SHAPE (genitals) and there an *end*.

Shallow is an ass and probably a pederast, as other puns in this speech indicate (TRIBUTE; LIAR). He 'came ever in the rearward of the fashion': Partridge calls this a 'vague charge of monosexuality', but in the listing 'Mandrake' says it 'perhaps' indicates that Shallow was 'monstrously perverted in his sexual practices'. Shallow comes (experiences sexual emission – C; P) in the rear WARD (compartment or division), as in *1H6*, III.iii.33: 'Now in the *rearward* comes the duke. . . . Fortune . . . makes him lag behind [BEHIND, the rear]' (italics added).

Shallow comes in the rearward of the fashion or tale (rump); in the rear of the *taille* or CUT (cunt – K; castrate – *OED*); in the rearward of the fashion or *rigle* (Cot), pun on RIDGEL–RIGEL, a male with one or no testicle, an effeminate. He comes in the rear of the 'rig' or rigol, rigil: (1) generic for wantonness; (2) a gelding; (3) style, rum rigging, fine clothes (F&H), i.e. fashion.

Fast(ing) Copulate; coition. Fast or fasten: obs., join in wedlock; lay hold of. *Ficher*: to fasten (Cot); to fuck (TWR). Feast/fast (K): 'feasts of love' (*LC*, 181) and 'fasting in his wantonness' (*TrC*, III.iii.137).

Oth, I.ii.11. Iago asks if Othello is 'fast married', for if the marriage is *consummated* Brabantio cannot annul it.

Cym, I.vi.120: 'A lady/ So fair, and fasten'd to an empery,/ Would make the great'st king double'. Despite a seeming loftiness, this sentiment comes from Iachimo, whose intent is to disillusion and to seduce: he uses (1) 'fasten'd' to mean in marriage and in copulation; and (2) DOUBLE, double up or couple, to imply a liaison, esp. homosexual – his next phrase is that her husband partners with TOMBOYS.

138. Iachimo asks to sleep with Imogen, saying he will 'continue fast to your affection,/ Still close as sure'. Instead of fast and loose (F&H 1500) he will CONTINUE fast and CLOSE (lecherous) as SURE/ a sewer (whore).

MM, v.i.210: 'the hand which, with a vow'd contract,/ Was fast belock'd in thine; this is the body/ That took away the match from Isabel,/ And did supply thee', says Mariana, who with a CONTRACT (sexual union) did SUPPLY Angelo and whose HAND (genitals) in so doing was fast in his, thus fulfilling their earlier vows.

In both *MM* and *Cym* above, the pun on fast–fasten–copulate is linked to a pun on the woman's cunt: CONTINUE; CONTRACT.

See CLOSE, *H5*.

Fat Ass-like. *Un fat*: a sot, an ass, a gull; *fat*: foppish, foolish (Cot). To 'fat' meant to fertilise (*OED*: 'If the sheepes dung did not fat the ground'). *Graissin*: 'Fat mould, or dung to manure ground with' (Cot).

TrC, v.ii.55: 'the devil/ Luxury, with his fat rump and potato finger'.

H5, III.vii.143: 'this king of England . . . with his fat-brained followers so far out of his knowledge!' In the context of a scene in which two *French* men and the effeminate Dauphin engage in anal-erotic and bestial bawdry, this line means that the *fat-brained* followers of the King are ass-heads, shit-heads (BRAINS/ Fr *bran*, a turd), and foppish.

See TABLE, *Ham*; DRAWERS; TITLE, *TrC*; EPHESUS, *MWW*.

Fault The arse and its flatus. A breach (pudendum – C; P), breech or buttocks. A flaw, crack (*pet*: tail crack, fart – Cot). A lost scent in hunting, as in *MV*, III.ii.304: 'Before a friend . . . Shall lose a hair through Bassanio's fault' – lose a hare (P; K) through a lost scent. Dekker, *The Shoemaker's Holiday*, II.iii.: 'Where's Cicely Bumtrinket . . . she has a privy fault, she f—ts in her sleep.' Also a sin, the act of intercourse (Hulme, p. 112).

KJ, IV.ii. King John opens the scene: 'Here once again we sit . . . looked upon, I hope, with cheerful eyes'. Wanting eyes full of CHEER (love), he *sits* there, and he *is* looked upon (*miré* – Cot; mire: to defecate upon – P) by critics who think his EYES (arse) full of CHEER/ *chier* (shit – Cot). Apropos of the *breach* between John and Arthur, the discontent that will 'break' out, Pembroke says, 'patches set upon a little breach/ Discredit more in hiding of the fault/ Than did the fault before it was so patch'd' (33). He then regards Hubert and sees 'The image of a wicked heinous fault' (he means murder) in Hubert's 'eye' (71) – the HEINOUS/ anus fault connoting buggery and castration of Arthur's little breech (see SHIP-BOY).

Ado, II.i.228:

Don Pedro. To be whipped! What's his fault?
Benedick. The flat transgression of a school-boy . . . .

For the flat/ flatus transgression of being an ass/ arse and telling Don Pedro about Hero, the 'bird's nest [vulva – P] he found', Claudio deserves an ass's whipping. This pun on his loose talking (the fault of farting) leads to the accusation that Don Pedro stole Hero's virginity and *he* ought be WHIPPED (castrated) with a 'rod' for *his* ass's more serious 'transgression' (Ps 89:31: 'If they . . . keep not my commandments; Then will I visit their transgression with the rod').

See BEAST, *MWW*; PRAYER, *MWW*; MISTAKE, *H5*.

Feather Penis. *Penard*: a feather or plume of feathers; 'also as the Latine Penis; a mans yard' (Cot). *Penne*: feathers; a man's privities (F). To feather: to tread, said of a cock, in coitus.

LLL, IV.i.96. Armado's absurd love-letter elicits from the Princess, 'What plume of feathers is he that indited this letter? . . . what weathercock?' PLUME (penis), feathers and cock – today's Princess would ask what kind of prick he is. She thinks of him as a WEATHER/wether cock. 'Indite' puns on indict or make a culprit of, which the letter did to its writer, who indited or penned it.

See JET, *TN*; HAGGARD, *TN*.

Feeble Of pimps; of sexual inadequacy. Pimping: lit. weak, feeble, puny. *Feble*, *foible*: feeble (Cot); *qui a le resort foible*: that wants erection.

2H4, III.ii.158. For the army, Falstaff is about to 'prick' (used 10 times), or tick off on a list, Francis Feeble, whose 'trade' (prostitution – C; P) is that of 'A woman's tailor', and whose name puns on his lechery and inadequacy. Shallow: 'Shall I prick him, sir?' Falstaff: 'if he had been a man's tailor, he'ld ha' pricked you.' See WINGS, *MV*, for the lechery of tailors.

Tim, I.i.107. Some editors call *Tim* one of Sh's most puzzling plays. If the sexual pathology revealed in the puns is given proper weight, much light can be shed on this misanthrope. The tying of homosexuality and cannibalism (see WOLF; WORD), as in Tennesee Williams's *Suddenly Last Summer*, has a long literary tradition. Some find the subplot concerning Alcibiades unsatisfactory. But in Plutarch's story Timon 'avoided and repelled the approaches of everyone but embraced with kisses and the greatest show of affection Alcibiades, then in his hot youth' – 'Life of Antony', in *Lives*, trs. A. H. Clough (Boston, Mass.: Little Brown, 1905). The sexual and business relationships between Timon and every 'suitor' – those who want professional favours and those who come to woo – are revealed in his saying of one, 'being enfranchised, bid him come to me./'Tis not enough to help the feeble up,/But to support him after.' He will ENFRANCHISE Ventidius: (1) see him freed and pay his debt; (2) punningly, mount him coitally. He will help the feeble, pimping, impotent Ventidius *up* and will support (Fr *soutenir*) him after (behind). *Souteneur* means a pimp – the whore's support or sustainer. In *R2*, V.iii.11, Bolingbroke describes the 'loose companions', the 'dissolute' crew his son, a 'young wanton and effeminate boy', *takes on* himself 'to support'.

Cor, III.iii.125. Coriolanus despises those who can be bought (like whores): 'Let every feeble rumour shake your hearts' – let the rumour of every pimp, i.e. their tribunes, SHAKE (coitally) their HEARTS (arses), screw them. The theme of people and tribunes as whores and pimps runs through the play. Earlier in the scene, a tribune had asked, 'Have you a catalogue/Of all the voices that we have procured/Set down by the poll?' He condemns himself with Coriolanus's conceit: he is the pimp who procured (16th c.) all the VOICES/VICES.

Fetch Cause ejaculation. Lit. draw forth. Sh's puns on fetching and bearing may have been influenced by biblical lines such as 2 Sam 11:27: 'David sent and fetched her to his house, and she became his wife and bare him a son.'

TGV, III.i.274. Launce describes the qualities of his mistress, a 'bare Christian': 'She can fetch and carry. Why a horse can do no more: nay, a horse cannot fetch, but only carry'. The horse can only bear or carry him but cannot, unlike his *bare* Christian, bear him in intercourse. The other horse (HORSE/whore) cannot fetch (of a commodity, bring in money or sell for) like his whore, who can 'milk': (1) get money out of (F&H); (2) fetch or draw forth MILK (semen), q.v.

TSh, Induction, i.11:

Sly. . . . go to thy cold bed, and warm thee.
Hostess. I know my remedy; I must go fetch the third-borough.

She means fetch him in order to get the money Sly owes her, but, coming immediately after his statement, hers sounds as if she must *fetch* him as remedy for her cold bed.

2H4, II.i.110. The Hostess says Falstaff promised to marry her: 'didst thou not kiss me and bid me fetch thee thirty shillings?' – kiss (coit – P) and fetch 30 shillings by playing the 'quean' (whore and bawd) he called her (51).

They kiss, yet he deceives her and she betrays him, bringing him before the Lord Chief Justice and his men to be condemned and arrested. One remembers the kiss of the betrayer Judas (Luke 24:47), Jesus taken before 'all the chief priests', and those 'thirty pieces of silver'.
See JAPHET, *2H4*; LAUGHTER, *AW*.

Fie An expression of disgust, akin to 'Shit!' P2 dates its smutty use from Thackeray; but *maistre fi fi* or *phy phy* was a cleaner of the privies or jakes (Cot); as Cotgrave charmingly observes, 'A jakes feyer (who hath often occasion enough to say phy).' Fi or Fie: an expression used when something disgusting had been said; it means dung and the anal orifice and is current still in Lincolnshire (B).

TSh, IV.i.1. Grumio enters with 'Fie, fie on all tired jades, on all mad masters, and all foul ways!' Fie, fie on all masters (Master Fi Fi) introduces his story of how Kate and Petruchio fell out of their saddles into the filth, she under the horse, in a 'miry' place (mire: defecate upon – P). More puns on his 'tale' and the horse's 'tail' (rump – *OED*; C; P) evoke the foul, the fi-fi they were all immersed in. His last words before telling Curtis the tale are 'every thing in order?' – for in his tale (rump – C; P) everything was in *ordure*. (1) Kate's 'bridle was burst' (*CE*, II.i.14: 'there's none but asses will be bridled so'). *Bride*: keeps in order (Cot). Kate's ass did not keep-in ORDER/ordure. (2) Grumio had a similar accident: he 'lost' (the contents of) his 'crupper' (1594, buttocks; *cropion*: 'rumpe, or crupper' – Cot).

Sir-reverence meant excrement or to shit; it was an apology for anything unmentionable (F&H; P). *RJ*, I.iv.42: 'we'll draw thee from the mire / Of this sir-reverence love, wherein thou stickest / Up to the ears [EARS/arse]'. The following link 'Fie, fie' with the unmentionable Sir-reverence or shit, and possibly with anal eroticism.

TGV, II.vi.14: 'Fie, fie, unreverend tongue! to call her bad, / Whose sovereignty so oft thou hast preferr'd'. Proteus berates his unreverend TONGUE (penis) for calling Julia, who in the next scene assumes masculine disguise, BAD (hermaphrodite; homosexual) – Julia whom he has so OFT/aft (behind) preferred.

Ado, IV.i.96: 'Fie, fie! they are not to be named, my lord, / Not to be spoke of'. Hero's sexual transgressions are unmentionable, like Sir-reverence. However, NAMELESS refers to the sin of sodomy.

Field Womb, vulva. Montaigne, Bk II, ch.11, on 'copulation with women', quotes Lucretius: 'the bodie doth light-joyes fore-know, / And Venus set the woman's fields to sow'. Weever, *Faunus and Melliflora*, 867: Faunus woos a nymph, 'Shall such a field lie leyes and not be tilled . . . . Women were borne to beare . . . . enjoy the spring-tide of your age, / These Aprill flowers in winter will asswage: / Spend that you cannot keep' – familiar message to readers of Sh's sonnets.

TSh, III.ii.233. Petruchio calls Kate 'mine own . . . my goods, my chattels . . . my house, / My household stuff, my field . . . My horse . . . my ass, my any thing'. She is his GOODS, CHATTEL, stuff (C; P), HOUSE and HORSE – five puns on fornication and whores; his OWN (ass), his field, his ass, his ANY (ass) thing (genitals – C; P)

LLL, IV.iii.366. The Lords are about to 'woo these girls of France':

King. Saint Cupid, then! and, soldiers, to the field!
Biron. Advance your standards, and upon them, lords;
Pell-mell, down with them!

Advance the standard (penis – P) of Saint CUPID (god of lust). Pell-mell to the field (as in *KL*, IV.vi.119) 'to't luxury [lechery], pell-mell'; and DOWN for intercourse.
See PRESENCE, *AW*; GREEN, *H5*.

Fine (1) Buttocks. Obs. for the end.
(2) Excrement. *Fine de pouls*: chicken excrement (Cot).

Ado, I.i.313: 'And thou shalt have her. Was't not to this *end* / That thou began'st to twist so *fine* a story?' (italics added). TWIST: a sign of sexual acquiescence; the crotch.

RJ, III.v.154: 'But fettle your fine joints 'gainst Thursday next' to get married. To fettle is not only to ready, but also to bind (OE *fetel*, a girdle) and to BEAT OR THRASH (both punning on copulate); hence there is no doubt which JOINTS (genitals), under which girdle, are Juliet's *fine* joints.

Ham, V.i.116. As the clown digs up skulls with a 'dirty shovel', Hamlet comments on whose they might be: 'is this the fine of his fines . . . to have his fine pate full of fine dirt [excrement – *OED*]?' See FANCY.

See HEINOUS, *1H4*; WIT, *TSh*; COPATAIN HAT; INFINITE, *AW*.

Finger Caress intimately, finger-fuck (C; P). *Fouquer*: to finger (Cot). *Little* and *potato* finger: penis (P).

R2, V.v.53: 'my finger, like a dial's point' – the prick (*OED*) on the round face of the dial (pudendum – P). Thus Richard describes how he, hermaphrodite-like, will 'people' and 'beget'. See FIX, *Oth*, for the same image.

1H6, II.iv.49: 'Prick not your finger as you pluck [deflower – F&H; P] it [the white rose] off' – lest *you* are the one to *bleed*.

3H6, I.iv.55. Clifford, called 'bloody' and 'blushing' by York, is warned, 'do not . . . prick thy finger . . . to wound his [York's] heart'. Here, and in *1H6* above, men are advised not to fuck themselves while hurting others.

Fist A blow: a stroke; flatulence. Fist, fise, feist: a flatus or breaking of wind. L *flatus*: a blow, blowing.

KJ, II.i.465. The Bastard comments on a Citizen's 'large mouth [that talks] . . . of roaring lions . . . not a word of his / But buffets better than a fist of France'. ROAR(ing) is farting; buffets, too, are blows, and *b*ut (butt) *b*uffets *b*etter (with its onomatopoeia) suggests anal blows or fists. These few puns on *break*ing wind introduce the Bastard's magnificent speech (561–95) on Commodity, the 'broker' that 'breaks the pate of faith' when 'kings break faith'.

Per, IV.vi.177. Marina tells Boult 'To the choleric fisting of every rogue / Thy ear is liable, thy food is such / As hath been belch'd on by infected lungs'. Working for diseased whores in the brothel, he is liable to *choleric* fisting: (1) angry blows on the ear; (2) fists or farts of whores and whoremongers, sick with *cholera*, of which diarrhoea and vomiting were characteristic symptoms; (3) fists or farts of those whose sickness is of the *culare* (arse-gut – F; a choler / colour pun). His food, too, is subject to wind or blowing of another sort, the belching of infected lungs.

Fistula Penis. A fistula is a long narrow pipe-like ulcer (L *fistula*, water-pipe).

AW, I.i.39: 'What is it . . . the king languishes of?' – 'A fistula, my lord.' This illness no one could cure was his impotence. The man who reputedly had known a cure was Helen's dead father, Gerard de Narbon, a pun on *Guerir* (to cure – Cot) *de Nar-bon*, of the nose-bone (nare is nostril; L *nares*, nose). A nose is a penis (P) and his skill 'had it stretched [STRETCH, coitally] so far, would have made nature immortal'!

(1) The King languishes of his fistula. 'Languish' is be inert, flag, drop (*WT*, II.iii.17: 'And downright languish'd').

(2) Asked if she believes in the cure that was 'set down', Helen says, 'Ay, madam, knowingly' (I.iii.256). A strange construction – but 'knowingly' is L *gnarus* and puns on *nares*, the nose that, like the remedy, is also set down.

(3) Lafeu asks the King to 'know her business [BUSINESS, coitus]': 'I am Cressid's uncle, / That dare leave two together; fare you well' (II.i.101). He is Pandarus (*TrC*), who brought Troilus and Cressida together for lechery. Lafeu: 'I'll fit you' – make him fit (able to coit – C; P).

(4) The King accepts help, adding (II.i.210) there is more to 'know' (*OED*; P), i.e. carnal

knowledge (Helen's 'knowingly'). If she proceeds as 'high' as her word, her reward will be matched by his 'deed' (TWR, s.v. Dede; P) or sexual performance.

(5) 'Why, your dolphin is not lustier' than the cured King (II.iii.31). Dolphin, an animal of the whale kind, suggests a second stunning pun on de Nar-bon and fistula: the male of the Nar-whal (whale) species has one enormous projecting tusk, called a horn (*OED*; horn: penis – C; P), and a fistula (1646) is the spout of a whale.

For more on the King's impotence, see BREATHE; OFFICE; OIL; UNDONE; RAISE.

Fix Fornicate. In Fr *fabliaux*, *foutre* meant 'fuck, for which the seventeenth century substituted the euphemism ficher' (TWR). *Ficher*: fix, thrust, set far in (Cot).

Cor, I.viii.4. Aufidius combines two common words for fuck, *foutre* and *ficher*, in his challenge to Marcius, whom he does 'abhor' (ABHOR/whore): 'Fix thy foot [FOOT/*foutre* – P].' See SLAVE.

Oth, IV.ii.54. Desdemona has made Othello 'A fixed figure for the time of scorn/To point his slow unmoving finger at!' Her sexual betrayal, her fixing or adultery, made him a fixed (screwed or cuckolded) figure at which Time will point his index FINGER (see *R2* for similar metaphor), his (s)low FINGER (penis), his 'gnomone . . . knowman of any diall' (F). That know-man, gnomon or index on a dial suggests that Time points his FINGER, his cock (1613, gnomon on a sundial; penis), in scorn at Othello, the *real* know-man or no-man, the cuckold (see TWELVE for a similar pun). *Se ficher*, to make game of: time makes game of or scorns the *fiché*, fixed, fucked and cuckolded figure (*figgere*, to fix, thrust in – F) of Othello. It SCORES/SCORNS or screws him. (See ANCIENT: Iago, the Jack of the clock, strikes the time, also in scorn.) For another pun on the gnomon, see PLAIN, *MND*.

V.i.5. Iago tells Roderigo (ANGER) that to 'enjoy' Desdemona, he must 'fix most firm thy resolution' and kill Cassio: fix firm his RESOLUTION (*fiché*, resolved on) or erectile ability; be phallicly firm in his fixing or fornicating.

MWW, II.ii.303. The jealous Ford says, 'my wife hath sent to him; the hour is fixed; the match is made'. The HOUR/whore that is fixed, Ford fears, is his wife, since he expects his 'bed shall be abused' in the 'match' (love-bout – C; P).

See DOOR, *TN*; STICK, *AW*.

Flea Being bitten by fleas was a common 16th c. conceit for fornication. Marlowe, *Doctor Faustus*, I.iv: 'a little pretty frisking flea . . . here and there and everywhere. O I'll tickle the pretty wenches' plackets'. Donne, 'The Flea': the lover says the same flea 'suck'd me first, and now sucks thee' – thus in that flea they are married ('Where wee almost, yea more than maryed are'). After she kills the flea and it has 'Purpled thy naile, in blood of innocence' (virginal defloration), he points out that she will lose no more honour 'when thou yeeld'st to mee' than 'this flea's death tooke life from thee'.

MWW, IV.ii.158. Ford believes Falstaff, whom he suspects of being his wife's lover, is in the clothes-basket. Mrs Ford: 'If you find a man there, he shall die a flea's death.'

Flew (1) Rectum. Pun on a flue that emits air, smoke. Tewel: flue, anus (*Cham*). Chaucer, 'The Summoner's Tale': the chimney 'tuwel', an anus (TWR).

(2) Was let loose (from the bowels: faeces or flatus).

1H6, I.i.124: 'Here, there, and everywhere, enraged he flew. . . . His soldiers . . . rush'd into the bowels of the battle'. 'Flew' rather than 'slew' (as some eds) for the following reasons: (1) the flew/flue–bowels quibble is the same one Sh makes in *TrC* (the following example), where he puns on breach/breech–flew; (2) Spenser's *Faerie Queene*, Bk III, c.i., st. 66, has a similar line: 'Wherewith enrag'd she fiercely at them flew. . . . Here, there, and every where about her swayd/Her wrothfull steele'.

TrC, IV.v.246: 'in which part of his body/Shall I destroy him? whether there, or there, or there?/That I may . . . make distinct the very breach whereout/Hector's great spirit flew.' The breach (female pudendum – P), pun on *breech* (buttocks – TWR) – Hector's anus out of which flew his great (chimney-grate) spirit (L *spiritus*, blowing), his great blowing, L *flatus* – that made DISTINCT/stink his breach.

H8, IV.i.74. Asked where he has been 'broiling', the man answers that the crowd, which included 'Great-bellied women . . . like rams [symbol of lechery – C; P; and of rank, rammish smells]', was such that he was 'stifled/ With the mere *rankness* of their *joy*' (italics added). For this odd phrase for joy, see FART. He adds 'such a noise arose . . . hats, cloaks, – / Doublets, I think, – flew up; and had their faces/ Been loose, this day they had been lost'. He didn't *see* them fly up, but he *thinks* it, because of the NOISE and smell of the flatus. He was stifled from the MERE (merry, wanton) rankness (sexual heat – *OED*); hence broiling. Had their FACES (buttocks) been LOOSE with diarrhoea, they would have lost their faeces, too.

The event is the coronation of Anne Bullen as Queen. 'No man living/ Could say "This is my wife" there; all were woven/ So strangely in one piece' – one PIECE, pejorative for woman and her pudendum. No man could distinguish his wife from the others, the great-bellied women like rams. This includes, of course, the already pregnant Anne Bullen. The metaphor develops (105–11) into an even more serious comment on the religious–political 'breach'/ breech in the kingdom and 'privy council' (a privy is also a latrine).

Flute Anus, one of Sh's 'wind-instruments' (P). Silent flute: penis (F&H; G). Doucet: flute-like instrument; deer's testicles.

MND, I.ii.46. The actors' names (CON) pun on their occupations and genitals: *Peter* calls on *Bottom*, then on 'Francis Flute, the bellows-mender', who 'must take Thisby on you', a suggestive way of saying play her part. The flute is a wind instrument; and the bellows, an instrument that furnishes a blast of air, is *le soufflet* (the bum – F&H).

AC, II.ii.200: 'the poop was beaten gold . . . The winds were love sick . . . the oars were silver,/ Which to the tune of flutes kept stroke, and made/ The water which they beat to follow faster,/ As amorous of their strokes . . . pretty dimpled boys . . . With divers-colour'd fans, whose wind did seem/ To glow the delicate cheeks which they did cool'.

It is difficult but helpful if one can overcome a reluctance to see bawdiness in this erotic poetry. Cleopatra the beautiful and alluring is also Cleopatra, 'triple-turn'd whore'; and the speaker is Enobarbus, whose views on women in general and Cleopatra (the 'Egyptian dish') in particular, are most cynical (I.ii). Kittredge (p. 1372) speaks of the seeming inconsistency of 'gorgeous poetry' coming from Enobarbus, who, he says, by l.230 has 'descended' to his usual tone. But that has been Enobarbus's level throughout.

These lines contain an implicit pun on flutes or flageolets/ flagellates (beats or strikes), esp. as a sexual perversion. In the context of 'beaten', 'beat', 'stroke' and 'strokes', all to the tune of flutes, the love-sick WINDS (coital embraces) and WINDS (farts – P) that are evoked (the winds from the sea and the *fans*) are those of the area most frequently BEATen and stroked (strike: fuck – C; P), the arse – or, as Enobarbus says, 'the poop'. Cf. Etherege, *The Man of Mode*, III.iii: 'That's one of the walking flageolets who haunt the Mall o' nights', said Belinda, of one who had said of her, 'I like the oily buttock'.

Note the COLOUR'd/*culare* (arse-gut – F) FANS/ fins (musical ends; buttocks) of these pretty dimpled boys (see VARY); and the wind that came from them and did COOL/ cul (arse) the CHEEKS or buttocks (see POOP).

Foot 1. Copulate (C; P): *foutre* (Cot); *fottere* (F). See DOOR, *TN*.

2. 'Foot', like 'fuck' and 'fuck up', also means hurt, destroy; 'screw' in the sense of make impotent, castrate physically or psychologically. Fr *fouetter*: to WHIP (*fouettage*, castration). See HEINOUS, *1H4*; BEGGAR, *R3*.

3. Bugger; like 'fuck', may be lit. or fig. Foot: *pied* (Cot); and 'pied' means variegated (see VARY, bugger). See BITE, *Tem*; SLAVE, *Cor*; STAND BACK, *1H6*.

H5, III.iv.54: 'le pied et la robe' are 'De foot et de coun [cunt]'. Alice calls the lesson EXCELLENT (lewd, esp. of buggery); Katherine agrees it is 'assez' – ass-y, ENOUGH.

4. A small penis (only part of a yard, i.e. penis – *OED*); a castrate. See INCH, *TSh*.

LLL, V.ii.674: 'Loves her by the foot' – 'He may not by the yard.'

3H6, III.ii.137. Gloucester is like one who 'spies a far-off shore where he would tread, / Wishing his foot were equal with his eye'. He would like to tread (copulate – *OED*; P), but his foot is not equal to his EYE (arse), his desire.

1H4, II.iv.388:

Falstaff. . . . Douglas, that runs o' horseback up a hill perpendicular, – . . .

Hal. Why, what a rascal art thou then, to praise him so for running!
Falstaff. O' horseback, ye cuckoo; but afoot he will not budge a foot.

Hal calls Falstaff a RASCAL (castrate), for praising a military runaway. Falstaff, in turn, calls him cuckoo or cuckold, and says he had meant (1) that Douglas runs (coits or ejaculates – C; P) on a HORSE / whore's *back*; and up a hill (hillocks: buttocks – C; P) perpendicular (L*latus rectum*, perpendicular side – *Cham*; perpendi*cular* may also have suggested *culare*, arse-gut – F); (2) that Douglas would BUDGE / bugger a foot, a castrate or male whore – not that Douglas would run or budge a foot of *ground*. Middleton, *A Mad World, My Masters*, V.ii, makes similar puns:

Constable. . . . They were all riding a-horseback, an't please your worship.
Sir Bounteous. Yet again! A pox of all asses still, they could not ride afoot unless 'twere in a bawdy house.
Constable. The ostler told me they were all unstable fellows, sir.

(See STAND BACK for others who will not budge a foot, i.e. bugger.)

Forest Forest: pudendum and pubic hair (F&H).

AYL, III.ii.354. The 'pretty youth' GANYMEDE–Rosalind dwells 'in the skirts of the forest, like fringe upon a petticoat'. This only seeming male lives in the skirts or petticoat (a female – *OED*; F&H) of Rosalind. A placket is a petticoat and the slit in it (*OED*); and it is the slit the placket covers, the pudendum (P). Ganymede dwells in *les ailes d'un forest*, 'skirtes of a Forrest' (Cot); *les ailes*: 'the sides of a womans privities' (Cot).

Fork(ed) (1) Crotch (F&H; *OED*; P). *2H4*, III.ii.334: 'naked' Shallow looked like a 'fork'd radish'.

(2) To coit. The 'forked plague' in *Oth*, III.iii.276, and the 'fork'd one' in *WT*, I.ii.186, refer to cuckoldry (P). Montaigne, Bk II, ch. 12: 'he had seene him graft the forked tree in her upon a table'. Cf. P: 'to get (or climb) on the old fork (to coit)'.

See ROUND, *AYL*.

Frail(ty) Lewd. Sensual weakness (P). Marston, *The Dutch Courtesan*, IV.v: the whore Franceschina is called 'catafugo Frank o' Frank Hall!' – 'Ah, my fine punks, good night. Frank Frailty, Frail o' Frail Hall, Bonus noches.'

Ham, I.ii.146: 'Frailty, thy name is woman!' Nothing in Hamlet's speech indicates that woman is fragile: the thrust is against things 'rank and gross' – rank, in sexual heat; and gross, large and obscene – specif. his mother, whose '*increase* of appetite [lust – P] had *grown*' (italics added).

Oth, IV.iii.100. Emilia says women also have 'Desires for sport, and frailty, as men have'. Delivered without stress on the comma, as context dictates, the line is a statement of women's desires for sport (amorous play – C; P) *and* frailty, just like men's.

1H4, III.iii.189: 'Thou seest I have more flesh than another man, and therefore more frailty.' The pun resolves a seeming contradiction: having more flesh (carnality – C; P), by def. Falstaff has more frailty.

See SHIN, *Tem*.

France, French Subject to the same scurrility as ITALY (home of VD and sodomy). Anon., 'The Women's Complaint to Venus' (1698): 'Till Mounsieur from France Taught Pego [penis

– F&H; G] a Dance To the tune of old Sodom's Embraces' (*Penguin Book of Restoration Verse*, p. 167). Wycherley, *The Country Wife*, I.i, of a man pretending impotence from VD: 'he's a sign [obs. mere semblance; a manifestation of disease] of a man, you know, since he came out of France' – 'Stinking, mortified, rotten French wether'. See LAME, Dekker.

AW, II.iii.291: 'France is a dog-hole, and it no more merits/The tread of a man's foot: to the wars!' France is a dog-hole, equiv. of an arse-hole: DOG (sodomist) hole (anus, pudendum – TWR; P). It does not merit a man's *tread* or FOOT, fucking (P). So, off to the Italian WARS/whores.

MND, I.ii.99: 'Some of your French crowns have no hair at all' – jest on the crown, a coin; and the crown of a head, bald from the French disease, syphilis.

H8, I.iii.1:

Lord Chamberlain. Is't possible the spells of France should juggle
 Men into such strange mysteries?
Sandys. New customs,
 Though they be never so ridiculous,
 Nay, let them be unmanly, yet are followed. . . .

 They have all new legs, and lame ones.

In France the English were juggled (fucked – P), they learned STRANGE (bisexual) mysteries (MYSTERY, whoring), new unmanly customs (sexual uses – C; P), and returned effeminate, impotent (LAME), and diseased.

1H6, III.iii.85. Pucelle's words 'battered' (BATTER, screw) the 'vanquished' Burgundy: 'Done like a Frenchman: turn, and turn again!' 'Turn' is a bout in bed (F&H; P), but Pucelle is not praising him for virility. He is a political whore who turns again, changes sides for profit, turns a gain. See PUNY for a 'maiden youth' she also 'vanquished'.

Frank Lusty, licentious. A pig-sty. To fatten for killing. Spenser, *The Faerie Queene*, Bk II, c.ii, st.37: 'Might not be found a francker franion,/Of her leawd parts to make companion'. Alexander Pope, *Moral Essays*, ii.71: 'Chaste to her husband, frank to all beside.'

Oth, III.iv.44. Othello holds Desdemona's hand, 'Hot, hot, and moist. . . . 'Tis a good hand,/A frank one.' GOOD: adulterous; moist: lustful (see HAND, *MWW*).

2H4, II.ii.160. Asking 'doth the old boar feed in the old frank?' Hal is told, yes, Falstaff sups with 'Ephesians' (EPHESIANS, licentious fornicators) and the 'parish heifers', Doll and Mistress Quickly, in the frank ('sty', i.e. brothel, in *Per*, IV.vi.104).

R3, I.iii.314, Gloucester: 'Clarence . . . is frank'd up to fatting for his pains'. Penned up in the Tower, like a fatted pig, Clarence will be killed for his PAINS/penis, for his royal power.

KL, III.iv.20. In context of metaphors on feeding ('Is it not as this mouth should tear this hand/For lifting food to't?'), Lear enters the hovel: 'O Regan, Goneril!/Your old kind father, whose frank heart gave all' – *but* as one gives to animals, possessions, fattening them for personal return. Recall I.i when his 'largest bounty' was given for exchanges, and Lear spoke of him 'that makes his generation messes/To gorge his appetite' – him who feeds on his own children as on franked pigs.

See DAINTY, *TrC*.

Fray Deflower, 16th c. Copulate: *frayer*, to spawn, as fishes (Cot). Lit. to rub (from L *fricare*). Frig and rub: 16th c. sl. for copulate, masturbate (F&H). Durfey, 'A Ballad of Andrew and Maudlin': the 'Fraysters and Friskers' who 'laid the Girls down' sweat 'more from their Arses' than their faces. Wilmot says man should not 'fuck in time of flowers [menses] . . . if after every close/My smoking prick escape the fray/Without a bloody nose' (p. 139).

See ACCOMMODATE, *2H4*; KNOCK, *TSh*; QUAINT, *MV*.

French See FRANCE. In battle, the French armies are denigrated as made up of impotents, effeminates, buggers: see CLIP, *H5*; BOB, *R3*.

Fresh With sexual prowess (TWR); shameless as a whore (P).

TrC, IV.iv.147: 'Yea, with a bridegroom's fresh alacrity'.

Per, IV.ii.10. Because their stock of whores 'with continual action are even as good as rotten', they need 'fresh ones' – for the CONTINUAL (cunt) action.

See WHITE AND RED, *TSh*.

Froth (1) Semen. Lit. foam and scum. Montaigne, Bk II, ch.12, discusses 'of what matter men are derived and produced one from another ... made of milkie slime or muddie.... Pythagoras [said] our seed is the scumme or froth of our best blood ... others, blood, concocted and digested by the heate of the genitories'.

(2) Masturbate: 'frot' is rub, caress ('th' and 't' interchange: throstle/trassel; Sathan/Satan; Goth/goat – K). Ben Jonson, *Every Man out of his Humour*, IV.iv: 'Let a man sweat once a week in a hot-house [brothel] and be well rubbed and froted, with a good plump juicy wench, and sweet linen, he shall ne'er have the pox.' Frottage: achieving orgasm by rubbing against someone; frotteur: practitioner of same (*Cham*).

Tim, IV.iii.433: 'Till the high fever seethe your blood to froth' – as in Montaigne above, the heated blood becomes semen (see BLOOD).

MM, II.i.214: 'Master Froth, I would not have you acquainted with tapsters: they will draw you, Master Froth, and you will hang them.' Pompey, the TAPSTER (bawd) (1) draws a frothy head on beer; (2) draws him into the whore-house; and (3) will *draw* him out, expose his sexual organ (C; P) and *mastur*bate *Master* Froth (ABUSE). Escalus warns him not to get ACQUAINTed with (have carnal knowledge of) tapsters, for his complicity will contribute to the fate of the pander whom the law will hang (Fr *pendre*: see HANG).

(Massinger, *A New Way to Pay Old Debts*, IV.ii: Froth is the wife of Tapwell, Alehouse Keeper: 'I see thee, Froth, already in a cart,/For a close bawd.')

Furnish(ed) Well-equipped sexually. In botany, having thorns or prickles; in heraldry, armed, with horns, talons, etc. Horns, thorns, *prick*les are all penis symbols (C; P).

AYL, III.ii.258. Celia describes the man Rosalind loves: 'He was furnished like a hunter.' 'Venery' means both hunting and sexual indulgence, and Orlando is furnished for both, as Rosalind's retort indicates: 'he comes to kill my heart'. Orlando is furnished to kill both HEART and *hart* (K): the female is a *hind* (see ACORN, DEAR).

Cym, I.iv.8. Iachimo says Posthumus had earlier not elicited his admiration, though he was of 'a crescent note, expected to prove' itself – a crescent or rising NOTE (prick), expected to PROVE (be virile), attest with testes. Philario says, 'You speak of him when he was less furnished than now he is with that which makes him both without and within.' What makes him *without* is probably the codpiece, the veneer (from F *fournir*, to furnish), pun on *venery*. L *penus* is that which is kept within, pun on the penis, *within* the codpiece.

TGV, II.vii.85. Julia, dressing as a man, is told she needs a 'codpiece' (56). Julia: 'go with me to my chamber/To take a note of what I stand in need of,/To furnish me upon my longing journey'. Her two uses of NOT in this speech, and an earlier reference to 'true-love knots', highlight the pun on the *note* or prick she stands (the erect penis – C; P) in need of, needs to be furnished with for her *long*ing journey – as well as the one she longs and makes the journey for, Proteus's.

See ALTAR, *1H4*.

G

Gait/Gate Gate: sluice-gate, vulva (P): 'the two-leaved gate of her chastity' (Nashe, *Selected Works*, p. 252). Man's sluice-gate: penis, anus. Gate: contrivance for regulating the passage of fluid (*OED*) – like a cock. Robert Burton, p. 53: 'welcomed lust at every gateway of his body'.

WT, I.ii.197: 'Whiles other men have gates and those gates open'd,/ As mine, against their will' – ptg to adulterous wives.

Ado, IV.i.106, Claudio (disillusioned): 'For thee I'll lock up all the gates of love'.

LLL, IV.iii.185, Biron: 'When shall you hear that I/ Will praise a hand, a foot, a face, an eye,/ A gait, a state, a brow, a breast, a waist,/ A leg, a limb?' A gait, a state would be out of place in this list of anatomical parts were it not for the puns: the gait/ gate or body entrance, vulva, anus; the STATE, seat of dignity and pun on the buttocks.

TN, III.i.93. Sir Toby vulgarly appraises the nature of Cesario's visit: 'Will you encounter the house? my niece is desirous you should enter, if your trade be to her' – encounter (make love – P) in this HOUSE (brothel, gaming-establishment), in which his niece is desirous to trade (sexual intercourse; pander – P). As the uncle (F&H), he is pawn-broker in the establishment (and so he is). Told to 'Taste' (TASTE, test sexually, q.v.) his legs and 'to go [copulate – C; P], sir, to enter', Cesario says, 'I will answer you with gait and entrance' (see DOOR for his sexual gait). He answers equally bawdily in a metaphor of fencing and sexual assault; he will ANSWER (return hit in fencing; a coital thrust) with his gait and will enter (coitally – C).

See DOOR, *MV*, *TN*; OTHER, *TN*; COURTIER, *MWW*; PORTER, *LLL*; RAISE, *H5*; TARTAR, *TN*; PLAIN, *TSh*.

Ganymede Eliz. shorthand for homosexuality (Richard Barnfield, the 'Ganymede' sonnets in *The Affectionate Shepherd*, 1594). The young boy in a homosexual relationship is a catamite, corruption of 'Ganymede', whom Zeus fell in love with. Rabelais, *Pantagruelian Prognostication*, ch. 5: 'ganymedes . . . ingles, fricatrices, he-whores, sodomites'.

AYL. Rosalind, seeking a name for her male disguise, chooses 'Ganymede', which proves appropriate for the later love-play with Orlando, who becomes quite carried away with his 'boy' substitute for his beloved Rosalind.

Her infatuation with Orlando does not negate the feelings between her and Celia before either fell in love with a man, a relationship that bears scrutiny. As Le Beau says, their 'loves/ Are dearer than the natural bond of sisters' (I.ii.288). In the 16th c. UNNATURAL (q.v. ptg to Lesbianism) meant not in accordance with the usual course of nature, outraging moral standards.

Celia's language is intense and passionate. In I.ii.8 she is jealously impatient with Rosalind's longing for her father: 'Herein I see thou lovest me not with the full weight [WEIGHT, ass/ arse] that I love thee' – the same vocabulary used by Orlando when he falls in love with Rosalind: 'What passion hangs these weights upon my tongue?' (269). In his case, the weights (L *as*, a weight, a pound) would seem to be the pounders (testicles – F&H), hung upon his TONGUE (penis).

When Rosalind asks, 'what think you of falling in love?' (27), Celia responds that love with a man is not to be taken seriously: 'to make sport [amorous play; whoring – P] withal: but love no man in good earnest; nor no further in sport neither than with safety of a pure blush thou mayst in honour come off again'. Go no further than you can with the *safety* of a PURE (homosexual) blush 'come off' (coitally – C). Give no GOOD (copulating) earnest (i.e. part payment to secure a bargain).

When her father banishes Rosalind (as a TRAITOR, whore), Celia says, 'we still have slept together,/ Rose at an instant, learn'd, play'd, eat together,/ And . . . like Juno's swans,/ Still we went coupled and inseparable. . . . I cannot live out of her company' (iii.75).

This is the bond (L *copula*) Le Beau spoke of. They were coupled, said Celia, a word Sh mocks in the coupling (*copula*) or sexual union of Touchstone and Audrey (MEETING). (In *1H6*, IV.vii.20, 'Coupled in bonds of perpetuity' – though meaning death – shows Sh's linking of these words.) Celia's list could not have included more intimacies: they slept together, ROSE (sexually, as in III.ii.117: 'He that sweetest rose will find/ Must find love's prick and Rosalind'), played (TWR; C; P) and eat (C; P), coital activities, together. In v.iv.148, 'Wedding' is described as 'O blessed bond of board and bed!' – just the bond (*copula*), the things, Celia said she and Rosalind shared.

When Rosalind does not immediately understand from this that Celia plans to share her banishment, Celia says, 'Rosalind lacks then the love/ Which teacheth thee that thou and I am one:/ Shall we be sunder'd? shall we part, sweet girl?/ No. . . . Say what thou canst, I'll go along with thee' (I.iii.98).

And when Rosalind marries Orlando, Celia marries his brother Oliver, with whom she had the following exchange (IV.iii.122) before she knew whom she was addressing:

Celia. O, I have heard him speak of that same brother;
And he did render him the most unnatural
That lived amongst men.
Oliver. And well he might so do,
For well I know he was unnatural.

So two young women with a love dearer than the natural bond of sisters marry two brothers, one of whom is that SAME (Gk *homos*, *homo-*) brother, the MOST (buttocks) UNNATURAL (homosexual), and the other of whom engaged in quite ardent love-play with Ganymede (see CATTLE; SISTER).

See TRAITOR, *AYL*; PERFECT, *AYL*; CUP; GIDDY, *AYL*.

Garden Female pudendum. Hortus: privy parts of a woman (Nathan Bailey, *English Dictionary*, 1728); L *hortus*: a garden. Boccaccio (*Decameron*) p. 136: 'I'll work your garden [l'orto] in a way it was never worked before', says a virile boy who works for the convent. Cotton, 'Forbidden Fruit': 'the bliss that I would tast,/ Is something lower than the wast,/ And in your Garden's Centre plact' (*Penguin Book of Restoration Verse*, p. 176). Song Sol 4:12: 'A garden inclosed is my sister, my spouse; a spring shut up, a fountain sealed'; 4:16: 'Let my beloved come into his garden, and eat his pleasant fruits.'

Oth, I.iii.323, Iago: 'Virtue! a fig! 'tis in ourselves that we are thus or thus. Our bodies are our gardens, to the which our wills are gardeners'. The *will* is the penis (C; P). This subtle pun links virtue, fig and garden – the fig-leaf that covers both the garden and the will after the loss of virtue in the original Garden of Eden.

Son 16. Sh advocates that his friend defy immortality through posterity: 'Now stand you on the top of happy hours,/ And many maiden gardens yet unset/ With virtuous wish would bear your living flowers'. He does stand (with phallic erection – C; P) on top (coitus – *OED*; P) of happy HOURS/ whores, instead of virtuous maidens, with unset virginal gardens.

See RESOLUTION, *Ham*.

Gate *See* GAIT.

General(ly) (1) Common; (2) upon the whole. Common: whore-like (*OED*; P). Whole/hole: pudendum and anus (K; P). Freq. counterposited to PARTICULAR (a whore).

Cor, v.i.2. Menenius says Coriolanus rejected Cominius, who 'was sometime his general, who loved him/ In a most dear particular' – perhaps in a MOST DEAR/ deer (pricket/ pricked) part. He concludes (38), 'I'll not meddle' (sexually – *OED*; P; as in IV.v.50: 'meddle with my master?' – 'Ay; 'tis an honester service than to meddle with thy mistress') – his metaphor for not prostituting himself to get Coriolanus to return.

MM, III.ii.106. Of 'lechery' the Duke says, 'It is too general a vice'.

TrC, II.i.3: 'Agamemnon, how if he had boils? full, all over, generally? . . . And those boils did run? say so: did not the general run then?' Thersites mocks the Greek general, generally covered with BOILS (VD symptom) and running (*gonorrhée*: a running of the reins – Cot). Agamemnon, diseased whore, by implication a coward, running.

AYL, III.ii.367. Rosalind says her uncle 'knew courtship too well' and she thanks God 'I am not a woman, to be touched with so many giddy offences as he hath generally taxed their whole sex withal'. She would not want to be touched (sexually caressed – C; P) with the GIDDY (lecherous; sodomitical) OFFENCES (sex-acts; buttocks-related) with which he generally taxed the whole/ hole of women, as in TRAITOR. But in IV.i.153 this GANYMEDE says that after marriage 'I will be . . . more giddy in my desires than a monkey'.

Tim, IV.i.7: 'Matrons, turn incontinent . . . to general filths/ Convert o' the instant, green virginity,/ Do't in your parents' eyes!' Timon exhorts virgins to convert into general filths, to whores, to do't (copulate – C; P) in their parents' eyes. See INDEED, *2H4*.

See SUBTLE, *Oth*; CREATURE, *TA*; GERMAN, *LLL*.

Gentry Gender (as in *MWW*, II.i.51, Folger ed, 1964) or sex; and engender or breed. See EXCEED, *Cym*; ALTER, *MWW*.

German Sperm (P). Germen or germs are generally thought of as the female reproductive element, opposed to the sperm: the ovary or egg. But *germe d'un oeuf* is the sperm, the little 'siring' on either side of a raw yolk (Cot).

Cym, II.v.16. The seducer Iachimo is 'Like all a full-acorn'd boar, a German one'. See ACORN (testicle; glans penis, 'full' of germen or sperm).

KL, III.ii.8: 'Smite flat the thick rotundity o' the world!/ Crack nature's moulds, all germens spill at once,/ That make ingrateful man!' Crack the MOULDS (wombs) of NATURE (generative organs); spill all the germens, male and female, that make for the rotundity of pregnancy (as well as of the world).

Ado, III.ii.35. Benedick 'in love' (LOVE, Fr *l'oeuf*, the egg) is mocked as 'a German from the waist downward, all slops'. SLOPS: (1) liquid waste (waist/ waste – K); (2) full, baggy breeches, partic. those supplied sailors or *seamen* (was Sh quibbling on *semen*?). Don Pedro says (63) a 'heavy tale [penis; rump – K; P]' can be told of Benedick. The various types of breeches were a regular source of humour to the period. Rabelais, Bk I, ch. 20: 'the martingal fashion of breeches, wherein is a spunghole with a drawbridge for the more easy caguing [cacking]' (Wallis says these were 'in fashion in 1579, among the court minions, who made them serve for a quite different use than what they were at first invented'); the 'fashion of the mariners [very full breeches]'; and the ones 'having in the seat a piece like a cod's tail'. Rabelais and Sh seem to be making similar quibbles on *German* SLOPS (q.v.).

LLL, III.i.192. Reluctantly and with disgust, Biron yields to what he calls 'love'. His cynicism (see an earlier DANCE, act of coition, with Rosaline) is evident in his calling CUPID the great GENERAL (whore) 'Of trotting 'paritors' (trots are bawds – C; P); the 'Dread prince of plackets, king of codpieces', both of which are covering for the genitals and the genitals themselves (C; P). It is scarcely romantic love that leads Biron to exclaim, 'I seek a wife!/ A woman, that is like a German clock,/ Still a-repairing, ever out of frame,/ And never going aright' and always having to be 'watch'd'. (A 'Dutch clock' was a wife – F&H n.d.) She is a *germen* clock, always repairing itself: her ovary with its monthly repairs, acquiring the new germen or egg. She must be watch'd, clocked; man's relations with her must be timed. She is the woman ever out of frame (1590, constitution or nature; service, shape or use), because of menstruation and pregnancy. A 'frame' is a travail, hence evoking the travail of childbirth. Cf. Middleton, *A Mad World, My Masters*, III.iii, in which the 'lust' of man leads him 'To dote on weakness, slime, corruption, woman!' who is 'Much like your German clock . . . They'll strike to ten when they should stop at one.' ('Ten' puns on the period of pregnancy, which Middleton also figures out as bringing 'forth fruit in forty weeks'.)

Perh., being *Germ*an, she is also diseased and needing medical repair. (See EYES, FACE, for Biron's further development of Rosaline as diseased.) How appropriate therefore that the punishment Rosaline imposes at the end of the play – on him who had said, 'I seek a wife!' – is that for one year he must seek the beds of people 'sick'.

Giddy Lecherous, deviating from accepted sexual norms. Fr *hanneton*: a giddy person, a cockchafer (one of Britain's common beetles, also called the dor or dung-beetle, scarab, tumble-bug or tumble-dung, which deposits its eggs in balls of rolled up dung – *OED*). Believed to be born in and fed on dung, it was an opprobrious term ('Battening like scarabs in the dung of peace' – Massinger, *The Duke of Milan*, III.i). See GREEN SICKNESS, *AC*, and PEGASUS for anal-erotic links. *Hanetons*: huge flies that engender like silk-worms, backwards, and hold onto each other's tails in hibernation (Cot; cf. SILK, effeminate). *Parentage d'hanetons*: lecherous, incestuous alliance.

AYL, IV.i.153. When GANYMEDE (homosexual) weds, he will be 'more giddy in my desires than a monkey' ('lecherous as a monkey' – *2H4*, III.ii.338; 'hot as monkeys' – *Oth*, III.iii.403).

TA, V.ii.78. Tamora (also called SEMIRAMIS, queen known for castration) will 'disperse [DISPERSE/dis-purse, castrate], the giddy Goths', earlier called 'Lascivious' (II.iii.110) and 'lusty' (V.i.19): Goth/goat, symbol of lechery (K). Monkeys and goats were also linked to sexual bestiality (see DILDO). Rabelais, Bk III, ch. 34: 'the women of Mendes, in Egypt', who copulate with goats in honour of Bacchus.

RJ, I.ii.48. Romeo's greeting of 'God-den, good fellow' and the servant's return 'God gi' god-den' may pun on God and *god*den/garden (*TN*, III.i.78: 'Dieu vous garde', or God guard you). This is part of the conceit on 'giddy', from OE *gydig*, insane, possessed by a god. The servant extends the tempting invitation to 'supper' where Romeo is to forget her who has had no 'match since *first the world began*' (italics added); and where he meets Juliet, the forbidden fruit, in her 'orchard', whose walls he climbs though 'the place death' if her kinsmen 'see thee' – Juliet and Romeo forgetting what Sh does not, that 'God saw him when he was hid in the garden' (*Ado*, V.i.181).

Juliet, the 'backward turning' remedy, supposed to cure Romeo who does 'Turn giddy' of his old love Rosaline ('Turn back', Romeo says, as he climbs into the orchard – II.i.2) – she, too, is giddy (and lecherous). As the vulgar Nurse's husband predicted (STINT), Juliet has learned to 'fall backward' instead of 'upon thy face' (I.iii.41). Later in the morning, Romeo tells the Friar, 'I have been feasting [on forbidden fruit in the orchard] with mine enemy,/ Where . . . one hath wounded me, That's by me wounded' (II.iii.49). Friar: 'Women may fall, when there's no strength in men' (80) – the fall from Paradise (WOUND, coit).

H5, I.ii.145. Henry fears 'the Scot, who will make road upon us'; 'We do not mean the coursing snatchers only,/ But fear the main intendment of the Scot,/ Who hath been still a giddy neighbour to us . . . pouring, like the tide into a breach . . . with hot assays'. How ironic that in his own assays in France, his first words on landing are 'Once more unto the breach, dear friends' (III.i.1).

The sexually evocative language, composed of familiar puns, condemns the Scots who make road (a whore – C; P) coursing (COURSE) and SNATCHing or whoring. INTEND puns on probe sexually; and 'breach', which means the breaking of waves and of a moral bond, puns on the *breech* or buttocks into which the giddy (backward engendering) Scots NEIGHBOUR (adulterer) makes his hot (lascivious – C; P) *assays*. The puns on (political) buggery continue in Canterbury's saying England's 'chronicle' (CHRONICLE, annal/anal) is '*as* rich with praise/*As* is the *ooze* and *bottom* of the sea/ With sunken wreck and sunless treasuries' (italics added).

See CUSHION, *Cym*.

Gift The sexual gift; genitals. Chaucer, 'The Wife of Bath's Prologue', 39: the 'yifte of God' is sex (TWR, s.v. Yifte).

Ham, I.v.41: Hamlet's uncle, 'that adulterate beast,/ *With wit*chcraft of his *wit*, *with* traitorous gifts, – / O wicked *wit* and gifts', seduced the 'will' (vagina – P) of the Queen (italics added). His were a traitorous, a TRAITOR's or whore's gifts – his WIT (penis) and his WITCHCRAFT (L *fascinum*: witchcraft; the penis). The Ghost continues that his 'natural gifts' (NATURE, lit. generative organs) had 'the power/ So to seduce!'

TGV, III.i.89. Valentine tells the Duke, 'Win her with gifts . . . Dumb jewels often in their silent kind/ More than quick words do move a woman's mind.' JEWELS, i.e. precious stones or testicles, in their silent KIND (1590, sex or gender) do more than words to MOVE (arouse sexual feelings) a woman's MIND (arse).

Ado, III.iii.15, Dogberry: 'to be a well-favoured man is the gift of fortune'. 'Favours' are sexual parts (P), and a WELL is the penis. In III.v (see HORSE) the 'Gifts that God gives' are Dogberry's penis and testicles, items that his friend Verges 'comes *too short* of' (italics added).

Son 11. Sh again urges his friend to immortalise himself through a child. Let others 'barrenly perish', but those whom NATURE (*natura*, genitals – F) 'best endow'd she gave the more;/ Which bounteous gift thou shouldst in bounty cherish'. As she 'carved' him for her 'seal' (SEAL, testes), endowed him with that gift, so should he 'print' more. Bounty, goodness: *bonté* (Cot); *des bontés*: the sexual favour (F&H, s.v. Kindness, n.d.).

See DOG, *MWW*.

Glass 1. Usually glossed as virginal membrane (P). *Per*, IV.vi.151: 'crack the glass of her virginity'.

TSh, Induction, i.7, Hostess: 'You will not pay for the glasses you have burst?' 'Crack' (*Per* above) or 'burst' – the pun adds meaning to Sly's activities in the alehouse–brothel (RED LATTICE) appropriate to the subsequent Induction bawdiness (Index: Sly).

2. However, it is also the penis and scrotum (suggested perhaps by the shape of an hour-glass and an alembic) or semen. Carew, 'A Rapture': the lover will 'ravished sweets distil/ Through love's alembic, and with chemic skill . . . one sovereign balm derive,/ Then bring that great elixir to thy hive'.

Son 5. The poet speaks of 'Sap [SAP, procreative juices] check'd with frost' and, as usual, urges procreation: 'Then, were not summer's distillation left,/ A liquid prisoner pent in walls of glass'. Son 6 continues to urge that the lover 'Make sweet some vial'.

Mac, IV.i.119. The hags show Macbeth the long line of Banquo's posterity, the eighth apparition bearing 'a glass/ Which shows me many more; and some I see/ That two-fold balls and treble sceptres carry'. The glass is a mirror, but a 'stone' is also a mirror (Sh – *OED*). This glass is the potent stone (testicles – *OED*), the TWO-FOLD *balls* and SCEPTRES (penises), the heirs of Banquo.

See GOLD, *MWW*.

Gold(smith) 1. Excrement. Gold-finder (F&H; *gadouard* – Cot): emptier of privies. Rabelais, Bk 2 II, Prol.: 'pouldre d'oribus' (powder of gold), 'powdered dung' or 'quack-shit powder'. Jonson, Chapman and Marston, *Eastward Ho*, v.i: 'there may be a pot of gold hid o' the back-side'. Commonly words meaning excrement or sewers also mean whores: *gens de voirie*, gold-finders, jakes-farmers (Cot); *voirie*, a whore (F&H, s.v. Barrack-hack); *gadoue*, a trollop, sewage, night-soil (manure).

JC, IV.i.21. Antony says they should get rid of Lepidus, whom they used only 'To ease ourselves of divers slanderous loads': 'He shall but bear them as the ass bears gold,/ To groan and sweat under the business . . . [now] take we down his load, and turn him off,/ Like to the empty ass, to shake his ears,/ And graze in commons'. To EASE themselves (through evacuation or sexual intercourse) they let him bear the LOAD (shit; semen). Now they relieve the four-legged ass of his load of gold, i.e. the two-legged one of his load of excrement – leaving an 'empty ass'. Lepidus is the ass or whore's ass/ arse they used for political dirty work. He groaned (GROAN/ groin) and sweated *under* the BUSINESS (17th c., screwing) they gave him (see GREEN SICKNESS). Now he can go and (1) shake his ears like an old ass put out to commons, i.e.

public grounds; (2) SHAKE (fornicate) his EARS/ arse like a cast-off common (whore – C; P). See PROPERTY.

Tim, v.i.103 – 15. Timon reviles as whores the Painter and the Poet who visit him in his cave: 'I'll give you gold. . . . I'll give you gold enough. . . . Hence, pack! there's gold; you came for gold, ye slaves. . . . You are an alchemist; make gold of that.' Timon flings at them from the cave his own waste, the 'gold enough' (ENOUGH, Fr *assez* / of the ass). He repeats III.vi.103 when he threw 'reeking villany' into their faces (see CHEER, PASSAGE). Also, in mod. sl., he will beat the shit out of them. 'There's payment for you': to pay is to smear the *bottom* of a vessel with *tar* (compare to *TN*, IV.i.21: 'There's money for thee: if you *tarry* longer, / I shall give worse [WORSE/ whores] *pay*ment' (italics added). Timon tells them to PACK (a bundle for pack animals – asses; and a strumpet). Like Lepidus above, they are whores (see GOUT).

MWW, I.iii.76. This exchange on Falstaff's intended seductions of two women who he thinks will financially reward his copular service illustrates the overlap of gold, excrement and whoring: of *voirie* (whore) and *gens de voirie* (gold-finders, jakes-farmers).

Falstaff says that Mrs Page examined his PARTS (genitals) with 'judicious oeillades; sometimes, the beam of her view gilded my foot . . . my portly belly'. Pistol: 'Then did the sun on dunghill shine.' The beam of the sun or Sol (gold) gilded his foot; just as the 'angels' (60, 64) or gold coins from her husband's purse will reward or gild his FOOT (fucking – P; K).

When Mrs Page's beam fell on his belly (ME, bowels), says Pistol, it shone on Falstaff the dunghill (*voirie*, city dung-heap), and Falstaff the whore (*voirie*). Cf. SERVANT, *2H4*, for similar pun.

Falstaff: 'her eye did seem to scorch me up like a burning glass . . . she is a region in Guiana, all gold and bounty. . . . I will trade to them both.' He of the *port*ly belly will trade (prostitute – C; P) with both these 'golden shores [SHORES/ sewers, whores]', Mrs Page and Mrs Ford. The former's EYE (arse) scorched him up like a burning-glass, i.e. a lens that focuses rays on an object; but connoting a burning (venereally diseased – *OED*) GLASS (pudendum) that would also scorch a man up. She is a REGION (*contrée* – Cot) or country (cunt – C; P); a region (L *ora*) of Guinea: (1) coast of Africa; (2) guineas or gold coins.

2. Goldsmiths were bankers, down to the 18th c., and they and their wives were the subject of puns on the *Bank*side, home of pimps and whores; they were considered financial prostitutes (usury: prostitution – C; P). See QUAINT, *AYL*; LOMBARDY.

CE, v.i.219. Antipholus E. accuses his wife of feasting 'with harlots'. And the 'goldsmith' Angelo (angel, an old gold coin) 'were he not pack'd with her, / Could witness it'. The goldsmith is her PACK (pimp), in collusion with her.

Good In the Fr *fabliaux*, from whom Chaucer borrowed many metaphors, to do *lor*(*s*) *bon*(*s*), to do their good(s) is to coit (TWR, p. 23). 17th c. use of 'good' was ironic. (1) A 'good man's is rarely virtuous (G); he is a good performer in the brothel (P2). *RJ*, II.iv.32: 'a very good whore!' (2) A 'good one' (F&H) is a 'whore, punke . . . good one' (Cot, s.v. *gaultière*). (3) A 'good fellow' is a thief (*OED*); 'A mad whoreson . . . good fellow' (Cot, s.v. *gaultier*); also a whore: 'She is now very needy . . . for lucre's sake will be a good fellow' (Rowse, p. 100); 'To looke like a whore (Venus the Goddesse of good-fellowship . . .)' (Cot, s.v. *marée*). (4) A 'good time' is a carouse, sexually enjoyable (Pepys). (5) 'Goodyear' is the pox (F&H), corruption of 'gougeer' (from *gouge*: soldier's trull – Cot); see *MWW*, I.iv.129; *KL*, v.iii.24.

Per, IV.vi.122:

Marina. The good gods preserve you!
Lysimachus. . . . Thou art a piece of virtue. . . .
  . . . here's more gold for thee,
  . . . die he like a thief,
  That robs thee of thy goodness! If thous dost
  Hear from me, it shall be for thy good.

God/ gold/ good pun. Marina, though in a brothel, is a PIECE (cunt) of virtue. He who robs her of 'goodness' is a thief ('good fellow' – *OED*). And when she next hears from him it *is* for her good, for he who had wanted to be brought to her 'private place [PLACE]' asks leave to 'woo' her (v.i.263).

WT, v.iii.33. Leontes's wife 'might have done,/ So much to my good comfort, as it [her statue] is/ Now piercing to my soul'. Comfort: coitus (P); instead of the discomfort piercing his soul, there would have been the *good* comfort or pricking of his SOUL/SOLE (arse). For past coldness, he is rebuked by the 'stone': her statue and his testes (stone – *OED*).

Tim, IV.ii.38. Timon was 'Undone by goodness! Strange, unusual blood,/ When man's worst sin is, he does too much good . . . bounty, that makes gods, does still mar men'. He is undone by bounty ('all goodness that consists in bounty' – *Per*, v.i.70): *bonté* (goodness – Cot); *des bontés*, the sexual favour (see GIFT, Son 11). One ought not be 'half [HALF, homosexual] so kind' to men as this 'kind lord' (KIND, sex), says Timon's STEWARD (q.v.).

See TWIN, *H8*; PARTICULAR, *H5*; FIELD, *TSh*; MIND, *Tim*; PRESENCE, *AYL*; ADVOCATE, *WT*; BULK, *WT*.

Gout Sl. for VD (*OED*): garden gout, French gout, *la goutte militaire* or 'ladies' fever' (F&H).

Cym, v.iv.5. Posthumus is put in 'locks' to prevent escape: 'yet am I better/ Than one that's sick o' the gout . . . [and fears] the sure physician, death, who is the key/ To unbar these locks'. Lock Hospitals were for syphilitic or 'Pockey Folks' (*OED*). Posthumus welcomes death, unlike one sick of the gout, who prefers suffering over the cure (like Falstaff: SCOUR). Not only is death a *sure* physician but, this suggests, as many died from the other sure/*suer* (to sweat – Cot) physician, in a sweating-tub. Nashe, *The Unfortunate Traveller*, p. 220: 'Mother Cornelius' tub, why it was like hell, he that came into it never came out of it.'

2H4, I.ii.273: 'A pox of this gout! or, a gout of this pox! for the one or the other plays the rogue with my great toe.'

Tim, IV.iii.46. Timon buries some 'gold', the 'common whore of mankind': 'thou'lt go, strong thief,/ When gouty keepers of thee cannot stand'. Syphilis causes impotence (164), but GOLD is a whore with undying (though buried) potency: it will *go*, or screw mankind (P), even when man, her gouty KEEPER (pimp and customer – F&H) can no longer achieve erection, no longer stand (P), because of his gouty toe!

TrC, I.ii.30: Ajax 'hath the joints of every thing, but every thing so out of joint that he is a gouty Briareus, many hands and no use, or purblind Argus, all eyes and no sight'. Ajax has the same gouty or erectile problem as in *Tim* above – he has every thing (penis – C; P), but out of JOINT (JOIN, copulate). He is a Briareus with HANDS (penises), but no use (the sex-act – C; P); an Argus or eunuch (*LLL*, III.i.201: 'Argus . . . her eunuch').

See RHEUM, *MM*.

Gown Cunt (gown/*con*/cunt – K, p. 75).

H5, III.iv.53. Katherine is shocked that 'la robe' is 'de coun' ('gown' as pronounced by Alice), hearing this as *con* (cunt).

Ado, III.iv.15. Describing wedding-gowns, Margaret repeatedly evokes the cunt. Hero's 'gown's a most rare fashion' – MOST (Fr *fin*) and RARE pun on buttocks and 'rear'; 'a fine, quaint, graceful, and excellent fashion' – a FASHION (Fr *taille* or cut) that is FINE (buttocks), QUAINT/cunt, graceful (filled with her GRACES, genitals) and EXCELLENT (L *excellere*, to rise high). Hero's gown displays her charms. See CLOTH.

TSh, IV.iii.101. Katherine 'never saw a better-fashion'd gown,/ More quaint, more pleasing'. As in *Ado* above, it has a fine FASHION (tail or rump), calculated to please (give sexual pleasure – F&H; P). No wonder Petruchio beats the tailor with his 'yard' (16th c., penis) for having 'cut it to pieces' (CUT and PIECE: cunt), having 'curiously [CURIOUSLY, shittily] cut' it. And there is much ado over taking up 'my mistress' gown for thy master's use [coitus – *OED*; P]'. The tailor insists he was told to make a 'loose-bodied gown' ('loose' means wanton, as in Middleton, *Michaelmas Term*, I.ii: 'dost dream of virginity . . . remember a loose-bodied gown, wench, and let it go'). See UP AND DOWN and VELVET for equally bawdy dismissal of Kate's cap.

MWW, IV.ii.70. The wives despair: 'no woman's gown big enough for him'. Falstaff begs them to devise 'something; any extremity' – ANY (ass) extremity, any thing (pudendum – P) that could fit him. After he has donned the gown, Mrs Ford wishes Mr Ford 'would meet him in this shape' – MEET (mate or coit) him in this SHAPE (genitals), which may be just what her husband does (OLD LADY).

2H6, *3H6*, *LLL*, *AW*. Many of Sh's gowns are black, common adj. for vulva and anus, as in 'it was as black as ever was Malkin's queme [female pudendum]' (F&H, s.v. Quim).

Grace (1) Penis. Gk *charis*: grace; *keros*: horn. Horn: erect penis (P).

(2) Vulva (TWR, citing *Troilus and Criseyde*: many Greek knights want 'to stonden in youre grace'), Chapman, *The Gentleman Usher*, II.i.: 'And women will ensue,/ Which I must tell you true . . . [are] pages made for need/ To fill up women's places/ By virtue of their faces/ And other hidden graces'. 'See the places where I enjoyed those graces/ The gods might move', Anon., 'A well-wishing to a place of pleasure' (*Signet Classic Poets of the 17th c.*, vol. II, p. 78).

TGV, v.iv.165, Duke: 'the boy hath grace in him' – 'more grace than boy', adds Valentine, who knows the 'boy' is Julia, wearing 'codpiece' (II.vii).

TrC, III.i.15.

Servant. You are in the state of grace.
Pandarus. Grace! not so, friend: honour and lordship are my titles.

The play on 'grace' and 'honour', both of which are titles (TITLE: penis, arse), points to the pun made clear by the Royal Shakespeare Company, London, June 1981, when the Servant looked pointedly at Pandarus's genitals as he said, 'You are in the state of grace.' 'Grace' is attractiveness (*OED*); and Pandarus, in the *state* (from L *stare*, *statum*, to stand) of grace, is horny, standing in erection.

H5, III.v.34. To the Dauphin's 'Our madams mock at us, and plainly say/ Our mettle is bred out', Bourbon adds, 'They bid us to the English dancing schools . . . Saying our grace is only in our heels,/ And that we are most lofty runaways'. Their madams (prostitutes – *OED*) bid them to English DANCING-SCHOOLS (q.v., brothels), saying plainly (*flat*ly) that their mettle (semen – F&H; P) is bred OUT, Fr *hors*/ whores. They are impotent, diseased; their grace/ grease (K) is in their heels: (1) grease: disease of horses' heels (*OED* 1674); (2) heel: 'crust of a loaf' (*OED*); CRUST: venereal lesion. Is a pun on *loaf* the reason they are *lofty*? for, certainly, they lack a lofty penis and semen (grace/ grease) for DANCING (coitus). They run away, ejaculate prematurely (C) or in coitus interruptus; cf. *AW*, III.ii.42: Bertram is safe 'if he run away . . . the danger is in standing to't . . . [which causes] the getting of children.' These Frenchmen cannot stand to it (effectively coit – F&H; P). There is a quibble on being *bred* out – whores' *bread* (and butter) – and saying grace (grease, butter) for daily bread. These 'runaways' are run-*à*-ways, run-to-whores (ways: whores – P) and they run with *gonorrhée*, running of the reins (Cot), a running nag (the clap – G).

See BUDGER, *TSh*; WELL, *AW*; TRULL, *TA*

Gracious Genitally well endowed, with all the GRACES (genitals, male and female).

TN, I.v.280. Olivia cannot love Duke Orsino, though he is 'in dimension and the shape of nature/ A gracious person'. His graciousness consists of his dimensions or bodily parts as in *KL*, I.ii.7: 'my dimensions are as well compact'; and his SHAPE (genitals – *OED*) of NATURE, lit. his sex.

TGV, III.i.6. Another duke, and as such entitled to be called 'your grace', is called gracious by the sexually ambivalent Proteus, whose name means of many SHAPES, lit. genitals. When the Duke asks, 'Now, tell me, Proteus, what's your will with me?', Proteus replies, 'My gracious lord . . . when I call to mind your gracious favours . . . My duty pricks me on to utter that . . . my friend . . . intends to steal away your daughter:/ Myself am one made privy to the plot.'

The gracious Duke of gracious favours (lit. attractions; genitals – P) asks what is Proteus's will (sexual desire; penis – K; C; P) with him. Proteus is thus *pricked on* to UTTER (a seminal ejaculation) what he is privy to: Valentine's plan to STEAL (make a stale of) the Duke's daughter, to steal Silvia AWAY/*a way* (a whore) – the *plot*, pun on scheme and plot of ground of which he is privy (cess-pool – F&H) and which he foully leaks. All these puns express the sexual anxieties and the criss-cross currents of (bi)sexuality.

See EYES, *H5*; BREAST, *TN*; CACKLE, *MV*; MEETING, *H5*.

Grapple Embrace coitally. Montaigne, Bk I, ch. 20: a heretofore lusty King of Egypt wedded and 'found himselfe so short, when he came to grapple with her' that he almost killed her, fearing 'sorcerie'. Boccaccio, p. 252: 'he wanted to grapple with such a buxom . . . and when the milling was over, she said'.

See SHEEP, *LLL*; TIGER, *TN*; STERN, *H5*.

Graze Be a prostitute. Free grazing for sheep, given in return for the shepherd's services, is 'pack'. PACK: 16th c., a prostitute.

LLL, I.i.238: 'About the sixth hour; when beasts most graze, birds best peck' is when Armado found Costard and Jaquenetta in 'that obscene and most preposterous event', in sexual intercourse. The HOUR/whore was about six (L *sex*), when SHEEP (the only animal in Sh that grazes, with the exception of one 'ass'), i.e. mutton (Fr *moton*: sheep; prostitutes – F&H) graze. 'Peck' (a kiss, a hole or prick) puns on the *pack* or free grazing that Costard had.

RJ, III.v.190. An enraged Capulet tells Juliet to marry Paris or 'Graze where you will, you shall not house with me. . . . An you be not [mine], hang, beg, starve, die in the streets'. Like a sheep or prostitute, she is free to graze or pack: she may HANG (Fr *pendre*/pander) herself; BEG or whore; die (in sexual orgasm – C; P) in the streets, be a walker of the streets. But she will not HOUSE (a brothel – C; P) with him. See GREEN SICKNESS.

JC, IV.i.27. When Lepidus leaves the room, Antony says he is 'Meet to be sent on errands' – he is MEET/MEAT (whore's flesh) to go on ERRANDS, to be a go-between, a pimp, help others get what they want. Now that Lepidus is not needed in the triumvirate, Antony and Octavius will discard him like an old whore and 'turn him off,/Like to the empty ass, to shake his ears,/And graze in commons'. His being a pander, grazing in commons, feeding on commons (whores – C; P), is repeated in his being 'one that feeds/On abjects . . . staled by other men'. He feeds on, his livelihood comes from, stales (prostitutes – *OED*; P).

Green Colour of love and copulation (F&H). Song Sol 1:16: 'Behold thou art fair, my beloved, yea, pleasant; also our bed is green' (see *H5* below). When the names of planets are used in blazoning, Venus denotes green (*OED*). Durfey, 'Ballad of Andrew and Maudlin': 'They laid the Girls down, and gave each a green Mantle,/While their Breasts and their Bellies went a-Pintle a-Pantle.' Jonson, *Bartholomew Fair*, IV.iii.: 'Fit 'em to their calling. Green gowns, crimson petticoats, green women! my lord mayor's green women! guests o' the game, [prostitution, common pun – P], true-bred.'

LLL, I.ii.86: 'Of the sea-water green, sir.' In myth, Venus sprang from foam of the sea.
90: 'Green indeed is the colour of lovers'.

H5, II.iii.18. The death of Falstaff as described by the Hostess is the description of his final sexual erection: 'A' made a finer end and went away an it had been any christom child; a' parted even just between twelve and one, even at the turning o' the tide: for after I saw him fumble with the sheets and play with the flowers and smile upon his fingers' ends, I knew there was but one way; for his nose was as sharp as a pen, and a' babbled of green fields. . . . So a' cried out "God, God, God!" three or four times. Now I, to comfort him [caress lovingly – P] . . . put my hand into the bed . . . felt to his knees, and they were as cold as any stone, and so upward and upward, and all was as cold as any stone' (stones: testicles – *OED*; P).

First there are the penis puns: the nose (C; P) as sharp as any pen (C; P) as he babbled ('the bable of a man' is his penis – Cot, s.v. *queue*) of green FIELDS (female pudenda), the green bed of Song Sol (above). Nor is the time of his parting 'between twelve and one' arbitrary: see TWELVE, the time of maximum erection for the recumbent man, the penis pointing straight up like the hand at twelve o'clock. He made a FINE end (fine: to bring to an end; 1540, consummate, i.e. complete by sexual intercourse).

Next, the flowers that he *played* with (amorously – TWR; C; P) as he smiled upon his fingers' (FINGER: finger-fuck – P; toy with genitals – C) ends (end: penis, prepuce – P), are less likely to be the decorations on the sheets, as freq. glossed, than the flowers or reproductive organs and their envelopes. These are the flowers of the green fields – the heraldic 'field' or surface of a shield, tinctured green or Venus in its blazoning, for this knight, Sir John, who is dying.

Rabelais, Bk I, ch. 39: 'N'est ce falotement mouru quand on meurt le caiche roidde' – he who dies with a stiff prick dies a good fellow.

Green sickness (1) Lechery, whoring. *Paillard(e)*: lecherous, whorish; a whore (Cot). *Paillarder*: haunt bawdy-houses (Cot). *Couleur paillarde*: a pale colour, the green sickness (Cot).

(2) Pox or syphilis. Anaemia of young girls at puberty or sign of love-sickness (P).

RJ, III.v.157. Romeo had told Juliet (II.ii.7) to cast off her sick and green vestal livery (of the Vestal Virgins), i.e. her virginity; and she may have. Now, her father's language is what he would use if ejecting a venereally diseased strumpet: 'Out, you green-sickness carrion! out, you baggage! You tallow-face!'

Her tallow or pale (*pasle* – Cot) face is a clue to the pun: Juliet is greensickness or *pasles couleurs*; she is carrion, i.e. corrupting flesh, offal or *rebut*; and she is a baggage, i.e. a strumpet. Lord Capulet's combined epithets are almost a lit. translation of *Madame de rebut*, a pocky whore (*les pasles couleurs de Madame de rebut*: the pox – Cot). OUT (Fr *hors*) you diseased whore!

Lady Capulet's 'what, are you mad?' shows that Juliet has been called more than anaemic or love-sick; as does Capulet's continuing that the 'young baggage' can 'hang, beg, starve, die in the streets [designation of life of prostitution – *OED*],/ For, by my soul, I'll ne'er acknowledge thee,/ Nor what is mine shall never do thee good:' (See GRAZE.)

This virulent rejection of Juliet, who can 'die in the streets'; Egeus's decision to 'dispose' of his daughter Hermia 'either to this gentleman/ Or to her death' (*MND*, I.i); Lear's egotistical casting off of Cordelia: 'Better thou/ Hadst not been born', and 'we/ Have no such daughter, nor shall ever see/ That face of hers again' (*KL*, I.i) – these are to be remembered as correctives to harsh judgement of Shylock when his daughter Jessica proves a thief and elopes with a man not of her religion, thus, by religious law, demanding that Shylock declare her 'dead'.

AC, III.ii.6. Since Pompey's feast, Lepidus 'is troubled/ With the green sickness'. Some say this means he has yellow skin, weariness and hangover symptoms, similar to the anaemia of young girls. Maynard Mack (Pelican ed, 1960) perceptively noticed that the first 18 lines are devoted to how much Lepidus 'loves' Caesar and 'loves' Antony, and he says Lepidus is likened to a girl 'in his relations to Caesar and Antony'. Actually the pederastic nature of that relationship (see Index) is even clearer in the next few lines.

Agrippa. Both he loves.
Enobarbus. They are his shards, and he their beetle.

'Shards' means dung, excrement; and Lepidus is the beetle that lays its eggs in dung and was also believed to live on, to eat, dung. The common dor, dung-beetle, cockchafer, May beetle, etc., is freq. referred to in the literature (Dryden, *The Hind and the Panther*, 321: 'Such souls as shards produce, such beetle things'). Hence the pun on Lepidus's anal eroticism, his green sickness or lechery: (1) his eating their shit; and (2) his laying his eggs in their dung. Cf. *chiard*, 'A shitten fellow; a stinking rogue' (Cot); and PEGASUS.

Shards are not the cases of beetle-wings, as trad. glossed. The *OED* says this is a mistaken definition that developed in 1755 from a misunderstanding of Sh's phrase in *Mac*, III.ii.42, about the 'shard-borne beetle' (in which he did not mean air-borne but where born: i.e. laid and born in dung). See GIDDY for more puns on the habits of this beetle.

Grief, grieve (1) Bowel-pains; the gripes (1601) or colic pains. *Grevé*: grieved; 'also, burst, or whose bowels are fallen into his cods' (Cot). *Griffes*: gripes, seizes greedily, violently, catches at wrongly (Cot). Anon., 'On Melting down the Plate: Or, the Piss-Pot's Farewell, 1697': 'Queens themselves are forc'd to stoop to thee;/To thee they cringe, and with a straining Face,/They cure their Grief by opening of their Case' (*Penguin Book of Restoration Verse*, p. 349). Their straining FACE (rump) and opening of their case (buttocks – C; P; K) cures their grief. See VEX (a flatus): 'grief . . . vexeth' (*JC*, IV.iii.115). Cf. dejection: 1605, faeces.

(2) To whore: GRIEVOUS/Fr *une grivoise*, a whore.

Cym, IV.ii.59: Imogen's grief is called 'the stinking elder' – stinking ELDER (arse).

III.ii.33. Imogen hopes the letter from Posthumus will relish of CONTENT (sexual joy) but not content 'That we two are *asunder*; let that grieve him:/Some *griefs are med'cinable*; that is one of them,/For it doth *physic love*: of his *content*' (italics added).

And soon (IV.ii) she will assume that Cloten, the 'ass' (as he is twice called), is her husband, and there will be many more puns on the ass/arse (see CUSHION).

RJ, III.v.199, Juliet: 'Is there no *pity sitting* in the clouds,/That sees into the *bottom* of my grief?' (italics added). If her marriage is not delayed her 'bridal bed [will be]/In that dim monument where Tybalt lies'. She means the lines innocently, but Sh does not: (1) the seat of pity was thought to be the *bowels* (*OED*); and (2), as the Friar had said, 'violent delights have violent *ends*' (II.vi.9; italics added). *Griffe*: catch at violently, wrongly (Cot). To an Eliz. audience it was clear that Juliet had done this and that her own grievous, sexual misbehaviour brought about her grief (see ANCIENT).

Sh comments ironically on that grief when (IV.v.128), as Juliet had predicted, the 'wedding cheer to a sad burial feast' is turned; and Peter sings, 'When griping grief the heart doth wound,/And doleful dumps the mind oppress,/Then music with her silver sound – '. Why 'silver sound' the musicians keep asking Peter, none of them knowing that this sad conclusion started the night her lover had said, 'How silver-sweet sound lovers' tongues by night,/Like softest music' (II.ii.166).

So Sh utilises an old song of the 1550s to parody griping grief – the *griffes* or gripes and doleful dumps (songs of lament; melancholy) of Juliet, 'dove trooping with crows', as Romeo on first sight described her. Juliet, DOVE (whore), now doleful (dole: a company of doves), full of dole (deceit) in this false burial, full of grief and doll (dung, esp. pigeons' [doves'] – *CD*). The oppressed (ravished – *OED*; TWR; P) MIND (arse) of Juliet, in her grave (oppressed, *grevé*), grievous (*grave* – Cot), accused by her father (GRAZE, GREEN SICKNESS) of being a *grivoise*, whore. Thus ends Lord Capulet's 'wedding cheer [CHEER/Fr *chier*, to shit]'.

The disobedient daughter who marries against her parents' wishes was not a sympathetic character to the 16th c. As punishment, Imogen's husband was 'banish'd' (*Cym*, I.i.8) and so was Juliet's (III.ii.112): BANISH, treat like shit. And Imogen was believed dead of 'melancholy', and Juliet, of 'grief'. See PARTICULAR, *Oth*, for another disobedient daughter and grieving father.

Ado, II.i.63. Beatrice. 'Would it not grieve a woman to be overmastered with a piece of valiant dust . . . ? . . . Adam's sons are my brethren, and . . . I hold it a sin to match in my kindred.' With her premise, to marry is to commit the sin of incest and, as such, would grieve or make a whore of her. Her uncle then turns to his daughter: 'if the prince do solicit you in that kind, you know your answer' – if the prince solicit (1591, court 'with immoral intentions') in that KIND (lit. sex) or sexual intercourse (P), Hero's father wishes her to accept (see HEART, OCCASION).

See BREAST, *LLL*; MELANCHOLY, *WT*; ROAR.

Grievous(ly) Of whores. Fr *grivoise*: obscene; *une grivoise*: Fr syn. for 'barrack-hack' (F&H). Lam 1:8, 9: the daughter of Zion, Jerusalem 'hath grievously sinned . . . all that honoured her despise her, because they have seen her nakedness. . . . Her filthiness is in her skirts'.

CE, V.i.206. When Antipholus E. complains, 'she shut the doors upon me,/While she with harlots feasted', the Duke responds, 'A grievous fault!'

See WORM, *R3*; OLD WOMAN, *MWW*; PARTICULAR, *Oth.*

Groan Groin. Erotic moan (C); cry on lost virginity (P). Tourneur, *The Atheist's Tragedy*, II.iii: 'Sh' had rather you would wake and make her groan'.

R2, v.ii.102, York: 'were he twenty times my son,/ I would appeach him' – to which the Duchess returns, 'Hadst thou groan'd for him/ As I have'. York would and does (see HEINOUS) appeach, peach or inform on his son (a PEACH: arse, pederast). The Duchess says his part in begetting Aumerle was easy: even were it TWENTY, i.e. a score of times, that he had to SCORE (coitally). But she endured the groans of intercourse and of travail as he left her groin.

See ANSWER, Son 50; KEEN, *Ham*; GOLD, *JC*.

Groom A degraded person. Varlet: a male whore (P); OFr *varlet*: groom. *Valetté*: made common, groom-ridden, 'prostituted unto the use of groomes' (Cot). *Valeter*: to stoop, crouch, submit too much. Abolished under George III, a groom-porter was an officer of the royal household, whose principal functions were 'to regulate gaming . . . to furnish cards and dice, and to decide disputes at play' (*OED*). It is easy to see the extension of his job to the arranging of illicit assignations, etc., as in Jonson, Chapman and Marston, *Eastward Ho*, II.ii: 'every trencher-bearer, every groom, that . . . crept . . . by panderism into his chamber . . . the groom of his close-stool'.

1H6, I.iii.14: 'dunghill grooms' (see STAND BACK).

Per, IV.vi.201: Marina tells the Pander, 'prostitute me to the basest groom/ That doth frequent your house [HOUSE, brothel]'.

H8, v.ii.18. Here the groom as the licentious, the pimp, the sexually debased emerges in several puns. Cranmer hopes *Butts*, the King's PHYSICIAN (q.v.) who is passing by, does not see his disgrace, how they 'would shame to make me/ Wait else at door, a fellow-counsellor,/ 'Mong boys, grooms, and lackeys. But their pleasures/ Must be fulfill'd, and I attend with patience.' He waits among BOYS (catamites) and grooms and lackeys (1556, camp-followers), like a fellow-COUNSELLOR (pimp). ''Mong' means among but it connotes mong or trade and traffic (a monger, from L *mango*, a slave-dealer), used allusively for discreditable traffic. He is kept waiting at the door (like a door-keeper, the pimp's job – C), among types who fulfil illicit pleasures (sexual – P); he waits with PATIENCE/ PATIENTS, homosexual passives (see VOICE, *H8*).

See CUP, *2H6*; DETESTED, *KL*.

Gull An emasculated or buggered male. Lit. a dupe, simpleton. *Fregare*: to masturbate; to gull (F).

See YELLOW, *TN*; BUNG-HOLE, *H5*; WIND, *1H4*.

H

H (1) 'Ache' was pronounced like the letter.

(2) The H- or aitch-bone is the rump bone; a 'nache' is the buttocks.

AC, IV.vii.7, Scarus: 'I had a wound here that was like a T,/ But now 'tis made an H' – (1) 'tis (*T's*) made an H; (2) WOUND (genitals), a nache that aches.

Scarus/ scars plans to attack the enemy who 'are beaten' ('R' – the arse): 'Let us score [pun on his name] their backs,/ And snatch 'em up, as we take hares, behind.' (1) Let us SCORE (coit) their *backs*; (2) let us SNATCH (a hasty act of intercourse) them *behind*; (3) let us (s)natch 'em (only one 's' is heard). Backs, behind, nache – three puns on the buttocks. Take (fuck – C; P) the enemy, as if they were hares (prostitutes – P; bawds – *OED*, s.v. Hare). Bugger 'em, says Scarus.

Antony's response is suggestive: 'Come thee on'; and this short scene of 16 lines ends with Scarus's saying he'll halt 'after' (behind).

Haggard A whore. *Hagard*: a falcon that preyed for herself before she was taken (Cot). Webster, *The White Devil*, v.i: 'Is this your perch, you haggard? fly to the stews.'

Oth, III.iii.260: 'If I do prove her haggard,/ Though that her jesses were my dear heartstrings,/ I'ld whistle her off'.

TN, III.i.71. Viola says the Clown gains his living by judging the mood and quality of the people 'on whom he jests' (jess, strap around the leg of a hawk). He 'must . . . like the haggard, check at every feather/ That comes before his eye'. Many eds emend 'And . . . check' to 'Not . . . check' – to give a more favourable picture of the Clown. But he had just rather bawdily dunned Cesario before bringing him to Olivia, and said he would 'play Lord Pandarus' (pander) in bringing one coin to another for breeding.

A hawk that checks is one that stoops to follow base game, deserting its proper quarry, like the whore who also stoops to every FEATHER (penis) for a living. See BOGGLER, *AC*, for a similar metaphor. Sir Toby had just said of Malvolio when he stooped to pick up Maria's letter, 'with what wing the staniel checks at it', checks at or follows the false game.

TSh, IV.ii.39. Hortensio, observing Bianca in intimacies with another man, concludes she is a 'haggard' and renounces her. More interesting is Petruchio's using the word for Kate (i.191), the SCOLD (whore), at the same time calling himself her 'keeper': the KEEP (pimp, ponce – F&H) of a whore. See RUFFIAN for similar name-calling.

Hags See WITCHES (HAGS, SORCERERS): whores, homosexuals, hermaphrodites, deformers of the body, specif. sexually.

KL, II.iv.281. Lear calls his daughters, who fig. castrate him, 'unnatural hags' (UNNATURAL, sexually disturbed): see TRAIN, *KL*.

Half (faced) 1. Homosexual: see ROUND for Plato's half-men, seeking their other halves for completion. L *semimas*: half male, hermaphrodite, castrated. See CONTENT, *MV*; PROMISE, *Cor*; GOOD, *Tim*; EVIL, *AYL*; PERFECTION, *KJ*.

2. Half-faced: half-assed/ arsed. FACE/ *fesse* (a buttock, one side of the breech – Cot).

1H4, I.iii.208. When Hotspur says his father and Worcester 'Did gage them both in an unjust behalf' (173) he sets the groundwork for the pun in his later remark, 'But out upon this half-faced fellowship!' The emotion behind that exclamation is far better served by its meaning half-arsed than by the usual explanation that 'half-faced' means half and half.

2H4, III.ii.283. Falstaff doesn't care for the '*big ass*emblance of a man!' (italics added). He wants men who present 'no mark to the enemy', like 'this same half-faced fellow, Shadow . . . the foeman may with as great aim level at the edge of a penknife.' His *ass*/ arse is no bigger to aim at than the edge (L *acies*) of a knife. Men who present no mark to be aimed at, i.e. a *butt* (*OED*) are really half-arsed creatures, especially this SAME (homosexual) one, SHADOW (q.v.; 'Who do you call shadows of men?' – 'Half-men').

See PAINS, *KJ*; FACE, *2H4*.

Hand(le) Genitals; phallic symbol (K, p. 59). Act of coition or masturbation (C; P). 'Hond': used erotically; 'holden hym in honde', hold the penis; 'The Wife of Bath's Prologue', 211: 'I hadde hem hooly in my hond'; 'hol' and 'hool', terms that often mean the genitals (*TWR*). Wilmot, 'A Song of a Young Lady to her Ancient Lover', p. 89: 'Thy Nobler part, which but to name . . . wou'd be counted shame,/ By Ages' frozen grasp possest . . . shall be releast: / And sooth'd by my reviving hand,/ In former Warmth and Vigor stand'.

RJ, II.iv.119: 'the bawdy hand of the dial is now upon the prick of noon'. NOON is TWELVE o'clock, time of the height of the erection ('let my needle run in your diall' – F&H, s.v. Needle).

MWW, II.ii.218: 'Have you received no promise of satisfaction [sexual – P] at her hands?'

Ado, II.i.124. The masked Antonio is identified: 'you were the very man. Here's his dry hand up and down'. A DRY hand was a sign of impotence. By contrast, *VA*, 143: 'My smooth moist hand, were it with thy hand felt,/ Would . . . seem to melt [in orgasm – P]'. UP AND DOWN: masturbate.

MND, II.i.244. Demetrius warns Helena not to commit herself 'Into the hands' of one who doesn't love her; her 'virginity' is in danger and he may do 'mischief'. She responds she'll follow him 'and make a heaven of hell,/ To die upon the hand I love so well'. Since he talked not of killing her but of doing her sexual violence, we assume she expects (hopes) to make (copulate – P) her heaven by dying (orgastically – C; P) *upon* the *hand* she loves.

See EASE, *TSh*; SLEEP, *1H6*; NOON, *KJ*; THIGH, *Oth*; REPREHEND, *R3*; EXERCISE, *Oth*.

Handiwork The human body, 'God's handiwork' (*R3*, IV.iv.51); and sexual fondling. Handie-Dandie: copulation (F&H). Plautus, *The Two Bacchises*, 70–80: to the courtesan's 'We'll have to soften you . . . I'll take you in hand myself – this way', Pistoclerus replies, 'your handiwork is too expensive' ('Malacissandus es . . . tibi do hanc operam' – 'nimium pretiosa es operaria').

KJ, I.i.238. The Bastard says his legal father was not man enough to have begotten him: 'We know his handiwork. . . . Sir Robert never holp to make this leg.'

See Introduction, p. xii, on *JC*, I.i.30.

Hang(ing) 1. Of genitals (C; P). Well-hung: large genitals (G); 'Well-hanged (betweene the legs)' (Cot, s.v. *couillatris*). Dryden, *Absalom and Achitophel*: 'well hung Balaam and cold Caleb'. Cremasters (Gk *kremastos*, hung): muscles suspending the testicles. Laurence Sterne, *Tristram Shandy*, vol. v, ch. 17: Tristram was circumcised by a careless nurse who 'did not consider that nothing was well hung in our family, – so slap came the [window] sash down like lightning upon us; – Nothing is left, – cried Susannah'. Anon., 'One Writeing Against his Prick': 'Base metell hanger by your Master's Thigh! / Eternall shame to all Prick's heraldry . . . what is't you lack' to 'stand stiff'? (*Penguin Book of Restoration Verse*, p. 184). See SCOUR, *2H4*.

TN, I.v.20: 'Many a good hanging prevents a bad marriage'. Both a hanging on a gallows and a good sexual hanging would prevent a bad marriage. See COLOUR.

AYL, III.ii.1: 'Hang there, my verse, in witness of my love' – his verse on a tree (Gk *stichos*, *sticho-*: line, verse) and his own verse or stick hang with his testicles as WITNESS (L *testis*) of his love. See ACORN.

LLL, IV.ii.4:

Sir Nathaniel. Very reverend sport . . . done in the testimony of a good conscience.
Holofernes. The deer . . . ripe as the pomewater, who now hangeth like a jewel in the ear . . . .

The sport (sex-play – C; P) is reverend because 'testimony' puns on (1) to bear WITNESS, a testicle; (2) the Mosaic Law (Ex 31:18: 'two tables of testimony, tables of stone'; (a stone is a testicle – *OED*, P). *Con*science: the cunt (P). The deer, a 'pricket', was RIPE (sexually ready) as the pomewater, an APPLE (testicle) that hangeth like a JEWEL (precious *stone*).

MWW, IV.i. After a few lines on Falstaff's visit to seduce Mistress Ford, the scene moves to the Latin lesson of Parson Hugh and a def. of 'lapis' as 'a stone' (testicle; adj., lustful – *OED*) and puns on 'genders', with interruptions from Mistress Quickly and her 'prabbles'. The lesson is a *parable* on fornication: (1) on 'hic, haec, hoc' – puns on *hick* (P) and *hack* (F&H; K), coitus; (2) 'focative is caret' – puns on *fuck* and *carrot*, penis (P); (3) 'Genitive, – horum' and 'Vengeance of Jenny's [*geni*tive] case . . . if she be a whore [*horum*]'; (4) 'accusativo . . . hang, hog' and ' "Hang-hog" is Latin for bacon' – hanging of bacon and of man's testes (his 'quods' or cods, 1.80– K), and of the fornicator himself. The lesson ends appropriately with 'Adieu' or *à dieu*: (1) to God; (2) to Hugh, parson; (3) to DUE (TWO, testes and stones). Thus a scene that began with Falstaff's attempted seduction, and a lesson that began with *lapis* or stone, ends with 'to God'. Leave punishment to God, let him who is without sin cast a *lapis* at Falstaff, adulterer. John 8:7: 'He that is without sin among you, let him first cast a stone at her' – 'For shame' the parson said when Mistress Quickly wanted vengeance on Jenny.

2. To pander, punning on L *pendere* and *pendre* (Cot), to hang.

Ado, III.ii.11: 'the little hangman' is CUPID, arranger of matches, pander.

MM, IV.ii.18: Pompey, 'unlawful bawd' (pander), wants to become a 'lawful hangman' or *pendeur* (Fr).

See SIXPENCE, *MND*; PAINT; FROTH, *MM*.

Hateful Of the anus or ass/arse. Hateful: *haineux*, *-euse* (Cot).

MND, II.i.258. Oberon's plan that Titania be 'full of hateful fantasies [FANTASY, sexual desire]' comes to fruition when she 'straightway [STRAIGHT] lov'd an ass', *Bottom* (III.ii.34).

IV.i.54,68. The 'hateful fool' is Bottom; the 'hateful imperfection of her eyes [EYES, arse]' is her love for him.

H5, V.ii.52. The MEAD (buttocks) conceives and 'nothing teems/But hateful docks'. Nothing TEEMS (gives birth) but/butt hateful docks (obs., buttocks).

2H6, III.ii.93. Margaret challenges Henry's love and remembers how once she prayed the winds would 'blow' her toward England or 'turn our stern upon a dreadful rock'. But 'Aeolus . . . left that hateful office unto thee'. The god of WIND (a flatus – C; P) left the *hateful* duty of the anus (to fart contemptuously) to Henry's 'flinty heart' – his HEART (arse), the flint 'rock' upon which her STERN (arse) is wrecked.

H5, II.i.52: Nym's 'I would have you solus' is answered by Pistol's ' "Solus", egregious dog? . . . The "solus" in thy most mervailous face . . . in thy hateful lungs, yea, in thy maw, perdy,/And, which is worse, within thy nasty mouth!/I do retort the "solus" in thy bowels'. Pistol is furious that Nym, the DOG (sodomite) would have him (carnally – C; P) for solus/solace (pleasure, entertainment; *solacier*, to make merry, recreate oneself – Cot) – all words that mean sexual pleasure (C; P). Having lost Nell to Pistol, Nym seeks solace and would make a SOLE (arse) of him. Enraged, Pistol gives him the solus in four places, all puns on the arse, as the last one makes explicit. First is Nym's mervailous face, one of his freq., usually bawdy, French errors: 'mervailous', meaning *merveilleux*, indicates that FACE is also French, is *fesse* (buttock), is a MOST (*fin*) mervailous face – the one in *la fin* (end, buttocks). Second, there are *two* mouths: the maw, perdy (more minced Fr: *per dieu*) and, what's worse, the nasty mouth, the *trou* (mouth, anus – Cot). In this context, there are prob. also two lungs, the bellows (F&H 1615) and the hateful ones, the bum (Fr syn. *le soufflet*, a pair of bellows – F&H),

another air-passage. Finally, Pistol retorts the solus overtly in Nym's bowels, saying, 'Pistol's cock is up'.

At this Nym says, 'If you grow foul with me, Pistol, I . . . would prick your guts a little' – with a sword, yes, but with a sword or prick up the guts or bowels. He 'will scour [Pistol] with my rapier'. SCOUR: cleanse, purge, empty out the bowels. See PAY and HOME for more on his pricking.

See CHEER, *TA*; MEAD, *H5*.

Head Prepuce (C; P). More freq. the testes or scrotum – pun on *teste* (head – Cot) and *teste* (heads; parts of the brain resembling the stones of man – F).

See DEWLAP, *MND*; BRAINS, *TA*; COLOUR, *RJ*; CROWN, *3H6*; DETESTED, *TA*; SHAME, *AW*; SNATCH, *MM*.

Hearer The young boy (Gk *aïte*) in the pederastic relationship; the lover was the inspirer (Wilkinson, p. 22; Norton, p. 124).

Ado, I.i.309. Don Pedro tells Claudio (293), 'My love is thine to teach: teach it but how,/ And thou shalt see how apt it is to learn/ Any hard lesson that may do thee good.' It is apt (sexually willing or inclined – C; P) to learn any hard (the erect phallus – C; P) lesson that does GOOD (coitus). Realising that Claudio may 'affect' Hero (AFFECTION: desire, esp. ptg to the buttocks), he says, 'Thou wilt be like a lover presently/ And tire the hearer with a book of words.' Whereas in the relationship with Don Pedro, Claudio is the hearer, now that he wishes to woo Hero (the young boy actor) he will become the lover and tire (prey on ravenously, sexually – C; fatigue himself on sexually – P) the hearer, Hero. He will be 'like a lover' – a LIKE (homosexual) lover. This conforms to the Greek pattern of catamite who becomes older and in turn becomes inspirer. See DRUM for another ref. to this change in Claudio's sexual preferences.

Don Pedro then offers to woo and win Hero for Claudio (see HEART).

See HERCULES, *Ado*.

Heart Arse. Bowel: by transf., heart (*OED*). Perh. punning on 'eart/ ART (L *ars*).

MND, III.ii.319:

Hermia. . . . who is't that hinders you?
Helena. A foolish heart, that I leave here behind.

Hinder: BEHIND; and a hart/ hind pun on the male and female deer.

MWW, III.i.111, Host: 'Boys of art . . . your hearts are mighty' – this ART/ 'eart quibble is one in a cluster of arse puns: see CONTRARY.

TSh, IV.ii.10:

Lucentio. I read that I profess, the Art to Love.
Bianca. And may you prove, sir, master of your art!
Lucentio. While you, sweet dear, prove mistress of my heart!

Master of *art*, mistress of *heart*: the DEAR/ deer pun – he, the hart; she, the hind.

LLL, III.i.36: 'learn her by heart' – 'By heart and *in* heart, boy' (italics added).

Ado, I.i.325, Don Pedro: 'I will assume thy part in some disguise . . . And in her bosom I'll unclasp my heart/ And take her hearing prisoner with the force/ And strong encounter of my amorous tale'. This sounds like the old rights of the Seigneur, who took the virginity or 'first fruits' of each new bride. (Plautus, *Casina* 838: 'meus fructus est prior' a gentleman tells his servant, in anticipation of the privilege. See BLISTER: James Shirley writes that women paid this price to be introduced to wealthy lords.)

In a speech filled with sexual images, 'heart' is no sentimental metaphor. Pedro will *ass*ume the younger Claudio's PART (private parts) and in her bosom (sexual part – P) he'll unclasp or open his *heart* (claspings: embraces – C; P). He will take prisoner Hero's hearing (HEARER, q.v.: young pederast); this boy actor's hearing he will take (sexually – C; P) with the *force* and encounter (sex-act – C; P) of his *amorous* tale (penis – C; P), his *heart*'s tale (Jer 4:4: 'Circumcise yourselves to the Lord, and take away the foreskins of your heart'). The CONCLUSION (coitus – TWR) is she shall be Claudio's: 'In practice let us put it' – he will *practise* putting (16th c., introducing male to female for breeding; putour: fornicator – TWR, *OED*; putery, putage: whoring). See GRIEF for the unfortunate advice Hero received from her father about this wooing.

III.iv.25:

Hero. God give me joy to wear it! for my heart is exceeding heavy.
Margaret. 'Twill be heavier soon by the weight of a man.

Hero certainly does not sound joyful, anticipating the wear (coital – P) of her wedding GOWN (cunt – K; P); it and her heavy heart, EXCEEDINGLY (full of seed) heavy, will soon be heavier by the weight of a man. Is it already heavy ('great with young' – *OED*) for this very reason? See TWELVE for more on this hypothesis.

See KEEN, *MND*; TIGER, *3H6*.

Heavenly Homosexual love, as distinguished from common or heterosexual love; a distinction Plato makes between the 'common' and the 'heavenly' Aphrodite: 'Common love is inferior because it is directed at women as much as youths . . . heavenly love is exclusively male'. This speech, says Wilkinson (p. 26), 'was probably intended to represent the justification for pedersty'. Urania (lit. the heavenly one): muse of astronomy. Uranism (Gk *ouranios*, 'Heavenly, taken to mean "spiritual" '): homosexuality (*OED* 1899).

VA, 793: 'Call it not love, for Love to heaven is fled,/ Since sweating Lust on earth usurp'd his name'.

AYL. Orlando daily makes mock (?) love to Rosalind, who is dressed as a boy and is called GANYMEDE (lit. catamite). Ganymede is his 'heavenly Rosalind' (I.ii.301). He writes, 'Heaven Nature charged/ That one body should be fill'd/ With all graces [GRACE: vagina, penis] wide-enlarged. . . . Thus Rosalind of many parts [PARTS: genitals]/ By heavenly synod was devised' (III.ii.149).

WT, I.i. This scene is mainly devoted to the 'affection' (AFFECTION, sexual desire) between the two kings; the interchange of 'gifts, letters, loving embassies; that they have seemed to be together, though absent . . . embraced, as it were, from the ends of opposed winds. The heavens continue their loves!' See SPIRIT for their answering 'heaven' (I.2). Cf. Fiedler, p. 151: 'In *The Winter's Tale* . . . (as I. A. M. Stewart has convincingly argued), Leontes is clearly, almost clinically, portrayed as the victim of unacknowledged homosexual desires directed toward his old friend Polixenes. These impulses he disguises as nostalgia for the "innocence" of their childhood' (see discussion under SPIRIT).

See FANTASY and ANCIENT, *Oth*; PHYSICIAN, *H8*; LIFE, *MV*; PERFECTION, *TGV*, *R3*; ROUND, *TSh*.

Heavy Pregnant, 'great with young' (*OED*).

R3, I.iii.231: 'Thou slander of thy mother's heavy womb!'

See TWELVE, *Ado*; HEART, *Ado*.

Hedgehog, hedge-pig Symbol of sexual bestiality. Hedge: despicable, mean (F&H; *OED*). Hog: 'A swine reared for slaughter; *spec.* a castrated male swine' (*OED*); 'A gelded pig' (*CD*). The hog and hedgehog (*herisson* – Cot) are bristly (*MND*, II.ii.10: 'thorny hedgehogs'). There may be a pun on *herissé* (horrid, standing up like bristles – Cot) and *heresy*: 'buggery' meant both 'abominable heresy' and 'sodomy' (*OED*).

R3, I.ii.102. The scene opens with a *hearse* proceeding to *Chertsey* (quibbles on heresy?). Anne attacks Richard's 'butcheries' (BUTCHER, bugger), calls him 'hedgehog' and puns on 'grant' and the grunt of a hog (Richard, the 'boar': see SWINE), a sound the 17th c. linked to bestial lust: 'each whore relieves her tingling cunt/ As hogs on goats do rub themselves and grunt' (Wilmot, 'The Imperfect Enjoyment', in *Signet Classic Poets of the 17th c.*, p. 383). *Subire*: 'to grunt as the sow doth for the bore [boar] to doe his kinde to long or lust for most beastly' (F).

Gloucester. I grant ye.
Anne. Dost grant me, hedgehog? then, God grant me too. . . .

Hedgehog or urchin (one deformed in body) fits the sexually deformed Richard (SHAPE; CROOKED). A hogback rises sharply in the middle (cf. RIDGEL, male with one testicle, the other being up in his ridge or spine). Fiedler, p. 49, speaks of the 'confrontation of male and female as "hog" and "hag" – for so Shakespeare calls' Richard and Margaret. See WITCH–HAG, *R3* (a sexual deviant).

Mac, IV.i.2, 2nd Witch: 'Thrice and once the hedge-pig whined.' She puns on (1) whine, a 'mean' (*OED*), 'unmanly' (*W*) complaint; and (2) whin, gorse ('pricking goss' – *Tem*, IV.i.180), a prickly shrub, like a prickly hedge-pig. The same witch then introduces Macbeth's entry with 'By the pricking of my thumbs,/ Something wicked this way comes.' This hermaphroditic WITCH, with her beard and her *prick*ing thumb, is in empathy with wicked Macbeth, whose anticipation of murder (I.iii.135) 'doth unfix my hair' – made it stand on end, *herissé*, like the hedgehog's; whose murder of a king was (political) heresy.

'Wicked' is L *nefandus*, *nefarius*: abominable, *not to be spoken of.* Macbeth asks these masculine women 'What is't you do?' and is told 'A deed without a name', standard epithet for sodomy (NAMELESS). Sh freq. uses BUGGERY as a metaphor for heresy. The witches' nameless deed prepares for Macbeth's deed, twice called UNNATURAL (deviating sexually): ' 'Tis unnatural,/ Even like the deed that's done' (II.iv.10); 'unnatural deeds [deed: coitus – P]/ Do breed unnatural troubles' (V.i.80). Macbeth, like Richard (above) is a butcher–bugger: 'this dead butcher and his fiend-like queen' (viii.69), who had called on 'murdering ministers' to 'unsex' her (I.v), who became witch or fiend-LIKE (Gk *homoios*, *homo-*), who suffered 'unnatural troubles' and who did unfix Macbeth's 'hair' and, more important, his *heir* (see COMPUNCTIOUS).

See BITE, *Tem*; PINCH, *Tem*.

Heinous Anus/'einous. The 'h' is often dropped in puns (Arden/harden, art/heart – K). *Haines, l'eine*: groin (Cot). Nashe, *Pierce Penilesse*: a Frenchman thinks it a favour to converse while 'sitting on his close stool'. He honoured some Englishmen, who accompanied him 'to the privy dore, set down the trash [paper]' and left, 'which he . . . took very hainously.'

R2, IV.i.131: 'plume-pluck'd Richard . . . his high sceptre yields'. Richard is impotent: his PLUME (penis) is plucked; his *high* SCEPTRE (penis) YIELDS (is gelded). Bolingbroke will 'Ascend his throne', 'ascend the regal throne' – *regal* throne of the RIGEL, lit. gelding. 'God forbid! . . who *sits* here that is not Richard's subject? . . . That in a Christian climate *souls refined* / Should show so *heinous*, *black*, obscene a deed!' (italics added). Emphasis on (1) *ascend*, the *ass-end*, (2) *soul*/ SOLE (bottom, buttocks) and (3) re*fine*d (FINE, end, buttocks) conveys how obscene a deed (a screwing – C; P) it was: the buggering of Richard, not permitted in Christian climate (cf. TURK, *Oth*).

V.iii.34:

Bolingbroke. . . . this fault
. . . how heinous e'er it be
To win thy after-love I pardon thee.
Aumerle. Then give me leave that I may turn the key,
That no man enter till my tale be done.
Bolingbroke. Have thy desire.

Aumerle *begs pardon* (ii.113) on his *knees* (see HOMAGE, *2H6*: buggery). His FAULT was a breach of loyalty: pun on *breech*, i.e. buttocks. Bolingbroke, political broker and bugger of men, will win his after- (behind) LOVE. He lets Aumerle turn the key (*chiavare*, lock with a key; also fuck – F) till his tale (arse – C; P), be done (fucked – P). Aumerle shall *have* his *desire*.

v.iii.59. York (GROAN) vows to 'appeach'/*a* PEACH (arse, bugger) Aumerle and bursts in, calling him TRAITOR (whore). Bolingbroke: 'O heinous, strong and bold conspiracy!'

TA, IV.i.80. Lavinia's double rape, a 'heinous, bloody deed' done by 'stern [STERN, buttocks] . . . hands [HANDS, penises]' (II.iv.16) was probably sodomy (METAMORPHOSED).

1H4, III.iii.213. Hal 'procured' (like a bawd – *OED*) Falstaff 'a charge of foot'. Falstaff: 'I would it had been of horse. Where shall I find one that can steal well? O for a fine thief of the age of two and twenty or thereabout! I am heinously unprovided.' Fastaff wants a HORSE/arse, whore that can STEAL/stale (K): 'stale' is horse urine and a whore; and Falstaff wants to find a FINE (lit. end; arse) *young* thief to PROVIDE (give sexual satisfaction) for his hind end. God be thanked for these rebels who 'offend none but the virtuous' (OFFENCES are of the rear end). 'Where shall I find one' is deliberately ambiguous in its reference (1) back to the horse/arse and (2) ahead to the thief – assumed to be a female by K, pp. 60, 150, through a pun on theave/thief. He–she is to be of TWO and TWENTY, a SCORE (in coitus), or thereabout (ABOUT/a butt) – Falstaff's redefinition of Hal's charge (sexual assault – P) of FOOT (coitus – P)!

The scene concludes: 'Rare words! brave world! Hostess, my breakfast, come!/O, I could wish this tavern were my drum!' DRUM (buttocks) was perhaps accompanied by a gesture indicating he wished the hostess's tavern/taborin (a drum that gets beaten with *one drumstick*) were the only drum he had to follow – not a military one. The whole scene has played on RARE/rear words, and fittingly ends with one.

Hem The cough made by or to whores. Dekker and Middleton, *The Honest Whore I*, IV.iii: 'not so much as a Bee, he did not hum; not so much as a bawd he did not hem; not so much as a Cuckold he did not ha'; Dekker, *The Honest Whore II*, IV.i: no whore can 'scape the hem' of passing men.

Oth, IV.ii.29: 'Leave procreants alone and shut the door;/Cough or cry "hem", if any body come'.

2H4, II.iv.33:

Hostess. . . . How do you now?
Doll. Better than I was: hem! [Her cough is better]
Hostess. Why, that's well said

– said like a WELL (a whore). A pun on the recovery of the whore, Doll *Tear-sheet* – well and mended, hemmed.

Hence Whore, bawd. 'Hence' was spelt 'hens' (Tyndale Bible, Luke 4). Hen(ne): hence (*OED*). Hen: a bed partner (P). *Uccellessa*: hen bird, 'cunnie-catching woman' (F).

Ado, IV.i.156. Leonato says the sea could not wash clean Hero's 'foul-tainted flesh!' He trusts Claudio, who 'speaking of her foulness,/Wash'd it with tears. . . . Hence from her! let her die.' A pun on foul/fowl makes the hence/hens pun clear. She is a hen, a strumpet: let her die.

To fowl, go birding or go wenching is *uccellare* (F); 'foul' means lewd and obscene (P); and ME 'foul', 'fowle' means tread, the treading or copulation of birds. 'Flesh' is the body of a prostitute (P); the flesh of his daughter, the hen, is foul with the 'foul disease' (syphilis–*OED*). Therefore the sea can not wash her flesh clean – i.e. free from defilement (Lev 12:8) and free from disease (1611). (See OLD LADY, *MWW* for a foul/fowl pun.)

CE, IV.iii.44. Antipholus S., repelled by the too free behaviour of the inhabitants of EPHESUS, hopes to leave: 'Some blessed power deliver us from hence!' – from here and from hens or whores. '*Enter a Courtezan*' is the immediately following stage direction, and he refuses the invitation from this 'light wench'.

H5, IV.v.13. Whereas Henry says French resistance means English soldiers, with 'foul' hand, will 'Defile . . . your shrill-shrieking daughters' (III.iii.34), Bourbon says he who does not resist is a pander in his country's ruin: let such a one 'go hence, and with his cap in hand, / Like a base pandar, hold the chamber-door / Whilst . . . His fairest daughter is contaminated'. Let this member of the hold-door trade (a pimp – C; P) go 'hence' and his own be the *foul* hand responsible for the *cont*amination of his daughter (her cunt).

See BARBAROUS, *H5*.

Hercules Hercules's bisexuality is a feature of Greek and Eliz. lit. In ancient Doric society, homosexual 'practices were especially attributed to their favourite god Apollo, and their favourite hero, Heracles' (Wilkinson, p. 21). RARE(LY), *MND*: Bottom wants to play Hercules and recites doggerel about Apollo. Marlowe, *Edward II*, I,iv: 'Hercules for Hylas wept; / And for Patroclus stern Achilles drooped'. In Greek and Latin comedy, he is a stock character, a fool and glutton. Plautus, *Curculio*, 345–73: a gluttonous parasite says, 'I . . . invoke my fostering nurse Hercules'.

Ado, II.i.260. Beatrice, 'infernal Ate' (cf. the Gk *aïte* or pederastic boy, the HEARER, q.v.), 'would have made Hercules have turned spit . . . and have cleft his club to make the fire too'. Aggressive Beatrice would (1) have made effeminate Hercules, who wore Omphales' clothes and did woman's work, turn (in coitus – P; in sexual betrayal – C) his SPIT, penis; and (2) have cleft (between the buttocks – TWR, s.v. Clifte) his club to make a fire, her 'infernal' fire, in her Hell (vulva – P; F&H). Don Pedro interrupts Benedick: 'here she comes' (the *hear*er), with 'her terminations [ends]' (256), *her cules* (rumps).

AC, I.iii.84. Antony believed he was descended from Hercules, loved and imitated his carriage and attire (Plutarch): ' 'Tis the god Hercules, whom Antony loved, / Now leaves him' (IV.iii.16). When Cleopatra calls Antony a 'Herculean Roman' she is not praising but taunting him, questioning the quality of his love. When (82) he swore 'Now, by my sword, – ', she added, 'And target', substituting for the masculine sword (penis – P) the feminine target or buckler. Cf. *Ado*, V.ii.17: Benedick boasts of a *manly* wit, conceding Margaret 'the bucklers', to which she retorts, 'Give us the swords; we have bucklers of our own.'

MV, III.ii.60. Apropos of a homosexual attachment between Bassanio and Antonio, we note Portia, to Bassanio: 'Go, Hercules!' In his answer he says many wear 'The beards of Hercules' and yet are 'cowards' (COWARD, effeminate).

Hide Human skin, a whore. See LEATHER.

Hiss 1. A flatus, expression of mockery or disapproval. Lit. sibilance of escaping air.

RJ, I.i.119. Accused earlier by Tybalt of having 'drawn among these heartless hinds' (the hinds, their behinds, and themselves as arses), Benvolio now retorts that Tybalt's sword 'cut the winds, / Who nothing hurt withal hiss'd him in scorn'. WIND (as from hinds), common pun on a flatus, *hiss'd* Tybalt in SCORN / SCORE (a cut). A CUT is an insult; a gelding: they mocked his impotent sword (penis – P).

2. A diseased, specif. a venereal, wheeze or hiss.

TrC, V.x.55: 'my fear is this, / Some galled goose of Winchester would hiss: / Till then I'll sweat and seek about for eases, / And at that time bequeath you my diseases'. The spirant sound of geese, like the hiss of disapproval from a Winchester goose (diseased whore – *OED*; P) in the audience. Pandarus will sweat in fearful anticipation of the hiss, and in sweating-tubs where one seeks for eases to cure venereal diseases.

KL, III.vi.17, Lear: 'have a thousand with red *burn*ing *spits* / Come hissing in upon 'em' and 'It shall be done; I will ar*raign* them'. This is punishment for his daughters – with whom nature had 'join'd [JOIN, copulate]. . . . O! 'tis foul!' (ii.22). Let a burning (venereally diseased – *OED*; P) SPIT (penis; copulate) hiss*in* upon them. It echoes what he invoked in ii.14. '*Spit*, *fire*! spout, *rain*!' (italics added). And it anticipates IV.iii.48, when Kent says a 'burning shame / Detains him from Cordelia'. Not only Lear's sense of shame but also his burning, diseased SHAME (genitals) makes him unwilling or unable to see her. As early as I.i.167 Kent had spoken of Lear's 'foul disease' (epilepsy, syphilis – *OED*), symbol of his moral sickness (see IDLE and LAME).

MWW, III.v.124. Falstaff was thrown into the Thames 'hissing hot [amorous – P]'; and diseased, like a 'horse-shoe' (HORSE/whore's shoe). Whores' shoes are diseased cunts (see Introduction, p. xii, *JC*).

Hoard Whored. See SQUIRREL, *MND*; WORM, *R3*.

Homage A sexual relationship; often homosexual. Feudal law: public ceremony by which a man acknowledges he is the man or vassal of a lord and exchanges services for protection. An obeisance, as in Heywood, 'Love's Mistress': 'Jove sometimes bends and Neptune bows,/ Mars homageth, and Phoebus will submit.'

CE, II.i.104, Adriana: 'I know his eye doth homage otherwhere . . . Since that my beauty cannot please his eye' – her 'I' and his EYE (vulva and penis) and the sexual homage her husband pays elsewhere since she cannot please (sexually satisfy – P) him with her beauty (body/beauty – K; as in *1H4*, I.ii.27).

III.ii.43. Homage is clearly sexual payment when Antipholus S. (mistaken for his twin, her husband) says, 'Nor to her bed no homage do I owe'. 'I owe': EYE and O, the pudenda.

2H6, III.ii.224. But for the King's presence, Warwick would 'on thy knee/Make thee beg pardon . . . And after all this fearful homage done,/Give thee thy hire and send thy soul to hell,/Pernicious blood-sucker of sleeping men!' He attacks Suffolk's bisexuality (CUP). 'On thy knee' and 'beg' are the obeisance of homage and the (sexual) position of the BEGGAR/bugger. Warwick would give him his hire as he would fee a whore, and send his SOUL (buttocks) to hell, where PERNICIOUS (sexually depraved) sodomites or penilingists, BLOOD- (semen) suckers of SLEEPING men (impotents, effeminates) go.

See INCH, *Tem*; BUDGER, *TSh*; PEASANT, *TSh*; PERFECTION, *TGV*.

Home Vulva; an orgasm. Etherege, *The Man of Mode*, I.i: the shoemaker's shoe fits 'as smooth as your mistress's skin does upon her; so, strike your foot in home'. Strike and FOOT: copulate (P). Middleton, *A Chaste Maid in Cheapside*, v.i: 'I have struck it home i' faith', says the man whose wife became pregnant.

TA, II,i.118. Aaron instigates the rape of Lavinia: 'single you thither then this dainty doe,/And strike her home by force, if not by words'. He is addressing Chiron, ironically named after a centaur known for wisdom and skill in hunting.

H5, II.i.103, Pistol: 'As manhood shall compound [fornicate – P]: push [PUSH] home.' A pushing-school was a fencing-school and a brothel (F&H). This overlap of sword-play and fornication is what the Hostess meant in saying 'we shall see wilful adultery and murder committed'.

See RECOVER, *CE*; OIL, *AW*; ANGRY, *Oth*.

Homo A man (L *homo*), but also a homosexual (Gk *homos*, *homo-*, the same). Fielding, *Tom Jones*, Bk VII, ch. 12, speaking of Homer: 'D—n *Homo* with all my heart', says Northerton, 'I have the marks of him in my a— yet.' *Double entendre* on carrying the '*Homo* in his pocket'. Dekker and Middleton, *The Honest Whore I*, I.v: 'is't possible that homo/Should be nor man, nor woman: not once moved' – said of a 'patient' man, who 'has not all the things belonging to a man'. A line in Lily's *Latin Grammar* ('*Homo* is a common name to all men') inspired many 16th and 17th c. jests (McKerrow, in Nashe, *Works*, vol. IV, p. 114); for example, 'The first (Meretrices) like *Homo*, common to all men' – a pun on 'common': (1) of a whore or meretrice (*OED*; P); (2) of gender, 'indeterminately either masculine or feminine' (*W*). See BITE, *1H4*.

LLL, v.i.9. After fanfare on how the 'knight' (I.i.179) Don Armado is to be 'intituled, nominated, or called', he is called 'hominem' (from L *homo*), pun on 'homonym', one name with different meanings, homonymous, ambiguous, equivocal – like his sexuality. He is 'picked . . . spruce . . . odd' (14; cf. the 'picked effeminate Carpet Knight under the fictionate person of Hermaphroditus' – Nashe, *Strange News*). He is further mocked: 'This is abhominable, –

which he would call abbominable'! Ab*homin*able (ABOMINABLE, sodomitical) plus 'strange without heresy' (6) indicates that in this satire the focus is on buggery ('a. Abominable heresy. b. Sodomy' – *OED*).

See MAN; LIKE; SAME.

Honey (1) Sexual bliss (F&H; P). Honey and honey-pot: semen and female pudendum (F&H). Durfey, *Wit and Mirth*, iii.342: 'when you have possession got,/ Of Venus' Mark, or Honey-pot'. Daedelus built a golden honeycomb for the Temple of Aphrodite.

(2) Loss of honey, impotence. Fr *chatrer*: to take honey away from the beehive; castrate. Geld: cut out the old comb from a bee-hive; castrate.

Ham, III.iv.93: 'honeying and making love/ Over the na*sty sty*' (italics added).

JC, v.i.35:

Brutus. Words before blows: is it so, countrymen? . . .
Cassius. Antony,
The posture of your blows are yet unknown;
But for your words, they rob the Hybla bees,
And leave them honeyless.
Antony. Not stingless too.
Cassius. O, yes, and soundless too. . .

'Countrymen' (country: cunt – P; coitus – K) evokes Antony's address to the Romans (III.ii) when, with his honeyed words, he showed his 'sweet friends' the citizens, 'sweet Caesar's wounds, poor dumb mouths'. At that time he cut out the old comb, castrated the hive of the conspiracy, leaving them powerless: stingless, without STING (prick or penis), and soundless, unable to SOUND (probe the bottom), soundless TOO/ two (testes). But this time they challenge him not with words but with blows (coital thrusts – C; P); and it remains to be seen what his posture is – how upright or erect he will be, how potent, in this battle.

See NOTE, *TrC*; OIL, *AW*.

Hood Prepuce. Rabelais, Bk IV, Prol.: 'Priapus doffed his hood, discovering a red flaming face' (Le Clercq); 'Priapus, standing up and taking off his Cowle, his Snout uncas'd and rear'd up, fiery and stifly propt' (1694 trs.).

MV, II.vi.51, Gratiano: 'Now, by my hood, a Gentile and no Jew.' This is generally glossed as an oath of no precise meaning. I suggest it is his 'hood', his Gentile uncircumcised penis, in contradistinction to the circumcised prepuce of the Jew, that forms the basis of the oath.

See CACKLE, *MV*.

Horrid *Whore-d.*

Ham, II.ii.589. An actor with his 'motive' would 'cleave the general ear with horrid speech'. Yet Hamlet 'Must, like a whore, unpack my heart with words,/ And fall a-cursing, like a very drab,/ A scullion!' Ironically, he succeeds in making his own speech horrid and whore-d: like a whore he does UNPACK (a whore) his heart with WORDS (whores) and curses like a drab or strumpet, a SCULLION.

III.iii.88. For killing Claudius, Hamlet waits for 'a more horrid hent:/ When he is drunk asleep, or in his rage,/ Or in the incestuous pleasure of his bed' – in rage (sexual activity – TWR; filled with lust – P) or in the incestuous pleasure (sexual – P) with the woman he 'whored' (v.ii.64), in a horrid hent or act of seizing, catching, i.e. in the sexual position.

See CROUCH, *Tim.*

Horse 1. Whores. Cf. hoarse/horse/whores (K). In Dekker, *The Honest Whore II*, Mrs Horseleech/*whores' leech* is 'a Bawde'; IV.iii: 'So this is for the bawd, the rogue, the whore' – 'An excellent team of horse!'

TrC, v.vi.7. Troilus tells Diomedes, who took from him first his mistress Cressida and then his horse, 'O traitor Diomed! turn thy false face, thou traitor,/ And pay the life thou owest me for my horse!' Cressida's betrayal, his loss of her, upsets him more than the loss of his horse, and it is she he refers to when he quibbles on Diomed, horse-trader and TRAITOR or whoremonger.

TSh, I.ii.81: 'marry him to . . . an old trot with ne'er a tooth in her head, though she have as many diseases as two and fifty horses'. Trot is a horse's pace, but also a whore or bawd (F&H; P); and the one he marries will have a whore's diseases. Cf. running horse: the clap (G); running nag: the penis (F&H).

AC, I.v.22. When Antony leaves for Rome, Cleopatra says, 'O happy horse, to bear the weight of Antony!' She is thinking of her own pleasure when bearing his weight (freq. metaphor for coitus, as in *Ado*, III.iv.26). But Sh is thinking of those political whores Antony is joining back in Rome – Caesar and others – and the previous scene, in which Caesar had said that while Antony takes 'a tumble on the bed of Ptolemy . . . *we do bear / So great a weight* in his lightness' (italics added).

KL, I.iv.359. An ambiguous antecedent for 'her' damns Lear's daughters, both of whom illicitly desire Edmund. Goneril: 'have you writ that letter to my sister?'; 'Take you some company and away to horse:/ Inform her full of my particular fear'.

'Her' (for which the last noun reference is 'horse') is her SISTER, of whom she has a PARTICULAR (a whore's) fear. AWAY/*a way* (a whore – P) to horse – *two whores*!

2. Buttocks. Horse/'orse/arse.

TN, II.iii.181: 'My purpose is, indeed, a horse of that colour' – 'And your horse now would make him an ass.' Maria's PURPOSE (end or butt) is a horse of that COLOUR/ Fr *culier* (of the arse) – to make an ass/ arse of Malvolio.

Ado, III.v.40, Dogberry: 'an two men ride of a horse, one must ride behind. An honest soul . . . by my troth he is. . . . But God is to be worshipped; all men are not alike'. 'By my troth' is a fitting oath for this exchange, for TROTH puns on *trot* like a horse and like a whore or bawd (C; P). If two men ride of a horse, one must ride BEHIND – on the arse (*dos d'asne*: back of an ass; ridgel-backed, i.e. high in the centre – Cot). Leonato agrees that Verges/ verge (a penis – *OED*) 'comes too short of you', short of the two testicles or GIFTS (genitals) God gives (see SHORT, *AC*). He is a ridgel, with imperfectly developed genitals, the undescended testicle(s) being, it was believed in the back, the ridge (see RIDGEL; CROOKED, *3H6*). Short-changed by God, Verges, honest SOUL/ SOLE or arse, is a eunuch or gelding. The *cheval qui porte derriere* (lit. horse who carries on his backside, the image we started with) is a double gelding or horse that will carry double (Cot). Since 'ride' is such a freq. analogue for copulate (F&H; P), this whole conversation would seem to have *double entendres*.

See HEINOUS, *1H4*; BEHIND, *Ado*.

Hose Penis. Lit. a flexible tube or pipe for conveying liquids. *Vagine*: a sheath, 'the hose, or cod of corne' (Cot).

TVG, II.vii.55. The 'round hose' is 'not worth a pin [PIN: erect penis – F&H; C]/ Unless you have a codpiece'. Sh makes many puns on 'doublet and hose' and 'hose and doublets' in which DOUBLET is the testicles.

LLL, IV.iii.58: 'wanton Cupid's hose;/ Disfigure not his shop' – the organ of generation and codpiece (as glossed in the Arden edn, 1966, which follows the First Folio).

Hour(ly) A whore (K; cf. *CE*, IV.ii.53; *MWW*, II.ii.38). Horel: a fornicator; horal: 1600s, hourly.

AYL, II.vii.26. A fool 'drew a dial from his poke' and looking at it said, 'And so, from hour to hour, we ripe and ripe,/ And then, from hour to hour, we rot and rot;/ And thereby hangs a tale' – the general decay of man from hour to hour, and the rot or disease as man goes from whore to whore on the RIPE or the Bankside, home of the stews. Perh. a pun on the common inscription on old church dials and clocks: *Vulnerant omnes, ultima necat* – 'All [hours] wound, the last [one] kills.' The *tale* that hangs could be a diseased, impotent penis (C). See SAKE, *Oth*, for a similar tale or penis (C; P).

KJ, III.i.56: 'Fortune, O . . . She adulterates hourly with thine uncle John. . . . That strumpet Fortune, that usurping John!' The strumpet adulterates (commits adultery) hourly or horal, like the horel or fornicator she is.

Ham, III.ii.135:

Hamlet. . . . look you, how cheerfully my mother looks, and my father died within these two hours.
Ophelia. Nay, 'tis twice two months, my lord.

His father died within these two hours or between (the actions of) these two whores, his mother and his uncle ('He that hath kill'd my king and whored my mother' – V.ii.64). Hamlet's inaccuracy reflects not only his perception of his mother's too-speedy re-entry into marriage, as usually annotated, but also his perception of the nature of the marriage, his feeling she and the King are two adulterous whores, who, between them, killed the former king. See TWO HOURS.

AW, IV.iii.35. His friends do not expect Bertram 'till after midnight; for he is dieted to his hour'. He will be with his whore, the young lady he 'perverted' till after MIDNIGHT (hour of phallic erection). He 'fleshes his will [sexual ingression – P] in the spoil of her honour'. 'Spoil' quibbles on *flesh*, spoiled, and the diet (cure for VD: see RHEUM). For his being venereally infected, see RING; VELVET.

See FACT, *2H6*; TOMBOY, *Cym*.

House(wife) (1) Codpiece, appendage to breeches or hose, 'often conspicuous' (*OED*). Dekker and Webster, *Northward Hoe*, IV.i: 'This goat's pizzle of thine' – 'I have no such implements in my house' (pizzle: penis; scourge made of a bull's pizzle – F&H). *Housé*: wearing hose (Cot).

(2) Penis, like HOSE. 'Codpiece' was cant for male genitals.

(3) Brothel. See GRAZE, *RJ*; GROOM, *Per*; RESORT, *MM*; OLD, *MM*.

(4) Huswife/housewife: hussy (K). *Putain*: light huswife, whore (Cot).

Oth, IV.i.95: 'A housewife that by selling her desires/ Buys herself bread'.

MWW, I.i.74. Evans puts forth Slender as candidate for marriage to Anne *and* her 'moneys', thus becoming another of the amateur bawds to visit the Page house:

Evans. . . . What hoa! Got pless your house here!
Page. Who's there!

Hoa, *house who's* – *house here*, *who's there*: wild punning on 'house' and 'hose'. Cf. Jonson, *Every Man in his Humour*, IV.viii: a woman seeks her husband's whore crying, '*Ho*! *who* keeps *house* here?' (italics added).

See ALL, *R3*; IDLE, *Cor*; CLOSE, *H5*; TRUNK, *Tim*.

Hungary, Hungarian Impotent; castrated. *Hongre*: a Hungarian; a gelded man or eunuch (Cot).

MWW, I.iii.23, Pistol: 'O base Hungarian wight! wilt thou the spigot wield?' How can 'withered [WITHERED, impotent]' (19) Bardolph be a TAPSTER (pimp – 17); how can a dry Hungarian wield a spigot, i.e. the cock of a cask, when he cannot wield his own spigot (F&H) or cock (P), his penis? The sounds in *wilt–wield* suggest the subject under discussion, Bardolph's wilted will or penis (P). He is *wit*hered, a 'wight', a whit (by-form of 'wight'), the smallest possible thing – like his WIT, penis.

MM, I.ii.5: 'Heaven grant us its peace, but not the King of Hungary's!' Any PEACE/PIECE (penis) but an impotent, castrated one. This fear continues in the use of 'scraped', 'razed' and the 'pair of shears between us'.

I

Idle Sexually wanton. 'Idleness begets Lust': 16th c. proverb – M. P. Tilley, *A Dictionary of the Proverbs in England in the Sixteenth and Seventeenth Centuries* (Ann Arbor: Univ. of Michigan, 1950). Henry VIII, 'Pastime with Good Company': 'idleness is Chief mistress/ Of vices all'.

H5, V.ii.51. In the 'best garden [GARDEN, pudendum], of the world,/ Our fertile France', the mead 'rank,/ Conceives by idleness'. The rank (in sexual heat – P) MEAD (buttocks) conceives *by* idleness, bringing forth 'docks, rough thistles, kecksies, burs' – like that garden where there was sin and, as punishment, God told Adam, 'Thorns also and thistles shall it bring forth to thee' (Gen 3:18).

Cor, I.iii.76. *Petegolare*: to play the 'idle slut' or strumpet, the *petegola*, 'idle huswife' or trull (F). Valeria coaxes Virgilia to 'play the idle huswife with me this afternoon'. Virgilia responds to the *double entendres* in idle and HOUSEWIFE (whore) and says she will 'not out of doors' – repeated verbatim by Valeria. She will 'not over the threshold till my lord return from the wars'. Two uses of 'not'/ KNOT (intertwine coitally) stress her maintenance of chastity and refusal to OUT (Fr *hors*) of doors and to OVER (O'ER/ whore) her THRESHOLD (point of entry for copulation). It is ironic ('you confine yourself most unreasonably', says Valeria) that she awaits her husband's return from the WARS/ whores.

KL, I.iii.16. Goneril complains that Lear 'flashes into one gross crime or other', his knights grow 'riotous' (dissolute, wenching – P); and when he 'returns from hunting' (venery: hunting and sexual pursuits), she will not speak with him: 'Idle old man,/ That still would manage those authorities/ That he hath given away!' Lear, out hunting and wanting to manage his affairs, could not be called indolent; his idleness is his indulgence in gross (lewd – *OED*; P) crimes, the sexual wantonness of himself (HISS) and his riotous knights.

Ignorant Lewd: obs., ignorant, implying reproach. Lewed: ignorant, lascivious (TWR).

LLL, IV.ii.52. Holofernes composes an epitaph on the death of a deer: 'to humour the ignorant, call I the deer . . . a pricket'. Beginning 'The preyful princess pierced and prick'd a pretty pleasing pricket', it doubtless humoured the lewd.

Oth, IV.ii.70. Desdemona, accused of adultery, asks, 'Alas, what ignorant sin have I committed [COMMIT, copulate adulterously]?' – an unfortunate choice of words answered by Othello's calling her 'whore'.

Ill Effeminate; sexually bestial. *Male*: ill, sickness; evil (F). L *male mas*: an ill or bad man; fig., effeminate, unmanly.

TN, I.v.162. Viola–Cesario, girl–boy, would speak with Olivia:

Olivia. What kind o' man is he?
Malvolio. Why, of mankind.
Olivia. What manner of man?
Malvolio. Of very ill manner. . . .

The question as to what KIND (gender, sex) o' man he is contains its own answer: ' 'oman' means a woman in *MWW*, IV.i.58. He is a MAN (L *homo*) of ill MANNER (coitally).

RJ, III.iii.113, Friar: 'Art thou a man? thy form cries out thou art:/ Thy tears are womanish;

thy wild acts denote . . . a beast: / Unseemly woman in a seeming man! / Or ill-beseeming beast in seeming both!' A perfect picture of the man–woman, the ill-beseeming BEAST – Romeo acting like an unseemly woman, seeming man, and beseeming beast; the hermaphroditic (bisexual) combination.

KL, II.ii.63. Kent tells the effeminate Oswald 'nature [NATURE, generative organs] disclaims in thee'; a tailor made him – only clothes (codpiece) make him a man: 'a stone-cutter . . . could not have made him so ill, though he had been but two hours at the trade'. Even a cutter (castrater) of stones (testicles, emphasised by TWO) could make so ill or unmanly a man.

See ANGEL, *2H4*.

Impudent Of a woman, mannish. From L *im-pudens*, without shame; pun on without *puden(t)s*, pudendum. Middleton and Dekker, *The Roaring Girl*, V.i: told his son married a woman who wears man's apparel and is 'As good a man as your son', the father responds, 'O monstrous impudence!' MONSTER: 1607, a hermaphrodite.

TrC, III.iii.217: 'A woman impudent and mannish grown / Is not more loathed than an effeminate man / In time of action.' Not just war, but action (the sex-act – C; P).

See PUDENCY; SHAME, *AW*; NAPLES, *3H6*.

Inch 1. The penis, relative to its length. Montaigne, Bk III, ch. 5: the Queen of Naples hanged her husband because 'neither his members nor his endeavours' met her hopes; 'I hate to see one for an inch of wretched vigor, which enflames him but thrice a week, take-on and swagger.' Jonson, *Bartholomew Fair*, I.i: old women need to be visited as a 'tomb, with a torch . . . flaming hot . . . so thou mayst help to make 'em feel thee, and after, come to inherit according to thy inches'.

AC, I.ii.59, Charmian: 'if you were but an inch of fortune better than I, where would you choose it?' Iras replies, 'Not in my husband's nose.'

TSh, IV.i.29:

Curtis. Away, you three-inch fool! I am no beast.
Grumio. Am I but three inches? why, thy horn is a foot . . . .

Grumio may call himself a 'little pot' but he resents Curtis's mentioning his size, esp. the size of his penis; so he retaliates (1) that Curtis's horn (C; P) is only one third of a yard (penis – *OED*; see FOOT, *LLL*, for the same jest); (2) that it is his horn of cuckoldry, that is the long one.

Tem, II.i.283, Antonio: 'this obedient steel, three inches of it, / Can lay [the King of Naples] to bed for ever'. Three inches of STEEL, his sword and penis. According to Prospero (I.ii.111), Antonio 'So dry [DRY, impotent, sodomitical] he was for sway', for ducal power, that he 'confederates . . . wi' the King of Naples / To give him annual tribute, do him homage . . . bend . . . To most ignoble stooping'. He paid the ANNUAL/anal price of HOMAGE (homosexual submission): he STOOPED for buggery. Now he can *lay* the King *to bed* forever (kill him with three inches of sword, instead of regularly laying him with three inches of penis). Sebastian suggests, 'Draw thy sword [expose the phallus – C; P]. One stroke [strike: coitus – C; P] / Shall free thee from the tribute which thou payest / And I the king shall love thee.' Freed from the old TRIBUTE i.e. geld, he PAYS (as pederast), he will have a new lover!

See CHEVERIL, *RJ*.

2. The inch-pin is defined as both bowels and sweetbreads, the latter overlapping in meaning with testicles (see DULCET): sweetbreads of a deer, lower gut (*OED*); fatgut (*CD*); sweetbreads (*W*); *gras boyeau* (lit. greasy, well-fed bowels – Cot). Jonson, *The Sad Shepherd*, I.ii: When Marian says she did not reward her hounds as well as she was rewarded, although she gave them 'All the sweet morsels call'd tongue, ears, and doucets [testes]', Robin asks, 'What? And the inch-pin?' He says he sees her *sports* then *pleased* her, and she calls him 'a wanton'.

Cym, V.v.52. The Queen had a 'mineral; which, being took, / Should . . . feed on life and lingering / By inches waste you . . . . But, failing of her end . . .'. The image of feeding and eliminating faecal waste – by inches or by way of the bowels – is reinforced in her having *but* / butt failed of her *end*. So she, this CRAFTY (q.v.), arse-like, woman, having failed to kill her husband, 'Despairing died' (DESPAIR: It *scitare* / to shit). A fitting end for her who did 'yield the world this ass', her son Cloten, between whom and his mother Imogen was almost destroyed.

Indeed In (the) deed (coitus – P): a simple pun, to lend support or piquancy to others.

TGV, I.i.74, Proteus: 'Indeed, a sheep doth very often stray,/ An if the shepherd be a while away.' SHEEP – or, as they are called a few lines later, 'mutton' and 'laced mutton', i.e. prostitutes (*OED*; P) – do *in deed* stray; as will Proteus when he does 'lose myself', 'lose' Julia, and 'lose' Valentine (II.vi.20) – i.e. is unfaithful to them all by wooing Silvia, because his 'shepherd' Julia (as she calls herself, IV.iv.97) is away.

Oth, III.iii.102:

Iago. I did not think he had been acquainted with her.
Othello. O, yes; and went between us very oft.
Iago. Indeed!
Othello. Indeed! ay, indeed: discern'st thou aught in that?

To arouse Othello's suspicions of Cassio, Iago uses the suggestive term ACQUAINTed (carnally). 'Went between us very oft' gives him another opportunity to jog Othello's unconscious, for to go between is the pander's job (P), 'Indeed!' OFT puns on 'aft', the behind.

2H4, III.ii.20. Shallow remembers being called 'lusty Shallow': 'By the mass, I was called any thing; and I would have done any thing indeed too, and roundly, too. There was I, and Little John Doit of Staffordshire . . . we knew where the bona-robas were' – there in the *doit* (OFr, conduit or sewer), underground where the brothels were (L *fornix*, vault, brothel). There *in deed* he was, he and his *Do-it* or fornicating (C; P) friend of the staff (penis); and he would have done ANY (ass) thing (genitals – P), and ROUNDLY (homosexually) too, just as he was called ANY (ass) thing. See GENERAL, *Tim*, for a 'Do't' pun.

Index (1) Penis. Lit. the gnomon, cock, pin (penis – F&H 1638; C; *LLL*, IV.i.138) of a sundial; the hand of a watch, 16th c.

(2) Fig. and by transf. that which is forbidden (*OED* 1611): 'the Inquisition was introduced into Italy (1542) . . . and the index of prohibited books was established' (B).

Ham, III.iv.52. Hamlet says his mother's 'act' (coitus – P) mocks 'religion' and sickens 'heaven's face'. Queen: 'Ay me, what act/ That roars so loud, and thunders in the index?' Usu. glossed as prologue, 'index' means the forbidden things, incl. her act of adultery, against which God's voice roars and thunders 'against the doom' (49) or Doomsday. Cf. Job 37:4: 'a voice roareth: he thundereth'; and Rev 9:21; 10:1–3: 'Neither repented they of their murders . . . nor of their fornication', after which an angel came down with 'a little book open' and cried 'as when a lion roareth' and 'seven thunders uttered their voices'.

Oth, II.i.263. Iago says Desdemona paddles with the palm of Cassio's hand. 'Lechery, by this hand; an index and obscure prologue to the history of lust and foul thoughts' – prologue *and* index that points to her paddling with his other HAND (penis – K), index, cock or pin.

Infinite In*fin*ite: in the *fin* (Fr) or end; in the FINE (obs., the end) or buttocks.

AW, III.vi.11. There is no redundancy in the French Lord's description of Parolles as 'a most notable coward, an *infinite* and *endless* liar' (italics added). The first word in italics tells where he is a LIAR (bugger) and the second tells when. He is a MOST (which to this French lord is *le fin* – Cot) notable COWARD (effeminate).

V.iii.215, Bertram: 'I liked her,/ And boarded her i' the wanton way of youth . . . and, in fine,/ Her infinite cunning . . . Subdued me to her rate'. He BOARDed (copulated, with specif. ref. to the arse) her in the wanton way of youth; and in fine, in the end, her CUNNING (*finesse*, *fin*), her in*fin*ite cunning SUBDUEd (seduced) him.

H5, V.ii.163: 'these fellows of infinite tongue, that can rhyme themselves into ladies' favours [sexual parts – P]'. They behave like the musicians Cloten hired to 'penetrate her [Imogen] with your fingering . . . we'll try with tongue too' (*Cym*, II.iii.15). TONGUE: penis

Tim, III.vi.108, Timon: 'Of man and beast the infinite malady / Crust you quite o'er!' CRUST is the venereal scab one gets quite o'er – from QUITE / coit(us) with the O'ER / whore. The malady is syphilis, the infinite malady one catches in the end. (SMOOTH.)

See FANCY, *Ham*; VARIETY, *AC*; TWIN, *H5*.

Innocence *In a sense, in no sense*; *incense* and *in sins.*

MND, II.ii.45. Lysander wants 'one bed' with Hermia, who says 'Nay'. He asks, 'O, take the sense, sweet, of my innocence!' – (1) take the sense sweet or sweet scents, the incense (i.e. flattery, adulation), the SWEET (sexually intimate) sense; (2) take (accept sexually – F&H; P) the sense (instrument for gratifying 'lusts of the flesh' – *OED*). His was innocence *in no sense.*

Son 35. Phrases such as 'faults', 'trespass', 'sins', 'Myself corrupting', and 'lawful plea' set the religious and legal framework: 'Excusing thy sins more than thy sins are: / For to they sensual fault I bring in sense – / Thy adverse party is thy advocate'. This not only puns on sins / sense / sensual (K), but says the advocate both *brings in* (to the court) *sins* of the lover and *brings incense* to the altar of his love (thus being a *censer*). He says he excuses his love's sins more than (he is) his *censor* – more than his *sins are*. The advocate says there is 'civil war' between his 'love and hate'. He is playing the role of Devil's Advocate, the Promoter of the Faith at the papal court, who proposes objections against a canonisation. (Sh parodies this practice in *TSh*, IV.iii. Petruchio finds fault with all things about Kate 'under the name of perfect love'. He calls, 'O mercy, God!', speaks 'i' devil's name' and uses such phrases as 'a censer' and 'demi-cannon'. The scene ends with religiously connotative phrases such as 'thy father's house', her still 'crossing' him and an aside that he 'will command the sun'.)

2H4, IV.i.45. Meeting him as representative of the opposing force, Westmoreland tells the Archbishop his 'white investments figure innocence, / The dove and very blessed spirit of peace', but he *means* the white investments figure *in no sense* the dove and spirit of peace. The Archbishop's answer that he is not 'an enemy to peace' tacitly acknowledges this meaning.

Westmoreland uses 'figure' and 'investments' (what Sh called priests' 'holy vestments' in *Tim*, IV.iii.125) for their financial implications. 'Investments' is used again only in *Ham*, I.iii.128, and then insultingly, with a pun on brokers, middle-men in business, esp. pimps: 'they are brokers, / Not of that dye which their investments show'.

The Archbishop is accused of whoring the church, having financial interests in it and the government. And he would not be with the rebellion were it 'guarded with rags, / And countenanced by . . . beggary' – he whose 'see is by a civil peace maintain'd' and whose beard 'the *silver hand* [that *main*tains him: "La main, de hand" – *H5*, III.iv.12] of peace hath touched' (italics added). The head of the see is silver; and the head (Archbishop) of the see has been touched by accepting silver bribes of silver hands.

See POOR, *MV*; POOP, *AC*.

Intend, intent(ion) Probe sexually. Tent; lit. probe; insert into a wound to keep it open.

MWW, II.i.181, 188. Page learns Falstaff plans to seduce the merry wives: they 'accuse him in his intent towards our wives'; 'If he should intend this voyage towards my wife, I would turn her loose to him' (turn: sexually – P).

I.iii.73. Falstaff says Mrs Page 'did so course o'er my exteriors with such a greedy intention': a COURSE is a sex-act; *coureuse*, a whore (Cot). O'ER / whore.

LLL, V.ii.155: 'There's no such sport as sport by sport o'er thrown . . . So shall we stay, mocking intended game', says the Princess of the lords' intended game (copulation – C; P) with the girls they intended to throw (tumble sexually – C; P). They will, instead, themselves be O'ER / whore thrown in the sport (amorous play – P).

V.ii.467. Biron learns that the men's amorous designs had been revealed: someone 'Told our intents before; which once disclosed, / The ladies did change favours'. Their sexual in*tents* (that keep WOUNDS, pudenda, *open*) were *disclosed.*

RJ, V.iii.37. About to enter Juliet's tomb, Romeo says, 'The time and my intents are savage wild'. The pun in 'intents' clarifies Paris's intriguing fear that Romeo planned 'vengeance' and 'some villanous shame / To the dead bodies' (53). What vengeance and shame can he fear that Romeo will do to two people already interred as dead, unless he fears some necrophilic perversion, the exhuming of corpses to see them, kiss them or mutilate them. (See MISUSE, *1H4*.) Cf. *The Bodley Version of Mandeville's Travels*, ed. M. C. Seymour (London: Oxford Univ. Press, 1963) p. 21: a story of necrophily (thus Seymour) about a young man who 'for the grete love and longynge that he hadde to that woman, he yede upon a nyght to here tombe and opened it and lay by here'.

First, what *shame* – a word used for fornication in play after play (*Oth*, v.ii.211: 'The act of shame' or coitus – P)? Specif., what *villanous* shame? In *MM*, v.i.96, seduction is the 'vile conclusion [CONCLUSION]' uttered with 'shame'. Next, what *savage wild* intents? Sh uses the same words in *KJ*, IV.iii.47, with ref. to the alleged killing of Arthur: 'the bloodiest *shame*, / The *wild*est *savagery*, the *vile*st stroke' (italics added). And Sh was familiar with the belief that Arthur was castrated, in the tradition of thus ensuring the end of a line of rival heirs for the throne (Saccio, p. 193); and he puns on it when speaking of Arthur's death (SHIP-BOY).

It sounds as if Paris fears that Romeo intends both the embrace and the mutilation of a necrophiliac, to embrace Juliet and to mutilate Tybalt; and, if so, he is not the only one who questions Romeo's intents.

(1) In v.i Balthasar fears 'misadventure' – Sh's only use of this word, which occurs three times in this scene. ADVENTURE is sexual union. And when Balthasar exits Romeo says, 'Well, Juliet, I will lie with thee tonight.' Only in death, or *lie* in sexual intercourse (C; P), in *mis*- (wrong, improper) adventure?

(2) Romeo tells Balthasar (iii.27) 'do not interrupt me in my course. / Why I descend into this bed of death' is to take 'A precious ring, a ring that I must use / In dear employment'. Some readers may think this sounds plausible, but Balthasar does not: 'his intents I doubt' (44). A COURSE is a bout of copulation. Romeo descends into the *bed* of death to take a RING (pudendum – P), for DEAR / deer (female: hind; male: pricket) use and employment (sexual use – C; P).

(3) Romeo fantasies (103) that 'death is amorous' and that the 'lean [LEAN, pimp] abhorred monster keeps [KEEPS, pimps]' his 'paramour' in this 'vault' or brothel (L FORNIX: brothel, vault; stem of 'fornicate'). In despite, Romeo will 'set up my everlasting rest'. So 'Eyes, look your last! / Arms, take your last embrace! and lips. . . . Thus with a kiss I die' – a presumably necrophilous embrace. Romeo has *set up* his REST, the erect penis ('The County Paris hath set up his rest / That you shall rest but little', the Nurse told Julie – IV.v.6).

The final irony is that, when, by chance, Romeo had seen the invitations to the Capulets' party and decided to go, the Servant had said, 'Rest you merry [MERRY, sexually wanton]!' (I.ii.86). And now in the tomb Romeo rests 'merry' (v.iii.89) and sets up his eternal rest (LIGHTNING).

See COMPUNCTIOUS; GIDDY, *H5*.

Intestine See INWARD for puns on the intestines, with ref. to those who are asses / arses and, sometimes, buggers.

Inward Pun on *innards*, bowels; sexually intimate.

LLL, v.i.102. After a series of anal puns (81–99) – 'dunghill, at the fingers' ends'; 'I smell false Latin; dunghill'; 'the posteriors of this day'; 'The posterior', a word 'well culled [cul: anus – *OED*] . . . I do assure you, sir, I do assure' – Armado says, 'Sir, the king is . . . my *familiar*, I do *ass*ure ye . . . for what is *inward* between us, *let it pass* . . . it will please his grace . . . sometime to . . . with his royal finger, thus, dally with my *excrement*, with my mustachio, but . . . *let that pass* . . . but *let that pass*. . . . I have acquainted you withal, to the *end* to crave your *ass*istance' (italics added). He ACQUAINTed them (gave carnal knowledge – TWR) with all that is inward between the King and him. But / butt let that PASS (like excrement or a flatus). The usu. gloss that excrement means no more than the mustachio that follows it ignores context. (1) The *finger* that dallies with *excrement* parallels the earlier *dung*-hill at the *fingers*' ends.

FINGER is caress intimately (P); it is also a penis, which the King dallies with (caresses amorously – TWR, s.v. Dalliaunce; P). (2) Excrement may grow out of the body, like a moustache, but more commonly it *passes* out of the body, specif. out of the inwards or innards, like faecal waste (as in *Tim*, IV.iii.445).

So the play ends with sexual intimations and dual mockery of the *effeminate ass* Armado, as it had begun I.i when the King said, 'I will use him for my minstrelsy' – use him (sexually – *OED*; P) as a MINSTREL (q.v.), an effeminate.

Ado, IV.i.12: 'If either of you know any inward impediment why you should not be conjoined . . . utter it.' Kittredge *et al*. note that Sh slightly rewords the English marriage service: 'If either of you do know any impediment why ye may not be lawfully joined'. But it is *what* he adds that is significant: *inward* and CON (cunt), which, plus JOINED (copulated), set the stage for the accusation that Hero is no virgin, has an impediment, physical defect (a ruptured hymen). 'Impedimenta' is baggage (a strumpet; bag: be pregnant). This may substantiate the possibility that Hero is pregnant (TWELVE). Such is the sexual intimacy the Friar charges (assails sexually – C; P) them to UTTER / L *utor* (be intimate): (1) discharge seminally; (2) *uter*us – the two components or agents of an inward impediment to marriage.

See BEGGAR, *MM*; BUTCHER, *1H4*; ABSOLUTE, *Oth*.

Italy, Italian Italy and France were referred to as the source of VD (the 'mal de Naples or French Pocks' – Cot) and the breeding-grounds of sodomy. Nashe, *The Unfortunate Traveller*, p. 284: 'Italy . . . From thence he brings the art of atheism, the art of epicurizing, the art of whoring, the art of poisoning, the art of sodomitry.' Middleton, *Michaelmas Term*, III.i: ' 'tis such an Italian world, many men know not before from behind'. Weever, 'The First Satyre of Juvenall': 'Italians should in fond loves take delight, / In stranger sinnes, sinnes which she was ashamed, / Among th' Italians rightly should be named . . . that lustfull venerie, / Should be the downfall of all Italie: / This is the cause Italians to this day, / Are ever readie, apt and prone that way.' These loves Italians delight in, the STRANGE (sodomitical) sins, and *that way* to which they are prone, in the next poem, 'A Prophecie of This Present Yeare, 1600', are explicitly identified with sodomy. Weever says he would not with 'malignant tongue / Teare out the *bowells* of sinnes hidden long, / Hooke out abhorring-nature *strange delights* / Drownd in the red sea with the *Sodomites*'.

See LOMBARDY (home of buggery); STRANGER, *Cym*; RAMP, *Cym*; VENICE.

J

Japhet The second son of Noah, whose descendants spread over the N. and W. regions of the earth, is probably the Japetus whom the Greeks considered the ancestor of the human race.

Instead of the conventional humour that we are all kin because we are all descended from Adam, Sh sees humorous possibilities in the name of Japheth (AV sp.), in Hebrew the 'extender' (Young) and the 'enlargement' (*W*).

2H4, II.ii.128. Poins says that Falstaff is like those who claim to be 'kin to the king; for they never prick their finger but they say, "There's some of the king's blood spilt." "How comes that?" says he, that takes upon him not to conceive'. Prince: 'Nay, they will be kin to us, or they will fetch it from Japhet.' FETCH (cause ejaculation) and 'conceive' are part of the quibble in the 'prick' and the spilt BLOOD (semen) that makes all men kin through Japhet, the extender and the enlargement!

See ENLARGEMENT.

Jest (1) The rear, behind. *Rire*: to jest; *rière*: behind (Cot). To jest is to make an ass of. To break or crack a jest: emit a flatus (*pet*, a crack, fart – Cot).

(2) Coitus. A jest is a notable deed (coitus – C; P).

2H6, I.i.132. A punning cluster on 'Suffolk's' and 'suffocate' (without air), and 'vantages' (from Fr *avant*, before, and connoting *ventages*; 1623, air-hole, vent-hole – *OED*; and *vent*, anus – *OED*), leads to 'A proper jest and never heard before' – only heard/aired *behind.*

TSh, IV.v.72, Vincentio: 'is it else your pleasure . . . to break a jest/ Upon the company you overtake?' (come up on from behind). Hortensio: 'I do assure thee, father, so it is.' He *ass*ures him of his son's marriage, the jest they broke.

Ham, V.i.204: 'infinite jest' (INFINITE: in*fin*ite, in the *fin* – Fr, end). See FANCY.

TA, IV.ii.26. Aaron mocks Chiron's failure to understand the threat in Titus's message: 'Ay, just; a verse in Horace; right, you have it./ (*Aside*) Now, what a thing it is to be an ass!/ Here's no sound jest! The old man hath found their guilt'. The introductory 'just' (1) stresses the 'jest'; (2) puns on JUST/ joust (coitus – the rape), on the verse/ L *versus*, turn (sex-act – C; P) in Horace/*her ass* (Lavinia's). RIGHT, you have it (L *rectum est*, it is right): Chiron is an ass/ arse. The jest (coitus) is not SOUND or healthy for the boys who raped: their sounding or probing of Lavinia's bottom has been sounded, fathomed, by her father, Titus.

See TRUE, *MWW*; DRY, *TN*.

Jet An erect penis; the sexual spasm (F&H n.d.). Lit. a jut, projection; to jut, jerk the tail up and down.

TA, II.i.64. Aaron asks if Demetrius and Chiron know 'how dangerous/ It is to jet upon a prince's right', to jet upon his RIGHT (L *rectum*), to rape his wife.

TN, II.v.36: 'Contemplation makes a rare turkey-cock of him: how he jets under his advanced plumes!' 'Turkey-cock' is used twice by Sh and each time it evokes the cock (penis – P). Here Malvolio jets like one; in *H5*, V.i.16, Pistol 'comes, swelling like a turkey-cock'. The pun on a turgid penis is furthered by the 'swelling' in one case, and, in the other, the 'advanced' PLUME, a large showy FEATHER (q.v.).

See ALL, *R3*.

Jewel/ Jule (1) A precious stone (testicle – *OED*).

(2) Maidenhead (C; P).

MV, II.viii.20: 'And jewels, two stones, two rich and precious stones,/Stolen by my daughter!' With this metaphor Sh indicates Shylock's loss of his manhood, his control over his house and daughter, who gave herself to her lover ('She hath the stones upon her' – 82).

See HANGING, *LLL*; GIFTS, *TGV*; TRASH, *Oth*; MODEST, *Tem*; STINT.

Join(er), Joint (stool) 1. Join: copulate. L *copulare*: to join together.

See PLAINLY, *MND*; SQUIRREL, *RJ*; TORCH, *1H6*; CROOKED, *R2*; SPIT, *Per*.

2. Joint: genitals. Chapman, *The Widow's Tears*, IV.ii: 'One joint of him I lost was much more worth/Than . . . thy entire body.' Waiting-woman: 'O, know what joint she means'.

R2, V.iii.105. The Duchess says of her husband, old York, 'His weary joints would gladly rise, I know' – not only from kneeling, but also in coitus, as she knows ('rise' is a common pun on phallic erection).

Oth, II.iii.328, Iago: 'this broken joint between you and her husband entreat her to splinter'. Cassio suffered a rupture in his friendship with Othello but also a physical injury, which may have been the broken joint of the genitals (see RAG).

See GOUT, *TrC*; SPIT, *Per*; TERMS, *1H4*.

3. Joined or joint stool: a close-stool, i.e. a chamber-pot enclosed in a stool or box. To close: 1551, to join; stool: a privy seat, the faeces. *Mac*, III.iv.68: 'Why do you make such *faces*! When all's done,/You look but on a *stool*' (italics added). Macbeth is a fearful ass, 'unmann'd in folly'. His 'fear' suits 'A woman's story', a 'grandam'; it is old womanish, anile/anal.

See THUNDER, *KL*; STATE, *1H4*; MOVE, *TSh*; SLIP, *MND* (a 'three-foot stool').

Just(ly) Coitus. 'Juste': joust, euph. for 'coit' (TWR). ME 'justen': copulate.

Ado, IV.i.82. Hero answers the 'charge' she is 'common stale' with 'Who can blot that name/With any just reproach?' – (1) who can justly reproach her (see GRIEF for her father's responsibility); (2) who can reproach her for fornication, or blot that name, i.e. Hero: who can blot Hero/her-'O' (pudendum – C; P) with the reproach of justing? The pun has antecedents in l.35: 'Behold how like a maid she blushes *here*! *O* . . .' (italics added). The blood of the blushing *maid* becomes the blot or stain of maiden blood if deflowered.

MM, II.iv. 52. Angelo asks Isabella if, to preserve her chastity, she would rather 'the most just law/Now took your brother's life' – the 'O just but severe law!' (II.ii.41) against fornication, justing.

R3, III.v.89: 'My princely father then had wars in France;/And, by just computation of the time,/Found that the issue was not his begot'. Exact computation of the time the just took place revealed the child was a bastard. It seems the husband, too, was an adulterer, since he *had* WARS/whores in France.

Oth, IV.ii.173. Roderigo berates Iago for failure to provide sexual *entrée* to Desdemona.

> *Roderigo.* I do not find that thou dealest justly with me.
> *Iago.* What in the contrary? . . .
>
> You charge me most unjustly.

Precisely, Roderigo charges him with not providing justly in the CONTRARY (cunt). Roderigo lacks the just, the 'comforts of sudden respect and acquaintance' he had been promised: the comforts (sexual satisfaction – P) of SUDDEN (lecherous) ACQUAINTANCE (sexual intimacy).

Justice A whore, a human sewer. *Voirie*: justice; the city's dung-heap (Cot). *Voirie*: a 'barrack-hack' or whore, lit. a common sewer (F&H n.d.). Jonson, *Bartholomew Fair*, IV.iv: 'I'le commit you upon my woman-hood . . . upon my Justice-hood' – 'Upon your Justice-hood? Mary shite o' your hood, you'll commit [COMMIT, copulate adulterously]? Spoke like a true Justice of peace's wife . . . turd i' your teeth for a fee, now.'

Sh parallels Fortune and Justice, both fickle whores.

R3, IV.iv.105, Margaret: 'I call'd thee then vain flourish of my *fortune* . . . [but] the course of *justice wheel*'d about' and it is Elizabeth's turn to 'Decline' (italics added). Justice wheels about, like the capricious wheel of Fortune (*H5*, *Ham*, *KL*, *AC*). The 'course of justice' is like the 'course of fortune' (*Ado*, IV.i.159), both of them the COURSE (embrace in bed) of a whore, a *coureuse* (Cot).

MM, V.i.35. Angelo says that Isabella 'hath been a suitor to me for her brother/ Cut off by course of justice – '. Isabella: 'By course of justice!' Her brother was cut off first by his own COURSE of justice or whoring, and then by Angelo's justice or screwing, which really doomed him (see SIEGE).

See GOLD, *MWW*; SERVANT, *2H4*; THUNDER, *KL*.

K

Keen (1) Sexually excited (P).
(2) Of the ass/arse. L *acies*: keenness, sharp edge; the eye, a piercing look.
Ham, III.ii.258:

Ophelia. You are keen, my lord, you are *keen*.
Hamlet. It would cost you a groaning to take off my *edge*.

(Italics added to indicate puns on *acies*.) Cf. GROAN/groin.

Luc, 9: 'bateless edge on his keen appetite!'

MND, II.ii.123. Helena is revolted at Lysander's saying (104) that the ART (L *ars*/arse) of NATURE (the genitals) enabled him to see the beauty of her HEART ('eart or arse); 'be content' (CON, cunt), she says, with Hermia. But 'Content [CONTENT, sexually satisfied] with Hermia!' he cannot be; for he is now 'ripe' (RIPE, sexually mature), at the 'point' (erect penis – C; prepuce – P) or peak of 'human skill [SKILL: L *ars*/arse]' and so is led from Hermia to Helena's 'eyes' (EYES, arse), where he can 'o'erlook/Love's stories' (its tales, arses).

These puns on the girls' arses lead Helena to ask, 'Wherefore was I to this keen mockery born? . . . Is't not enough, is't not enough [ENOUGH, Fr *assez*/asses] . . . That I . . . never can,/Deserve a sweet look from Demetrius' eye . . . ? . . . I thought you lord of more true [TRUE: *trou*, arse – Cot] gentleness . . . [I am] abused!'

Sh's keen mockery of sexual excitement includes many other puns on L *acies*: the look and O'ER/whore look; eyes and eye, and 'I' used 10 times in 20 lines. Helena concludes that this keen mockery ABUSED (sexual misuse of the arse) her, buggered her; she is being screwed by them all. Cf. SKILL, *LLL*.

Keep(er) Pimp (F&H); maintain a whore. Defined freq. as one who salaries a mistress, keeper loses its characteristic 16th c. vulgarity. Wycherley, *The Country Wife*, I.i: 'Is not keeping better than marriage?' – 'A pox on't, the jades would jilt me. I could never keep a whore to myself.' See HOUSE (4).

MM, III.ii.211: 'Mistress Kate Keepdown', whore.

Oth, IV.ii.137. Emilia defends Desdemona: 'Why should he call her whore? who keeps her company?/What place?' See KEY.

TrC, II.ii.81. In the debate over whether to return Helen to her husband, Troilus asks, 'Why keep we her? . . . Is she worth keeping?'

See GOUT, *Tim*; O'ER, *Ado*; LODGER, *H5*.

Key Allusive to coitus and genitals (F&H); keys/case/cods (K). The Crossed Keys was a famous 15th c. brothel. 'Turn the key' meant fuck (*chiavare*: to lock with a key; to fuck – F). It was also the job of bawd or pimp.

MWW, II.ii.285: 'I will use her as the key of the cuckoldly rogue's coffer', says Falstaff of Mrs Ford, whom he plans to use (exploit sexually – *OED*; P) and from whom he plans to take two *keys*: hers and that to her husband's coffer (*quaisse* – Cot).

R3, I.ii.5. The corpse of Henry VI, who had been notoriously cuckolded by Margaret, is described as 'Poor key-cold figure of a holy king!' The usual gloss of 'key-cold' as a proverbial expression for cold as metal overlooks the pun on *cuckold* (*MWW* above). The holy king and 'holy load [LOAD – used twice]' had been made an ass/arse: 'holy' puns on the anus (TWR, p. 106; K, p. 117).

Oth, IV.ii.94, Othello: 'there's money . . . turn the key and keep our counsel'.

MM, I.iv.8: 'Turn you the key, and know his business of him' – see SISTER for the BUSINESS (sexual intercourse).

KL, II.iv.53, Fool: 'Fortune, that arrant whore,/Ne'er turns the key to the poor' – Lear's daughters have closed their doors to him and his men, now that he is penniless. Like the whore Fortune, they won't turn the key (*chiavare*) or bestow favours on those who cannot pay. Twice Regan tells Gloucester (II.iv) 'Shut up your doors' (308) against Lear; her husband adding, 'My Regan counsels well' (COUNSELLOR, bawd; WELL, fornicate).

See SMOOTH, *2H4*.

Kind(ly), Kindness Lit. sex, gender. Kindness: 1728, the sexual favour (F&H). Rabelais, Bk IV, ch. 38: 'nothing could serve him [Jupiter] but he must give her a touch of his Godship's kindness', after which the woman conceived. 'Kindly' puns on 'kindle', to inflame the passions, to conceive, to make warm (P).

KL, IV.vi.166: 'Thou hotly lust'st to use' the whore 'in that kind/For which thou whipp'st her'.

Per, IV.vi.63. Marina, having refused to do 'the kindness of our profession', is now asked by the Bawd, 'without any more virginal fencing, will you use him kindly?'

Tim, II.ii.226. Of the ingrates who refuse him money, Timon says, 'Their blood [BLOOD, semen] is caked, 'tis cold, it seldom flows;/'Tis lack of kindly warmth they are not kind'. This lack of kindly/kindle warmth (sexual ardour – C; P) that would conceive or bring forth young is another punning indicator of the new cold (sexual and) business relationships between Timon and his sycophants. See STIR; FEEBLE.

Cor, II.iii.81. Coriolanus recognises that political prostitution is the price of a consulship: 'What must I say? "I pray sir". . . . I cannot bring/My tongue to such a pace (55)' – the *pace*, sexual gait of a whore (P). Told 'The price is to ask it kindly', he submits: 'Kindly! Sir, I pray, let me ha't.' His TONGUE (see BEGGAR) has been brought to the whore's pace, to ask kindly. But not for long: 'Better it is to die . . . Than crave the hire which first we do deserve./Why in this woolvish toge should I stand here' (120) – the hire and dress of the WOLF (whore).

See ALL, *H8*; ENLARGEMENT, *3H6*; EPHESUS, *CE*; GRIEF, *Ado*.

Knit(ter) Unite sexually. Form fruit (ME); conceive (*OED* 1732). Tie in or with a KNOT (coit; genitals).

Ado, IV.i.45: 'Not to be married,/Not to knit my soul to an approved wanton.'

MWW, III.ii.76. Page says Fenton shall not marry his daughter: '*No*, he shall *not knit* a *knot* in his fortunes with the finger of my substance' (italics added) – not with FINGERing (pricking) of Page's daughter.

See SPINSTER, *TN*; MIDNIGHT, *KJ*; LIPS, *MND*.

Knock (1) Coit. Knocking-house: brothel (F&H). *Coignaufond*: knocking, lechery (Cot). Marston, *The Dutch Courtesan*, IV.vii: 'I knew your wife before she was married, and since I have found your . . . dore open and I have knockt, and God knows what I have saved.'

(2) Knock: penis (F&H). *Cunno*: 'a woman's nocke or privy parts' (F). Nock: posteriors (F&H); 'aperture of the fundament' (John Ash, *Dictionary*, 1775).

Cym, III.v.148: 'when my lust hath dined . . . to the court I'll knock her back, foot her home again . . . be merry in my revenge'. Cloten could mean beat her up, but more likely this epicene's idea of MERRY (lascivious) revenge is to knock her back or *nock* (anus), and FOOT (fuck – K; P) her HOME (vulva) again.

R3, V.iii.5. Out in the field, Richard calls for Norfolk.

Richard. Norfolk, we must have knocks; ha! must we not?
Norfolk. We must both give and take, my gracious lord.

Richard's 'ha' is the give-away that he hears (even if he does not intend) the double meaning in 'knocks' as buffets of battle and sexual buffets. 'Give' and 'take' (C; P) represent the active and receptive roles in any encounter, including a sexual one, and are therefore a safe answer to 'must we not [/ KNOT, intertwine coitally – C; P; K]'.

TSh, I.ii.5–42. Though Petruchio has just pointed out the house at which he wants his servant (a RASCAL, man with one testicle – 37) to 'knock', Grumio asks 'whom' and 'is there any man has rebused your worship?' Why this play on ABUSE (sexually misuse)? The rebus, an enigmatical representation of a word by a figure or picture ('we must' preceding a picture of a sun-dial: 'we must die all'), was popular and was a word in literary use (Jonson, *The New Inn*, I.i). Grumio has visualised 'this is his house' and 'knock' as a rebus of a knocking-house or brothel. At Petruchio's rewording his request as 'knock me', Grumio becomes truly excited, hearing that he rap his master and also an indecent suggestion, which is reinforced when Hortensio opens his door and Petruchio asks, 'come you to part the fray?' FRAY: lit. a quarrel and the sexual act. See PLAIN for details.

See DOOR, *CE*; DISDAIN, *CE*; SLAVE, *Cym.*

Knot/not 1. Intertwine coitally (C; P). 2. Sex-organs. Lit. a hard lump, protruberance.

Oth, IV.iii.70. Emilia would 'do such a deed' as adultery, would 'do't as well i' the dark'. Desdemona replies, 'In troth, I think thou wouldst not [/ Knot].' Emilia: 'In troth, I think I should: and un-do't when I had done.' *Un-do't* or untie the knot, when she had *done*. Emilia's DARK well (brothel) where she would do't, would TROT(H), trot like a whore or bawd, echoes Othello's 'cistern' for 'toads/To knot and gender in!' (ii.62).

Per, IV.ii.160: 'Untied I still my virgin knot will keep'.

AW, IV.iii.359. Parolles has been (fig. ?) screwed and castrated (SHAME): 'You are undone, captain, all but your scarf; that has a knot on't yet.' Pun on (1) their unbinding him; (2) his being UNDONE as a man – only his scarf, i.e. bandage for a wound, still has a knot. See CATERPILLAR, *1H4*.

III.ii.23. Bertram puns on the 'nuptial knot' (as it is called in *3H6*, III.iii.55) of his marriage-in-name-only: 'I have wedded her, not bedded her; and sworn to make the "not" eternal.' His mother: 'This is not well, rash and unbridled boy' – not WELL, his being un-*bridal*-ed (BRIDLE), his having a rash, being ill (see RING).

3. A pack of whores, pimps.

MWW, IV.ii.123. Ford thinks his servants are hiding the adulterer, Falstaff: 'O you panderly rascals! there's a knot, a ging, a pack [PACK, pimp] . . . against me.'

R3, III.iii.6: 'God keep the prince from all the pack of you! A knot you are of damned blood-suckers.' BLOOD: semen; blood-suckers: buggers (see PUNY).

Tim, III.vi.99: 'You knot of mouth-friends!' – Timon's blood-suckers.

See FURNISH, *TGV*; IDLE, *Cor*; KNOCK, *R3*.

L

Lady-bird A prostitute (*OED* 1656). '1690. B.E., *Dict. Cant. Crew*, s.v. LADYBIRDS. Light or Lewd women' (F&H).

RJ, I.iii.3: 'Now, by my maidenhead, at twelve year old,/I bade her come. What, lamb! what, lady-bird!/God forbid! Where's this girl? What, Juliet!' These lines introduce the bawdy Nurse, whose choice of endearments flows naturally out of the reference to her own maidenhead (lost at twelve?). A lamb is a young SHEEP or 'mutton', two common terms of opprobrium for loose women. Hence her hasty adding of 'God forbid!' Perhaps there is a quibble on lamb, young *ovis* (L) and bird, *avis*: 'Courtesans . . . oves' (F&H, s.v. Mutton, 1569).

The symbol of Juliet as a wanton lady-bird is persistent. (1) In the balcony scene she bids Romeo farewell, wishing him 'gone:/And yet no further than a *wanton's bird*' (II.ii.177). (2) Nurse: 'your love/Must climb a *bird's nest* soon when it is dark' (v. 75) – pun on the pudendum and pubic hair (P). (3) Nurse: 'Now comes the *wanton* blood up in your cheeks' (72). (4) Friar: '*Lady*, come from that *nest*/Of death' (v.iii.151) – the vault in which both the lady-bird and her bird die. (All italics added.) See ANCIENT.

Lame Impotent; often as a result of venereal infection. Dekker, *The Shoemaker's Holiday*, III.iv: returning from the war, Ralph is greeted by Hodge, 'Why, how now, lame?', and by Margery, 'Trust me, I am sorry, Ralph, to see thee impotent. Lord, how the wars have made him sunburnt [syphilitic – C]! The left leg is not well; 'twas a fair gift of God the infirmity took not hold a little higher, considering thou camest from France [source of the French disease, syphilis].' In IV.ii Firk (fuck – C; P) says, 'Thou do for her? then 'twill be a lame doing, and that she loves not. . . . I would have yearked and firked your Priscilla. Hey, down a down, derry.'

Oth, II.i.162: 'O most lame and impotent conclusion [CONCLUSION: arse; coitus]! Do not learn of him, Emilia, though he be thy husband.'

KL, II.iv.166. Talking of Goneril (pun on *gonorrhoeal*: see BOILS), Lear (himself in a 'rash mood' – 172, pun on venereal rash) says, 'Strike her young bones,/You taking airs, with lameness!' Not that she is to be made halt, but that those taking-*heirs*, those who render sterile, are to strike her bones with bone-ache (VD – C; P), make her barren and impotent. Her eyes already 'burn' (175), i.e. have VD (*OED*; P).

R3, I.i.22. Richard complains that he is 'curtail'd' (tail cut short; castrated) and 'Deform'd, unfinish'd . . . scarce half made up,/And that so lamely and unfashionable/That dogs bark at me as I halt by them'. He is *un-*FASHION-*able*, *not able* with his *fascinum* (L, penis).

See NOTHING, *Ado*; PLUM, *2H6*.

Land Vulva, womb. *Landie*(*s*): the two 'wings within the lips of a womans privities' (Cot).

AW, I.iii.47. The Clown wants 'friends for my wife's sake' – her SAKE, womb. 'He that ears my land spares my team and gives me leave to in the crop; if I be his cuckold, he's my drudge.' He wants friends to ear (copulate – P), be the EAR (plant part containing seeds) or testes for him, and ear (plough – *OED*) his land, his wife and her vulva, so sparing his TEAM, i.e. a pair (of testes), and his TEEM, outpouring (of semen). The other can be the drudge (penis and lover – P); the Clown will in the crop, reap the brood and sit around pouring food and drink into his crop, throat.

Oth, I.ii.50. Iago says Othello 'hath boarded a land carack. . . . He's married.' The sea hero this time BOARDed (mounted sexually – P) a land CARACK (ship of burden; prostitute). Davenant, *The Tragedy of Albovine*, III: 'I must be furnished too' – 'With a mistress?' – 'Yes . . . some old land-carack.'

Mac, V.iii.51: 'If thou couldst, doctor, cast/The water of my land, find her disease,/And purge it to . . . health'. Macbeth wants the doctor to 'Cure' two lands: (1) to cast his wife's water (urine – *OED*) and 'cleanse [her] stuff'd bosom [lap and sexual parts – P]'; (2) to empty Scot*land* of the English (see ECHO), to purge it of the intruder.

Laugh(ter) 1. Man's rear end. *Rire*: to laugh; *rieur*: a laugher (Cot).

AW, III.vi.44: 'O, for the *love* of *laughter*, *hinder* not the honour of his design: let him fetch off his *drum* in any hand' (italics added). A masturbatory image: FETCH, cause ejaculation. See DRUM (buttocks) for puns on the rear end of this ass.

2. Make love. Loffe: obs. sp. of 'laugh'. *TrC*, I.ii.140–50: a cluster of puns on 'love', 'egg' (Fr *l'oeuf*) and 'laugh'. Dekker and Middleton, *The Honest Whore I*, III.i: to arouse a husband's jealousy Fustigo tells his wife, 'we had good sport [the sex-act – F&H; P] ifayth, had we not? and when shals laugh agen?'

MV, I.i.65. Antonio bids two friends farewell: 'I take it your own business calls on you/And you embrace the occasion to depart' – he takes it (receives it coitally – F&H; P) their own BUSINESS (copulation) is the reason they *embrace* OCCASION (genitals) to depart. The arriving Bassanio greets them: 'Good signiors [GOOD fellows, fornicators] both, when shall we laugh? say when?'

WT, II.i.198. Believing his pregnant wife an adulteress who means him harm, Leontes says 'she should be confined' (pun on her confinement), 'for this business/Will raise us all' (as her BUSINESS, fornication, *raised* her). Antigonus: 'To laughter, as I take it' (see *MV* above). He puns on the pregnancy as a laughter, i.e. a clutch of eggs laid by a fowl: in *Tem*, II.i.33, 'A laughter' is the 'wager' bet on a competition between an 'old cock' and a 'cockerel'.

3. Fart. Loffe (obs. sp. of 'laugh') and *loffe* (farts – F).

JC, I.ii.251, Casca: 'for mine own part, I durst not laugh, for fear of opening my lips and receiving the bad air', presumably Caesar's, but a condemnation of Casca himself and his part in the conspiracy, through puns on the bad air or *loffe* he'd receive from his OWN (arse) PART (split in the buttocks) and LIP (anus) were he to *laugh* too vigorously.

See BUDGE, *TSh*; DRAWERS, *1H4*; TRUE, *MWW*; APPLAUSE.

Lean Pimp. L *leno*: pimp, seducer. Lena, leno: bawd, as in 'my lean lena' (Webster, in *CD*).

H5, V.i.91. Pistol's wife is dead, his 'rendez-vous [RENDEZ-VOUS, revenue] is quite cut off. . . . Well, *bawd* I'll turn,/And something *lean* to cutpurse' (italics added).

MV, II.vi.19. Gratiano compares the ardour of Lorenzo and Jessica to a scarfed bark that leaves the bay 'Hugg'd and embraced by the strumpet wind' and like a prodigal returns 'Lean, rent and beggar'd by the strumpet wind!' Returns BEGGARed (whored) and rent: torn and a source of revenue (used specif. for coition – P).

Ado, III.iii.155. Borachio has wooed Margaret, who 'leans me out at her mistress' chamber-window, bids me a thousand times good night' (the same farewell Juliet gave Romeo). Margaret *leans* him out and so convinces the distant viewers that he is a leno and seducer and that she is Hero who leans OUT (Fr *hors*/whores) in this 'amiable encounter [sexual engagement – C; P]'.

JC, I.ii.194. In view of this pun, the 'lean and hungry' look of Cassius might be Sh's early comment on the conspiracy and on the political seduction of Brutus by the pimp Cassius: 'Brutus, I have much mistook your passion' – 'Into what dangers would you lead me, Cassius . . . ?' (48, 63).

Leather Whore; female pudendum. L *scortum*: hide, leather; a prostitute. Hide: human skin (F&H). Leather: female pudendum, as in 'It is half ane yeir almaist,/Sen ever that loun laborde my ledder' (F&H 1540). Chapman, *All Fools*, IV.i, of a man flirting with his friend's wife: 'What huge large thongs he cuts/Out of his friend Fortuno's stretching leather.'

See BOTH-SIDES, *TrC*; NEIGHBOUR, *H5*; Introduction, p. xii, *JC*.

Leek Also called the Welsh onion, chibol or scallion (*OED*), the latter perhaps a pun on 'scullion', an abusive epithet, and 'cullion', a testicle (*OED*; P). It is always defined in terms of the onion, to which it is related; the leek, however, lacks the full, rounded bulb: 1601, 'it hath in maner no distinct head at all, but only a long neck'; 1731, 'The Welch Onions . . . These never make any Bulb' (*OED*, s.v. Leek). Jonson, *The Case is Altered*, IV.v: 'if I be not revenged on him, let Peter Onion (by the infernal Gods) be turned to a leeke or a scalion!' (If he fails to get revenge, let him be turned into a thing with no bulb, no balls.) The leek is a symbol of inadequacy, the salaciousness of the impotent, lechery. In Chaucer's 'Reeve's Prologue', 24, the Reeve says that old men 'have an hoor heed and a grene tayl,/ As hath a leek; for thogh oure myght be goon,/ Oure wyl desireth folie evere in oon'.

H5. Bawdy punning on the *leek* and the S*alique* law provide commentary on the famous battle of Agincourt. In I.ii, Henry's bishops, for venal reasons, urge him to fight France, saying the French cannot use 'the law Salique' to bar his claims to France. Henry decides in favour of war and says history shall 'with full mouth' praise him, or else his grave, 'Like to a Turkish mute shall have a tongueless mouth', an image connoting the victor with phallic TONGUE as opposed to the deprived, mutilated Turkish mute (cf. *TN*, I.ii.62:'Be you his eunuch, and your mute I'll be'). His remark is followed by the entrance of the French ambassadors with their insulting TENNIS-BALLS and the implication that these are what Henry lacks in bed (balls, testicles) and on the field (potent cannon-balls). Sh's scorn for religious and political hypocrisy and the mistaken idea of manhood that can be measured by 'balls' and 'gun-stones' (282) underlies the puns.

There are parallels between Henry and the Salique *law*, and Fluellen and 'martial law'; Henry and his balls, and Fluellen and his leek; Henry who lands in France saying (III.i), 'Once more unto the breach [breach; female pudendum – C; P; breach/ breech, buttocks] dear friends [DEAR/ deer, arse]', and Fluellen, whose first words in the play and on landing are 'Up to the breach, you dogs . . . you cullions' (ii.21); Henry 'in his rages', and Fluellen in his 'rage' (lust – TWR; P), to whom Pistol says, 'Abate thy rage . . . thy manly rage'; and Henry's concluding, 'I am Welsh . . . good countryman' (IV.vii.110), Welsh like Fluellen, who had traced Henry's ancestry to Edward the Black Prince of Wales who 'fought a most prave pattle here in France' – a prave pattle (L *prave*, crookedly, ill, wrongly), a depraved battle – like the brave battle for title in France, which the bishops had justified, also by tracing Henry's ancestral claims. (See GIDDY for further insight into Henry's self-condemnatory 'unto the breach'.)

In V.i, Sh introduces the oral eroticism of Fluellen's asking Pistol to eat the leek, as Henry fig. made the French eat the Salique law. Henry was angered by the French gift of (tennis) balls; and Fluellen was angered because Pistol had brought him 'pread and salt . . . and bid me eat my leek' – the offensive salt and leek, the Fr *Sal* (salt) + *lique*. Pistol is told, if he can mock a leek, he can eat a leek, but Pistol is 'qualmish at the smell of leek'; his 'digestions' do not agree with it. However, Fluellen has still 'another leek in my pocket' and 'more sauce to your leek' (SAUCE: semen, a gonorrheal leak). Pistol's 'gleeking' (78) had back-fired.

At the end of the scene, Pistol, soldier and fornicator ('Pistol's cock is up,/ And flashing fire will follow' – II.i.55) who had arrived 'swelling like a turkey-cock', has a 'broken coxcomb'. He reads a letter that his Nell has died of syphilis, 'Of malady of France' – a tragic and cynical comment on all those who died of the prave (*prave*, ill) pattle in France. As for Henry's famous speech (IV.iii.47) that the hero who 'comes safe home' can 'strip his sleeve and show his *scars*,/ And say "These wounds I had on Crispin's day",' it is Pistol, with his 'ploody coxcomb', the last man in the play to speak from '*The English camp*', who has the concluding word: 'Well, bawd I'll turn,/ And something lean to cutpurse of quick hand./ To England will I steal, and there I'll steal:/ And patches will I get unto these cudgell'd *scars*,/ And swear I got them in the Gallia wars' (italics added). Pistol, with his mouth full of leek, turning bawd; and history with its 'full mouth'. Was history, too, given a 'Welsh correction' (82), a symbolic Welsh onion or leek to eat?

See BITE, *H5*.

Leer Loin (obs.); flesh, partic. of the thigh (TWR); cheek; complexion (obs.).

AYL, IV.i.67. It 'pleases' (satisfies sexually) Orlando to call Ganymede his 'Rosalind', but 'he hath a Rosalind of a better leer'.

TA, IV.ii.119: 'Here's a young lad framed of another leer' from that of his half-brothers – he is of Aaron's loin and complexion.

MWW, I.iii.50, Falstaff: 'I do mean to make love to Ford's wife: I spy entertainment in her . . . she gives the leer of invitation . . . and the hardest voice of her behaviour . . . is "I am Sir John Falstaff's" '. Mrs Ford's leer or loin and VOICE / VICE (closed thighs and pudendum – P) are the source of the entertainment (sexual hospitality – C; P) Falstaff spies in her.

See APPROACH, *2H4*; TUTOR, *2H4*.

Lend (1) Buttocks (*OED*). Lendes: loins, possibly buttocks, as in Chaucer, 'The Miller's Tale', 118: Nicholas 'thakked [patted amorously] hire bout the lendes weel'.

(2) Yield or bend sexually: 'lend' means prest and puns on *pressed* (coitally – P). *Prester*: lend, yield, give (Cot; cf. *MV*, IV.i.425: 'You press me . . . I will yield'). L *lento*: I bend (*MM*, V.i.442: 'kneel by me . . . lend a knee').

VA, 315: 'his tail that . . . Cool [COOL / cule, rump] shadow to his melting buttock lent'.

AW, IV.ii.40. Asked for his 'ring' (L *anus*), the RING (arse) with which he hopes to seduce her, Bertram says he can only 'lend it thee, my dear; but have no power / To give it from me'. No one has the POWER (potency of the arse) to *give away* his arse; one can only *lend* it. 'My dear' means (1) Diana, his DEAR / deer (hind); (2) his own DEAR (arse).

Diana then claims that her 'honour's such a ring: / My chastity' – another body part, and one she has no power to give (*prester*) and will not lend (prest) or have pressed coitally.

MV, V.i.249, Antonio: 'I once did lend my body for his wealth' (see SUBJECT for erotic implications). Lending his body was followed by 'losses, / That have of late so huddled on his back, / Enow to press a royal merchant down' (IV.i.29). Two things went down: (1) his ship (his 'bottom' – I.i.42), a merchant (a trading-vessel – *OED*; cf. *Tem*, II.i.5, apropos of a 'loss' at sea: 'The masters of some merchant and the merchant / Have just the theme of woe'); and (2) himself, another merchant who went DOWN (in coitus), another bottom (he lent). Antonio has losses that *huddled on his back*.

See BEAT, *AW*; BITE, *1H4*; CUP, *AC*; ADVENTURE, *RJ*.

Leprosy Linked to moral defilement, and often confused with venereal infection. In 1321 Edward II founded Lock Hospital as a Leprosarium, but so many so-called lepers really had gonorrhoea and syphilis that later Lock Hospital concentrated on VD (*OED*). The foul disease or evil meant '(a) epilepsy, (b) syphilis' (*OED*, s.v. Foul). John Ford, *'Tis Pity She's a Whore*, I.i: 'the leprosy of lust'; IV.iii: the 'lust-be-lepred body' of a 'strumpet, famous whore'.

Tim, IV.iii.35. Timon says 'gold' will 'Make the hoar leprosy adored' – punning on the venereally infected hoar / whore (K) and on the hoar or white scales characteristic of the leper's skin. Gold will make the white adored (*dorer*, to do over with gold – Cot).

AC, III.x.10. Scarus describes the fight: 'like the token'd pestilence, / Where death is sure. Yon ribaudred nag of Egypt, – / Whom leprosy o'ertake! – '. He asks that Cleopatra, the ribaudred (ribald, a harlot) nag (1598, whore) be overtaken (like an old tired nag or HORSE / whore) by leprosy, the whore's disease. The death of the sewer (see SURE) is to O'ER- / whore take the whore.

See CRUST, *Ham*.

Liar See LIE.

Libya An impotent. L *Libys*, Libyan; pun on 'libs', i.e. castrates. Dryden's trs. of Vergil's *Pastorals*, ix.31: 'O Tityrus, tend my herd . . . And 'ware the Libyan ridgel's butting head.' A RIDGEL is a male with one or no testicle.

TrC, I.iii.328. Nestor mocks Achilles: 'were his brain as barren / As banks of Libya, – though

Apollo knows,/'Tis dry enough'. He is barren of wit: his BRAIN (testes) is barren as the BANKS (lit. seats) of Libya, barren as DRY (barren) ENOUGH, Fr *assez*/asses.

AC, III.vi.69. Antony has 'given his empire/Up to a whore; who now are levying/The kings o' the earth for war'. This WAR/whore will be lost, for the impotency of his defence is typified by the first on the list of *ass*embled kings: 'Bocchus, the king of Libya' – pun on Bacchus, also known as Liber, the god whom Ovid called 'a boy, as pretty as a girl'; 'Bacchus . . . with the soft delicate limbs of a woman, was the type of disgraceful effeminacy' (Lecky, *Rationalism*, in *CD*). *Up* and *levying* (raising) imply a phallic energy belied by *given up*. As Caesar accurately says (87), 'the *high* gods . . . make them ministers/Of us' (italics added): the (phallic) superiority is Caesar's.

See SLEEP, *TrC*.

Lie, liar Copulate ('lie' – C; P; like today's 'lay', i.e. fuck). *Frotter*: 'Se fier une fille? Allez vous y frotte' ('Rely on a maid? not I; you may lie on her if you will') – Cot. Cf. *Oth*, IV.i.36: 'Lie with her! lie on her! We say lie on her, when they belie her.' The copulator or liar may be a bugger or buggered. Bugiard: liar (*CD*); It *bugiardo*, from *bugiare*, lie (F).

Tim, IV.iii.292: 'Where liest o' nights, Timon?' – 'Under that's above me.'

2H4, III.ii.325, Falstaff: 'I do see the bottom of Justice Shallow. Lord, Lord, how subject we old men are to this vice of lying! [He] . . . hath done nothing but prate to me of the wildness of his youth . . . and every third word a lie . . . . a' came ever in the rearward of the fashion . . . . and there an end.' (1) 'Bottom', PRAT(E), 'rearward' and 'end' – all are the buttocks, focus of buggery and syns of arses. (2) Old men are SUBJECT (the pathic or woman in a sex-act) to the vice of lying – the VICE (fornication, closed thighs) – and every third WORD/whore a bugger. To come in the rearward is sodomy (P, s.v. Mandrake), and he came in the rearward of FASHION (q.v.), Fr *taille*/tail (buttocks – *OED*; P).

Tem, III.ii.25–54:

> *Trinculo* . . . but you'll lie like dogs and yet say nothing neither. . . .
>
> Thou liest, most ignorant monster. . . . Why, thou deboshed fish . . . Wilt thou tell a monstrous lie, being but half a fish and half a monster? . . .
>
> *Caliban* . . . I do not lie.
> *Stephano.* Trinculo, if you trouble him any more in's tale . . . .

Double talk on sexual roles: they don't run or go; they lie (prone, like DOGS: whores, sodomites) and yet say nothing (except with that 'backward voice', VOICE/VICE, from 'thy other mouth' – II.ii.95). Caliban is an IGNORANT (lewd) MONSTER (hermaphrodite, bisexual), a word used seven times in 20 lines. He is 'half . . . and half' (a hermaphrodite, bisexual), and he tells a monstrous (monster's) lie. He is half fish (prostitute – P), a deboshed fish (*desbauché*: deboshed, lewd, seduced – Cot). He protests he does not lie and Stephano tells Trinculo not to trouble him any more in's tale – the one he's telling and his own tale (rump – C; P).

The end of *Tem* evokes the end of Rev: Prospero, generally regarded as a sort of Providence, drowns his 'book' – the 'books' from his 'library' (I.ii.167; Bible: lit. books, a library). He starts his last speech with 'I'll deliver all'. Rev 22:15: 'For without are dogs and sorcerers, and whoremongers, and idolators, and whosoever loveth and maketh a lie.' The three *Tem* dissolutes are each of these: (1) Trinculo compares them to dogs; (2) Caliban says he is 'subject [SUBJECT, a pathic; see BITE] to a . . . sorcerer' (III.ii.48); (3) by def. they are idolators, Caliban kneeling to 'kiss thy foot: I prithee, be my god' (II.ii.153) and calling Stephano 'my lord' (III.ii.34); (4) each of them certainly 'loveth and maketh a lie'. It only remains that they be whoremongers, and that the puns reveal.

See APPLAUSE, *TrC*; LOLL, *TrC*; SLAVE, *Cor*; SWINE, *R3*; INFINITE, *AW*.

Life Penis; vulva. *Vita*: life; *vitto*: food; in jest, man's penis (F). *Vit*: penis; *vite*: vulva (Cot).

Vie: life; *viedaze*: penis of an ass (F). The punning cluster often includes Fr *vite*, fast. 'O not so fast! my ravished mistress cries,/ Lest my content, that on thy life relies,/ Be brought too soon' (Nashe, *The Choice of Valentines*).

Oth. Bianca and Desdemona each maintain the honesty (chastity) of their life, their genitals, in regard to Cassio.

v.i.122, Bianca: 'I am no strumpet; but of life as honest/ As you'.

ii.59, Desdemona: 'I never did/ Offend you in my life, never loved Cassio . . . . I never gave him token [TOKEN, genitals].'

AC, I.i.46: 'Now for the love of Love and her soft hours . . . There's not a minute of our lives should stretch/ Without some pleasure now.' The lives of both Antony and Cleopatra will pleasurably STRETCH (in coitus).

MV, III.v.79: 'It is very meet/ The Lord Bassanio live an upright life . . . He finds the joys of heaven here on earth'; and

v.i.214, Bassanio: 'Even he that did uphold the very life/ Of my dear friend'.

It is very MEET, coit/ MEAT, penis (K; *vitto*: food, penis), that Bassanio live a (phallicly) up-right life, says Jessica, who then, in bawdy 'table-talk', tells her own husband, 'I'll set you forth'. Perhaps the joys of HEAVEN (homosexual love) are what *Lord* Bassanio finds on earth through Portia's *upholding* the life of his DEAR friend. Table-play: sex act (Hulme, p. 137).

See ALTER, *MV*; OFFICE, *AW*; TIGER, *TA*.

Lightning Sexual orgasm. A 'flash' is lightning, as in the 'lightning flash' of *TA*, II.i.3: *JC*, I.iii.52; *Per*, III.i.6. 'Pistol's cock is up,/ And flashing fire will follow' (*H5*, II.i.56): (1) flashing fire follows when the cock is up and the pistol discharges; (2) seminal ejaculation follows when the cock (penis – TWR; P) is up and the Pistol/ pizzle (penis – K) discharges.

RJ, v.iii.90, Romeo: 'How oft when men are at the point of death/ Have they been merry! which their keepers call/ A lightning before death; O, how may I/ Call this a lightning? O my love! my wife!' Romeo, in a fury, desperate, having just killed a man and believing he is writ in 'sour misfortune's book!' is hardly MERRY except as it meant lusty and wanton. In 'This vault . . . full of light [venial, of a sin]', this L *fornix*, vault and brothel, he says, 'O here/ Will I set up my everlasting rest [REST, the erect penis]'. To *die* is to experience an orgasm (TWR; P). Romeo has a phallic erection and discharge, 'a lightning', as he embraces Juliet. See INTEND.

Like Homosexual. Gk *homoios*, *homo-*: the same, alike, like.

See SHED; VERY, *AYL*; EVIL, *AYL*; HEARER; WITCHCRAFT, *CE*; PROMISE, *Cor*.

Linguist A linguist is a man of more than one tongue. Such a man can also be (1) a deceiver (*MND*, III.ii.72: 'with doubler tongue/ Than thine, thou serpent, never adder stung'); (2) an intimate kisser as in Plautus, *Comedy of Asses*, 690: a man asks the courtesan to kiss him, saying, 'make a reptile of me and let me have a double tongue in my mouth'.

AW, IV.iii.265. Parolles is a 'linguist': he is a double-talker and deceiver. It is likely this is also bawdy punning on his sexual practices, for he is a 'manifold linguist' and 'manifold' is the intestines or bowels (*OED*). Cf. *KL*, II.i.49: 'with how manifold . . . a bond/ The child was bound to the father' – the bond of the bowels, as in *MM*, III.i.29 ('thine own bowels, which do call thee sire') and Gen 15:4 ('he that shall come forth of thine bowels shall be thine heir').

Parolles is an apologist, an arse-kisser, or, as he was called 15 lines earlier, a 'both-sides rogue' (BOTH-SIDES), hypocrite and pederast; a 'cat' (prostitute – F&H) whose 'offences' (OFFENCES, fornications) are 'many' – a *mani*fold linguist (see TWO-FOLD). The only other 'linguist' in Sh is the bisexual Valentine (PERFECTION, *TGV*).

Lip *Labia pudendi*, 'lips of a womans Privities' (Cot, s.v. *landies*). Robert Burton, p. 844: 'it is the husband's first business to cut apart the fettered nether lips of the maiden' (a practice that preserved chastity). The 'lip' of any orifice is the rim (lips: 'puckered skin around the anus' – Rodgers). To lip: to caress genitally.

Oth, IV.i.71: 'O, 'tis the spite of hell . . . To lip a wanton in a secure couch,/ And to suppose her chaste!' To 'lie in those unproper beds' and lip in secure couches certainly implies more than kissing (kiss: coit – P).

WT, v.i.54. Had he not lost his wife, leaving himself 'heirless' (10), Leontes would 'Have taken treasures from her lips – ', and Paulina adds, 'And left them/ More rich for what they yielded.' He would have taken her treasure (vulva, chastity – P) and left her lips more rich, i.e. with child, with yield, to replace what they yielded.

Per, v.iii.42: Pericles wishes 'That on the touching of her lips I may/ Melt and no more be seen' – a ref. to the melting (of the orgasm – P) after the lips, in which he disappears, touch (copulate – F&H; P).

Oth, II.i.178: 'Yet again your finger to your lips? would they were clyster-pipes for your sake!' Iago compares Cassio's courtly gesture to the approach of an enema tube to the other lips (of the rectum), tubes for his SAKE/ sack or bag-like cavity.

MND, v.i.192, 203. A combination of bawdry and scatology, Pyramus played by *Bottom*:

> *Thisbe.* My cherry lips have often kissed thy stones,
> Thy stones with lime and hair knit up in thee [the wall]. . . .
> *Pyramus.* O, kiss me through the hole of this vile wall!
> *Thisbe.* I kiss the wall's hole, not your lips at all.

Her CHERRY lips have often kissed the stones (testicles – *OED*; P) of the WALL (buttocks), the stones KNIT up (coitally) with lime (L *limus*, slime, mud) and hair. Now she kisses the hole (anus – P; K, p. 117) of the vile/ villus (shaggy hair) WALL – and not Bottom's lips at ALL (genitals).

See NETHER; FANCY, *Ham*; BOARD, *TSh*; LAUGHTER, *JC*.

Little The arse. The suffix -cule or *-culus*, which means little, puns on cule (*W*; *OED*) or L *culus*, the rump.

MND, II.i.166. The juice of 'a little western flower' will make man or woman dote on the next creature it sees. And the 'liquor' (178) of that *little* flower from the WEST (arse) makes Titania liquorish or lecherous and she dotes on *Bottom*, 'an ass' (III.ii.33) with an ass's head.

See PRETTY, *LLL*; CAMEL, *R2*; DRAWERS; ABOUT, *KJ*; MONSTER, *MND*; YELLOW.

Load 1. Of the bowels, full of undigested food or faeces (*W*).

See BRAINS, *Ham*; GOLD, *JC*; KEY, *R3*.

2. Semen (P).

Luc, 734. The raped Lucrece 'bears the load of lust he left *behind*,/ And he the burthen of a guilty *mind*' (italics added) – BEHIND and MIND (arse).

WT, IV.iv.360: 'when I was young . . . I was wont/ To load my she with knacks; I would have . . . pour'd it/ To her acceptance'. 'Knacks' and *knocks*: the penis and coition (F&H). He would have poured the silken 'treasury' (female pudendum – F&H; C; P; semen – P).

H8, II.iii.39. Anne is asked if she would prostitute herself for a title (see ANNUAL): 'have you limbs/ To bear that load of title [TITLE, penis]?'

Lobby Latrine. Man's sewer, the anus. Fr *couloir*: lobby, passage, corridor; *culare*: arse-gut (F); *culier*: of the arse (Cot). See PASSAGE.

2H6, IV.i.61. Suffolk demeans the Captain: 'Remember . . . How in our voiding lobby hast thou stood/ And duly waited for my coming forth?' Pun on that which is voided, specif. excrement, and this CAPTAIN (pimp) waiting in the voiding-lobby or anteroom. See CUP.

Ham, IV.iii.39. When the King asks, 'where's Polonius?' Hamlet answers, 'At supper'; 'Not where he eats, but where he is eaten'. After a series of puns on eating and evacuation, Hamlet concludes, 'a king may go a progress through the guts of a beggar'. Repeating 'Where is Polonius?' the King is told, 'you shall nose him as you go up the stairs into the lobby'.

This scatological metaphor began when Hamlet said (III.iv.212), 'I'll lug the guts' of Polonius (who had hid 'Behind the arras'; guts, BEHIND, ARRAS/ arse – three words signifying intestines), a brutal phrase, made clear by its pun on the *lug*worm or *lob*worm (lobby worm) – a large, 8–10 inch worm, used for bait ('A man may fish with the worm . . .' – IV.iii.28). It 'crawls through sandy and muddied soil, eating its way as it goes, and leaving in its wake coiled casts of the soil thus passed through its body' (*CD*).

See TABLE, *Ham*, for the details of this, mankind's, fate.

Lodge(r) Coit; a whore, a whorehouse. Lit. a house in the forest occupied in the hunting-season; hunting is a freq. pun on sexual indulgence, both being venery (*AYL*, IV.iii.18; *TN*, I.i.16; *TA*, II.ii.25). See UP AND DOWN for Radcliffe's 'Bawd' who led wives 'To lodge with Squires of high renown'.

TN, III.iii.40: 'Hold, sir, here's my purse./In the south suburbs at the Elephant,/Is best to lodge . . . there shall you have me.' The *suburbs* of London was the brothel district (*OED*: C; *JC*, II.i.285). A house in the suburbs (a brothel – F&H) is where it is best to lodge. There Sebastian shall have (carnally – P) Antonio, whose 'desire/More sharp than filed steel, did spur' him forth (4), 'pure for his [Sebastian's] love' (V.i.86), into a city where he shall 'pay dear' if lapsed (PAY, coitally; DEAR/deer, hind: the deer pun is esp. pertinent to the hunting-lodge). STEEL: penis; SPUR: prick (penis – *OED*); PURE: homosexual love.

H5, II.i.33:

Pistol. . . . Nor shall my Nell keep lodgers.
Hostess. No, by my troth . . . for we cannot lodge . . . fourteen gentlewomen that live honestly by the prick of their needles, but it will be thought we keep a bawdy house straight.

Ham, I.v.87: 'leave her to heaven/And to those thorns that in her bosom lodge,/To prick and sting her'. Each word adds to the Ghost's saying Hamlet's mother is adulterous: thorns (penises – P) that lodge in her bosom (genitals – C; P) and *prick* and STING her (sensual desire – C; P).

See COPATAIN HAT; REST, *TGV*.

Loll Engage in sexually dubious activity. Johnson's *Dictionary* proposes that loll 'might be contemptuously derived from lollard, a name of great reproach before the reformation; of whom one tenet was, that all trades not necessary to life are unlawful'. Dryden's trs. of Juvenal's *Satires*, vi, 'The Vices of Women': 'But wanton now, and lolling at our Ease . . . No Crime, no Lustful Postures are unknown'. Loll: stick the tongue out in derision (F&H). Loll-tongue: to be salivated for syphilis (G; F&H).

TrC, I.iii.162. Achilles 'in his tent/Lies mocking our designs: with him Patroclus/Upon a lazy bed . . . on his press'd bed lolling'. Achilles, with his 'male varlet' or 'masculine whore' (V.i) LIES (buggers) on the lazy (to lazy: to loll) bed, press'd (weighed down coitally – P) with the lolling lovers.

R3, III.vii.72. Gloucester 'is not lolling on a lewd day-bed,/But on his knees at meditation:/Not dallying with a brace of courtezans,/But meditating with two deep divines' (see PART).

RJ, II.iv.96, Mercutio: 'drivelling love is like a great natural, that runs lolling up and down to hide his bauble in a hole'. UP AND DOWN (whore-like) he runs to HIDE (whore, cover with skin) his bauble (penis – C; P) in a hole (female pudendum – C; P; anus – TWR, p. 106, and K., p. 117). 'Drivel' also meant a dirty, foul person.

Lombardy, Lumbert 'The sin of Buggery brought to London by the Lombards' (Bugger, *OED*, s.v. 1617). Lombardy is the setting of *TSh*: see BUDGE, last para.

'Lumbert street' (SMOOTH, *2H4*) is believed a corruption of 'Lombard Street', home of bankers, pawn-brokers, money-changers. 'Usury' puns on sexual indulgence (C; P); 'lumbar' means of the loin. Thomas Randolph, 'An Ode to Master Anthony Stafford': the poet had rather 'gain a kiss' from 'country girls' than meet 'The beauties of the Cheap and wives of Lombard Street' (*Signet Classic Poets of the 17th c.*, vol. II, p. 181). See QUAINT, *AYL*.

Loose To relax or loosen the bowels (*OED*). Troubled with a loose behind, beshitten (*foireux* – Cot).

See PURGATION, *LLL*; FLEW, *H8*; PRAYER, *MWW*.

Love 1. A flatus; mockery of the speaker (and his hot air). *Loffa, -e*: a close-fart (F).

TSh, I.ii.179. Hortensio will 'no whit be behind in duty/To fair Bianca, so beloved of me', though ' 'tis now no time to vent our love'. He won't *be* BEHIND his *be*loved, not one WHIT/WHITE, pun on the fair or white (It *bianca*) Bianca, and on the white target usually placed on the *butt* (*OED*). It is not the right moment to *vent* that hot air (*loffe*) he calls love. Vent: to discharge by natural evacuation; the anus, and the power of tracing by scent, as hounds in pursuit (*OED*).

LLL, III.i.17: 'sometime through the nose, as if you snuffed up love by smelling love'. V.ii.415:

Biron. . . . My love to thee is sound, sans crack or flaw.
Rosaline. Sans sans, I pray you.

A reflection on the quality of Biron's love. He says it is SOUND (probe the bottom). Rosaline seems to think it is 'soun' ('the musical tone of a fart' – TWR) and not sans crack (*pet*: a crack or fart – Cot) or flaw, i.e. a crack or sudden short blast. She would prefer to do without (Fr *sans*) the souns or farts; without (*sans*) L *sens*, one of the five senses, here the *sens* / scents of smell. 'I pray you' is the third pun of this French lady: *après*, behind, after (Cot) – *après vous*, behind you. Without scents after or behind you. (See PRAYER, *CE*, for similar pun.)

2. Nothing. *L'oeuf*: egg; *l'oeuve*: spawn (Cot). Egg: 1589, oval; hence an 'O' or nothing. In games, 'love' means no score, nothing.

MV, III.iv.13. In an elaborate conceit on the yoke of love Antonio and Bassanio share, and the yoke or 'bond' they share with Shylock, Portia says their 'souls do bear an equal yoke of love. . . . If it be so,/How little is the cost' she pays for 'purchasing' Antonio from his bond. An equal yoke of love or yolk of *l'oeuf* is the golden yolk. The *little cost* is the 'gold/To pay the *petty debt*' (III.ii.309; italics added) for purchasing Antonio and Bassanio: 'Since you are dear bought, I will love you dear' (315) – a *little* cost and yet *dear* bought, because both LITTLE (-cule, pun on *cule*, rump) and DEAR/deer (K) pun on the hind or arse, and the hart/HEART, arse, the heart or love. Portia's gold will pay the petty DEBT, L *aes alienum* (lit. another's money; pun on another's ass/arse). Perhaps it will buy Bassanio from that yoke of love shared by the SOULS (buttocks) of him and Antonio, 'the bosom lover of my lord' (bosom: to clinch amorously – C; the private parts – P). This may be another punning affirmation of the homosexual relationship. See a similar word-cluster in *TA*, IV.i.109: 'bad bondmen to the yoke' – at a time when there were bondmen, BAD (*OED*) meant effeminacy (in *TA* it referred to Tamora's sodomitical sons, Chiron and Demetrius: see Index).

KL, I.i.94. Lear asks Cordelia what she can say to draw a more 'opulent' share than her sisters.

Cordelia. Nothing my lord.
Lear. Nothing!
Cordelia. Nothing!
Lear. Nothing will come of nothing. . . .
Cordelia. . . . I cannot heave
My heart into my mouth. I love your majesty
According to my bond. . . .

She offers nothing, i.e. her love; her heart (of gold – *1H4*, II.iv.307: 'hearts of gold'; *H5*, IV.i.44: 'heart of gold') – the golden yolk (i.e. the core or heart) of the egg she cannot heave (an *oeuve* pun?) into her mouth; she loves him according to her bond or yoke/yolk. This metaphor of eating love (*l'oeuf* or egg) continues (118–20) in Lear's 'barbarous Scythian,/Or he that makes his generation messes/To gorge his appetite', who eats his children. This BARBAROUS/Gk *borboros* (mud, a bog) Scythian makes them his messes, lit. (1) what he eats, and (2) his filth, what he excretes (FRANK).

Lear says nothing opulent will come from this nothing, not understanding that the nothing ('O') or love she offered is *l'oeuf* or the egg from which everything *does* come, the *yolk* or core (*OED*).

*Cor*delia had offered herself, L *cor*, Fr *coeur*, her heart (a common pun; cf. *Ham*, III.ii.78: 'In my heart's core, ay, in my heart of heart').

See MOVE, *TGV*; *TrC*, I.ii.146–9 (love–egg–laugh).

Lubber(ly) (1) Sexually wanton. *Lubre*: filthy, lubric (1490, lascivious) – Cot. Dryden, 'To the Pious Memory of Mrs Anne Killigrew': 'This lubrique and adult'rate age'. 'Your lubberly legs would not carry your lobcock [a large, relaxed penis – F&H; G] body' (F&H).

(2) The epicene: lubric is SLIPPERY (third sex).

MWW, V.v.195. Slender came 'to marry Mistress Anne Page, and she's a great lubberly boy'. Page: 'Upon my life, then, you took the wrong.' Slender took (carnally – C; P) the WRONG (a penis) took the BOY (catamite) counterfeiting Anne.

TGV, II.v.47, for another (sexually) mistaken 'lubber' and 'lover' ('this lubber–lover' – F&H), see SWINGE and MISTAKE.

TN, IV.i.14. The Clown, mistaking Sebastian for Cesario, says, 'I am afraid this great lubber, the world, will prove a cockney.' Past experience tells him Cesario–Viola is an effeminate lubber: see COCKNEY (effeminate milksop). In 'lubber' plus 'cockney' Sh means Lubberland (*Cucagne* – F; *CD*), the land of Cockaigne (London – B), imaginary land of dissolution, mocked by Jonson, *Bartholomew Fair*, III.ii: 'will it [the pig] run o' the spit into our mouths . . . as in Lubberland'. Cf. *2H4*, II.iv.251: Falstaff, the 'whoreson little tidy Bartholomew boar-pig'.

TrC, III.iii.139: 'the lubber Ajax' (effeminate, impotent: GOUT; BAD; CAMEL).

KL, I.iv.101: 'If you will measure your lubber's length again, tarry', says Kent to Oswald, the DOG (sodomite), 'mongrel', 'cur' and 'Lady the brach', a *bitch* hound – i.e. Oswald, the pathic (like the 'brach' in *TrC*, II.i.126 – P).

M

Madonna A most important pun, made in Act I, repeated in Act V, and clue to the allegory in *Twelfth Night*. A madonna or mad *donna* (woman, wife, lady, mistress, dame – F). *Ma donna*: my wife, mistress, dame. A mad or foolish woman, even an ass.

TN, I.v.64, Clown: 'Good madonna, give me leave to prove you a fool.' She, whom he calls 'madonna' nine times in this scene, he also calls 'my mistress' and 'My lady' (III.i.46, 63). The pun on *mad* donna is exposed in l.145: 'He is but mad yet, madonna; and the fool shall look to the madman' (mad donna and mad man). The same pun is made in V.i.300:

Clown. . . . 'By the Lord, madam – '
Olivia. How now! art thou mad?
Clown. No, madam, I do but read madness. . . .
Olivia. Prithee, read i' thy right wits.
Clown. So I do, madonna. . .

It is usually assumed her violent reaction is to his reading in a loud voice. But Olivia, remembering the joke he played on her once before (ELDER), is alert to potential impudence in 'madam' or mad dame, as we see from her questioning whether *he* is not mad and her advocacy of his using his right wits. She may also be evening the score: his RIGHT (L *rectum*) wits would be those of an arse. When the Clown persists and calls her 'madonna' – not used since I.v, when he proved her a fool DEXTERIOUSLY (L *dexter*, right), q.v. – the infuriated Olivia takes the letter away from him.

The letter is from 'The Madly-Used Malvolio', who Maria had said 'turned heathen' and is 'no Christian'. See YELLOW for puns on the pagan goddess Cybele, whose festivals were celebrated with music, dancing and orgiastic excesses; so, too, on Twelfth Night, *festival* of the Epiphany, a time of merry-making, *Feste* (the Clown), Toby and Andrew sing, dance, get drunk and engage in lewdness (see EXCELLENT; BREAST). They are a travesty of the three wise men: 'Three merry men be we', says Toby and breaks into song, 'O, the twelfth day of December, – ' (II.iii.81–91).

As a 'puritan' (151), Malvolio regards Christmas festivities as pagan and refuses to participate in the merry-makers' frivolity. He asks them if they are 'mad' and chastises them for making 'an alehouse of my lady's house' – for desecrating the house, the church of my lady, *ma donna*, Olivia, the Madonna (see III.i.1–10 for the house–church quibbles). It is not he who is 'heathen' but they who are pagan (see YELLOW) and worship the lascivious Cybele, also called Great Mother of God. It is the Mother of Jesus Christ, the Madonna, whose steward he is, stewardry being the individual's function in the practical work of the Christian church. Malvolio is the 'steward' (II.iii.77) of Olivia, of that Madonna.

Malice Testicles; potent evil. L *malus*, apple (APPLE, testicle); bad, wicked.

KJ, II.i.251. Yield and 'Our cannons' malice vainly shall be spent' – the cannons' balls will be spent (exhaustion of semen – *OED*; P), shooting at the sky. The men will 'bear home that lusty blood again / Which here we came to spout against your town' – they, too, will not expend their balls, their BLOOD (semen) against the 'town . . . children, wives'.

Mac, II.iii.138: 'Look to the lady: / And when we have our naked frailties hid, / That suffer in exposure, let us meet. . . . In the great hand of God I stand; and . . . fight . . . treasonous malice.'

A biblical conceit: look to the Lady Macbeth (Eve). Sin, death, mortality have entered, through the treasonous malice (*malus*, the apple); and now the nakedness of the sinners must be covered.

H8, I.i.105: 'The cardinal's malice and his potency' – see DART; SIZE.

V.iii.44: 'Men that make/Envy and crooked malice nourishment/Dare bite the best' (as in *Mac* above, a ref. to biting the apple of sin).

Man A homosexual. L *homo*: man. See HOMO.

See PLAINLY, *MND*; SAME; STRANGER, *Tem*; CONTENT, *MV*; OLD WOMAN, *MWW*; ILL, *TN*; PASSAGE, *Tim*; SHADOW; OTHER, *MND*.

Manner (1) The *man*ner of man, his sex. 'In the mainour [manner]' (1530) means in the act of doing something unlawful, *in flagrante delicto*, while the crime is blazing – used for catching someone in fornication: 'He comes i' the middle of their sport . . . Took the poor Lovers in the Manner' (F&H, s.v. Sport, 1673). Num 5:13: 'And a man lie with her carnally . . . and there be no witness against her, neither she be taken with the manner'.

(2) Manure.

These two uses sometimes overlap and suggest sexual entry from the rear and, perhaps, sodomitically.

See SUCH, *MV*; MATTER, *LLL*; PERNICIOUS, *R2*; DRY, *MWW*; CURIOUSLY, *AW*.

Marriage, marry An unpleasant binding, hardly a new idea (Montaigne, Bk III, ch. 5: 'A good marriage (if any there be) refuseth the company and conditions of love'; it is 'shackles', a bird's 'cage', and, as Socrates says, whether you do or don't take a wife, you'll regret it). But Sh's puns are his own: a marriage/*amarrage* (the cordage of a ship, used to tie or moor – Cot); marry/*amarrer* (to tie or moor – Cot).

AC, II.vi.127. Menas says the marriage of Antony to Octavia has KNIT (joined sexually) not the married pair but 'Caesar and he for ever knit together. . . . that purpose made *more* in the *marriage* than the love of the parties.' Enobarbus then predicts the 'band' (in logic, the copula) meant to 'tie' will be found a 'strangler of . . . amity'.

Oth, I.ii.67. Desdemona's father denies that she willingly married Othello, the Moor. 'If she in chains of magic were not bound . . . So opposite to marriage' was she that she never would have 'Run from her guardage to the sooty bosom/Of such a thing' as Othello. Only magic chains that bound, magic *moor*ing of the Moor who 'enchanted' her, would have made her leave her guard*age* and run into this marri*age*, this *amarrage* or *moor*ing.

See MERE, *Oth*; SHEEP, *LLL*; HANG, *TN*.

Mask, visard, visor A prostitute, by whom (as by loose women) they were worn to conceal identity. See Sir Charles Sedley, 'To Nysus': 'If we write Plays, few see above an Act,/And those lewd Masks, or noisie Fops distract' (*Penguin Book of Restoration Verse*, p. 290). Etherege, *The Man of Mode*, II.ii: 'A lady masked in a pretty dishabillie whom [he] entertained with more respect than the gallants do a common vizard'.

RJ, I.v.25. Lord Capulet boasts of past sexual exploits: he, too, has 'seen the day/That I have worn a visor and could tell/A whispering tale in a fair lady's ear,/Such as would please'. 'Worn' cannotes coital wear and tear (C; P); and the tale (penis – K; P) he remembers so fondly that pleased (amorously – P) the lady's EAR (pudendum) is his own. He concludes, 'foot it, girls' (FOOT: common pun on fuck) and tells his cousin, 'you and I are past our dancing days:/How long is't now since last yourself and I/Were in a mask?' Now past DANCING (fornicating – TWR), it was twenty-five years ago, at a nuptial, that they were in a mask or *in* a strange woman. *Loup*: a half-mask; *danse de loup*: lechery (Cot).

I.iv.30. Mercutio's sentiments about the ball were: 'Prick love for pricking. . . . A visor for a visor!' The parallel doublets suggest that the second, too, is bawdy. A visor for a visor, i.e. one who wantonly pricks (coits – P). Cf. FAN: Mercutio again speaks of an obscene 'prick' and something hiding the face of a 'bawd' (the Nurse).

JC, v.i.62. Cassius condemns Octavius Caesar (and Sh the triumvirate): 'A peevish schoolboy . . . Join'd with a masker and a reveller!' JOIN'd (coitally) with Lepidus, the masker or pimp ('Meet to be sent on errands' – ERRAND-goer, pimp); and with Antony, the reveller (copulator and adulterer – TWR; revel: joyous love-making – P). To these, Caesar, school-BOY (catamite), is joined.

Matter 1. Pandering. Métier or trade (harlotry, pandering – P). 2. Female pudendum. Matrice: the womb.

TrC, I.i.86: 'I have had my labour for my travail . . . gone between and between but small thanks for my labour', so 'I'll meddle nor make no more i' the matter.' The labour and travail of Pandarus's womb–matrice, his pandering–métier, did not give birth to the matter or harlotry in which he was go-between (pander – P). He will *meddle* and *make* (coit – P) no more in the matter.

MWW, v.i.11: 'Master Brook! Master Brook, the matter will be known tonight, or never.' After several frustrated attempts on Mrs Ford, Falstaff says her matter or pudendum will finally be known (carnally – P); and he will deliver her to Brook for his presumably also lecherous designs. 'Deliver' (like 'labour' in *TrC* above) reinforces 'matter' as womb and harlotry. Eight repetitions of 'Master' Brook (in only 34 lines) are a Fr *maistre / maître* / master / matter pun. 'Master' was a title given all tradesmen (bawds – P), the sorry occupation of both men who planned to whore Mrs Ford: Falstaff, the 'pander' (v.v.176) who would break her in and then hand her over to the customer, Master Brook. Falstaff had promised BROOK (a pimp; lit. to enjoy) 'you shall . . . enjoy Ford's wife' (II.ii.265).

LLL, I.i.203. Costard was caught 'in the manor-house' and in the MANNER (sex-act): 'The matter is to me, sir, as concerning Jaquenetta. The manner of it is, I was taken with the manner.' The matter, i.e. legal allegation, pertains to him who was caught 'with the manner' (*in flagrante delicto – OED*). 'As concerning' means in the matter of and *in re* (L *re*, thing). Costard's matter is concerning, is in the matter or in the thing (genitals – P) of Jaquenetta. See RE.

3. Penis and semen.

TGV, II.v.21: 'Why, then, how stands the matter with them?' – 'Marry, thus; when it stands well with him, it stands well with her.' Pun on marry / marrow (semen – P) – the matter needed to make *it* stand (erect – P) and well.

LLL, III.i.119:

Costard. . . . I, Costard, running out, that was safely within,
 Fell over the threshold, and broke my shin.
Armado. We will talk no more of this matter.
Costard. Till there be more matter in the shin.

Puns on (1) Costard's running out of the safety of the manor-house and falling over the THRESHOLD (point of entry for threshing or copulation); (2) the running out of his semen, *that* had been safely within him and / or Jaquenetta, and his post-coital falling, as in Son 151: 'flesh . . . rising at thy name . . . is contented . . . To stand in thy affairs, fall by thy side . . . for whose dear love I rise and fall'. Freeing Costard from custody, Armado says 'no more [talk] of this matter' – legal or sexual. Costard agrees, at least until he has more matter in the SHIN (penis): renewed virility.

AYL, IV.i.74, Rosalind: 'speak first, and when . . . gravelled for lack of matter, you might take occasion to kiss . . . good orators, when they are out, they will spit; and for lovers lacking . . . matter, the cleanliest shift is to kiss.' GOOD ORATORS (male whores) will SPIT (penetrate sexually) when they are OUT (Fr *hors*). But when they run out of or lack matter, semen and erection, they take OCCASION (genitals) and kiss (in bowls, said of one ball touching another when both are in motion – *OED*). Speakers out of matter are *gravel*led, have a problem with their *stones* (testicles – *OED*), for which the cleanliest shift (sexual strategem – P) is to kiss (osculate or masturbate): (1) *cleanliest*: other writers had jested that actors blow their noses, cough or spit when they are *non plus*; (2) *shift*: 'When there is no more ink in the pen,/I will make a Shift as well as other men' (F&H, s.v. Pen, 1547) – an 'indelicate figure which occurs in jest books and other early literature' (Hazlitt, ibid.).

4. Faecal matter. Fielding, *Jonathan Wild*, ch. 13, puns on matter, MANNER/manure: 'the matter . . . the unmannerly word . . . thrown in our faces [/faeces] . . . this mighty matter of philosophy, this heap of knowledge, which was to bring such large harvests . . . to those who sowed it, and . . . to enrich the ground on which it fell'. (See MELANCHOLY, *AYL*.)

AC, II.ii.179, Maecenas: 'matters are so well digested. You stayed well by't [the BITE: cunt, coital grip; of the WELL, cunt, whore] in Egypt.' Puns on a 'matrass', chemical vessel for digesting (*OED* 1605). The usual ambivalence concerning Cleopatra: *cuict* is digested, fit to be eaten (Cot), but *matiere cuict* is often used for *matiere fecale* (excrement – Cot). The 'matter of feast' (187), the 'Egyptian dish', Cleopatra, in her 'mattress' (II.vi.71)/matrice (womb), is all these things. See THRONE.

Mead(ow) Prat or buttocks. L *pratum*: meadow. Pratal: growing in meadows.

TA, III.i.125. Titus asks his mutilated, raped daughter, how may I 'do thee ease:/Shall [we] sit around . . . Looking all downwards, to behold our cheeks/How they are stain'd as meadows, yet not dry,/With miry slime left on them'. Each word stresses Lavinia's HEINOUS/anus/rape. *Stain'd* is sexual and bloody violence, defiling (C; P); the stain'd as(s) meadows/the defiled prat of Lavinia. How can he do her EASE (relieve the ass/arse): shall they empathetically *sit* around and *down*wards look (*mirer* – Cot) at the miry slime (mire: defecate – P) on their not yet dry CHEEKS (buttocks)? How shall they 'Pass the remainder of our hateful days?' – PASS (defecate) the remainder of HATEFUL (Fr *haineuse*/anus) days – in their total identification with her, possibly sodomitical, rape (see SPURN). He expects the 'brinish bowels' (97) of the sea will swallow him. Laurence Sterne, *Tristram Shandy* (see RIGHT): an extended metaphor on a woman's 'Backside' quotes 'Aristotle's Master Piece' as saying 'when a man doth think of any thing which is past – he looketh down upon the ground' – just so Titus, in his extended metaphor on Lavinia's backside, sits *looking all downwards.*

H5, V.ii.48. Burgundy says only 'rank' (offensive smelling) things now grow, and contrasts this, or thinks he does, with the old 'fertile' France, 'The even mead, that erst brought sweetly forth/The freckled cowslip'. But his language makes a mockery of France and himself.

He is French-speaking and the Fr equiv. of 'freckles' is *bran de judas* (Cot), lit. sandy-coloured (*de judas*) excrement (*bran*), flecked on the face of the cowslip (lit. cow-dung or SLIP – *OED*). This is what the meadow sweetly brought forth (*Mac*, I.vii.72: 'Bring forth men-children only') – precisely what one would expect a *meadow* to give birth to, a *prat* to bring forth: dung. See HATEFUL: and the same pun four lines further on; IDLE.

As for Burgundy, he is a traitor, a Judas (sandy-coloured) who will desert Talbot and be seduced by Pucelle into fighting for FRANCE (q.v.): he, too, is dung.

Means A pander; money earned by or used for whoring.

MM, II.i.84. Had Elbow's wife been 'a woman cardinally given' she might have 'been accused in fornication, adultery' in the 'naughty house'. 'By the woman's means?' – 'Ay, sir, by Mistress Overdone's means: but . . . she spit in his face'. She might have been accused by Mistress Overdone's *means*, Pompey the pander; accused of the *woman's means* ('way of women-kind' – *Per*, IV.vi.159), of whoring.

III.ii.22, Duke to Pompey: 'Fie, sirrah! a bawd, a wicked bawd!/The evil that thou causest to be done,/That is thy means to live.'

CE, I.ii.18. Antipholus S. is 'stiff and weary' (STIFF, erect phallicly), but gives Dromio money to 'Get thee away.' Dromio S.: '*Many* a *man* would take you at your word,/And go indeed, having so good a *mean*' (italics added; mean/men – K). Antipholus is a good master, a GOOD man (a fornicator), a good mean or pander. He has given Dromio the means to go (copulate – C; P) INDEED (in the deed or sex-act – P), the means to get AWAY/*a way* (whore).

Ham, II.ii.216. Polonius, the 'fishmonger' (seller of fish, i.e. pander of whores – C; P), as Hamlet has just called him, will 'suddenly contrive the means of meeting between him and my daughter'. He will SUDDENLY (lewdly) *con*trive the means, he will be pander, for a MEETING (L *coitus*).

See ANCIENT, *Oth*; ADVOCATE, *Oth*.

Meat See MEET.

Meet(ing)/meat (1) Coitus. L *coitus*, *coetus*: a meeting, assemblage. (2) Meat: flesh of a whore (P). The penis.

Ado, II.i.206: ' 'twas the boy that stole your meat' – Hero, allegedly whored, stolen from Claudio (see STEAL).

TN, II.iii.44: 'Trip [succumb sexually – C; P] no further, pretty sweeting;/Journeys end in lovers meeting,/Every wise man's son doth know.'

MWW, II.i.97. The two wives Falstaff is interested in BOARDing (fornicating) decide to 'appoint him a meeting; give him a show of comfort in his suit'. So Mrs Ford makes the appointment for the meeting or love-making, gives him a show or pretence of comfort (sexual solace – P).

AYL, III.iii.36. Touchstone tells Audrey that 'to cast away honesty upon a foul slut were to put good meat into an unclean dish' (see VELVET, *TSh*). 'But be that as it may be, I will marry thee . . . the vicar . . . promised to meet me in this place . . . and to couple us' (46). Jaques jests, 'I would fain see this meeting' – pun on 'fain' and *fane*, i.e. the 'temple' (50) where they will be coupled (a word used for animal copulation) with no 'assembly [L *coitus*] but horn-beasts'.

H5, v.ii.1, 13. Introducing the final scene and his proposal to Katherine, Henry says, 'Peace to this meeting, wherefore we are met!' Queen Isabella: 'So happy be the issue . . . of this gracious meeting'. Presumably speaking politically, both are punning on the issue, i.e. offspring, of this GRACIOUS (genitally well endowed) *meeting* of his grace, the King – the boy Henry hopes (221) he and Kate will 'compound' (procreate – P).

See SUDDEN, *Ham*; WEATHER; ASSEMBLY, *Ado* and *AYL*.

Melancholy, melancholic Bowel disorder; shitty. *Scitare*: to fall into a depression, despair; to ordain, decree (F). 'Melan-cholic' (lit. having black bile) puns on *melan* (black) *colic* (griping belly pains, arising from the bowel). A 'malady associated . . . with the solitude of the close-stool' (C, p. 110). Jonson, *Every Man in his Humour*, III.i: 'Oh, it's your only fine humour, sir; your true melancholy breeds your perfect fine humour, sir, I am melancholic myself . . . and then I do no more but take pen and paper . . . and overflow you half a score or a dozen sonnets at a sitting.' Melancholy is a fine (the end – *OED*) humour; melancholic Matthew uses *paper* for the *overflow* of sonnets he produces at a *sitting*. Stephen asks, 'have you a stool [a chamber-pot; bowel-evacuation] there, to be melancholy upon?' Weever, *The Whipping of the Satyre*: 'in the melancholike nature is,/So closse conceald . . . At last bursts out into some sodaine ill,/Or mitigates by phisickes soveraigne skill'. Jonson, *Volpone*, v.iv: 'My lady's come most melancholy home,/And says, sir, she will straight to sea for physic.'

WT, IV.iv.790: 'The king . . . is gone aboard a new ship to purge melancholy and air himself . . . [he] is full of grief.' Polixenes is flatulent (full of *air*, gas) and must purge (evacuate the bowels) melancholy. He is full of GRIEF (colic), over his missing son, and has gone on ship to *air* himself and to find his *heir*.

AYL, III.iii.74. The name of the 'melancholy Jaques' (as he is called nine times) puns on a *jakes* or privy (a jakes/Ajax – K). Touchstone fastidiously refers to him as 'Master What-ye-call't'.

1H4, I.ii.88:

Prince. What sayest thou to a hare, or the melancholy of Moor Ditch?
Falstaff. Thou hast the most unsavoury similes and art indeed the most comparative, rascalliest, sweet young Prince.

Kittredge (p. 550) says many dramatists used the hare sitting on its form as a symbol of melancholy: 'Hares flesh' is of 'hard digestion, and breedeth melancholy . . . for it maketh a very dry, thicke, and melancholike blood' (1620).

Sh, however, puns that, being hard to digest, it makes a dry, thick and melancholic (black-bowel-like) turd; and he links it with Moor Ditch, an open sewer freq. mentioned in conjunction with melancholy by Sh's contemporaries (Kittredge), and with the savour or odour that arose from ditches used as privies, especially Moor ('coal-black Moor' – *TA* III.ii.78), or black ditches. A DITCH (L*scrobis*, a ditch; the vulva), pun on vulva and anus, often described as black (see GOWN, *MWW*).

TN, III.iv.28: 'Not black in my mind, though yellow in my legs. It did come to his hands, and commands shall be executed.' Pun on shit and both meanings of *scitare*: (1) *black in my mind* or despair; (2) *commands* or decrees. Also a pun on 'come . . . hands' and *com-mands* (Fr *mains*, HANDS: genitals). Malvolio is not depressed, not black in MIND (arse); he is YELLOW (excrement colour) in his legs. See TARTAR and DRY.

LLL, I.i.234. Armado's letter – 'So it is, besieged with sable-coloured melancholy, I did commend the black-oppressing humour to the most wholesome physic . . . and, as I am a gentleman, betook myself to walk' – suggests the reason this gentleman betook himself to walk to find the privy. He was besieged (SIEGE: excrement, a privy – *OED*) with melan-choly the COLOUR (It *culare*, the arse) of *sable* (the colour black in blazoning – Cot), and needed wholesome physic. The hole/whole/wholesome complex was 'almost exclusively used for bawdy puns' (K).

See CUSHION, *Cym*; MUD/MOOD, *CE*; GRIEF, *RJ*.

Mercury Cure for VD. Wycherley, *The Country Wife*, I.i: a man posing as a 'eunuch' (his loss attributed to VD caught in France) is mocked by another, 'I'll plague him'; 'Hah, hah, hah! Mercury, Mercury!'

TrC, II.iii.13, Thersites: 'Mercury, lose all the serpentine craft of thy caduceus . . . the vengeance on the whole camp! or rather, the bone-ache!' As usual, Thersites calls on syphilis, here 'bone-ache' (P), to punish lechery. Mercury, god of medicine, is to lose his 'craft'; and mercury, the medicine, is to lose its powers. 'Serpentine' is part of the conceit, deriving from L *serpens*, creep, root of the 'serpigo' (syphilis – P) he invokes in l.81 – 1493, 'el mal serpentina' (Richard Burton, p. 89).

WT, IV.iii.25. Autolycus is now 'out of service [prostitution – C; P]', probably impotent from his 'three-pile' (THREE-PILE, VD) and 'tumbling in the hay' with 'aunts' (whores and bawds – *OED*; P). He was 'littered under Mercury'. 'Litter' puns on (1) bedding for animals ('the straw and dung together' – *OED*), and on mercury or quicksilver ('the basest kind of Quicksilver, made of dung and hay' – Cot, s.v. *vulgal*); (2) to bring forth in birth; (3) framework of a sick bed, perhaps that of his venereally diseased mother; and (4) the straw or hay in which he caught and communicated disease.

See CRUST, *Ham.*

Mere(ly) Lecherous. Puns on MERRY–MERRILY (lusty – *OED*; P); 'mere' (obs.) and *mer* (Cot), the sea; *marée*, salt water, the sea, the tide (Cot). *Sentir la marée*, 'To look like a whore (Venus the Goddesse of good-fellowship was bred of the sea-foame)' (Cot).

AC, III.vii.9. Enobarbus rails against women's being at the wars: 'If we should serve with horse and mares together,/The horse were merely lost; the mares would bear/A soldier and his horse'. His prediction that the mares would *bear* the horse (i.e. be mounted by the stallion), the merely/merrily (lustfully) lost horse, when they should instead be bearing the soldier in battle, is exactly what happened: Antony's loss at sea (*marée*) when he followed Cleopatra's deserting ships. Glossing 'merely' as 'utterly' misses Enobarbus's goad that Antony would be merely/merrily lost to Cleopatra – lost to his mare (16th c., contemptuous epithet for a woman), to his 'nag' (x.10) or whore (1598) – lost because of lechery.

Ham, I.ii.137. Hamlet reviles the 'stale [a prostitute; horse urine] uses [sexual intercourse – *OED*]' of this world: 'things rank and gross in nature/Possess it merely'. The pun in 'merely' (lecherously) goes to the heart of the soliloquy: (1) the 'salt' of his mother's tears, her 'salt' or salaciousness; (2) the speed with which his mother did 'post' (the gait of a HORSE/whore) to incestuous sheets. Hamlet's mother (1460, mere; *mère* – Cot), the mare, posted. A 'beast' would have mourned longer, but – as Hamlet says twice – his mother *'married'* (italics added). The world is possessed by things gross (obscene) in NATURE (female pudendum, esp. that of a mare – *OED*).

Oth, II.ii. This scene of only 12 lines tells of Othello's victory at sea (*mer*) and the merriness or lustfulness of his nuptial celebration: the 'pleasure' (P; 'pleasaunce' – TWR), 'dance' (TWR; P) and 'sport' (C; P) – all puns on copulation. The town had received 'tidings . . . importing the mere perdition of the Turkish fleet' – tidings (to moor, to tie; the tide, *marée*) of the *mere* perdition (or loss) at *mer*. But perdition also means the future of the wicked; or hell. And *mere* perdition foreshadows Othello's use of 'perdition' (III.iv.67) or death that would follow upon the loss of the handkerchief (which he later believes lost through Desdemona's lechery): 'Damn her, lewd minx . . . death/For the fair devil' (iii.475).

IV.ii.89: 'I took you for that cunning whore of Venice/That married with Othello' – *marri*ed with Othello the *Moor* (*marer*, to moor – Cot). He took her for a *whore* of *Venice*: *sentir la marée*, to look like a *whore*, like *Venus*, goddess born of sea-foam!

See RHEUM, *MM*.

Mermaid (siren) Prostitute. Dekker and Middleton, *The Honest Whore*: a whore dressed as a man is called a mermaid (*I*, III.v); a man says of a whore, 'I love no Maremaids' (*II*, I.ii). Jonson, *Volpone*, IV.ii: a jealous wife thinks her husband's male companion is a transvestite whore, a 'land-syren here . . . Sporus . . . hermaphrodite' (Sporus, Nero's castrate whom he married).

CE, III.ii.45. Antipholus, approached by a stranger who called him 'husband' and with whom he did 'entertain [enjoy sexually – P] the offer'd fallacy', is now urged by her sister to show 'A husband's office' to the first; so that he logically thinks they are prostitute and bawd: 'train me not, sweet mermaid, with thy note'. Preferring the sister, he asks, 'Sing, siren, for thyself'.

TA, II.i.23. Aaron will 'wanton with this queen', this SEMIRAMIS, 'mount aloft with [his] imperial mistress,/And mount her pitch' – this 'siren, that will charm Rome's Saturnine/And see his shipwreck and his commonweal's'. Pitch: (1) image from falconry, height to which a bird of prey rises before swooping; (2) the musical note of the siren; (3) PITCH, infectious whore. Mounting (copulating – *OED*; P) with this QUEEN/quean, this siren, results in fathering her child.

See SPREAD, *Ham*; ORATOR, *3H6*.

Merry, merrily Sexually wanton (F&H); of sexual intercourse (Chaucer, 'Wife of Bath's Prologue', 42: King Solomon on 'The firste nyghte [of marriage] had many a myrie fit'). Mirth ('myrthe'): sexual intercourse (P; TWR). Beaumont and Fletcher, *The Maid's Tragedy*, III.i: 'What odds, he has not my sister's maidenhead tonight? . . . She's merry enough of herself; she needs no tickling [tickle: masturbate – F&H; P]'.

Cym, I.vi.60. Iachimo tries to incite Imogen to sexual retaliation by calling her absent husband 'Exceeding pleasant . . . So merry and so gamesome: he is call'd/The Briton reveller'. He is EXCEEDING (virile) pleasant ('pleasaunce': sexual joys – TWR; please: enjoy sexually – P; rape – C); gamesome (sexually promiscuous – C; P); a reveller ('revelour': copulator – TWR; revel: indecent carousal – F&H).

III.v.150. Cloten plans to sate his lust on Imogen by dressing in her husband's clothes (see CLOTH) and raping her: 'I'll be merry in my revenge'.

MM, III.ii.6: ' 'Twas never merry world since, of two usuries, the merriest was put down'. Usury: financial usury and prostitution (C; P).

Tim, II.ii.105. The Fool speaks of the two kinds of usury (*MM* above): 'When men come to borrow of your masters, they approach sadly, and go away merry; but they enter my mistress' house merrily, and go away sadly.' They enter lustfully and leave with post-coital sadness. 'Aristotle says, *Omne animal post coitum est triste*' (G, s.v. Gib cat).

MV, II.viii.43: 'Be merry . . . employ your chiefest thought/To courtship and . . . love'.

TSh, III.ii.25: 'Though he be merry, yet withal he's honest'. Tranio defends Petruchio as being cheerfully but not wantonly merry: he is honest, i.e. chaste, and 'means but well' by Katherine.

MWW, IV.ii.107: 'Wives may be merry, and yet honest too'.

See NOTE, *TrC*.

Metamorphosed Transformed in shape or character. In lit., freq. used with ref. to the metamorphosis of male and female into one body, as in Ovid's stories of Hermaphroditus and Salmacis, merged into the original 'hermaphrodite', and Pyramus and Thisbe, metamorphosed into the purple mulberry tree (*MND*, v.i.149: 'Thisbe, tarrying in mulberry shade'). Sydney, *The Countess of Pembroke's Arcadia*, Bk II, chs 16 and 17: Pyrocles calls his disguise as Zelmane, an Amazon or masculine woman, an 'unused metamorphosis'. Like TRANSFORMED, metamorphosed connotes a transvestite or a homosexual. Sh uses it only three times, once in direct ref. to Ovid and twice to describe the ambisexual Proteus and Valentine in *TGV*.

TA, IV.i.42. Lavinia turns the pages of 'Ovid's Metamorphoses', seeking a clue that can alert her family to her rape by Chiron and Demetrius. In Greek mythology, Chiron had transformed himself into a stallion and impregnated Philyra, who then gave birth to Chiron, king of the CENTAURS, half man and half beast, symbols of sexual bestiality (see NORMAN). This is one of the indications that the rape of Lavinia had been sexually bestial.

TGV, I.i.66, Proteus: 'Thou, Julia, thou has metamorphosed me'. Proteus, whose name means many shapes and forms, is speaking of Julia, who spends most of the play in boy's clothes.

II.i.32. Speed tells Valentine that he has become like his friend, 'like Sir Proteus', and 'now you are metamorphosed with a mistress, that, when I look on you, I can hardly think you my master'.

(See Index for puns on the androgynous characteristics of these two gentlemen of Verona.)

Midnight Height of a phallic erection. Marlowe, *Doctor Faustus*, III.iv: 'hast any mind to Nan Spit, our kitchen-maid, then turn her and wind her to thy own use as often as thou wilt, and at midnight'. See TWELVE; NOON.

MM, v.i.281: 'I will go darkly to work with her' – 'That's the way; for women are light at midnight.' Women are light (wanton), show the way, when men go DARKLY (illicitly) to work (copulation – TWR; P) at midnight.

KJ, IV.i.45. In a speech full of time-related puns ('watchful'), the 'Young boy' (BOY, catamite) Arthur, with his 'innocent prate' (PRAT(E), buttocks) pleads for his EYES (eye-*balls*). For the historical rationale of these puns, his being made blind (bot., sterile), emasculated, see SHIP-BOY.

When your head did but ache,
I knit my handkerchief about your brows . . .
And with my hand at midnight held your head,
And . . . cheer'd up the heavy time,
Saying . . . 'Where lies your grief?'
Or 'What good love may I perform for you?'
Many a poor man's son would have lien still
And ne'er have spoken a loving word . . .
But you at your sick service had a prince.

When Hubert's HEAD (prepuce – P; testes) did *but ache* / buttock, Arthur KNIT (united sexually) his handkerchief (his hand; the kerchief, lit. head-covering) about Hubert's brow (over the EYE-balls). Cf. *RJ*, II.iv.119: 'bawdy hand . . . upon the prick of noon'. With his HAND at midnight, he held Hubert's HEAD. Many a POOR (a pederast) MAN'S (L *homo*'s) son (L *puer*) might have lien still (LIE, coit – *OED*; P) lovelessly, but Hubert had at his SICK (It *male*) service (coital – *OED*; P) a prince to cure his GRIEF (bowel-pain) and to CHEER (love) *up* and perform (sexually – P) GOOD love (fornication). Arthur concludes, 'If heaven be pleased that you must use me ill,/Why, then you must' – if HEAVEN (homosexual love) dictate he be used (coitally – *OED*; P) ILL (*male*), homosexually, it must be. See NOON for the next scene.

Milk (1) Masturbate. Jonson, *The Alchemist*, III.ii: 'For she must milk his epididimis. Where is the doxy [sl., prostitute – *OED*]?'

(2) Genital secretions. See FROTH for 16th c. syns for semen, incl. 'milkie slime'. 'Cream' or milk (F&H 1610). *Latte*: milk; soft roe of fish, i.e. milt or semen (F). Creamstick: penis (F&H); Port syn., *bacamarte*: milk-giving gun.

TGV, III.i.278. Launce is in love: she is a 'maid' in that she serves for wages, but not a virginal maid, since she has had 'gossips' (those who attend baptismal services) for her bastards. She is 'better' than a 'horse' (HORSE/whores) or a 'jade' (woman of low morals and horse in bad shape) and has the virtue of the young lady in the Jonson quote above: ' ". . . . She can milk"; look you, a sweet virtue in a maid with clean hands'. See FETCH (she can draw forth).

AC, IV.xv.74. Antony dies. Cleopatra: 'The crown o' the earth doth melt. . . . No more, but e'en a woman, and commanded/By such poor passion as the maid that milks/And does the meanest chares . . . good cheer! . . . Ah, women, women, look,/Our lamp is spent, it's out!' See CROWN for the eroticism of this scene and the likelihood it describes Antony's last amorous embrace. 'Melt' is experience an orgasm (P), and 'spent' means completed a seminal emission (*OED*; P). Cf. 'lanterne' for the metaphor of the quenched light, the 'folk wisdom of the candle and the lantern' (TWR).

This is no ordinary milkmaid. MEAN (coital) *chares* pun on *charesse* (hugging – Cot) and *c(h)aresser*, 'make good cheere unto' (Cot), like Cleopatra's 'good cheer!' CHEER: love.

Cleopatra is commanded by the same passion as any who milk (cause ejaculation by masturbation), who *com-mand* with a hand. (*H5*, III.iv.12: 'La main, de hand'; *Oth*, II.i: hand–main–command; *Ham*, IV.iv: commands–main: *H5*, IV.iv: *commande—mains*–hands.)

The main/mean (K) chares and GOOD (fornicating) CHEER include milking, making love, masturbating.

AW, IV.iii.124. Parolles has sat in the stocks all night and 'weeps like a wench that had shed her milk; he hath confessed himself' to a supposed friar. Terrified, he pours out of every orifice: his eyes, his mouth; he wets himself and prob. spends his semen.

Milking a cow, masturbating a male and a male's urinating were three related ejaculations. *Pisser*: to piss; *le laict pisse*: 'the milke spinnes out of her breasts' – lit. the milk pisses (Cot). Wilmot 'The Disappointed': 'May'st thou ne'er piss that did'st refuse to spend' (spendings: semen – F&H). Rabelais, Bk III, ch. 27, warns that, if nurses 'desist from giving suck . . . they lose their milk; and if continually thou do not . . . exercise and keep thy mentule [penis] going, thy lacticinian [milky] nectar will be gone, and it will serve thee only as a pipe to piss out at' (1694 trs.); ch. 28 addresses the 'withered cod . . . skimmed of its milk . . . empty of sperm' (Le Clercq trs.). See TIGER, *Cor.*

Thus Parolles weeps or is as wet as the wench who SHED (ovulated or menstruated) her milk; he is 'as leaky as an unstanched wench' (UNSTANCHED, *Tem*, I.i.51).

Mind Buttocks; physical passion. Sh would have known the first word of the *Iliad*, 'Menis' (L *mens*), root of 'mind' and 'Minerva', who sprang from the head of her father – 'a paradox that has impregnated male minds to this day' (Günter Grass, *Headbirths*, trs. Ralph Manheim (New York: Harcourt Brace Jovanovich, 1982) p. 5) – his mind that sired her, fig. his bowels (*MM*, III.i.29: 'thine own bowels, which do call thee sire'). Middleton, *Michaelmas Term* , II.iii: 'methinks it does me most good when I take it standing: I know not how all women's minds are'. Father: 'I think they are all of thy mind for that thing.'

Cym, II.i.69. A Lord hopes Imogen will withstand 'this ass' Cloten: 'The heavens hold firm/The walls of thy dear honour, keep unshak'd . . . thy fair mind'. May the WALLS (buttocks) of her DEAR/deer (hind) honour or chastity hold firm; may her *mind* not be SHAKEN (in coitus; a shaker: a lecher) or become in*firm*.

LLL, IV.i.4: 'Whoe'er a' was, a' show'd a mounting mind', says the Princess of 'the king that spurr'd his horse so hard/Against the steep uprising of the hill'. (1) As the man disappears on his mount, the mounted part he SHOWED (*monstre*: show; something unnatural – Cot), this king who rejected women for three years, was his rump. (2) In the context of man's sexual attributes – SPUR (prick); HORSE/arse; hard (erect penis – P); mounting (copulating – P) – the King's mounting mind or arse is analogous to the steep (L *ar-rectum*) *up-rising* of the hill; the croup, i.e. rounded top of a mountain, buttocks.

Tim, IV.ii.49. The mad Timon has lost his *mens* or mind and the men or sycophants who fawned on him ('Undone by goodness!' – do GOOD, copulate). He is 'flung in rage from this ingrateful seat/Of monstrous friends'. They are MONSTROUS (homosexual; sexually bestial) because half human, half animal: in rage (lust – TWR; P) these mad (L *amens*) HORSES/whores – like lustful Centaurs – flung him off the seat on which he rode (copulated – P). These ingrates are gone but Flavius will 'ever serve his mind with my best will;/Whilst I have gold, I'll be his steward still'. Flavius, his STEWARD (pimp) will continue to serve (coitally, esp. of *stallions* – *OED*; P) Timon's passions (1) with his own will (penis – C; P); (2) as long as he has *gold* (a whore). For more on this metaphor of man's screwing of man, see STIR and STEWARD.

See TRANSFORMATION, *CE*; ABSOLUTE, *Mac*; GIFTS, *TGV*; LOAD, *Luc*.

Mingle Copulate (C; P); esp. homosexually, with ref. to the male and female elements mingled in one person. Perh. a pun on mingle/ingle, ningle (catamite). There was a link between (1) the mingler or blender of alcoholic spirits; (2) the pot-boy in an inn or tavern, cup-bearer in a great household; and (3) Zeus's cup-bearer and young lover, Ganymede. Cf. F&H, s.v. Ganymede: (1) a sodomite; (2) a pot-boy, a *mescitore* ('a filler of wine . . . a mingler, a Ganimede' – Florio–Torriano, *Vocabolario*).

AC, I.v.59. Antony, 'not more manlike/Than Cleopatra' (iv.5), is again, one scene later, not wholly one thing or the other, 'not sad . . . not merry . . . but between both:/O heavenly mingle!' See HEAVENLY: Plato's conception of homosexual love.

IV.ii.27. The previous scene had opened with Caesar's saying, 'He calls me boy [L *puer*]', and closed with his saying, 'feast the army . . . they have earned the waste' and predicting victory over 'Poor Antony!', whom he will reduce to POOR/*puer*, BOY. Caesar gave his army feast (*mangeaille* – Cot), waste (*mangeaille pour les pourceaux*: swillings, hogs' wash). And Sh started his *mangeaille*/mangle/mingle conceit.

In the contrasting scene ii, Antony also invites his men to be 'bounteous at our meal' but tells his cup-bearers ('wait on me tonight:/Scant not my cups – 20) that tomorrow he may be a mangled shadow [SHADOW, half-man]'. See CUP and SCANT for puns on homosexuality.

See CAPER, *1H4*.

Minstrel(sy) Derisive term; may connote effeminacy. In 1597 in England, minstrels were by statute classed with rogues, beggars and vagabonds. Old sps 'menstral', 'menestral' led to puns on *menstrual*. *Menestral*: a minstrel; menstrual, woman's monthly flow (Cot). In alchemy, the *menstrual* element was 'added to metal in its conversion into gold' (*OED*).

LLL, I.i.164–78. The effeminate Armado is mocked in terms of alchemy: he is 'refined', has a 'mint' of phrases, is a man of 'fire-new' words, and the King 'will use him for my minstrelsy'. He will be the feminine, menstrual element in the otherwise all male court.

Tim, II.ii.170. Flavius defends his 'husbandry': 'when every room/Hath . . . bray'd with minstrelsy,/I have retired me to a wasteful cock,/And set mine eyes at flow'. Sh compares Timon's sycophants, seeking his gold, to minstrels – diseased, begging whores. Every room bray'd (bray, *braye*: 'crie, like an asse' – Cot). A *braye* is also (Cot) a 'trusse . . . worne by such as are burst', a close linen breech or under-slop, a diaper (and doubtless a menstrual cloth). Every RHEUM (gonorrhoeal discharge) brayed like a leaky ass. At such times, Flavius retired (re-tired, re-dressed) him to a wasteful cock (wine-spigot, but also penis – C; P) and set his own EYES (arse) at flow.

See 'ZOUNDS; RE, *RJ*.

Mistake Take: possess carnally (C; P). '*Mis*take' meant (1) adulterously (PLACE, *MWW*); (2) homosexually. It follows the pattern of 'use' (sexually – *OED*; P) and MISUSE.

TN, II.ii.36. Of Olivia's infatuation with her, another woman (dressed as a man), Viola says, 'And she, mistaken, seems to *dote on me*' (italics added) – she imagines a dot (a 'prick' – *OED*) on the 'i', on I, Viola: see TITLE.

TSh, IV.v.45. Petruchio calls an elderly gentleman 'gentle mistress' and tells Kate to 'embrace her'. Hortensio: 'A' will make the man mad [lunatic; carried away by desire – *OED*], to *make a woman* of him' (italics added). Kate embraces this 'lovely bed-fellow' and later asks pardon for her 'mad mistaking', saying the sun made everything look 'green' (GREEN, colour of sexuality) to her 'mistaking eyes [EYES, arse]'. Petruchio concludes he–she is a 'wither'd' (WITHERED, buggered, castrated) man; and the mistaken man calls the episode a 'strange [STRANGE, sodomitical] encounter [sexual engagement – C; P]'. See COPATAIN HAT: Vincentio calls his imposter a sodomite; is told 'You mistake, sir, you mistake' – you are a 'mad ass'; and he concludes 'Thus strangers may be . . . abused [ABUSE, sexual misuse]'.

H5, III.ii.148:

Macmorris. I do not know you so good a man as myself: so Chrish save me, I will cut off your head.
Gower. Gentleman both, you will mistake each other.
Jamy. A! that's a foul fault.

FAULT: breech; a homosexual mistaking (C). See BEASTLY, *MWW*, for a 'foul fault' of sexual bestiality.

TGV, II.v.50. To Speed's 'sayest thou, that my master is become a notable lover?' Launce replies, 'I never knew him otherwise' – than the 'notable lubber, *as* thou reportest him to be' (italics added). Speed: 'thou whoreson ass, thou mistakest me'. Speed's anger with the whoreson ass who mistakes him is based on a pun on lover/LUBBER (effeminate). See LUBBER, *MWW*, where Slender tried to marry a 'lubberly boy'. He mistook or 'took the wrong' BOY (catamite), a transvestite.

See UNKIND, *AW*.

Misuse Use: employ sexually (*OED*; P). '*Mis*use' is any deviation from the accepted sexual norm.

1H4, I.i.43: 'A thousand of his people butchered; / Upon whose dead corpse there was such misuse, / Such beastly shameless transformation, / By those Welshwomen done as may not be / Without much shame retold or spoken of' – BEASTLY (sexually bestial), SHAME-(genitals) less TRANSFORMATION (sex-alteration) on those they butchered and then castrated. Necrophilism: mutilation of dead bodies, 'sometimes accompanied by kissing, embracing . . . cannibalism' (*CD*). See BOTCHER for antecedent puns on butchery/buggery.

AYL, IV.i.205. Celia says that in the love-play and 'love-prate [PRAT(E): the buttocks; to act the ass]' between Orlando and the other presumed male, GANYMEDE (a catamite), the disguised Rosalind had 'misused our sex'. Rom 1:26–7: 'for even their women did change the natural use into that which is against nature: And likewise also the men, leaving the natural use of the woman, burned in their lust one toward another'.

Celia continues, 'we must have your doublet and hose plucked over your head, and show the world what the bird hath done to her own nest'. Nest: the vulva (P); and to defecate (F&H 1670). (1) Removing her doublet and hose would show the shit, so to speak, with which her prate and love-prate had soiled its nest. (2) If her DOUBLET AND HOSE (testes and penis, i.e. her assumed codpiece) were removed, the world would see how she had demeaned her sex, had misused her femininity.

Modest(y), modestly Of the pudenda. Pudic: (1) modest, chaste; (2) pudendal. Used freq. with words for the anal–genital area, such as 'end' (penis – P) or CONCLUSION (buttocks, coitus).

Tem, III.i.53, Miranda: 'by my modesty, / The jewel in my dower' – her modesty, JEWEL (maidenhead – P).

MND, III.ii.285: 'Have you no modesty, no maiden shame [privy members – *OED*] . . . you counterfeit, you puppet'. This must have amused an audience who knew that this female counterfeit, this puppet (obs., actor) was no 'maiden'.

AC, IV.xv.27: 'Your wife Octavia, with her modest eyes/ And still conclusion'. Modest EYES (arse) is Cleopatra's dig at Octavia's womb. In III.iii.24 she had jealously questioned a messenger and, when he said Antony's wife 'shows a body rather than a life,/ A statue than a breather', Cleopatra exulted, 'I do perceive't: there's nothing in her yet': Octavia has no *life*, no child, in her, is not a BREATHER/ breeder; has nothing in her *yet*, her still (pantry)/ style (part of the gynaeceum), is perchance wife in name only. She has had no LIFE (penis), no thing (penis – C; P) in her yet/ yett, yate (Spenser, a gate), her GATE (vulva). Now again Cleopatra speaks of Octavia's modest arse, her still (inactive) CONCLUSION (passionless coitus); her still, lit. dead before birth, births.

TrC, IV.v.222. Hector speaks 'modestly': 'the end crowns all . . . Will one day end it'. Will (penis – P), end (penis – P), CROWN (genitals), ALL (penis) – he speaks modestly (see BLOOD).

Monster, monstrous (1) A homosexual. Lit. an imaginary animal compounded of elements from two or more animal forms; fig. combining two opposites. *TrC*, III.iii.266: 'he's grown a very land-fish . . . a monster'. Hermaphrodite: 1607, used loosely and fig. for a homosexual; Addison, a catamite (*OED*). Colette, *The Pure and the Impure* (New York: Farrar, Straus & Giroux, 1967) ch. 8: her homosexual and lesbian world, 'the world of my "monsters" . . . . Tenderly, then, I recall the monsters who accompanied me for a long way'. Jonson, *Sejanus*, IV.v: 'He is our monster, forfeited to vice . . . he hath his boys and beauteous girls . . . dealt away/ Unto his spintries [male whores], sellaries, and slaves,/ Monsters of strange and new commented lusts/ For which wise nature hath not left a name.' The 'deviant sexuality which most Ovidian scholars have treated as "stories of monstrous or forbidden love" – namely, tales concerning homosexuality' (Wilkinson, p. 53).

(2) A castrate. Thomas Heyrick, 'The Battle between the Cock and Capon': the capon is 'Not Male, nor Female, but a sort between./ *Monster*! . . . Whose sex the carefull *Housewife* did impart' (*Penguin Book of Restoration Verse*, p. 272).

(3) A cuckold. *Oth*, IV.i.63: 'A horned man's a monster and a beast.'

TN, II.ii.35. Viola disguised as Cesario: 'my master loves her dearly;/ And I, poor monster, fond as much on him;/ And she, mistaken, seems to dote on me . . . . As I am man . . . As I am woman . . . .' She is the POOR (catamite) girl–boy monster. See MISTAKE (sexually).

MND, I.ii.54. Bottom wishes to play both Pyramus and Thisby: 'An I may hide my face, let me play Thisby too. I'll speak in a monstrous little voice, "Thisne, Thisne"; "Ah Pyramus, my lover dear!"' This *Bottom* will hide his face so that he may play both PARTS (genitals), both sexes. He will speak in a *monstrous little* voice (VOICE/ VICE), the humorous contradiction stressing the pun: a 'monster' (1556) was a monstrous example of some particular vice. The LITTLE (-cule) voice of Bottom: the *cul* (arse – Cot); the cule (obs. for 'rump' – *W*).

Oth, III.iv.161: ''tis a monster/ Begot upon itself, born on itself'. The hermaphroditic monster jealousy, who performs both the male begetting and female bearing roles. Cf. Spenser, *The Faerie Queen*, Bk IV., c. x: the *Venus biformis* or Hermaphroditic Venus 'hath both kinds in one,/ Both male and female, both under one name:/ She syre and mother is her selfe alone,/ Begets and eke conceives, ne needeth other none'.

See WITCHES, *R3*; SIZE, *AW*.

Mood(y) See MUD(DY).

Most Buttocks. *La fin*: the end; *fin*: most (Cot). Often clustered with such words as 'bottom', 'end', 'extremes', 'breeches', which it seems intended to emphasise.

Tem, III.i.3. Talking of 'sports' (coitus – P), 'labour' (copulation – TWR) and 'delights' (*aises* – Cot: the same pun on asses is made in SLIP, *MND*), and how his 'mistress' makes his labours 'pleasures' (sexual delights – P), Ferdinand says some 'baseness' is nobly *under*gone and 'most poor matters/ Point to rich ends' – the 'rich gift' of Miranda (IV.i.8). See AFFECTION.

H5, III.vii.27: 'most absolute and excellent horse' – the horse the Dauphin also calls 'my mistress'. Absolute has no degrees, but this horse, object of his sexual bestiality, is *most* ABSOLUTE (of the ass/arse); an EXCELLENT (lewd, sodomitical) HORSE/arse.

MV, I.i.131, Bassanio: 'to you, Antonio,/I owe the most, in money and in love'. A significant pun for the thesis that these two men shared a homosexual love.

See PREPOSTEROUS, *LLL*; TRIBUTE, *Tem*.

Mould(y) The womb. Coit, esp. to whore (*ruffa*: mouldiness, a harlot – F). Diseased venereally (*ruffa*, *ruffola*: morphew, i.e. scurfy or leprous eruption – F).

Per, III, Gower, 11: 'Hymen hath brought the bride to bed,/Where, by the loss of maidenhead,/A babe is moulded.'

Cor, III.ii.103. Possessed by some 'harlot's spirit' (113) Coriolanus goes to the market place to sell himself for office. 'This mould of Marcius, they to dust should grind it'. Pun on *mouldre* (grind – Cot) and 'grind' (copulate – F&G). *Macinio*: grinding of grist; carnal copulation (F).

V.iii.22. She who had urged him on in III.ii ('He must, and will'; and whom he finally quieted with 'be content:/Mother, I am going to the market-place') he now describes as 'the honour'd mould/Wherein this trunk was framed' – an ambiguous phrase, since he recognises (190) that in this, her final victory over him, 'Most dangerously you have . . . prevail'd,/If not most mortal . . . . I'll frame convenient peace.' Again he'll play the whore at her behest, and frame (mould) a convenient – a whore's – PEACE/PIECE. Etherege, *The Man of Mode*, III.iii: 'Dorimant's convenient [mistress] Madam Loveit'.

2H4, III.ii.115. Falstaff chooses Mouldy ('Prick him') for the army: it is time he was 'spent', his semen discharged (C; P). But *Mould*y says he 'was pricked well enough before' See ABOUT.

II.iv.132 and 158. Doll calls Pistol a 'scurvy companion' and a 'mouldy rogue' who 'lives upon mouldy stewed prunes'. Prunes: a staple in the diet of venereal patients (C), served in stews (brothels); cf. *MWW*, I.i.296; *MM*, II.i.103, 111. Dekker and Middleton, *The Honest Whore I*, IV.iii.35: 'Peace, two dishes of stew'd prunes, a Bawde and a Pander'. Pistol also 'lives upon' or by exploiting such women as Doll: he tears a 'whore's ruff [pudendum – P]'; he is a RUFFIAN (pimp), a 'scurvy', 'mouldy', diseased, *ruffoloso* one (see CAPTAIN).

See GERMAN, *KL*.

Move (1) Arouse sexually. Motion (P) and 'mevynge' (TWR): erotic movement.

(2) Cause bowels to act (B. E., *Dict. Cant. Crew*, 1700, in *OED*).

(3) Provoke a discharge. 'Camels haie . . . mooveth the tearmes' (*OED*, s.v. Move, 1597). TERMS are the menstrual flow.

TSh, II.i.195:

Petruchio. Myself am moved to woo thee for my wife.
Katherina. Moved! in good time: let him that moved you hither
Remove you hence.

She continues that he is a 'moveable' or 'A join'd stool' (JOINED STOOL, chamber-pot).

Petruchio. Thou hast hit it: come, sit on me.
Katherina. Asses are made to bear, and so are you.

TGV, I.ii.27. Lucetta feels 'passion' (16) at mention of Proteus – it is a 'passing shame [SHAME, genitals – *OED*]'. Julia asks, 'And wouldst thou have me cast my love on him?' when 'he, of all the rest, hath never moved me'. CAST is evacuate waste; shed spawn or eggs. Should she cast her LOVE/*l'oeuf* (egg – Cot) or *l'oeuve* (spawn – Cot) on him? See TERMS: having one's menes was a prerequisite for marriage.

IV.iv.175. Julia riddles that a woman, 'passing fair', was 'passioning' for the 'perjury' of a lover (cf. the 'perjury' of Proteus – V.iv.103) and was 'moved therewithal'.

MM, I.ii.189. Claudio's life was 'lost at a game of tick-tack' (a game in which pegs are put into holes; 1550, copulation – F&H). His only hope is Isabella, who has 'a prone and speechless dialect/Such as move men' – (1) move the pieces, i.e. the 'men' in the game of tick-tack; (2) move men in the sexual game of tick-tack or copulation. Eventually his life does depend on her willingness to lie prone (flat; eager for action) for Angelo, whom she STIRS (sexually) as no strumpet had ever done (II.ii.185).

Ham, I.v.53: 'But virtue, as it never will be moved,/Though lewdness court it in a shape of heaven,/So lust . . . Will sate itself in a celestial bed'.

AC, I.v.22, Cleopatra: 'O happy horse, to bear the weight of Antony!/Do bravely, horse, for wot'st thou whom thou mov'st?' Her sexual longing emerges also in *bear the weight* and *do* (P), freq. puns on the sex-act.

See DESPAIR, *2H6*.

Mud(dy)/mood(y) Excrement. Shitty. Weever, *Faunus and Melliflora*, 57: 'No muddy mind no slimie dunghill slave,/But hates with Pickt-hatch t'have his name defaced' – even a *mud*dy, *dung*hill slave hates to be deFACED (have more faeces flung on him) by being called a Pickt-hatch (brothel – F&H) whore.

AW, v.ii. 'Muddy'/'mood' (K) form part of a conceit on excrement or faeces.

Parolles: 'Good Monsieur Lavache, give my Lord Lafeu this letter. . . . I have held familiarity with fresher clothes; but I am now, sir, muddied in fortune's mood, and smell somewhat strong of her strong displeasure.' (Possibly Lavache is a corruption of Fr *lavage*, slops, puddle, water-pool.)

Clown: 'fortune's displeasure is but[*t*] sluttish, if it smell so strongly. . . . Prithee, allow the wind [WIND, a flatus]' – let him get to windward side.

Parolles: 'Nay, you need not to stop your nose . . . I spake but by a metaphor' – he used 'but' metaphorically (for *butt*).

Clown: 'if your metaphor stink I will stop my nose. . . . Prithee get thee further.'

Parolles: 'Pray you . . . deliver me this paper [his letter].'

Clown: 'Foh! prithee, stand away: a paper from fortune's close-stool' – a paper from the chamber-pot of Fortune, who was *but* sluttish. Parolles has, he tells Lafeu, 'fallen into the unclean fishpond of her displeasure; and . . . is muddied withal'. He fell into the *piscina* (fishpond; pissing-place – F) of Fortune, whom Elizabethans considered a slut.

The repeated use of 'prithee' and 'pray you' suggest the pun on PRAY(ER) and a flatus.

CE, v.i.79. The Abbess tells Adriana jealousy drove her husband mad: 'The venom clamours of a jealous woman/Poisons'. His sleep 'hinder'd', his sports 'hinder'd', what 'ensued' was 'ill digestions' and a 'moody and dull melancholy,/Kinsman to despair'.

Adriana is a venomous serpent (*scitala* – F) who *hinder*ed (the posteriors) – fig. shit on (see DISDAIN) – his sleep and sport (sexual play – C; P). Is she also the viper who kills its mate? What ensued or issued forth was ill digestion and moody/muddy MELANCHOLY (black bile) and DESPAIR (excrement). *Scitare* (pron. 'shit-'): despair, fall into a depression (F).

Mule/Muli An emasculated or cuckolded male. Lit. a hybrid generated between the ass and the horse; biol., a sterile hybrid. One who is 'neither one thing nor another' (Jonson, in *OED*). 'Muley' are *hornless* cattle.

Cor, II.i.263. Brutus says the people must be told Coriolanus would have taken all power away from them, emasculated them: 'For an end . . . he would/Have made them mules . . . holding them/In human action and capacity,/Of no more soul nor fitness for the world/Than camels in the war'. For an end – as for their end or buttocks – Coriolanus would make sterile mules of them, fit only for 'bearing burdens, and sore blows/For sinking under them' (268). It is the feminine role to bear burdens, as in *RJ*, II.v.78, the Nurse to Juliet: 'you shall bear the burden soon at night'. They will be mules and CAMELS (passive male homosexuals) who sink *under* the blows (coital thrusts – C; P). In action (copulation – C; P), their fitness (for sexual activity – C; P) assigns them the degraded role. See VOICE for similar puns on the emasculation of the people.

TA, IV.ii.152. Aaron, the Moor, must dispose of his child, born illegitimately to Tamora, the Empress. He will send it to a countryman, a Muli, a word Sh chose for its punning possibilities:

'one Muli lives, my countryman;/ His wife but yesternight was brought to bed' and she, too, delivered a child that was not of her husband's complexion (paralleling Tamora's plight). The Muli had been cuckolded: he, a Muli (a *muley* or animal without a horn), without a horn or potent penis, was given the horn of cuckoldry; and his wife (L*mulier*, wife) had given birth to a hybrid. Aaron's solution, that the children be exchanged so that each mother would have a child of the proper colour, would make his own child a mulier (eccl. law, a child legitimised by marriage) – make him appear the legitimate child of these adopted parents, these Mulis.

In making Aaron a Muli with whom Tamora mated, Sh was thinking of his puns on SEMIRAMIS (the name Aaron gives Tamora), queen who mated with a horse.

See SLAVE, *MV*.

Mutual(ity) Intimate; reciprocal. A meaning now incorrect ('Pertaining to both parties; common' – *OED*) lent itself to a description of homosexual intimacy. Cf. Donne, 'Sapho to Philaenis': the Lesbian Sappho speaks of the 'likenesse' of her parts and the beloved's 'brest' and 'thighs'. Heterosexual love lacks this mutuality: 'Plaies some soft boy with thee, oh there wants yet/ A mutuall feeling which should sweeten it'.

TGV, V.iv.173. See PEASANT for full discussion of the line in which the two couples will share 'One feast, one house, one mutual happiness'. Cf. Montaigne, Bk I, ch. 27, in which he says woman's love is inferior to masculine friendship, in which 'all things being by effect common between them; wits . . . goods, wives, children, honour, and life', and 'their mutuall agreement, being no other than one soule in two bodies, according to the fit definition of Aristotle'.

AC, I.i.37. The first embrace of Antony and Cleopatra is accompanied by his saying, 'when such a mutual pair/ And such a twain can do't'. Repetition stresses the point: they are a mutual pair, alike as a twain (1580, twins): he, the effeminate male and she, the masculine woman (see SUCH). As Caesar says (I.iv.4): 'he . . . is not more manlike/ Than Cleopatra; nor the queen of Ptolemy/ More womanly than he'. TWIN: homosexual love.

Mystery Prostitution. Pandering. Jonson in 'An Execration upon Vulcan', refers to the brothels on the Bankside: 'Bred on the Banck, in time of Poperie,/ When Venus there maintain'd the Misterie'. Aristophanes, *Lysistrata*, 880–901: Cinesias begs his wife to return and make love, saying, 'And Aphrodité, whose mysteries you have not celebrated so long? Oh! won't you please come back home?' *Fottisterio*: a bawdy-house, the mystery of fucking (F).

Oth, IV.ii.30. Othello, acting as if his home were a brothel, addresses Emilia as the bawd: 'Some of your function, mistress;/ Leave procreants alone and shut the door. . . . Your mystery, your mystery: nay, dispatch.'

See PAINT, *MM*; FRANCE, *H8*.

N

Name(less), no name, without a name Not fit to be spoken of, unmentionable, not to be named; lewd, wicked, nefandous (from L *ne fari*, not to speak).

The unspeakable, not-to-be-named sexual activity has traditionally been sodomy, 'denounced by Justinian as devil-inspired. . . . From then until our time in Christendom sodomy has been what the Law has called "that abominable crime, not to be named among Christian people". Hence the wording of Housman's poem, which he never ventured to publish, evoked by the trial of Oscar Wilde: "Oh, they're sending him to prison for the colour of his hair . . . The nameless and abominable colour of his hair" ' (Wilkinson, p. 31). ABOMINABLE is also a standard epithet for homosexuality: 'The Parson cannot bring himself to name this terrible sin – "thilke abhomynable synne, of which that no man unnethe [scarcely] oghte speke ne write" ' (TWR, s.v. Abhomynable synne). Jonson, *Sejanus*, IV.v: kidnapped boys are 'dealt away/ Unto his spintries, sellaries, and slaves,/ Monsters of strange and new commented lusts/ For which wise nature hath not left a name'. ('Spintries' and 'sellaries' are male whores.)

Mac. See HEDGEHOG for the witches' 'deed without a name'.

Ado. See POOR and FIE for Don John's insinuations that Hero's sexual transgressions that 'are not to be named, my lord,/ Not to be spoke of' include adulterous sodomy.

TGV, II.i.111, Valentine: 'I have writ your letter/ Unto the secret nameless friend of yours' – the letter Sylvia actually intends for the writer himself, the ambisexual Valentine (see PERFECT; PEASANT). Speed continues to pun on the see-sawing role-switching that is a frequent concomitant to Sh's metaphors for bisexual relationships: 'My master sues to her, and she hath taught her suitor/ He being her pupil, to become her tutor.' TUTOR: older male in a pederastic relationship.

See SHIP-BOY, *KJ*; MIS-USE, *1H4*.

Naples Connotes the disease (syphilis) and habits of whores. *Napleux*, *-euse*: full of the (French) pox (Cot). Neapolitan bone-ache: syphilis (P). 'The frenchmen at that siege got the buttons of Naples (as we terme them) which doth much annoy them at this day' (*OED*, s.v. Naples, 1596).

Oth, III.i.4, Clown: 'Why, masters, have your instruments been in Naples, that they speak i' the nose thus?' The instruments (P), like the nose (P) are penis symbols, eaten away by syphilis. Massinger, *The Guardian*, IV.111: 'An hospital only for noseless bawds'. Middleton and Dekker, *The Roaring Girl*, IV.ii: 'His hair sheds off, and yet he speaks not so much in the nose as . . . before' – baldness resulted (C) from syphilis ('make curl'd pate ruffians bald' – *Tim*, IV.iii.160).

3H6, II.ii.139. Queen Margaret called Richard a 'foul mis-shapen stigmatic': from the 'foul disease' (syphilis – *OED*) he is mis-shapen (SHAPE, genitals – *OED*), STIGMATIC (sexually deformed). Richard's riposte is an exact *quid pro quo*: Margaret is 'Iron of Naples hid with English gilt,/ Whose father bears the title of a king, – / As if a channel should be call'd the sea, – / Shamest thou not'. A two-pronged attack.

First, Margaret, daughter of the King of Naples, came from France and her nose is eaten away by syphilis, is *napleuse*, full of the French pox, and she has an iron one. Dekker and Massinger, *The Virgin Martyr*, IV.ii: 'No, sir, nor the bridge of her nose fall, tiss full of iron works'. 'Syphilitic deterioration of the nose could be so complete as to cause rich patients to wear false noses made of various metals' – John Aubrey, *Brief Lives* (Harmondsworth: Penguin, 1962) p. 178. Fielding, *Joseph Andrews*, ch. 9: 'where, in some Men of Pleasure, the natural and artificial Noses are conjoined'. Margaret's iron work is hid with English gilt (gold), her father is a channel, and she is a *navire begue*, a ship whose 'nose is pointed with yron or brasse' (Cot). *Begue*: speak imperfectly, like the masters in *Oth* above, whose instruments have been 'in Naples, that they speak i' the nose thus'.

Second, Margaret is a whore. This *navire begue* with the iron nose is a 'beggar' (154), a BEGGAR/bugger, whore. Having denigrated Richard sexually, she becomes his butt: her father may have the title of a king but not the TITLE/tittle (prick): as if a little channel were called the sea. He has a regal title but is only a rigol, i.e. water-channel or gutter; and a pun on RIGEL, a male with only one or no testicle.

Edward picks up the attack: Margaret, who is iron (Fr *fer*), wronged her husband even more than the strumpet 'Helen of Greece', who was '*fairer far*' (italics added), wronged hers. Margaret, the 'shameless callet' (like Richard's 'call'd . . . Shamest'), is SHAME (genitals) -less, is gilt/gelt, unfeminine.

York's earlier speech commencing at I.iv.111 contains all the same elements: Margaret is a 'She-wolf' (WOLF), Fr *louve* or L *lupa* (she-wolf and prostitute), a *loup* (wolf, malignant ulcer of the skin – Cot), a lupus (L, wolf), ulcerous skin condition commonly affecting noses. She is an 'Amazonian trull' (Amazonians were masculine women and TRULLS sodomites); her 'face [FACE, arse] . . . Made impudent with use of evil deeds' – IMPUDENT (spayed pudenda, mannish), perh. with diseased pudenda, from use (fornication – *OED*; P) of deeds (fornications – C; P) that were EVIL (It *male*) or sodomitical. She is 'flinty': Sh links flint to STEEL (penis) and to rocks, stones (i.e. testes).

So, this Margaret, iron of Naples hid with gilt, is a syphilitic whore, a mannish woman (see Index).

Nature, natural Generative and excretory organs (*W*; F&H); semen, menses, female pudendum, esp. that of a mare (*OED*). *La natura*: woman's 'quaint' (cunt) and 'privie parts of any man or beast' (F).

See TRUNK, *Tim*; WITCHCRAFT, *Oth*; GIFT, *Ham*; ACCESS, *Mac*; PARTICULAR, *Oth*.

Neigh(bour) Invite fornication (pun on the cry of a horse). An adulterer. Jer 13:27: 'I have seen thine adulteries, and thy neighings, the lewdness of thy whoredom'. Jonson, *Volpone*, IV.v, Corvino: "This woman . . . is a whore,/Of most hot exercise, more than a partrich . . . Neighs like a jennet.' Cf. William Cowper's 'Adultery neighing at his neighbour's door' (*OED*, s.v. Neigh).

MND, II.i.46. Puck describes his pranks: 'When I a fat and bean-fed horse beguile,/Neighing in likeness of a filly foal'. Puck, who can assume any shape, seduces a stallion. Cf. Jer 5:8: 'They were as fed horses in the morning: everyone neighed after his neighbour's wife.'

AYL, IV.i.171. Rosalind warns Orlando, 'you might keep that cheek . . . till you met your wife's wit going to your neighbour's bed. . . . to say she came to seek you there.'

WT, I.ii.195: 'And his pond fish'd by his next neighbour – his wife fish'd (seduced – P) by an adulterer.

H5, IV.ii.8:

> *Constable.* Hark, how our steeds for present service neigh!
> *Dauphin.* Mount them, and make incision in their hides . . .

The steeds neigh for service – 'serve', esp. of stallions, is mount coitally. 'Mount them' repeats the image. To make incision, cuts, in a horse's hide is something one normally tries to avoid; but these steeds include the horse of the Dauphin, who had earlier (III.vii.47) told the Constable 'my horse is my mistress', and in whom, therefore, a CUT is a cunt (C; K). Make incision in the HIDES (L *scortum*: hide; prostitute – his 'mistress').

Oth, III.iii.351. Believing Desdemona a 'whore' (359), Othello says, 'Farewell the neighing steed. . . . Othello's occupation's gone!' 'Occupy' is fuck (C) and possess a woman (P). In Rabelais, Bk III, Prol., *occupation* is a pun on *au-cul-passion* (passion in the rump), pron. similarly in Fr. Othello's wife and his career are gone; no more neighing for Othello, the steed. It is a trim metaphor in that his wife is a 'whore' (HORSE/whore).

Neither/nether Lower part of the body, covered by 'nether-stocks' or breeches (*1H4*, II.iv.130). The 'nether ye' (rectum, in Chaucer, 'The Miller's Tale' – TWR) and 'nether lips' (vulva: see LIP) are in the Netherlands (anal–pubic area – C; P). 'Nether', 'nather': ME sps of 'neither'.

Oth, IV.iii.40, Emilia: 'I know a lady in Venice would have walked barefoot to Palestine for a touch of his nether lip.' This lady from VENICE, a byword for sexual immorality, would have made the traditional penitential journey for Lodovico's touch (sexual caress – C; P). Unless this is a fetish, we assume the nether LIP is his groin: *groin*, mouth; *faire le groin*, pout, 'hang the lip' (presumably the lower lip) – Cot.

(Is this 'Lodovico' a 17th c. in-joke – the same as the Lodowick or 'meddling [fornicating – *OED*; P] friar' of *MM*, V.i.127; the Lodowike of Montaigne's *Essays*, Bk I, ch. 19: 'some men like Lodowike . . . end their daies between womens thighs'?)

See ENOUGH, *Cor*, *MND*; DAMSEL, *LLL*.

Nimble Lusty. ME 'nimel': quick at seizing. Marston, *The Dutch Courtesan*, II.i: 'a puncke . . . smooth thigh, and the nimble Divell in her buttocke'.

LLL, V.ii.16. Katherine says Rosaline is sexually precocious; had her sister 'been light, like you,/Of such a merry, nimble, stirring sipirt,/She might ha' been a grandam ere she died'. Had she been light (*OED*; P), MERRY (F&H; P), STIRRING (C; P), i.e. sexually wanton; had she been 'nimel' or quick (at seizing), been *vite* (Fr, quick) with her *vite* (pudendum – Cot), then she would certainly have been quick, that stage of pregnancy at which the foetus stirs, and an early grandam.

See DEXTERITY, *1H4*.

Noise A fart; used fig. for contempt. A quibble on 'noisome', i.e. ill-smelling. Jonson, *Bartholomew Fair*, IV.iv: 'A turd i' your teeth' – 'Turd, ha turd? a noysome vapour'.

Ado, V.ii.53: 'Foul words is but [/butt] foul wind [WIND, a fart], and foul wind is but foul breath, and foul breath is noisome'.

MND, III.i.93. *Bottom* exits 'to see a noise that he heard' during the rehearsal of the 'play', in which there is confusion about the 'odious savours sweet', 'Odours, odours', and 'odours savours sweet' – a quibble on sweet/*suitte* (the issue – Cot), the fart that issued. Cf. Chaucer, 'The Summoner's Tale', in which a deliberate 'fart' is called an 'odious' mischief to a friar and his 'Order'.

See ABOMINATION, *AC*; ROAR, *Cor*; SAKE, *Oth*; FLEW, *H8*; OFFENCE, *Cor*; BANISH, *Tim*.

Nonny The vulva. *Fossa*: 'a grave, pit. . . . Used also for a womans pleasure-pit, nony-nony, or pallace of pleasure' (F). *Nanni*: name men call their tame assess by (F). Nan-boy: effeminate man (F&H 1691); nanny-house: brothel; nanny: whore (F&H n.d.). A refrain used to cover indelicate allusions (*OED*; F&H: 'Cupid bidds itt shold bee soe, because all men were made for her hinononino').

KL, III.iv.103. Edgar's speech on having been a SERVING-MAN who 'served the lust of my mistress' heart' advises keeping 'thy foot [FOOT: fucking – C; P] out of brothels' and 'thy hand [HAND, penis] out of plackets [vagina – C; P]', and concludes with a 'nonny' refrain and 'let him trot by' (trot: whore, bawd – C; P).

See DOVE, *Ham*; ASS, *KL*.

Noon The culminating point (*OED* 1600). Man's phallic erection at its height. See TWELVE o'clock and MIDNIGHT.

RJ, II.iv.119: 'the bawdy hand of the dial is now upon the prick of noon'.

3H6, I.iv.34: 'Now Phaethon hath tumbled from his car,/ And made an evening at the noontide prick.'

KJ, IV.ii.151: 'ere the next *Ascension*-day at *noon*,/ Your *high*ness should deliver *up* your crown', said Peter, 'a prophet' (italics added). Religious allusions aside, the sentence anticipates his *high*ness's political decline, his loss of potency after noon, as is developed in v.i.1, when John hands his crown to Pandulph, symbol of his submission to the Pope: 'Thus have I yielded up into your hand/ The circle of my glory.' He is then informed that some 'damn'd hand' has taken the life of Arthur, rival claimant to the throne. These two events, expressed with the symbol of a HAND (the phallus – K) start the decline of John's popularity and power. As the Bastard immediately says, 'wherefore do you droop? . . . Be stirring as the time'. But it is past noon and John can no longer STIR (rise up erotically – C; P): he has yielded up his circle/ cercal (of the *tail*: penis – K; P). See YIELD/ geld.

Norman(dy) A bugger. '*Qui fit Normand il fit truand*: Prov [erb]. Hee that made a Normand made a begger'; *truand*: beggar, filthy or lewd fellow; *truande*: 'A filthie beggarlie queane [whore]' (Cot). See BEGGAR/ bugger.

Ham, IV.vii.91:

King. . . . a gentleman of Normandy . . .
And they can well on horseback; but this gallant
Had witchcraft in't; he grew unto his seat . . .
As had he been incorpsed and demi-natured
With the brave beast. . . .
Laertes A Norman was't?
King. A Norman. . . .
Laertes. I knew him well: he is the brooch indeed . . . .

Three times the point is made that he is a Norman; and men of Normandy can WELL (whore, fornicate) on HORSE/ whore's *back*. He had WITCHCRAFT (L *ars magic*a) in it. He grew unto his *seat*, was demi-natured (*natura*, privy parts of man or beast – F: NATURE) with the horse: he was in other words, a CENTAUR – in art a complete man to whose body were attached, behind, the barrel and hind-quarters of a horse; symbol of sexual bestiality (METAMORPHOSED, *TA*). Centaurs were given 'to pouncing on anyone of either sex'; and under *céntaur* one lexicographer listed 'wild', 'brigand', 'arse' and 'pederast' (Dover, p. 38). Laertes says this Norman is the brooch, the same word as 'broach' (stick into, as in coitus; lit. to brooch or broach a cask or *butt* – C; P), and Laertes knew him WELL, this Norman who is a brooch INDEED (in intercourse).

These puns on sexual bestiality may be by way of introducing the end of the play, when Hamlet, 'fat, and scant of breath' (v.ii.298) – FAT (ass-like, foppish) and scant (SCANTY, castrated) of BREATH (breeding) – will be (like that gentleman of Normandy) in*corpse*d, will be buggered and screwed by the King's poisoned cup; scanted, cut down, by Laertes's poisoned sword, on which he *broaches* Hamlet – Hamlet who tells Laertes 'you but dally . . . you make a wanton of me' (308). 'Dally' means to wanton, in the way of amorous caresses; and Laertes but/ butt(?) dallies.

See BUCKRAM, *2H6*.

Not See KNOT/ NOT.

Note (1) Penis (if one note). A 'prick' is a musical note; 1592, a penis. *RJ*, II.iv.21: 'prick-song'.

(2) Testicles (if two). Note/ nut (K), as in *MWW*, I.i.171: 'if you run the nut-hook's humour on me; that is the very note of it'. NUTS: testicles.

(3) Noting or pricking, i.e. fornicating.

TSh, III.i.77. Hortensio asserts his masculinity: 'one clef, two notes have I' – one penis and two testicles. Clef or key: penis (F&H 1700s). Clef was occ. used loosely for the musical stave or staff (penis – F&H), as in *Ado*, v.iv.125: 'staff . . . tipped with horn' – symbol of cuckoldry. See RE.

H5, IV.ii.35. The Constable contrasts the impotent English ('husks of men') with the virile French who 'shall today draw out,/ And sheathe for lack of sport'. Pun on *draw* the sword and uncover the penis (C; P); and sheathe the sword in flesh for lack of the other sport (coitus – P). So 'let the trumpets sound . . . the note to mount . . . That England shall couch down in fear and yield'. The French musical note or the prick *mounts* (man's coital position – C; P) and the effeminate English *couch* (lie down in intercourse – P).

TrC, v.x.45: 'Full merrily the humble-bee doth sing,/ Till he hath lost his honey and his sting;/ And being once subdued in armed tail,/ Sweet honey and sweet notes together fail.' The bee sings MERRILY (lustfully) until he loses his STING (prick; tail). And *once* sub*due*d in tail, he loses his one and DUE (two – F): his two notes or testicles and his HONEY (semen) fail. Cf. *MM*, IV.i.38: 'a due and wary note'; *LLL*, v.ii.929: 'Tu-who, a merry note'.

See ANNUAL, *H8*; FURNISHED, *Cym*.

Nothing Copulating (pricking). Pun on noting (K). Music in which the notes are pricked is called prick-song (*RJ*, II.iv.21: 'He fights as you sing prick-song'). 'To my chamber to prick out my song' (Pepys, in *OED*).

Much Ado about Nothing is much ado over (sexual) pricking.

I.i.65. In its first use, 'nothing' is pricking in fencing (to skirmish: to fence):

Leonato. [Beatrice and Benedick] never meet but there's a skirmish of wit between them.
Beatrice. Alas! he gets nothing by that. In our last conflict four of his five wits went halting off, and now is the whole man governed with one; so that if he have wit enough to keep himself warm, let him bear it for a difference between himself and his horse . . . .

In the skirmish of WIT (genitals – a freq. pun in this play) when they MEET/ mate or coit – mate or match their wits – it is Benedick and not Beatrice who makes no score or gets *nothing*, gets pricked. 'To prick' (1500s) meant to lame a horse during shoeing, and four of Benedick's wits went halting off (to halt, be lame). His fifth wit, his penis, with luck not LAME (impotent), is the one to keep him warm or *chaud* (Cot). Let him bear (L *ferre*) it for the difference between him and his shoed (*ferrer*: to shoe a horse – Cot) horse. (A *chaud*/ shoed quibble, like show/ shew, alt. sp.)

II.iii.59:

Don Pedro. . . . if thou wilt hold longer argument,
Do it in notes.
Balthasar. . . . There's not a note of mine that's worth the noting.
Don Pedro. Why, these are very crotchets that he speaks;
Notes, notes, forsooth, and nothing.
Benedick. . . . Well, a horn for my money, when all's done.

Puns on not/ note and the size of a man's NOTES (genitals) – the whole notes, *longer* notes, musically speaking, versus crotchets: (1) short, quarter notes; (2) whimsical *not*ions, worth *nothing*; (3) CROTCHETS (partial men) like short NOTES.

These crotchets or quarter notes tie in with the earlier puns of Beatrice on the 'whole man' (a whole note) and the other 'four' (quarter notes or crotchets) that went limping off, because impotent, partial men.

Balthasar, who speaks crotchets or quarter notes with *crooks* or *hooks* on the stem to show their musical length, also sings crochets (Donne, 'Jealousie': 'The nimblest crocheting Musitian') in a song of 'deceivers' and 'fraud' (hook and crook). And all the men set out to deceive Benedick; as Claudio says (114), 'Bait the hook well; this fish will bite' (*crochet*: a fish-hook – Cot). It all ties together in the basic pun on NOTE or prick – and all the 'notes, forsooth, and nothing'.

Son 20. Sh says, 'And for a woman wert thou first created; / Till Nature, as she wrought thee, fell a-doting, / And by addition me of thee defeated, / By adding one thing to my purpose nothing. / But since she prick'd thee out for women's pleasure, / Mine be thy love and thy love's use their treasure.' 'Nothing' and 'doting' are an end-of-line rhyme, and both of them pun on pricking. Just as 'nothing' sounds like *noting*, so 'doting' quibbles on *dotting*. 'To prick' is to mark by or with pricks or dots (*OED*); and nature fell a-dotting – she added a dot or prick, and prick'd him out for women's pleasure. 'Use' is also part of the same conceit, for 'note' meant use (*OED*): 'thy love's use [note or prick] their treasure'.

See OLD, *AW*; SHAKE, *TGV*.

Nuts Testicles (F&H n.d.); the glans penis (*OED*). *Pennache de mer*: a sea creature resembling 'th'uncovered nut of a mans yard [penis]' at one end (Cot).

TrC, II.i.108. Thersites says 'Hector shall have a great catch, if he knock out either of your brains: a' were as good crack a fusty nut with no kernel'. Neither Ajax nor Achilles is a great CATCH/*caiche* (penis – Cot) or fornicator. Their BRAINS (testes) are like stale-smelling nuts with a shrivelled kernel (seed or soft part within a stone-fruit – *OED*). Cf. KNOCK, CRACK, verbs ptg to copulation.

RJ, III.i.21. Benvolio starts with 'The day is hot . . . these hot days'; and Mercutio responds 'an there were two such [as he], we should have none shortly, for one would kill the other . . . thou wilt quarrel with a man for cracking nuts, having no other reason but because thou hast hazel eyes.' But this is good reason: the hazel-nut consists of a single pendulous seed composed of two equal fleshy hemispherical cotyledons enclosed in two large and fleshy bracts – two separate but joined nuts (as in the scrotum) – and Benvolio doesn't like them cracked, for he has hazel EYES (testicles). Sh makes every possible pun on Benvolio's hazel-nuts: (1) the day is hot or *hasle* (the scorching sun of summer heat – Cot); (2) the hazel-nut is L *corulus*, and six times we are told Benvolio *quarrels* if a man merely coughs and awakens his dog: hazel-nut oil was a remedy for coughs (*CD*), and to be anointed with hazel-nut oil meant to be soundly drubbed (*OED*).

AW, II.v.47. Lafeu, who belittles Parolles in every encounter ('I write man: to which title age cannot bring thee' – iii.209), now says, 'there can be no kernel in this light nut; the soul of this man is his clothes'. He is a *light* nut, without weight, or stone in his scrotum. Stone: unit of weight for a man; a testicle. Only his clothes – his codpiece – give the misleading impression that he is a man of SOUL (bottom).

See SQUIRREL, *MND*.

O

Oaths/oats Testicles. Sh puns on 'oath' and 'oat': 'oaten straws' (*LLL*, V.ii.913); 'oaths are straws' (*H5*, II.iii.53); 'a horse's health . . . a whore's oath' (*KL*, III.vi.21) – a delightful switch on the age's concern for the whore's health (*Per*, IV.ii.27) and the horse's oats (HORSE/whores). Oats are grains: *les grains*, Fr syn. for cods (testicles – F&H). This pun is still current: cf. Le Clercq's trs. of Rabelais, Bk III, ch. 18: talking of fellatio, Panurge says his 'asparagus stalk' is 'succulent' and will not 'suckle her in vain; she'll not look for oats in the nosebag I clap over her pretty snout, nor for negus in my ballocky bumper' (ballocks: testicles). Sow wild oats: 1576, indulge in dissipation (*CD*; F&H).

MND, IV.i.36. When Bottom, with his ass's head, says he wants 'good dry [L *assus*, DRY] oats', Titania's offer to send out for 'new nuts' is not a *non sequitur*, but recognition *Bottom* needs an ass's oats, new NUTS or testicles (see SQUIRREL).

Cor, V.vi.95. In this final exchange, in which each says the other is a passive homosexual, a bugger (SLAVE), Aufidius calls Coriolanus 'Marcius' (his boyhood name), a 'boy' (BOY, catamite) whose broken oath and RESOLUTION (testicles) symbolise effeminate weakness: 'He has betrayed your business . . . Breaking his oath and resolution like/ A twist of rotten silk'. Coriolanus's cods (lit. scrotum, a cocoon) are rotten (venereally diseased – P) like a SILK (effeminate; the female organ of corn, which in Scotland and Ireland means oats – *Cham*) TWIST (crotch). This baby (because of his 'nurse's [mother's] tears') 'betrayed', made fools of, them all, masturbated himself (*coglionare*: to deceive; play with one's stones – F).

JC, II.i.114:

Cassius. And let us swear our resolution.
Brutus. No, not an oath.

As in *Cor* above, the resolution and oath combine to signify manhood. Brutus adds they need no 'spur' (SPUR: penis, dildo; artificial spur added to the legs of fighting *cocks*) to 'prick' them on: their 'performance' (virility – P) never 'Did need an oath' besides their own two. Only 'Such creatures as men doubt' need the addition of an oath to establish their potency. Only SUCH (L*sic*/sick) CREATURES (sodomites) as 'priests and cowards [COWARD, effeminate] . . . and such suffering souls [SUFFER, the passive male's role; SOUL, arse]' need the addition of a spur or dildo (*let us (s)wear*: pun on *let us wear*).

And the idea of being sick, which runs through the scene ('is Brutus sick'), in fact, through the play (see SUCH), is part of the metaphor. They need no spur or ergot (Fr *ergot*, a spur), a 'diseased transformation of the seed of rye and other grasses', resembling a cock's spur (*OED*). Brutus wants no weaklings, no diseased seed, no 'rotten silk' as in *Cor* above, no venereally diseased cocoons, cods or oats, to stain their enterprise.

MM, V.i.241: 'foolish friar . . . think'st thou thy oaths,/ Though they would swear down each particular saint,/ Were testimonies against his worth and credit,/ That's seal'd in approbation?' (1) the friar's *oaths* don't count as *testi*monies against one whose worth has SEALS (testes – F&H) in approbation; (2) the friar's may swear down each *saint* but they don't count against *Angelo*'s.

Per, I.ii.120: 'I'll take thy word for faith not ask thine oath;/ Who shuns not to break one will sure crack *both*:/ But in our *orbs* we'll live so *round* and safe' (italics added). Pericles and Helicanus, though forced to inhabit two separate *worlds*, will live, potent and safe, in their *round orbs*. The two testicles, the ROUND (homosexual) orbs in one scrotum, are symbol of their love. He who would break faith would crack oath, would crack *both*: note that Sh uses 'crack' for *nuts* (*TrC*, II.i.111) and *egg*-shells (*Cym*, III.i.28). Cf. Fielding, *Jonathan Wild*, ch. 3: Wild, a rake (wild oats: a debauchee or rake – Bacon, in F&H), had been delivered by his mother 'in an house of an orbicular or round form in Covent Garden [brothel area] . . . [and was] baptized by the famous Mr Titus Oates'.

See EAR, *Cym*; BARBER, *MND*.

Occasion (1) Genitals. Lit. an instance or case. Case: privy parts (K; P).

(2) Necessities of nature (*OED*). Smollett, *Peregrine Pickle*, vol. III, p. 77, tells of hermaphrodites who wait on ladies, clean their tooth-brushes and 'soften waste paper for your occasions'.

2H6, III.i.3. Gloucester is late. King: 'I muse my Lord of Gloucester is not come: / 'Tis not his wont to be the *hind*most man, / Whate'er occasion keeps him from us now' (italics added). Suffolk then accuses him (47) of being 'privy' (latrine) to his wife's faults. See EASE.

Ado, I.i.151. The young men say that Leonato 'heartily prays some occasion may detain us longer' – the *occasion* of either his unmarried daughter or niece to detain the men *longer*, evoking the ardent phallus (*RJ*, II.iv.104: 'I was come to the whole depth of my tale; and meant . . . to occupy the argument no longer'; *MM*, V.i.370: 'till my tale be heard, / And hold no longer out'). He prays too *heart*ily, perh.: see HEART and GRIEF for his advice to Hero.

MM, IV.ii.60: 'if you have occasion to use me for your own turn, you shall find me yare . . . for your kindness I owe you a good turn'. He is YARE (sexually ready) to be used (coitally – *OED*; P) for a turn (in the bed – C; P), if Abhorson has occasion. He owes him a GOOD turn for past KINDNESS (sexual favours – F&H). What is presumably an offer to pimp sounds also suspiciously like an offer of himself, Pompey *Bum*, to the other's occasion.

MV, I.i.139, Antonio: 'My purse, my person, my extremest means, / Lie all unlock'd to your occasions'. His purse (scrotum – *OED*; P), reinforced by the pun in *pers*on (*2H4*, II.i.127: 'made her serve your uses both in purse and in person'; K), awaits Bassanio's occasions. His *extremest means* are his finances but also his body, since Sh is punning on his extremities (*OED* 1598), the *extremes* as opposed to the *mean*. These puns on coital and financial MEANS, prostitution (1) define their relationship; (2) connote the venality of Bassanio's new sexual venture; and may (3) reflect on Antonio's means of earning a living, his ships that go to Tripolis and Barbary ('You have among you many a purchased slave' – IV.i.90).

O'er, over Whore. Weever, *Epigrammes*, The Fourth Weeke, ix: 'that old trot [whore] every day / Wafts *o're* the water for to see a play, / And there a withered *ore-worn* face she shows' (italics added). Hour / whore / o'er (K).

Ham, II.ii.57. The Queen tells Claudius that the source of Hamlet's distemper is 'His father's death, and our o'er hasty marriage'. 'Our' and 'o'er' pun on *whore*: as Hamlet says (V.ii.64), Claudius 'kill'd my king and whored my mother'.

TrC, V.ii.160, Troilus: the 'orts of her love . . . greasy relics / Of her o'er eaten faith' are Diomed's. Left-over scraps of Cressida's love; greasy, i.e. obscene and defiled, RELICS (parts of a saint's body; pun on arse, excrement) – digested remains of her *whore-eaten* faith, these are Diomed's. 'Eaten' as consumed coitally (C; P) continues in 'My sword [penis – P] should bite it' – BITE (coitally) Diomed's helmet bearing her sleeve. Thersites ends the scene, referring to Cressida as 'whore'.

1H6, I.i.36. Gloucester describes Winchester's political manipulations: 'None do you like but an effeminate prince, / Whom, like a school-boy, you may overawe.' He puns on L *terrere*, to awe ('awe and terror' – *2H4*, IV.v.177), and *terere*, to rub, wear away. Rub: caress fricatively, masturbate (F&H; P). Winchester, whom Gloucester never omits to call whore (SCARLET; STAND BACK) is lover, manipulator, of an effeminate school-boy whom he can, like a whore, rub, over-awe.

Ado, V.ii.9: 'To have no man come over [coitally – P] me! why, shall I always keep below stairs?' Does Margaret deserve only to serve (sexually – *OED*; P) someone else, 'below stairs', i.e. as servant? Shall she never have her own love come over (whore) her – only KEEP (play bawd or whore), like the night she pretended to be her mistress, Hero (UTTER)? Is this another aspersion on Hero, and from one who ought to know?

See BOIL, *MM*; LEPROSY, *AC*; IDLE, *Cor*.

Offence 1. Copulation. Offend in a dream: have an amorous dream (P). *Effoncer*: to beat the bottom (of a vessel) – Cot. *Cas*: an offence, the privities (Cot); Fr sl. for arse. *Foigner*: to be offended at; *foigne*, *foine*: a fish spear (Cot). Foin: copulate (C; P).

MM, I.ii.90: 'what's his offence?' – 'Groping for trouts in a peculiar river.'

MWW, V.v.238: 'The offence is holy that she hath committed'. Anne COMMITTED (copulated) a holy (of the hole or pudendum – P; anus – TWR) offence in having been 'contracted' to Fenton (CONTRACT: a betrothal; the cunt).

KJ, I.i.257. The Bastard's mother admits Richard Coeur-de-lion had 'seduced' her and 'Thou art the issue of my dear offence'. He is issue of her DEAR/ deer (*hind*) offence or *cas*, of the *beating* of her *bottom* or hind (pun on *effoncer*).

AW, IV.iii.271. 'My life, sir, in any *case*: not that I am afraid to die, but that, my *offences* being many' (italics added). One of many puns on Parolles's attempt to find a DRUM (Fr *caisse*/*cas*, arse) and on his ignominy that started in II.vi with the plan to 'case him' and that ends here with his admission he has been 'found an ass'. See BEAT.

2. Being related to the buttocks, offences have offensive odours.

Ham, III.iii.36: 'O, my offence is rank, it smells to heaven' starts a soliloquy in which the King uses 'offence' four times and quibbles on the rank smell of the murder of a king and the rank he acquired in 'crown . . . ambition and my queen'.

Cor, V.i.28: 'Of noisome musty chaff . . . to nose the offence' – 'You are the musty chaff; and you are smelt'.

Per, II.iv.5. The 'incest' between Antiochus and his daughter is called a 'heinous [HEINOUS/ anus] capital offence' for which they were burnt by heaven and 'they so stunk' no one would bury them.

See RELIC; COURSE, *MM*.

Office Copulation. One's duty, therefore marital duty. Shirley, *The Lady of Pleasure*, III.ii: the bawd can 'satisfy you madam; I have a thousand ways to do sweet offices'.

CE, III.ii.2: 'you have quite [QUITE/ coit] forgot/ A husband's office?'

Oth, I.iii.394: ' 'twixt my sheets/ He hath done my office'.

AW, IV.iv.5: 'Time was, I did him a desired office,/ Dear almost as his life', says Helena, who cured the King's FISTULA (sexual impotence) – a (sexually – P) desired office, dear as his LIFE (Fr *vie*) or penis (*vit* – Cot).

AC, I.i.5. Antony is a 'strumpet's fool' who cools 'a gipsy's lust'; his 'goodly eyes' that once did a soldier's office 'now turn,/ The office and devotion of their view/ Upon a tawny front'. His EYES (genitals) now turn (perform sexually – C; P) their office to cool (P) the sexual heat of the TAWNY (vulva) of Cleopatra.

See DOWN, *TSh*; FACE, *H5*.

Oft The rump: pun on 'aft' (behind; naut., in the stern), as in *AYL*, III.iv.50: 'you have *oft* inquired/ *After*'; and *AC*, III.vi.18: '*oft before* gave audience'. (Italics added.)

TrC, III.iii.20. Calchas asks a favour of the Greeks: 'You have a Trojan prisoner, call'd Antenor,/ Yesterday took: Troy holds him very dear./ Oft have you – often have you thanks therefore –/ Desired my Cressid in right great exchange,/ Whom Troy hath still denied: but this Antenor. . . .' By correcting 'oft' to 'often', Calchas says two truths: (1) they had, in the past, desired Cressid *aft*, desired her sexually in her aft, *in* RIGHT (L *rectum*) exchange (exchange flesh: copulate – C; P); (2) they had often asked for her return. (She will be exchanged for *Ante*nor: L *ante*, before.)

MV, I.iii.107, Shylock: 'Signior Antonio, many a time and oft/ In the Rialto you have rated me . . . Still have I borne it with a patient shrug'; and now that Antonio wants money 'Should I not say "Hath a dog money? . . ." ' Like Calchas (above) he distinguishes between 'many a time' and 'oft'. Antonio had screwed or buggered him, RATED (copulated, i.e. fucked) him, in which buggering Shylock had the PATIENT (q.v.) role of the passive male in the sex-act. Now Shylock asks Antonio, hath a DOG (sodomite) money?

H8, II.iv.164. Wolsey denies he encouraged Henry's divorce and Henry responds in double-talk: 'you ever/Have wish'd the sleeping of this business; never desired/It to be stirr'd; but oft have hinder'd, oft,/The passages made toward it'. He incorrectly depicts Wolsey's attitude toward divorce but accurately portrays his feelings about Henry's amorous PASSAGES and BUSINESS with Anne Bullen. 'Oft' surrounds 'hindered' (hinder: the hind part) in this metaphor of the screwing of both Katherine and Anne. SLEEP and STIR pun not only on arousing sexual desire, but also on buggery.

See FANCY, *Ham*; COPPER, *1H4*; PLAY-THE-SIR, *Oth*.

Oil Semen. *Potage de la bite*: 'the oyle of man; an oyle which a woman should not (unlawfully) tast of' (Cot).

MWW, v.v.39. The women Falstaff hopes to seduce run off: 'I think the devil will not have me damned, lest the oil that's in me should set hell on fire'. In light of his sexual frustration and the pun on not being 'damned' (DAMN) or *dam*-ed, not physically possessing a dam or woman, the oil Falstaff speaks of is not merely his fat.

II.i.65: 'this whale, with so many tuns of oil in his belly . . . I think the best way were to entertain him with hope, till the wicked fire of lust have melted him in his own grease.' Falstaff is the sperm-whale, filled with spermaceti, fatty substance used for candles, etc., who, when entertained (sexually – P), even merely with hope, melts (experiences an orgasm – F&H; P) in sheer anticipation. Melt/milt (spawn of the male fish).

AW, I.ii.59. The King, suffering from impotence (FISTULA), who 'nor wax nor honey can bring home' (HOME: the vulva; without HONEY: impotent), quotes an old friend: 'Let me not live . . . After my flame [lust – P] lacks oil'.

AC, I.ii.53. On the subject of child-bearing Charmian says, 'Nay, if an oily palm be not a fruitful prognostication'. (1) The palm-tree was a source of oil; (2) a moist hand was believed to be a sign of potency (see HAND, *Ado*); (3) oil (semen) is a fruitful token of fertility.

1H4, II.iv.575:

Hal. This oily rascal is known as well as Paul's . . . . call him forth.
Peto. Fast asleep behind the arras, and snorting like a horse.

Oily Falstaff, snorting like a HORSE (arse; whore) BEHIND the ARRAS/arse or palls (curtains), is known as well as PAUL'S, meeting-place of the dissolute.

Old Ptg to a whore. Hoar (OHG *hêr*, old): ancient, venerable. Hoary: 1609, ancient. Rabelais, Bk IV, ch. 25 (1694 trs.): 'Macreon signifies in Greek an old Man . . . I believe the Name of Makerel (that's a Bawd in French) was deriv'd from it; for procuring is the Province of the old, as Buttock-riggling is that of the young'. Old man: theol., unregenerate human nature (*OED*).

2H4, III.ii.219. Shallow asks about a 'bona-roba' (prostitute – P) whom he and Falstaff knew: 'Doth she hold her own well?' 'Hold', of a female animal, is hold to the male; hold seed or conceive. 'Hold-door trade' is prostitution.

Falstaff's answer quibbles on a dropped 'h' in hold ('old) – like the puns on Arden/harden, art/heart, ear/hear, etc. (K, p. 308).

Falstaff. Old, old, Master Shallow.
Shallow. Nay, she must be old; she cannot choose but be old; certain she's old; and had Robin Nightwork by old Nightwork before I came to Clement's Inn.

Shallow oozes impatience with Falstaff's failure to reply to whether she is still lusty, whether she doth hold. Four repetitions of 'old' – plus the force of 'must be', 'cannot choose but be', 'certain she is' – mean, of course she's old, and of course she was a whore: she long ago had her child Robin by *old* night-work as well as by Mr Nightwork. Cf. old, *vieille*; and night-labour, *veille* (Cot). Veal/well (K; *LLL*, v.ii.247). WELL is a brothel, and Falstaff has failed to answer his question as to how *well* she is doing.

MM, IV.iii.4. Describing a prison, whose executioner is appropriately named Abhorson (a whore's son – P), Pompey says, 'one would think it were Mistress Overdone's own house, for here be many of her old customers'. The prison is like her HOUSE (brothel), for in its 'holds' (91) or cells (comparable to the whores' quarters) are many of her old (former) and old (whores') customers.

AW, II.iv.19:

Parolles. . . . O, my knave, how does my old lady?
Clown. So that you had her wrinkles and I her money, I would she did as you say.
Parolles. Why, I say nothing.

Parolles denies saying she *did* anything; he had meant only how *is* she. But the Clown plays on 'does' as do (fornicate – C; P); and 'old' as further implication that the lady is a whore. Cf. *chizza*: old, 'wrimpled' (i.e. rimpled or wrinkled), and a strumpet (F). Therefore the Clown wished the *old* lady or strumpet *did* or fornicated, as long as Parolles had the WRINKLES associated with both age and whoring, and he, the Clown, had the money.

However, even Parolles's denial puns on whoring, since NOTHING (like NOTING, as it was pronounced – K) puns on copulation.

Cf. the preceding lines 1–10, in which the same old lady is 'not well' and yet has her health; is 'very well and wants nothing i' the world, but she is not well'. She is not WELL (a whore), but has her health; she is well (healthy) and wants NOTHING (copulation).

Old lady, old woman Whore, bawd; prob. a bugger. L *anus*: old woman. Ptg to an old woman is 'anile', which lends itself to a pun on 'anal'.

H8, II.iii. The 'Old Lady' (given no other name) or the 'old cat [prostitute] that appears with Anne Bullen' (George Steevens, *Shakespeare*, 18th c. – as quoted by White) is a self-professed 'courtier beggarly' (COURTIER, bawd; BEGGARLY/buggerly) whom one could 'hire' to 'queen it' (QUEEN/quean, a whore), and who is jealous of Anne, the 'fresh fish' (FRESH fish or whore – P), who will 'have your mouth fill'd up/Before you open it'.

MWW, IV.ii. Falstaff escapes from the house of Mrs Ford (whom he's been trying to seduce) disguised as her 'maid's aunt', the 'old woman of Brentford [or Brainford]', a place about 14 miles from Windsor and known for furtive sexual assignations (Massinger, *The City Madam*, II.i: 'pleasures stolen . . . raptures of being hurried in a coach to Brainford'). Sh puns on Brent*ford* and *Brain-ford*: *Ford* is told his wife's lover exists only 'in your *brain*' (italics added).

Disguised as an 'aunt' (a bawd or whore – *OED*; P) and called a 'quean' (whore) and 'baggage' (whore), there is no doubt that the 'old woman' (used five times) is thought of as a whore. However, he–she is also called a 'witch' (WITCH, hermaphrodite) and 'Mother Prat': 'Mother', familiar name for any old woman and (F&H) slang for a bawd; and PRAT, 16th c. sl. for the buttocks. These simple puns on Falstaff's acting the old woman or *anus* – as he says at v.iv.121, 'I do begin to perceive that I am made an ass' – may also intimate buggery (it most certainly is punning on the confusion in sexual roles).

(1) Ford, who was 'Hard by' and then 'hard at door' (hard: the erect penis – C; P) beats Falstaff with his cudgel, while Falstaff is wearing the 'gown' (GOWN, cunt) of the 'fat woman', because it is large enough to 'serve' (coitally – *OED*; P).

(2) Falstaff says (v.i.16), 'I went to her . . . like a poor old man; but I came from her . . . like a poor old woman' – Ford 'beat me grievously in the shape of a woman. . . . I'll tell you strange things of this knave. . . . Strange things in hand'. Ford BEAT him (sexually), GRIEVOUSLY (obscenely, like a whore) beat him in the SHAPE (genitals – *OED*) of a woman, an old woman or

anus. He went like a POOR / L *puer* (boy or unmarried man; partner in a pederastic relationship) MAN (L *homo*), and he returned like a POOR old woman.

(3) Falstaff says (IV.v.121) he was saved by his 'dexterity' (DEXTERITY, of the rectum) or manual skill ('Strange things in hand') and by his 'counterfeiting the action of an old woman': 'action' is sexual intercourse (P), and he counterfeited the action of an *anus*. See STRANGE (pederasty).

Jupiter, Falstaff and Ford (alias Brook) each disguised themselves for purposes of wooing. Jupiter committed the 'beastly fault' (BEASTLY, ptg to sexual bestiality); and Falstaff asks, 'When gods have hot *backs*, what shall poor [POOR, pederastic] men [MAN, *homo*] do?' (v.v.12; italics added).

Open Sexually available (P).

TrC, v.ii.24: 'A juggling trick, – to be secretly open.' A seeming paradox: be *open* in her *secrets* (private parts – P), a *trick* in *juggling* (terms for fornication – P).

R3, III.v.30: 'his apparent open guilt omitted, I mean, his conversation with Shore's wife'. By open guilt he does mean conversation, 16th c. word for sexual intimacy (P).

MWW, II.ii.175. Ford pretends to want a woman's sexual favours: 'they say, if money go before, all ways [prostitutes] do lie open'.

See PEAR, *RJ*.

Opinion (1) A whore. A doxy: an opinion, esp. in theol.; a prostitute (F&H; *OED*).

(2) A penis. A 'pinion' is a FEATHER (penis).

MV, IV.i.157. He 'is furnished with my opinion' writes Bellario, introducing Portia, who is FURNISHED (equipped sexually) with both his legal opinion and his masculine dress: 'they shall think we are accomplished / With that we lack', she has told Nerissa (III.iv.61).

1H4, II.iv.444. Imitating the King, Falstaff mocks Hal's parentage: 'That thou art my son, I have partly thy mother's word, partly my own opinion'. Two PARTS (genitals) are evidence: (1) WORD (pudendum) of his mother (a bawd – F&H 1690, *Dict. of Cant. Crew*); (2) his own opinion.

AC, II.i.36. Pompey fears Antony's return: 'I did not think / This amorous surfeiter would have donn'd his helm / For such a petty war. . . . let us rear / The higher our opinion, that our stirring / Can from the lap of Egypt's widow pluck / The ne'er-lust-wearied Antony.' He describes himself as in competition with Cleopatra: for such a petty WAR / whore as his (as he), Antony left the lap (pudendum – TWR; P) of Cleopatra. Pompey's stirring (sexual provocation – C; P; STIR, bugger) has lured him: this gives Pompey a *higher* opinion, which he will *rear* – a feeling of potency and power. He is able to pluck (despoil – P) the ne'er-lust-wearied Antony of his FEATHER (penis or pinion), bring him down.

Cor, I.i.169. Coriolanus repeatedly airs his view that the citizens are poor specimens of men: masturbators, diseased whores, buggers. 'What's the matter, you dissentious rogues, / That, rubbing the poor itch of your opinion, / Make yourselves scabs?' (1) The opinion that itches and that they rub (masturbate – F&H; P), and that forms a SCAB (syphilitic sore – *OED*) is their penis – their POOR (pederast's) penis. (2) Since they are dissentious and make *themselves* scabs (16th c., scoundrels), the other opinion is prob. heterodoxy.

See BOTH-SIDES, *TrC*; BAD, *TrC*.

Oppress(ion) Rape (TWR); obs. ravish, violate. Press (coitally – TWR; P).

TrC, IV.v.241. Achilles had expressed 'a woman's longing . . . To see great Hector' (see SICK). Now the meeting takes place.

Achilles: 'Now, Hector, I have fed mine eyes on thee . . . And quoted joint by joint.' His eyes have fed (amorously – C; P), imaginatively quoted / coited with Hector, JOINT (penis) by (alongside) joint. (Quote / coat and coat / cod – K.)

He continues, 'I will the second time, / As I would buy thee, view thee limb by limb.' (1) As if buying a whore, a piece of flesh, a limb, (2) he will coit him a second time, as he would if *by* him, joint by joint, limb by limb.

Hector: 'there's more in me than thou understand'st./Why dost thou so oppress me with thine eye?' Hector feels the visual rape of Achilles' EYE (penis; arse; his 'I', used six times in eight lines). UNDERSTAND: a coital position.

RJ, I.i.190. Benvolio weeps at Romeo's 'good heart's oppression'. Romeo: 'Why, such is love's transgression' (love's sin, that of oppression). He continues that he has grief 'Which thou wilt propagate, to have it prest/With more of thine'. Coital pressing results in propagation of offspring. Likewise, one grief oppressed by another will propagate more GRIEF (q.v.). And so Benvolio *does*, for it is he who instigates, who urges, Romeo's attendance at the Capulets' ball.

KJ, II.i.177. Constance's language anticipates the rape of her son Arthur (SHIP-BOY), 'this oppressed boy'.

III.i.88. Constance: 'Lewis marry Blanch! O boy, then where art thou?' (34). By this political convenience, she says, Arthur will be buggered or screwed out of the crown. 'This day of shame, oppression . . . on this day let seamen fear no wreck' ('seamen' links this oppression to the rape and subsequent death of Arthur, in a SHIP-BOY's costume).

See WIND, *1H4*; GRIEF, *RJ*.

Orator(y) Whore, bawd. Nashe, *The Choice of Valentines*: entering the 'house of venerie' the lover is asked for a penny, because 'in our oratorie' none enters 'to do his nicarie' without an 'offertorie'. Dekker and Middleton, *The Honest Whore I,* III.ii: a reformed whore condemns her 'bawd, Lust's Factor, and damnation's Orator'.

2H6, III.ii.274: 'you . . . were glad to be employ'd,/To show how quaint an orator you are'. Suffolk says that in delivering a message from the 'commons' (whores – P; *OED*), the 'hinds', Salisbury was glad to be employ'd (P), bought like a woman for sexual use; glad to SHOW (manifest bisexuality) what a QUAINT (cunt – F&H) cunt-orator he is (L *volva*, vulva; *volvo*, of orators whose words flow ceaselessly). Aristophanes, in *The Knights*, mocks the orator who is 'fit to wrangle with harlots and bathmen' (1402) and calls him an 'Inspector of Arses' who is against 'pederasty . . . for sheer jealousy, knowing it to be the school for orators' (879).

3H6, III.ii.188. Gloucester 'can smile . . . murder. . . . I'll drown more sailors than the mermaid . . . slay more gazers than the basilisk . . . play the orator as well as Nestor,/Deceive more slily than Ulysses . . . set the murderous Machiavel to school. . . . I'll pluck it [the crown] down.' He will kill more than a MERMAID (prostitute – *OED*), a basilisk, i.e. cockatrice (whore – *OED*), or the murderous Machiavel. He will deceive better than the slyest; he'll pluck (ravish – F&H; P) the crown. In such context, 'orator' must be derogatory.

R3, III.v.95. Buckingham promises to sell Gloucester to the populace: 'I'll play the orator/As if the golden fee for which I plead/Were for myself'. He will prostitute himself verbally (1) as if the golden fee (gold crown he wants to procure for Gloucester) were a fee (sexual reward – P) for himself; (2) as if the *oratore* (gold coin called a guilder – F) were for himself, the bawd. See TROTH for his being a bawd.

vii.20. He reports back to Gloucester that, when 'mine oratory grew to an end', unsuccessfully, he 'reprehended' them. REPREHEND: masturbate.

AW, v.iii.254. Parolles (whose name puns on Fr *paroles* or WORDS/whores) is 'a naughty orator' – a naughty (bawdy – P) one (naughty house: brothel – F&H; P), i.e. a whore.

See MATTER, *AYL*; SUBTLE, *3H6*.

Order Ordure, excrement. Nashe, *Pierce Penilesse* (in *Works*, vol. I, p. 168): the mice 'encountred . . . with a cod-peece, wel dunged and manured with greace . . . not a flea or a cricket . . . would stay there after ha had once tasted the order of their fare'.

R2, III.iv.46. A servant says England is a neglected garden, 'fruit-trees all unprun'd . . . knots disordered' – dis*order*ed, not manured by the 'wasteful king' (55), who instead wastes (in) Ireland (II.ii) or Bogland (*W*; P), the buttocks (C; P, s.v. Ireland).

MWW, v.v.65, Mrs Quickly: 'The several chairs of order look you scour'. This is customarily glossed as the stalls of the Knights of the Order of the Garter. But it is equally fitting, and more characteristic, of this bawd and housewife that she be concerned with scouring the chairs of ordure, or privy seats and chamber-pots, a prime sanitary concern of the 17th c.: 'Maids need no more their Silver Piss-pots scoure' (*Penguin Book of Restoration Verse*, p. 349). Later emendations give this speech to the bride, ANNE, who would be equally likely to want the seats scrubbed for the wedding-guests.

See RIGHT, *1H4*; FIE, *TSh*; NOISE, *MND*.

Other The arse.

Tem, II.ii.98. Stephano pours wine into a 'monster' with two voices: a 'forward voice' and a '*backward* voice . . . to utter *foul* [full of mire – *OED*] speeches' (italics added). Twice Stephano says 'open your mouth', but the third time he says 'open your chaps again' – *chiappe* (buttocks – F), his 'other mouth'. The anal conceit continues with his pulling Trinculo out and calling him the 'siege' (excrement – *OED*) of this monster who can 'vent' (evacuate; anus – *OED*) Trinculos. Both men marvel that they ' 'scaped' (118), did ' 'scape' (122); SCAPE: fart (F&H). See BUNGHOLE, *2H4*, for another pun on the chaps/*chiappe*.

H8, I.iii.58. The Chamberlain does '*ass*ure' (italics added) Lovell that the Cardinal is 'noble;/He had a black mouth that said other of him'. He then leaves in his 'barge' (63). Cf. foist: a barge (*OED*); a fart (F&H). See POOP, *AC* for similar pun.

TN, v.i.198. Andrew tells Cesario that, if Toby 'had not been in drink, he would have tickled you othergates than he did'. Not other*wise*, which Sh otherwise always uses, but otherGATES (sluice-gates – C; P), tickled him in the rectum or anus – with his sword!

MND, III.i.69, *Bottom*: 'Some man or other must present Wall' – some MAN or arse must present WALL (*MND*, buttocks). They have just arranged for 'moonlight' or 'moonshine' to be presented. (Is the current jest about showing moons, i.e. buttocks an old one?)

See TURK, *Oth*; BUCKRAM, *1H4*; BOLT, *TrC*; WARD, *MWW*; Introduction, p. xvi.

Out (of door) Whore (ME sp. 'hor'). *Hors*: out, out of doors (Cot). 'To get outside of' is to copulate (F&H n.d.). Jonson, *Bartholomew Fair*, IV.iv:

Puppet Damon. Mistress Hero's a whore.
Master Lantern. Is she a whore? . . . Sir knave, out of door.
Puppet Damon. Knave out of door?
Puppet Hero. Yes, knave, out of door.
Puppet Damon. I say, whore, out of door.
Puppet Hero. Kiss the whore o' the arse.
Puppet Pythias. Yes, so say I too.

AW, I.i.158. Parolles says virginity becomes 'withered', loses its 'by't' (buy-it and BITE: coital grip): 'Keep it not; you cannot choose but lose by't; out with't! within ten year it will make itself ten . . . away with't.' Out, Fr *hors*/whore with it; AWAY/*a way* (a whore) with it; make money 'while 'tis vendible' (168).

AYL, IV.i.163. Orlando says his wife would be faithful 'For ever and a day.' Rosalind: 'Say "a day", without the "ever". . . . make the doors upon a woman's wit and it will out at the casement; shut that and 'twill out at the key-hole; stop that, 'twill fly with the smoke out at the chimney. . . . till you met your wife's wit going to your neighbour's bed.' Puns on (1) *ephemeral*, existing for a day; (2) *femerell*, outlet for smoke, part of a chimney; (3) *femoral*, ptg to the thigh; (4) *femora*, woman's privy parts (F). Rosalind is specific: doors, casement, key-hole, and chimney are four ways *out* – four openings – and woman's WIT (genitals) will out or whore at every opening, every opportunity, and wind up in the bed of a NEIGHBOUR (adulterer). The openings: (1) DOORS or vulva; (2) casement window, *ventiera* (F), pun on *venter* or womb; (3) chimney or anus – 'tewel' and 'tuel' ('tuwel' – TWR) means anus, rectum, chimney, flue, smoke-outlet (Rosalind's four uses of ' 'twill' plus 'till' and ' 'twill fly [flue]' probably pun on the tewel); (4) KEY-hole, vulva (F&H). See PRAT.

RJ, II.iii.84. Romeo defensively tells the Friar, who feared he was with Rosaline all night, that he has a new love: '[you] bad'st me bury love'. Friar: 'Not in a grave,/To lay one in, another out to have.' (Cf. Lyly, *Endymion*, v.ii: 'digge an old wife out of the grave that shall be answerable to his gravity'.) The Friar had said (10), 'What is her burying grave that is her womb' (*R3*, IV.iv.423: 'in your daughter's womb I bury them'; *fossa*: grave, female pudendum – F). A grave is a womb: the Friar did not intend Romeo to lay (fuck – P) Rosaline in her grave, her pudendum, and then have (carnally possess – *OED*; P) out (*hors*) another wanton girl.

As the following examples show, often 'out' or 'out of door' is part of a cluster where it functions better as an additional epithet for whoring than as a directive to leave or go out.

1H6, v.iv. A shepherd claims to be the father of La Pucelle (which means both a slut and a virgin), whom he ultimately calls a 'drab'. His first speech says 'this kills thy father's heart *out*right! . . . I sought . . . to find thee *out*' (italics added). And so she is, when he finds her. His second speech, after she denies his paternity, begins, 'Out, out!' These puns are part of the larger picture: Pucelle's declaring she is pregnant by a 'married man', being accused of 'juggling' (fornication – P), and being condemned as a 'strumpet'.

MWW, IV.ii.194: 'Out of my door, you witch, you hag, you baggage, you polecat, you ronyon! out, out!'

WT, II.iii.67. 'Out! A mankind witch! Hence with her, out o' door: A most intelligencing bawd!' (see WITCH).

Ado, IV.i.57: 'Out on thee!' says Claudio to Hero, who he says is not a maid and talked with a lover 'Out at your window betwixt twelve and one' (see TWELVE).

See IDLE, *Cor*.

Over See O'ER/whore.

Own Ass/arse. Sc sp. 'ain' (*CD*) or 'ane', pun on Fr *âne*, ass. (See AN for the silent 's' in *asne* – Cot.)

MND, III.i.120, *Bottom*: 'you see *an ass*-head of your *own*' (italics added).

AYL, IV.i.16. Jaques (a *jakes* or privy – C; P) says, 'I have . . . a melancholy of mine own' – a MELANCHOLY (bowel disorder) of his arse.

See AN; CROOK-BACK, *3H6*; BOG(GLER), *AC*; DANCE, *Ado*; FIELD, *TSh*.

P

Pacify Ptg to sexual bestiality. In Greek mythology Pasiphae mated with a bull and gave birth to the Minotaur, which her husband imprisoned in the Cretan labyrinth. *1H6*, v.iii.188: Suffolk admonishes himself not to 'wander in that labyrinth;/There Minotaurs and ugly treasons lurk'.

1H4, III.iii.195: 'Thou seest I have more flesh than another man' says Falstaff: 'thou seest *I am pacified* still'. The Prince responds, 'O, my sweet *beef*' – beef or flesh of the ox (bull or cow, but esp. the castrated male of the species). (Italics added.) See HEINOUS/anus for the rest of this exchange on the sexual nature of Falstaff, who in *2H4*, II.ii.172, is called 'the town bull', and in *MWW*, v.v.3, likens himself to Jove when he was 'a bull' (see ANGEL, *MWW*).

Pack(ing) A whore; pimping (F&H, s.v. Naughty pack). Richard Hakluyt, *Voyages*: 'The women of the place are . . . the most of them naughtie packes' (in *CD*).

Cym, III.v.80. Cloten thinks Pisanio was confederate to Imogen's flight: 'What, are you packing, sirrah?/Come hither: ah, you precious pandar!'

CE, IV.iv.105. Antipholus E.: 'Dissembling harlot, thou art false in all/And art confederate with a damned pack'.

2H6, IV.ii.51. Cade, claiming descent from an honourable mother, is mocked by his listeners in asides, such as 'But now of late, not able to travel with her furred pack, she washes bucks here at home.'

AC, IV.xiv.19. Thinking he has lost Cleopatra's 'heart', Antony says she 'Pack'd cards with Caesar' – not merely connived, as usually glossed, but packed CARDS/cods with him. Caesar's gain is repeated in Antony's loss: 'She has robb'd me of my sword [penis – P]' – the virility of Caesar contrasted with the impotence of Antony.

See GOLDSMITH, *CE*; AWAY, *MWW*.

Paid See PAY.

Pains (1) Penis; (2) to take pains: to coit. *Pene*: pains; *penne*: penis and pens (F). Smollett, *Humphrey Clinker*, p. 261: 'our new footman . . . laboured exceedingly, that she may bring forth fruits of re*pen*tance . . . he will take the same *pains* with . . . all of you . . . to *pene*trate . . . into your most inward parts' (italics added). *H5*, v.ii.25: Burgundy, likewise, 'labour'd' with his 'pains' and asks why there are no 'joyful births' in 'fertile' France. Dryden, 'Rondelay': she 'Kiss'd him *up*, before his dying;/Kiss'd him *up* and eas'd his pain' (italics added). Anon., 'An Amorous Dialogue between John and his Mistress . . . on how he pleased her so well, that she rewarded him with fifty broad pieces for his pains' (*Penguin Book of Restoration Verse*, p. 154).

KJ, I.i.78. The Bastard is 'well begot . . . Fair fall the bones that took the pains for me!' King John repeats the metaphor (121): 'my brother,/Who, as you say, took pains to get this son'. The Bastard asks (219), 'who comes in such haste in riding-robes?/What woman-post is this? hath she no husband/That will take pains to blow a horn before her?' This woman rides (copulates – F&H; P) but no husband takes pains, or blows (coits – C; P) the horn (erect penis – C; P), the post-horn (a long straight horn – *Cham*). On the contrary, she is the POST (penis); she must do the man's job. A horn is also a symbol of cuckoldry; and the woman is the Bastard's mother, who in begetting him had cuckolded her husband with Richard Coeur-de-Lion. So there was another, earlier time when her husband did not take pains to blow a horn, and was, consequently, given one.

In ll. 129–33 Richard's pains are implicitly contrasted with another penis symbol, the Bastard's legal 'father's will' (C; P), which is 'of no more force to dispossess me, sir,/ Than was his will to get me'. He considers his father (and brother) HALF-FACED (used three times in as many lines), i.e. half-arsed.

AYL, II.iii.65. Orlando, inconsolable lover, calls Adam a 'good old man', who 'prunest a rotten tree,/ That cannot so much a blossom yield/ In lieu of all thy pains and husbandry'. Adam may be 'strong and lusty' and his 'age' be as a 'lusty winter', but all his *lust* and *pains* and *husbandry* cannot make Orlando, the rotten tree, conceive.

2H4, IV.v.79. King Henry says Hal's perfidy is helping 'to end' him. Fathers are like 'the bee . . . Our thighs pack'd with wax, our mouths with honey,/ We bring it to the hive, and, like the bees,/ Are murdered for our pains'.

Though biologically incorrect (it is the worker–neuter who makes honey and not the male drones, the 'fathers' or impregnators), the metaphor successfully compares (1) the destruction of their father by the 'sons' who 'revolt' to achieve the 'gold' crown; and (2) the murder of the male bee for his pains after he has brought HONEY (sexual bliss – F&H), impregnated the queen bee and produced heirs.

Wanting power, the (young bee) son helps to 'end' (penis – P), to prick the 'ending father' and murders him for his pains – his penis, symbol of potency and power.

MV, V.i.182: 'the boy, his clerk,/ That took some pains in writing, he begg'd mine'. This feeble excuse for giving away his ring (*bague* – Cot) to the clerk that *begg*'d it puns on the clerk's taking pains or pens in writing, and there is no ambiguity about what the pens are when Gratiano says (237) 'I'll mar the young clerk's pen [penis – C; P]'. In her disguise of boy clerk, Nerissa had taken pens and penis (codpiece): as Portia said (III.iv.61), they shall see us in 'such a habit,/ That they shall think we are accomplished/ With that we lack' – with pens.

See CON, *MND*; POST, *TN*; FRANK, *R3*.

Paint 1. Pander. *Peindre* (Cot), to paint. Dekker and Middleton, *The Honest Whore I*, II.i: 'When you are old, and can well paynt no more,/ You turne Bawd'. Cosmetic paint or 'fucus' (Jonson, *Cynthia's Revels*, V.ii) may have connoted 'fucks' (F&H; *fottarie* – F). Painted brothel panels (Dekker's 'painted cloth rhymes' – *CD*) bore cheap sentiments: 'traders in the flesh, set this in your painted cloths' (*TrC*, V.x.46).

MM, III.ii.83. Pompey, 'bawd' and 'bawd-born', is taunted, 'Does Bridget paint still, Pompey, ha?'

IV.ii.38. Pompey, 'unlawful bawd', tells Abhorson, executioner, 'Painting . . . is a mystery; and your whores . . . being members of my occupation, using painting, do prove my occupation a mystery; but what mystery there should be in hanging, if I should be hanged, I cannot imagine.' Painting is a MYSTERY (prostitution). Whores prove pandering a mystery by *using* paint (fucus) and pander. But to hang is also L *pendere*, Fr *pendre*, so Abhorson, *pendeur* (Fr), can also call his hanging trade a mystery, one that – through a pun – panders.

Cym, III.iv.52. Imogen believes her husband thinks her a 'strumpet' because 'Some jay of Italy/ Whose mother was her painting, hath betray'd him. . . . And, for I am richer than to hang by the walls,/ I must be ripp'd: – to pieces with me!' Some jay or flashy, loose woman (*OED*; F&H; *MWW*, III.iii.44) falsely ripped Imogen to PIECES (whores). Her mother (bawd – F&H; cf. Middleton, *A Mad World, My Masters*, I.i: 'The close courtesan, whose mother is her bawd') was her painting. Imogen cares nothing for a physical resemblance, but is saying that the mother was the bawd, painting (Fr *peinture* / pander) of this jay.

2. Excrement, faeces. See RELICS, Chaucer: 'thyn olde breech . . . with thy fundament [arse] depeint!'

LLL, V.ii.648. Dumain mocks Armado's portrayal of Hector, who 'was not so clean-timbered' (timber: legs; tail-timber: toilet-paper – F&H): 'He's a god or a painter; for he makes faces.' This is not meant to be a compliment: he makes faeces/ FACES, for he is an ass

(like Holofernes, just mocked for his portrayal of 'Jud-as', 'the ass to the Jude'). See SLIP, *MND*, for puns on the scatological painting that ends this scene.
See WORSE, *Ado*.

Pair See PEAR.

Paradise Genitals. See DICE, L *tales*.

Pard The leopard is *lepered* (LEPROSY, confused with syphilis). Weever, *Faunus and Melliflora*, 65: 'Foretell that brutish sensuality,/ Leopard-skind, soul-polluting Sodomy,/ Dogges appetite, and damn'd impiety'.

Tem, IV.i.262: 'more pinch-spotted make them/ Than pard or cat o' mountain'. These spots (see AGE) are the running sores of pox or syphilis. Cf. Lyly, *The Man in the Moon*, IV.iii. where fairies punish Corsites for lechery: 'For the trespass he hath done,/ Spots o'er all his flesh shall run'; they 'pinch him blue and red' and he looks 'more like a leopard than a man', his face 'now too foul for lover'. The spots that *run* are oozing venereal sores (of the 'foul disease', syphilis – *OED*) of this *lover*: (1) *Laufer*, lit. runner (*lauferich*, in heat, lecherous), Ger syn. for syphilis (F&H, s.v. Ladies fever, n.d.); (2) *gonorrhée*, running of the reins (Cot); (3) a running horse, gonorrhoea (G).

Parrot Known for the vulgarity of the language it was taught. Lyly, *Midas*, I.ii: she has the 'tongue of a Parrot' and 'every hour she will cry, "Walk, knave, walk!" ' – 'Then will I mutter, "A rope for parrot, a rope." ' These are phrases taught parrots, punning respectively on (1) the sex-act; (2) a hangman's rope and a penis (Lancashire edn, p. 90). Cf. Butler, *Hudibras*, Pt I., c.i.540: 'Could tell what subtlest *Parrots* mean,/ That speak and think contrary clean;/ What *Member* 'tis of thom they talk/ When they cry *Rope*, and *Walk*, *Knave*, walk.'

Oth, II.iii.281: 'Drunk? and speak parrot? . . . swagger? swear? and discourse fustian with one's own shadow?' 'Speak parrot' and 'fustian' are usu. glossed as meaning nonsense, but both words have fouler connotations: 'fust' is a winecask and a mouldy, stale smell; Sh uses 'fustilarian' for a low fellow (*2H4*, II.i.66); a 'fustilug' was a 'Beastly, Nasty Woman' (F&H). It is the vulgar swearing typical of drunks, parrots, and SWAGGERERS (pimps) that Cassio regrets.

Ado, I.i.139. Similarly, when Benedick tells Beatrice 'you are a rare parrot-teacher', it is not that she spoke unintelligibly or merely parroted his words – as freq. glossed – but that he very well understood her RARE/ rear bawdiness. She says a bird of her tongue is better than a BEAST (eunuch, bugger) of his TONGUE (penis). She impugns the sexuality of any 'gentleman' (term of opprobrium to Sh) who does not want a 'scratched face [FACE, arse]' at her hands. 'Scratching [manual caressing – C; P] could not make it worse an 'twere such a face' as his. A scratch was a hermaphrodite (F&H). See DEFORMED: Beatrice would swear that 'if fair-faced . . . the gentleman should be her sister'.
See DELICATE, *Mac*.

Part (1) Euph. for private parts (ME). Nashe, *The Unfortunate Traveller*, p. 229, quoted Ovid on eunuchs: 'Who first deprived young boys of their best part,/ With self-same wounds he gave he ought to smart.'
(2) Division in the buttocks.

Cym, I.iv.162. Iachimo boasts that he will enjoy 'the dearest bodily part of your mistress' – perhaps her DEAR/ deer (hind). Donne, 'The Indifferent': 'Venus heard me . . . And by love's sweetest part . . . she swore'.

MND, I.ii.20: 'Name what part I am for, and proceed' – 'You, Nick Bottom, are set down for Pyramus.' When Nick (nick: a slit or breach – K) *Bottom* is *set down* for a part, that part can only be an arse; with the part, nick or slit, in the breech.

III.i.102: 'you speak all your part at once, cues and all' – cues/ *queues* (*queue*: 'the bable [penis] of a man' – Cot), and ALL/ AWL (penis).

R3, III.vii.51, Buckingham: 'stand betwixt two churchmen. . . . Play the maid's part, still answer nay, and take it.' Richard is to divide the two, play (amorously – P; TWR, s.v. Pley) the *part* and take it (admit to sexual congress – F&H; P). Sh added 'part' to the old saying 'Do as the maids do, say no, and take it' (Ray's *Proverbs*, in F&H, s.v. Take). Richard concludes, 'we'll bring it to a happy issue [birth – after he takes it]'.

LLL, IV.ii.28:

Dull. I said the deer was . . . a pricket.
Nathaniel. . . . he is only an animal, only sensible in the duller parts. . . .

Nathaniel pricks two birds with one stone, the *prick*et and Constable *Dull*.

See RARELY, *MND*; WALL, *MND*; APPROACH, *RJ*.

Particular A loose woman. *Particulière*: Fr syn. for a tart (F&H). Jonson, *The Alchemist*, I.i: Dol Common (a whore, as both her names indicate – F&H; P) shall 'sit in triumph . . . the longest cut at night,/ Shall draw thee for his Dol Particular'.

H5, III.vii.50. The Dauphin has a 'good and particular mistress': 'my horse is my mistress'. His mistress is a GOOD one (a slut) and certainly particular (special or noteworthy). For his sexual bestiality, see C, s.v. Horse; P, p. 49; BEAST, VARY.

Oth, I.iii.55. Brabantio has a 'particular grief . . . of so flood-gate and o'erbearing nature'. Asked what is the matter, he says only, 'My daughter! O, my daughter!' A GATE, esp. a sluice or flood-gate, is the vulva, anus; and NATURE is generative organs, Desdemona's being o'erbearing – O'ER/ whore, whore-bearing. He grieves (GRIEVOUS/ *une grivoise*, a whore – Cot) she was 'corrupted', 'abus'd' (ABUSED, seduced – P), i.e. has become a particular.

Ado, IV.i.3. Hero's father tells the Friar, 'be brief; only to the plain form of marriage, and you shall recount their particular duties afterwards'. But, instead of there being a ceremony, Hero is called a whore, who knows particular duties already.

H8, II.iii.101. Anne tells an OLD LADY or court courtesan who asked if she'd prostitute herself to be a QUEEN/ quean (whore), 'Good lady,/ Make yourself mirth with your particular fancy/ And leave me out on't.' Make herself mirth (enjoy sex – P; TWR, s.v. Myrthe) with her own particular (whoring) FANCY or sexual desires, but leave Anne out (OUT, Fr *hors*/ whore).

Pass The ass; that which passes out of it: excrement, a flatus. To excrete. Anon., 'On Melting down the Plate: Or, the Piss-Pot's Farewel, 1697': the 'Silver Piss-pots' are melted down, 'new coin'd' and will 'pass as currant, pleasant and as free,/ As that which hath so often pass'd in thee' (*Penguin Book of Restoration Verse*, p. 349). Pun on 'currant', sterling as opposed to counterfeit; *currents* or streams of fluids (urine); and *courance*, diarrhoea (Cot).

MND, III.ii.33: 'it came to pass,/ Titania waked and straightway loved an ass'. The rectum (L *rectum*, STRAIGHT) derived its name from its relatively straight way in some animals.

AW, IV.iii.371: 'it will come to pass/ That every braggart shall be found an ass'.

AYL, II.v.52: 'If it do come to pass/ That any man turn ass'.

MWW, IV.ii.127, Page: 'Why, this passes, Master Ford; you are not to go loose any longer; you must be pinioned', i.e. (1) bound because he is 'mad'; (2) pinned up like a baby in diapers because he goes LOOSE (diarrhoea), is spluttering vulgarities – as we say today, has verbal diarrhoea (see PRAYER).

JC, IV.iii.68: 'they pass by me as the idle wind'. Cassius's threats are as the IDLE (vulgar) WIND (a flatus) – offensive but impotent.

See STIR, *AYL*; PHYSICIAN, *H8*; ASSAIL, *RJ*.

Passage Genital and excretory orifices. *Vulva*: 'privy passage' (F). *Meat*: an open passage; a hole in the body (Cot). Meat: lust-fodder (C; P). See LOBBY.

Tim, III.iv. Timon's liberality bankrupts him; his 'friends' refuse loans. Anal metaphors symbolise the shit they requite him with. In III.iii.11 they are described as 'physicians' (PHYSICIAN: arse; sodomite). One pretends jealousy that for his 'occasions' (OCCASIONS, toilet functions – *OED*) Timon had not 'woo'd me first', for he was 'the first man [MAN, L *homo*]/That e'er received gift [GIFT, genitals] from him:/And does he think so *backwardly* of me now . . . ? . . . Who bates mine honour shall not know my coin [penis – P; K]' (italics added). Thus an old love is rewarded.

Timon's servant says that 'in the end' that which is 'foul' shall be 'clear' and Timon's 'Doors' must be shut to protect him from creditors. Scene iv opens with the milling servants of the creditors: 'Well *met*' – 'What, do we *meet* together?' Timon's steward rues that their 'false masters [*mets* – Cot] eat of my lord's *meat*'. (Italics added.)

Timon enters and sees the never-before-closed iron doors: 'are my doors opposed against my passage? . . . The place which I have feasted, does it now,/Like all mankind, show me an iron heart?' He plans revenge: he will 'once more feast the rascals' – 'let in the tide/Of knaves once more; my cook and I'll provide [PROVIDE sexually; pimp for]'.

Naut. terms, the *tide* of *knaves* (L *navis*, ship: the same pun in ANCIENT, *Oth*), indicate that the cook is a *coq* (Fr, ship's cook) – Timon's *cock* (penis – F&H; cf. 'my cook and I [EYE, penis, anus]') and his *cack* (excrement – *OED*) – for it is his cock and cack that will provide the contents of the feast (SPUR; CHEER; GOLD).

The metaphor is the cannibalistic consuming of food and of people; both may be avoided and voided; both may, as Hamlet says (*Ham*, IV.iii.33), 'go a progress through the guts of a beggar' (see LOBBY, *Ham*, and TABLE, *Ham*, for similar puns on the buggers of mankind).

So Timon opens his iron HEART (arse), his doors, his passage or *meat*, and in III.vi invites 'Each man to his stool [seat; matter excreted from bowels]', tells them not to let the 'meat cool', and ends by throwing containers of his urine and faeces into their faces.

See VELVET, *LLL*; OFT, *H8*; COMPUNCTIOUS, *Mac*.

Patience, patient '. . . the male feminism whereby man becomes patiens as well as agens, the woman a tribade [Lesbian]' (Richard Burton, p. 207).

RJ, I.v.73,91. Capulet angrily tells Tybalt that Romeo must 'be endured': 'be patient, take no note of him:/It is my will'. Tybalt must endure Romeo, be patient, take no NOTE (a penis, a prick), no pricking Romeo with his sword. He must submit to Lord Capulet's will (penis, potency – C; P; carnal desire – K). Tybalt: 'Patience perforce with wilful choler meeting /Makes my flesh tremble in their different greeting. I will withdraw'. It is not the internal conflict but the enforced role of patience or patiens, male feminism, in confrontation with his uncle's wilful (full will) CHOLER/It *colere* (desire), *culare* (arse-gut). 'To draw' is both to draw a sword and to expose the sexual organ (C; P); and Tybalt can do neither. On the contrary, he must withdraw – in this MEETING (L *coitus*) or symbolic coital act.

MV, I.iii.110. A metaphor of buggering, of rendering helpless sexually–financially. Shylock: 'Signior Antonio, many a time and oft/In the Rialto you have rated me . . . Still have I borne it with a patient shrug,/For sufferance is the badge of all our tribe'. Now that Antonio wants money 'Should I not say/"Hath a dog money?"' OFT/aft (behind) Antonio had RATED (screwed) him, had vented on him his *rate* ('Spleene, or Milt', i.e. spermatic organ of fish and its secretion – Cot). Shylock has *borne* it, the submissive sexual role (*2H4*, II.i.36, Mistress Quickly: 'I have borne, and borne, and borne'). To SUFFER (sexually receptive role) is the badge of his tribe. Now Antonio wants money from one whose purse (scrotum – *OED*; F&H) he tried to empty (render impotent – F&H) by bringing 'down' the 'rate of usance'; from one he treated like a DOG (bugger).

IV.i.12, Antonio: 'I do oppose/My patience to his fury, and am arm'd/To suffer with a quietness of spirit,/The very tyranny and rage of his'. The roles are reversed: (1) Antonio has an ARM (penis) ready to suffer (passively); (2) he opposes *his* patience to Shylock's fury – an avenging deity or spirit; (3) *he* will suffer Shylock's rage (sexual lust – TWR; P) with QUIET/*coit*al SPIRIT (semen, *rate*). It is useless to say to him *Ayez bonne rate* (pluck up your spirits – Cot).

See TAWNY, *AC*; GROOM, *H8*; TIGER, *CE*; TAME, *R2*; BEAST, *H5*.

Paul('s) Centre for loungers and illicit assignations. To go to Paul's for a wife: to go whoring (F&H). Old St Paul's Cathedral was a rendezvous for men of the baser sort; a Paul's man and a

Westminster woman had similar reputations (White, vol. VI, p. 533); a Westminster Wedding: 'A match between a whore and a rogue' (G). Jonson, *Every Man out of his Humour*, III.v: 'A pimpe . . . he comes every morning to emptie his lungs in Paules here.' Cf. Plautus, *Curculio*, 462–89: 'If you want to meet wealthy, wasteful husbands, seek round the Basilica. There too will be the haggard harlots, and the men who habitually haggle for them'.

2H4, I.ii.58, Falstaff: 'I bought him [Bardolph] in Paul's, and he'll buy me a horse in Smithfield: an I could get me but a wife in the stews, I were manned, horsed, and wived.' Three kinds of HORSE/whores, from three similar kinds of places: (1) Paul's; (2) Smithfield: 'He that . . . buys a horse in Smithfield . . . shall likely have a jade' (Richard Burton, in F&H); (3) stews, i.e. brothels.

R3. 'Paul' is used twice with ref. to Falstaff (*1H4*, II.iv.576; and *2H4*, above). The other eight uses are in this play, running through Acts I–V: see BEGGAR.

I.iii.45. Gloucester asks who complains that he is 'stern and love them not?' (STERN: sexually potent; lit. the buttocks). 'By holy Paul, they' who spread such rumours just because he cannot 'Smile in men's faces, smooth, deceive and cog,/Duck with French nods and apish courtesy' are 'silken, sly, insinuating Jacks' – perfect descriptions of the men of St Paul's: effeminates, whores, pimps (COG; FRENCH; SILK; SMOOTH).

See OIL, *1H4*.

Pay, paid 1. Copulate. Lit. thrash, satisfy (1500s). *Emplir une femelle*: to serve, give a woman payment, get her with young (Cot). Chaucer, 'The Shipman's Tale', 424: the wife says, 'By god, I wol nat paye yow but abedde'. In 'The Monk's Prologue', 72, the Host says women go to church for sex because churchmen 'mowe better paye/Of Venus paiementz than mowe we'. See GOLD, *Tim.*

Tem, IV.i.96: 'no bed-right shall be paid/Till Hymen's torch be lighted'.

2. A pederast (Gk *pais* or *paid*, boy + *erastis*, love). See BOY: the passive partner is called *pais*, pl. *paides*.

TGV, V.iv.77. Proteus apologises for having loved Silvia: 'I do as truly suffer,/As e'er I did commit [COMMIT, fornicate adulterously – P]'. Valentine: 'Then I am paid . . . . And, that my love may appear plain and free,/All that was mine in Silvia I give thee.' For their masculine love (that it may APPEAR, q.v.), he gives up the woman he has sought throughout the play. Proteus SUFFERS (is a pathic); Valentine is *paid*, his love is PLAIN (pederastic) and free – unlike the (sexual) service of the Greek SLAVE (a *paid*) for whom one paid.

H5, II.i.98. Near the end of a quarrel involving a sexual misunderstanding (HATEFUL), Nym asks, 'You'll pay me the eight shillings I won of you at betting?' – or *at bedding*. (Sh makes this quibble freq., as in *Tem* above, with ref. to paying a *bed*-right; and in *Oth*, I.iii.344, 383, when Iago sends Roderigo 'to bed', saying, 'I could never better stead [/*bed-stead*] thee', Roderigo says on departing, 'I'll be with thee betimes [/*bedtimes*].') Pistol: 'Base is the slave that pays.' In Athens, the SLAVE was hired out by his master or kept by a brothel to serve as a whore. Some owners 'kept *paedeagogia*, regular establishments of beautiful boys . . . for the delectation of guests as well as masters' (Wilkinson, p. 29). Pistol refuses to be the slave (*pais*) who pays.

1H4, I.ii.60:

Falstaff. . . . thou hast called her to a reckoning many a time and oft.
Prince. Did I ever call for thee to pay thy part?
Falstaff. No, I'll give thee thy due, thou hast paid all there.
Prince. Yea, and elsewhere, so far as my coin would stretch . . . .

The coin/quoin (penis – K) that STRETCHes (coitally) grows logically from the preceding suggestive remarks that the hostess and bawd, Mistress Quickly, was called to a reckoning many a time *and* OFT (behind); that Falstaff never had to pay his PART (genitals); that the Prince paid ALL (the penis) his DUE (the two testes). See TRIBUTE, *2H4*; Son 134: 'He pays the whole'.

See ANGEL, *1H4*; SCANT, Son 117; PLACE, *TGV*.

Peace Genitals. PIECE (of flesh, male or female). Piece/peace (K), as in *KJ*, IV.iii.93: 'Cut him to pieces' – 'Keep the peace, I say' (CUT: cunt; castrate).

LLL, V.ii.83. Boyet warns the French ladies, 'Arm, wenches, arm! encounters mounted are/Against your peace'. The ARMS (penises) of the lords are mounted (the coital position – *OED*; P) against their peace. (See RUSSIAN.)

TSh, V.ii.163. Katherina teaches the wives what a woman 'oweth to her husband': be 'obedient to his honest will' and 'kneel for peace'. Woman *o*wes ('O': the vagina – C; P) *o*bedience and should kneel to man's honest (chaste) will (penis and carnal desire – C; K; P). She should kneel to her 'king' (138), her 'sovereign' (147) for peace: (1) his piece (of flesh – P); (2) his piece, lit. a coin (*OED*), his sovereigns (gold coins).

Son 75. Like *TSh* above, this has a pun on 'peace'/piece (coin): 'And for the peace of you I hold such strife/As 'twixt a miser and his wealth is found'.

TN, II.iii.73. Sir Andrew tells the Clown to begin the 'song' or 'catch' (CATCH/Fr *caiche*, penis): 'Begin, fool: it begins "Hold thy peace".' Clown: 'I shall never begin if I hold my peace.'

2H4, I.ii.233, Falstaff: 'all you that kiss my Lady Peace at home [HOME, sexual goal]'.

TGV, V.ii.18. Thurio asks how Silvia likes it 'when I discourse of love and peace?' Julia: 'But better, indeed, when you hold your peace.'

See HUNGARY, *MM*; RUSSIAN, *LLL*; BREATHE, *1H6*; DAMSEL, *1H6*.

Peach *Pesca*: 'A young man's bum, a peach'; *pesco*: a man's bum, a peach-tree (F). *Dare le pesche* (lit. to give peaches): 'To give ones taile, or consent to unnaturall sinne' (F). *Scuotere il pesco*: shake the peach-tree well, i.e. commit lechery with boys (F).

MM, IV.iii.12. A customer of Mistress Overdone's brothel is in gaol 'at the suit of Master Three-pile the mercer, for some four suits of peach-coloured satin, which now peaches him a beggar'. A mercer is a dealer in fabrics and 'occas. a small-ware dealer' (*OED*), merchandise of any sort: Master THREE-PILE (a bawd; VD; piles or haemorrhoids) sold small boys. He is suing for four unpaid-for suits of peach-colour *satin*; and four peach COLOUR (*culare*, the arse – F) arses, also unpaid for (and *sat-in*). For a satin-merchant who is a pimp, see SMOOTH, *2H4*.

The gaoled customer is a beggar, broke, impeached for inability to pay; and he is a BEGGAR/bugger, whose peach-coloured satin suits peaches or informs against him as a shaker of the peach-tree, one who commits lechery with boys.

2H4, II.ii.19. Prince Hal is ashamed of knowing Poins: 'What a disgrace is it . . . to know thy face tomorrow! or to take note how many pair of silk stockings thou hast . . . and those that were thy peach-coloured ones! . . . But that the tennis-court keeper knows better than I'. Poins's SILK (sign of prostitution and effeminacy) peach-coloured stockings are something the KEEPER (pimp) of the TENNIS-COURT or brothel would best know.

See HEINOUS, *R2* ('appeach').

Pear/pair, appear/a pair *AC*, III.x.12: 'like *a pair* of twins *appear*ed' (italics added).

(1) Testicles. Pear-tree ('pyrie' – TWR): penis, as in Chaucer, 'The Merchant's Tale', where May, wanting 'peres', climbed up the tree to her waiting lover.

(2) Copulate (L *copula*, sexual union, from *co(m)*-, with *apere*, to fasten). Pair: a mated couple; to match, couple. *Aperire*: to open (F).

H5, IV.viii.38, Fluellen: 'saving your majesty's manhood . . . I hope your majesty is pear me testimony and witness'. To save *both* manhoods, he hopes his majesty will ap*pear* for him as *testi*mony and WITNESS (L *testis*: witness; testicle).

MWW, IV.v.103. Falstaff has been 'transformed' (TRANSFORM, alter sexually) and if his 'transformation' were to become known his fat would melt drop by drop till 'I were as crestfallen as a dried pear'. This is not a mixed metaphor but a neat pun on the fallen *crest* of the *cock* because of a dried pair (of testes). See WITCHES for Falstaff's 'peard'. Rabelais, Bk III, ch. 28: 'withered cod . . . shaped like a weary pear; O dejected and downcast' (LeClercq trs.).

RJ, II.i.38: 'O, Romeo, that she were, O, that she were/An open et caetera, thou a poperin

pear!' An open (*aperto* – F) 'O' (vagina – P); 'et caetera' (pudendum – P); and a *pop-her-in* pear (P)/pair.
  See CLOSE, *H5*.

Peasant Peasant, an Eliz. insult (1500s, a low fellow, base – *OED*), is always used contemptuously by Sh, usually suggesting the arse, and sometimes buggery. *Le pedzouille*: lit. a peasant, fig. the arse (F&H, s.v. Bum). *Paisant*: peasant, hind (Cot). A hind: a peasant; the rear or posterior. Connotes effeminacy when used for a man, since the hind is the female deer/DEAR, the hart being the male.

2H6, IV.iv.33. Cade's army is a 'multitude/Of hinds and peasants' who are given 'heart'.

CE, II.i.81. Dromio E., no peasant in any rustic sense, is addressed by his master, 'Hence, prating peasant!' He is peasant (hind) and PRATE (prat: buttocks).

TGV, V.iv. This much criticised final scene in which the women are unsentimentally bandied back and forth between the men may be better understood in the light of the play's sexual ambivalence, of which one clue is the Duke's phrase 'that peasant Valentine' (V.ii.35). A well-to-do young man who has a servant and sets out to see the world, whose friend's father readily believes he is visiting 'an emperor's court', is hardly a peasant, unless it be sexually. He becomes reconciled to his close male friend because Proteus says he SUFFERS (male homosexuality) and feels 'repentance' and 'penitence' – both containing the element *pen*, a penis, as in 'penance' (C; P) – and he accepts Proteus's apology, saying, 'Then I am paid [PAID/Gk *paid*, a young boy in the pederastic relationship]'. After a final mention of Proteus's 'penance' (sexual compliance, as in *H8* – P), the play concludes with the dubious arrangement 'our day of marriage shall be yours;/One feast, one house, one mutual happiness'! MUTUAL: descriptive for homosexual love; HOUSE: brothel; penis; fornicate. See PERFECTION for the sexual love of Proteus and Valentine.

TSh, Induction i.135: 'how my men will stay themselves from laughter/When they do homage to this simple peasant'. Sly is a tinker and no peasant but for his being treated like a bugger (see BUDGER) by this lord for the entertainment of his dissolute companions: Sly is called 'husband' by a page dressed as his wife, is given 'kind [KIND, sex] embracements, tempting kisses' and told he is not the kind of BEGGAR/bugger he thinks. HOMAGE, (homo)sexual duty, is done this peasant.

KL, III.vii.80, Regan: 'Give me thy sword. A peasant stand up thus! (*Takes a sword, and runs at him behind*.)' The sword (common penis symbol – P) and 'stand' (the erect penis – C; P) colour our understanding of the stage direction and the label 'peasant' for this servant, whom Regan earlier called 'dog' (DOG, bugger) after he had spoken of the 'service' he rendered her husband, whom he had 'served' ever since he was a child. 'Serve' (*OED*) and 'service' (P) refer to sexual serving or copulation.

MWW, V.v.218. Dr Caius eloped with a boy dressed in Anne's costume.

> *Caius*. Vere is Mistress Page? By gar, I am cozened: I ha' married un garçon, a boy; un paysan, by gar, a boy; it is not Anne Page.
> *Mrs Page*. Why, did you take her in green?
> *Caius*. Ay, be-gar, and 'tis a boy! Be-gar, I'll raise all Windsor.

Asked if he took (P) Anne in GREEN (venery – P; F&H, s.v. Greens), he answers, yes, that is how he discovered he had taken a BOY (catamite), a peasant, by gar, be-gar (BEGGAR/bugger). See STRANGE.

Pegasus A winged horse was (B2) the standard and emblem of ancient Corinth (city known for licentiousness). The flying horse or 'le cheval volant' (*H5*) is Sh's symbol for bestial love and sodomy. He is a HORSE/whore, with WINGS (penis), a male whore; he is a horse *volant* (a capon – Cot), a gelding. Sh is not the first to mock this steed of the muses. Aristophanes, *Peace*, 1–94: a man wants to ascend to Zeus (trad. 'he who descends in thunder', *kataibatos*; by adding 's' and creating *skataibatos*, Aristophanes makes him 'he who descends in ordure'). For the trip he nurtures a giant 'dung beetle' who lets 'off some foul smell' and whom he names 'my little Pegasus, my noble aerial steed'. His favourite food is a cake, not 'made of ass's dung' but 'of the dung of a boy-catamite; for he says he likes it beaten up' (trs. W. J. Hickie); the 'stool of a fairy's favourite' because 'he likes it well ground' (trs. Oates).

H5, III.vii.15. The Dauphin, who calls his horse 'le cheval volant, the Pegasus', also says 'my horse is my mistress' (see BEAST).

See COPATAIN HAT; ANGEL, *1H4*.

Pepper Infect venereally (G). B. E., *Dict. Cant. Crew*: 'Peppered off, Damnably Clapt or Poxt'. Stephens, *Essays and Characters* (1615): 'You snarle . . . As if you had been peppered with your wench' (F&H, s.v. Pepper).

TN, III.iv.159:

Sir Andrew. . . . I warrant there's vinegar and pepper in't.
Fabian. Is't so saucy?

Vinegar and pepper makes it saucy (SAUCE, gonorrhoea).

1H4, III.iii.9: 'I am a peppercorn, a brewer's horse', says Falstaff, who fears he is 'withered' (WITHERED, impotent) and dwindling away, and asks for a consoling 'bawdy song' as he recollects going 'to a bawdy-house not above once in a quarter – of an hour'. A peppercorn: a corn or *corne* (Cot) is a horn, a horny excresence (pun on the horn or penis). Falstaff is a diseased, peppered penis; a brewer's horse (HORSE/arse), old, worn out, not fit for riding. A pun on his penis or corn and the corn or grain used in brewing. See *MWW* below.

MWW, III.v.149. Ford says Falstaff, the 'lecher' is 'at my house' and cannot escape for he cannot 'cree*p* into a half*p*enny *p*urse, nor into a *pepp*er-box' (italics added). This tongue-twister must emerge sounding like *a pepper-pox*. Ford's house – unlike a HOUSE or brothel (P) – has no pepper-box (Fr *poivrière*: pepper-box; infected woman; *poivre*: pepper; infect with VD), has no diseased whore for a peppercorn (see *1H4* above) to creep into. Even 'creep' connotes VD: L *serpere*, to creep, stem of 'serpigo' (syphilis – P). Cf. William Cooke, 'The Cheating Age': 'Or else from the Spittle, half cur'd of the pox,/But I'll careful be, lest he pepper my box' (in National Theatre programme for Middleton and Rowley, *A Fair Quarrel*, 1979). Jonson, *Bartholomew Fair*, I.iii.: 'a pox o' your boxe'.

See WORM, *RJ*.

Perfect(ion) In bot. said of a flower having both stamens and pistils; a hermaphrodite. A hermaphrodite: a person or thing in which two opposites are combined; having parts belonging to both sexes; used loosely for a bisexual, for homosexual love (Addison used it to mean a catamite – *OED*). Cf. Donne, 'Sapho to Philaenis': the Lesbian Sapho tells her beloved, 'Thy body is a naturall *Paradise*,/In whose selfe, unmanur'd all pleasure lies,/Nor needs *perfection*; why shouldst thou then/Admit the tillage of a harsh rough man?' Puns on (1) the beloved's body, though *un-man*ur'd, not needing the tillage (1538, husbandry of a *man*; (2) the Lesbian, in whom all pleasure lies, herself embodying the male element, not needing (lacking) perfection. Bacon, 'On Love': 'nuptial love maketh mankind, friendly love perfecteth it'.

KJ, II.i.440. The citizen who wants Lewis and Blanch to be 'made one' vividly portrays the perfection of the hermaphrodite:

Such as she is, in beauty, virtue, birth,
Is the young Dauphin every way complete:
If not complete of, say he is not she;
And she again wants nothing, to name want,
If want it be not that she is not he:
He is the half part of a blessed man,
Left to be finished by such a she;

And she a fair divided excellence,
Whose fulness of perfection lies in him.

TN, I.v.315. Olivia says, 'Methinks I feel this youth's perfections'. The youth has the perfection of a she–he, Viola–Cesario. Then she sends Malvolio after 'that same peevish messenger,/ The county's man'. The peevish (i.e. perverse) county's man or cunt-man (see Introduction, p. xv; coun (P) and count (C): cunt). See SAME (Gk *homos*, *homo-*).

TGV. An atmosphere of ambisexuality pervades the play (see PEASANT). Valentine ascribes to his dear friend Proteus, a sea-*god* who assumed various shapes, 'angel-like perfection . . . He is complete in feature and in mind' (II.iv.66) – perfection of the ANGEL (catamite). Julia, too, describes him as 'Of such divine perfection' (vii.13).

And when (IV.i) Valentine is captured, one 'outlaw' says, 'a king for our wild faction!' Because 'you are beautified/ With goodly shape and by your own report/ A linguist and a man of such perfection/ As we do in our quality much want', the outlaws want him to be 'of our consort [CONSORT, bed-fellow]'; indeed, to be their 'general' (GENERAL, whore) and 'captain' to whom they will do 'homage' (HOMAGE, homosexual service) – and if he refuses, they will kill him! BOTH-SIDES (ambisexual) Parolles (see *AW* above) is Sh's only other LINGUIST; and he, too, is a CAPTAIN (pimp). It may be relevant to this wild faction that a lexicographer lists 'wild', 'brigand' and 'pederast' under the one heading of 'centaur', CENTAURS being 'creatures of ungovernable lust, given to pouncing on anyone of either sex, whose beauty aroused them' (Dover, p. 38); these outlaws are attracted by the 'banish'd' (BANISH: linked to dung; whoring; prob. sodomy), beautified Valentine, a MAN (L *homo*, to whom they will do homage) of such perfection.

Both friends are sexually ambivalent: both are men of SUCH (*tale* – F) perfection. Proteus, lit. of all SHAPES (genitals – *OED*), is complete (hermaphroditic), *angel-like* and *divine* (i.e. beatified – *OED*). Valentine has a *goodly* (OE *god*) shape and is *beautified*. (Apropos of the beautified/ beatified pun, we note that Middleton, in *The Roaring Girl*, a comedy based on transvestite humour, introduces Sir Beauteous Ganymede – GANYMEDE, lit. a catamite.) The parallels would seem deliberate; I suggest Sh was thinking of Plato's *Symposium* and the distinction between the 'common' and the 'heavenly' Aphrodite. 'Common love is inferior because it is directed at women as much as youths . . . heavenly love is exclusively male'. This speech, says Wilkinson (p. 26), 'was probably intended to represent the justification for pederasty.' (See FANTASY, *Oth* for the two types of love.) Cf. *AYL*, I.ii.76: Le *Beau* (another of the *beau*tified, beatified men) insinuates a kind of *heavenly* love when he tells Orlando, '*Hereafter*, in a *better world than this*,/ I shall desire more love and knowledge [arch., sexual intercourse] of you' (italics added).

R3, III.vii.80, Buckingham: 'By heaven [HEAVEN, homosexual love], I come in perfect love to him'.

Pernicious Sexually depraved. Lit. wicked and speedy.

MM, II.iv.150. Angelo's 'words express my purpose' ('express', like 'pernicious', means speed: 'How I have sped . . . shall express' – *KJ*, IV.ii.142. Isabella: 'most pernicious purpose [PURPOSE: arse, fornication]!' – sexual villainy towards her.

V.i.241. Mariana's claim that 'in's garden-house' Angelo 'knew me as a wife' establishes her as a 'pernicious woman'.

Ham, I.v.105. The ghost tells Hamlet of the 'couch for luxury and damned incest' of his uncle and mother. Hamlet: 'O most pernicious woman!' In I.ii.156 he had spoken of the 'wicked speed' (each word one aspect of pernicious) with which she posted to the incestuous sheets.

R2, III.i.4. Bolingbroke describes the 'pernicious lives' of Bushy and Green, who 'misled a prince' and 'in manner with your sinful hours/ Made a divorce betwixt his queen and him,/ Broke the possession of a royal bed . . . by your foul wrongs [WRONG, penis]'. They had pernicious lives (LIFE, penis). In MANNER (in the sex-act) with sinful HOURS/ whores, they broke (broker: pimp) possession of his bed and divorced Richard from his wife. Ironically,

Bolingbroke (V.i.71) is one of the 'Bad [BAD, homosexual] men' who are accused of having 'Doubly divorced' Richard from his 'crown' and 'wife'. DOUBLY: homosexual love; used fig. for buggering, ruining.

1H6, III.i.15: 'Thy lewd, pestiferous and dissentious pranks . . . . Thou art a most pernicious usurer ... Lascivious, wanton'. The pernicious usurer (usury: sexual intercourse – P), Winchester (owner of brothels – C; P), profits from and contributes to lewd pranks (sexual congress – P), as well as to pranks of political dissension.

Phrygian Pertains to sexual activity. Phrygians were known for orgiastic worship (*W*). Montaigne, Bk I, ch. 25: 'that effeminate shepherd of Phrygia'. Marston, *The Scourge of Villanie*, Satyre iii: 'Before some pedant Tutor in his bed/ Should use my frie [son] like Phrigian Ganimede [GANYMEDE, symbol of homosexuality]'. 'Frigging' is masturbation (F&H). Cf. Martiall's *Epigrams*, trs. R. Fletcher, Bk XI, no. cv: 'The Phrygian Boyes in secret spent their seed [semen – F&H]/ As oft as Hector's wife rid on his steed.' *TN*, III.i.58: 'I would play Lord Pandarus of Phrygia'.

The connection between the pouch and purse, i.e. the scrotum or testicles (pouch: purse; purse: scrotum – *OED*), and masturbation was a frequent one: (1) *coglioni* means the stones or testicles, and *coglionare* to play with one's stones (F); (2) Jonson: 'Claw a churl by the culls [testes], and he'll shite in your fist' (F&H, s.v. Culls).

MWW, I.iii.97. Pistol refuses to play 'Sir Pandarus of Troy' for Falstaff, who then tells him to vanish like 'hailstones'. The word 'stones' (testes) triggers off Pistol's 'Tester I'll have in pouch when thou shalt lack,/ Base Phrygian Turk!', punning on (1) he'll have a TESTER, standard pander's fee, in his purse when Falstaff has none in his; (2) he'll have testicles (stones) in his scrotum when Falstaff, the bottom-frigging TURK (castrate or bisexual) has none in his. 'No money in the purse' means to be impotent (F&H). See BRAINS, *Cym*, for Cloten's empty, impotent purse.

TrC, IV.v.186. The pouch–Phrygian link in *MWW* above is made here, too: 'I have seen thee [Hector],/As hot as Perseus, spur thy Phrygian steed' – a Perseus/purse pun. SPUR means a penis, a prick. See BEAST, *H5*, in which a steed, a 'beast for Perseus', is used in sexual bestiality.

See BLOOD, *TrC*.

Physician An arse. Puns on (1) the physic and its function; (2) *mire* (a physician – Cot) and 'mire' (urinate, defecate upon – P). QUAGMIRE: buttocks.

H8, V.ii.11: ' 'Tis Butts,/ The king's physician: as he pass'd along,/ How earnestly he cast his eyes upon me!/ Pray heaven, he sound not my disgrace!' Cranmer fears that Butts, who passed along – PASS (excrete) from the butt (buttocks – *OED*) – and is a physician who administers physic (both a theory of medicine and a cathartic for cleansing the bowels) may have SOUNDED (probed to the *bottom*) the depths of Cranmer's degradation (see GROOM). Butts CAST his EYES (arse): to cast or diagnose excreta was a function of the physician (LAND, *Mac*).

MWW, III.iv.101. Mistress Quickly asks Anne's mother, 'will you cast away your child on a fool, and a physician?' Since acquiring a physician for son-in-law is not usually considered casting away one's daughter, Sh is punning on this particular French physician or *mire*, and on 'mire' as filth: see CAST (evacuate waste). This Dr CAIUS/ Fr *cas* (buttocks) is a fool, an ass, and perhaps a sodomite, seeking ANNE/ Fr *âne* (an ass) for his bride. (See CONTRARY and DRY.)

See PASSAGE, *Tim*.

Piece (1) Whore, pimp. Pejorative for women (C; P); for either sex (F&H).

(2) Genitals.

TrC, IV.i.62. Helen of Troy is a 'flat tamed piece' with 'whorish loins'.

TN, I.v.30. Maria is 'as witty a piece of Eve's flesh as any in Illyria'.

Ado, III.iii.179. Borachio the 'ruffian' (IV.i.92; RUFFIAN: prostitute's bully – *OED*) is partner to a 'dangerous piece of lechery'.

IV.ii.86. Dogberry is 'as pretty a piece of flesh as any is in Messina', and an 'ass'.

RJ, I.i.34, Sampson: 'I am a pretty piece of flesh'. Both Sampson and Dogberry (*Ado*, above) are PRETTY/prat-y pieces of flesh.

Cym, IV.ii.127. Cloten, 'an arrogant piece of flesh', is 'a fool, an empty purse [an empty, impotent scrotum – F&H]' (113).

H8, III.ii.280. Surrey calls Wolsey 'a piece of scarlet [SCARLET, a whore]'.

Tim, I.i.202. Apemantus calls the sycophantic painter 'a filthy piece of work [sexual activity – TWR, s.v. Werke; P]' – the painter prostitutes his work (and himself).

Pin 1. Penis (C; F&H 1635).

LLL, IV.i.138. Costard jests on hitting the mark with the 'prick' in it: 'Then will she get the upshoot by cleaving the pin' – *upshoot* or seminal ejaculation of the pin (C). Shoot and shot: coitus (F&H).

2. DILDO. Marston, *The Scourge of Villanie*, Satyre viii, tells of a 'busk-poynt (which in secrecie I fear was conscius of strange villany)'. It belonged to Publius's mistress and, 'if he get her itch-allaying pinne,/O sacred relique, straight he must beginne/To rave . . . thus . . . Her haire imbrac'd it, o thrice happy prick/That there was thron'd, and in her haire didst stick'.

WT, IV.iv.228. The servant announces a pedlar selling 'dildos', and Autolycus enters crying his wares, 'Pins and poking-sticks of steel,/What maids lack from head to heel'. See ROOF, Dekker quote of an 'ingendring' poke. See DILDO.

See WITCHES, *CE*.

Pinch 1. Penis. The male 'member' or 'pricke' is *pinge* and *pinche* (Cot).

H8, II.iii.1. Sh plays on these sounds and meaning in the 'pang that pinches'. This is just prior to the puns (see ANNUAL) on whether Anne would stretch her 'cheveril conscience' (CHEVERIL; *con*science, cunt) for Henry's 'title' (TITLE, prick); and the next scene, in which Henry's 'conscience . . . received a . . . prick' telling him to divorce Katherine.

II.iii.17. Anne, the Queen's maid-of honour, pities Katherine's 'sufferance panging/As soul and body's severing' – ironically anticipating the sentiment of her own woman when Anne, by then herself Queen, is delivered of a child: 'her sufferance made/Almost each pang a death' (V.i.68). And the labour pangs she suffers are forerunners of her pangs of death (like Katherine's 'soul and body's severing') for having, like Katherine, delivered only a female heir. Thus the scene that began with the pang that pinches – the *pinche* or prick (penis) that led to her pangs of labour – ends with her saying, 'pray, do not *deliver*' (italics added) to the Queen the news of her newly acquired title (with its implicit acquisition of Henry's TITLE, prick). And, through the puns, Sh comments on the pinches and pricks of the King's conscience and of Anne's *con*science (cunt – P) that end in Anne's execution.

2. To caress (P). To coit, in the sense of to screw someone out of something; to bugger; to render impotent through VD or castration. Pinch: lit. nip off the bud in pruning.

WT, II.i.51. Leontes rues the escape of his wife's alleged lover: 'and I/Remain a pinch'd thing' – his plan for revenge nipped in the bud and his bud, too, his thing (penis – F&H; P), pinched or pruned; he cuckolded and impotent to revenge.

2H4, I.ii.258: 'A man can no more separate age and covetousness than a' can part young limbs and lechery: but the gout galls the one, and the pox pinches the other'. AGE and COVETOUSNESS (lust), and youth and lechery: GOUT (syphilis) and pox (syphilis – C; P) pinch and curtail – play the rogue with man's 'great toe' (274)!

Tem, I.ii.328. Caliban: 'a south-west blow on ye [Prospero]/And blister you all o'er!' Not just heat blisters, but disease and impotence from the syphilitic BLISTERS and the south-west wind (L *Libs*) that *libs*, i.e. castrates. Prospero retaliates that Caliban will 'be pinch'd/As thick as honeycomb, each pinch more stinging/Than bees that made 'em'. Prospero's 'urchins' (syn. for HEDGEHOGS, sodomites), whose 'pricks' Caliban fears (BITE), will 'exercise' (EXERCISE, sexually) on him and pinch him thick (L *pinguis*), each pinch (Fr *pinche*, prick) a STING (prick, penis).

Honeycombs, in which bees store not only honey but also eggs, are made by *neuter* bees, who also have the stings (Sh freq. mocks the males or drones who 'eat honey' from 'others' labours' – *Per*, II., Gower, 18). The ' 'em' that bees made has an ambiguous antecedent: it refers back to (1) the pinches (or pricks); (2) the thick (*pinguis*) honeycomb. But both are made by *neuter* bees and, just so, it is *neuters*, urchins or HEDGEHOGS, who shall pinch, sting – or bugger – Caliban, and give him syphilis (see AGE; PARD).

See SINGE, *CE*; WRINKLE, *AC*.

Pink The genitals. Coitus. *Pinco*: the prick; *pinca*: the vulva (F). Ger *Pincke*: prick (F&H). *RJ*, II.iv.61:

Mercutio. Nay, I am the very pink of courtesy.
Romeo. Pink for flower.
Mercutio. Right.
Romeo. Why, then is my pump well flowered.

The trad. annotation of a well-flowered pump or shoe as decorated with pinked flowers, and the pink as the flower of excellence, ignores the pun in pinking, i.e. *pricking* of decorative holes (*OED*; *W*), is atypical of the boys' usual bawdy humour, and isolates these four lines from their context. (1) Romeo's reply to where he had spent the night was 'my business was great' (BUSINESS: sexual intercourse – F&H). (2) The case (genital area – P; K) was such as 'constrains a man to bow in the hams [1552, thigh and buttock]', in which case 'a man may strain courtesy' – may strain, i.e. stretch beyond proper length (to man: to copulate, as in III.ii.14 – P). Man also *strains* at a bowel-evacuation (*OED*); see COURTESY. (3) The boys go on to jest on phallic stretching; and the 'bauble', 'tale', 'gear' and 'prick' all pun on the penis (C; F&H; P).

If the above four lines are seen as integral to the whole, then (1) Romeo's pump (F&H 1730) is his prick; (2) the flowers, lit. organs of generation, are the *pinco* (prick) and *pinca* (vulva), and a pun on deflower ('Flower as she [Juliet] was, deflowered by him [Death]' – IV.v.37); and Romeo is boasting that last night his *pump* was WELL (a penis; a whore) flowered, pinked, and pricked. Cf. Day, *Humour Out of Breath*, II.i: 'she's a pink, Board her'.

Pit Female pudendum (F&H). *Fossa*: pit; woman's pleasure-pit; grave; ditch (F). Cf. DITCH.

See CHERRY, *TN*; PUSH, *JC*.

Pitch To whore. Lit. to thrust in. *Pegola*: pitch; an infectious whore (F).

H5, II.iii.51. Almost the last words Pistol addresses to his wife (see CLOSE), Mistress Quickly, bawd, who (V.i.87) dies in the spital 'Of malady of France' (syphilis) are 'the word is "Pitch and Pay [PAY, fornicate]" ' – the WORD (whore) or motto of the whore.

2H6, II.i.196. Gloucester responds to the Queen's warning about 'the tainture of thy nest [pudendum – P]', 'if she [his wife] have forgot/Honour and virtue and conversed with such/As, like to pitch, defile nobility,/I banish her my bed'. 'Conversation' meant sexual intimacy (*OED*). See FACT.

LLL, IV.iii.3: 'The king he is hunting the deer; I am coursing myself; they have pitched a toil; I am toiling in pitch, – pitch that defiles [violates sexually – P].' Both men are engaged in venery: the King in hunting, Biron in sexual indulgence. The King hunts the deer, and Biron the DEAR/deer (hind). He COURSES (whores) and curses himself for his entanglement with this diseased and wanton woman. He blames 'her eye . . . but for her eye, I would not love her; yes, for her two eyes'. See FACE (the rump and its two eyes) for his earlier, similar diatribe.

See EVIL, *MM*; MERMAID, *TA*.

Place Pudendum (TWR; F&H) or anus. 'The Women's Complaint to Venus' (1698): having learned 'Sodom's Embraces' in France, the 'Souldiers . . . But at the wrong place will be thrusting' (*Penguin Book of Restoration Verse*, p. 167).

MWW, II.ii.226. Brook (i.e. Ford) claims to have got no satisfaction at Mrs Ford's hand: his love was 'Like a fair house built on another man's ground; so that I have lost my edifice by mistaking the place where I erected it.' A phallic erection in the wrong *place*: Ford admits to a MISTAKE (adultery, sodomy) in place.

KL, v.i.11. Regan, sexually jealous of her sister, asks Edmund 'have you never found my brother's [i.e. brother-in-law's] way/To the forfended place?' She suspects he has 'been conjunct/And bosom'd with her'. Bosom: clinch amorously (P).

Per, IV.vi.98. Lysimachus, customer in a brothel, tells Marina he is ready: 'Come, bring me to some private place: come, come.' PRIVATE: genitals (*OED*); come: orgastically (P).

TGV, II.v.6: 'man is never . . . welcome to a place till some certain shot be paid and the hostess say "Welcome!" ' Pay the shot: copulate, as in 'He laid her on her Back, and paid her the shot/Without ever a stiver of mony' (F&H 1630).

See SCREW, *TN*, *Mac*; SUPPLY, *TSh*; CONTRARY, *MWW*.

Plain(ly), plain-song (1) Of copulation 'Pleyn': amorous play (TWR). Plain-song or chant, *cantus planus*, as distinguished from prick-song or descant, the highest part of the score, sung or played above plain-song. These terms were linked (as in 'plainesong and priksong' – *OED* 1545) and lent themselves to freq. puns on the cunt and the prick playing on it. Richard Edwards, *Damon and Pythias* (1566): 'the ladies . . . do plainly report/That without mention of them you can make no sport:/They are your playne song, to singe descant upon' (*CD*, s.v. Plainsong). Plain, plane, flat: recumbent partner, as opposed to the *pricker*; if male, he is flat because impotent. Plain: belly, perhaps back (P).

(2) Of sodomy. Sodom and Gomorrah are the biblical 'cities of the plain' (Gen 25; Marcel Proust, *Cities of the Plain*).

Ado, III.iv.80.

Margaret. Get you some of this distilled Carduus Benedictus, and lay it to your heart . . . .
Hero. There thou prickst her with a thistle. . . .
Margaret. . . . I meant plain holy thistle.

Sh juxtaposes thistle that pricks and thistle that is plain, holy/*hole*-y (the cunt – P). Beatrice will lay (coitally) the thistle of Benedictus, prick of Benedick, to her HEART (arse): she will be plain-chant (*chant*, a lay or song – Cot) to his prick-song.

MND, III.i.47: ' ". . . I am a man as other men are"; and there indeed let him name his name, and tell them plainly he is Snug the joiner'. Snug (lying close) is to say plainly, flatly, that he is a joiner (one who does delicate, ornamental carpentry), who physically unites things (L *copulatio*, JOIN, copulate). But, no matter what he says, Snug is *not* a man as other men are, any more than he is a lion. He is to name his name (L *nomen*, pun on his *gnomon*, a carpenter's square, and his being *no man*). As a joiner his tools are a gnomon and a plane – flat. And, once he speaks 'to the same [SAME, Gk *homo*-] *defect*' (italics added), the 'Ladies' assuredly will not 'fear' or 'tremble', for Snug is a MAN (L *homo*) who won't hurt women; that is what he must tell them *plain*ly. (See FIX, *Oth*, for another gnomon pun.)

3H6, III.ii.69:

Lady Grey [knows what] Your highness aims at . . . .
King Edward. To tell thee plain, I aim to lie with thee.
Lady Grey. To tell you plain, I had rather lie in prison.

He tells her *plain* or *flat*ly, he aims to lie with her. And she tells him *plein* (pregnant – Cot) she would rather lie in prison than in the other confinement (child-bed). He says she wrongs her 'children' and she says his *highness* (used several times, maybe as pun on his prick-song, highest part) wrongs (WRONG: prick; seduce) both them and her by screwing them of their land.

TSh, I.ii.40. Three times Petruchio asks Grumio to KNOCK (copulate – F&H): 'knock me at this gate [GATE, anus]'. Grumio, like the audience, hears a pun on his being asked to assail Petruchio (and sexually): 'Spake you not these words plain, "Sirrah, knock me here, rap me here, knock me well, and knock me soundly"?'

SOUNDLY puns on (1) to sound or heal: knock me *well* and *soundly*; (2) to examine (as lungs) by percussion, striking one body against another with force; (3) to penetrate the *bottom* (fundament, arse). So, Grumio asks, did you not speak *plain*, in the language of Sodom, and ask me to knock (16th c., fuck – F&H) you? Did you not say 'rap *me*' (*raper*, knock at a door – Cot), *rape* me? (italics added). A 'nock' was the posteriors or 'aperture of the fundament', anus (F&H); and a rap, esp. with knuckles, is a similar pun, since it was a 'con' (*OED*) and a pun on CON (genitals). Everything was conducive to Grumio's misunderstanding his master's intent. Petruchio's last words were 'Now, knock when I bid you, sirrah villain!' and Grumio not only KNOCKED (q.v.) but also knuckled down, as we know from Hortensio's greeting, 'Rise, Grumio, rise.'

'Soundly' introduces the music puns. Petruchio: 'I'll ring it; I'll try how you can sol, fa, and sing it'. Talk of knocking changes to ringing, as he wrings Grumio's ears. RING: encircle; the genitals (L *anus*, ring). Petruchio will try (test sexually – C; P) – perh. a pun on cunt/cun(ne), try, test – how Grumio can/CON (cunt), sol, fa, or sing (take someone on coitally – C; P); sing prick-song, perh., since Petruchio spoke *plain*. No wonder Grumio called, 'Help, masters, help! my master is mad.' 'Mad', with desire as well as lunatic (*OED*; P), puns on *mated* (K) and *maid* (K), several times in *TSh*.

H5, III.ii.6. Bardolph urges 'On, on, on, on, on! . . . to the breach!' And Fluellen urges, 'Up to the breach, you dogs! avaunt, you cullions!' But Nym and Pistol cannot avaunt or advance, they can neither *on* or *up* to the breach (female pudendum – C; P) or to the breech (buttocks; part of a fire-arm): 'that is the very plain-song of it' and 'The plain-song is most just'. They are not men.

Boy: 'I am boy to them all three: but all they three, though they would serve me, could not be man to me; for indeed three such antics do not amount to a man.' Though they would (if they could) serve (coitally – *OED*; P) this BOY (catamite), they can't be MAN (older male pederast) to him INDEED/*in* (the) *deed* of coitus – for all they (and their) THREE (penis and testes) do not *amount* (assume superior position coitally, rise in erection – *OED*; P).

Pistol: 'God's vassals drop and die [in war]', but in an 'alehouse' Pistol's 'purpose should not fail [fall, drop]' – there 'would I hie'. Pun on vassals/vessels: he can raise high alehouse vessels ('pots'), but his PURPOSE (penis), the other vessel (tube for body fluids), *that* drops and dies.

See CACKLE, *KL*; PAID, *TGV*; TRAITOR, *LLL*.

Planks Buttocks. *Asse* (F) and *ais* (Cot): plank or board.

AC, III.vii.63. A Roman soldier tells Antony 'do not fight by sea;/Trust not to rotten planks'. Don't trust rotten ships, i.e. bottoms (as in *MV*, I.i.42); don't trust rotten planks, corrupt, putrid arses – let 'the Egyptians/And the Phoenicians go a-ducking'. But Antony does not listen, and it is he who goes a-ducking: he 'Claps on his sea-wing, and, like a doting mallard [a duck],/Leaving the fight in height, flies after her' (III.x.20) – after his mate, Cleopatra, a rotten plank or 'whore' (III.vi.67). *Clap* and *rotten*: venereally diseased; debauched (P).

Play the sir *Le jeu de ser*: 'close-buttock play; lecherie' (Cot, s.v. *serrecropière*). Pun on *le jeu*, play, the *ser*.

Oth, II.i.175. Observing Cassio conversing with Desdemona, Iago interprets his gestures as sexual overtures: 'it had been better you had not kissed your three fingers so oft, which now again you are most apt to play the sir in'. By l. 263 Iago rephrases 'play the sir' as 'Lechery, by this hand', just as Cotgrave's *jeu de ser*, play the sir, is 'lecherie'. See SAKE.

AC, II.v.5:

Cleopatra. Come, you'll play with me, sir?
Mardian. As well as I can, madam.

This is Sh's only mention of 'billiards' (3), a game that needs a cue and balls, yet is being played

– as well as he can – by her eunuch and Cleopatra, the 'whore' (III.vi.67). *Truccare*: to play billiards; *trucca*: a whore (F).

TGV, IV.iv.1, Launce: 'When a man's servant shall play the cur with him, look you, it goes hard'. The pun in play the *cur* and play the *sir* is anticipated in the extended jest (II.iii) in which Launce, the *ser*vant, confuses himself with his 'cur' (11) and his DOG (bugger): 'I am the dog: no, the dog is himself, and I am the dog – Oh, the dog is me, and I am myself'. Such puns on the sexual ambivalence of Launce and Speed (see MISTAKE; Index) mirror the androgyny of their two masters. Whether one plays the *s*ir or *c*ur, in lechery 'it goes hard', said of an erect penis (P): Gk *skiros*: hard; a hard swelling. Cf. *MWW*, I.i.97: 'A cur, sir'; and *LLL*, V.i.35: 'Quare chirrah, not sirrah?'

Plenty, plentiful Plenty or 'copia' puns on 'cope' (copulate – C; P); and on Fr *assez* (plenty).

R3, V.v.34, Richmond (to be Henry VII): 'And let their heirs [his and Elizabeth's], God, if they will be so, / Enrich the time to come with smooth-faced peace, / With smiling plenty'. Like so many other closing speeches of plays, this one is ironic. 'Smooth-faced' (SMOOTH) describes flatterers and effeminates – the smooth FACES (arses) of a PEACE / PIECE (genitals and whores); and the SMILE (Fr *rire* / rear) of plenty. Historically, those whom Richmond calls 'The true succeeders' (30) suffered from 'relative infertility. . . . Only one of Henry VII's sons survived to adulthood. None of Henry VIII's did' (Saccio, p. 185). Richmond's *peace* and *plenty* – whores and asses / arses – bred impotents or effeminates. Cf. *Cym*, III.vi.21: 'Plenty and peace breed cowards: hardness ever / Of hardiness is mother.' See COWARD (effeminate).

Plum(e) (1) Plums: testicles (P; cf. SILK, *RJ*). Plum-tree: legs and female pudendum (F&H; P). Plum-tree shaker (F&H; *hoche-prunier* – Cot): penis.

(2) Plume: the penis. *Penard*: a plume of feathers, also a man's yard, i.e. penis (Cot). Women poets are deposing men: 'Each snatches [snatch: vulva] the male quill from his faint hand . . . He to her fury the soft plume doth bow – / O pen! ne'er justly slit [vulva] till now!', Lovelace, 'On Sannazar's being honoured . . .' (*Signet Classic Poets of the 17th c.*, vol. II, p. 259.

2H6, II.i.97. A man who climbed a 'plum-tree' to get his wife plums became 'lame' (LAME, impotent) from 'a fall off a tree'. This is a variation on I.ii, in which the Duchess jabs at Duke Humphrey's masculinity, asking why he 'droops' and whether his hand [HAND, penis – K] is 'too short'. The Duke himself dreams his 'staff [penis – F&H] . . . Was broke in twain' and predicts his wife will 'tumble down' her husband in her desire to have him climb politically. The scene ends with a prediction of 'Humphrey's fall'.

Oth, I.iii.399. Alleging Othello acted ' 'twixt my sheets' and Cassio supplanted him in Othello's affections, Iago plans 'To get his place and to plume up my will / In double knavery'. He will get simultaneous revenge on both, be more the man than either – will plume *up* his will (penis – C; P) in double knavery: DOUBLE or didymous, pun on Gk *didimos* (a twin, a testicle). Perhaps his scheme resulted in sexual injury to Cassio (JOINT; RAGGED).

See JET, *TN*; FEATHER, *LLL*; TRAIN, *1H6*; ALTAR, *1H4*; HEINOUS, *R2*.

Poop Buttocks (*OED*); vagina, tail (Hulme, p. 114). To fart (TWR, s.v. Horn). Poop-noddy: fornication (F&H). *Poupe*: cankerous disease of the nose, Noli me tangere (Cot); which is the pox, French disease, i.e. syphilis (F&H). *Poupée*: 'barrack-hack', i.e. whore (F&H n.d.).

Per, IV.ii.23. A poor man 'that lay with the little baggage' is dead. 'Ay, she quickly pooped him; she made him roast meat for worms.' She screwed him (QUICKLY), made him a syphilitic corpse (C, s.v. Poop) for WORMS (VD).

1H4, III.iii.28: 'thou art our admiral, thou bearest the lantern in the poop, but 'tis in the nose of thee; thou art the Knight of the Burning Lamp.' Bardolph's nose may be lit from drink, usual gloss, but *varole* is pimples as in drunkards' faces *and* the pox (F). Bardolph's lantern is in the poop, buttocks, or, speaking nautically, since he's an 'admiral', in the stern. It is in the nose (*nez* or *naze* – Cot), pun on *le naze* (the bum – F&H) and the nose (penis – P). He is burning (symptom of VD – *OED*; F&H; P) in the nose on his FACE / Fr *fesse* (rump). Bardolph is knight of the burning, not to be touched, lamp (Noli me tangere, 'Touch me not' – John 20:17). He reminds Falstaff of 'Dives . . . burning, burning' (Luke 16:19); and, doubtless, of Lazarus, in the next verse, 'full of sores'. His poop has the *poupe*.

AC, II.ii.197. One is reluctant to see the pun on disease in this, Sh's third and last use of 'poop', but it is there and it serves a purpose. Ackn)wledging Cleopatra's dissipation and disease even while praising her beauty is what one ought expect from the cynical Enobarbus (FLUTE), who concludes his speech, 'vilest things/ Become themselves in her; that the holy priests/ Bless her when she is riggish [rig: a strumpet]' – just as Enobarbus does: 'The barge she sat in like a burnish'd throne,/ Burn'd on the water; the poop was beaten gold;/ Purple the sails, and so perfumed that/ The winds were love-sick with them'.

Many of the puns in *1H4* above are repeated: she sat in a barge that like a *burn*ish'd throne *burn'd*, burning with VD (*OED*) – suggestive of a fire-ship (sufferer from VD – *OED*; a tainted whore – F&H); her purple sails evoke 'Dives that lived in purple . . . in his robes, burning, burning'. The sails are perfumed (L *perfumis*, smoke) with smoke – from the burning fire (sexual heat and disease – C); the wind is love-sick or venereally sick (Venus: goddess of love; venereal: exciting sexual desire) like the men in *Tim*, IV.iii.207, who hug their 'diseased perfumes' or whores. 'A strange invisible perfume hits the sense [/ scents; the cense or incense used for fumigation of diseases]/ Of the adjacent wharfs. The city cast/ Her people out upon her'. This is an awkward way to say only that the city emptied out to see her, but Sh is punning: (1) a 'casting' bottle was used to sprinkle perfume, as in Marston, *Antonio and Mellida*, III.ii; (2) the city cast or vomited, CAST (ejected waste) on her. 'Cast urine' is diagnose disease; and she whom Enobarbus said custom (whoring – C; P) could not stale (a whore; urine) is like the 'wappen'd' (sexually stale – C; fucked – F&H) widow in *Tim*, IV.iii.40: 'She, whom the spital-house and ulcerous sores/ Would cast the gorge at'. Both sick women elicit vomiting: that wappen'd, lit. beaten, widow with her beaten poop; and Cleopatra who *sat* on her poop of beaten GOLD (excrement; a whore), sat on her burning or venereally diseased THRONE (toilet).

Cleopatra, 'triple-turned whore' (IV.xii.13) is a symbol of ravage and disease, as is borne out also in her other name, 'serpent of old Nile' (I.v.25). 'El mal serpentina': 1493, syphilis (Richard Burton, p. 89); 'serpent' and 'serpigo' (VD – P) both stem from L *serpere*, to creep. Cleopatra, serpent of old Nile, is like that serpent of Gen 3:1–5, and, like him, she brings about another downfall of man, of Antony. It is fitting that she dies, symbolically, from her own disease, the bite of a serpent that she calls a 'worm' (WORM: syphilis; moral decay). See LEPROSY; THRONE; SURE.

Poor/pure (1) Of harlots. Rabelais, *Pantagruelian Prognostication*: 'Blowings, tits, pure ones, concubines' (1694 trs.).

(2) Of homosexual love, pure in that it is unmixed, involves only one sex. L. *puer*: boy. Cf. *MV*, II.ii.130: 'Not a poor boy, sir, but the rich Jew's man' – prob. a play on his being not the BOY (young male homosexual) but the MAN (L *homo*) – not the buggered, but the buggerer; he has run away, screwed Shylock. (3) *Puir*: to stink (Cot). See FANCY, *Ham*; POWER, *MM*.

VA, 736. Venus tells of Adonis's 'pure perfection' (PERFECTION: the hermaphrodite – a perfect flower combines male and female sex organs), the combination of opposites that in Eliz. lit. symbolised the homosexual, the male–female combination. Earlier (9) she had called him 'The field's chief flower . . . more lovely than a man'. Adonis rejected the love of Venus (woman) and will 'not know it [love],/ Unless it be a boar'. His death by a kiss from the boar was a metaphor for copulation (see WOUND; Introduction, p. x).

AC, I.ii.146, 152, Enobarbus: 'I have seen her die twenty times upon far poorer moment. . . . her passions are made of . . . the finest part of pure love.' The pure love of Antony 'not more manlike/ Than Cleopatra' nor she 'More womanly than he' (I.iv.5).

MV, I.i.145. Bassanio says that what follows is 'pure innocence', is '*child*hood proof': he, a 'wilful youth', wants Antonio to lend him more money (italics added). This is obviously *puer* INNOCENCE, but pure in-no-sense.

Ado, IV.i.105. Unions of opposites – 'But fare thee well, most foul, most fair! . . . Thou pure impiety and impious purity' – describe the presumed strumpet Hero, who bears a name given men, particularly *intermediates* between gods and men, *demi*-gods. And she has just been accused not only of adultery, but also of sodomy (see NAMELESS).

1H6, II.i.20:

Burgundy. . . . But what's that Pucelle whom they term so pure?
Talbot. A maid, they say.
Bedford. A maid! and be so martial!
Burgundy. Pray God she prove not masculine ere long. . . .

Even 'Pucelle', name of this *masculine maid*, means two opposites: virgin and whore.

Tim, IV.iii.203. Apemantus says Timon suffers from 'a poor unmanly melancholy . . . Why this spade?' A cluster of puns on his emasculation: poor/*L puer* (boy); unmanly; spade/spado (a castrated man, impotent person – *W*; *OED*).

See ROUND, *AYL*; TIGER, *TN*; BOTCHER, *Cor*; CHEER, *TA*; BARBAROUS, *H5*; POVERTY, *KL*; OLD WOMAN, *MWW*; LODGE, *TN*; MONSTER, *TN*; MINGLE, *AC*.

Porter 1. Pimp. Both are (1) doorkeepers: the bawd Boult in *Per* is twice called 'doorkeeper' (IV.vi.125, 175); (2) keepers of the keys (KEYS, *2H4*). Congreve, *Love for Love*, I.i: 'like a decayed porter, worn out with pimping'. Dekker and Middleton: *The Honest Whore I*, I.ii, 'better men than Porters are bawds'.

CE, II.ii.213. Adriana wants to embrace the man she mistakes for her husband: 'let no creature enter. . . . Dromio, play the porter well.' Be the pimp who keeps the door locked till whore and customer finish, as in *Oth*, IV.ii.94.

RJ, I.v.10: 'let the porter let in Susan Grindstone'. The porter–pimp lets in the young lady with the revealing name. *Macinio*: grinding corn; the sex-act (F).

MWW, II.ii.181. Ford (alias Brook) asks Falstaff to seduce Mrs Ford, who then won't be able to refuse him, her reputation as whore having been established. Ford has 'a bag of money here troubles me: if you will help to bear it, Sir John, take all, or half, for easing me of the carriage'. A bag is the scrotum (TWR; P), and Ford's needs EASING (intercourse). Falstaff: 'I know not how I deserve to be your porter' – (1) to carry his money-bag; (2) to ease his cods of *their* load by procuring a whore for him, pimping.

2. Pederast. Oldham, 'Upon the Author of a Play Call'd *Sodom*': the paper of the play should 'to th' publick Jakes be lent . . . There bugger wiping *Porters*, when they shite,/ And so thy *Book* it self turn *Sodomite*'.

TrC, II.ii.170. Achilles (who has a male lover) is 'a porter, a very camel.' He carries on his back, being (1) porter, (2) CAMEL (pederast) – a VERY (the arse) camel.

LLL, I.ii.75, Armado: 'what great men have been in love?' Moth (who hears 'great men' as *grate men* or porters who stand at door grates) says HERCULES (bisexual) and Samson, a man of 'great carriage, for he carried the town-gates on his back like a porter'. Carried the town-GATES (sluice-gates) on his *back*: 'carriage' is bearing the lover's weight in intercourse (P), and he bore on his back. (See RAISE, *H5*.)

Post Penis (TWR), like stake (C) and pole (P). Gk *posthe*: penis. 'Worst part of me . . . the common fucking-post/ On whom each whore relieves her tingling cunt' (John Wilmot, p. 37). In Chaucer's 'General Prologue' to *The Canterbury Tales*, 214, the wanton Friar, dallying, at his own cost finds husbands for ex-mistresses: 'Unto his ordre, he was a noble post'.

MV, v.i.46: 'there's a post come from my master, with his horn [erect penis – F&H; P] full of good news'.

TN, I.v.303:

Olivia. . . . let him send no more;
Unless, perchance you come to me again . . . .
I thank you for your pains: spend this for me.
Viola. I am no fee'd post, lady; keep your purse:
My master, not myself, lack recompense.

Enchanted with Viola–Cesario, Olivia asks her–him to come again and offers money for his PAINS (coitus, penis) – but Cesario is no post that can be fee'd or bought by her purse. In fact, as the audience knows, Viola has no post to need a fee (gratification of lust – C; P). It is her master whose PAINS lack Ophelia's re-com-pense: (1) an invitation to re-come, come again or *back*, as messenger, a post (L *post*, behind) or lover; (2) her recom*pense* or pence, i.e. pennies or fee; (3) her RECOMPENSE (physical love).

See PAINS, *KJ*.

Postern Buttocks, anus. Lit. 'Latter or hinder part. Rare' (*W*); back door, entrance other than the usual, honourable one (*OED*). Cf. Dekker and Middleton, *The Honest Whore I*, II.i: the sodomitical 'Back-door'd Italian'. Postern: the fundament (F&H). Cf. Charles Cotton, *Virgil Travestie* (1678): 'And thrice her latest breath did roar,/In hollow sound at Postern-door'. See DISCHARGE, Rabelais.

See CAMEL, *R2*; EASE, *WT*.

Poverty Impotence, effeminacy: from POOR/L *puer* (boy, catamite). See POOR, *Tim*; SICK, *LLL*.

KL, III.iv.26: 'In, *boy*; go first. You *houseless poverty*, – /Nay, get thee in. . . . *Poor* naked wretches' (italics added). When Lear, in RAGS (q.v.), fig. emasculated, finishes, Edgar emerges from the 'hovel' a 'poor, bare, forked animal' – bare fork (i.e. crotch), no HOUSE/HOSE (breeches, codpiece, penis): he, too, fig. impotent (UNNATURAL, NAIL). Lear starts to 'unbutton here' (BUTTON, on codpiece or breeches), another loss of HOUSE/HOSE, the fate predicted by the Fool (ii.27; see ASS, CRUM).

The 'hovel' contrasts with Gloucester's house, taken over by Lear's daughters: 'this hard house – /More harder than the stones whereof 'tis raised' (ii.63). A figure of arrogant potency: a HOUSE (codpiece) harder than the stones (testicles) that *raise* it; a HOUSE (brothel: see KEY) made harder by the 'hard commands' (82) of the children Lear *raised* (to power), now subjecting him to 'wind and rain', the 'hard rein' of his sons-in-law, 'borne' against him (I.ii.27). Jests on exaggerated codpieces were common (see DULCET, HOUSE).

In III.iii.26, the contrast of children with power and helpless parents is encapsulated in Edmund's phallic metaphor: 'The younger rises when the old doth fall.'

Power Potency, of the male or female arse. Lit. potence (1500). It *pote*: power, be able; *potte*: cunts (F). *Potuto*: powered; *pottuta*: 'cunted' (F).

MM, I.iv.76:

Isabella. Al*as*! what poor ability's in me
 To do him good?
Lucio. *Ass*ay the power you have.
Isabella. My power? Al*as*, I doubt –

(Italics added.) Lucio tells her to *assay* her power, for she has *assez* (Fr. enough) power to sway Angelo. It is, unfortunately, just that, her *ass* / arse or cunt – the POOR/ Fr *puir* (stinking) ability *in* her – that will have power to seduce Angelo.

1H6, I.iv.103: 'la Pucelle . . . new risen up,/Is come with a great power to raise the siege'. Pucelle (whose name means virgin and slut) is come with her great power (*potuto*), virgin and whore 'cunted' (*pottuta*) – to raise the *siege* (rectum – *OED*). A well-known episode in Rabelais, Bk I, ch. 17, contains a series of Parisian oaths, including 'Pote de Christo!' ('Christ's power!'). Samuel Putnam, in his edn (p. 106), explains 'Pote' as 'sometimes power and sometimes the feminine pudenda'.

See FANCY, *AYL*; RAISE, *H5*; LEND, *AW*; QUICKLY, *Oth*.

Prat(e) Buttocks (P; F&H): Those who prate are commonly revealed as asses. Peele, *The Old Wives' Tale*, 774: 'Why, what a prating ass is this!' Anon., 'Robin Hood and Little John': 'Thou dost prate like an ass' (F. J. Child, *Ballads*, vol. V, in *CD*).

H5, IV.i.79: 'If the enemy is an ass and a fool and a prating coxcomb, is it meet, think you, that we should also, look you, be an ass and a fool and a prating coxcomb?' Gower's answer, 'I will speak lower', accentuates this quibble on the ass/arse or prat, i.e. the 'lower part' of *AW*, II.iii.267.

Ham, III.iv.215. Hamlet takes the dead Polonius, who had hidden 'behind the arras' (BEHIND; ARRAS/arse), and says he'll 'lug the guts [bowels]' of this '*fool*ish*prat*ing knave. . . . to draw toward an *end* with [him]' (italics added).

See LIE, *2H4*; PEASANT, *CE*; AFFECTION, *AYL*; MISUSE, *AYL*.

Prayer A flatus. Putting the palms together in prayer is compared to the meeting of the palms that produces a clap or burst of sound, as in APPLAUSE (farting) and THUNDER (clap) or flatus. *MM*, IV.iii.43: 'I would desire you to clap into your prayers'. Perhaps also a pun on *I pray* and *après* (behind, after – Cot).

CE, I.ii.53. When Dromio E., speaking of stomachs, says, 'we . . . Are penitent for your default today' (FAULT: lit. a crack; *pet*: a crack or fart – Cot), Antipholus S. answers, 'Stop in your wind, sir: tell me this, I pray' – stop in your WIND (flatus); tell me this *après* (after): such hot air should come not from the mouth but from the behind. See LOVE, *LLL*.

MWW, I.iv.13. John Rugby's 'worst fault is, that he is given to prayer; he is something peevish that way: *but* nobody *but* has his fault; *but* let that pass' (italics added). A fit of peevishness is a pet (*CD*), and a *pet* is a fart or crack; a *pet de masson*, 'A fart in syrup, a squittering fart' (Cot). Mistress Quickly says but/butt everyone has that FAULT (fart), but let that PASS or leave behind, discharge from the body.

Ado, II.i.108. Margaret has Rugby's fault (above): she has many 'ill qualities' of which one is 'I say my prayers aloud'.

See MUD, *AW*; CAIUS, *MWW*.

Preposterous Of the posteriors; of sexual entry from the rear. L *posterus*: coming after, hinder. Preposterously: inverted; with bottom upward, hind part foremost. Arsy-versy: polite use 16th c., backside foremost, preposterously. Henry King, 'An Exequy': 'No wonder if my time go thus/Backward and most preposterous' (*Signet Classic Poets of the 17th c.*, vol. II, p. 172). Montaigne, Bk I, ch. 22: 'more by custome than by nature doe men meddle and abuse themselves with men. . . . Plato undertaketh to banish unnaturall and preposterous loves of his time. . . . To wit [a list of incestuous matings].' Jonson, *Every Man in his Humour*, IV.v: 'for more instance of their preposterous natures. . . . They have assaulted me as I have walk'd alone in divers' 'skirts i' the town' – men with preposterous NATURES (generative organs) *ass*aulted him as he walked *in 'skirts* (and in the outskirts, the suburbs, area of licentious practices in the 16th c.).

TSh, III.i.9. Hortensio is a 'Preposterous ass'.

TrC, V.i.27. Thersites hopes venereal infections 'take and take again such preposterous discoveries' as Patroclus, Achilles' 'masculine whore'. The key to what is recognised as a puzzling phrase (connoting buggery – C) lies in the breakdown of 'discoveries' into *dis-* (prefix meaning *two ways*) and *cover* (mount sexually – P; *OED*). Therefore Thersites says it *twice*: 'take and take again' (take: have sexually – C; P). These dis-coveries are preposterous for they refer to two ways to take, have or cover, including from the rear.

LLL, I.i.244. Armado surprised Costard and Jaquenetta in intercourse, in an 'obscene and most preposterous event'. His descriptives indicate the position: (1) MOST – of the buttocks; (2) preposterous – with the bottom upward. Its having occurred at the hour when 'beasts *most* graze [GRAZE, copulate]' (italics added) suggests entry (like animals) from the rear. See DAMSEL; GRAZE.

See ANY, *MWW*; BUNG-HOLE, *H5*.

Presence, present(s) Genitals. See GIFT.

AW, II.iii.158, 306. The King forces Bertram to marry Helena: 'Here, take her hand . . . scornful boy, unworthy this good gift'. The coerced Bertram flees to the war in Italy: 'his present gift/ Shall furnish me to those Italian fields,/ Where noble fellows strike!' He contrasts the *present gift* of Helena to Italian FIELDS (genitals) in which happier fellows strike (copulate – F&H; P). FURNISH: equip sexually.

H5, I.ii.260: 'His present and your pains we thank you for;/When we have match'd our rackets to these balls,/ We will, in France . . . play a set'. Henry means the present of TENNIS-BALLS (q.v.) or testicles.

AYL, I.ii.130:

Celia. . . . Bon jour, Monsieur Le Beau. . . .
Le Beau. . . . you have lost much good sport.
Celia. Sport! Of what colour?
Le Beau. What colour, madam! how shall I answer you?

Puns on *bon* and *beau*, good and goodly (Cot); on GOOD (copulation) sport (love-making – C; P). Being French, Le Beau knows COLOUR/*culier* means of the tail or arse, so he describes the wrestlers *and* their equipment:

Le Beau. *Three* proper young men, of excellent *growth* and *presence*
Celia. . . . 'Be it known unto all men by these *presents.*

(Italics added.) THREE: male genitals.

Pretty Of the prat, buttocks. Praty: obs. and dial., pretty. Pretty: orig. tricky, from OE *praett*, a trick. See Introduction, p. xiv, for 16th c. pun on 'pretty, prattling . . . pig [/ Gk *pyge*, rump]'.

LLL, I.ii.21: 'Thou pretty, because little' – 'Little pretty, because little.' Moth is little (slightly) pretty, little praty, a little arse, because little. LITTLE (sfx, L *-culus*, -cule) puns on L *culus*, and 'cule', the arse (*OED*; *W*). Moth/ mote (K), pron. *mote*, puns on *motte* (groin – Cot): 'I pretty, and my saying [*mot* – Cot] apt? or I apt, and my saying pretty?'

Cym, II.iv.102. Iachimo boasts he achieved Imogen's chastity and her bracelet, a JEWEL (chastity; pudendum) she stripped from her arm. When he adds, 'Her pretty action did outsell her gift', this taunter does not mean her grace (an alien sentiment for such as he) but the *pretty* action (sexual activity – C; P) of her *prat* that did merit higher praise and price than her GIFT (pudendum). See TOMBOY and RAMP for his taunting of Imogen with Posthumus's infidelity (and sodomy).

Ado, v.i.202: 'What a pretty thing man is when he goes in his doublet and hose and leaves off his wit.' Without wit, man is an ass/ arse.

Private The genitals, the 'privates' (*OED*; P).

TN, III.iv.100. Having concluded Olivia loves him, Malvolio imperiously dismisses everyone: 'Go off; I discard you: let me enjoy my private: go off.' He wishes to enjoy his private, his new potency, and he believes Olivia's instructions were to humble the others – hence he dis*cards* or castrates them: CARD/ cod (scrotum); go *off*, go *off*.

Per, IV.vi.98. Believing Marina is a new, fresh whore, the brothel customer says, 'Come, bring me to some private place: come, come.'

TGV, v.iv.71. Valentine, wounded in love, says, 'The private wound is deepest'. Cf. Ford, *'Tis Pity She's a Whore*, I.ii: Putana (*puttana*, a whore – F) dismisses soldiers as lovers because they usually have 'some privy maim or other that mars their standing upright [erect penis – F&H; P]'.

See ASSEMBLY, *CE*.

Privily Connotes the arse; a privy or latrine. Lit. be privy to. Chaucer, 'The Miller's Tale', 616: 'And up the wyndowe dide he hastily,/ And out his ers [arse] he putteth pryvely/ Over the buttok, to the haunche-bon'.

KL, III.iii.15. Gloucester has a letter about Lear locked in his 'closet' (short for 'water-closet

– *OED*). He will 'seek' Lear and 'privily relieve him. . . . the king my old master must be relieved': (1) relieve him privately; and (2) provide the relief one gets in the privy (to relieve nature, i.e. evacuate the bowels). Anyone asking for Gloucester is to be told he is 'ill'. SEEK/SICK and *ill*. The metaphor, based on the pun in 'seek him' and *caecum* (pron. *seek-um*) – part of the large intestine that includes the colon and rectum; or the *blind* gut (*OED*) – serves two important functions: (1) it anticipates Gloucester's being blinded, as the result of his seeking to aid Lear; and (2) it introduces the next scene, considered the turning-point of the play. Here Lear talks (iv.8) of 'malady', tells Kent (23) to 'seek thine own east'. Like 'relief' EASE means evacuation of excrement. Then follows (32) the first sign that Lear is aware of the kingdom's ills and his responsibility for them: 'O, I have ta'en/Too little care of this! Take physic, pomp; / Expose thyself to feel what wretches feel, / That thou mayst shake the superflux to them'. Flux: an abnormally copious flow of excrement from the bowels (*OED*) – symbol of the superfluity of wealth (GOLD, excrement). Lear recognises the need to take a physic (a physical and a moral cathartic) to shake the kingdom's illness and his own, and the responsibility of pomp to share its superfluity of goods.

Progress Fornication. Lit. go forward.

MM, II.ii.97. Angelo anticipates the end of future evils (fornications) 'by remissness new-*conceived*, / And so in *progress* to be *hatch'd* and *born*' (italics added).

LLL, IV.ii.144. A love-letter 'by the way of progression, hath *miscarried*' (italics added). In the Royal Shakespeare Company's production, London, April 1979, Holofernes accompanied delivery of this line with bumps and grinds.

Promise *Puttaneggiare*: promise carelessly, not keep one's word, play the whore (F).

AYL, IV.i.43: 'Break an hour's promise in love?' The HOUR/ whore pun (K) was made in II.vii.26.

Cor, I.viii.2:

Marcius. I do hate thee
Worse than a promise breaker.
Aufidius. We hate alike:
Not Afric holds a serpent I abhor
More. . .

WORSE/whores than a whore: both hate and ABHOR/whore alike – *a* LIKE (Gk *homoios*, *homo-*); therefore, 'Let the first budger die the other's slave, / And the gods doom him after!' See BUDGER/bugger and SLAVE (eunuch whore). Their homo-eroticism is a constant theme: 'were I any thing but what I am, / I would wish me only he' (I.i.235); 'Were half to half the world by the ears and he / Upon my party, I'ld revolt, to make / Only my wars with him; he is a lion / That I am proud to hunt.' Pun on 'party' and *parti-* (half) and HALF (homosexual love) and the sexual PART. He is proud (pride: sexual heat – *OED*; P; a *pride* of lions) to hunt him: hunting, common metaphor for the eager pursuit of the sexual object (venery). Marcius would WAR/ whore only with Aufidius, just as Antony 'Makes only wars on thee [Cleopatra]'.

Mac, V.viii.21. Another pair of adversaries struggle to see who shall be the victorious man and who the fucked or buggered. Macbeth: 'it hath cow'd my better part of man! / And be these juggling fiends no more believed, / That . . . keep the word of promise to our ear / And break it to our hope.' The juggling (fornicating – C; P) fiends dared 'To trade and traffic with Macbeth / In riddles' (III.v.4): *trade* and *traffic* (in sexual commerce – P; whores were called 'Traffick' – Dekker, *The Belman of London*, p. 145). They used him like a whore, cow'd (*vaccheggiare*, to play the cow or whore – F) his better PART (penis) of a man. The 'weird women promised' (III.i.2) a future and an invulnerability he misunderstood: they kept the WORD/ whored of promise only – Macduff was not born of woman. Macbeth, who was 'too full o' the milk of human kindness' has been cowed by those same spirits who took his wife's 'milk for gall' (I.v.49). 'Lay on, Macduff' (lay on coitally – TWR; P). We shall see who will be 'damn'd' (DAMN/dam – K), made a woman of; who will cry 'Hold, enough!' (hold; of an animal, to hold to the male, to conceive). (See TERMS.)

Proof, prove Attest to virility, with testes.
TSh, I.ii.177:

Gremio. Beloved of me; and that my deeds shall prove.
Grumio. And that his bags shall prove.

Grumio mocks the deeds (coital acts – C; P) and bags (scrotum – TWR; P) of this impotent old fool, who has only *money bags* to prove his love.
2H4, II.iv.127. Pistol will 'discharge' with 'two bullets' (testes – C; P) on the Hostess, who says, 'Come, I'll drink no proofs nor no bullets' (a hint of penilingus? – P).
See TASTE, *TrC*; COCKNEY, *TN*; SHAPE, *R3*; FURNISH, *Cym*; BREATH, *1H4*.

Property The ass/arse. L *aes meum*: my property.
JC, IV.i.40. Antony and Octavius compare Lepidus to an 'ass', an 'empty ass' and a 'horse': 'do not talk of him,/But as a property' – but/butt; as/ass; property (ass). See GOLD.
See WITCHCRAFT, *Oth*.

Proportion Penis. *Proportion*: Fr syn. for the prick (F&H). *Taille*: the proportion, size or stature of man or beast (Cot); tail: penis (F&H; P). Marston, *The Dutch Courtesan*, I.ii, where Malheureux, who boasts of sexual virtue, is suddenly seized with desire for a whore he meets: 'A courtesan? (*Aside.*) Now cold blood defend me! What a proportion afflicts me!'
RJ, III.v.182. Capulet says Paris would be a husband 'nobly train'd,/Stuff'd, as they say, with honourable parts,/Proportion'd as one's thought would wish a man' – a noble TRAIN (penis and testicles); stuff'd (in intercourse – C; P) with stuff (semen – C; P); proportion'd as one would wish a man, with honourable PARTS (genitals).
See SHAPE, *R3*; SIZE, *H8*.

Provide Pander, whore; provide sexual satisfaction. Fr *caser*: to provide for. *Cas* (Cot) and 'case' (K; P): genitals. Case: a casa, brothel (F&H n.d.).
TrC, III.ii.220: 'Cupid grant all . . . maidens here/Bed, chamber, Pandar to provide this gear [private parts – F&H; *mozza* – F]!'
MND, I.i.45. If Hermia refuses the man of her father's choice, he will dispose of her as 'Immediately provided in that case'. The Duke asks if she can 'endure the livery of a nun' and 'live a barren sister all your life'. There seems to be a play on two extreme ways to provide for her case, since both 'nun' and SISTER meant a prostitute (F&H).
TGV, III.ii.53: 'as you unwind her love from him . . . You must provide to bottom it on me'. Proteus as go-between (pander) is to provide (*caser*) that Silvia UNWIND herself from, not copulate with, Valentine; and instead bottom (lit. to wind thread on a bottom) her love on Thurio, the ass, on his bottom (*cas*, buttocks): see WIND, *MND*.
See SISTER, *R2*.

Pudding The penis and coition, as in 'He Rumbl'd and Jumbl'd me o'er and o'er/Till I found he had almost wasted the store/Of his pudding' (F&H 1682). Anon., 'Robin Hood and the Beggar': 'I know no use for them so meet/As to be pudding pricks' (F. J. Child, *Ballads*, vol. v, in *CD*). This ballad also puns on MEET/MEAT and the BUTCHER's prick (q.v.). 'Pudding' meant (1) bowels, guts; (2) sausage (penis – F&H). Putting: fornication (F&H; P); put-in: fornicate (P); *putain*: whore (Cot). 'Sweetheart and bag-pudding': a girl got with child (F&H).
MWW, II.i.32. Falstaff wants to 'assay' Mrs Page, who thinks there ought to be a bill 'for the putting down of men . . . his guts are made of puddings' – the putting down (of erections) of pudding. *Ass*ay leads to her reversal of the usual word-order, that *puddings* are made of *guts*. Yet, in both cases, puddings are stuffed into guts, into the sausage-skins or into those who eat

them. If one thinks this is a jab not only at Falstaff's obesity but also at anal eroticism, then there are three cases.

MM, IV.iii.17. Many customers of Pompey the bawd were gaoled, incl. 'young Drop-heir that killed lusty Pudding'. To 'drop' is to let fall in birth, give birth to; and young Drop-heir killed lusty Pudding who (which) also dropped heirs.

AW, II.ii.29. The Clown compares a 'barber's chair [whore – F&H] that fits all buttocks' to the fit of 'the nail to his hole . . . the nun's lip to the friar's mouth, nay, as the pudding to his skin'. Pudding is stuffed into its skin, entrails or bowels, as the put-in is stuffed into the SKIN or whore (L *scortum*: skin; prostitute), the *putain*.

Oth, II.i.258. Iago scoffs at the idea of a chaste Desdemona: 'Blessed fig's end! . . . Blessed pudding!' See WINE.

Pudency The feminine pudendum, L *puden(t)s*. See IMPUDENT (spayed; mannish).

Cym, II.v.11. Posthumus, believing his wife has been 'mounted' by another man, says, 'Me of my lawful pleasure she restrain'd/ And pray'd me oft forbearance; did it with/ A pudency so rosy the sweet view on't/ Might well have warm'd old Saturn'. Her rosy pudency is customarily glossed as the blush of modesty, but the sight of her rosy *pudenda* – ROSE itself means pudenda (P) – would far more likely have warmed the heart of Saturn, who is known not only for his cold temperament, but also for the Saturnalia, a mid-December festival synonymous with an orgy. Posthumus's fury is occasioned not by remembering his wife's modesty, but by the thought of those charms she had asked him to forbear and was now freely granting to others.

Puff A libertine. Fornicate. Lyly, *Galathea*, V.i: 'a pretty wench come to his shop, where with puffing, blowing, and sweating he so plied her that he multiplied her' – 'How?' – 'Why he made her of one, two.' Double talk on alchemy and sex: puff is third in a list of 16th c. puns on sexual exertion, blow (P) and sweat (P). Nanny-shop: brothel (F&H), Ger *Puff* (also the sex-act). Paphian: from Paphos; unlawful sexual action. A sodomist: homosexual (F&H n.d.), today's 'poof', 'pouffe', 'puff'. Marston, *Antonio and Mellida*, III.ii: an effeminate 'treble minikin' is called 'musk-cod' and 'puff-paste'.

Ham, I.iii.49, Ophelia: 'Do not, as some ungracious pastors do,/ Show me the steep and thorny way to heaven;/ Whiles, like a puff'd and reckless libertine,/ Himself the primrose path of dalliance treads' ('tread' and 'dalliance': amorous toying – *OED*; TWR; P).

Cor, II.i.230. To view Coriolanus, the populace crowds for seats: 'seld-shown flamens/ Do press among the popular throngs and puff/ To win a vulgar station'. Puns on L *flamen*, a priest, a blowing, a wind. What puffing would win one a space? Do they blow and puff, abruptly emit air (*vescieggiare*, 'to puffe, fiste [fart]' – F)? Do they emit an offensive flatus and so win/ WIND (flatus) a station? (*Ham*, V.ii.298: 'Our son shall win' – 'He's fat, and scant of breath', i.e. he will wind himself.)

The flamens press close to the people, as in coitus: (1) 'press' (coitally – C; P), and THRONG, lit. press forward, specif. the thrust of the penis (TWR); (2) 'popular' (*popolare*: popular; to populate – F) and 'vulgar': the popular, populating throng, thronging as in coitus. Sh's only other flamen is in *Tim*, IV.iii.155: Timon tells two whores to 'hoar the flamen,/ That scolds against the quality of the flesh,/ And not believes himself'. We see that flamens, like pastors (*Ham* above), do not practice the chastity they preach, are not above puffing.

MWW, V.v.160. Falstaff was asked if he actually thought the merry wives would have 'thrust virtue out' of their hearts and given themselves to 'A puffed man' who was 'slanderous as Satan' and 'given to fornications'. In such context, 'puffed' is not only the opposite of slender; it is the fornicator.

Puny A whore; a bugger. Pun on the bed-bug: a punice or punese (*CD*), a puny or punaise (*OED*). Fr *punaise*: a bug, a public woman of lowest grade (F&H, s.v. Barrack-Hack); 'The noysome, and stinking worme, or vermine called, a Punie or the bed Punie' (Cot). Butler, *Hudibras*, Pt III, c.i: the thief who stole a '*Talismanique Louse* . . . his *Flea*, his *Morpion*, and *Punese*' is also he who 'drove/ A kind of Broking-Trade in Love . . . [he is] Procurer . . . Pimp

. . . a Puiney-Imp it self' – pun on puisne/puny: a junior, a tyro. Cf. *zanzere*: gnats; *zanzeri*: young male homosexuals (F).

1H6, IV.vii.36:

Charles. . . . We should have found a bloody day of this.
Bastard. How the young whelp of Talbot's, raging wood,
  Did flesh his puny [Folio, 'punie'] sword in Frenchmen's blood!
Pucelle. Once I encounter'd him, and thus I said:
  'Thou maiden youth, be vanquish'd by a maid':
    But . . .
    He . . .
    rushing in the bowels of the French,
    He left me proudly . . . .

Blood evokes the blood-sucker; and young Talbot's raging wood or madness the wooden furniture or walls in which the raging (lustful, sexually active – TWR; P) female lays her eggs. Just as the bedbug fleshes its proboscis-sheathed sucker, so Talbot's whelp fleshed his sword (achieved coitus – C; P) – his puny sword (penis – P) – in the Frenchman on the field; he rushed into the *bowels* of the French. A fig. (?) description of his buggery and destruction of the French.

Pucelle claims she encountered him (engaged sexually – C; P). Her claim that she, a maid (Fr *pucelle* means both maiden and slut), would have vanquished the maiden (virgin? effeminate?) youth suggests another parallel: that she, a *puce* (louse – Cot), would vanquish him, a punie or bedbug (with a puny sword). See FRANCE, where Pucelle again 'vanquished' or buggered.

R2, III.ii.86. Richard is 'pale', the 'blood' (he twice says) drained from him: Bolingbroke, 'a puny [Folio, "punie"] subject strikes/ At' his glory. Bolingbroke, the bedbug or bugger, the SUBJECT (pathic), strikes (screws, rapes – F&H; P) him.

1H4, II.iv.33. Francis, butt of the humour, is a 'puny drawer', a bedbug in the drawers – 1537, the furniture and breeches. See DRAWER.

See TWENTY, *MV*.

Pure See POOR.

Purgation Purging the bowels or the soul.

Ham, III.ii.318, Guildenstern: the king is 'distempered' with 'choler'. Hamlet: 'Your wisdom should show itself more richer to signify this to his doctor; for, for me to put him to his purgation would perhaps plunge him into far more choler.' It would be wiser for Claudius to submit to a doctor's physic or purge his bowels for his CHOLER/It *culare* (arse-gut). Hamlet would only make him more distempered – more angry or choleric and with a higher temperature – for Hamlet would *purge* his soul and plunge him into *purg*atory and hot hell.

LLL, III.i.128. Armado sets 'bound' Costard free. Costard: 'True, true; and now you will be my purgation and let me loose.' TRUE/Fr *trou*: bung-hole or anus – Armado is the purgation or laxative to let the bound, i.e. costive, Costard LOOSE (L *laxus*) in the bowels.

Purpose Buttocks, genitals; fornication. *But*: a purpose, an end; a prick in a bowling alley (Cot). A butt: the target on which the prick is set in archery; a buttock.

MM, I.iii.4. The Duke has 'a purpose/ More grave and wrinkled than the aims and ends [penises – P]/ Of burning youth'.

TN, II.iii.181:

Maria. My purpose is, indeed, a horse of that colour.
Sir Andrew. And your horse now would make him an ass.
Maria. Ass, I doubt not.

Maria's purpose is a HORSE/arse, of that COLOUR/It *culare* (arse) – to make an ass/arse of Malvolio.

TGV, II.vi.42: 'Love, lend me wings to make my purpose swift'. See QUICK and LIFE for puns on Fr *vite*, swift, and *vit*, man's yard or penis.

MWW, IV.vi.3: 'Assist me in my purpose', Fenton asks the Host, who agrees to keep his *coun*sel (coun: cunt – P). Fenton 'acquainted' (ACQUAINT, have carnal knowledge) the Host with his 'dear love' (DEAR/deer, hind) for Anne and with the '*con*tents' of her letter, stating that, though she 'hath given *con*sent' to elope with another, she really loves him (italics added; CONSENT and CONTENT both pun on fornication and on the CON, cunt). The Host tells him to 'husband' his 'device' and agrees to *ass*ist in his purpose.

AW, III.vii.29. Helena plans to deceive the 'count' into winning Diana's 'consent' but into sleeping with her, Helena. Diana's mother sees 'The bottom of your purpose'.

See NOTHING, Son 20; SLEEP, *TrC*.

Pursy See CROUCH, *Tim*.

Push Copulate (F&H n.d.); push-pin: copulation (F&H); pushing-schools: brothels (G); *jeu de poulse-avant*: 'Any thing that thrusts another forward', 'lecherie' (Cot). Chapman, *The Widow's Tears*, V.iii: 'I ever wished you to withstand the push of that soldier's pike, and not enter him too deep into your bosom'.

JC, V.v.25, Brutus: 'Our enemies have beat us to the pit;/It is more worthy to leap in ourselves,/Than tarry till they push us . . . . Even for that our love of old . . . Hold thou my sword-hilts, whilst I run on it.' The opposition of leap and push – *pushing*-schools and *leaping*-houses (*1H4*, I.ii.9) are brothels – introduces the familiar concept of the roles in fornication (or BUGGERY), in which it is worthy to be the fucker, not the fucked; the buggerer, not the buggered. He will run on a sword, not have a sword thrust into him. He will leap (mount the female – *OED*) into the PIT (female pudendum), not let someone push him.

See BOYS, *LLL*; HOME, *H5*; CAPER, *1H4*.

Q

Quagmire Buttocks; excrement. Mire: urinate, defecate upon (P). Dekker, *The Shoemaker's Holiday*, IV.ii: 'why our buttocks went jiggy-joggy like a quagmire'. Jonson, *Bartholomew Fair*, I: Ursula, 'mother o' the bawds' and 'mother o' the pigs [Gk *pyge*, rump]' is a 'quagmire' and 'bog' in which one 'might sink' and never be found. She, in return, hopes they get pox from 'lean playhouse poultry' with 'bony rump'. See BOG, *KL* ('bog and quagmire').

1H6, I.iv.109. Talbot will be revenged on the French: 'Your hearts I'll stamp out with my horse's heels,/ And make a quagmire of your mingled brains'. He'll make a quagmire of their BRAINS (excrement) – their (Fr) *bran*, *bren* (man's excrement – Cot). He'll make shit of them, these whores' shits, these mingled brains – mingle (eyes, bloods): coit (C; P). His HORSE/ whores heels will stamp out (engender – C; P) or fuck their bloody HEARTS/ arses – their mingled brains or mixen (*OED*), 'mixne' (TWR), i.e. a dunghill.

Quaint, acquaint 1. Cunt (F&H; 'queynt' – TWR). *Conno*: a woman's quaint (F).

MV, III.iv.69. Portia and Nerissa will dress like men, as if 'accomplished/ With that we lack'. Portia will 'speak of frays/ Like a fine bragging youth, and tell quaint lies,/ How honourable ladies sought my love'. She will wear a 'dagger' and in her *braguette* (Fr) or codpiece she will BRAG (*braguerie*: wanton 'tricking', lascivious 'pranking') of FRAYS (*OED*), acts of defloration. She will belie her own woman's quaint, as she tells quaint lies about the quaints of the honourable ladies.

TSh, IV.iii.102: 'I never saw a better-fashion'd gown,/ More quaint'. GOWN: cunt (K).

MWW, IV.vi.41: 'mask'd and vizarded,/ That quaint in green she shall be loose enrobed'. The language expresses everyone's deception. Anne will 'deceive' both her father and a 'plot' of her mother and elope; the Host will 'procure' (pander) a vicar. Anne will wear MASK and VISARD (like loose women): that quaint/ cunt in GREEN (for coitus – F&H; P), loose enrobed (as in GOWN, *TSh*) – 16th c. for strumpets' garb.

2. 'Acqueyntaunce': knowledge of woman's private parts (TWR). *Vezzegiare*: to wantonise, to quaint it (F).

MM, IV.iii.1, Pompey the pimp: 'I am as well acquainted here as I was in our house of profession . . . Mistress Overdone's own house [HOUSE, brothel]'.

AYL, III.ii.288:

> *Jacques.* . . . Have you not been acquainted with goldsmiths' wives, and conn'd them out of rings?
>
> *Orlando.* Not so, but I answer you right painted cloth, from whence you have studied your questions.

Pun on wives of GOLDSMITHS being, like women of the *Bank*side, 'ladies of more compliance than virtue' (F&H). Jaques implies Orlando is intimate with wealthy, loose women whom he conned (CON, cunt) of rings and RINGS (pudenda). In return Orlando says Jaques's questions come from painted cloth (brothel hangings – PAINT, *TrC*) or from whores (CLOTH) themselves: he is the one who cons (studies) RINGS.

Queen Quean, quene (F&H; TWR) and quine (Sc form of 'quean' – *CD*): harlot, as in *2H4*, II.i.51: 'throw the quean in the channel'. Ford, *Perkin Warbeck*, II.iii: 'I never was ambitious/ Of using congees to my daughter-queen – / A queen! perhaps a quean!' Heywood, *A Woman Killed with Kindness*, III.ii, Woman: 'I am a queen' – to which her husband, knowing she is unfaithful, returns, 'A quean, thou should'st say'.

H8. This pun reflects on the King's decision to deny the legitimacy of his marriage to the Queen (thus making her a quean) in order to marry Anne Bullen, new queen.

I.i.177: 'Charles the emperor,/ Under pretence to see the queen his aunt'. He, too, has a pretence to see the Queen an aunt (prostitute – F&H; P). The first clue that Katherine's marriage will be declared unlawful and her daughter not legitimate.

II.iii.37. An OLD LADY asks Anne Bullen if she'd not venture maidenhead to be a queen: 'a three-pence bow'd would hire me,/ Old as I am, to queen it . . . . What think you of a duchess? have you limbs/ To bear that load of title?' To play quean: to whore (F&H). See PARTICULAR.

V.iv.27. The Porter's man reviles the lascivious rabble – the 'fry of fornication', the 'cuckold or cuckold-maker' – pressing in to see the christening of the Queen's baby: 'Let me ne'er hope to see a chine again;/ And that I would not for a cow, God save her!' Outrageous quibble on 'God save her' and 'God save the Queen', in which the antecedent for 'her' is 'cow' (term of opprobrium – F&H; P; *vaccheggiare*: 'to play the cow or whore – F). Puns on (1) *chine*, a piece of the back for cooking, which he would never see again were it not for *kine* (cows); (2) *kine*/ quine: cows or whores (the rabble), whom he hopes never to see again even for a *queen*; (3) Anne *Bull*en, *Queen*, and according to many also a *quean*, being pregnant before marriage (Saccio, p. 225). For a ' "chine", "penis" equation', see Hulme, p. 129.

TrC, II.ii.77, Troilus: 'And for an old aunt whom the Greeks held captive,/ He brought a Grecian queen, whose youth and freshness . . . makes stale the morning'. An even exchange: for an aunt (whore – F&H; P), Queen Helen, the 'whore' (II.iii.78), quean or stale.

See ADVOCATE, *WT*; SCOLD, *KJ*.

Quick (1) Of genitals. Fr *vite*, *viste* (see AN for silent 's'): quick. *Vit*, *vite*: penis and vulva (Cot). Quick: endowed with life (*vie*). Middleton, *A Mad World, My Masters*, I.ii, Courtesan: if a husband enters when his wife is reading a 'stirring pamphlet', she ought 'convey it/ Under your skirt, the fittest place to lay it' and that way 'outvie suspect'. Husband: 'She puts it home, i' faith, ev'n to the quick'. Both courtesan and wife put it (fornicate – C; P; TWR, s.v. Putour) HOME (q.v. for Middleton's use as the vulva), under the skirt, to the quick.

(2) Of fornication. Rape: obs., hasty, quick.

MWW, III.iv.91: 'I had rather be set quick i' the earth/ And bowl'd to death with turnips!' Rather than marry Caius, Anne would prefer to be (1) buried quick (immediately; alive); (2) BOWL'd to death with rape (turnips – *OED*).

Oth, II.i.80: 'Make love's quick pants in Desdemona's arms'.

313: 'this poor trash of Venice, whom I trash/ For his quick hunting' – his (sexual) chase of Desdemona. Roderigo is POOR (stinking) TRASH (purse and scrotum) of Venice/ Venus or Venere, whom Iago trashes for his *venery* (hunting and sexual intercourse).

CE, II.ii.132, Adriana: 'How dearly would it touch thee to the quick,/ Shouldst thou but hear I were licentious/ And that this body, consecrate to thee,/ By ruffian lust should be contaminate!' It would touch him to the quick or genitals, were her body, *con*secrate (CON, cunt) to him, to be *cont*aminate to a RUFFIAN's (pimp's) lust or rape ('he rubbed and pricked and pierced her . . . Now diving deep he touched her to the quick' – Broadbent, p. 73).

See YARE, *AC*.

Quickly A *quick lay* (quick fuck). Mrs Quickly's name (*1H4*) puns 'on lie and -ly' (K). Quickly: *vite*; 'a man's yard': *vit*; 'a woman's &c': *vite* (Cot). 'Rape' (Chaucer): quickly.

1H4 and *2H4*. Mistress Quickly and Doll Tearsheet (bawd and whore), 'parish heifers' to Falstaff, 'town bull' (*2H4*, II.ii.171).

Oth, IV.i.109: 'if this suit lay in Bianca's power,/ How quickly should you speed'. If the suit *lay in* the POWER (potency) of Bianca, Cassio's mistress (whom Iago calls a whore), then Cassio should quickly speed (prove potent – P).

RJ, I.i.7: 'I strike quickly, being moved.' Once MOVED (aroused sexually), Sampson strikes (copulates – F&H; P) quickly, and with his 'naked weapon' cuts off 'maidenheads' – quickly, prob. by rape.

II.iv.166. Peter, another oaf, assures the Nurse that had he seen any man 'use you at his pleasure' his weapon, too 'should quickly have been out'. (Tourneur, *The Atheist's Tragedy*, II.v: 'husband . . . he was ready even to have drawn his naked weapon upon me'.)

H5, v.ii.145: 'If I could win a lady at leap-frog . . . I should quickly leap into a wife.' 'Leap' and 'leap-frog' mean copulate (P). Butler, *Hudibras*, Pt II, c.i: love can make a man woo his own sister and 'Set popes and cardinals agog,/ To play with pages at leap-frog'. Since Henry woos a French princess, it is tempting to see a pun on 'frog' and Frenchman; according to F&H, the earliest dating I have found, 'frog' is a Parisian, 'a jest common at Versailles before 1791'.

Ham, III.i.143: 'To a nunnery, go, and quickly too.' This pun may help resolve reservations on the question of whether the 'nunnery' is a brothel (*OED* 1503). See DOVE.

Quit(e) Coit. 'Quite', obs. form of 'quit': discharge a duty. Marston, *The Dutch Courtesan*, I.i: in 'fleshly entertainment', women 'will give you quite for quo . . . doe you rise, theyle fall, doe you fall, they'l rise'. A play on *quid pro quo*, in which the *quid* or 'quite' is coition.

TN, v.i.329, Duke: 'Your master quits you . . . you shall from this time be/ Your master's mistress.'

CE, III.ii.1. Luciana believes she talks to her libertine brother-in-law, who sexually 'feeds from home': 'And may it be that you have quite forgot/ A husband's office?' He has forgotten 'quite' to quit his coital OFFICE or duty as husband.

MM, II.ii.186: 'never could the strumpet . . . stir my temper; but this virtuous maid/ Subdues me quite'. STIR is arouse sexually (C; P), and Isabella surpasses the strumpet. She SUBDUES (deceives, seduces – *OED*) him quite/*coit*ally, substituting Mariana for herself in the dark.

IV.iv.23: 'This deed unshapes me quite, makes me unpregnant/ And dull to all proceedings.' Angelo's guilt about the deed (coitus – P), having 'deflower'd' a maid, leaves him impotent: dull (sexually torpid – P), unpregnant, and unshaped quite – in no SHAPE (genitals – *OED*; F&H) for coitus.

TGV, II.iv.195: 'Even as one heat another heat expels,/ Or as one nail by strength drives out another,/ So the remembrance of my former love/ Is by a newer object quite forgotten.' One heat (amorous ardour – P) has driven out another. Proteus's former love is quite forgotten/*forgotten coitus*, a forgotten affair.

See RENDEZVOUS, *H5*.

Quiver Pudendum (F&H); rump; codpiece.

RJ, II.iv.171, Nurse: 'I am so vexed, that every part about me quivers'. Her PARTS (genitals) are a-quiver and are a quiver or case for arrows or any straight pointed missile. ABOUT: a *bout* is the *end* of anything, and the head of an arrow (Cot).

Her remark is reminiscent of Rosaline's 'quivering thigh' (i.19) and the 'demesnes that there adjacent lie'.

See ABOUT, *2H4*; VENICE, *Ado*.

R

Rags, trash (1) A castrated scrotum (pl. scrota). L *scruta*: rags, trash. A 'rag' is (1) a hard, rough stone (*TA*, v.iii.133: 'ragged stones'); (2) a fragment. 'Trash' is that which is lopped off, loppings. The combination lends itself to puns on castrates, left with a fragment of their stones (testicles – *OED*; P), with ragged, torn scrota. See SILK, *KJ*.

(2) A whore.

KL, II.iv.48. The Fool contrasts children's behaviour towards 'Fathers that wear rags' and towards 'fathers that bear bags' – the rags of poverty versus the bags of wealth: impotent fathers, divested of their money-bags and their 'bagge of the genitras' (scrotum – TWR, s.v. Bagge), emasculated, left with rags, like Lear; and powerful fathers who kept their purse, their money-bag and scrotum (*OED*; TWR; P), their power and virility. See TRAIN.

R3, I.iii.233. In one of her many diatribes against Richard's lack of virility, Margaret calls him, 'Thou rag of honour! thou detested – '. DETESTED: de*tested*, testes removed.

TSh, IV.iii.112. Petruchio belittles the Tailor (the 'rag trade' was tailoring – F&H), 'Thou yard, three-quarters, half-yard, quarter, nail! . . . Away, thou rag, thou quantity, thou remnant'. As he whittled away the size of the tailor's yard (penis – *OED*), so he diminished his testicles, his scrotum or rag, his stone, of which only a remnant is left.

Oth, III.iii.157: 'Good name . . . Is the immediate jewel . . . Who steals my purse steals trash'. The purse or scrotum is trash or *scruta*. Iago's metaphor on stealing is calculated to arouse fear of sexual loss and it succeeds, for Othello concludes (1) Desdemona has 'stol'n hours of lust' (338) and lost *her* JEWEL (chastity); (2) he has been 'robbed' (342) and lost *his* JEWEL (stone, testicle), his manhood as well as the jewel of his good name; (3) he will 'tear her all to pieces' (431), make a rag of her, a PIECE or whore, trash.

II.i.313, Iago: 'If this poor trash of Venice, whom I trash/For his quick hunting, stand the putting on'. Interpretations differ as to whether Iago trashes (restrains) or traces (encourages) Roderigo's hunting of Desdemona. Either way, he makes *trash* or a *purse* of Roderigo, whom he milks of 'jewels' (IV.ii.188) or stones, never delivered to Desdemona; Roderigo, whose stones he takes, leaving him fig. castrated, without sexual satisfaction. 'Thus do I ever make my fool my purse' (I.iii.389): Iago, like the 'putter on' (*WT*, II.i.140) who makes a husband suspect his wife's fidelity (putery: harlotry – *OED*).

V.i.85. Cassio is 'spoil'd, undone', his 'leg is cut in two', he is 'mangled'. Iago says he suspects the 'strumpet' Bianca, '*this trash*/To be a party in *this injury*. Patience awhile, good Cassio' (italics added). Since this 'trash' was earlier linked to stones and purses (scrota), both the nature of this injury (a leg cut in *two*) and the advice that Cassio be PATIENT (the passive male homosexual) indicate that Iago stabbed Cassio in his genitals: he was cut (CUT: a gelding – *OED*) in TWO, in the testes, and sustained castration or, at least, injury to his genitals.

Iago succeeds where Roderigo had failed. Cassio: 'That thrust [Roderigo's] had been mine enemy indeed,/But that my coat is better than thou know'st:/I will make proof of thine' (24). The thrust would have been an enemy INDEED (in the deed of intercourse), but Cassio's coat/cod (scrotum – K) escaped. His codpiece saved him, but in revenge he made PROOF or test of Roderigo's *test*es.

In II.iii.262, Act V was anticipated. Cassio feared he had 'lost my reputation! . . . the immortal part of myself, and what remains is bestial. My reputation, Iago, my reputation!' 'Reputation' (putation: the act of pruning trees, lopping off buds) is said six times. And so, in Act V, Iago inflicts that loss on him, the loss of 'Good name . . . the immediate jewel of their souls' – the SOUL/SOLE (bottom)'s immortal PART (genitals), the JEWEL (stone, testicle) that enables man to be immortal through posterity (recurring theme of the Sonnets). On Cassio's castration, see JOINT; PLUME; TURK.

See STRIPE, *WT*.

Raise 1. Erect phallicly.

AW, II.iii.118. The King, whose FISTULA (impotence) Helena had cured, gives her in marriage to Bertram, who does not want her.

King. Thou know'st she has raised me from my sickly bed.
Bertram. But follows it, my lord, to bring me down
Must answer for your raising?
. . .Disdain
Rather corrupt me ever.
King. 'Tis only title thou disdain'st in her, the which
I can build up.

Helena's different sexual effect on the two men is seen in all the raising and bringing down, building up and DISDAINing. She renders Bertram impotent (UNDONE). The King promises that, just as Helena had *raised* him when he was in a SICK (impotent) bed, so he will *build up* (1) Helena's TITLE/tittle (a small dot), her *dot* (marriage-portion – Cot), dote or dowry; and (2) Bertram's lowered TITLE/tittle (a prick).

2. 'Raise a siege' means lift or end it. SIEGE: bowel movement; rectum (*OED*; P).

H5, III.iii.47, Governor: 'Our expectation hath this day an end:/The Dauphin . . . Returns to us that his powers are yet not ready/To raise so great a siege. Therefore, great king . . . Enter our gates; dispose of us and ours'.

The Act opened with 'Once more unto the breach' (i.1) and 'On, on, on, on, on! to the breach, to the breach!' (ii.1) – the breach/breech (buttocks). Now the Governor says, enter our GATES (arses). The town is defeated (BUGGERED), their expectations have an *end*. The Dauphin lacks POWERS (potency; arse) to raise the siege; so the *great* king (see FLEW, *TrC*) will dispose of *us* and *ours* (*ass* and *arse*: 'ours' rhymes with 'progenitors' – K). Anal metaphors mock this war (LEEK).

1H6, I.ii.53: 'Methinks . . . your cheer [CHEER/Fr *chier*, shit] appall'd. . . . A holy maid . . . Ordained is to raise this tedious siege'.

130, Pucelle: '*Ass*ign'd am I. . . . This night the siege *ass*uredly I'll raise' (italics added; see Pucelle's POWER).

Ramp(alian) Whore or wanton woman ('a rampe of such boldnesse, that she would . . . do thynges that other young maidens both abhorred and were ashamed to do' – F&H 1548); a 'wild-living whore; a low, vicious wanton'. 'Ramp' meant leap aggressively; Sc and Ir, rank, excessively large or gross. Marston, *The Dutch Courtesan*, I.ii: a lover says she is 'none of your ramping cannibals that devour man's flesh'.

Used specif. for deviations from sexual norms. Ramps are identified with roaring girls and viragos (men-like women – *OED*; women with masculine qualities – *W*). 'Shameless double-sex'd hermaphrodites,/Virago roaring girles' (*CD*, s.v. Roaring, 1630). Middleton and Dekker, *The Roaring Girl*, III.iii: 'the bouncing ramp, that roaring girl' is Mad Moll, who dresses 'in man's apparel', incl. 'codpiece'; who tells one father-in-law, 'you should be proud of such a daughter,/As *good a man as your son* . . . . you've a roaring girl to your son's wife' (italics added) – 'a devil rampant', thinks the father-in-law. Moll was based on the real Mary Frith, described by writers as 'A very Tomrig or Rumpscuttle'; 'lewd impudent . . . man or woman . . . but I think rather, neither'.

Cym, I.vi. 134. To entice Imogen to sexual revenge and infidelity, Iachimo compounds the voluptuousness of her husband's alleged offence by saying he hires deviants as whores: is 'partner'd/With tomboys hired' (120) – with masculine girls or with catamites (see TOMBOY).

Why does she 'Live, like Diana's priest, betwixt cold sheets,/ While he is vaulting variable ramps'? VARIABLE does not mean various (their plurality was established in 'tomboy*s*' and 'ramp*s*') but a biological deviation from a type. Imogen calls Iachimo a 'saucy stranger' come 'to mart/ As in a Romish stew and to expound/ His beastly mind to us' (151). This SAUCY (lascivious, diseased) STRANGER (sodomite)'s MIND (arse) is BEASTLY (used for bestiality, unnatural connection with man or beast) – and she will tell her father of his '*ass*ault' (italics added).

See SCULLION.

Rare(ly) Of the rear, the arse; a pederast. *Germe d'un oeuf*: 'a raw, or a reare, egge' (Cot). 'Rear' means (1) rare; (2) the back part. Marston, *Antonio's Revenge*, III.ii: Feliche greets the arrival of the despised, effeminate Castilio with, 'what treble minikin squeaks there' and, aside, 'Plague on thee for an ass!' When the next fop enters, '*backward*', Feliche says, 'More fools, more rare fools!'

MND, I.ii.31. Bottom 'could play Ercles rarely, or a part to tear a cat in, to make all split'. For *Bottom* to play Ercles *rarely* reminds us that for the Greeks and Sh's contemporaries HERCULES was also a buffoon, glutton and bisexual. To demonstrate his ability, Bottom recites doggerel about Apollo ('Phibbus' car'), also known for homosexual loves (HERCULES). Bottom would play the part rarely, like the rear-end or ass/ arse he is. Hercules, being cleaner of the Augean stables (BRAINS, *Ham*), is linked to rears and their products, hence should be played rarely. Bottom sees the role as a PART (genitals) to make all *split* – both PART (*MND*) and 'split' suggesting the division in the buttocks.

IV.i.210. Bottom awakens, remembers his ass's head and announces he 'had a most rare vision', but 'man is but an ass' were he to expound it – but/ butt AN/ Fr *âne* (ass) ass/ arse.

Cor, IV.v.169. Two servants praise Coriolanus: 'he had, sir, a kind of face', and 'he is simply the rarest man i' the world'. His KIND (sex-organs – *OED*) of FACE (buttocks) is most rare/ rear. Their own general, Aufidius, too, is 'excellent' – 'Ay, and for an assault too.' He, too, is EXCELLENT (lewd; pederastic) and good for AN *ass*ault (sexually – P). For their homosexual attachment, see ANNUAL; and Aufidius's lines 107–30.

TN, III.i.96, Sir Andrew: 'That youth's a rare courtier'. The rare youth is the boy–girl Cesario–Viola, in love with a man and loved by a woman. And in III.ii.60, Andrew, 'a dear manikin' (like Marston's 'minikin' above), writes 'a rare letter'.

See ANY, *Cym*; TRAIN, *KL*; ENGINEER, *TrC*; AFFECTION, *Tem*.

Rascal A castrated or impotent man. 'Originally meaning a lean shabby deer, at the time of changing his horns, penis &c., whence . . . is conceived to signify a man without genitals. . . . Some derive it from *rascaglione* . . . man without testicles, or an eunuch' (G). Lean or inferior deer distinguished from full grown antlered bucks (*OED*). Rabelais says 'Jews snip off that parcel of the skin in circumcision, choosing rather to be called clip-yards [yard: penis] and rascals than. . .' (Bk III, ch. 18; Nock and Wilson edn). Fielding, *Tom Jones*, Bk VIII, ch. 7: a woman belittles her second husband, whom she had married 'for certain purposes, which he had long since desisted from answering', by saying her first 'was a husband to me, he was . . . I never called him rascal'.

AYL, III.iii.58, Touchstone: 'the noblest deer hath them [horns] as huge as the rascal'. The noble, i.e. a full-antlered deer, of course has horns as huge as (much huger than) the rascal's; but Touchstone means the horns of cuckoldry, from which no deer – and no man, even the best equipped sexually (with horn, i.e. penis) – can escape, any more than the least well equipped, i.e. the rascal. The same jest prob. underlies the rascal's *huge* horns and the 'genitivo, hujus' in the Latin lesson on 'articles' that 'declined' (*MWW*, IV.i.45).

TN, I.v.92; V.i.383. Malvolio calls the Clown 'a barren rascal' – as must all rascals be. See BRAIN.

2H4, II.iv.135. Doll calls Pistol 'cut-purse rascal' – not because being called a thieving rascal would incense him, but because he would resent the slur in her calling him a CUT (cunt – C; K; castrated) purse (scrotum – *OED*) and *therefore* a rascal. See BUNG.

v.iv.34, Doll: 'Come, you thin thing; come, you rascal.' Like the lean inferior deer or rascal, the beadle, too, is a thin thing, a eunuch – with a thin thing (penis – F&H; P).

Rate Fornicate. Price of hire for a courtesan (C). *Rate*. milt, i.e. in fish, the male reproductive glands and their secretions (Cot).

AW, v.iii.217. Bertram bought Diana 'At market-price'; 'Her infinite cunning . . . Subdued me to her rate'. Her INFINITE (in the end and buttocks) CUNNING (*fin, finesse* – Cot), her end, SUBDUED (seduced – *OED*) him to her rate – both the action and the price.

RJ; III.v.170. When Capulet calls Juliet 'carrion' (prostitute – F&H; used for Mistress Quickly, *MWW*, III.iii.205, and Helen of Troy, *TrC*, IV.i.71), 'young baggage [strumpet]' and 'hilding' (good-for-nothing woman), the Nurse says he ought not so 'rate' her: (1) scold her, (2) evaluate her so basely, as a whore.

v.iii.301. The mercenary vulgarity of Capulet and Montague emerges in their final exchange.

> *Montague.* . . . I will raise her statue in pure gold . . .
> There shall no figure at such rate be set. . . .
> *Capulet.* As rich shall Romeo's by his lady's lie;
> Poor sacrifices of our enmity!'

Language of the market-place – *raise*, *gold*, *figure*, *rate*, *rich*, *poor* – for Juliet, whom her father had rated as a whore (GRAZE; GREEN SICKNESS).

3H6, II.ii.84. Margaret tells Edward, 'Go, rate thy minions, proud insulting boy! Becomes it thee to be thus bold in terms . . . ?' (bold in TERMS: period of sexual heat, the menses). Do not scold her but rate or screw his male minions, his paramours (Marlowe, *Edward II*, I.iv: 'The king is lovesick for his minion [Gaveston]'. She, the 'proud insulting' queen of II.i.168, and he, the proud insulting BOY (catamite) – both full of pride (sexual heat – *OED*; P), swelling and lascivious.

See PATIENCE, *MV*.

Re Sex-organ. *Re* is the ablative of L *res*, thing. Thing: sex-organ (F&H; P). Re is the second note of the musical scale (NOTE: testicle, penis; fornicate).

TSh, III.i.74. Hortensio asks Bianca to read his ' "Gamut" . . . ground of all accord', his ground or base/*bass* of all *a chord* (alt. sp. of 'cord', which is an old literary pun on penis: see ROPE). ' "A re". to plead Hortensio's passion . . . "D sol re", one clef, two notes have I'. D sole/*desolé*, desolate (Cot), re: one clef or key (penis – F&H 1700s) and TWO NOTES/nuts, testicles, that ask 'pity, or I die'.

RJ, IV.v.121. Peter calls the musicians MINSTRELS (effeminates; pimps). The First Musician retaliates he is a 'serving-creature' (SERVING-MAN, whore), a *serve-* (coitally – C; P) *in-*CREATURE (whore, sodomite). Peter: 'Then will I lay the serving-creature's dagger on your pate. I will carry no crotchets: I'll re you, I'll fa you; do you note me?' He will *lay* on him (screw – C; P) the dagger (another of Sh's phallic weapons). The dagger or obelisk is also the *second* mark of reference for footnotes, used when a page already has one; it is kin to re, the *second* note (see COAT/cod for similar pun).

Part of the conceit is a pun on NOTES or musical pricks. Peter will carry no CROTCHETS or half-men: crotchets are lit. short notes, not whole ones. Peter will *re* the First Musician, give him a second (his missing) note, make a man of him. As he said (115), he will give the musicians 'the gleek': (1) a jest; (2) a trio, *three* of *anything*. He'll also *fa* the First Musician (1) 'fa', Sc for 'fall' – he'll knock him down; (2) fa, one's share or due – he'll give him what's DUE him – a beating and *two* testes. Do you *note* me? asks Peter: no, I screw you.

The *Second* Musician takes him at his punning word: 'put up your dagger and put out your wit'. Putage, putery: fornication (TWR); put: fornicate (C; P). *Up* with your dagger and *out* with your WIT (penis). Peter: 'I will . . . put up my iron dagger. Answer me like men' – ANSWER, return thrust in fencing and in coitus. 'What a pestilent knave is this same!' says the First Musician. He calls them *men* (MAN, L *homo*); they call him SAME, homo(sexual).

See MATTER, *LLL*.

Recompense Love-making. Cotton, 'Sonnet': 'we might/Love here, or there, to change delight,/And ty'd to none, with all dispence,/Paying each Love its recompence'. Quibble on the fee or pence.

Cym, II.iii.97. Cloten offers Imogen's servant gold if she will 'sell' him her good report, speak well of him to Imogen. She quips that he has made a sexual request of her. Being informed of his offer, Imogen enters and tells him he does 'lay out too much pains/ For purchasing but trouble'. For but/butt (?) trouble, he lays out (sexually – C; P) too much PAINS: (1) *pence* and gold, (2) his *penis* – neither of which, Imogen tells him, will receive 'recompense' from her (as they had not from her servant).

See POST, *TN*.

Recover (1) Cover again (K), as in *CE*, II.ii.73–6, where one who cannot recover his hair can recover his head with a wig. Since, however, the baldness was caused by VD, there is a second pun in that his recovery means he is once more able to cover (mount sexually – *OED*; C; P).

(2) Procure or pander. *Recouvrer*: to recover, procure (Cot); puns on 'procure' (pimp – *OED*).

CE, V.i.41. Adriana, wife of Antipholus, tells the 'Lady Abbess' that she wants to take her husband out 'And bear him home for his recovery'. She will *bear* him (Sh's freq. pun on the woman's bearing in the sex-act) HOME (her vulva); there he will have a recovery, will re-cover her, Adriana's dream of reviving their marital relationship.

TN, II.iii.200, Sir Andrew: 'If I cannot recover your niece, I am a foul way out' – (1) recovery (law) or obtaining possession by legal means; (2) recovery or obtaining possession of Olivia by immoral means, through Sir Toby's procuring her, for which service Toby had just again financially dunned Andrew; (3) recovery or having Olivia 'i' the end' – in *the* end being in *her* end – without which Andrew is a foul way *out* and Toby says you may 'call me cut' (CUT: a cunt, a castrate).

Red lattice Brothel sign. A 'red lattice' is the sign of a tavern (F&H); a 'red grate' is the sign of a tavern or brothel or combination of both (F&H): 'a licensed and licentious dispensary for the sensual pleasures of this world . . . . In the morality plays . . . the den of temptation was usually a tavern . . . . In the Digby *Mary Magdalene* . . . the heroine is seduced on her harlot's progress . . . in a tavern in Jerusalem . . . so the tavern scenes of Shakespeare have behind them a rich backlog of dramatic convention' – Harry Levin, 'Falstaff's Encore', *Shakespeare Quarterly*, vol. 32, no. 1 (Spring 1981). Dekker and Massinger, *The Virgin Martyr*, III.iii: 'I see then a tavern and a bawdy-house have faces much alike; the one hath red grates next the door, the other hath peeping-holes within-doors.'

MWW, II.ii.28: 'To your manor of Pickt-hatch! Go . . . your cat-a-mountain looks, your red-lattice phrases'. The Pickt-Hatch ('Pickt-Hatch and Shoreditch courtizans' – F&H 1618) was a common brothel-sign. In Sh's time it was a notorious tavern frequented by harlots. Jonson, *Every Man in his Humour*, I.ii: 'From the Bordello . . . The Spittle, or Pict-Hatch'. Falstaff is berating Pistol's manor and manner, his CAT O' MOUNTAIN (a whore) looks and language.

2H4, II.ii.86. Here, too, 'red-lattice' is usually annotated merely as ale-house, despite its context: 'Come, you virtuous ass, you bashful fool, must you be blushing? . . . Is't such a matter to get a pottle-pot's maidenhead?' – 'A' calls me e'en now, my lord, through a red lattice . . . at last I spied his eyes, and methought he had made two holes in the ale-wife's new petticoat and so peeped through.' Cf. 'bawdy-house . . . peeping-holes' above. Following this exchange, Page is told to 'away' (AWAY, fornicate) and is given 'sixpence' (SIXPENCE, fee for a whore or VD treatment).

Region A whore; the cunt. *Contrée*: a region (Cot). Country: 'the pudend and adjacencies' (P).

See GOLD, *MWW*; CONTRARY, *WT*.

Relics The arse; excrement. Lit. that which is left behind, remains. Relict: relic; 'Leavings; refuse (rare)' (*OED*). Chaucer, 'The Pardoner's Tale', 949: the Host tells the effeminate Pardoner (a 'gelding'), 'Thou woldest make me kisse thyn olde breech,/ And swere it were a relyk of a seint,/ Though it were with thy fundement depeint!/ But . . . I wolde I hadde thy coillons [testicles] in myn hond/ In stide of relikes or of seintuarie'. Interpretations differ as to whether breech is his arse or breeches; but in 'The Nun's Priest's Tale', 627 ('I-blessed be thy breche, and every stoon!'), it definitely means the arse (TWR), and it is again used with testicles.

AW, v.iii.25: 'The nature of his great offence is dead,/ And deeper than oblivion we do bury/ The incensing relics of it'. (1) The King will bury all incensing or exasperating relics or memories; (2) NATURE: a generative or excretory organ or process, and the matter issuing from such a process (*W*; as to relieve nature, evacuate urine or faeces – *OED*). The King will bury the incensing relics – incense, a fumigating perfume, connotes sick odours – of Bertram's OFFENCE (specif. those made by the arse). See OFFENCE, *Per*, for one that 'stunk' and also required burying.

See O'ER, *TrC*.

Rendezvous Meeting-place of lechers. Dekker, *The Honest Whore II*, IV.i: 'And there's lust's Rendez-vous, an Hospital'. John Lyly: 'A taverne is the Randezvous . . . for good fellowes [GOOD fellows: thieves, whores]' (*OED*, s.v. Rendezvous). Lit. a place for the assembly or meeting of soldiers (Cot); however, both ASSEMBLY and MEETING are L *coitus*. A rendezvous is where men fuck (harm) men.

Ham, IV.iv.4. Following on the heels of Claudius's plan to kill Hamlet with the connivance of 'England, if my love thou hold'st at aught' (IV.iii.60), comes another political arrangement: Fortinbras's march on Poland. In this short eight-line scene, a cluster of dubious words raises our doubts about this other son of a dead king, with whom Hamlet compares himself. Fortinbras sends a 'captain' (CAPTAIN, pimp) to greet Claudius, by whose 'license' (freedom from moral, esp. sexual restraint – P) he is there. He craves the 'conveyance' (an underhand, clandestine removal) of a march over Denmark. Convey meant steal: ' "Convey" the wise it call', says Pistol (*MWW*, I.iii.32). Fortinbras continues, 'You know the rendezvous./ If that his majesty would aught with us' – the same 'aught' Claudius just used for his relationship with England.

H5, v.i.88. Pistol, humiliated on the fields of France (LEEK), hears that 'my Nell is dead i' the spital/ Of malady of France;/ And there my rendezvous is quite cut off'. His tavern – with its irregular forms of entertainment (RED LATTICE) – being closed, and Nell, his wife, being dead, all fornication there is QUITE/*coit*us cut off, finished. He will turn elsewhere to earn a living, will be 'bawd' and 'cut-purse'. His own rendezvous 'cut off', he will be a *cut*-purse and cut off others' rendezvous or revenues (one of his many French Malapropisms). He'll 'steal' to England 'and there I'll steal' (STEAL/ stale, whore).

Reprehend Masturbate; grasp sexually. L *reprehendere*: (1) to censure; (2) to take, seize.

R3, III.vii.27. As part of the charade that led up to Richard's unlawful grasping of the crown, Buckingham offered to 'play the orator [ORATOR, whore]' for him (v.95). And so he did: he spoke to the crowds and 'left nothing fitting for the purpose/ Untouch'd or slightly handled . . . And when mine oratory grew to an end,/ I bid them . . . Cry "God save Richard, England's royal king!" ' but they stood dumb, so he 'reprehended them' for their 'wilful silence' and urged the mayor to 'tell my tale again'.

He compares his attempt to manipulate the sentiments of the crowd to a whore's masturbating her client: he left undone nothing fitting (appropriate to the prostitute – C; P); HANDLED (masturbated – P) everything; but, when his ORATORY (prostitution) *grew* to an *end*, they still remained in *wil*ful (will: the penis – C; P) silence, i.e. stillness. So he reprehended them, regrasped them; and, still failing to arouse them, told the mayor to tell the tale (penis – C; P) again, redo the job of arousing the citizens.

See ASSEMBLY, *CE*.

Resolution, resolve (1) Fornication. *Fiché*: resolved on (Cot); 17th c., fucked (TWR, p. 23): see FIX, *Oth.* Lit. convert to liquid state, soften hard tumours, dissipate swellings – defs that lend themselves to puns on coitus.

(2) Genitals, esp. the testicles, on which sexual resolution depends. *Luc*, 352: Tarquin, about to rape, says 'My will [penis – C; P] is backed with resolution'. In ancient prosody, resolution was the use of *two* short syllables for a long.

TSh, I.i.49. Baptista says of the marriage of his two daughters, 'how I *firmly* am resolved you know' (italics added). One line in the light-hearted television play of *Mycenae and Men* (BBC2, 23 March 1979), by Frederic Raphael and Kenneth McLeish, translators of Aeschylus, was 'My resolution all stiffened.'

TN, I.v.25. The Clown is not 'resolute' but is 'resolved on two points', of which, 'if one break, the other will hold; or, if both break, your gaskins fall'. These puns follow directly those on a sexually well-equipped male with a 'good hanging', i.e. testicles (see COLOUR and HANG).

KL, I.ii.108. Gloucester says he 'so tenderly and entirely loves' his son Edgar that 'I would unstate myself, to be in a due resolution.' Hearing the three puns on testicles (TENDER; ENTIRE; DUE), his other, jealous son Edmund mocks man's blaming 'spherical predominance' (the stars) instead of his own spheres (balls or testicles), his own 'goatish disposition', for what befalls him. To be resolved on Edgar's love, Gloucester would unstate himself, i.e. undo his man's state (1580, manhood) – his own STATE (L *stare*, to stand), or arse, his stand (erect penis – F&H; P). And he *does* lose his stare, his two eyes; and he does learn of Edgar's love: he finds his *due* resolution after the loss of his two (It *due*) EYES (eye-balls, testicles).

Ham, I.ii.130:

> O, that this too too solid flesh would melt,
> Thaw and resolve itself into a dew!
> Or that the Everlasting had not fix'd
> His canon 'gainst self-slaughter! O God! God!
> How weary, stale, flat and unprofitable,
> Seem to me all the uses of this world!'

The puns convey Hamlet's inability to see a resolution, his feeling of impotence and concomitant revulsion against sexuality, his own and his mother's, the 'garden [GARDEN, vulva]/That grows to seed'; and perhaps a desire to resolve the one (her second marriage: 'man and wife is one flesh' – IV.iii.53) into its component parts, into two. He focuses immediately on the Queen's *uses* (sexuality – *OED*; P) – her *stale* (whore's) uses.

His verbs mean fornicate and each also means resolve: (1) *melt* (experience an orgasm – F&H; P), cf. *fondre* (melt, resolve 'as snow', i.e. thaw – Cot); (2) *resolve*; and (3) *fix'd*, or resolved on and fucked (see above: *fiché*, fixed, fucked, resolved).

Hamlet is obsessed by the TWO/TOO, DEW/adieu, testicles, the power behind fornication and resolving, symbols of potency: the *too too* solid flesh that resists resolving in*to* a *dew* (exuded moisture, evocative of orgiastic melting); the two (It *due*, Fr *deux*) mentions of God – L *deus*, Fr *dieu* (*H5*, IV.iv.7: 'Seigneur Dieu' and 'Signieur Dew'); and his own earthly father 'But two months dead' ('Nay, 'tis twice two months, my lord', III.ii.136).

Hamlet desires resolution (1582, death, as in *AC*, IV.xv.91); but that is forbidden by God, by Dieu. Tortured, he asks, 'Must I remember?' (I.ii.143). Unfortunately, he must; for the 'word' between him and the Ghost (V.111) is 'Adieu, adieu! remember me' – *adieu*, said twice, and re*member* (member: penis – F&H; 'membres': genitals – TWR). He has still another dilemma to be resolved: is the Ghost his father or a 'potent' 'devil' (II.ii.631, 628) – another deuce (the devil is a Deuce; and so is the number two). See ABUSE: Hamlet fears the Devil will effeminise him, render him helpless, bugger him.

Resort Brothel. Sexual intercourse. 'Resorters' are brothel-frequenters (C); *un homme à ressorts*: a whore-monger (F&H, s.v. Mutton-monger).

MM, I.ii.104. Fearing a new proclamation, Mistress Overdone, 'a bawd', asks, 'shall all our houses [HOUSE, brothel] of resort in the suburbs [brothel area – *OED*; F&H] be pulled down?' *Qui a le ressort foible* is one 'That wants erection' (Cot).

Per, IV.vi.86:

Lysimachus. Why, the house you dwell in proclaims you to be a creature of sale.
Mariana. Do you know this house to be a place of such resort, and will come into 't?

Ham, II.ii.143. Polonius says he saw Hamlet's 'hot love on the wing', and gave Ophelia prescripts 'That she should lock herself from his resort'.

Rest Erect penis in its desired place of rest. A lance in rest is erect, in the loop that keeps it in position for the charge: 'And when I charge, my lance [penis – F&H; P] in rest, / I triumph in delight' (F&H, s.v. Lance, 1622). Dekker, *The Comedy of Old Fortunatus*, IV.i: 'set your heart at rest, for I have set up my rest . . . . I could get a young king or two . . . of you'. He has set up his rest (*RJ* below) to beget a child.

TGV, III.i.144. Valentine, whose 'thoughts do harbour with my Silvia nightly', wishes he could 'lodge where senseless they are lying! / My herald thoughts in thy pure bosom rest them'. 'Herald', one who conveys challenges in a joust, establishes the context for his nightly/ knightly thoughts that harbour in her bosom (pudendum – C; P), where he would like to LODGE (coit) and be at rest. Harbour: pudendum (F&H), as in Cotton, 'Epistle to John Bradshaw Esq.', where the lover 'saw the light . . . and fanci'd . . . swimming . . . To my long long'd-for Harbour of delight' (*Penguin Book of Restoration Verse*, p. 266).

CE, IV.iii.25–33. Dromio S. tells of an officer who 'rests them'; who 'sets up his rest to do more exploits with his mace than with a morris-pike' (pike: penis – K; C); who 'thinks a man always going to bed and says, "God give you a good rest!" ' Puns on arrest and the two kinds of resting in bed.

RJ, IV.v.6, Nurse: 'Sleep for a week; for the next night, I warrant, / The County Paris hath set up his rest, / That you shall rest but little.' Rest is, as in *TGV* above, in the context of knight/night (K). At the ball Romeo asked, 'What lady . . . doth enrich the hand / Of yonder knight?' (I.v.43). He himself becomes her 'true knight' (III.ii.142); and now the Nurse calls Paris her 'next night', next knight or jousting partner (JUST/ joust, coit).

LLL, V.ii.831. Rosalind's penance for Biron, that he 'never rest, / But seek the weary beds of people sick' (SEEK/ SICK) has been interpreted lit. But she has imposed a year of no rest, of sexual abstinence (SEASON), more fitting the tone of the play and her usual flippancy, and paralleling the similar punishment meted out by the Princess to the King, who must be remote from 'the pleasures of the world' (pleasure: sexual – TWR; P; 'worldly pleasures' having always meant sensual gratification – *OED*).

Rheum VD symptom. Dekker and Middleton, *The Honest Whore I*, II.i: 'I have a whoreson salt rheume, that I cannot hold my water'. Marston, *The Dutch Courtesan*, I.ii: 'panderess, supportress of barber-surgeons and diet-drink!'; II.ii: 'De diet is very goot for de rheume'.

TrC, V.iii.105. Pandarus has 'A whoreson tisick . . . a rheum in mine eyes too, and such an ache in my bones'. A *whores*on tisick, rheum, and bone-ache: syphilis (C; P).

MM, III.i.31. His 'bowels . . . The mere effusion of thy proper loins, / Do curse the gout [GOUT, VD], serpigo [syphilitic skin lesions – P] and the rheum [running of eye and nose], / For ending thee no sooner'. Venereal diseases of the anatomical end (genitals – P), capable of ending one and characterised by oozing and running, *curse* him (L *cursus*, running), like a 'running horse' (gonorrhea – G; *gonorrhée*: running of the reins – Cot). The disease is a product of the MERE/MERRY (lecherous) effusion (semen – P) of his loins.

Ridgel, rigel, rigol A ridgel is a male with one testicle; it was thought the second testicle remained, undescended, in the back, the ridge. Rig(il): a half or whole gelding, as in 'I hate a base cowardly Drone,/Worse than a Rigil with one Stone' (F&H 1678). Fletcher, *Women Pleased*, II.vi: 'A pox o' yonder old rigel.' Ger dial. *Rigler*: a half-castrated cock (*W*, s.v. Ridgeling). 'Rigole' means to indulge wantonly (*OED*, obs., rare); and 'rigoll' is obs. and rare for 'regal': a prince, ruler (*OED*).

TrC, Prol.:

From isles of Greece
The princes orgulous . . .
. . . their ships
Fraught with the ministers and instruments
Of cruel war: sixty and nine, that wore
Their crownets regal . . .
Put forth toward Phrygia . . .
To ransack Troy, within whose strong immures
The ravished Helen, Menelaus' queen,
With wanton Paris sleeps; and that's the quarrel.

In this second sentence of the play, the WAR/whore ('war . . . wore') is reduced to a quarrel over Helen, a QUEEN/quean (whore). And the fighting-men are also diminished in stature by being ministers: 'L. *minister* servant, f. **minis-*, *minus* less', 'An underling' (*OED*). They are Menelaus's ministers, doing his work, getting his wife back (in *TA*, V.ii.61, 'Rapine and Murder' are the 'ministers' of 'Revenge'). The 'argument is a cuckold and a whore' (II.iii.79): Menelaus, 'both ox and ass' (V.i.65), ox, castrated male of a species; Menelaus, 'a herring without roe' (69), no semen, impotent. They are ministers of a rigel and instruments of his war: instrument (penis – TWR; P) for this rigel. These princes, rigolls (prince: *regolo* – F; L *regulus*), are orgulous or *rigoglio* (F), 'proud as mans flesh' (*rigoglioso* – F); and they wore their crownets regal, i.e. their rigols as they are called in *2H4*, IV.v.36: 'this golden rigol'. See BOLT for similar puns in these lines.

See CROOK-BACK, *3H6*; DEFORMED, *Ado*; HORSE, *Ado*; FASHION, *2H4*.

Right The rectum. L *rectum est*: it is right. Sterne, *Tristram Shandy*, vol. II, ch. 7: discussing his wife's 'Backside', Tristram's father tells Uncle Toby he ought know 'the right end of a woman from the wrong'. 'Right end!' says Toby, fixing his two eyes 'upon a small crevice, formed by a bad joint in the chimney piece – Right end of a woman! . . . (keeping his eye still fixed upon the bad joint).' The father then tells Toby to consider 'all the parts . . . of that animal, called Woman, and compare them analogically'. 'I never understood rightly the meaning of that word', says Toby. Backside, right end, small crevice, bad joint, chimney-*piece* (Chaucer, 'tuwel': chimney or anus – TWR): *anal*ogically, rightly!

TA, IV.ii.26. Aaron calls Chiron an ass: 'right, you have it. (*Aside*.) Now, what a thing it is to be an ass!' See JEST.

1H4, III.8.70, Glendower: 'shall we divide our right/According to our threefold order' – a continuation of the anal metaphor (ORDER/ordure, excrement) in which he gets the 'fertile' (well-ordured) land, and Hotspur is robbed of 'so rich a bottom'. See BANK.

See VELVET, *AW*; OFT, *TrC*; ABOUT, *KJ*; STRANGE, *MWW*; JET, *TA*.

Ring 1. Vulva (TWR; F&H; P). *AW*, IV.ii.61: Diana: 'on your finger in the night I'll put/Another ring'. 2. Buttocks, anus (L *anus*, ring, the rump). See Introduction, p. xv, *1H4*. 3. Prepuce. 'Virole' is a ring: around a horn (heraldry); iron circlet around end of a cane, knife-handle. The last two meanings explain how there may be an exchange of rings between lovers of different sexes, clarifying the puzzlement expressed by Ross (TWR, s.v. Pley), who asks how in 'pleyinge' (the sex-act) Troilus and Criseyde 'interchange their rings'. He realises 'her gift to him represents the vulva', but asks 'what it means for Criseyde to receive Troilus' ring, except in the literal sense'. See a similar 'interchangement of your rings' in *TN*, v.i.162 (Introduction, p. xv).

Cym, I.iv.98. Iachimo wants Posthumus's ring more than Imogen's chastity – the latter is merely a means to the former. His first speech in the play commented on Posthumus's body, of 'crescent note' (2) – growing NOTE (penis) – but not then as worthy of admiration. Posthumus had been 'less furnished [FURNISHED, sexually equipped] than now'.

Now Iachimo tells Posthumus, 'Your ring may be stolen too . . . . a cunning thief, or a that way accomplished courtier, would hazard the winning both of first and last.' A CUNNING (*fin* – Cot) or rear-end thief, a COURTIER (whore), who was accomplished *that way* (sodomitically: see ITALY), could STEAL (make a stale or whore of) both his wife's chastity (ring) and Posthumus's ring (his chastity) – see STRANGE.

II.iv.42. Iachimo returns with (false) proof he seduced Imogen, her bracelet (OFr *virole*), saying 'the ring [virole] is won' – her vulva (see CUNNING) that entitles him to ask for *Posthumus*'s ring.

Posthumus. The stone's too hard to come by.
Iachimo. Not a whit,
Your lady being so easy. . . .

. . . I now
Profess myself the winner of her honour,
Together with your ring; and not the wronger
Of her or you, having proceeded but
By both your wills.

Iachimo parallels their sought-after genitals: (1) Posthumus's stone (testis), not a WHIT/ WHITE (a target, butt) TOO/ TWO (testes) *hard* to hit because Imogen was 'so' (*tale* – F) EASY (arse); (2) her honour (pudendum – C; P), his ring. Iachimo did not WRONG (related to 'wring' – *OED*; man's prick – K) either; he proceeded *but* by *both* their wills (male and female genitals – C; P).

4. Syphilis.

AW, IV.iii.20. A lord says that 'this night he [Bertram] fleshes his will [achieves coitus – C; P] in the spoil' of a 'chaste' girl: 'he hath given her his monumental ring, and thinks himself made in the unchaste composition'. Lords are not apt to be impressed with a ring's size, and the gloss that a monumental ring is inherited, comes from an ancestral monument, seems strained. I suggest that his large ring, gross virole, is his *grosse verole* (the French pox, i.e. syphilis – Cot). 'Monumental' means serving as a memento, as in *Ado*, v.ii.81. Bertram is giving a French (pox) memento to the Italian girl. In IV.ii.35 he had asked Diana to 'give thyself unto my sick desires,/ Who then recover'. He meant not only his passion but lit. his *sick* desires, for it was believed a virgin heals gonorrhoea in transmission (Richard Burton, p. 87); and Diana is named after the goddess of virginity. Donne, Satire iv: 'burnt [venereally infected – *OED*: P] venome Leachers do grow sound/ By giving others their soares'.

The 'memento mori' was a 16th c. ornament decorated with reminders of death (*OED*); 'a Death's head or a memento mori' – *1H4*, III.iii.34; 'A Death's face in a ring' – *LLL*, v.ii.616. Marston, *The Dutch Courtesan*, I.ii: 'how can it [a bawd's death] be bad, since their wickedness is always before their eyes, and a death's-head most commonly on their middle finger?' This then may be the ring Bertram would have given Diana: a memento of whoring, disease, death.

Ripe Sexually ready, lit. marriageable. Sexually wanton (a 'ripe', 15th–16th c. was the bank of a river, such as the Bank in Southwark, where the brothels were). Heywood, *A Woman Killed with Kindness*, IV.iii: knowing his guest will cuckold him, Frankford says, 'in my absence use/ The very ripest pleasures of my house!'

Per, IV., Gower, 17. Philoten (Gk *philo-*, love) was a 'wench full grown,/Even ripe for marriage-rite'. 'Wench' most freq. implies loose morals (P).

RJ, I.ii.11: 'Let two more summers wither in their pride,/Ere we may think her ripe to be a bride.' A simple pun on *ripe bride* and *summer pride* (sexual heat, esp. in female animals) anticipates Capulet's attack on Juliet as a 'baggage', a HORSE/whore he will turn out to GRAZE (q.v.). A *sommier* is a sumpter ('pack or baggage horse' –*OED*) and a groom (Cot). Juliet is a baggage horse, who in her pride desired Romeo instead of her father's choice of groom. And two grooms will wither and die in their summers' pride or sexual desire for Juliet before she is ripe or ready, 'Ready to go ["to church"] but never to return . . . Flower as she was' (IV.v.33): (1) Paris ('Verona's summer hath not such a flower' – I.iii.77) and (2) Romeo ('This bud of love, by summer's ripening breath' – II.ii.120).

MV, I.iii.64. Antonio borrows money 'to supply the ripe wants' of Bassanio, off to woo Portia of the 'sunny locks . . . like a golden fleece;/Which makes her seat of Belmont Colchos' strand'. Portia's seat (buttocks) is the strand (land bordering a river) or the ripe river BANK where Bassanio hopes to become rich. In the parting scene Antonio says, 'Slubber not business for my sake, Bassanio,/But stay the very riping of the time' (II.viii.40). Jealous of this new relationship, Antonio uses quite ugly imagery. Don't slubber, i.e. (1) soil (with slubber, mud, slime) the BUSINESS (sexual intercourse), (2) deal in a slovenly way with the *business* aspect, but stay the riping of the time or tide (i.e. time – *OED*) of that ripe, that *bank*, that seat of Portia's.

See SISTER, *AYL*; BOTCHER, *R2*; HOUR, *AYL*; KEEN, *MND*; HANG, *LLL*.

Roar The sounds of evacuations and farting. 'On Melting down the Plate: Or, the Piss-Pot's Farewell, 1697': 'Presumptuous Piss-Pot! . . . Queens themselves are forced to stoop to thee . . . And oft to ease their Ailments made thee roar' (*Penguin Book of Restoration Verse*, p. 349). A rank breaking of wind, what Swift called a 'roarer' (F&H, s.v. Fat-un). See POSTERN.

Cor, II.i.85. Menenius calls a tribune an 'ass' (ENOUGH): 'if you chance to be pinched with the colic [bowel spasm, with flatulence] . . . and, in roaring for a chamber-pot'.

II.iii.60. Coriolanus despises the citizens; he got his 'wounds' when their 'brethren roar'd and ran/From the noise of our own drums' – no sign of the foe, just the sounds of their own fear, the NOISE (farts) of their OWN (ane/Fr *âne*, ass) DRUMS (buttocks). He repeats the same insult (see DESPAIR).

1H4, II.ii.118. Prince: 'Got with much ease . . . . The thieves are all . . . possess'd with fear . . . Each takes his fellow for an officer.' Poins adds, 'How the rogue roar'd!' The booty was got with, accompanied by, EASE, a bowel evacuation, done in fear. So soiled were they that each mistakes the other for an officer (informant – G; but also a quibble on 'office': out-house – *OED*; obs. except dial., voiding of excretions – *W*). Later Hal again jokes about Falstaff's roaring or farting (DEXTERITY). Cf. Patrick White, *Flaws in the Glass* (New York: Viking Press, 1981, p. 229: 'rorty old, farting Falstaff'.

See APPLAUSE, *TrC*; FIST, *KJ*.

Robin One who is morally lax. *Robin a trouvé Marion*: 'A notorious knave hath found a notable queane' (Cot). Robin is Falstaff's page and 'go between' (pander – P) – *MWW*, II.ii.130. Robin is the child of the 'bona-roba' (whore – *OED*; P) Jane Nightwork – *2H4*, III.ii.217; and 'Robin Goodfellow' is another name for Puck, 'knavish sprite' – *MND*, II.i.33. A 'good fellow' is a Puck (B); a GOOD fellow is a thief or a loose woman (*OED*).

Ham, IV.v.187: 'For bonny sweet Robin is all my joy' follows Ophelia's other bawdy snatches (NONNY; DOWN; STEWARD). Seng, p. 153, suggests there could be 'sexual implications' in this line, which prob. came from a lost Robin Hood ballad (C, p. 141).

Through Ophelia's mad snatches runs the thread of the 'tumbled' and deceived 'maid' no more: 'Young men will do't . . . By cock, they are to blame' (61). *Bon Robin* is the English ragged robin (Cot); and, when Ophelia dies by the WILLOW (for unchaste maids), with its 'hoar'/whore leaves, she is carrying (vii.170) 'crow-flowers [ragged robins] . . . and long purples . . . our cold maids do dead men's fingers call them' (FINGER: penis). (Ophelia's next song is travestied by Jonson, Chapman and Marston in *Eastward Ho*, III.ii: a deceived daughter *Gertrude* has a footman named *Hamlet*.)

Roof (1) Female pudendum (a ruff – P). 'Elizabethan prostitutes wore particularly large ruffs' (C). Dekker and Middleton, *The Honest Whore I*, II.ii: 'Your ruff, your poker, are engend' ring together upon the cupboard'.

(2) Harlot. *Ruffa*: harlot; *ruffola*: 'as Ruffa', dandruff, morphew (scurvy disease) – F.

MM, I.ii.45: 'Madam Mitigation comes! I have purchased as many diseases under her roof as come to . . . three thousand dolours a year . . . A French crown more.' Madam Mitigation is a *roffiana* (female bawd – F), under whose roof/ ruff and *ruffa* (whore) he purchased three thousand *dollars* worth of dolours (diseases – *OED*), plus one more dollar/ dolour (K; as in *Tem*, II.i.19), the French crown (*AW*, II.ii.21): a coin, and a bald head, symptomatic of VD and *ruffola*.

Tim, IV.iii.144. Timon tells two whores to 'burn' man up (burn: infect with VD – *OED*); and he gives them gold with which they can 'thatch your poor thin roofs/ With burdens of the dead . . . wear them . . . . Whore still!' 'Roofs', usu. glossed as their heads, balding from VD, should include their ruffs or pubes, where the hair is also thinning. Burdens of the dead, or wigs, would then include the merkin, 'counterfeit hair for the private parts of a woman' (F&H; TRUE, *H5*). For other 'burthens', see DILDO, *WT*.

Rope A derisive cry (*OED* gives *1H6*, I.iii.53). The following is offered as another dimension to the derision (as in SCARLET, *1H6*, and ALTER, *MV*) beyond an allusion to one's being hanged at the end of a rope. 'Rope-ripe chiding (of very foul and abusive language)' (F&H 1533).

(1) A sexual union is a copula (L *copula*, rope). Rape: obs., rope.

(2) Penis. Aristophanes, *The Wasps*, 1341–74: an old man carrying a torch tells a flute-girl she is obligated to him for saving her from fellators, so, 'Mount up there, my little gilded cock-chafer; take hold of this rope's end in your hand. Hold it tight, but have a care; the rope's a bit old and worn. But . . . it still has its virtues.' This rope is the same as the 'piece of hanging leather, thick and reddened at the end [worn] to cause laughter among the children' in *The Clouds*, 535–83. Sp *poya*: hemp; syn. for the prick (F&H). See the rope-ladder in ENFRANCHISE.

(3) Rectum, excrement. 'Rope' means intestine, gut; 'ropy' means viscid, stringy threads. Aristophanes, *The Ecclesiazusae*, 339–73: Blepyrus, who 'needed to crap', is asked by a neighbour, 'What are you doing, making well-ropes?'

(4) VD. Rabelais, *Pantagruelian Prognostication*, ch. 5: 'chancres, claps, virulent gonorrhoeas, chordees [painful, curved erection of the penis, attending gonorrhoea – *CD*; L *chorda*, a chord, alt. sp. "cord"]'. Wilmot: 'Cordes are shankers and buboes' (Burford. *'Orrible Synne*, p. 200). Sh alternates cords and ropes ('Take up those cords: poor ropes, you are beguiled' – *RJ*, III.ii.132). Wooden figures of 'men with a cord around the neck' signified syphilis (Richard Burton, p. 29). See SAUCY, *RJ*. Ropesick (herrings): the back infested with parasitic worms.

(5) Whore. Sp *rabiza*: end of a rope; sl., procuress, low-down whore (Rosensweig).

CE, IV.iv.16,46:

Antipholus E. To what end did I bid thee hie thee home?
Dromio E. To a rope's end, sir; and to that end am I returned.
Antipholus E. And to that end, sir, I will welcome you. (*Beating him.*) . . .
Dromio E. Mistress, 'respice finem', respect your end; or rather the prophecy like the parrot, 'beware the rope's-end'.

So Dromio greets his mistress, who enters accompanied by his master's courtesan. Puns on (1) his master's end or purpose; (2) his own beaten end; (3) the end of her life or *finem*; (4) the rope's end (L *funem*); and (5) the Courtezan, another kind of rope's-end. See PARROT for the vulgar language they were taught, incl. these particular puns. See RE for another cord (penis) pun.

Rose A conventional symbol for the pudendum and maidenhead (C; P), but it is also, by transf., a whore – just as 'cunt', meaning vulva, has become an epithet for the woman who uses hers indiscriminately. It is also applicable to men's genitals. Dekker, *The Comedy of Old Fortunatus*, v.ii: 'Andelocia is a nettle: if you touch him gently, he'll sting you' – 'Or a rose: if you pull his sweet stalk he'll prick you.'

Per, IV.vi.38. Marina refuses to be 'ravished'.

Bawd. We have here one, sir, if she would – but there never came her like in Mytilene.
Lysimachus. If she'ld do the deed of darkness [copulation – P] thou wouldst say.
Boult. For flesh and blood, sir, white and red, you shall see a rose; and she were a rose indeed, if she had but –

He, too, interrupts himself instead of finishing, as he had in 1.21, 'if the peevish baggage would but give way to customers'. Again what is left unsaid is that Marina would be a rose INDEED/*in* the *deed* – would be a whore – if she'd but consent. The audience hears the unmentioned concomitant of the rose: the prick (*AYL*, III.ii.118; *AW*, IV.ii.19). WHITE AND RED puns on her complexion, the colours of roses, the colours linked to whores. The profession accounted for the number of Rose Streets in certain parts of London (Burford, *Queen of the Bawds*, p. 32).

AC, III.xiii.39. Cleopatra complains of Caesar's lack of ceremony: 'See, my woman!/ Against the blown rose may they stop their nose/That kneel'd unto the buds.' They no longer kneel for her fragrance but stop their nose against the putrid 'strumpet' (I.i.13) and 'whore' (III.vi.67). She is now the rose, blown (coitally penetrated – P) as by the blowing wind, a favourite image (VELVET, *LLL*). Middleton, *Women Beware Women*, IV.iii: 'the bud of commendation . . . . I am blown, man . . . I've buried my two husbands'.

A *blown* rose in context of 'stop their nose' also suggests nose-blowing. She is the rose against whom they blew their nose (penis – P; as in I.ii.63).

In the following, Richard's being a rose is linked to puns on phallic erection and detumescence, symbols of power and its loss.

R2, v.i.8. The Queen sees Richard going to Caesar's '*ill-erected* tower . . . . But *soft*, but see . . . My fair rose wither [WITHER/wether, a castrate] yet look *up*' (italics added).

1H4, I.iii.175. Hotspur attacks those who 'put down Richard, that sweet lovely rose,/ And plant this thorn, this canker, Bolingbroke' – who put *down* the lovely *rose* and instead plant the thorn (penis, prick – P), the canker (dog-rose – *OED*).

Round Homosexual. Cf. Plato, *The Symposium*: the three types of original man were all round and when they rolled they were so powerful that Zeus, to weaken them, sliced them down the middle. From the all-male being came the male homosexual who seeks to embrace his other male half and become whole again; from the all-female came the Lesbian; and from the male–female came those who seek the other sex and who are, incidentally, the adulterers and adulteresses. Pausanias continues that exclusively male love is 'heavenly', as opposed to heterosexual or 'common' love. See PERFECTION, *TGV*; EVIL, *AYL*.

TSh, Induction, i.47. In preparation for the homosexual game at the expense of Sly, the BEGGAR/bugger, the Lord's page is to go to the 'fairest chamber/ And hang it round with all my wanton pictures . . . Procure me music . . . To make a dulcet and a heavenly sound . . . be ready straight/ And with a low submissive reverence'. He is to HANG (pander), q.v., the chamber *round* with wanton pictures of homosexual love; and to be ready *straight* (L *rectum*), be a ready arse, with a low submissive reverence, and play the part of Sly's wife, in transvestite clothing. Round and straight are juxtaposed but not opposed (like 'jade' and 'scarlet', seeming opposites but both meaning whore: SCARLET, *H8*). He is to procure (obtain for gratification of lust – *OED*) music, to make a DULCET (lit. testicles; symbol of homosexual love) and HEAVENLY (homosexual love) SOUND (probe the bottom).

AYL, II.i.25. It irks the Duke that the deer, 'poor dappled fools,/ Being native burghers . . . Should in their own confines with forked heads/ Have their round haunches gored'. To gore (OE *gor*, dirt, dung), pierce and bloody, the haunch (loin, buttock) might not kill but would bugger the 'poor deer' (47). These native *burghers*, as opposed to the intruding *buggers*, are POOR/ L *puer* (BOY, catamite) DEAR/ deer (hinds and prickets). Their *round* haunches are gored by the men of this all-male forest society, in their OWN (arse) CONFINES (CON, cunt; FINES, buttocks). Gored with forked heads is usu. annotated as by two-pronged arrows, though these appear nowhere else in Sh, while there are freq. puns on FORK as the crotch and to coit. More likely their haunches are gored with the *heads* of penises (C; P), with the forked heads of their neighbours' (confines: 1598, neighbours) crotches. They are killed 'In their *ass*ign'd and native [inherent, inborn] dwelling-place [PLACE: pudendum, anus]' (63; italics added). Jaques is left in '*con*templation' (italics added) and the Duke says, 'Show me the place: / I love to cope him in these sullen fits . . . full of matter.' Show him the PLACE (latrine) where Jaques/ a *jakes* (latrine – K) is. He loves to cope him (sadistic verb of copulation – C; P) in these fits (coital – C; P), full of (faecal) MATTER. 'I'll bring you to him straight [STRAIGHT, L *rectum*]', says a lord.

Sh leaves no one unscathed – buggers of mankind, all: this duke usurps (27) 'more . . . Than doth your brother that hath banish'd you' (BANISH: treat like dung). For details of the buggery in this scene, see BUDGE.

See INDEED, *2H4*; WITCHCRAFT, *Oth*; OATS, *Per*.

Ruffian The prostitute's bully (*OED*). *Ruffien* (Cot), Gk *roufianos*: pimp; *ruffianelle*: a young bawd, ruffian (F). Middleton, *The Roaring Girl*, IV.2, Mistress Gallipot: 'He having wasted them [£30] comes now for more,/ Using me as a ruffian doth a whore'.

TN, IV.i.60. Olivia speaks of the 'many fruitless pranks/This ruffian hath botch'd up'. Pranks are sexual (Oth, II.i.143; III.iii.202), and these suitors are not the first Toby has drained of money and promised amorous access to Olivia. *Ruffienner*: to make lecherous matches (Cot).

1H4, II.iv.500. Falstaff, called 'that reverend vice, that grey iniquity, that father ruffian', admits he is 'old' and has 'white hairs', but 'a whoremaster, that I utterly deny'.

TSh, II.i.290. When Petruchio says he hears they call her 'Kate', Katherina rebukes him: 'They call me Katherine that do talk of me.' What they did call her (I.i.54) was 'too rough' (*ruffa*: a harlot – F) and worthy of a 'cart', such as removed whores (probably to St Katherine's reformatory for fallen girls, mentioned in Jonson, Chapman and Marston, *Eastward Ho*, IV.i.79); at which she asked if her father intended to 'make a stale [whore] of me'. Eleven times Petruchio calls her 'Kate', century-old name for whores (P; as in *MM*), and says he means to keep warm 'in thy bed', and she calls him 'A madcap ruffian'. The whore and her bully! (See HAGGARD.)

KL, II.ii.67. To Oswald's calling him 'ancient ruffian', Kent's *quid pro quo* is to call Oswald his whore, the 'whoreson zed!' the 'goose' (whore – P) he will drive to sale (see CACKLE).

2H6, I.i.188. Salisbury has seen the cardinal, the Bishop of Winchester (C; P), who owned most of the land in the Bankside brothel area, 'Swear like a ruffian and demean himself/ Unlike the ruler of a commonweal'. A double slap: he acts like a lowly pimp and not like the ruler of the COMMONWEALTH (brothels) that he is.

See QUICK, *CE*; MOULDY, *2H4*.

Rural Ptg to the cunt. Lit. of the country (cunt – C; P).

WT, IV.iv.448. Polixenes warns Perdita, who he thinks was free with his son, never more 'These rural latches to his entrance open,/ Or hoop his body more with thy embraces'. 'Rural' and 'hoop' (P) connote the en-circl(e)-ing embrace of cunt and arms.

AC, V.ii.233: 'Here is a rural fellow/ That will not be denied your highness' presence: / He brings you figs.' He brings figs (female pudendum – F&H; *fica*: a fig; a woman's quaint, i.e. cunt – F). It is a country (L *rus*), rural ruse, for under the figs lies the 'worm' (WORM, serpent – that introduced sex and death into the garden): 'My resolution's placed, and I have nothing/ Of woman in me.' Her RESOLUTION (death and fornication) is placed, *placé* (fixed –

Cot; FIX: fuck, from Fr *ficher*, to place, resolve, fix, fuck – TWR). As the Clown says, 'the worm will do his kind' – do (P) the deed of KIND (sex – P), fornicate. Everything contributes to Cleopatra's final erotic scene, her act of death.

Russian Lecherous. *Roussiner*: 'To whinnie after Mares, like a rammish, or lecherous Jade; also, to leape a Mare' (Cot). *Roussin*: a horse (Cot).

LLL, v.ii.121. In their wooing of the Princess and her three ladies, the King and his three lords come 'apparell'd' like 'Russians'. It is a pity to explain this away, as is done, by saying that to Sh's audience the garb meant little more than exotic or strange.

The bilingual pun on Russians/*roussins* as horses, whinnying lecherously and eager to leap them, would be known to these French ladies. It started with Boyet's warning to the women (82) that 'encounters mounted are / Against your peace', with the quibbles on 'mounted' for copulation and on horse-back (C; P); and PEACE/PIECE, pejorative term for women (C; P). And, of course, the idea of masking themselves also was a ruse – *Russe*, Russian (Cot) – by which, Boyet says, the men hope 'every one his love-*feat* will advance' (italics added). These Russians hoped to *roussiner*, to leap a mare, just as in *Ado*, v.iv.50, a bull 'leap'd' and begot a calf in that love feat.

S

Saffron Sign of male effeminacy. A deep orange–yellow powder, made from stigmas (ovaries or pollen receptors) of the crocus: 'Capons that ben coloured with saffron' (*CD*). The crocota was the saffron-coloured mantle worn for the ceremonial of the cult of Bacchus (Dionysus), worn by Bacchus himself, by women, and by men considered effeminate (*CD*). Aristophanes, *The Frogs*, 42–56: Hercules mocks Dionysus, 'the lion-skin on a robe of saffron silk! How comes my club to sort with high-heeled shoes?' Is Dionysus coming from 'making love to Clisthenes [notorious Athenian homosexual]'? *Thesmophoriazusae*, 95–140: Agathon, in saffron tunic, surrounded by female toilet articles, is called an 'androgyne'.

Hickie, in his edn, says 'a saffron vest . . . was a mark of effeminacy among Romans also'.

CE, IV.iv.64: 'Did this companion with the saffron face/Revel and feast it at my house today. . . ?' (as at Dionysian revels), asks Antipholus E., speaking of Dr Pinch, whom he later castrates (SINGE).

AW, IV.v.3. Bertram was misled by 'a snipt-taffeta fellow there, whose villanous saffron would have made all the unbaked and doughy youth of a nation in his colour'. Parolles is the snipt (cut, castrated) TAFFETA (whore) who would have corrupted all the unbaked, doughy (as yet unrisen? virgin?) youth in his COLOUR/Fr *chaleur* (amorous heat)/It *culare* (arse-gut). '. . . if ye pinch me like a pasty, I can say no more' (iii.140). Pasties (SIXPENCE, Dekker) are whores; PINCHed (castrated) like a male whore, excess dough trimmed off, pricked so steam can escape, he still can say no more.

Sake Womb, scrotum, bowels; anatomical sacks or bags. Gk *sakkos*, L *saccus*: a bag. Margery 'lay still/And bid me fill, fill . . . Her sack, her sack . . . But 'twas all in vain/For I had spilt my grain' (Broadbent, p. 430). See ALTAR, *VA*; LAND, *AW*.

RJ, III.iii.89: 'For Juliet's sake, for her sake, rise and stand'. The Nurse's injunction has two often-noted puns on phallic erection: *rise* and *stand* (P). What is overlooked is the also double reference to the inspiration for the erection: Juliet's *sake*, for her *sake*.

MM, V.i.495: 'for his sake/Is he pardon'd; and for your lovely sake/Give me your hand and say you will be mine'. Claudio is pardoned for his *sake*, for (1) consideration of his person; (2) 15th c., a lawsuit or sin; (3) his bag (scrotum – P); and (4) its having bagged, i.e. impregnated, Juliet. And Isabella is proposed to for her *love*ly sake.

Oth, II.i.179. Enemas freq. elicit bawdry. Rabelais, Bk IV, ch. 68: 'an apothecary – I mean a suppository or clyster, thrust into royal nockandro' (1694 trs.). Cassio's kissing of his fingers while speaking to Desdemona elicits Iago's aside, 'would they were clyster-pipes for your sake!' He sneeringly likens Cassio's fingers placed at the opening of his mouth to clyster-pipes that inject liquid into the opening of the bowel (Cassio's *sake* or sack). *Cul de poule*: lit. chicken's arse, means bringing finger tips together (Cot). See PLAY THE SIR.

III.i.13. The rectal image of pipes and bags is repeated when Cassio hires musicians to serenade Desdemona. Told they are using 'wind instruments' (anus – C; P), that make L *ars musica*/arse music, or farts, the Clown says, 'thereby hangs a tail' – or *tale* (penis – K; P). He says Othello so likes their music that he begs they make 'no more noise [NOISE, farts]', 'for love's sake' – the anatomical sack (bowels) of LOVE/*loffe* (farts – F). He concludes, 'put up your pipes in your bag': take your unwanted music and stick it up your arse, so to speak. (Note:

some eds. say 'of all loves' instead of 'for love's sake', in which case the metaphor continues minus the pun on 'sake' and the 'bag' for their pipes.)

Same Homosexual. Gk *homos*, *homo-*: the same; L *homo*: man. 'Sam', cognate with 'semi': half, as in 'sam-sodden'. See ROUND and HALF for Plato's homosexual half man or half woman, who seeks an identical half to love. ME 'sam': mutually (MUTUAL, homosexual love). For an interesting constellation, cf. F&H, s.v. Sammy (a fool): 'I'm a ruined homo, a muff, a flat, a Sam, a regular ass' (1843).

2H4, III.ii.283: 'this same half-faced fellow, Shadow' – same HALF-FACED (half-arsed) SHADOW. See BOY for 17th c. use of shadows as half-men.

MWW, IV.v.37: 'the very *same man*' (italics added) and 'the woman herself' are both Falstaff, who had been disguised as 'an old fat woman' (28) – a FAT (Fr *un fat*, foppish, an ass) old woman (L *anus*).

TN, I.v.319: 'Run after that same peevish messenger,/The county's man: he left this ring behind him.' Each word puns on the bisexuality of the messenger (L *angelus*, messenger, angel; pun on ANGEL, bisexual): Viola–Cesario, girl–boy, posing as 'an eunuch' (ii.56) is the county's man or cunt-man (count: cunt – K, s.v. Gown; coun: cunt – P). Malvolio is to run *after* the peevish (perverse) messenger, who left a RING (L *anus*) BEHIND. Viola–Cesario is *that same* messenger, who says, when Malvolio throws the ring at her–him, 'I am the man'; 'I, poor monster'. She is the MAN (*homo*); the POOR/L *puer* (BOY, catamite) MONSTER (hermaphrodite, bisexual).

1H4, I.ii.209. Hal and Poins put on 'cases' (genitals – K; P) of BUCKRAM (sign of buggery) to hoax Falstaff and his friends. Poins: 'Well, for two of them, I know them to be as true-bred cowards *as ever turned back*; and for the third [/turd – K]' (italics added). See COWARDS (effeminates) for this line. Hal says the 'virtue of the jest [JEST, make an *ass* of]' will be the 'lies that this same fat rogue will tell us' – the LIES (tales of buggery) this *same* FAT (*un fat*, an ass) rogue will tell.

See PERFECTION, *TN*; BUNG-HOLE, *H5*; CONTENT, *MV*.

Sap Procreative juices, male and female.

See WINE; BOWL, *AC*.

Sauce, saucy Used 'Occas. with the notion: Wanton, lascivious' and 'In Shaks. as a term of serious condemnation' (*OED*). Cf. the 'saucy sweetness' of fornication (*MM*, II.iv.45) and the 'saucy stranger. . . . As in a Romish stew' (*Cym*, I.vi.151). Sauce: (1) the clap or pox (F&H); (2) semen. Boccaccio, *The Decameron*, pp. 129, 393; one lady squeezed her husband's 'cold pestle' (*pestello*) but it made no sauce (*salsa*); another would not let a priest ever again pound 'sauce in her mortar' (*non pesterete mai più salsa in suo mortaio*).

AC, II.i.25. Pompey wants Antony kept in Egypt with 'Salt Cleopatra'; wants the 'libertine' tied up in a 'field of feasts'. Let 'Epicurean cooks/Sharpen with cloyless sauce his appetite' – the *cloy*less sauce or lasciviousness of Cleopatra, 'his Egyptian dish' (vi.134), unlike 'other women [who] cloy/The appetites they feed' (ii.241).

2H4, II.iv.139. Doll will thrust her 'knife in your mouldy chaps, an you play the saucy cuttle with me.' This puns (1) on *sauci*ate: to hurt, wound, *cut* (*OED* 1656); (2) on the cuttle-fish, which ejects a black fluid or sauce from a sack. Doll is not only calling Pistol a cut-purse but also saying that his MOULDY (venereally diseased) chaps/It *chiappe* (a buttock; see BUNG-HOLE for this speech) or bowels are incontinent, which is why a few lines earlier she had called him a 'lack-linen' mate.

In the following, Sh pairs 'saucy' with words that mean disease, specif. venereal.

AC, V.ii.214: 'saucy lictors/Will catch at us, like strumpets; and scald [infect venereally – P; scabby, scurvy – *OED*] rhymers'.

MM, V.i.135: 'a saucy friar,/A very scurvy fellow'.

RJ, II.iv.153, Nurse: 'what saucy merchant was this . . . so full of his ropery? . . . Scurvy knave!' Saucy and lascivious, diseased and scurvy (see WORM), and full of his ropery (ROPES, lit. intestines) or, in mod. sl., *full* of his *foul*, sick shit (fool/full/fowl and fowl/foul – K).

See BITE, *H5*.

Scab Skin disease, 'spec. . . . syphilis' (*OED*). Whore or pimp. Lit. 16th c. syn. for a scoundrel. Middleton, *A Mad World, My Masters*, III.ii: 'An itching scab, that is your harlot . . . a running, your promoter . . . but a white scab, that's a scald knave and a pander'.

2H4, III.ii.296. Falstaff chooses Wart for his army: 'O, give me always a little, lean, old, chapt, bald shot . . . . thou'rt a good scab: hold, there's a tester for thee.' Wart is a LEAN/leno (pimp) scab, OLD, hoary/of whores; and bald (from syphilis – C) – and Falstaff gives him a TESTER (standard tip for the pimp).

See OPINION, *Cor.*

Scant(y), scantling (1) A homosexual, The *Lex Scantinia* (alt. sp. *Lex Scantina* or *Scautinia* – Norton, p. 363) was a Roman law against homosexual practices (Wilkinson, pp. 29–30). Marston, *The Scourge of Villanie*, Satyre i: 'Thou sayst Law Julia,/Or Catoes often curst Scatinia/Can take no hold on simpering Lesbia' (the *Law Julia* regulated marriage, discouraged celibacy). *Monstre*: a scantling, an example; a deformed creature, fashioned contrary to nature, a monster (Cot). See MONSTER (hermaphrodite; homosexual).

(2) Castrate.

KL, II.iv.178. Lear tells Regan, ' 'Tis not in thee/To grudge my pleasures, to cut off my train . . . to scant my sizes,/And in conclusion to oppose the bolt/Against my coming in'. See TRAIN for his daughters' whittling away at Lear's potency, power. Here is the same idea in the puns on his 'pleasures' (sexual – P) not being grudged; his TRAIN (penis) not being cut off; his SIZES (Fr *tailles*/tails, penises – his and those of his followers) not being scanted; and in CONCLUSION (coitus), no bolt opposing the 'coming in' (coitus – C; P) of his own BOLT (penis).

Son 117:

Accuse me thus: that I have scanted all
Wherein I should your great deserts repay, . . .
That I have frequent been with unknown minds
And given to time your own dear-purchased right;
That I have hoisted sail to all the winds
Which should transport me farthest from your sight.

Whether one hears Sh's having *scanted all* as a statement of homosexual loves and infidelities might depend on to whom one believes the sonnets are addressed and acceptance of the following puns: (1) repay: PAYS/Gk *pais*, the young partner in a homosexual relationship; (2) the MINDS (arses): the unknown minds, virgin or hitherto unknown to him arses that he frequents, comparable to the 'unknown bottom' of Ganymede, a catamite (*AYL*, IV.i.212) and the 'unknown loins' of the BEGGAR/bugger (*Ado*, IV.i.137); (3) his having ignored the DEAR/deer (hind) purchased RIGHT (L *rectum*) of the lover; (4) while he hoisted sail/*saillir* (to leap as the male does the female – Cot) in beastly fashion (Fr *sale*, foul, beastly); with (5) all the WINDS (farts) that transported him *far*thest (see TRULL: trullo, a fart, an anus) – all the WINDS (copulative acts; pun on to wind on a *bottom*, as of thread); (6) all those who transported him from the lover's sight (L *acies*; see KEEN for puns on sight and ass/arse).

See CUP, *AC*; MINGLE, *AC*.

Scape A flatus (F&H). *Pettare*: to let a scape or fart (F); and *pet*: a scape or fart (Cot). Middleton, *A Mad World, My Masters*, III.ii:

Courtesan. Bound? No, no, I'ld a very comfortable stool this morning.
Harebrain. I'm glad of that . . . that's a good sign, I smell she'll 'scape it now.

See THUNDER, *KL*; SIXPENCE, *MND*; FART; OTHER, *Tem.*

Scarlet Symbol of whoredom. 'Most Elizabethan playwrights whose plots touch the church of Rome (to keen Protestants, the scarlet whore of *Revelations*) exploit the . . . symbolic effects of the red robes worn by cardinals' (Saccio, p. 205). Isa 1:10,18,21: 'Hear the word of the Lord, ye rulers of Sodom . . . ye people of Gomorrah . . . though your sins be as scarlet. . . . How is the faithful city become an harlot!'

1H6, I.iii.42,56. Gloucester attacks the hypocrisy of the Bishop of Winchester, a cardinal who wears 'scarlet robes' and gives 'whores indulgence to sin'. A three-pronged attack on (1) the church's selling of indulgences; (2) Winchester's ownership of the districts within which brothels were situated (C; P); (3) the similarity between him who sells indulgence for sin and the whore who sells her body for indulgence in lust. He concludes, 'Winchester goose, I cry, a rope! a rope! . . . thou wolf in sheep's array./ Out, tawny coats! out, scarlet hypocrite!'

The thrust of the speech is that this *Winchester goose* is a whore (*OED*): a WOLF (whore) in the scarlet array of the SHEEP (a filthy dolt; whore). He is a male whore, this hypocrite with his TAWNY (vulva), i.e. effeminate COATS/cods (testes – K). To cry is to call out, hawk in the market-place; and Gloucester cries him a ROPE (lit. intestines): an arse, a whore; out, out (OUT, Fr *hors*/whores)! See STAND BACK.

H8, III.ii.255, 280. Cardinal Wolsey is 'scarlet sin'; and Surrey refuses to be 'jaded by a piece of scarlet'. 'Jade' and 'scarlet', seeming contrasts, are synonyms. Surrey refuses to be made a jade (worn out whore of either sex – F&H) by a scarlet PIECE (whore). He concludes with a pun on startling Wolsey 'Worse than the sacring bell, when the brown wench/ Lay kissing in your arms' – the sacring bell, the church bell that announces the *raising* of the eucharist, the *Elevation* of the *Host* (as Wolsey's guest, the brown girl, lay in his arms).

See COPATAIN HAT, *TSh*.

Sceptre Penis (F&H; TWR). Chaucer, *The Parliament of Fowls*, 256: Priapus, his plans for sexual intercourse interrupted, stood there with 'his sceptre in honde'.

Mac, III.i.62: 'And put a barren sceptre in my gripe'. See ACCESS.

IV.i.121: 'and some I see/ That two-fold balls and treble sceptres carry'. Whereas his own sceptre is 'barren', the apparitions of 'Banquo's issue' carry these symbols of potency, including the TWO-FOLD balls.

See HEINOUS, *R2*; CLIP, *H5*.

Scold Whore. Scald (alt. sp.): also, to infect venereally. Anon., *The Woman Taken in Adultery* (medieval miracle play), 149: 'Come forth, thou quean . . . thou scold! . . . thou slut!' Jonson, *The Poetaster*, IV.iii: 'She's a curst quean . . . plays the scold behind his back'. *Petegolare*: to play the common scold, strumpet (F).

AW, II.ii.27: 'as a scolding quean to a wrangling knave'.

KJ, II.i.191. Queen Elinor and her daughter-in-law call each other adulteresses. Elinor: 'Thy bastard shall be king,/ That thou mayst be a queen and check the world!' (122). (HAGGARD: a hawk that *checks*, follows, base game, deserts its proper chase.) Constance will be QUEEN/ quean or whore to the world. Constance: 'His father never was so true begot'; and 'this is thy eld'st son's son,/ Infortunate in nothing but in thee:/ Thy sins are visited in this poor child;/ The canon of the law is laid on him,/ Being but the second generation/ Removed from thy sin-conceiving womb' (177). She means the law of Deut 5:9, 18: 'visiting the iniquity of the fathers upon the children unto the third and fourth generation' and 'Neither shalt thou commit adultery'. Elinor is a venereally diseased adulteress whose grandson is 'plagued for her sin . . . her sin and her the plague . . . plagued for her/ And with her plague'. At this point Elinor calls Constance, 'Thou unadvised scold', which in context makes more sense as an imprudent strumpet than as merely an abusive, loud-mouthed woman.

3H6, V.v.29. Gloucester calls the adulterous Margaret a 'captive scold', the implication of harlotry being political dynamite in that it impugned the legitimacy of her son – whom he and his brothers murder on the spot. To call her merely a user of lewd language would meet neither the virulence of the occasion nor his needs.

H8, V.i.173. An old court prostitute tells the King that Anne gave birth to a daughter as 'like you / As cherry is to cherry'. Upon receiving only 'an hundred marks', she testily complains, 'I will have more, or scold it out of him. / Said I for this, the girl was like to him? / I will have more, or else unsay't'. If she unsays it, then the child does *not* look like him, by implication he is *not* the father, the child is a bastard and the mother a scold or strumpet. This is more like the bitterness of an old whore, disappointed with her payment, and a more likely meaning than that she expects she can scold or use abusive language to dun a king.

Score, Scorn (1) Female pudendum (K, p. 133), like nick and cut, 16th c. Score, tally, tale (penis – K; P).

(2) Fornicate. A score was a cut or notch, to keep tally. Chaucer, 'The Shipman's Tale', 414: 'For I wol paye yow wel and redily / Fro day to day; and, if so be I faille, / I am your wyf; score it up-on my taille' – 'By god, I wol nat paye yow but a-bedde.'

(3) Score a man, make him a cut (gelding – *OED*). Scar / scorn (K): ' 'tis but a scar to scorn' – *TrC*, I.i.114.

AW, IV.iii.257. Bertram is a 'lascivious boy, who is a whale to virginity' and 'After he scores, he never pays the score.'

Oth, IV.i.131. Othello observes Cassio mock his own mistress, but mistakenly thinks Desdemona is the subject: 'Have you scored me?'

Cym, III.ii.69. Believing Imogen guilty of 'adultery', her husband asked Pisanio to kill her *en route* to him. Thus to Imogen's 'How many score of miles may we well ride', Pisanio replies, 'One score . . . Madam's enough for you: (*aside*) and too much too.'

Tim, I.ii.38:

Timon. . . . let my meat make thee silent.
Apemantus. I scorn thy meat; 'twould choke me. . . . O you gods, what a number of men eat Timon. . . .

Pun on to *scorn* meat instead of to *score* or make parallel cuts for cooking. Metaphor for the whores who eat (consume coitally – C; P) Timon: the number (ME 'tale' – *OED*) or tale (penis – K; P) of men who consumed, screwed, him till his wealth was gone.

TGV, I.i.29: 'To be in love, where scorn is bought with groans. . . . With twenty watchful'. TWENTY, i.e. a score, stresses the pun on *love* (also a score – in games, meaning nothing), where scorn and scoring (coiting) are *bought* with groans, as in *Ham*, III.ii.259: 'It would *cost* you a groaning [GROAN / groin] to take off my edge' (italics added).

See FIX, *Oth*; CAPER, *MV*.

Scour (1) Purge the bowels, with the aid of a clyster (an enema and occ. a suppository). See HATEFUL, *H5*: Nym will 'prick his [Pistol's] guts' and 'scour him with my rapier'.

(2) Be scoured clean in the process of the VD cure, i.e. sweating in tubs.

(3) Scourers, or street roisterers, were associated with physical and sexual violence: 'scourers, and Alsations' (F&H, s.v. Debauchees). Oldham, 'The Streets of London': 'the drunken Scowrers of the Street, / Flush'd with success . . . Of Constables subdu'd and Brothels storm'd'.

2H4, I.ii.246. The Chief Justice calls Falstaff physically and morally sick. Falstaff ends the mutual acerbity with 'I were better to be eaten to death with a rust than to be scoured to nothing with perpetual motion.' In Sh it is always 'weapon', 'sword', 'rapier', 'dagger' – all penis symbols – that are consumed by rusty ravages of disease or disuse. Alexander Radcliffe, 'A Call to the Guard by a Drum': the foot soldiers 'With trusty Pike and Gun, and the other rusty Tool [penis]' come with 'Pox in the Breeches', and 'their Wenches run hither . . . To behold 'em wear Pikes rusty just like their Whores' (*Penguin Book of Restoration Verse*, p. 256). Rabelais, Bk III, Prol. (1693 trs.): 'Every Man exercis'd his Weapon, every Man scour'd off the Rust from his natural Hanger' and the women likewise 'furbish'd' their gear, for 'the Corinthian Women of old were reputed very couragious Combatants' – in the Venereal combat of Corinth (a brothel – G; see CORINTHIAN).

Falstaff is going to war but means 'not to sweat extraordinarily' (sweating: treatment for, and symptom of, VD; cf. *TrC*, v.x.54) nor to 'brandish any thing but a bottle' – no *thing* (genital – C; P), neither sword nor penis, to be subjected to danger. He fears less the rust of degeneration (from lack of morals and lack of use) and the rust of disease than he does the cure: the purge (moral), and the purge or scouring in the sweating-tub; as well as the perpetual motion (1598, bowel-evacuation) that would reduce him to nothing: see GOUT, *Cym*.

See ORDER, *MWW*.

Screw Copulate (G). 'Internal' and 'external', feminine and masculine 'screws' (*vite femina* and *maschio* – F), were contemporary phrases; and 'screw' meant penetrate windingly, worm one's way.

TN, v.i.126: 'I partly know the instrument/ That screws me from my true place in your favour'. The Duke knows Cesario is the instrument (tool, penis – P) that screwed him out of Olivia's favour (sexual parts – P), out of his TRUE/*trou* (the bung-hole, fundament – Cot) place. He knows what partly (PART, genitals) screwed him from his screwing-PLACE (pudendum).

Mac, I.vii.60: 'But screw your courage to the sticking-place,/ And we'll not fail' is Lady Macbeth's injunction to Macbeth to be a man; as in her previous speech she had said, 'then you were a man . . . Be so much more the man'. Emphasis on manhood continues in his response, 'Bring forth men-children only'. The sticking-place has been glossed as 'to its height', with ref. to a bent crossbow; however STICK is copulate (Fr *foutre*, to stick, to fuck – P; TWR) and a stick (L *talea*) puns on tale/ tail (penis – K; P). It is a dagger (penis – C, s.v. Weapon), not an arrow or stone, that Macbeth will stick Duncan with, when he does 'bend up/ Each corporal agent to this terrible feat' of murder – and also, fig., this *feat* of coitus (*Ado*, v.iv.50: some bull 'leap'd your father's cow,/ And got a calf in that same noble feat'). Macbeth's sticking-place will be achieved with a corporal (body part) agent, and he will accomplish his murderous feat, screwing (his courage) like a man. But Macbeth's screwing fails to produce heirs: it kills.

Scrubbed Of the vulva or a hole (L *scrobis*). 'Scrob': ME form of 'scrub'.

MV, v.i.162, 261. Nerissa, who had been disguised as the doctor's clerk, is described by her husband as 'A kind of boy, a little scrubbed boy . . . A prating boy that begg'd it [the ring]'. And she later calls herself 'that same scrubbed boy'. Editors offer many explanations of 'scrubbed': stubbed, scrubby like a shrub; stunted. I suggest Nerissa (disguised as a boy) is precisely what Sh says, only a *kind of* boy, a girl–boy, a scrubbed/*scrobis* (vulva) boy, a prating boy with evasive PRATE and ambiguous PRAT, buttocks. And she begg'd the ring: *bague* (a ring – Cot), *bagos* (a man-bawd, ribald – Cot). She was, in her male disguise, a BEGGAR/ bugger of her husband's RING (L *anus*): she made an ass of Grat*iano* (*ano*: a man's bum – F).

Scullion Whore; linked to foul anal smells. An 'abusive epithet' (*OED*). *Souillon*: a scullion; also, a 'greasie, filthie, nastie' fellow (Cot). (In sculling, the oar is worked over the stern or rear.)

2H4, II.i.65:

Falstaff. . . . throw the quean in the channel.
Hostess. Throw me in the channel! I'll throw thee in the channel. . . .
Thou wo't, wo't thou? thou wo't, wo't ta? . . .
Falstaff [or *Page*]. Away, you scullion! you rampalian! you fustilarian! I'll tickle your catastrophe.

The hostess, quean or whore, is to be thrown into the filthy channel (gutter – *OED*) – in which humans and animals defecated and urinated; the filthy *water* – the *wo't* and *wo't ta* – in which a scullion washes pots (and probably chamber-pots). She is a rampalian and fustilarian – words composed of fancy comic endings added to RAMP (whore, associated with anal acts) and 'fusty'

(foul-smelling). And Falstaff will tickle (masturbate, copulate – F&H; P) her catastrophe (posterior – C; P).
See BRAINS, *Ham*.

Scum Shit, dung. *Trullare*: to shit, skommer (F). Scummer: scumber, dung; scumber: to void excrement.
2H6, IV.ii.130: 'Rebellious hinds [boors, the posteriors], the filth and scum of Kent'.
2H4, IV.v.124: 'Now, neighbour confines, purge you of your scum'. 'Confines', 16th c., meant neighbours. The repetition emphasises the pun in CONFINES (in the arse), in the FINES (buttocks) that will purge or empty by defecation those who, like Hal's companions, are scum.

Seal (1) Male genitals. Chapman, *All Fools*, III.i: woman is the 'light sex' because she 'is an unfinished creature, delivered hastily to the world before Nature had set to that seal which should have made them perfect' (the *membrum virile* is lacking). Seals: testicles (F&H, s.v. Cods, n.d.).
(2) To stamp: engender (C; P).
Ham, III.iv.61. Hamlet shows his mother the picture of his father, 'A combination and a form indeed,/ Where every god did seem to set his seal,/ To give the world assurance of a man'.
MND, I.i.84. Theseus, the impatient bridegroom of ll. 1–6, speaks quite literally when he anticipates his wedding-day, 'The sealing-day betwixt my love and me'.
TrC, III.ii.204. Similarly, the lewd Pandarus, who had urged Troilus and Cressida to 'go to, go to' and 'Come in, come in', again pushes them toward each other with 'Go to, a bargain made: seal it, seal it; I'll be the witness.' WITNESS (L *testis*: witness; testicle) is a testicle; therefore everything is said *two* times: go *to*, go *to*; come in, come in; seal it, seal it (TWO, testes).
MV, II.viii.18. Jessica fled and in so doing destroyed Shylock, the man. 'A sealed bag, two sealed bags of ducats,/ Of double ducats, stolen from me by my daughter!/ And jewels, two stones, two rich and precious stones,/ Stolen by my daughter!' Shylock has been kicked in the groin; every word expresses the pain: (1) *bag* (scrotum – P; 'bagge of the gentras' – TWR, s.v. Bagge); (2) TWO and DOUBLE, shorthand for 'testes'; (3) *stones*, testicles (*OED*); (4) JEWELS, testicles.
See SURE(TY), *TA*; Introduction, p. xvi.

Season (1) Seisin: confiscate (K); possession (*OED*). Pun on *seize on*: 'Time is a very bankrupt and owes more than he's worth to season' (*CE*, IV.ii.58). See CACKLE, *MV*.
(2) Impregnate, copulate with (*OED*).
Tim, IV.iii.85: 'Be a whore still. . . . Make use of thy salt hours: season the slaves/ For tubs and baths'. The salt, i.e. salacious, HOURS/ whores season/*seize on* and copulate with men, communicating diseases for which the salt tub was treatment.
LLL, V.ii.63. Rosaline plans to 'torture' Biron: to 'make him fawn and beg and seek/ And wait the season and observe the times . . . And shape his service . . . And make him proud to make me proud'. He must beg for the sexual favour, observe her woman's times or periods (see GERMAN), and wait the season, i.e. that time when the female animal is in heat. He must SHAPE (sex-organs – *OED*; to mould in conception) his service (copular – *OED*; P), be proud or full of pride (sexual heat – *OED*; P), to make her proud. See REST.

Seek/ sick See GERMAN, *LLL*; REST, *LLL*; PRIVILY.

Semiramis Assyrian queen famed for voluptuousness and sexial bestiality. 'Semiramis with a horse, Pasiphae with a bull' – two women who mated with animals (Robert Burton, p. 651). Butler, *Hudibras*, Pt II, c.i, 715: 'Semiramis of Babylon, who first of all cut men o' the stone' (castrated them).
TSh, Induction, ii.41. The Lord, planning to seduce Sly with a Page dressed as a woman, tells

him, 'we'll have thee to a couch / Softer and sweeter than the lustful bed / On purpose trimm'd up for *Semiramis* . . . thy *horses* shall be trapp'd' (italics added).

TA. The incest of 'Semiramis with her own sonne' (Nashe, *The Anatomie of Absurditie*, in *Works*, vol. I, p. 11; cf. Boccaccio, *De Claris Mulieribus*, p. 15) is relevant to the sexually bestial Tamora and her sons (see CARD, TRUNK). Tamora is twice called 'Semiramis' (II.i.22; iii,118), queen who mated with a horse; and Sh names one of her sons (who raped Lavinia) after Chiron, mythological centaur, half man and half horse – an ironic choice, for, unlike his wild brothers, Chiron was known for gentleness (see HOME for further irony).

See BARBAROUS, *TA*; TAME, *TA*.

Servant, serving-man Lover; stallion and pimp (F&H). Massinger, *The Fatal Discovery*, II.ii: the 'distinction between a husband and a servant is the first will lie with you when he pleases, the last shall lie with you when you please'. Marston, *Antonio and Mellida*, V.i: Rosaline's gallants are 'thirty-nine servants, and my monkey that makes the fortieth'.

KL, III.iv.87: 'A serving-man . . . that . . . served the lust of my mistress' heart, and did the act of darkness with her'.

R3, III.v.82. Gloucester reviles Edward's 'hateful luxury, / And bestial appetite in change of lust; / Which stretched to their servants, daughters, wives, / Even where his lustful eye or savage heart . . . listed to make his prey'. His savage heart made prey with a BESTIAL (sodomitical) appetite. His luxury (lasciviousness, its only meaning in Sh) was HATEFUL (Fr *haineux* / of the anus), and it STRETCHED (coitally) to servants, daughters and wives.

2H4, V.iii.12. Falstaff visits the 'squire' (as he calls him, III.ii.344) in his 'orchard', where he grows the 'pippin' ('pippin squire', n.d., or 'apple-squire', 1500s: a pimp – F&H).

> *Shallow.* Barren, barren, barren; beggars all, beggars all, Sir John: marry, good air. Spread, Davy, spread, Davy; well said, Davy.
> *Falstaff.* This Davy serves you for good uses; he is your serving-man and your husband.

The language of these two old lechers is sexually charged. His place is 'barren', 'marry'. There is good air, Folio sp. 'ayre', pun on *herre* or beggar (Cot) and *herry* or arse-gut (Cot), as in BEGGAR, *TrC*. It BEGGARS / buggers him, it beggars all. Davy, who is to spread (presumably a TABLE, itself a far from innocent practice) is merely told to SPREAD (of men, to lay out for copular service – F&H). Davy serves (coitally – *OED*; P) for GOOD (wanton) uses (sexual pleasures – C; P). He is Shallow's husband in more ways than one (see VARLET).

V.i.76. CON and count: the cunt (K; C; P). Davy, 'Well*con*ceited', does twice 'beseech' or beg Shallow to '*coun*tenance' (COUNTENANCE, said three times, is a doublet of continence, sexual restraint – *OED*) a certain 'Visor' (VISOR, whore). Shallow replies the 'knave' (lit. boy servant) 'shall have no wrong [WRONG, prick – K]'. Falstaff says that Master Shallow 'by *con*versing with them [his servants], is turned into a justice-like serving-man: their spirits are so married in *con*junction [CONJUNCTION: coitus; see under *KJ*] . . . they flock together in *con*sent like so many wild-geese'. (Italics added.)

This JUSTICE- (whore) LIKE (Gk *homoios*, *homo-*) serving-man and his servants ('beggars all') are like wild (licentious – TWR; *OED*) geese (whores – C; P). Cf. Dekker, *The Bel-man of London*, pp. 85, 107: 'Wild-geese' are a rank of canting beggars, whose sexual habits include 'Incest . . . laughed at, Sodomy made a jest'. And with tales of them Falstaff hopes to keep Hal 'in continual laughter' (CONTINUAL, cunt).

See VIRTUE, *WT*; RE, *RJ*.

Shadow Homosexual, who mates with his LIKE. One of Plato's homosexual half-men, created when Zeus cut original men in half (see ROUND). Wycherley, *The Country Wife*, I.i: 'Who do you call shadows of men?' – 'Half-men' (see BOY). Tyndale, *Obedience of a Christian Man*: 'better to have a tyrant unto thy king than a shadow; a passive king that doth nought himself but suffreth others to do with him what they will . . . A king that is soft as silk and effeminate, that is to say turned unto the nature of a woman'.

2H4, III.ii.137: 'prick him' for the army, says Falstaff, who wants 'to sit under' Shadow, this 'half-faced' (HALF-FACED, q.v.), half-arsed, fellow, one of the 'half a dozen sufficient [*assez* – Cot] men'.

Falstaff. Shadow, whose son art thou?
Shadow. My mother's son, sir.
Falstaff. Thy mother's son! like enough, and thy father's shadow.

He is his mother's son, her sun Shadow – *like* ENOUGH (an ass/arse).

AYL, IV.i.220. Rosalind – GANYMEDE (a catamite) 'cannot be out of the sight of Orlando. I'll go find a shadow, and sigh till he come.' Maybe the shadow (another HALF-man like himself) he'll *go find* is one that will tell time, the shadow of the gnomon as it moves over the pricks on the sun dial (see FIX for gnomon/no-man puns). This conceit has an antecedent in III.ii.118: 'He that sweetest love will find/Must find love's prick and Rosalind.'

See CROOKED, *3H6*; CUP, *AC*.

Shake 1. Coit. A 'schakere', *lascivus*: person of loose life (*OED*, s.v. Shaker). Cf. Rabelais *Pantagruelian Prognostication*, ch. 5: 'Those whom Venus is said to rule, as . . . Wenchers, Leachers, Shakers' (also in *OED*). Heywood, *A Woman Killed with Kindness*, I.i: 'The Shaking of the Sheets . . . the dance her husband means to lead her'. 'From what Dunghill didst thou pick up this shakerag, this squire [pimp or stallion] of the body?' (F&H, s.v. Squire, 1665).

JC, I.ii.9. Caesar asks Antonius in his 'speed' (sexual potency – C; P) to be sure to 'touch' (caress erotically – F&H; P) Calpurnia, because it was believed 'the barren' so 'touched' could 'Shake off their sterile curse'.

TGV, II.v.37. Asked if it will be a match between Julia and Proteus, Launce says, 'Ask my dog . . . if he shake his tail and say nothing, it will' – shake his tail (penis – K; P) or penis and say NOTHING (fornication).

Oth, V.i.118. Iago calls Cassius's injury 'the fruit of whoring' and asks his mistress Bianca, 'What, do you shake at that?' Bianca: 'He supp'd at my house; but I therefore shake not.' 'I am no strumpet'.

H5, II.iv.134. Angered at the gift of 'Paris balls', Exeter says Henry will 'make your Paris Louvre shake for it,/Were it the mistress-court of mighty Europe'. The Louvre (OFr *lover*) will shake like a mistress, as in III.vii.52: 'methought . . . your mistress shrewdly shook your back'.

2. Shake the head connotes castration, impotence. Rabelais, Bk III, ch. 45, mocks prophets who shake their heads like the gelded eunuch priests of the goddess Cybele. In *Ado*, II.i.123, Ursula recognises the masked Antonio: 'I know you by the waggling of your head'; 'Here's his dry hand up and down' – Antonio's old HAND (phallus – K), DRY (impotent) and shaking UP AND DOWN, like his head.

KJ, III.i.20. Constance asks the meaning of Salisbury's 'shaking of thy head' and looking 'sadly on my son'. This, plus 'fall and die', three uses of 'tale' (penis – C; P) and the HEINOUS/anus harm she fears, anticipates her son's castration and death (see SHIP-BOY for the same implication in 'shake their heads').

KL, I.iv.319. Lear is 'ashamed/That thou hast power to shake my manhood thus' – he is a-shamed, without SHAME (genitals), has been emasculated by his daughters (TRAIN).

See AGE, *Cor*; MIND, *Cym*; ACCESS, *Mac*.

Shame (1) Privy members (*OED*). L *pudendum*: the shameful thing. *Vergogne* (F), *vergongne* (Cot): shame; the privy parts. Isa 47:2–3: 'make bare the leg, uncover the thigh . . . . Thy nakedness shall be uncovered, yea, thy shame shall be seen'.

(2) Castrate. *Che(s)mer*: to decrease, fall away (Cot).

MM, IV.iv.35. Angelo fears Claudio might seek revenge if his life be spared 'With ransom of such shame' – at the cost of his sister's being 'deflower'd' – a ransom of SUCH (*tale* – F) *shame*, his sister's tale (pudendum – K; P).

AW, IV.iii.363. A soldier mocks Parolles's impotence (KNOT): 'If you could find out a country where but women were that had received so much shame, you might begin an impudent nation.' If he could find a country (cunt – C; P) where the women had received his shame – psychological or actual castration or circumcision ('off with his head [HEAD, prepuce, testes]' – 343) – they could start an IM-PUDENT (without pudenda) nation.

KJ, IV.iii.97. Hubert is told they will 'Cut him to pieces', CUT (castrate – *OED*) him, make a CUT (cunt – C; K) of his PIECE (penis), a CUT or gelding of him. Salisbury threatens to sheathe a sword in the SKIN (scrotum) of this 'dunghill' and then turns on the Bastard, who warns him, 'If thou but frown on me, or stir thy foot,/ Or teach thy hasty spleen to do me shame,/ I'll strike thee dead. Put up thy sword betime;/ Or I'll maul you and your toasting-iron'. They cannot threaten him as they did Hubert. If Salisbury thinks his hasty/ L *hasta* (sword) SPLEEN (anger and semen) will do the Bastard shame, decrease or curtail (*chemer*), castrate or screw him, he is wrong; for the Bastard will first strike Salisbury dead or maul *his* toasting-iron.

See MODEST, *MND*; TORCH, *MV*; MISUSE, *1H4*.

Shape Sex-organs, male and female, now exclusively the female (*OED*; TWR, s.v. Shap). To create, as in Ps 51:5: 'Behold, I was shapen in iniquity; and in sin did my mother conceive me.'

AYL, V.iv.126. Phebe learns Ganymede is really a woman: 'If sight and shape be true,/ Why then, my love adieu!' If the only shape Ganymede has is TRUE/ *trou* (an anus; gap or hole – Cot; hole: pudendum – P), then there is nothing in it for Phebe.

Tim, II.ii.119. The Fool says a 'whoremaster' is a 'spirit' that appears 'generally, in all shapes that man goes up and down in'. He is the SPIRIT (penis; semen) that goes UP AND DOWN (whores) in all shapes.

AW, I.i.71. Bertram's mother: 'Be thou blest, Bertram, and succeed thy father/ In manners, as in shape!' (See MANNER, sex.) Cf. *Tem*, V.i.290, in which the 'mis-shapen knave' Caliban (268) 'is as disproportion'd in his manners/ As in his shape'.

R3, I.i.14: 'But I, that am not shaped for sportive tricks . . . that am curtail'd of this fair proportion . . . unfinish'd . . . scarce half made up . . . cannot prove a lover'. The deformity as Richard describes it sounds less like a hunch-back than a sexual inadequacy: *curtail'd* of this fair PROPORTION (penis) – his tail (penis – C; P) cut short or off; not *shaped*, his genitals inadequate for *sportive tricks* (each word meaning love-making – C; P); incapable of *proving* a lover (to PROVE: attest to manhood with the testes, exactly the area in which Richard is DEFORMED (q.v.).

See GRACIOUS, *TN*.

Share (1) Fork of the body (*OED*; F&H).

(2) Coit. Lit. possess or occupy with others.

RJ, I.iii.93. Lady Capulet tells Juliet to provide a 'cover' (mount coitally – *OED*; P) for Paris's book of love: 'So shall you share all that he doth possess,/ By having him, making yourself no less'. She may mean Paris's wealth and social status, but the Nurse hears the coital implications in *share*, *possess*, *having*: 'No less! nay, bigger; women grow by men.'

MND, III.ii.198. Helena rebukes Hermia, one of the '*con*federacy', who '*con*joined', '*con*spired', '*con*trived', and forgot 'all the *coun*sel that we two have shared' (italics added) – the shared CON (cunt) or feminine love. She appeals to their early love, in which 'our hands, our sides, voices, and minds' – HANDS, sides (loin – *OED*; buttocks – TWR), VOICES and MINDS, each of which means shares – 'Had been incorporate. So we grew together,/ Like to a double cherry' – LIKE (Gk *homoios homo-*) to /TWO a DOUBLE (q.v. *MND*): to fall in love with a double is shorthand for homosexual love. And certainly this sounds less like friendship than a Siamese creation to be physically 'rent' or cut: 'will you rent our ancient love asunder . . . . Our sex, as well as I, may chide you for it,/ Though I alone do feel the injury.' The speech, with its ambiguous 'our sex', is quite as 'passionate' as (Hermia calls it so, l.220) – and quite similar to – an earlier one of Lysander's (II.ii.41): (1) he wanted 'one turf' to be 'pillow' (cod: pillow, scrotum) for them both; Helena and Hermia sat on 'one cushion [CUSHION, buttocks]'; (2) he, like Helena, spoke of 'one heart', though two bosoms; (3) his heart was 'knit' to Helena's, and Helena and Hermia with 'needles' created one flower.

Renting their *ancient love* asunder evokes Plato's 'ancient woman' (ROUND), who had two sets of everything, like the *incorporate* Helena and Hermia, incl. two sets of genitals, like the double CHERRY. Jove sliced them in half to lessen their power *vis-à-vis* the gods, and from these rent women came Lesbians, who seek other women for completion, for love. It 'is not friendly [Platonic]'. Helena says, 'to join [JOIN, copulate] with men'.

MWW, III.ii.40. Another close feminine relationship (see above) is feared by the jealous Ford. Mrs Page is on her way (11) 'to see your wife. Is she at home?' Ford answers, 'Ay; and as idle as she may hang together . . . . I think, if your husbands were dead, you two would marry.' Mrs Page: 'Be sure of that, – two other husbands.'

Ford calls them IDLE (sexually wanton) women who HANG (Fr *pendre* / pander) together. She retaliates that he can be SURE (a bawd; a betrothal) of that; and she adds 'two other husbands', rejecting the implication in Ford's *you two* would marry, the idea of an intimacy between the women themselves, which this jealously obsessed man insinuates again in l.40: 'and our revolted wives share damnation together'. Ford anticipates forbidden sexual sharing for which they will share damnation (Sh puns freq. on DAMN / dam, woman, wife). Perh. he means their joint forthcoming adulterous sharing with Falstaff, or perh. he means *they* will share.

The 'monster' he invites his friends to see (they agree 'to see this monster') may be himself, the cuckolded MONSTER with horns; the MONSTER (hermaphrodite) Falstaff dressed as Mother Prat (PRAT, buttocks), a man–woman whom Ford (more accurately than he realises) calls a WITCH (hermaphrodite); or his wife, a MONSTER (homosexual), following his original insinuation that the merry wives have an initimate, Lesbian relationship (see SHOW).

Another man who is sexually frustrated by these two women also anticipates their sharing damnation, and again there may be another masculine imputation of their sexual irregularity (to explain the man's own failure): 'The devil take one party and his dam the other! so they shall be both bestowed' (IV.v.108). The devil and his dam will each take (carnally – C; P) one of the two women, who will then both be BESTOWed in sexual bestiality: the DEVIL was known as a hermaphrodite and bisexual.

Shed 1. Ejaculate semen; of plants, cast seed out of receptacle. Chaucer, 'The Parson's Tale', 575: those who 'dooth unkyndely synne, by which man or woman shedeth hire nature in manere or in place ther as a child may nat be conceived'.

TrC, I.iii.319. Ulysses has a 'young conception in my brain; / Be you my time to bring it to some shape'; 'the seeded pride . . . In rank Achilles must or now be cropp'd, / Or, shedding, breed a nursery of like evil, / To overbulk us all.' Achilles must be stopped from spreading his influence in the camp. The metaphor is of cropping the seeded pride (sexual heat, esp. in a female animal) of rank (sexual heat, as in the 'rank' ewes who 'turned to the rams' – *MV*, I.iii.81) Achilles; of cropping (cutting off the terminal part of a plant) this effeminate male before he sheds his seed and breeds a plant that will overbulk (BULK, conceive) them all. Else he will breed a nursery of LIKE (Gk *homoios*, *homo-*) EVIL (*male* – F): of L *male mas*, effeminate males, who will lie around as he does with his lover Patroclus and refuse to fight. (See EVIL and CATERPILLAR, *R2*, for a similar conceit on homosexual weeds.) To counter that breeding, Ulysses has his own conception in his BRAIN (testicles), which he wants to bring to SHAPE (genitals – *OED*), to flower.

2. To ovulate, which in women is accompanied by menstruation. A 'shedder' is a female salmon after spawning.

See MILK, *AW*.

Sheep / ship Whores: 'Courtesans . . . oves' (F&H, s.v. Mutton, loose women). *Pecore*: sheep; a filthy dolt (Cot). Puns on SHIP, a knave (shape / sheep / ship – K).

MV, III.ii.317. Antonio writes, 'my ships have all miscarried' and his bond to Shylock is forfeit. Lost ships that miscarried connotes sheep who aborted and thus directly contrasts his fortune to that of Shylock, who made gold and silver 'breed as fast' as Jacob's 'conceiving' ewes (I.iii.96).

But in the end it is Antonio's 'ships/ Are safely come to road [a low prostitute – P]' (V.i.287). His are the ships/sheep that are like Jacob's 'rank' (in heat) ewes who 'turned to the rams' (I.iii.81). It is Antonio's 'ventures' (i.42; VENTURE, whore) that were not in one 'bottom' trusted, that proved to be like what he had called Jacob's 'venture' (iii.92) with sheep. The overlapping of sexual gratification and monetary success is repeated when Portia turns to Lorenzo, who is obviously despondent, with 'How now, Lorenzo! My clerk hath some good comforts too for you' (V.i.288). Some comforts (sexual pleasures – P), some GOOD comforts (see *WT*) or screwing (of Shylock) for him *too*, as there had been for Antonio's ships/sheep (and for Antonio himself, in court? – see CACKLE); and Lorenzo is handed the deed entitling him to 'all he [Shylock] dies possess'd of'. These puns (see SUCH) provide important insights into all these dubious love-affairs.

LLL, II.i.220:

Boyet. I was as willing to grapple as he [Biron] was to board.
Maria. Two hot sheeps, marry.
Boyet. And wherefore not ships?

Maria chooses to hear the two nautical terms GRAPPLE and BOARD as puns on the coital mounting or boarding of two knaves, two SHIPS (L *naves*); and compares the men to two hot sheeps, in sexual heat or oestrus. Boyet asks why she changed his metaphor, since ships, too, MARRY, i.e. Fr *marer*, moor, get tied or fastened.

TGV, I.i.108. See STICK (fuck) for puns on sheep or 'lost mutton' (whores – C; P).

See UNSTANCHED, *Tem*; INDEED, *TGV*; WHISTLE, *WT*; ANCIENT, *Oth*; SCARLET, *1H6*; YARE, *AC*.

Shin Penis (like CHIN).

Tim, IV.iii.152. Timon tells whores to 'burn' men (infect them venereally – F&H; P); 'quell/ The source of all erection. . . . And ditches grave you all!' – quell (obs. for 'kill') the source of erection, bring men to impotence and death: may they who lived in DITCHes (whores' vulvas) die in ditches. The familiar list of venereal symptoms (plague, baldness, nose eaten away) includes 'strike their sharp shins,/ And mar men's spurring'. Timon is not interested in horsemanship (except as it, too, is a metaphor for intercourse); he wants men's SPUR (lit. a prick) or penis marred; he wants the whores to strike (copulate – C; P) the *sharp* shins and render them diseased and impotent.

Tem, IV.i.181. Ariel puns on 'chins' (CHIN, q.v.), 'shins' and the prick (penis – *OED*): 'they prick'd their ears' and 'pricking goss and thorns . . . enter'd their frail shins'. 'Shins' could mean shank-bones, but FRAIL (lewd, unchaste) indicates that these morally weak, lecherous men are being pricked in the shins that deserve it.

See MATTER, *LLL*.

Ship A knave; a whore. L *navis*: ship; *navire*: ship (Cot); navire: ship (*OED*, rare). Sh freq. puns on knave and ship: 'O royal knavery!' (*Ham*, V.ii.19); 'let in the tide/ Of knaves' (*Tim*, III.iv.119); 'knaves . . . Harbour more craft' (*KL*, II.ii.107). See SHEEP/SHIP.

Ship-boy A castrate; perh. a buggered lad. *Mozzo di nave*: ship-boy; *mozzo*: cut off, curtailed, a boy, a woman's quaint (cunt), a bawd (F). *Mousse* has the same overlap and means a ship-boy, blunt, edgeless, pointless (Cot) – words connoting impotence.

KJ, IV.iii.4. Arthur's fate as described by him and others evokes castration (and perh. buggery). The historical belief that Arthur was castrated, in the tradition of thus ensuring the end of a line of rival heirs for the throne (Saccio, p. 193) is incorporated in Sh's puns. (See TENDER, *R3*, for castration of two other imprisoned princes.) For buggery of prisoners, cf. the King's death in Marlowe, *Edward II*.

The young Arthur's appearance in 'ship-boy's semblance' must raise a question: these are hardly the clothes he wore on his return from France, and would this royal child *ever* have been dressed like a ship-boy; how, in prison, did he procure such garb? Perhaps when he leaps to his death saying, 'my uncle's spirit is in these stones', he is speaking not only of the stones on the ground but the stone (lustful, lascivious – *OED*), the stones or testicles and SPIRIT (passion; semen) that buggered him of his life; and is linking his condition to his treatment at the hands of the gaolers and the ultimate responsibility of his uncle. And the Bastard means his castrated state when he says, 'They found him dead and cast into the streets,/ An empty casket, where the jewel of life/ By some damn'd hand was robb'd and ta'en away' (v.i.39). He was *cast* into the streets, a *cast*rate, like an empty *cas*ket (or Fr *casse*, pun on 'case' and *cas*, genitals – C; P; K; Cot) from which the JEWELS (precious stones or testicles), his jewel of life, had been removed. This is what Arthur intended when he said the 'ship-boy's semblance hath disguised me quite [QUITE/ for *coit*us]'.

In the previous scene, ll.185–end, in falsely reporting the death of Arthur, whom affection had kept him from killing, Hubert said the people were against it 'And when they talk of him, they shake their heads [emasculation symbol: see SHAKE]. . . . [One stood] With open mouth swallowing a *tail*or's news . . . . Another . . . *Cuts off his tale* and talks of Arthur's death' (italics added; tail/ tale: penis – C; P; K).

John regrets Hubert let his 'hand to act/ The deed, which both our tongues held vile to name', i.e. the NAMELESS (sodomitical) *act* and *deed*, both meaning coitus (C; P). Upon hearing this welcome news, that John regrets Arthur's castration and/ or murder, Hubert says, 'This hand of mine/ Is yet a *maiden and* an *innocent* hand' and not the 'butcher [BUTCHER/ bugger] of an innocent child' (italics added).

But it is too late: Arthur has leapt from the walls, and (iii.42) those who saw or 'read' or 'heard' or 'think' about the 'wildest savagery' that ever 'wall-eyed' wrath presented call it murder 'so sole and so unmatchable . . . this heinous spectacle'. It is a 'graceless action'.

Again the intimations of something more than murder: 'The wall is high', Arthur said before he leaped: *wall – high* and a *wall-eyed* crime ('any work irregularly or ill-done' – J. C. Halliwell, *A Dictionary of Archaic and Provincial Words*); murder so SOLE (the buttocks) and so *unmatchable* – no two such, suggesting no TWO (testicles); a *graceless* action, without GRACE (genitals). And Hubert, believed the culprit, is a 'dunghill' (87), 'hateful' (77; HATEFUL, Fr *haineux*) and 'heinous' (ii.71; HEINOUS/ anus) – all anal insults. See SHAKE and OPPRESS for Constance's anticipation of the event.

Shore Whore; female pudendum. Lit. a sewer. Dekker and Middleton, *The Honest Whore I*, II.ii: 'Your body/ Its like the common shore, that still receives/ All the townes filth. The sin of many men/ Is with you.' Nashe, *Pierce Pennilesse*, in *Works*, vol. I, p. 216: 'Lecherie . . . examine how every second house in Shoreditch is maintayned'. Shoreditch Fury: a harlot (F&H).

MWW, I.iii.89. Falstaff sends Robin with letters to the merry wives, who he thinks are sexually available and will open up their husbands' purses in reward for his services! 'Sail like my pinnace to these golden shores'. A ship sails off to bring back gold, and his pimp, also a pinnace ('punk, pinnace, bawd' – Jonson, *Bartholomew Fair*, I.i), sails off to the two golden shores or whores from whom Falstaff will get their husbands' gold. See GOLD; AWAY.

R3, II.i.73, Clarence: 'By heaven, I think there's no man is secure/ But the queen's kindred and night-walking heralds/ That trudge betwixt the king and Mistress Shore' – only her relatives and those who arrange the assignations between the King and Mistress Shore, his *Mistress–whore*, are safe from the tower. TRUDGE: bawd.

III.iv.72: 'that harlot strumpet Shore'.

See ADVENTURE, *RJ*; THRONG, *R3*.

Short Refers to length of penis and duration of coitus (C; P): see GRAPPLE, Montaigne. *Scortare*: shorten (F); L *scortari*: associate with harlots. Jonson, 'Fragmentum Petron. Arbitr.

The Same Translated': 'Doing, a filthy pleasure is, and short; / And done, we straight repent us of the sport [copulation]' (F&H, s.v. Sport). Cf. the 'momentary trick' (*MM*, III.i.113).

RJ, I.i.170:

Benvolio. . . . What sadness lengthens Romeo's hours?
Romeo. Not having that, which, having, makes them short.
Benvolio. In love?
Romeo. Out –

Romeo is 'out of her favour'; he does not have that which shortens (*scortare*) hours, sexual intercourse or *scortari*. *Lengthens* insinuates that not only time would be made short were he to be *in* and not *Out* of her favour [the private parts – P]' (italics added). (*KL*, I.v.66: 'She that's a maid now . . . Shall not be a maid long, unless things be cut shorter.')

II.vi.35, Friar: 'Come, come with me, and we will make short work; / For . . . you shall not stay alone / Till holy church incorporate two in one.' *Come, come* (the sexual emission – P) indicates the short work (the sexual activity – TWR, s.v. Werke; P) and the incorporating of two individuals into one body that the Friar fears will take place before *he* makes short work and incorporates them with an immediate betrothal.

Cym, II.iv.44. Iachimo reports his alleged seduction: 'I'll make a journey twice as far, to enjoy / A second night of such sweet shortness'.

AC, II.v.8. Cleopatra consoles her eunuch, 'when good-will is show'd, though't come too short, / The actor may plead pardon'. Partridge calls this a short penis; but the eunuch has a *good* will (penis – C; P); his problem is that it comes too short, i.e. minus the TWO testicles, characteristic of the eunuch. Fr *leger de deux grains*: lit. light by two grains; a eunuch (F&H, s.v. Cods, n.d.). See HORSE, *Ado*, for the same pun.

Show(n) Manifest hermaphroditism, homosexuality, or something unnatural. *Monstre*: (1) show; (2) a monster, deformed creature, a thing fashioned contrary to nature (Cot).

Mac, I..iii.54, Banquo to the *Witches*: 'Are ye fantastical, or that indeed / *Which* outwardly ye show?' (italics added) – these women with beards.

IV.i.107:

1st Witch. Show!
2nd Witch. Show!
3rd Witch. Show!

V.viii.24: 'live to be the show and gaze o' the time . . . as our rarer monsters are', says Macduff to Macbeth. See HEDGEHOG for the 'unnatural deeds' done by Macbeth, one of the RARER / rear monsters.

AC, IV.xii.36, Antony: 'like the greatest spot / Of all thy sex; most monster-like be shown'. This to Cleopatra, whom he had just called a 'Triple-turn'd whore' and a 'witch' (WITCH, bisexual bawd) who (he said twice) 'sold' him to Caesar. To spot, to haunt whore-houses: *chiassare* (F). For the androgyny of these lovers, see Index.

MWW, III.ii.82. Master Ford invites friends to his home: 'besides your cheer, you shall have sport; I will show you a monster'. Shallow and Slender go another way: 'we shall have the freer wooing at Master Page's'. They hear *sport* as copulation (F&H; P) and, almost certainly, as *spot* (whore-house sport, which is *not* free: see *AC* above). The likelihood the 'r' is silent (K, p. 316), thus explaining their otherwise strange answer, is increased by their preferring the cheer (viands, food – *OED*) at Master Page's over the *food* at *Ford*'s. Food / Ford (K): 'my belly full of Ford' (v. 36); 'must have food' – 'Which of you know Ford . . .?' (I.iii.38). See ALTER and SHARE for the kind of sexual sport 'monster' evokes for these three: Ford, Shallow, an aging pederast, in *2H4*; and Slender, an effeminate.

Oth, III.iii.108. Othello says Iago acts 'As if there were some monster in his thoughts / Too hideous to be shown'. And so there is, the hermaphroditic 'green-eyed monster' (see MONSTER) that will make Othello a beast: 'A horned man's a monster and a beast' (IV.i.63).

See ORATOR, *2H6*.

Sick (1) Confined to child bed; parturient (*OED* 1828). Of fish in the spawning-stage (*OED* 1728).

(2) Effeminate. ILL: effeminate (*male*: ill – F; L *male mas*: effeminate, unmanly man).

TrC, III.iii.238. Patroclus (Achilles' lover) blames himself and his '*little stomach* to the war' that Achilles has become 'an effeminate man/ In time of action' (italics added). Achilles: 'Go call Thersites hither . . . invite the Trojan lords after the combat/ To see us here unarm'd: I have a woman's longing,/ An appetite that I am sick withal . . . . (*Enter Thersites*.) A labour saved!' Jonson, *Bartholomew Fair*, IV.i: pregnant women have a 'naturall disease of women; call'd/ A longing to eate Pigge' – 'Verily, the disease of longing . . . a carnall disease, or appetite, incident to women . . . naturall'. See DAINTY for Achilles' appetite for pig. With the arrival of Thersites, Achilles' labour (delivery; cf *Oth*, II.i.128) and that of Patroclus, messenger (and father) is saved.

Achilles and Patroclus will be un-ARM'd – militarily and sexually. In the Royal Shakespeare Company production, London 1981, Achilles, in a skirt, seductively led Hector to his tent, to satisfy another longing he is sick withal (a corrupt appetite: see TABLE).

LLL, V.ii.417. Biron is proved 'a fool, and full of poverty': (1) 'poverty in wit' (269); (2) POVERTY or state of being POOR (/L *puer*, a boy), not manly – in the King's womanless 'Academe' (I.i.13), a parody of Plato's Academy (where homosexual love was extolled over heterosexuality: see HEAVEN; ROUND; PERFECTION). Biron: 'these summer-flies/ Have blown me full of maggot ostentation' (fly-blow: the depositing of eggs in meat by flies; to blow (up): to inject semen into – P). He renounces his maggots (fly larvae, caprices), 'so God help me, la!', but his language smacks of his still being a *fool* and *full* of hot air (see LOVE for Rosaline's next line, a pun on his flatus) and of effeminacy (*la*!). He asks Rosaline to 'bear with me, I am sick'. She is to bear, as in pregnancy, with him who is impregnated with ostentation, 'full' of 'abstinence [that] engenders maladies [male ladies]' (IV.iii.295). See *TGV*, II.i.32–43: 'malady'/ 'my lady'/ 'metamorphosed' male lady; PROGRESS, where Biron's love letter 'miscarried'.

See WORD, *Tim*; BREAST, *2H6*; TAFFETA.

Side Female seat of generation. Loin, buttocks (TWR, s.v. Syde); womb (Milton).

AC, II.ii.130. To achieve peace, Antony marries Octavia, Caesar's 'sister by the mother's side'. But she cannot keep him away from 'each side' of Cleopatra (206) or from his death 'o' the other side' of Cleopatra's monument (IV.xv.8).

See SHARE, *MND*; ANSWER, Son 50; COMPUNCTIOUS; WEST, *MM*.

Siege Lit. excrement; a privy, rectum, anus. Jonson, *Sejanus*, I.i.315: 'Why, sir, I do not ask you of their urines,/ Whose smells most violet? Or whose siege is best?/ Or who makes the hardest faces on her stool?'

Tem, II.ii.111: 'How camest thou to be the siege of this moon-calf? Can he vent [the anus; discharge] Trinculos?'

MM, IV.ii.101. Angelo cannot 'countermand' Claudio's execution, for he had 'upon the very siege of justice . . . Profess'd the contrary'. He made the seat of JUSTICE (Fr *voirie*) a VERY (It *assai*) privy where he pro-fess'd (Fr *fesse*, buttocks) the *con*trary, *pro*- (stood for) FACES/ faeces. Angelo had shit on JUSTICE (q.v.), a whore, sewer, says Sh through the Provost. His attempted sexual violation of Isabella echoes in CONTRARY and *coun*termand (coun, count; cunt – P; K).

See RAISE; MELANCHOLY, *LLL*; STERN, *H5*; ANY, *MWW*; ASSAIL, *RJ*.

Silk(en) Of whores, effeminates, disease. Middleton, *Michaelmas Term*, I.ii: 'welcome silks, where lie disease'. Silky: 1599, effeminate. Lyly, *Endymion*, I.iii: 'silks, milksops'. Shirley, *The Lady of Pleasure*, III.ii: two 'poor silken vermin' have 'the shapes [SHAPE, genitals – *OED*] of gentlemen' but couldn't 'charm a woman' even of eighty. Silkworms were believed to engender backward, tail to tail (see GIDDY, bisexual). Sarcenet: a fine soft silk used for linings, incl. codpieces; Sp *sarassa*: effeminate man; cf. 'as rancke bougers [buggers] with mankind, and with beasts, as the Saracens are' (*OED* 1555). See SHADOW, Tyndale.

TrC, II.ii.69. They ought not return the slut, Helen: 'We turn not back the silks upon the merchant,/ When we have soil'd them'.

KJ, v.i.70: 'a beardless boy,/ A cocker'd silken wanton' (an example of 'silken' as effeminate, luxurious in *OED*). This BOY (catamite) is Lewis, who leads an army of SWINE (buggers). Dekker, *The Shoemaker's Holiday*, III.v: don't marry 'a boy that has no more hair on his face than thou . . . those silken fellows are but painted images, outsides, outsides, Rose; their inner linings are torn'; marry a 'grocer', who has 'plums, plums' (PLUMS: testes – P).

2H6, IV.ii.136. Cade calls the *two* Stafford brothers (who enter and exit together) 'silken-coated slaves': SLAVES (eunuchs) with silken, effeminate COATS/ cods (K). See OATS, *Cor* and *JC*, for other silken scrota, effeminate, diseased.

174: 'Lord Say hath gelded the commonwealth, and made it an eunuch'. Lord *Say* (a silk cloth) took all power from the COMMONWEALTH, made it a society of eunuchoid whores like himself (BUCKRAM).

RJ, II.iv.24. Mercutio calls Tybalt a lisping effeminate, a 'very butcher of a silk button' – 'The pox of such antic, lisping, affecting fantasticoes . . . a very good blade! . . . a very good whore!' – whose real aim is to BUTCHER (bugger) the silk BUTTON on his opponent's breeches.

See EPHESIAN, *CE*; PEACH, *2H4*; COPATAIN HAT.

Singe Effeminise a male. Trad., women removed unwanted (and pubic) hair by singeing. Cf. Aristophanes, *The Clouds*, 1083, for punitive depilation of male adulterers by a hot coal.

CE, v.i.171. In Ephesus, the mistreated Antipholus S. and his servant break loose and bind the 'doctor', whose 'beard they have singed off with brands of fire;/ And . . . they threw on him/ Great pails of puddled mire to quench the hair:/ My master preaches patience to him . . . while/ His man with scissors nicks him like a fool . . . they will kill the conjurer'. (In Aristophanes' *Thesmophoriazusae*, 235–45, the singed Mnesilochus is 'afire' and screams for 'Water' to protect his 'tool'.) As they singe the doctor's beard (pubic hair – F&H; P), they throw *puddled* mire (urine – P; cf. *AC*, I.iv.62: 'The stale of horses, and the gilded puddle') on him to quench the (pubic) hair (P). Quench: abate love (P); it and its preterite 'queynte' (TWR) pun on *cunt*. They preach PATIENCE to him: (1) he doctors patients (294); (2) he is to be PATIENT, one to whom something is done (patiens, passive homosexual). The scissors nick him like a fool in the femininising process (nick: a fool; vulva – F&H; C; K). They will kill the CONJURER (fornicator: by cutting off his CONGER, eel, penis). They will do to Dr PINCH what his name means: castrate (verb); penis (noun).

183. Antipholus will singe Pinch, who he believes cuckolded him (SAFFRON) and his own wife: he plans 'To scorch your face and to disfigure you'. He will scorch, singe, the FACE/ *fesso* (woman's quaint or water-box – F), of her he called adulterous 'harlot' (IV.iv.104).

MV, II.ix.79. Having chosen the wrong casket, the Prince may never 'woo a maid in way of marriage'; he is, fig., emasculated. 'With one fool's head I came to woo,/ But I go away with two' – his second HEAD (prepuce, testicles) is also now like a fool's, *nicked* (see *CE* above).

Portia: 'Thus hath the candle singed the moth' – he is singed, effeminised. *Moth* (pron. 'mote' – K) puns on his *motte* (pubes – Cot): they made a *mot* (wench – F&H; G) of him. Nerissa extends the conceit: 'The ancient saying is no heresy' – the saying (Fr *mot*) is no heresy, historically punished by burning. (See WORD for puns on *mot*.)

Siren A loose woman, like the bawd, a 'notable Siren', in Chapman's *All Fools*, IV.i, and the adulterous wife in *The Widow's Tears*, II.ii: 'Sing to me no more, siren, for I will hear thee no more'. See DEVIL, Jonson.

See MERMAID.

Sister(hood) Sisters of the bank: 1550, prostitutes. Dekker and Webster, *Westward Hoe*,

III.ii: 'The serving-man has his punk, the student his nun . . . the Puritan his sister'. Massinger, *The Guardian*, IV.iii: 'An hospital only for noseless bawds . . . myself the governess of the sisterhood'.

TrC, V.x.52: 'Brethren and sisters of the hold-door trade [prostitution – C; P]'.

MM, I.iv.5, Isabella: 'a more strict restraint/ Upon the sisterhood'. Hearing someone call, Francisca says, 'It is a man's voice. Gentle Isabella,/ Turn you the key, and know his business of him'. We assume the nunnery (1513, brothel) is not a brothel and that the puns in 'sisterhood', 'Turn you the key' (i.e. It *chiavare*, also to fuck: see KEY) and BUSINESS (fornication) indicate the business Lucio came about, Claudio's adultery; and that they foreshadow Angelo's attempted seduction of Isabella. The man's voice is Lucio's, a VOICE/ VICE pun on this libertine who ends marrying his own 'whore'.

AYL, IV.iii.88. Orlando describes Ganymede: 'The boy is fair,/ Of female favour, and bestows himself/ Like a ripe sister'. A RIPE (wanton) sister of the bank (the ripe or Bank in Southwark, home of brothels), a homosexual whore bestowing favours (sexual – P), is how he sees Ganymede's provocative conduct in their love-games. BESTOW: sexual bestiality.

R2, II.ii.105. In addressing the Queen, York makes an error that reflects his feelings on the illegitimacy of the King and Hereford: 'How shall we do for money for these wars? / Come, sister – cousin, I would say, – pray, pardon me. / Go, fellow, get thee home, provide some carts'. WARS, punning on *whores* and like them requiring money, triggers York's slip of the tongue, his misnaming the Queen 'sister' – for which he begs pardon and uses 'pray' as if speaking this time to a pure sister of a religious order. But substituting 'cousin' reflects the same doubts, since cousin/ cozen is deceive (K). He associates sister with PROVIDE (pander) and *cart*, in which whores were removed from brothels (*OED*; C).

See ACCESS, *MM*.

Sixpence, sixpenny A whore or pander's fee. Barber's price for VD treatment. Dekker, *The Honest Whore, II*, V.ii: Bots is a 'Pander – a Dog that will licke up sixe pence'; the whore is 'a sixe-penny Mutton Pasty, for any to cut up'. Dekker and Webster, *Westward Hoe*, V.iv: 'go saile with the rest of your baudie-traffikers to the place of sixe-penny Sinfulnesse the suburbes'. See TESTER (sixpence).

TN, II.iii.26: 'I sent thee sixpence for thy leman [paramour]: hadst it?'

MND, IV.ii.20. Flute reprimands Quince for calling Bottom a 'paramour': 'O sweet bully Bottom! Thus hath he lost sixpence a day during his life; he could not have 'scaped sixpence a day; an the duke had not given him sixpence a day for playing Pyramus, I'll be hanged; he would have deserved it: sixpence a day in Pyramus, or nothing.'

Repeated four times, 'sixpence' is obviously intended for humour. *Bottom* could not have 'SCAPED or farted a sixpence (*pet*: 'A fart; scape' – Cot) but *bully* Bottom could have earned it as Pyramus, the lover. A *bully* is a lover; also in a bad sense (*OED*). Cf. Etherege, *The Man of Mode*, I.i: 'These young women apprehend loving . . . as the young men do fighting at first, but once entered, like them too, they all turn bullies straight', says Dorimant of a 'baggage'. Hence, bully Bottom, paramour, like a bully-back (pimp or bawdy-house ruffian – F&H 1626; G) could have earned sixpence a day in Pyramus, or Flute says *he* will be hanged (HANG, Fr *pendre*/ pander).

2H4, I.ii.26. Falstaff mocks Hal for lacking that symbol of virility, hair on the CHEEK (buttocks): 'a barber shall never earn sixpence out of' it: (1) a BARBER or It *barbiera*, she-barber and strumpet; (2) any BARBER, since it was barbers who treated venereal infections (Jonson, *The Silent Woman*, III.v: 'barbers cure botches and burnes'; carted bawds employ the barber's 'bason').

II.ii.102. After jests on brothels and maidenheads (RED LATTICE), Poins says the young Page should 'be kept from cankers [syphilitic chancres]' and gives him 'sixpence to preserve thee' – the barber's fee for the VD cure, the salt tubs to preserve, to salt or cure, him.

Size Penis. *Taille*: size (Cot). Tail (*OED*; P) and tale (C; P): arse, pudendum, penis.

AW, II.ii.35. The Countess puts her Clown 'to the *height* of your *breeding*' (italics added;

taille: 'stature of man, or beast' – Cot). He then jests on the 'manners' (MANNER, coitus) of 'man': 'for me, I have an answer will serve all men'. He has an ANSWER (penis; coital thrust – lit. return thrust in fencing) that will serve (coitally – C; P) all men and 'fits all buttocks'. The Countess concludes it 'must be an answer of most monstrous size' if it fits 'all demands'. His size (*taille*) or penis is monstrous, not merely in size, but also in that, if it fits *all* buttocks and serves *all* men (all manner of MAN, L *homo*), it is that of a MONSTER (bisexual).

H8, v.i.135. Henry tells Cranmer the forces against him are potent: 'Your enemies are . . . not small; their practices/ Must bear the same proportion . . . . You are potently opposed; and with a malice/ Of as great a size.' His enemies are great, of large PROPORTION (penis) and size (*taille*: 'proportion, size, stature of man, or beast' – Cot) and they have MALICE (testicles) also large and potent – symbols of political power.

See SCANTY, *KL*; DILDO, *WT*.

Skill The arse. L *ars*: skill, art.

LLL, v.ii.396: 'Here stand I: lady, dart thy skill at me . . . Cut me to pieces with thy keen conceit'. Biron is her target in archery (a butt on which the prick is set – *OED*); there he stands (an erect prick – P; F&H), ready for the love-DART (q.v.) of Rosaline's skill or arse. There may be a quibble on her skill, L *ars*, at d*arts* (ART, *ars*). Cf. Son 139: slay me not 'by art' or 'with cunning' (CUNNING, *ars* – Vergil) but 'dart' your injuries elsewhere.

Biron is her butt: (1) buttocks; (2) ass or object of ridicule. And she does just as he asks (as do all the ladies, with their *con*ceits, their cunts and wits, to all the lords and their PIECES, genitals). *Cut me to pieces* or cut my two pieces: she makes him a CUT or gelding (*OED*). The men *are* horses: see RUSSIAN. Rosaline renders Biron impotent in the love-game of darts. See REST for the year of chastity imposed on the lords.

See COMPASS, *TGV*; TRUE, *MND*; DOVE, *Per*.

Skin 1. Scrotum ('perhaps a transposed form' of L *scortum*, skin – *CD*). *Scroto*: 'outward skin of the cods wherein are the stones of a man' (F). *Codica*: a man's skin (F).

1H4, III.iii.5, Falstaff: 'do I not dwindle? why, my skin hangs about me like an old lady's loose gown: I am withered like an old apple-john'. Falstaff, whom Bardolph calls 'Sir John', compares an old lady's loose GOWN (cunt – K; P) to his loose, WITHERED (like a wether or castrate) cods, which are like apple-johns (apples that are ripe when withered), his Sir John's APPLES (testicles). Cf. *vizzo*: 'wrinkled . . . soft, flappie, or saplesse as old womens dugs be' (F).

2. Prostitute. L *scortum*: skin, prostitute.

3H6, III.i.22. The First Keeper recognises the disguised King: 'Ay, here's a deer whose skin's a keeper's fee.' For a fee (reward and sexual satisfaction (C; P)) this KEEPER (pimp – F & H) will betray and sell the King as if he is a deer's skin or his whore.

See SHAME, *KJ*; PUDDING, *AW*.

Slave Boy kept for sodomy, a bardash (from Arabic *bardaj*, captive, slave; *bardache*, *bardascia*: a buggering boy – Cot; F). Athenian brothels were served by slaves hired out by their masters or kept by brothel-owners. 'Flesh-monger' meant both slave-dealer and pimp (Cham). Doul (from Gk *doulos*, slave): a very young gay boy (Rodgers). Plautus, *Pseudolus*, III.i: wanting a few comforts, the 'young Slave' or the 'Boy' of a pimp rues he 'can't find any *galant* [or "any admirer"] to love me'. IV.vii: Ballio, the pimp, insults the 'slave of the soldier': 'At night, when you and the soldier stood watch together, did his sabre fit your sheath?'

TGV, III.i.393. Launce tells Speed to run to his 'master', for 'thou hast stayed so long that going will scarce *serve the turn* [copular service – C; P; 'serve' and 'turn both mean to coit]' (italics added). Launce: 'Now will he be swinged. . . . an unmannerly slave, that will thrust himself into secrets! I'll after, to rejoice in the boy's correction.'

Speed will be SWINGED (thrashed and fucked – F & H) for being UNMANNERLY (unmanly), forgetting his place: a slave ought not *thrust* himself into secrets (genitals – C; P); on the contrary, he is the recipient of thrusting. Launce will *after* (behind) to rejoice in the BOY's (catamite's) correction (arch., flogging), his being swinged or buggered.

Cor, v.vi.104: 'Measureless liar . . . Boy! O, slave!' You dare to call me BOY (bardash), he tells Aufidius – you, a LIAR, a bugiard (*bugiare*, to lie – F)/a buggered! without measure (penis – P): a slave! Bugger him, Coriolanus tells onlookers: 'give this cur the lie . . . *thrust* the lie unto him' (italics added). *Boy*! *O*, slave, punning on *boyau-* (bowel – Cot) slave (see BOY, *LLL*). I.viii.5:

Aufidius. . . . Fix thy foot.
Marcius (Coriolanus). Let the first budger die the other's slave . . . .

Thus Act I starts what Act V finishes. The language of sexual submissiveness becomes the metaphor for cowardice (BUGGER): FIX and FOOT (*ficher* and *foutre*: two common words for fuck – C; P; TWR, p. 23). The BUDGER (Sh's only use of this word) or *bugger* will be the slave of the OTHER (arse) – will die (experience orgasm – TWR; P) a slave.

TrC, II.i.52. Given the vile title of 'Mistress Thersites', Thersites retaliates that Ajax is an 'ass' whom an 'assinego' could 'tutor' (TUTOR, older male in a pederastic relationship); a thing 'bought and sold . . . like a barbarian [BARBARIAN, dirty arse] slave'.

MV, IV.i.90, Shylock: 'You have among you many a purchased slave,/Which, like your asses and your dogs and mules,/You use in abject and in slavish parts,/Because you bought them'.

Why is this salient fact not glossed? Shylock parallels their purchased slaves, their flesh, with that 'pound of flesh' he bought. They use (common word for sexual exploitation – F&H; P) these slaves in abject (cast down, low-lying) PARTS (the genitals – *OED*; F&H). They were bought and are used like asses (in both senses), like DOGS (sodomites) and MULES (castrates). Shylock wants a *pound* of flesh, Antonio's pestle. 'Pestle': pound, beat (*OED*); penis (F&H); pounder, 'mans toole' (F, s.v. *Pestello*). Pound: fuck (see Boccaccio quote). If he does not get the pounders (testes – F&H) nearest Antonio's HEART (arse), then (101) 'fie upon your law!' He wants the Mosaic law, the *two* tables of *stone* (testes – *OED*). Antonio's immediate response is to call himself a 'wether'. They cannot 'rail the seal [SEAL, genitals] from off my bond', says Shylock: 'I stand here for law.' He will 'cut the forfeiture', CUT (1475, castrate) the *forfeiter*: Antonio is his purchased slave or cut (gelding – *OED*). (See DEAR.)

Cym, IV.ii.73. To Cloten's 'Soft! What are you . . . ? . . . What slave art thou!' Guiderius answers, 'A thing/More slavish did I ne'er than answering/A slave without a knock.' To Cloten, Queen's son, the other is a barbarian slave, with soft phallus. To Guiderius, Cloten is the slave, the eunuch without a knock (penis – F&H); and he, Guiderius, is slavish only in that he answers verbally instead of with a physical knock; gives ANSWER (return hit in fencing; coital thrust) to this castrated slave.

Sleep, slumber (1) Cohabit in sexual intimacy (TWR, s.v. Slepynge); lie with, have intercourse with (P).

(2) Castrate; be rendered impotent or effeminate. Lit. be dormant, inoperative. Lib: sleep, castrate (*OED*; F&H).

TrC, I.iii.327, Nestor: 'But that Achilles, were his brain as barren/As banks of Libya . . . will . . . find Hector's purpose/Pointing on him.' 'And wake him to the answer, think you?' asks Ulysses. Though Achilles' BRAIN (testes) were as barren as LIBYAN (L *Libys*, Libyan: pun on *libs*) BANKS (buttocks), Nestor says he can be roused to fight. He can be wakened from inaction, from his sleep of impotence, by Hector's PURPOSE (penis) pointing (in erection – C; P) on him. The potent Hector will wake him to an ANSWER (coital thrust), to a combat. But in II.iii.147 he is still a 'sleeping giant' and Agamemnon says (276), 'Let Achilles sleep' (and 'with him Patroclus/Upon a lazy bed' – I.iii.147; Patroclus, his male lover, who recognises that Achilles is 'loathed' for being 'an effeminate man/In time of action' – III.iii.218).

1H6, V.iii.41. Pucelle's soliloquy sets the stage for her castration threat: she calls on 'spirits, that are cull'd [culls: testes – F&H]', offering to 'lop a member ["='privy member'" – *OED*] off' if they help her. When the entering York calls her 'witch' and 'hag' (WITCH or HAG: hermaphrodite, castrater), Pucelle (whose name means whore) responds, 'A plaguing mischief light on Charles and thee!/And may ye both be suddenly surprised/By bloody hands, in sleeping on your beds!' She evokes the same plaguing mischief – impotence, castration, sterility – that Timon does (*Tim*, IV.iii.163) when he tells two whores to 'plague all . . . quell/The source of all erection', make men impotent; and, when they ask for money, says, 'more mischief first'.

This is no threat of death but the usual WITCH's mischief, to *light on* the victim and to *lighten* him – of his genitals (Fr *leger de deux grains*, light by two grains – F&H, s.v. Cods, n.d.). Lying on their beds, they will be SUDDENLY (lustfully) surprised, will be castrated or libbed while sleeping or libbing, and so, be surprised by bloody HANDS (the 'phallic symbol' – K), by their own bloody, castrated phalluses.

See TAME, *TrC*; DETESTED, *TA*; ANGEL, *R3*; HOMAGE, *2H6*.

Slip 1. Dung. Cowslip: OE *cú-slyppe*, cow-dung.

MND, v.i.340. Thisbe describes the dead Pyramus, played by *Bottom*: 'These yellow cowslip cheeks' – his CHEEKS (buttocks) are YELLOW (excrement colour). Cf. *LLL*, v.ii.906: 'cuckoo-buds of yellow hue / Do paint the meadows with delight'. The cuckoo-bud (cowslip – *OED*) is of the YELLOW hue (COLOUR/It *culare*, arse-gut) of excrement. Like slip (from *OE slypa*, slime), a creamy paste for coating and decorating pottery, it paints the meadow with delight (*aise* – Cot), as if the MEADOW is an *aisance* or privy, covered with cuckoo-buds or cowslip (i.e. cow-dung).

II.i.53: 'The wisest aunt . . . for three-foot stool mistaketh me;/Then slip I from her bum, down topples she'. Puck, mistaken for the stool (commode, chamber-pot), slips out from under her bum; and her stool (excrement) slips (*slyppe*, dung) from her bum as she *topp*les *down* in fright.

See MEADOW, *H5*; SLOP, *RJ*.

2. Slip meant (1) a counterfeit coin; (2) miscarry, abort, drop prematurely.

RJ, II.iv.50:

Mercutio. . . . You gave us the counterfeit fairly last night.
Romeo. . . . What counterfeit did I give you?
Mercutio. The slip, sir, the slip; can you not conceive?

Romeo gave them the slip, fairly (a *fere* is a mate, companionship). He slipped from their companionship to be, instead, with a mate. He gave them the slip, their plans *miscarried* – can't Romeo *conceive*, asks Mercutio.

Unfortunately, he can't: (1) Prol.: 'the *fatal loins* of these two foes'; (2) Friar: 'if aught in this/*Miscarried* by my fault, let my old *life* / *Be sacrificed, some hour before his time*' (v.iii.267; italics added) – almost a literal translation of the miscarriage of Romeo's love and life ('we shall come too late' – 'I fear, too early': I.iv.106).

Slippery Of a third sex; bisexual. George Chapman, *All Fools*, II.i: a gallant wrote verse 'In any rhyme, masculine, feminine,/Or sdrucciola, or complete blank verse'. Masculine; feminine; or a third gender, sdrucciola (It, slippery); or a blank verse (Gk *stichos*), a blank stich (pron. stik). Cf. Ger *Stich*, a prick, a thrust; and stichel, a term of contempt: 'Barren stichel! that shall not serve thy turn' (F&H, c. 1620).

See EXERCISE, *Cor*; TRUNK, *Tim*.

Slop(s) Liquid refuse; a mud-hole; full, baggy breeches. Under-slop: a child's diaper (Cot, s.v. *braye*). It was common to associate both the under-breeches and full, baggy breeches with excrement: Peele, *The Old Wives' Tale*, 45: 'why we make faces for fear; such as if thy mortal eyes could behold would make thee water the long seams of thy side slops'.

RJ, II.iv.48, Mercutio: 'there's a French salutation to your French slop'; 'The slip, sir, the slip'. See SLIP – like slop, a soft semi-liquid mass. Both words, connoting defecation, are prelude to the scatological jests that follow (COURTESY).

See GERMAN, *Ado*.

Slumber See SLEEP.

Smile 1. To smile: Fr *rire*, pun on the *rear* or arse and *rear* or rise (coitally). See LAUGH. See SMOOTH, *Tim*; VARY, *AC*.

2. Prob. puns on smell (ME 'smellan', 'smyllen'; 'smel', 'smil'). A 'smelt' or 'smilt' is an olive-green fish that emits a peculiar odour; also a simpleton or gull. Cf. Dekker and Webster, *Westward Hoe*, IV.iii: 'plain-dealing women can pull downe men: Moll, you'le helpe us to catch Smelts, too?' See YELLOW, *TN*: Olivia (olive-green?) and Malvolio, the smiling gull.

Cor, I.i.111–50. Menenius tells the rebellious citizens a story of a rebellion of all the 'body's members' against the 'belly' and 'The belly answer'd –'

1st Citizen. Well, sir, what answer made the belly?
Menenius. Sir, I shall tell you. With a kind of smile,
Which ne'er came from the lungs, but even thus –
For, look you, I may make the belly smile
As well as speak – it tauntingly replied. . . .

A belly that speaks, growls. But belly is 'bowels ME' (*OED*), and this organ, which the Citizen calls 'sink/O' the body' – a sink being a sewer – makes a noise that Menenius can '*As* well' make (italics added), i.e. a flatus with its smile/smell, *taunting reply*. Despite his claim, Menenius, usu. not slow with words, has difficulty in saying what the belly tauntingly replied – i.e. he has difficulty in making a fart. So the Citizen asks again what the belly answered.

Menenius: 'I will tell you;/If you'll bestow a small – of what you have little –/Patience awhile, you'll hear the belly's answer.' Now 'small' is added to the play on smile/smell; the Citizen is to bestow a small/smell of the LITTLE (L *-culus*; pun on *culus*, arse) arse he has. Angered, the Citizen does just that: he farts, and taunts Menenius, 'Ye're long about it' (Fr *abouti*, brought to an end: ABOUT).

Finally Menenius achieves the fart: '. . . "all/From me do back receive the flour of all,/And leave me but the bran." What say you to't?' Impersonating the belly, he has finally given *back* the flour (the corn the citizens had demanded), the *flour* or 'scent of the fart' (TWR) and left *but* bran or *bran* (a turd – Cot). In a final insult he turns to the citizen who had preempted him and said he was long about it: what say *you to't – you tout*, you buttocks or arse (TWR; F&H).

Smooth 1. Licentious. Ford, *'Tis Pity She's a Whore*, II.ii: 'This smooth, licentious poet'. *Lice*: smooth, sleek; a bitch, a whore (Cot). Lubric: smooth, lascivious (*OED*). 2. Effeminate. Castrated. Glib: smooth, slippery; to castrate. Docked smack smooth: amputation of the penis (F&H, n.d.).

KJ, II.i.573: 'That smooth-faced gentleman, tickling Commodity . . . this Commodity,/This bawd, this broker' – Commodity, the tickling (P; F&H; *fricciare*: frig and tickle – F), i.e. frigging, masturbating bawd and broker (pander), with his smooth face.

2H4, I.ii.43. Falstaff called the satin-merchant a 'whoreson Achitophel' (ACHITOPHEL, pimp): 'The whoreson smooth-pates do now wear nothing but high shoes and bunches of keys at their girdles'. KEYS were the equipment of pimps, whose smooth, lewd and filthy, heads were bald (from VD – C; as in *CE*, II.ii), and whose high shoes indicated effeminacy: see (1) the 'chopine' worn by 'my young lady and mistress', the boy-actor of women's roles in *Ham*, II.ii.447; (2) SAFFRON for 'high-heeled boots' and effeminacy. See PEACH, *MM*, for another satin-merchant who was a pimp.

II.i.31. The Hostess complains of Falstaff's financial and sexual dealings: 'he is indited to dinner to the Lubber's head in Lumbert street, to Master Smooth's the silkman. . . . There is no honesty in such dealings; unless a woman should be made an ass and a beast, to bear every knave's wrong.' Master Smooth (beardless – *OED*) the SILK-man (1599, effeminate, luxurious) lives in Lumbert, i.e. Lombard, Street, home of bankers and money-lenders; the LOMBARDS were said to have brought buggery to England (a woman should be made an *ass* and a *beast*, to bear every knave's WRONG, i.e. penis – K, s.v. Rung/wrong). 'Lubber's head' is usu.

annotated as *libbard's* or *leopard's head*: cf. PARD or leopard for puns on lechery, sodomy, disease. See LUBBERland (*TN*), which Sh's contemporaries used to mean a place of idleness and dissolution.

3. In the following, a nice opposition of smooth and crusted shows how smooth (*lice*) or lewd people are vulnerable to CRUST (VD), through an additional pun on 'lice', meaning not only (1) parasites that infect the head, but also (2) *crust*aceans that infest animals and plants.

Tim, III.vi.104: 'Most smiling, smooth, detested parasites . . . the infinite malady/ Crust you quite o'er'. Timon dismisses his sycophantic, bowing, buttocks-rearing (MOST, buttocks; SMILE, Fr *rire*/rear), DE-TESTED (without testes), parasitic, lascivious companions, hoping they are crusted QUITE/coit O'ER/whore – through coitus with whores – and succumb to the INFINITE malady (syphilis). See SHIN.

Ham, I.v.73. The Ghost tells Hamlet 'a most instant tetter bark'd about,/ Most lazar-like, with vile and loathsome crust,/ All my smooth body'. His father's smooth body adds to the picture of the dissolute king, the contradiction of Hamlet's unreal glorification of him (see CRUST).

See DISTRESS, *AYL*.

Snatch Act of copulation (F&H). Cf. Robert Burton, p. 814: 'I could not abide marriage, but as a rambler . . . I took a snatch where I could get it'. A hasty act of kind (C). A woman's genitals: see PLUME.

TA, II.i.95. Aaron learns the boys desire Lavinia: 'it seems, some certain snatch or so/Would serve your turns' – serve (coitally – P) their turns (sexual bouts – C; P).

MM, IV.ii.7. Pompey's talk of cutting off a man's and a woman's head is bawdy (as in *RJ*, I.i.27: 'I will be cruel with the maids, and cut off their heads', i.e. maidenheads). So, too, is the Provost's response: 'Come, sir, leave me your snatches and yield me a direct answer.'

This scene parodies II.iv (STRIPE), when Isabella would not 'yield' her body to save her brother's life and falsely believed he would accept castration or death, would 'tender down' (180) and 'yield [YIELD/geld] . . . up' 'twenty heads' to save her virginity – would TENDER, offer sexually (tenderings: a deer's stones) TWENTY (a score, i.e. a cutting or castration of his) HEADS or testicles (It *teste*: heads, parts of the brain that resemble a man's stones). The puns suggest Sh has reservations about the priorities of sister and brother, neither of whom would sacrifice chastity, sexuality or life for the other.

See WILLOW, *Ham*.

Sodomy See BUGGER(Y).

Sole/soul Buttocks. Sole: the bottom of a thing. Rabelais used *asne* (ass) in one edn of Bk III, ch. 22, and changed it to *âme* (soul) in a 'corrected' edn, in order to save his life (in ch. 23 he made the same pun): 'His soul goeth . . . under Prosperine's close-stool . . . within which she . . . voided the fecal stuff of her stinking clysters' (1693 trs.).

1H4, IV.i.50. Hotspur says his father 'writes' he has 'inward [INWARD, intestine] sickness' (31), but in this Hotspur does not 'read/The very bottom and the soul of hope'.

H5, II.ii.97: 'That knew'st the very bottom of my soul' – see BUNG.

TGV, II.iii.19. Looking at two shoes, Launce decides that the 'worser sole', the one 'with the hole in it', is his mother; the other, his father.

R2, II.ii.64: 'thou art the midwife . . . And Bolingbroke my . . . heir;/Now hath my soul brought forth her prodigy,/And I, a gasping new-deliver'd mother' – birth metaphor in which the Queen's soul (arse), not womb, delivers no baby but a prodigy, i.e. something monstrous, unnatural (see DESPAIR).

Cym, I.i.138. Cymbeline says Imogen could have married the 'sole son of my queen!' – an only son and an 'ass' of a son (II.i.58: 'That such a crafty devil as is his mother/Should yield the world this ass!').

Cor, I.iv.36. Marcus calls the Romans 'souls of geese,/That bear the shapes of men'. Geese or whores (*gueuse* – Cot; goose – P), who bear/bare the SHAPES (genitals) of men: the cowardly

Romans are whores' arses, 'All hurt behind: backs red, and faces pale/With . . . agued fear!' Hurt BEHIND, with red (or bloody) backs; and with FACES/faeces pale from sickly fright.

KL, IV.i.47. Blind Gloucester says, 'bring some covering for this naked soul' – ironically calling the unrecognised Edgar, his son, a soul (see *Cym* above) – pun on *sol*, sun (sol/sole/soul and son/sun – K). Edgar is the naked soul who plays the naked ass or fool, the 'fool to sorrow' (40), to help his father, a man of 'huge sorrows!' (IV.vi.288).

Sorcerers See WITCHES.

Soul See SOLE/SOUL.

Sound(ly) Bawdy and scatological pun on sounding or probing the bottom (buttocks). Chaucer, *Troilus and Criseyde*, 535: 'That to myn hertis botme it is ysounded'.

See CUSHION, *Cym*; DRAWERS; JEST, *TA*; HONEY, *JC*; PHYSICIAN, *H8*; ROUND, *TSh*; PLAIN, *TSh*.

Spain, Spaniard, Spaniel Epithets for farting and arse-licking. Orig. Spaniards were Spaniels, *Espaigneuls. Espagnol*: Spaniard; spaniel (Cot). A fise dog and fisting hound meant a small spaniel, or other pet dog, named from the fise and fist (a breaking of wind, i.e. a fart). Marston, Jonson and Chapman, *Eastward Hoe*, II.ii: Told that 'the bloodhound Securitie will *smell out* ready money' for him, Petronell makes plans, 'And alledging urgent excuses for my stay *behind*, *part* with her *as pass*ionately *as* she would from her foisting-hound' (PASS, excrete from the body). (Italics added.) Gk *spanos*: beardless.

CE, III.ii.133. Dromio S. anatomises the 'beastly creature' in the kitchen according to national characteristics: Ireland is 'in her buttocks' as he knew 'by the bogs'; he felt 'the hot breath of Spain; who sent whole armadoes of caracks to be ballast at her nose'. Whole (anatomical hole – P; 'hol': rectum – TWR) armadoes of CARACKS, cracks (farts – F&H). *Pet*: crack, fart, tail-shot (Cot). She is a BEASTLY (sexually bestial) CREATURE (whore; sodomite).

Per, IV.vi.133. If Marina stays chaste, may Boult 'be gelded like a spaniel'. Wycherley, *The Country Wife*, IV.iii: 'harmless a man as ever came out of Italy with a good voice', i.e. a castrato; a 'kiss of his' has 'no more hurt in't than one of my spaniel's'.

2H4, V.iii.124: 'fig me, like/The bragging Spaniard'. BRAG/Sp *da bragado*: of depraved sentiments.

H5, III.vi.62: 'The fig of Spain': see F&H for legend about extracting with one's teeth a fig from the fundament of a mule, and its use by Sh and contemporaries (Jonson, *The Alchemist*, I.i: 'Lick figs/Out at my –').

H8, V.iii.126. Henry tells the Bishop flattery cannot 'hide offences' (OFFENCE: sexual misbehaviour, with emphasis on the arse): 'To me you cannot reach, you play the spaniel,/And think with wagging of your tongue to win me'. The spaniel wags his *tail*; the Bishop wags his TONGUE or penis (cunilingus or penilingus in *TGV*, II.iii.53; *TSh*, II.i.213–19; *Cym*, II.iii.14). LOLL tongue: dissolute; wagtail: a dissolute man; harlot (*OED*; P). *Culetage*: buttock-stirring, tail-wagging, lechery (Cot). And a few lines later the Bishop is forbidden to 'wag his finger [FINGER, penis]'.

JC, III.i.43. Caesar tells a kneeling Metullus, 'Be not fond,/To think that Caesar' will be swayed by 'Low-crooked court'sies and base spaniel-fawning'. *Low* and *base* action of his bottom or buttocks; fawning ('wagging the tail' – *W*; *OED*). Metullus wags his tail (arse – F&H; P) like a CROOKED (castrated) bugger, an inviting spaniel, making court'sies (COURTESY, bow for fornication). 'Couchings' (lying down, esp. in intercourse – P), says Caesar, 'Might fire the blood of ordinary men' but cannot seduce Caesar.

Spin(ster) Coit (C; P). Whore, male or female. Rowse, p. 26: an earl rounded on some nuns with, 'Out, ye whores, to work, to work! Ye whores, go spin!' Coffey, *The Devil to Pay*, V: 'Come, and spin, you drab, or I'll tan your hide for you'. 'Spin(ning)-houses' were houses of correction for loose women; a 'spinster' was a harlot (F&H). Spintry (L *spintria*): a male prostitute, as in Jonson, *Sejanus*, IV.v: 'Ravished hence . . . dealt away/Unto his spintries, sellaries, and slaves'.

TN, I.iii.110: 'I hope to see a housewife [HOUSEWIFE, hussy, loose woman] take thee between her legs and spin it off'.

II.iv.45. Orsino asks for the song that 'The spinsters and the knitters in the sun/And the free maids that weave their thread' used to sing, a silly one that 'dallies with the innocence of love'. Spinsters, KNITTERS (copulators) and free (liberal, loose – P) girls sing of dallying and dalliance (leisurely love-play – P; 'dalliaunce': illicit sex-play – TWR).

Oth, I.i.24. Iago's jealousy of Cassio, who supplanted him in Othello's favour (ANCIENT), prompts him to compare Cassio to 'a spinster'.

Spirit (1) Penis. Gk *keras*: horn (erect penis – C; P); *keres*: spirit. Conjure down 'the standing [stand: phallic erection] spirit of my lord the king/That your good mother there, the Abbess, uses/To conjure down the spirit of the monk' (F&H, s.v. Stand, 1601).

(2) Semen (P), as in Son 129: 'The expense of spirit in a waste of shame/Is lust in action'. Bacon: 'much use of Venus doth dim the sight. . . . The cause of dimness of sight is the expense of spirits'. Thomas Heyrick, 'The Battle between the Cock and Capon': the 'Castrate' has a 'want of generous spirits and active fires,/Which Love inspires [and has instead a] useless Tail' (*Penguin Book of Restoration Verse*, p. 272). But with guile he defeats the 'Cock', who 'those fiery spirits want,/Which he so prodigally spent to please/The Lust of all his Mistresses'. For different reasons, the Castrate and the prodigal Cock both want or lack spirits.

2H6, III.ii.308. The Queen calls Suffolk 'coward woman' (COWARD): 'Hast thou not spirit to curse thine enemy?' – no spirit, *keres* (or horn, *keras*), with which to CURSE (screw) the enemy?

MWW, IV.iv.63. Mrs Page wants the fairies to interrupt Falstaff when he attempts seduction and ask why 'In their so sacred paths he dares to tread/In shape profane' – why he treads (copulates – *OED*; P) in so profane a SHAPE (penis) as the stag-horns he is wearing. They are to 'dis-horn the spirit,/And mock him home'. And they do: dis-horn and fig. emasculate him.

Actually, it is she who is profane, punning on (1) the profanity of his wearing horns (the attributes of deities, demons, Moses; emblems of power, the horn of salvation used of God and Christ); (2) his phallic horn; (3) his being a spirit they must dis-horn – the Holy Spirit of which *Mary* conceived, and Falstaff's spirit that attempts the chastity of the *merry* wives (marry/merry – K).

AYL, I.i.23. Orlando tells *Adam*, 'the spirit of my father . . . within me, begins to mutiny'. The spirit (mettle and semen) of his earthly father, and the Holy Spirit of Our Father, mutiny at 'helping' his brother 'mar that which God hath made'.

WT, I.ii.72. Polixenes and Leontes 'were as twinn'd lambs. . . . Had we pursued that life,/And our weak spirits ne'er been higher rear'd/With stronger blood, we should have answer'd heaven/Boldly "not guilty"; the imposition clear'd/Hereditary ours.' Had their *spirits* never been *higher rear'd* with stronger BLOOD (semen; sexual passion – P) they could have answered HEAVEN not guilty of original (L *origo*, origin, from *oriri*, to rise) sin. 'If you first sinn'd with' your wives, adds Leontes's wife ironically; 'By this we gather/You have tripp'd [lost chastity – C; P] since.' Possibly as boys they shared a homosexual love (see HEAVEN); they were as TWIN (like homosexual) lambs, who did 'bleat [/bleed] the one at the other'.

Ham, II.ii.631: 'The spirit that I have seen/May be the devil [who] . . . hath power/To assume a pleasing shape [and] . . . is very potent with such spirits'. The spirit or ghost may be the DEVIL (a bisexual), with his attribute, the horn, and his power to assume any pleasing (sexually – C; P) SHAPE (genitals). Being potent with SUCH (*tale* – F) spirits (tale: a penis – TWR; C; P), he will ABUSE (q.v.) Hamlet.

See CONJURE, *RJ*; STRETCH, *KL*.

Spit (1) Penetrate sexually (F&H n.d.). Rabelais, Bk IV, ch. 53: it was common to 'Burn 'em [heretics] . . . spit 'em at the bung-hole' (1694 trs.). This punishment may be related to an identification of heretics and buggers (buggery: heresy; sodomy – *OED*). Marlowe, *Edward*

II, v.v: planning to intrude a 'red hot' spit into the King's rectum, the murderer says 'ne'er was there any/So finely handled' (Marlowe perhaps punning, as Sh does, on ANY/*âne*, ass, and FINE, the end).

(2) A penis. Spit white: seminal emission (P). See HERCULES, *Ado*; HISS, *KL*.

TSh, III.i.40. Hortensio says his 'instrument's in tune', and when Bianca disagrees Lucentio mocks, 'Spit in the hole, man, and tune again.' Some eds say he spits in his hands before applying himself to the task a second time. But the scene abounds in puns and 'spit' would seem inescapably one: (1) Bianca is to 'touch' (caress erotically – P) his instrument; (2) he is to spit in the hole (pudendum, arse – C; P).

Per, IV.ii.142. The pander's servant who procured Marina asks, 'if I have bargained for the joint [JOINT, crotch]'; and the Bawd grants his request: 'Thou mayst cut a morsel off the spit.'

TA, IV.ii.146. Aaron had threatened Demetrius that 'this sword shall plough thy bowels up' (TAPER). He uses the same image in killing the Nurse: 'Weke, weke! so cries a pig prepared to the spit.' The Nurse is the pig/Gk *pyge* (buttocks), bowel, that he spits on his sword (penis – C; P).

Aristophanes, *Acharnians*, 777–97, Megarian peddles his little daughters as sows (*choiros*: sow, female genitals): 'the flesh of my sows will be excellent on your spit'. And when he tells the girls to 'Cry quickly, wee sowlet', they respond 'Wee-wee, wee-wee!' L *volva*: womb; a sow's womb was a favourite Roman delicacy (Horace).

Spleen Penis and semen. Spleen is milt, male generative organ of fishes and its secretion.

AYL, IV.i.217: 'wicked bastard of Venus that was . . . conceived of spleen'. Pisces: a constellation, the Fish or Fishes, 'the exaltation of Venus' (*W*). Chaucer, 'The Squire's Tale', 272: 'Now dauncen lusty Venus children dere,/For in the Fish hir lady sat ful hye'.

See BUDGE, *JC* and *TSh*; SHAME, *KJ*; TEEM, *KL*; TRULL, *TA*; STING, *2H6*.

Spread To open for copulation: of women, to open up; of men, to lay out for service (F&H 1798). Juvenal, *Satires*, vi, trs. Dryden: 'Many a fair nymph has in a cave been spread/And much good love, without a featherbed'.

RJ, III.ii.5: 'Spread thy close curtain, love-performing night'. Juliet's amorous impatience is conveyed in (1) the spreading of the CLOSE (genitals) curtain; (2) the love-performing (sexually active – F&H; P) *night*, her 'knight', as she calls Romeo in the last line of the scene.

Ham, III.iv.151. Hamlet begs his mother not to go to his uncle's bed: 'do not spread the compost on the weeds,/To make them ranker' (in sexual heat). No com*post* to be spread on *rank* weeds: this to the woman he spoke of when he said that in the world's garden grew 'things rank' (I.ii.136) on which her appetite had so grown that she did 'post . . . to incestuous sheets' (156).

IV.vii.176. The Queen's language lends support to the thesis of an unchaste Ophelia, held by Rebecca West (Hoy, p. 257) and others (Grebanier, p. 278). Ophelia died beside a WILLOW (symbol of lechery) that showed its 'hoar [/whore – K] leaves'; and there she brought 'long purples/That liberal shepherds give a grosser name/But our chaste maids do call them' dead men's fingers. She 'Fell in the weeping brook. Her clothes spread wide;/And, mermaid-like, awhile they bore her up'. On the 'pendent boughs' (of a weeping willow), hanging her weeds, she fell (a fall from virtue – C; P) into the WEEPING (whoring) BROOK (a pimp), which for a while bore her up like a MERMAID (whore).

Ophelia's *clothes spread*; Juliet (above) says *spread* thy *close*. The similar sounds suggest a clothes/close quibble (K, p. 321), and that Ophelia's clothes spread wide as, previously, her CLOSE (genitals) had. She had sung a little song on the loss of virginity (and rhymed 'rose' and 'clothes'): 'Then up he rose, and donn'd his clothes,/And dupp'd the chamber door;/Let in the maid, that out a maid/Never departed more' (v. 52).

See SERVANT, *2H4*; COLOUR, *1H6*.

Spur (1) Penis. Lit. a prick. *Penne*: a spur (Cot); a man's privities (F). Middleton, *A Mad World, My Masters*, III.ii: 'Ha, ha, I have fitted her; an old knight and a cock o' the game still; I have not spurs for nothing, I see.' In bot., the spur is often the nectary or honey-secreting organ.

(2) Dildo. A spur is lit. a prick; a hard, sharp projection on the leg of a fighting cock, and the artificial substitute for such a projection.

JC, II.i.123, Brutus: 'What need we any spur but our own cause,/ To prick us to redress?' They are not like the cock who needs an artificial spur or gaff in order to fight. Their own cause (*cas*: a cause; the privities – Cot) is spur, prick, penis enough. They need no other cause or case; their own cods (balls) give them the strength to fight like men. Brutus uses this metaphor again in OATHS.

Tim, III.vi.73: 'Each man to his stool, with that spur as he would to the lip of his mistress' – (1) each man to his table stool with the same eagerness with which he would approach the lip of his mistress; (2) each man to his stool (chamber-stool or pot) with that same spur (penis) he would use at the LIP (vaginal orifice) of his mistress. The quibble on 'stool' indicates what Timon is serving them, the seeming 'lukewarm water' in the covered dishes, which turns out to be stool or excrement. And when they try to leave, he says, '*Soft*! take thy *physic* first' (see CHEER and PASSAGE for similar behaviour by Timon). (Italics added.)

See COMPUNCTIOUS; LODGE(R), *TN*; ANSWER, Son 50; COPPER, *MM*.

Spurn Penis, copulate; obs. var. of 'spur' (*W*; *OED*). See SPUR. Spenser, *Faerie Queene*, Bk III, c.i, st.5: 'The Faery . . . sharply gan to spurne/ His fomy steed'. 'Folly it is to spurne against a pricke' (William Camden, in *OED*).

TA, III,i.101, Titus: 'It was my deer; and he that wounded her/ Hath hurt me. . . . But that which gives my soul the greatest spurn,/ Is dear Lavinia, dearer than my soul.' Titus's identification with his daughter's misery is absolute (MEADOW): Lavinia, his DEAR/ deer, hind ('this dainty doe' – II.ii.117), was raped; so, too, was his SOUL/ SOLE (bottom) violated, spurned.

Cym, IV.i.20. Cloten plans rape (KNOCK): Imogen shall be 'enforced' and then he will 'spurn her home to her father' – prick her HOME (vulva) and spurn or kick her home.

See DOG, *R3*, *Tim*; BEGGAR, *R3*.

Squire Pimp (F&H). In contemptuous use, 16th c.; a lover. Middleton, *A Mad World, My Masters*, III.i: 'That man's her squire . . . her pimp. . . . She's of the stamp'.

See CLOTH, *Cym*; BOY, *TGV*.

Squirrel Harlot (F&H; G). Con: 1600, a squirrel; CON (*con* – Cot): a cunt. Dekker, *The Comedy of Old Fortunatus*, IV.i: the 'pick-purse' who also does 'for gold sell her love' shall be transformed into a 'squirrel' to 'pick out a poor living here among the trees'. Lyly, *Pappe with an hatchet, Alias a figge for my God sonne Or cracke me this nut*; 'obscenitie? Naie, now I am too nice, squirrilite [scurrility] were a better word.'

MND, IV.i.40. Titania has a 'venturous fairy that shall seek/ The squirrel's hoard, and fetch thee new nuts'. The venturous fairy (VENTURES, whores – C) will fetch NUTS (testicles) for Bottom. They will come from the whore's HOARD but will be new and not old and *hoared* (hoary – *OED*; OATHS).

RJ, I.iv.68. Queen Mab's chariot is 'an empty hazel-nut/ Made by the joiner squirrel'. Mercutio is not building a doll's house for children; this is a bawdy, bitter speech, in which 'hazel-nut' (see NUTS) foreshadows the scene of his death, where it is used again. QUEEN Mab is a quean or slut; her chariot is made of NUTS, which (esp. hazel-nuts) are testicles; nuts that are emptied of seed (semen – P) by the joiner (JOIN, copulate) or fucking squirrel, who, like Dekker's whoring squirrel above, picked out a living by emptying (men's) nuts.

To see 'joiner' only as cabinet-maker is to ignore the tenor of Mercutio's speech, just as if one saw the 'wagon-spokes made of long spinners' legs' as meaning only a spinner of threads or a spider, and overlooked the possibility they were the same kind of spinning legs as in *TN*, I.iii.110: 'I hope to see a housewife [hussy] take thee between her legs and spin it off' (SPINSTER, whore).

See BOY, *TGV*.

Stale See STEAL.

Stand back (1) Sodomise. Stand (with erect penis – F&H; P) *back*. Cf. Gen 19: 4–9: the men of Sodom surrounded Lot's house and cried, 'bring them out unto us, that we may know them [carnally]'; and when he refused, they said, 'Stand back . . . now will we deal worse with thee, than with them. And they pressed sore upon the man, even Lot, and came near to break the door.'

(2) Perh. related to the back of an ass, or a man with one testicle, a RIDGEL, the other believed to be up in his back or ridge (*OED*). *À dos d'asne*: 'Ridgill-backed' (Cot), resembling the back of an ass, high-ridged, highest in the middle. The standing back (?) of Winchester?

1H6, I.iii.33, 38. Gloucester, who called Winchester's men 'dunghill grooms [GROOM, male whore]' (14), now tells Winchester, 'Stand back. . . . I'll canvass thee in thy broad cardinal's hat, / If thou proceed'. He will canvass – (1) shake amorously in a pair of sheets (P); (2) solicit or pander – this BROAD (obscene, effeminate) carnal / cardinal (K), just as, a few lines later (SCARLET) he says he will cry or hawk him through the streets. To the implication he is a whore who can be sold, Winchester responds, 'Nay, stand thou back; I will not budge a foot'. He will not BUDGE / bugger for Gloucester, even if he is canvassed, solicited, and threatened with beating, as were Lot and the ANGELS in his house threatened by the Sodomites. *Gloucester* may; *he* will not stand *back*, will not budge a FOOT (fornicate). (See FOOT, *1H4*, for another man who will not budge a foot.)

See BEGGAR, *R3*.

State A privy seat; man's seat or arse. Lit. a throne (THRONE, privy seat); like 'stool', another word that means both chair of state and seat for evacuating the bowels, as well as the evacuation itself.

1H4, II.iv.415. To Falstaff's 'this *chair* shall be my *state*', the Prince returns, 'Thy state is taken for a joined-*stool*' (italics added). See JOINT STOOL for the stool that held the chamber-pot. In this mockery of the throne and King, Falstaff tells the Prince, 'Stand *aside*, nobility' (italics added).

MV, IV.i.354, Portia: 'the other half / Comes to the *privy* coffer of the state' (italics added) – Sh again manifests scepticism about the court-room justice and mercy.

Cor, III.i.151. Coriolanus, whose metaphors are always brutal for the 'rank-scented many' (encompassing both their common rank and rank scent), says that those who would give free corn '*nourished* disobedience' (connoting digestion and elimination) in people who are 'well *ass*ured' they don't deserve it. How would the 'multitude digest' such courtesy? They'd say the Senate acted in fear and 'we debase / The nature of *our seats*' in so doing. But 'You [the Tribunes] . . . That love the *fundamental* [the fundament or buttocks] part of the *state* . . . and wish / To jump a body with a dangerous *physic*' must deny the people (italics added). The fundamental PART: the division in the buttocks.

See CRUST, *Ham*; ASSAIL, *3H6*; GAIT, *LLL*; RESOLUTION, *KL*.

Steal, stale, stole 'Stale' (obs.) and 'stole': past tense of 'steal'. Stale / steel (K). When a man 'stole' a girl, he often made a stale (whore – *OED*; P) of her.

Ado, II.i.206. Claudio is angry because Benedick told him to go to the 'willow' (WILLOW, symbol of lost virtue, lechery): 'the prince hath got your Hero'. Benedick continues, ' 'twas the boy that stole your meat, and you'll beat the post' – the Prince stole (made a 'common stale' of – IV.i.65) Hero, the meat (whore's flesh: female pudendum – F&H; P), so don't berate Benedick, only a messenger.

238. Benedick tells Don Pedro, 'you . . . have stolen his bird's nest [female pudendum – P]'.

ii.25. Hero is a 'contaminated stale' – has the cunt of a stale.

JC, II.i.238. Portia's 'You've ungently, Brutus, / Stole from my bed' lays the ground-work for l.287, when she says, 'Portia is Brutus' harlot, not his wife'.

See STEWARD, *Ham*; BOY, *TGV*.

Steel Penis. Lit. an *instrument* or *weapon* (two puns on penis – C; P) made of or like steel. Nashe, *The Choice of Valentines*: the dildo 'stands as stiff as if he were made of steel'.

RJ, III.i.120: 'Thy beauty hath made me effeminate/ And in my temper soften'd valour's steel!' Elasticity is imparted to steel by tempering. Having just left Juliet (after the Friar did 'incorporate two in one'), Romeo is 'soften'd' and 'effeminate' and loathe to use the other steel, the sword, on Tybalt, who, like Juliet, is a Capulet, 'which name I tender'. Cf. CHEEKS, *Tim*.

AC, IV.iv.33. Conversely, Antony creates an image of virility: 'To business that we *love* we *rise* betime,/ And *go to't* with delight'; and 'I'll leave thee/ Now, like a man of steel' (italics added). See BUSINESS (the sex-act).

TN, III.iii.5: 'I could not stay behind you: my desire,/ More sharp [L *acies*, sharp edge] than filed steel [Fr *acier*], did spur [SPUR, prick] me forth;/ And not all love to see you, though so much/ As might have drawn one to a longer voyage'. Antonio could not stay BEHIND Sebastian, whom he loves so much *as*/ass (?) might have drawn him (draw: expose the sex-organ as a sword – P) to a *longer* voyage.

See TAME, *TGV*; DEBT, *Cym*; PIN, *WT*; INCH, *Tem*.

Stern(age) Buttocks; hinder part of anything.

MM, II.ii.66. Isabella calls Angelo 'stern' and wishes she had his 'potency' – unfortunate phrases foreshadowing the attempted seduction.

H5, III., Prol., 18. Evoking both the impressive power and waste of the war is this series of puns on male buttocks and the sex-act. We are asked to visualise '*fan*ning' streamers and to 'Play with your *fan*cies' (FAN, buttocks; FANCY, amorous desire); to behold 'the huge *bottoms* . . . Breasting [L *sternum*, breast-bone] the lofty surge'; to 'Grapple your minds to *sternage*' of the navy (italics added). One who follows sees the stern and we are to 'follow/ These cull'd and choice-drawn cavaliers'. *Cull'd* and *choice* remind us of 'The posterior . . . culled, chose' (*LLL*, V.i.98), with its pun on *cul* (Cot), cule: rump; and Fr *chose*: a woman's thing (F&H; P). 'Play' (P; 'pley' – TWR) and GRAPPLE mean have intercourse.

Then, however, our thoughts are told to 'Work' signifying sexual activity (TWR, s.v. Werke; P) but also act as a purgative, and 'therein see a siege' (SIEGE: lit. anus, rectum, faecal matter – *OED*; F&H). 'And down goes all before them' begins the final couplet, followed by Henry's opening line of scene i: 'Once more unto the breach [/ breech, rectum]'.

2H6, III.ii.213. Deriding Warwick for mental and physical impotence, Suffolk calls him 'Blunt-witted lord' – BLUNT (impotent), WIT (penis) – whose 'mother took unto her blameful bed/ Some stern untutor'd churl . . . whose fruit thou art'. He is the fruit of some arse, a *stern un*tutor'd churl (TUTOR: initiator into sex; older male in a pederastic relationship).

JC, III.ii.97: 'on the Lupercal' [Roman fertility festival]', says Antony, Caesar had refused the crown: 'Ambition should be made of sterner stuff' – which Caesar apparently lacked in several ways. He lacked potency or stuff (semen – P) in his stern and had no children, though he blamed Calpurnia's 'sterile curse' (I.ii.8), for which he wanted 'Antonius,/ To touch Calpurnia' on the festival. 'Touch' meaning copulate (F&H; P), it might have worked. See STING.

See CHEER, *TA*; BUTCHER, *R2*.

Steward Pimp. Stewards wore the house keys on a chain (as did pimps: KEY); in *TN*, II.iii.129, Malvolio is told, 'rub your chain with crums'. Middleton, *A Mad World, My Masters*, III.iii: a 'quean' and her 'leash of pimps' is met by the 'steward', the 'chief gentleman i' th' chain of gold. That he should live to be a pander' – the quean (whore) with her leash and the steward with his chain.

2H4, V.iii.137. Elizabethans commonly called Fortune a whore (*KJ*, III.i.61: 'That strumpet fortune'). Falstaff: 'I am fortune's steward' – her pimp, who also steals ('Let us take any man's horses [HORSE/ whores]').

This strumpet's usual attribute is her wheel, symbol of caprice (*H5*, III.vi.29: 'Fortune's furious fickle wheel'). Falstaff's calling himself her steward evokes the bawdy scene (II.iv) when Hal called him (278) 'this nave of a wheel' (*knave* of a wheel, knave and steward of Fortune) and Poins added, 'Let's beat him before his whore.'

Ham, IV.v.173. The mad Ophelia sings bawdy songs: 'Hey non nonny, nonny' and 'You must sing a-down a-down,/ An you call him a-down-a,/ O how the wheel becomes it! It is the false steward, that stole his master's daughter.' To gloss 'wheel' as a spinning-wheel from whose workers Ophelia learned her songs, adds little to our understanding of a difficult section. To gloss it as a refrain has the virtue of stressing the refrains: NONNY (vulva – F) and DOWN (to whore). In such context the steward that stole may be a pimp like 'fortune's steward', who also stole (*2H4* above); and the wheel, a whore's, like the one in Dekker and Massinger, *The Virgin Martyr*, II.iii: 'what thred spins that whore Fortune upon her wheele now'. Then 'O, how the wheel becomes it!' is integral to its bawdy context.

A fascinating possibility is that 'wheel' puns on *weel*, a trap for fish. After Polonius says (II.ii.162), 'I'll loose my daughter to him' (the loosing of female cattle for breeding – Hoy, p. 194), Hamlet calls him 'fish-monger' (pimp – C; P). Fishmonger Polonius used a weel or trap to catch Hamlet, in which Ophelia was the stale (lit. a decoy, a whore – as in WARDROBE). He is the steward pimp who STOLE, made Ophelia a stale. Polonius was 'Jephthah' (422, 428), like the biblical Jephthah (Jgs 11:34–40) who sacrificed his daughter. Polonius, 'lord chamberlain', is a chamberlain (steward – *OED*).

Ophelia's madness focuses on him ('Conceit upon her father' – IV.v.45): 'She speaks much of her father; says she hears/ There's *tricks* i' the world; and *hems*'; hearers guess at the meaning of 'her *winks*, and *nods*, and *gestures*' (italics added). The *tricks* or trap: the weel or wheel of the strumpet; and the HEMS/ sounds of a bawd. This sounds like another sexually violated maid in *TA*, III.ii, Lavinia, who (43) shall not '*sigh* . . . Nor *wink*, nor *nod* . . . nor make a *sign*' but her father will 'learn' her 'meaning' (italics added). Ophelia's mad songs may be recognition of her own role in what she believed to be Hamlet's madness and her father's death. See Rebecca West's brilliant analysis of Polonius's exploitation of Ophelia for his own position: 'that army of not virgin martyrs, the poor little girls who were sacrificed to family ambition' (Hoy, p. 259). See ROBIN.

Tim, IV.iii.505. Timon, gone mad from mankind's cupidity, realises his steward honestly cares for him: 'I do proclaim/ One honest man . . . and he's a steward.' Sh's phrasing conveys the irony; and Timon immediately wavers in disbelief and asks if the steward's is not a 'kindness subtle, covetous,/ If not a usuring kindness'. KINDNESS is the sexual favour (F&H) – and Timon suspects his steward's is SUBTLE (that of sutler, pimp), COVETOUS/ covetise (lust), and usuring (prostituting, sexual indulgence – C; P), the kindness of the steward's profession.

The sexually co-operative steward is a character in Roman comedy. Plautus, *Casina*, 450–70: 'Get off my back' ('apage te a dorso meo') says a steward or head slave to his master, rapturously kissing, hugging him. Onlooker: 'that's the reason he made him overseer' and once wanted to make me his chamberlain, steward ('atriensim').

Stick (1) Fornicate (C). Fr *ficher*: 17th c. euphemism for fuck (TWR, p. 23); lit. to stick (Cot). Fr *foutre*: to stick; (Cot) to lecher. Alexander Radcliffe, 'Upon Mr Bennet, Procurer Extraordinary': 'If Men of Honour wou'd begin,/ He'd ne'er stick out at any Sin,/ For he was still for Sticking't in' (*Penguin Book of Restoration Verse*, p. 226).

(2) The clap (F&H n.d.). Marston, *The Dutch Courtesan*, I.i: 'employ your money upon women [and they] . . . will bestow that on you which shall stick by you as long as you live . . . give them the French crown, they'll give you the French – '.

AW, III.vi.46: 'this drum *sticks sore*ly in your disposition' – 'A *pox* on't' (italics added).

Luc, 317: 'Lucretia's glove, wherein her needle sticks . . . griping it, the needle his finger pricks'. A needle *sticks* her *glove* (Venus's glove: pudendum – P) and *pricks* his FINGER (penis).

KJ, III.iv.67: 'Like true, inseparable, faithful loves,/ Sticking together in calamity'. *Calamite*: magnet stone; *calamité*: misfortune (Cot).

AW, V.iii.45. Bertram remembers Maudlin: 'I stuck my choice upon her . . . Where the impression of mine eye infixing' made him scorn Helena. Note the parallel *I* stuck and EYE (penis) in*fix*ing (FIX, fuck). The I/ eye pun is relevant to her name Maudlin, from Magdalen, the reformed prostitute, often depicted with eyes red from WEEPING (whoring), q.v. This raises questions about their past relationship.

TrC, III.ii.130. Pandarus's kindred 'are burrs' who 'stick where they are thrown [tumbled sexually – C; P]'. Like another whore, Helen, who was compared to garbage some do 'throw in' a 'sieve' (II.ii.71), Cressida also is garbage (O'ER) and is *thrown*.

See VARLET, *2H4*.

Stiff Erect, of the penis (TWR, s.v. Stif). Rabelais, Bk I, ch.11 (trs. 1653): Gargantua's 'Governesses' would take 'you know what between their fingers . . . till it did . . . creep up to the bulk and stiffenesse of a suppository' and call it their 'stiffe and stout'.

1H4, v.iii.42. Hal contrasts Falstaff's lack of manhood with the courage of the dead: 'stand'st thou idle . . . ? lend me thy sword;/Many a nobleman lies stark and stiff . . . unrevenged'. Even in death, as these noblemen lie on the field with the phallic erection of rigor mortis (a recognised physiological phenomenon), they show more virility than Falstaff. Hal asks for the sword (penis symbol – C; P) of Falstaff, who *stands*, capable of erection (F&H; P), capable of fight, yet inactive and IDLE (lewd).

AC, I.ii.104. The Messenger confronts Antony with the enemy's potency: 'Labienus – / This is stiff news – hath, with his Parthian force,/Extended Asia from Euphrates;/His conquering banner shook from Syria/To Lydia'. *Stiff* news: the foe is *extended*; his banner or standard (penis – C; P) shook (SHAKE, in coitus) potently.

See MEANS, *CE*.

Stigmatic Sexually deformed. L*stigma*: a mark, prick, brand. Prick: penis (*OED*; P). Stigma: bot., plant part that receives the pollen, comparable to ovary.

2H6, v.i.215: 'Foul stigmatic', says Clifford of Richard, whom his father had called 'As crooked in thy manners as thy shape!' (158). Richard himself admits he is 'not shaped for sportive tricks' (*R3*, I.i.14). He lacks the SHAPE (sex-organs – *OED*) for sport (F&H; P) or tricks (P), love-making. He is CROOKED (sexually inadequate), q.v., in his MANNERS (coitus), rather than the controversial hunch on his back. Is this also a pun on the stigma, ligature in ancient Greek type, and ligature or impotence supposed to be induced by magic (*CD*), as in Beaumont and Fletcher, *The Coxcomb*, II.iii: 'coole your Codpiece . . . or I'll clap a spell upon't shall take your edge off with a very vengeance.' Cf. WITCHES, *R3*.

3H6, II.ii.136. Margaret makes the same slur: 'But thou art neither like thy sire nor dam;/But like a foul mis-shapen stigmatic,/Mark'd by the destinies to be avoided'. The enmity between destinies and love is an Eliz. concept (*MND*, I.i.151); and Richard was marked (*pricked*) by them in a way not destined for love. Unlike his mother (lacking feminine stigma) and unlike his father – lacking a proper stigma (prick) – he is foul (obs., disfigured, as in *R3*, I.ii.57: 'thou lump of foul deformity') and mis-shapen.

Richard was born of a dam (a mother, but also a wall that confines water or the water itself) and a sire (Sc for gutter and sewer – W). Sh puns on 'sire' and the human *sewer* in *MM*, III.i.29: 'thine own bowels which do call thee sire'. To be born of the bowels is a biblical phrase to which no stigma is attached. 2 Sam 16:11: 'my son, which came forth of my bowels'. But Richard, born of the bowels, is 'an indigested and deformed lump' (v.vi.51), an indigested turd, meant to be 'avoided' (voided – *OED*): (1) as excretion; (2) in abortion: he is an 'elvish-mark'd, abortive, rooting hog' (*R3*, I.iii.228). See CRAFTY, *Cym*: the despicable Cloten was also born from the arse.

See BLUNT, *CE*.

Sting Prick, penis; phallic potency. Sexual urge (C; P). Tail: penis (C; P); MHG *zail*: tail, sting. Wycherley, *The Country Wife*, III.ii: the impotent Horner yet keeps 'company with women'. His 'sting is gone' and 'Yet he must be buzzing amongst 'em still'.

JC, II.i.16, Brutus: 'And then, I grant, we put a sting in him,/That at his will he may do danger with.' So far, Caesar's political and sexual will (penis – C; P) lacks potency (he is childless: STERN). Brutus fears to put political sting in him; Antony, however, will exploit Caesar's 'seal' (SEAL, testes), 'will' and 'testament' (III.ii.133).

2H6, III.ii.127: 'The commons, like an angry hive of bees/ That want their leader, scatter up and down/ And care not who they sting in his revenge.' The 'spleenful' (128) commons (whores – C; P) is made up of political whores, who parade UP AND DOWN (in sexual movement), scattering their SPLEEN (seed – *OED*), like angry bees, stinging, pricking anyone.

See TONGUE, *TSh*; NOTE, *TrC*; VELVET, *H5*.

Stint Breed, conceive; used of mares and ewes (*OED* 1823). In W. England it meant in foal. Despite *OED*'s recent date, as a pun it seems much older.

Tim, V.iv.83: 'Make war breed peace, make peace stint war'. 'Stint' is usu. glossed as meaning stop; nevertheless it is juxtaposed to 'breed', which it seems to have elicited in the way 'stop' would not have.

H8, I.ii.76. Similarly, when Wolsey says, 'We must not stint . . . in the fear/ To cope', 'stint' is juxtaposed to 'cope' (coit – P) and the subject under discussion is his role in Henry's *divorce* and *marriage*; Wolsey concludes, 'The grieved commons Hardly *conceive* of me' (italics added).

RJ, I.iii.48, 57. The Nurse quotes her husband, ' "dost thou fall upon thy face?/ Thou wilt fall backward when thou hast more wit;/ Wilt thou not Jule?" . . . And, pretty fool, it stinted and said "Ay." ' She then repeats the story almost to the word: ' "fall'st upon thy face?/ Thou wilt fall backward when thou comest to age;/ Wilt thou not, Jule?" it stinted and said "Ay." ' ('Jule' puns on Juliet's JEWEL, chastity.)

If there is no pun, it is difficult to see a point in the almost verbatim repetition in the very bawdy story. Perhaps the humour lies in her not only using 'stint' to mean stop (as usu. glossed), but also knowing 'stinted' meant conceived or received into the womb and using it to mean that Juliet, who could not understand what the husband meant, i.e. could not conceive yet in either sense, still said 'Ay', thus amusing the adults. 'Ay', 'ey', 'eye' meant egg; so all the Ay/ I puns are relevant to stinting, conceiving or breeding. It then became Juliet's turn to pun on her having 'said "Ay" ' as a child; and she asks that the Nurse this time 'stint . . . say I'.

Stir Copulate (C; P). To sodomise (*bouger*: 'To stirre'; *bougre*: 'A Buggerer, a Sodomite' – Cot). Dover, p. 140, discusses Aristophanes, *Clouds*, 1104: 'Right's despairing cry to the audience, ō kīnoumenoi, "you who are stirred"; kīnein, "stir", "move", is a slang equivalent of bīnein, "fuck".' Oates translates 'you are stirred' (addressed to those who have been called 'wide arse' or 'broad arse', in Greek comedy common terms of abuse for the seduced young male) as 'Debauchees!'

KJ, II.i.415. The Bastard is pleased that in the attack on Angiers, a '*con*temptuous [cunt?] city' (386; italics added) made up of 'jades' (strumpets), John will make his 'assault' from the 'west'; and 'From north to south:/ Austria and France shoot in each other's mouth:/ I'll stir them to it'. The bawdry expresses his contempt: England will *ass*ault from the WEST (the posteriors); and he will stir Austria and France to shoot (to copulate – F&H) in each other's mouth.

AYL, I.iii.116. Both girls disguise themselves, hoping they can pass through the forest without provoking *any* kind of sexual attack (Rosalind is disguised as a boy). Rosalind: 'Beauty provoketh thieves sooner than gold.' Celia responds that they will 'with a kind of umber smirch' their FACES (arses; faeces); 'so shall we pass along/ And never stir assailants' – not stir *ass*ailants (ASSAIL, assault sexually). The GOLD (excrement) pun suggests the repellent appearance their disguise will assume: the umber with which they will smirch (*Ado*, IV.i.135: 'smirched thus and mired') their faces as they PASS, i.e. discharge from the intestinal canal, mire (excrement – P) and faeces (see EVIL for the end of this metaphor).

Sh knew that masculine disguise alone could not protect, that it could, indeed, arouse passion in three groups: men who would see through the disguise; men who were fond of youths and would be aroused by the girlish boy; and even women who would be attracted by a gentle youth (as was Phebe). See Kott, p. 314, for discussion of this theme in the literature of Sh's contemporaries.

AC, I.i.43. To Cleopatra's 'Antony/Will be himself', Antony responds, 'But stirr'd by Cleopatra . . . What sport tonight?' *Butt* stirred, in sport (copulation – F&H; P). See TAWNY for more on their games.

Tim, III.iv.53. Flavius tells Timon's debtors, 'You do yourselves *but* wrong to *stir* me *up* . . . . my lord and I have made an *end*' (italics added). When they complain, 'but this answer will not serve', he says, 'If 'twill not serve, 'tis not so base as you; / For you serve knaves.' His ANSWER (coital thrust) will not serve because it is not as base (the *bottom*) as they who serve (coitally – *OED*; P) knaves (sodomitically). Cf. the Clown's 'answer [that] will serve all men . . . like a barber's chair [whore – F&H] that fits all buttocks' (*AW*, II.ii.14).

They respond that no one is in a position to 'speak broader' than he. This last pun on BROAD (obscene and effeminate language) and on broader / Fr *brodier* (the arse) concludes the attack and counter-attack on buggery (see BROAD-arse, a fucked male). Flavius had said they do but/butt WRONG (penis – K): they prick the butt or stir. But they chose the wrong butt (target and buttocks) in approaching him, for he no longer serves Timon, to whom he had been STEWARD (pimp), q.v.

See OPINION, *AC*; OFT, *H8*.

Stole See STEAL.

Stoop Bow, lower oneself, for the sex-act.

Cor, V.vi.29. The political acts of Coriolanus are described in sexual terms: he had asked for a 'harlot's spirit!' (III.ii.112) and intended to prostitute himself for the consulship, but in the end he could not 'stoop to the herd' (32) or keep the promise to his mother to 'perform a part' (109) – perform (the sex-act – C; P) a PART (division in the buttocks), play the ass / arse.

Plutarch speaks of Coriolanus's utter devotion to his mother: 'He took a wife, also, at her request and wish, and continued even after he had children, to live still with his mother' as one family (vol. II, p. 56); 'it was the weakness and womanishness of his nature that broke out . . . in these ulcerations of anger [and he] retired, full of fury . . . against the people' (p. 69).

Aufidius says, 'I raised him' and he 'heighten'd' and 'Seducing so my friends . . . to this end, / He bow'd his nature' (NATURE: privy parts; sex). But a Conspirator reminds him that Coriolanus 'did stand for consul' but 'lost by lack of stooping – '. He did stand (erect penis – F&H; P), did not stoop to be buggered by the public, the herd. See BEGGAR / bugger.

See ABHOR, *MM*; WINGS, *H5*; INCH, *Tem*.

Straight, strait Rectum (L, straight), so named because of its straight path in some animals; like an arse. Thomas Carew, 'From "A Rapture" ': 'Yet my tall pine shall in the Cyprian strait / Ride safe at anchor and unlade her freight' (*Signet Classic Poets of the 17th c.*, vol. II, p. 164). Cyprus: birthplace of Venus.

MND, III.ii.34: 'Titania waked and straightway loved an ass', i.e. *Bottom* (see HATEFUL).

Oth, V.i.1. Iago's language (see ANGRY) manifests his sexual obsessions and connivings. He tells Roderigo, whose lust for Desdemona he promises to gratify, that Cassio, whom he is sexually and professionally jealous of, must be killed: 'Here, stand behind this bulk; straight will he come: / Wear thy good rapier bare, and put it home . . . . fix most firm thy resolution.'

He believes he will make asses / arses of all these men: hence, BEHIND, BULK (rump) and *straight.* He believes he will screw, bugger them: hence, (1) stand (with erect penis – F&H; P); (2) will (penis – C; P) come (ejaculate – P); (3) wear (coitally – C; P) his GOOD (fornicating) rapier (phallus) and put (place sexually – F&H; P) it HOME (a sexual orifice); (4) *firm*ly FIX (Fr *ficher*: fix, fuck – TWR) his RESOLUTION (balls).

See LODGE, *H5*; PASS, *MND*.

Strait strossers No (s)trossers or trousers: bare skin. Beaumont and Fletcher, *The Coxcomb*, II.iii: 'And trossers made of thy skin to tumble in'. STRAIGHT–STRAIT: the rectum.

H5, III.vii.57. The Dauphin and Constable insult each other's sexual habits (TRUE). One's mistress is 'not bridled' and the other's 'horse is my mistress'. The Dauphin says the Constable needs no bridle when he rides (fornicates – F&H; P), for his mistress is 'old and gentle; and you rode, like a kern of Ireland, your French hose off, and in your strait strossers'. French hose were 'loose, wide breeches'; strait strossers were 'tight trousers. This is of course a humorous reference to the bare legs of the Irish kerns who "wear no Breeches, any more than the Scotch highlanders do" ' (New Hudson edn).

Dauphin: 'they that ride so and ride not warily, fall into foul bogs'. In the context of their sexual bestiality and the fact of the bare-legged and bare-arsed Irish kern, the Dauphin's saying that all who ride un*warily* (wearing nothing) are apt to fall into bogs suggests falling into the BOGS (buttocks – P) of a BOG (whore) in buggery (the brilliant and rarely prudish ed. Rolfe omits these lines). For a similar conceit, cf. Sir John Denham, 'News from Colchester . . . Ballad of Certain Carnal Passages betwixt a Quaker and a Colt': the Quaker 'turns *Italian* [ITALIAN, sodomite]', takes a mare 'by force', 'us'd her like a Sister [SISTER, whore]' and 'when in such a Saddle / A Saint will needs be riding / Though we do not say / 'Tis a falling away, / May there not be some back-sliding?' He concludes the 'Filly Foal' is a 'Martyr' to '*Sodom*'.

To two Frenchmen, riding in strait strossers puns on *chausses à la bougrine*, strait venetians, strait hose without codpiece, which Cotgrave explains got their name from *bougrin*, fit for buggery. See TRUE for restatement of the pun 12 lines later; and BUCKRAM for possible puns on these same hose and buggery.

Strange(r) (1) Of fornication. Strain : embrace (F&H; P); from L *stringere*, to squeeze. Beaumont and Fletcher, *Knight of the Burning Pestle*, I.i: the wife, 'a stranger', told not to 'strain' herself too much, calls someone else an 'old stringer [fornicator – CD]'. A strange woman: 1535, harlot.

(2) Of homosexual acts. Aristophanes, *The Wasps*, 1142–86: 'God no! he is not fond of strangers . . . for he who says "Philoxenus' [lit. fond of strangers] means a pederast.' Philoxenus was a noted Athenian pederast (Oates, p. 1228). Marston, *The Scourge of Villanie*, Satyre iii: 'no strange lust can sate Messaline', Roman woman of infinite vices. See ITALY for the 'strange delights' of the 'Sodomites'. Jonson, *The Devil is an Ass*, V.iii: 'These gallants in these shapes [dressed as women] have done strange things, sir, / One as the lady, the other as the squire.' Middleton and Dekker, *The Roaring Girl*, IV.i: 'How strange this shows, one man to kiss another!'

AC, I.iv.67. Caesar says the ambisexual Antony (see Index) 'is not more manlike / Than Cleopatra' (5) and did 'eat strange flesh' (67). Jude 7: 'Even as Sodom and Gomorrha . . . giving themselves over to fornication, and going after strange flesh'.

MWW, V.v.224. Caius complains, 'I ha' married un garçon, a boy; un paysan, by gar, a boy'. Ford: 'This is strange. Who hath got the right Anne?' Marrying a transvestite BOY (catamite) *is* strange. See PEASANT for who got the RIGHT (L *rectum*) ANNE (Fr *âne*, ass).

Cym, II.i.38. The epicene Cloten, 'capon' and 'ass', wonders that a 'stranger' (used four times in nine lines), an 'Italian' (ITALIAN, sodomite), had arrived in court without his knowing. 2nd Lord: 'He [Cloten]'s a strange fellow himself, and knows it not.' The Italian is Iachimo, 'saucy [SAUCY, lascivious] stranger' of I.vi.151 (see RAMP).

TN, I.iii.120. Sir Andrew, who has the 'back-trick' (EXCELLENT), is 'a fellow o' the strangest mind [MIND, arse] i' the world'.

AYL, I.iii.130. Rosalind adopts the name GANYMEDE (catamite), and Celia chooses 'Something that hath a reference to my state; / No longer Celia, but Aliena'. Her STATE (arse) is like her new name, a pun on (1) L *alienare*, banish – as she and Ganymede have been; (2) L *aliena*, the (f.) stranger – a word Sh often links to UNNATURAL (deviant) sexual behaviour. Aliena, whose love for Rosalind is 'dearer [DEAR / dear, a hind] than the natural bond of sisters' marries Oliver, who is also 'unnatural', 'most [MOST, *fin* – Cot; arse pun] unnatural' and 'stranger as I am' (IV.iii.123,153).

IV.iii.52. Phebe loves the girl–boy Rosalind–Ganymede, this 'god' who has a 'strange effect' on her. 'Meaning me a beast [BEAST, bestial love]', says Ganymede.

Ado, V.iv.49: 'some strange bull leap'd your father's cow'. This bull was not only adulterous but also likened to 'Bull Jove', a god who, transformed to an animal, mated with a human and was, therefore, strange.

Tem, II.ii.28, 32. Following Caliban's being buggered (BITE), Trinculo finds him 'flat' (PLAIN, lit. flat: a sodomite): 'A strange fish! Were I in England . . . there would this monster make a man; any strange beast there makes a man'. Fish: female genitals; whore (F&H; P) – as opposed to male flesh. Any MONSTER (homosexual) or BEAST (sodomite) makes (makes love to – C; P) a MAN (L *homo*). He decides to 'creep under his gaberdine. . . . misery acquaints a man with strange bed-fellows.' ACQUAINT: know carnally.

See OLD LADY, *MWW*; COCKNEY, *TN*; THIGH, *1H4*.

Stretch Coital stretching of male and female genitals. In Chapman's *All Fools*, IV.i, a man flirts with his friend's wife: 'What huge large thongs he cuts/ Out of his friend Fortuno's stretching leather [LEATHER, L *scortum*: hide; prostitute]'.

1H4, I.ii.61: 'so far as my coin would stretch'. Coin: coit (P); coin/ quoin: penis (K).

KL, IV.ii.23, Goneril: 'this kiss, if it durst speak,/ Would stretch thy spirits up into the air:/ Conceive, and fare thee well'. His SPIRIT (penis) would stretch *up* – into the air (an heir?): *conceive*.

See FISTULA; CHEVERIL, *RJ*, *H8*; LIFE, *AC*; SERVANT, *R3*.

Strip(e) Deflower, emasculate. Lit. remove fruit from a tree (ME); 1697, seed from grain. Sh puns on strip/ stripe. *KL*, IV.vi.165: 'Why dost thou lash that whore? Strip thine own back' – (1) strip his own clothes off; (2) stripe his own back.

AC, III.xiii.152. After having the messenger castrated (see WHIP), Antony says, 'Hence with thy stripes, begone!' Be *gone*: 1598, ruined; striped by the whip and stripped of his seed, testicles.

MM, II.iv.102, Isabella: 'were I under the terms of death,/ The impression of keen whips I'ld wear as rubies,/ And strip myself to death, as to a bed . . . ere I'ld yield/ My body up to shame'. Her speech evokes the blood of TERMS (menstrual flow), hymenal blood of defloration, and, last, the ruby blood of stripes, which she would wear rather than be stripped of her chastity or her sexuality (YIELD/ yeld, be barren; see SNATCH for the irony of this speech).

WT, IV.iii.60. Autolycus was 'robbed', 'beaten', and 'detestable things' were put upon him. Their loathsomeness 'offends me more than the stripes I have received'. He is off-*end*ed (end: penis – P), stripped, robbed of his testes (see VIRTUE). Detestable/ DE-TESTED things (genitals – F&H; P) were put on him, 'rags' (RAGS, L *scruta*), he says, as he picks the Clown's purse (scrotum – F&H; P; see YIELD). The 'horseman's coat' he is wearing – the COAT/ cod (testicle – K) of a HORSE/ whore's man – has seen 'hot service' ('A plague on her for a hot whore' – Marlowe, *Doctor Faustus*, I.v): an exact description of his past copular service and venereal infection (MERCURY) that really robbed him, emptied his purse (syn. for impotency – F&H).

Subdue Seduce. Used with meanings of L *seducere*, to deceive, seduce (*OED*).

See RATE, *AW*; INFINITE, *AW*; EXCEED, *Cym*; BOY, *LLL*; QUITE, *MM*.

Subject A female or pathic. Lit. one who submits; placed beneath. Katherine Philips addresses many poems to Lucasia, the 'dear object of my love's excess' (from 'Orinda to Lucasia Parting', in *Signet Classic Poets of the 17th c*., vol. II, p. 348). In 'Friendship's Mystery, to my Dearest Lucasia' (p. 346), she writes that they are 'Both princes and subjects too./ Our hearts are mutual victims laid'. As Broadbent says (p. 317), 'we are bound to think of her work as lesbian'. MUTUAL: homosexual.

TSh, V.ii.155: 'Such duty as the subject owes the prince/ Even such a woman oweth to her husband . . . vail your stomachs . . . place your hands below your husband's foot'. A subject owes the prince and a woman owes a husband SUCH (*tale* – F) duty of the tale/ tail as placing the HANDS (genitals) beneath his FOOT (coitus – K; P).

CE, II.i.19:

Luciana. O, know he is the bridle of your will.
Adriana. There's none but asses will be bridled so.
Luciana. . . . The beasts, the fishes, and the winged fowls
Are their males' subjects and at their controls;
Men . . .
Are masters to their females, and their lords.

(1) Puns on *bridal* (a bride is a spouse of either sex) and BRIDLE, curb on a horse and on Adriana's will (vulva – C; P). Cf. the idiom, *brider l'asne par la queue*, bridle the ass by the tail, 'goe the wrong way to worke, to doe a thing by contraries' (Cot). Only *asses* will be so bridled, says Adriana (cf. Rabelais, Bk IV, ch. 30: 'The Colon, like a Bridle' – 1694 trs.). Is there a pun on the bridle bit that is put in the mouth? (2) Is there a deliberate ambiguity: men are masters to their females and (are) their lords – or men are masters to their females and (to) their lords (the asses/ arses that will be so bridled)?

MV, v.i.238: 'I am the unhappy subject of these quarrels', says Antonio, the same 'sad' (I.i.1) Antonio who had said 'let . . . my love . . . Be valued 'gainst your wife's commandment' (IV.i.151) and had urged a reluctant Bassanio to give away his wife's ring (vulva – TWR; P) – which he now calls Portia's 'husband's ring [L*anus*]' (250). Antonio is the subject (one 'bound' to a superior – *OED*) who 'once did lend my body for his wealth;/ Which but for [Portial],/ Had quite miscarried; I dare be bound again'. This is the 'bankrupt', Shylock says (III.i.47; IV.i.122), who had *hind*ered him. Cf. *monter sur l'asne*, a phrase derived from ancient custom whereby bankrupts had to ride backward on an ass, *holding his tail in their hands*, as a bridle (Cot). (The Antonio in *CE*, above, was also 'arrested' for 'debt' and compared to a 'bankrupt' – IV.ii.43, 48, 58.)

Antonio once did LEND (press coitally; loins) his body for Bassanio; now again he dare/ *dare* (to give – F) or gives it in bondage, as subject. Antonio's body (OE *bodig*, OHG *botach*) or genitals (P), his buttock or arse, had QUITE/ *coit*ally miscarried, in homosexual bondage, until Portia came on the scene, and his flesh would equally have miscarried legally had she not come on that scene. Portia has told Bassanio (136), 'You should in all sense be much bound to him,/ For . . . he was much bound for you' – pun on *cense* (valuation of an income) and *sense* (faculty for gratifying 'lusts of the flesh' – *OED*; P). Antonio: 'No more than I am well acquitted [QUIT/ coit] of.'

In another part of the stage, Gratiano is simultaneously confessing to Nerissa that he, too, has given away a ring, albeit it was 'paltry' (of the nature of refuse or TRASH: scrotum), to one he wishes 'were gelt'.

See LIAR, *2H4*.

Subtle, sutler A sutler follows an army and sells provisions. By extension, a whore who serves thousands. Middleton, *The Changeling*, II.ii: 'if a woman/ Fly . . . from him she makes a husband,/ She spreads and mounts then like arithmetic . . . Proves in time sutler to an army royal'; *Michaelmas Term*, I.i: Shortyard, who is to 'flatter, dice, and brothel to' the victim, 'be his bawd for once', 'creep into bed with him', 'kiss him, and undo him' says, 'What subtilty's in man that is not in mine?'

Oth, IV.ii.21. Othello calls Desdemona 'a subtle whore', meaning a whore for his whole army. In III.iii.345 he made the same point: 'I had been happy, if the general camp . . . had tasted her sweet body,/ So I had nothing known.'

TA, I.i.392: 'How comes it that the subtle Queen of Goths/ Is of a sudden thus advanced in Rome?' The very language of the question contains the answer: Tamora, the subtle QUEEN/ quean or whore of the Goths/ goats (symbols of lechery – K; C) is of a SUDDEN (for lasciviousness) so advanced in Rome.

3H6, III.i.33. King Henry says that Warwick, who went to France 'to crave the French King's sister/ To wife for Edward', will succeed, 'For Warwick is a subtle orator'. He is an ORATOR (pimp), a subtle one, pimping for a French wife for Edward. When news arrives that Edward has married Lady Grey, Warwick reviews the self-abasing things he has done for this Edward (iii.181–91), a list that substantiates his having been subtle and an orator in their worst sense and explains why he is now 'guerdon'd at the last with shame'.

Such(like) (1) Sick: Sc sic and L *sic* mean such. Symbol of moral decay.
(2) *Tale*: such(like), such a man, woman or thing (F). Tale: pubic–anal area (K; P).
3H6, I.i.215:

King Henry. Be patient, gentle queen. . . .
Queen Margaret. Who can be patient in such extremes?

Pun on being a patient and sick; the such (*tale*) extremes are the 'entail' of the crown to York, the denying his own son's 'birthright'. See CROWN.

JC, IV.iii.89. Sickness is a theme running through the scene: Cassius says a friend would not see 'such faults' as his 'infirmities'; he tells Brutus to mind his 'health' (36) and asks 'Upon what sickness' Portia died (150). Brutus notes Cassius's 'rash choler' [CHOLER, arse, tail]' (39) and 'spleen' (47) and says he, too, is 'sick of many griefs [GRIEF, illness of the tail, bowel]' (142). Another conspirator, Ligarius, was a 'sick man' (II.i.310). Caesar was right when he said of Cassius '*such* men are *dangerous*' (I.ii.195). Ironically, it is Caesar who is sick and who says, 'danger knows full *well*/That Caesar is more *dangerous* than he' (II.ii.44): Caesar with his 'fever' and 'fit', who cried like a '*sick* girl' and amazed Cassius that a man of '*such* a feeble temper' should rule (I.ii.119–29). (Italics added.)

MM, II.i.114. Pompey discusses the brothel-frequenters: 'Why, very well . . . such a one and such a one were past cure of the thing you wot of, unless they kept a very good diet'; 'Why, very well, then, –'. WELL (whores; prostitution) is the reason they are *sick* and need a diet, a VD cure (see RHEUM). *Such* a one *and such* a one – pl. of 'such', L *tales* – are the sick tails of the whores and their customers.

MV, V.i.1: 'In such a night' is the phrase (repeated eight times) with which Lorenzo and Jessica introduce a series of tales of illicit loves, of betrayed lovers and deceived parents. In such a night, she says, he did STEAL her soul (made a stale, a whore, of her). The arriving Portia describes it as 'This night methinks is but the day-light *sick* . . . 'tis a day,/*Such as* the day is when the sun is hid' (124; italics added).

There was another betrayal on a day when the sun was hid: 'and it was about the sixth hour, and there was a darkness over all the earth until the ninth hour. And the sun was darkened' (Luke 23:44).

Jessica says she 'would out-night' Lorenzo (OUT, Fr *hors*/ whores) – but 'hark, I hear the footing of a man'. She hears the *foot*ing of the messenger, *Step*hano. Footing, i.e. prick, track of a hare (Jonson, *The Sad Shepherd*, II.ii: 'prick her footing hence'). Jessica says 'hark' (hunting call of attention) and Launcelot says 'Sola, sola! wo ha, ho!', the same call. Jessica does *hear* the footing of a *hare*. Sadly for all, FOOT means lechery and fuck (TWR; F&H; P) and *hare* means a bawd; and this conclusion to 23 lines of 'such a night' informs us that the talk has been of *both* kinds of venery (pursuit of game and of sexual pleasure) and will continue to be, with a new cast of characters, whose arrival Stephano and Launcelot announce (the post 'with his horn full of good news' – footing, POST, and horn: three pricks). See Introduction, p. xi, *VA*.

This is a group not of happy, true lovers, but of betrayers and betrayed, who are feeling what Goddard (p. 84) calls 'vague discontent, an unexplained sense of something wrong', who quarrel (playfully?) about wedding-RINGS (genitals – F&H; P) – 'a paltry ring' (147); but 'You swore . . . you would wear it till your hour of death' – and about cuckoldry; whose greatest joy is in Antonio's ships that 'Are safely come to road [a whore – C; P]' (288) and in the 'special deed of gift,/After his death, of all he [Shylock] dies possess'd of' – Shylock, who had left the court-room saying, 'I am not well' and 'you take my life/When you do take the means whereby I live'. Shylock is *sick* on *such* a night. Jessica and Lorenzo are the heirs (hair/heir/here/hare – K).

Lorenzo greets Portia's statement with 'Fair ladies, you drop manna in the way/Of starved people'. A 'way' (C; P) and the 'way of women' (P) – ladies – is whoring. The wanton frivolity of these people is further insinuated in 'you drop manna in the way of' or you drop *manna* in the *manner* of: the fair ladies are doing something in the MANNER (q.v.) of, the act of doing something unlawful – neither fair, nor lawful, nor merciful.

The 'quality of mercy . . . droppeth as the gentle rain from heaven' and so did manna (Ps 78:24: 'And had rained down manna upon them to eat'). Was this Portia's mercy? Manna for the rich group at Belmont, Lorenzo and Jessica – hardly starved, except spiritually.

We need no more to condemn this group and to tell us that Act V is repeating what Sh had said in I.ii.6: 'they are as sick that surfeit with too much as they that starve with nothing'. For other puns on Sh's view of the world at Belmont, see BANK; CACKLE; SHIP.

See WITCHCRAFT, *CE*; TOMBOY, *Cym*; WORD, *Tim*; MISUSE, *1H4*; SHARE, *MM*.

Sudden Lustful; incontinent, i.e. unable to contain passion (or bowels, as in *KJ*, V.vi.30: 'Whose bowels suddenly burst out'). *Subito*: suddenly; *subire, subito*: to grunt for the boar as the sow does when in heat; to 'lust for most beastly' (F). *Soudainement*: suddenly, incontinently (Cot).

Mac, IV.iii.59. Malcolm calls Macbeth 'bloody,/ Luxurious, avaricious, false, deceitful,/ Sudden, malicious, smacking of every sin', in which list 'sudden' means lustful and *incontinent*, for Malcolm continues that his own 'voluptuousness', 'lust' and 'desire/ All *continent* impediments would o'er bear' (italics added).

Oth, IV.ii.192. Roderigo gave Iago jewels for Desdemona and was assured in return 'expectations and comforts of sudden respect and acquaintance' – at face value not what he hoped for, but comforts (P) and respect (P) are coitus, and theirs will be sudden or lustful. ACQUAINTANCE: carnal knowledge.

Ham, II.ii.215. Polonius, who had planned to 'loose' (163) – put the female to the male for breeding – Ophelia to Hamlet, now says he will 'suddenly contrive the means of meeting between him and my daughter'. He will be the MEANS (pander) for the sudden MEETING (coitus).

AYL, V.ii.32: 'there was never any thing so sudden but the fight of two rams . . . they looked . . . loved . . . made a pair of stairs to marriage which they will climb incontinent, or else be incontinent before marriage: they are in the very wrath of love and they will together'. The first 'incontinent' means immediately; the second, yielding to lust; and both are encompassed in 'sudden'.

A sudden *fight* of two rams (symbols of lechery – C) to parallel the *wrath* of love felt by Celia and Oliver is interesting in light of the play's ambisexuality. Aliena–Celia (see STRANGER for her sexual ambivalence) has been living in a *sheep*cote with GANYMEDE; and she and her husband-to-be are compared to two rams or two *male* sheep.

See SUBTLE, *TA*.

Suffer Be a pathic, one upon whom sodomy is practised (Sh's metaphor for sufferance). Lit. one who suffers or undergoes something. Jonson, *The Alchemist*, II.iii: 'Some do believe hermaphrodeity,/ That both do act and suffer'.

CE, III.i.16:

Antipholus E. I think thou art an ass.
Dromio E. . . . so it doth appear
By the wrongs I suffer and the blows I bear.

Dromio compares himself to an *ass* that bears the blows (coital thrusts – C; P), suffers the WRONGS (penises – K) of others; the passive sexual partner, who bears (is recumbent in the sex-act – C; P).

Cor, III.i.303. To kill Coriolanus 'Were to us all, that do't and suffer it,/ A brand'. Another example of the opposition of those who do't (do: copulate – C; P) or perform the sexual act, and those who suffer it or have it done to them

Oth, V.ii.256. Gratiano tells Othello, 'Thou hast no weapon, and perforce must suffer'. He speaks of Othello's impotence in the situation: having no arms, no weapon (penis – C; P), he is reduced to playing a passive role. The *double-entendre* continues in Othello's answer: 'naked as I am, I will assault thee'; 'Behold, I have a weapon; / A better never did itself sustain / Upon a soldier's thigh'. Othello claims to be capable of assault (an onslaught of passion – P), saying that for that he has a better weapon that any on a soldier's thigh ('naked' and 'weapon' evoke the 'naked weapon' – the pun on sword and penis in *RJ*, I.i.39); however, with his weapon, his sword, though he wounds Iago, he fails to kill the man who wronged or buggered him: it is only *ass*ault he is capable of.

See PATIENCE, with which SUFFER is freq. linked.

Supply Satisfy sexually, as in Nashe, *The Choice of Valentines*: 'My little dildo shall supply their kind', i.e. replace inadequate men.

MM, V.i.212. Mariana says it was she who slept with her husband Angelo, though in the dark he had assumed he was seducing Isabella: 'this is the body / That took away the match from Isabel / And did supply thee at thy garden-house'.

TSh, III.ii.251. When Petruchio and Kate do not stay for their marriage celebration, poor Baptista unwittingly says, 'Lucentio, you shall supply the bridegroom's place; / And let Bianca take her sister's room'. This is welcome *carte blanche* to these lovers, as Tranio knows when he quips, 'Shall sweet Bianca practise how to bride it?' One is only left to wonder whether Lucentio did indeed supply the PLACE (pudendum); and whether Bianca did take (common euphemism for accept sexually – P; F&H) and use her sister's room before her own secret wedding.

Sure(ty) 1. Of whores, fornication. Sure–cure rhyme (K); pun on 'sewer'. Venus Cloacina, goddess of sewers: Roman epithet for Venus, the purifier. Gay, *Trivia*: 'Cloacina, goddess of the tide . . . the town she roved / A mortal scavenger she saw she loved.' See SHORE. 2. A betrothal (obs.).

TrC, V.i.83, Thersites: 'Sweet draught: "sweet" quoth a'! sweet sink, sweet sewer [Folio sp. "sure"].' Three SWEET sewers: *draught* (sink, privy), *sink* and *sure* – 'The tide' (90).

MM, I.ii.72, Mistress Overdone: 'I am too sure of it: and it is for getting Madam Julietta with child.' (1) As bawd, she is by def. *sure*; she is *too* sure, *Over*done (do: fornicate – C; P). (2) She is *too* sure the *two* fornicators will be punished, though they were sure, betrothed (151).

Oth, I.iii.396: 'It is thought abroad that, 'twixt my sheets / He hath done my office. . . . I, for mere suspicion in that kind, / Will do as if for surety'. The unusual use of 'surety' is freq. said to mean Iago will behave as if sure. But in the context of what has been *done* to him, it seems Iago in that KIND (in coitus) also will do (screw – C; P) as if for surety, for sewer whores. He plans to make Othello think he is a cuckold. Cf. Jonson, Chapman and Marston, *Eastward Ho*, I.i: 'I had the horn [cuckold's] of suretyship ever before my eyes.'

TA, IV.ii.72. The Nurse holds Tamora's illegitimate child, 'black' like its father: [Tamora] 'sends it thee, thy stamp, thy seal, / And bids thee christen it with thy dagger's point'. Aaron: ' 'Zounds, ye whore! is black so base a hue? / Sweet blowse, you are a beauteous blossom, sure.' Editors say 'blowse', a 'ruddy faced wench', a def. from Johnson's *Dictionary*, is ironic, since the child is neither. I suggest it is a verbal caress for the SWEET blowse (beggar's slut – F&H); *blows*: coitus (P) and blossoms (*OED*). His child is a beauteous 'blossom, sure', a *sewer blossom*, born of a whore. Being black, it is of his stamp (begetting – C; P), of his SEAL (penis), that which warrants it is his, makes sure. The anger in 'whore' may be for both the Nurse and Tamora, who wants her (his) child killed. 'ZOUNDS are God's wounds, but there will be no stigma (stigmata: Christ's wounds) on his son; this father will not let them kill his son.

Tem, I.ii.475, Miranda: 'I'll be his surety' – to which Prospero returns, 'Silence! . . . An advocate for an imposter!' Miranda, who means she will be surety for Ferdinand's good behaviour, is the smitten girl soon to be his sure or betrothed. Prospero takes 'surety' to mean she will go between the men, be ADVOCATE (pimp, go-between); perh. 'advocate', one who espouses, puns on espousal, betrothal, becoming sure. Though his anger is pretended (?), the sudden brutality and vulgarity of what Miranda calls his 'unwonted' speech (497) suggests a possessive father's jealousy at having to share with this young, handsome arrival what had been her exclusive love for him: 'Thou think'st there is no more such shapes as he,/ Having seen but him and Caliban.' SUCH (*tale*- F) SHAPES (genitals) reveals his fear.

3. Sure/*suer*, to sweat (Cot), i.e. with VD and its cure, the sweating-tub. See GOUT, *Cym.*

AC, III.x.10. Scarus compares Antony's loss at sea, when he followed the diseased whore Cleopatra (LEPROSY), to a 'sure' death.

See AGE, *Cor.*

Sutler See SUBTLE.

Swagger(er) Bawdy-house bully or pimp. *Ruffa*: harlot; *ruffo*, swaggerer, ruffian; minion (F). Linked closely to RUFFIAN (pimp). *Ruffiano*: bawd; swaggerer (F). Scott, *The Fortunes of Nigel*, ch. 3: 'I was disturbed with some of the night-walking queans and swaggering billies.'

TN, V.i.408. The Clown concludes the play singing, 'But when I came alas! to wive . . . By swaggering could I never thrive'. We had seen him swagger – play (bawdy) house bully and try to get more coins in return for taking Cesario in to his mistress Olivia: 'I would play Lord Pandarus . . . to bring a Cressida to this Troilus' (III.i.58).

2H4, II.iv. 'Ancient [ANCIENT, pimp] Pistol', the 'swaggering rascal' and 'ancient swaggerer', is thrown out by Doll, the whore, and Mistress Quickly, the Hostess, who will have no swaggerers or swaggering (these words used 12 times) in her house. See MOULD.

Sweet (1) Sexual intimacy (P). Marston, *Antonio's Revenge*, I.i: 'you have disturb'd the pleasure of the finest dream. O God, I was even coming to it, la . . . 'twas coming of the sweetest'. *Faire le sucré* (lit. make sweetness): masturbate (Cot).

(2) Genitals. Marston, *Antonio's Revenge*, I.i: 'He won the lady . . . And from her sweets/ Cropp'd this Antonio', his son. Testicles. *Suites*: wild boar's cods (Cot); doucet/ DULCET: deer's testes; sweet. Playing with testes was a masturbatory image: see *MND* below.

TGV, II.vii.28. *En route* to a lover, Julia envisions their embrace as a current whose 'fair course' if 'not hindered . . . makes sweet music with the enamell'd stones,/ Giving a gentle kiss to every sedge'. The *fair* COURSE/ Fr *corser* (embrace sexually) *makes sweet* music or *fait le sucré* (makes sweetness) with the stones (testes – *OED*) and kisses every sedge (*balls* kiss when they touch gently in billards – F&H; *OED* 1579). Bisexuality pervades the scene: Juliet is disguised in 'such weeds'/ *sedge weeds* (such, *tale* – F) as 'breeches' with a 'codpiece' and 'round hose'; she, transvestite, is off to Proteus, whose name means trans-shape, alter SHAPE. (*Ado*, V.i.172: 'trans-shape' is used for Benedick, whom Beatrice said 'with a sigh' was the 'properest man [MAN, L *homo*] in Italy [ITALY, land of sodomites]' – 'For the which she wept heartily and said she cared not.' See DEFORMED.

MND, V.i.175: 'O sweet . . . O sweet and lovely wall. . . . O wicked wall . . . Curst be thy stones for thus deceiving me!' *Coglionare*: to 'play with ones stones. Also to cogge or deceive one' (F). The *stones* of the sweet WALL (buttocks) deceived *Bottom*.

TrC, V.x.45. Pandarus's direful views on fornication, disease, and impotence end the play: the bee loses 'his honey [HONEY: semen; potency] and his sting [STING: penis; potency]', and is 'subdued in armed tail' (ARM and *tail*: penis). 'Sweet honey and sweet notes together fail' – the honey of his *suites* or testicles, his sweet NOTES (genitals) fail and fall.

Tim, I.ii.102. Friends we don't 'use' (coitally – C; P) 'resemble sweet instruments hung up in cases that keep their sounds to themselves'. Sweet instruments (genitals – F&H; P) hung (see HANG) up in cases or codpieces do not SOUND (probe the bottom). Packed away they do not make music – or love. Timon's false friends develop his conceit of genitals and love-making: 'Joy had the like conception in our eyes/ And . . . like a babe sprung up.' Cf. a similar pun in Middleton, *The Roaring Girl*, IV.i: Moll never lets 'his instrument hang by the walls'.

R2, I.iii.68. About to fight, Bolingbroke embraces his father: 'The daintiest last, to make the end most sweet . . . author of my blood . . . with a two-fold vigour lift me up . . . steel my lance's point' that he 'may . . . furbish' their family name in his 'lusty haviour'. A metaphor for his becoming potent, virile, strong from this embrace, this physical contact with the author of his

BLOOD (semen). His father with his dainties (DAINTY, testicle), his TWO-FOLD (testes) vigour, will *lift* him *up*, make the *end* sweet – will STEEL (like an erect penis) the point (erection – C; P) of his lance (weapon and penis – P). However, Bolingbroke and his father both suffer a defeat: see CROOKED, where the same metaphor expresses deterioration.

See TRAIN, *KL*; DRAWERS; SWINE, *TSh*.

Swerve Be sexually unfaithful. Lit. deviate from a course.

Son 87. Losing his lover, Sh says 'And so my patent back again is swerving' – an ambiguity: (1) his patent or licence is swerving back again to its owner; (2) his patent, i.e. open to public use (*MND*, I.i.77: 'virgin patent'), sexually open or available, *back* is again swerving, in infidelity.

See CREATURE, *WT*.

Swine A bugger. Fr *cochon*: a pig; adj., beastly, lewd. *Bougre*: a bugger; *bougre de cochon*: an epithet (F&H, s.v. Brick). *Cochonner*: to pig; as a sow to bring forth a litter; to cocker, nourish daintily.

KJ, v.ii.142. The Bastard denigrates the French led by the Dauphin: 'This apish and unmannerly approach. . . . This unhair'd sauciness and boyish troops . . . this dwarfish war, these pigmy arms'. These French will be made to 'hug with swine'. The apish and UNMANNERLY (unmanly) APPROACH/broach or pierce (sexually), esp. a butt; the unhair'd and BOYISH, i.e. effeminate, troops, led by a dwarfish WAR/whore, who in the previous scene was called a 'beardless boy' and 'cocker'd' (*cochonné*). The *pig*my (anything small of its kind; Gk *pyge*, rump) ARMS (penises) of the French, who will be made to hug with swine – embrace or bugger swine, be *bougres de cochon*.

R3, v.ii.10. Richmond urges his men on: 'Thus far into the bowels of the land/Have we march'd. . . The wretched, bloody, and usurping boar/That . . . makes his trough/In your embowell'd bosoms, this foul swine/Lies now even in the centre of this isle'. Into the bowels they went, seeking the trough in which the swine Richard (the boar is his crest) LIES (buggers/It *bugiare*, to lie). He makes his *bauge* (muddy 'place wherein a wild bore hath wallowed or lien' – Cot) in their bosoms (laps – C; P), their em*bowel*l'd bosoms. He lies in the CENTRE (pudendum; external genitalia).

TSh, Induction, i.34, Lord: 'O monstrous beast! how like a swine he lies!' Almost every word puns on buggery (MONSTROUS, homosexual; BEAST, sodomite; LIE, bugger), in anticipation of the Lord's immediately conceived plan to wrap Sly in 'sweet clothes' (odd use of sweet, but SWEET is sexually intimate), feed him a 'delicious banquet', in other words cocker him (*cochonner*). The conceit on buggery (see BUDGER) culminates in his being sexually aroused by a page dressed as a woman, whom he attempts to bed.

Swinge Copulate (F&H). Beaumont and Fletcher, *The Beggar's Bush*, III.i: 'Give her cold jelly/To take up her belly,/And once a day swinge her again'. Lit. lash the tail (or somebody with the tail).

MWW, v.v.199. Slender mistakenly eloped with a boy: 'she's a great lubberly boy. If it had not been i' the church, I would have swinged him, or he should have swinged me. If I did not think it had been Anne Page, would I might never stir!'; 'If I had been married to him, for all he was in woman's apparel, I would not have had him'. Puns on the two modes of swingeing (F&H), beating and copulating. The boy in woman's apparel was LUBBERLY (lascivious, homosexual) or might Slender never STIR (fornicate, bugger). See SLAVE, *TGV*, for another BOY (catamite) who will be swinged.

2H4, III.ii.24. Shallow boasts of the days when he was 'lusty Shallow' and would 'have done any thing indeed'. He and Pickbone and Doit/do-it, etc. – 'you had not four such swinge-bucklers in all the inns o' the court . . . we knew where the bona-robas were'. They used to swinge the bucklers (pudenda – C; P) of the bona-robas (whores – *OED*; P); and were themselves four swinge-bucklers or fucking whores (buckler: It *brochiere*, root of *brocchiera*, whore – F&H, s.v. Barrack-hack). JUSTICE (the arse) *Shallow*, cousin to *Slender* in *MWW* above (names that suggest a coital inadequacy), would have done 'any thing indeed' (see INDEED).

TSh, v.ii.104: 'Go, fetch them hither: if they deny to come,/ Swinge me them soundly forth unto their husbands.' Ordered to come (sexual spasm – P), two wives 'cannot come', 'will not come' – only Kate 'comes'. When FETCHED (for coitus), wives are to come or be swinged (*tail* lashed) SOUNDLY (to the bottom) forth/*for't*.

T

Table Serve at table or satisfy lust. A 'sewer' is one who superintends table service; a channel for carrying off excreta; anat., the cloaca; and an epithet for whores (SHORE). See LIFE, *MV*.

TrC, II.iii.45. After Thersites mocks the pederasty of Achilles (ENGINE) and his lover Patroclus, the entering Achilles greets him, 'Art thou come? why, my cheese, my digestion, why hast thou not served thyself in to my table so many meals?' Probably a pun on 'my cheese' and *cissa*, pron. chissa ('longing or lust of a woman with child'; a 'corrupt appetite', i.e. desire to eat trash – F), since in III.iii.234 (SICK) Achilles says, 'call Thersites . . . I have a woman's longing' (a *cissa*). Why has Thersites not *served himself* (coitally – C; P) *in* to Achilles's table? The primary meaning of 'table' (*OED*) is a board (*CE, MND*, *2H6*), and Sh puns on BOARD (*asse* – F; *ais* – Cot) as the ass/arse.

Ham, IV.iii.26. Asked where Polonius is (LOBBY), Hamlet says, 'At supper', where 'he is eaten' by worms: 'your fat king and your lean beggar is but variable service, two dishes, but to one table: that's the end'. Hamlet's vitriol is to remind the King he is mortal, like Polonius, whom he can 'nose' as he goes into the 'lobby' (LOBBY: privy; arse). It is also a searing reflection that both men are asses, both buggerers of mankind: (1) the FAT king (*fat*: foppish, an 'asse' – Cot); and (2) Polonius, the LEAN (pimp: as also in SUDDEN; COUNSELLOR) BEGGAR/bugger. Both king and beggar are *but* VARIABLE (fit for buggery) service – 'but [/butt] to one table: that's the end' – that, i.e. the table, is the end, arse, sewer or server.

'. . . a king may go a progress through the guts of a begger' – be eaten by worms that are fed to fish that are eaten by beggars and then excreted: these are the *lug*worms or *lob*worms used for bait (Hamlet said he would 'lug the guts' of Polonius to the *lob*by – III.iv.212). A king may also go another PROGRESS (fornication) through the guts of a BEGGAR/bugger.

2H4, II.ii.190. To see Falstaff 'bestow himself to-night in his true colours, and not ourselves be seen' Hal and Poins will 'Put on two leathern jerkins and aprons, and wait upon him at his table as drawers.' Falstaff will BESTOW (in beastly fashion) himself on Doll and Mistress Quickly, 'the parish heifers'. And these two voyeurs will wear jerkins of LEATHER (L *scortum*: leather; a whore) and aprons (*tabliers* – Cot) and will (1) wait upon him as drawers, i.e. TAPSTERS (pimps); (2) as drawers, those who draw (expose the phallus – C; P); (3) wait upon him at table or BOARD (*asse*, *ais*); (4) in other words, will be as close as, will wait *upon* him like DRAWERS (1567, garment for the lower part of the body).

Taffeta Whores' dress (C). Dekker, *Lanthorne and Candle-light*, ch. 9: 'Harlots in Taffeta gownes' (in *The Guls Hornbook etc*, p. 241).

AW, II.ii.23: 'your taffeta punk [prostitute]'.

1H4, I.ii.11: 'bawds' and 'leaping-houses' (brothels) and a 'fair hot wench in flame-coloured taffeta'.

LLL, V.ii.406. Biron will 'never come in vizard [VISARD, mask worn by whores] to my friend'; he renounces his effeminate hypocrisy: 'Taffeta phrases, silken terms . . . three-piled hyperboles, spruce affectation' – false and diseased sentiments: SILKEN (effeminate) TERMS (the menses); THREE-PILED (piles, VD symptom; tuftaffety: taffeta with tufted pile) hyperboles. He admits he is SICK (q.v.) with 'plague' (EYES). Substitution of 'affectation' for the 'affection' of the folios and quartos has unfortunately lost the associated meanings of AFFECTION (sensual desire, and infection).

See SAFFRON, *AW*.

Tame Castrate, make impotent; effeminate. To carve, cut, prune: 'Tayme that crabbe'; 'Then he tameth his stacks of corn' (*CD*). Opposes 'wild' (yielding to sexual ardour – *OED*; TWR). Chaucer, 'The Monk's Tale', 301: be her husband 'wilde or tame', Zenobia will mate only once, to engender a child.

TA, II.iii.118: 'Semiramis, nay, barbarous Tamora'. See SEMIRAMIS, who mated with animals and castrated men; BARBAROUS *Tamor*a, too, is a *tamer*.

TrC, I.i.10: 'weaker than a woman's tear,/ Tamer than sleep'. Troilus feels impotent: (1) weaker than a woman's tear (K): her tear (tēr) and her tear (tār), a hole (female pudendum – F&H; P); (2) tamer than SLEEP (lib: sleep; a castrate), a eunuch. By l.110, he gives a 'woman's answer' to explain his 'womanish' absence from the field.

I.iii.391: 'Two curs shall tame each other' – the two 'mastiffs', Achilles and Ajax, two pederasts; the Greeks are 'dogg'd' (366; DOG: sodomite).

R2, I.i.52: 'Yet can I not of such tame patience [PATIENCE, the female or passive male role] boast'.

TGV, III.ii.80. The lute of Orpheus (who, after his wife's death, 'preferred to centre his affections on boys of tender years' – Ovid, Bk x, 68–106) 'was strung with poets' sinews,/ Whose golden touch could soften steel and stones,/ Make tigers tame' – make soft (1593, effeminate; 'grows soft and effeminate' – Francis Bacon, *Vicissitude of Things*, in *CD*, s.v. Soft) both STEEL (penis) and stones (testicles – *OED*). The golden touch is the bloody one (*Mac*, II.iii.118: 'golden blood'; ii.56: 'If he do bleed,/ I'll gild the faces') of castration. It is (1) the touch (i.e. stripe – *OED*; STRIPE: geld) that tames the tiger; (2) the touch (copulative caress – P) that lures the effeminate male – the golden, bloody, striped TIGER (stripped of testes), the eunuch, the tame, cut tiger.

Taper Penis. A wax taper was a 'pricket'. A visual and verbal pun on the prick (1592, penis).

R2, I.iii.223, Gaunt: 'My oil-dried lamp . . . Shall be extinct with age . . . My inch of taper will be burnt and done'. No more OIL (semen), a small INCH (penis); AGE/ ague (syphilis) has burnt (venereally – *OED*; P) him out (see CROOKED).

TA, IV.ii.89:

> *Demetrius.* I'll broach the tadpole on my rapier's point. . . .
> *Aaron.* Sooner this sword shall plough thy bowels up. . . .
> Now by the burning tapers of the sky
> That shone so brightly when this boy was got . . . .

Demetrius's threat to broach (spit; deflower – *W*; P; pierce a butt) Aaron's infant son, the tadpole (*boug*, frog or toad – Cot) on his rapier's point elicits a like threat from Aaron: his sword will plough (fuck – P) Demetrius's bowels (bugger, make a *bougre* of, him). These images lead to Aaron's boast that his – and the heavens' – tapers (*bougies* – Cot) burned the night he begot a son upon Tamora; and he who touches Aaron's boy will die upon his 'scimitar's sharp point [head of the penis – C; P]'. Bougies are (1) tapers; (2) flexible tubes introduced into rectum, urethra, etc. (*OED* 1754). Benjamin Disraeli, in *Coningsby*, calls two political schemers Tadpole and Taper. See SPIT.

When Saturnine chose Tamora for his bride, he, too, swore that 'tapers burn so bright and every thing/ In readiness for Hymenaeus stand' – *every* thing (penis – F&H; P), his *and* that of his cuckolder Aaron, did stand (the erect penis – F&H; P), the burning tapers or prickets on earth and burning tapers in the sky. Cf Vergil, *Aeneid*, Bk IV, 167–8: 'fires flashed in Heaven, the witness to their bridal' ('fulsere ignes et conscius aether/ connubiis'). See Introduction, pp. ix (*Cor*) and xiv (*MND*).

Tapster Broacher of casks, butts; came to mean a broker, pimp, bawd.

MM, I.ii.112. Mistress Overdone, bawd, to Pompey: 'What's to do here, Thomas Tapster? let's withdraw.' Bawd and tapster–pimp both (with)draw: (1) draw liquor from a cask; (2) draw: of men, expose the phallus; of women, incept the man (P).

II.i.232: 'you are partly a bawd, Pompey, howsoever you colour it in being a tapster'. Pompey Bum, whose 'bum is the greatest thing about you', COLOURS/It *culare* (arse-gut) it.
See APPROACH, *Tim*; FROTH, *MM*.

Tartar General term for Tartars, Turks, Mongols. Used opprobriously, as in *MV*, IV.i.32: 'stubborn Turks and Tartars' (see TURK). 'Tartar' is a purgative: Nathaniel Ward, American divine, 1600s, puns on tartar/Tartarus (Hell), 'When I want physick for my body, I would not have my soul tartared' (*CD*). Fecula (L *faecula*, dim. of *faex*, pl. *faeces*): tartar; feculent: covered with faeces (Spenser, *The Faerie Queene*, Bk II, c.vii, st. 61).
TN, II.v.226:

Maria. . . .If you will see it, follow me.
Sir Toby. To the gates of Tartar, thou most excellent devil of wit!
Sir Andrew. I'll make one, too. (*Exeunt*.)

The jest at Malvolio's expense is two-pronged: scatological and directed at his effeminacy (see YELLOW).
In II.iii.188. Maria conceived a plan: 'I know my physic will work with him. I will plant you two, and let the fool make a third' – (1) the Fool may make a third but (2) the fool or 'ass' (182), Malvolio, will make a turd (cf. CAIUS: 'If dere be one or two, I shall make-a the turd').
This explains Andrew's strange exit line, usu. glossed as meaning he will accompany them, too weak an explanation for a final tag and far too lacking in humour to fit the context. Andrew will make one or ane (*OED*), too; he will make *âne* (Fr, an ass) too (DRY: Maria had made '*an* ass' of him already – I.iii.79; italics added).
Toby says Malvolio 'must run mad' (have the runs, diarrhoea). Maria: 'Nay, but say true; does it work upon him?' (214) – but/butt say TRUE/Fr *trou* (anus), does it (her plan, the physic) work (as purgative), for, if so, he will come in 'yellow [YELLOW, excrement colour] stockings'. Maria is the devil of wit (WIT/WHITE), *devil* of the white crystals of tartar or cream of tartar, as the purgative is known. And Toby will follow her to the gates of Hell (Tartarus), the GATES (sluice-gates: excretory orifices – C; P) of Tartar. He ends the scene going to 'burn some sack': (1) tartar, sediment in wine-casks; (2) f(a)ecula, burnt tartar or salt of tartar. He is going to burn in Tartarus with Maria, this devil of *wit*, i.e. *salt*.
See BUNG-HOLE, *H5*.

Taste Enjoy or test sexually (C; P). Connotes the testes.
TN, III.i.89: 'Taste your legs, sir; put them to motion [movements of physical desire – P]'. See GAIT.
TrC, III.ii.98:

Cressida. . . . lovers swear more performance than they are able . . . .
Troilus. . . . such are not we: praise us as we are tasted, allow us as we prove . . . .

PROVE: attest to manhood through the use of testes. Troilus claims he is *teste*d and will prove able (*potere*, to be able – F) or potent in performance (virility – C; P).
See ACORN, *AYL*; ADVENTURE, *Per*.

Tawny Of the vulva. L *fulva*: fulvous or tawny.
AC, I.i.5. The adulterous Antony dotes on Cleopatra's fulvous 'tawny front' and not on his wife's, Fulvia's, vulva. See OFFICE.
II.v.12. Cleopatra and her eunuch discuss how they can entertain themselves, given his limitations. She decides they will 'to the river: there,/My music playing far off, I will betray/Tawny-finn'd fishes; my bended hook shall pierce/Their slimy jaws; and, as I draw them up,/I'll think them every one an Antony'. This *betrayal* of tawny fins, of fulvous fins (fin: obs. sp. of 'fine', the end, esp. of a musical piece) harks back to her conversation with Antony

when he left. Since he had been 'false to Fulvia' for her (I.iii.29), it is natural that now she should be, she said, 'betray'd' by his returning to Fulvia. He need 'seek no colour', no excuse for leaving. She knows he returns to Fulvia: that is the COLOUR/It *culare* (arse) he seeks, that *fulva* colour, Fulvia's vulva.

There is no bar in that the fishes are Antony and hers is the, presumably, male role of piercing. These two often entertained themselves with an exchange of roles (STIR; Index). Her next speech tells how she 'laugh'd him out of patience . . . laugh'd him into patience' (LAUGH, copulate; PATIENCE, passive male role); and 'drunk him to his bed;/Then put my tires and mantles on him, whilst/I wore his sword [penis – C; P] Philippan'. This scene parallels Hercules's enslavement to Omphale, who made him wear her clothes while she donned his lion-skin and carried his club. Antony is supposed to have been descended from Hercules: ' 'Tis the god Hercules, whom Antony loved,/Now leaves him' (IV.iii.15). (*Ado*, II.i.261: with ref. to Omphale's sexual humiliation of Hercules, Benedick says Beatrice would have done worse.)

This is also tied to IV.xii.10: 'This foul Egyptian hath betrayed me' – the tawny Egyptian has betrayed again; and when he is carried to her monument, dying, she tells her women to help for 'we must draw thee up' – the poor fish is drawn up for the last time.

See SCARLET, *1H6*.

Team/teem (1) Be fertile (P), as in *KL*, I.iv.303: 'If she must teem,/Create her child of spleen'. Lear wants 'sterility' for Goneril, but, if she does have a child, let it be created of SPLEEN (generative organ and semen of a fish), let it be a fish (a female pudendum and a whore – F&H; P), like herself. One of Kent's virtues (18) was that he did 'eat [coitally – P] no fish' (see SPLEEN).

(2) Of men, to teem, pour forth from his team OR PAIR, his testicles.

See LAND, *AW*; HATEFUL, *H5*.

Tender (1) Effeminate: tender (ME), tenderling (*OED*), *tenero* (F).

(2) Of testicles. *Daintiers*: tenderings, stones of a deer (Cot); see DAINTY for homosexual relevance.

(3) Offer sexually: ALL, *H8*; ADVOCATE, *WT*, IV.iv; *Ham*, I.iii.100.

RJ, III.i.75. Romeo won't fight Tybalt, whose 'name I tender/As dearly as my own' (as DEAR/deer as his own tenderings). This 'submission' (Mercutio calls it) he soon rejects as 'effeminate'.

R3, IV.i.99, Queen Elizabeth: 'Pity, you ancient stones, those tender babes'. She looks at the stones of the 'Tower' – the 'old . . . playfellow/For tender princes' – and compares the two tender babes with a pair of testes, tenderings, and 'bids your stones farewell' – the Tower's *and* the children's. A historical tradition of castration ensured the end of a line of rival heirs for the throne (Saccio, p. 193). (SHIP-BOY, *KJ*: Arthur met a similar fate.)

IV.385. Queen Elizabeth accuses Richard of murdering the 'two tender playfellows' – the 'children thou hast butcher'd': he is both murderer and BUTCHER/bugger, Richard who violates, castrates, and kills (see EAR).

There is a pun on the *two tender* playfellows and the old playfellow or wall of stones (above), the latter like the 'Old, wither'd plants' (IV.iv.394), the *Plant*agenets, the WITHERED parents whom Richard also buggered or destroyed, they being too old to have other children.

III.iv.65. Told by Hastings of 'The tender love I bear your grace [GRACE, genitals]', Richard responds, 'Then be your eyes the witness of this ill' – let his *tender* love, his EYES (eye-*balls*) be WITNESS (L *testis*), of this ILL (effeminate male); and he holds up his ARM (penis), 'wither'd up' by WITCHCRAFT (a castrating art).

TN, V.i.129. The Duke adds to the ambisexual ambience when he speaks of Viola–Cesario whom Olivia and he both love: 'whom, by heaven I swear, I tender dearly'. By HEAVEN (homosexual love), he tenders Cesario dearly – the DEAR/deer (hind).

See UNNATURAL, *KL*; SNATCH, *MM*.

Tennis (balls) (1) House of ill fame. Fr *tripot*: tennis; house of ill fame. Hall, *Virgidemiae*, IV.i.95: 'as neare, as by report,/ The stewes had wont to be the Tenis-court'. Chapman, Jonson and Marston, *Eastward Ho*, I.i: the master greets an apprentice, a 'drunken whore-hunting rake-hell' who is hiding sword, dagger and racket under his cloak, with 'Heyday, Ruffians' hall . . . here's a racket indeed!' He points to the good apprentice: 'does he pump [copulate – F&H] it, or racket it. . . ?'

(2) Testicles. Middleton, *Women Beware Women*, III.iii: 'I have catched two [balls] in my lap at one game'.

H5, I.ii.258. A 'tun of treasure [semen – P]' and 'Tennis-balls' are sent by the Dauphin, to symbolise Henry's lack of what it takes to perform on tennis-court, in brothel, or in war. Henry answers in kind: 'When we have match'd our rackets to these balls,/ We will, in France . . . play a set/ Shall strike his father's crown into the hazard.' England will match (a love-game – C; P) its rackets to the balls (racketeers: whore-mongers, spreesters – F&H; Fr *raquette*: syn. for 'prick' – F&H n.d.; cf. Rabelais, Bk IV, ch. 31: 'His Genitals . . . erecting Muscles, like a Racket' – 1694 trs.; 'Testicle-muscles like a tennis-racquet' – Putnam). Henry will turn 'his balls to gun-stones', i.e. cannon-balls and virile stones (testicles – *OED*). See EYES.

Ham, II.i.59. Polonius tells Reynaldo to cast aspersion on Laertes: ' ". . . There falling out at tennis"; or perchance/ "I saw him enter such a house of sale."/ Videlicet, a brothel'. Polonius makes an easy transition from falling out, perh. *tripping*, at tennis (*tripot*) to the house of sale or brothel (*tripot*); from falling out, perh. a fault, a tennis (a bisk, bisque), to a brothel (*bisca* – F).

See PEACH, *2H4*.

Term(s) The menstrual period or discharge. Samuel Purchas (1575?–1626): 'In times past . . . no young man married before he slew an enemie, nor the woman before she had her termes, which time was therefore festivall' (in *CD*).

TN, V.i.74: 'terms so bloody and so dear'.

Mac, V.viii.8. This pun is part of the conceit on Macduff's having been 'from his mother's womb/ Untimely ripp'd', his mother's not having experienced labour or gone her full term (time); and on Macbeth's being effeminised, 'cow'd' (see PROMISE):

Macbeth. . . . my soul is too much charged
With blood of thine already.
Macduff. . . . My voice is in my sword: thou bloodier villain
Than terms can give thee out!
Macbeth. Thou losest labour . . . .
I bear a charmed life, which must not yield
To one of woman born.

Macduff boasts of virility: his sword (penis – C; P) will further bloody Macbeth, so deep in others' blood that he is even bloodier than terms. But Macbeth is not afraid; he must not YIELD/ yeld, become barren or gelded by the sword of one whose mother came to her term (of pregnancy).

1H4, I.iii.46. Hotspur expresses contempt for an effeminate 'lord . . . perfumed like a milliner. . . . With many holiday and lady terms/ He question'd me . . . . and talk[ed] so like a waiting-gentlewoman . . . [with] bald unjointed chat' – this 'popinjay' with his holiday ('festivall' – Purchas) terms; bald, lacking hair, the male symbol of virility; and with no JOINT: penis.

LLL, I.i.37. Biron reviews the rules of his approaching all-male existence, the 'three years' term to live with' the king, a 'three years' fast' from women: 'But there are other strict observances;/ As, not to see a woman in that term,/ Which I hope well is not enrolled there . . . . O, these are barren tasks'. Cf. Lev 15: 19–33 on not lying with a woman who is menstruating. This is an aspect of woman's sexuality that seems to obsess Biron (see GERMAN; TAFFETA).

See STRIP, *MM*; MOVE, *TGV*.

Tester(ned) Fee for the pander. See its equiv., the SIXPENCE.

TGV, I.i.153. Speed has delivered Proteus's letter to Julia, whom he calls a 'laced mutton' (prostitute – *OED*; F&H). In return for being go-between, he is 'testerned' – given the usual fee.

See PHRYGIAN, *MWW*; SCAB, *2H4*.

Thigh Source of erotic pleasure: vagina, rump. Anon., 'No True Love between Man and Woman': ' 'Tis Priapus inspires the Talkative Engine,/ And all for the sake of her lilly white Thighs' (*Chorus Poetarum*, 1694).

Oth, III.iii.425. Iago tells Othello he 'lay with Cassio lately' and the dreaming Cassio would 'gripe and wring my hand,/ Cry "O sweet creature!" and then kiss me hard/ . . . then laid his leg/ Over my thigh, and sigh'd, and kiss'd'. TWIST or wring the HAND (penis – K) is a sign of sexual acquiescence, and lay a leg over (F&H 1719) is copulate. 'Kiss' (coit – P) was used in billiards (1579) of a ball touching another when both are in motion, a meaning this position evokes. Iago's repeated 'then' and 'then' implies continued action, and his unembarrassed recounting that Cassio kissed him hard suggests willing participation and lays open to conjecture the sexual relationships among all these men (ANCIENT). Intending to make Othello jealous by saying Cassio called out *sweet* CREATURE (whore – IV.i.98; and sodomite), as if to Desdemona, he implicitly defines himself. 'The Greek vocabulary for homosexual relations distinctly implies that coitus per anum, or at least inter femora, was the normal form' and 'the boy stood and was taken from behind between the thighs' (Wilkinson, p. 24).

JC, II.i.301. Portia asks for her husband's 'secrets': 'I grant I am a woman; but . . . I have made strong proof of my constancy,/ Giving myself a voluntary wound/ Here, in the thigh: can I bear that with patience,/ And not my husband's secrets?' The bizarre self-infliction of a wound to illustrate fortitude borders on the pathological, since to prove anything it would have to be appreciable, and if so its not having been noticed by her husband is further confirmation of what is really wrong. Is this not a symbolic reminder of her sexuality, of their closeness, which he has forgotten, since he does not 'eat, nor talk, nor sleep' and she needs ask, 'Make me acquainted with your cause of grief'. ACQUAINT is copulate; and 'cause', *case* and genitalia are *cas* (Cot). Knowing that 'secrets' are genitals (C; P), and 'bosom' is the pudendum and amorous embrace (C; P), and that after her speech Brutus says Portia's 'bosom shall partake/ The secrets'; noting the use of *coun*sels, *con*stancy, *con*strue, which within 10 lines must suggest CON and 'coun' (P), the cunt; and knowing that the 'knocks' and 'knocking' that interrupt them could be KNOCKS (16th c., coition) – one can then hope the WOUND Portia has is her pudendum, which bears with patience (PATIENCE, female sexual role) and longs to be reacquainted with his cause of grief (that which presses heavily) and his secrets; to *partake*, i.e. *take* (coitally – C; P) of his secret PARTS (genitals – C; P). See QUIVER, *RJ*, and WOUND, *PP*, for another possible thigh–pudendum pun.

1H4, V.iv.131,155. Seeing what he assumes is a dead Falstaff, Hal *says* (109), 'Embowell'd will I see thee by and by'. And this may be exactly what an angered and fearful Falstaff *does* – to what he, in turn, assumes is a dead Percy.

On Hal's exit, Falstaff '*Rising up*' (!) says, 'Embowelled! if thou embowel me today, I'll give you leave to powder [salt] me and eat me too tomorrow.' Bowels (from L *botulus*, sausage or cylindrical roll) is the root of the humour: a sausage was meat enclosed in a short length of intestine (*OED*; Aristophanes, *The Knights*, 363–88: 'And I will pull out your arse to stuff like a sausage'). There are hints of penilingus or sodomy: (1) to *eat* is consume coitally (C; P); (2) 'I gave him this wound in the thigh; if the man were alive and would deny it, 'zounds, I would make him eat a piece of my sword [penis – C; P]'; (3) Lancaster's summation, 'This is the strangest tale [penis – C; P] that ever I heard', and Hal's answer, 'This is the strangest fellow'. See STRANGE (of fornication and sexual deviations); 'ZOUNDS.

Falstaff: 'Therefore, sirrah (*stabbing him*) with a new wound in your thigh, come you along with me.' WOUND (lit. prick), stab coitally. 'Stab' (P) or 'get stabbed in the thigh' (F&H, s.v. Greens): copulate. The next line is Hal's congratulating of John in the suggestive imagery of 'full bravely hast thou flesh'd/Thy maiden sword' ('flesh one's will' and 'sword': coital stab – P).

Several alternatives suggest themselves for the new wound in the thigh. 'Embowel' means (1) convey into the bowels – an act of (symbolic) sodomy with the sword (penis – P); (2) disembowel: fig. castration (BOWELS, arse; perh. balls, testes).

In the previous scene, Falstaff had boasted (iii.46) that 'Turk Gregory never did such deeds in arms as I have done this day. I have paid Percy, I have made him sure.' It is assumed that *Turk* Gregory is *Pope* Gregory VII, detested for ultra-pontifical views and 'unbending assertion of . . . the celibacy of the clergy' (*OED*, s.v. Hildebrandic). Falstaff, however, calls him TURK (known for sodomy and castration) and boasts of his own similar or worse deeds. What better way to ensure celibacy than by castration ('If Percy be alive, I'll pierce him' – 59; Percy/pierce – K); he pierced Percy in his purse (scrotum – *OED*). He PAID (an act of pederasty) Percy; he made him SURE/sewer (a cloaca, a whore). For antecedents of Falstaff's (mis)behaviour, see MISUSE.

I neither suggest nor exclude actual necrophilia. But it is not out of the question that Sh is using puns on aberrant behaviour as commentary on the betrayals and violence that ended in the tragic slaying of young Hotspur by young Hal; and on the difficulty of assigning ultimate responsibility for Hotspur's death, whether it should be laid at the door of those relatives and friends who had let him down, of Hal, who slew him – or of Falstaff, who claims the credit.

Thrash, thresh(old) 'Thrash' and 'thresh' are the same word and both pun on copulate. Dekker and Massinger, *The Virgin Martyr*, II.iii: 'she-thrasher', i.e. whore. See BATTERY.

TrC, II.i.50. Thersites calls Ajax a male whore: 'an *ass*inego may *tutor* thee; thou scurvy-valiant *ass*! thou *art* here but to thrash Trojans; and thou *art* bought and sold . . . like a *barbarian slave*'. The italicised words (except 'ass' and 'assinego') are in this dictionary and are related to the ass/arse and to pederasty.

LLL, III.i.118. Costard was surprised in the sex-act, having fallen over the 'threshold', point of entry, and broken his SHIN (penis), after which his MATTER (semen), q.v., ran out.

See IDLE, *Cor*.

Three The proverbial three, the male genitals, penis and testicles – what the Two Ronnies (BBC comedians) meant in referring to the characteristically skin-tight trousers of pop singer Tom Jones: 'Tom Jones flew a plane, wearing tight trousers and made a remarkable three-point landing.' Durfey, *Wit and Mirth*, vi.329: 'This accountant will come without e'er a Fee,/And warrants a Boy by his rule of three.' Rule of Three: copulation; penis and testes (F&H).

LLL, I.ii.51:

Armado. It doth amount to one more than two.
Moth. Which the base vulgar do call three.

See BOOT, *TrC*; PRESENCE, *AYL*; PLAINLY, *H5*; WOUND, *VA*.

Three-pile Three-pile or rich VELVET, worn by whores, bawds. VD. Jonson, *Bartholomew Fair*, II.v: 'I'le see 'hem pox'd first, and pil'd, and double pil'd.' Elizabethans associated pox or VD and piles or haemorrhoids.

MM, I.ii.33: 'thou art good velvet; thou'rt a three-piled piece, I warrant thee: I had as lief . . . be piled, as thou art piled, for a French velvet'. Lucio was infected by a French VELVET (vulva) or PIECE of whore from a WARRANT/warren (brothel – *OED*).

IV.iii.11. Pompey's old brothel customers are in gaol. A 'Master Rash' is 'in for a commodity of brown paper' (syphilitic joints were wrapped in brown paper: 'Do penance in a paper lantern' – Butler, *Hudibras*, Pt II, c.I.870). Another is in 'at the suit of Master Three-pile the mercer' – Messrs Rash and Three-pile, venereally diseased.

See MERCURY, *WT*.

Thresh(old) See THRASH.

Throne Toilet seat, 17th c.; chamber-pot. Throne (*trône*): Fr sl. for toilet (Leitner), as in Montaigne, Bk I, ch. 3: 'Princes, who to dispatch their weightiest affaires make them often their close-stoole, their regall Throne or Councel-chamber.' Smollett, *Humphrey Clinker*, p. 289: 'Enthroned on an easing chair' (ease: evacuate the bowels).

TN, II.iv.22. The tradition of the musical FART is old; it is the *ars musica* (G) of WIND-instruments (rectum and anus – C; P). And it is an undercurrent in the Duke's request for a song from Feste to 'relieve' (as of the bowels – F&H; *1H6*, I.i.133: 'bowels . . . behind/ With purpose to relieve') his passions: *Feste*, a pun on the *festi*val of the *Twelfth Night* of Christmas, and on FIST and *feist*, a fart. Viola says his tune 'gives a very echo to the seat/ Where Love is throned'. Feste's tune or feist gives an ECHO (fart) to the toilet seat (VERY, arse) where LOVE/*loffa* (a fart – F) is throned. For similar images see (1) *WT*, IV.iv.185: 'he utters them ["tunes"] as he had eaten ballads' – he eats ballads and UTTERS (discharges, farts) musical tunes; (2) *KJ*, V.ii.166: 'drums' (DRUMS, buttocks) that 'being beaten . . . but [/ butt] start/ An echo' and 'reverberate' like 'thunder' (THUNDER, flatulence).

Sh never intended us to take the Duke's love for Olivia too seriously. The Duke (I.i.1) called music 'the food of love' and wanted 'excess of it', 'surfeiting', that 'The appetite may sicken'. Music, he said, is a 'strain' (a song; an effort to evacuate the bowels) and a 'sweet sound' (like Chaucer's 'soun or savour of a fart', its music or perfume – TWR). It comes 'Stealing and giving odour!' This sound that both steals and gives odour is a pun on the foist: (1) one who steals; (2) a fart (F&H). The Duke concluded that Olivia 'purged the air': purged or emptied the bowels of *air*, the final pun on the fart and its song, another kind of air (cf. LOVE, *LLL*).

AC, II.ii.195: 'Matters are so well digested', said Mecaenas, starting the puns on anal evacuations (see MATTER 4: faecal matter) in Enobarbus's description of the first meeting of Antony and Cleopatra. She came on her 'barge' (foist: a barge, a musty smell – *OED*; and a close fart – F&H). It was like a 'burnish'd throne' with its 'poop' (stern of a ship; buttocks of a man) of 'beaten gold'. From this barge came a 'strange invisible perfume'. It *is* a STRANGE perfume (L*stringere*, to strain), from a strain of bowels evacuated; and it is in*vis*ible (are not all perfumes), a pun on 'fist', 'fise' and *vesse* (a fart – Cot). Cleopatra's arrival was 'O, rare for Antony!' RARE and *rear* are doublets.

Concomitantly, Antony, who was 'Enthroned i' the market-place, did sit alone,/ Whistling to the air' – a strange image, but intended to mock Antony, the ass/ arse, on a throne, with the hissing or sibilance of his escaping flatus. Both lovers were throned – to be *thrown* meant to be tumbled sexually (P) – and both were diseased. The 'winds [WIND, flatulence – P] were love-sick'; Cleopatra's throne 'burned' and was 'burnish'd' (burn: symptom of VD – *OED*; P); and Antony WHISTLES or siffles/ syphilis. See POOP.

Throng Fornicate. Past tense of 'thring', thrust forward; vulgarity for the 'movement of . . . Damyan's penis into the . . . pudendum of May' in Chaucer, 'The Merchant's Tale' (TWR).

Ado, I.i.305: 'in their rooms/ Come thronging soft and delicate desires . . . Saying, I liked her [Hero] ere I went to wars'. Thronging and DELICATE (voluptuous) desires for Hero replace Claudio's 'war-thoughts' (303). He liked her ere he went to WARS/ whores.

R3, IV.iv.435, Ratcliff: 'to the shore/ Throng many doubtful hollow-hearted friends' – political whores like the prostitutes and whore-mongers who throng at the SHORE or Bankside brothels.

Tim, IV.iii.21. Timon addresses the 'breeding sun' on the earth's 'rotten [L *putere*] humidity', the *putery* (prostitution – TWR; *OED*) on earth: 'be abhorr'd/ All feasts . . . and throngs of men!' 'Destruction' to all throngs or fornications of men: may they be ABHORred/ whored and diseased. He concludes damning 'earth,/ Thou common whore of mankind'.

Per, I.i.101: 'the earth is throng'd/ By man's oppression'. The earth is thronged: (1) fig. screwed by man's tyranny; (2) propagated by man's oppression (rape – *OED*; TWR; press: coit – P).

Throstle A turd. A male effeminate. The genus *Turdus*; the Song-thrush or *Turdus musicus*. *Trossula*: a delicate wench; *trossulo*: a dainty, spruce fellow (F).
See ANGEL, *MND*; CAPER, *MV*.

Thunder A fart. Chaucer, 'The Miller's Tale', 620: Nicholas 'leet fle a fart,/ As greet as it had been a thonder-dent'. Jonson, *Every Man in his Humour*, V.i: 'Saturn . . . Disrobed his podex, white as ivory,/ And through the welkin thundered all aloud.'

KL, III.ii.6. The maddened Lear out on the heath: '*Blow*, *winds*, and *crack* your *cheeks* . . . . And thou, all-shaking thunder,/ Smite *flat* the thick rotundity o' the world!' (italics added). These are all puns on the flatus (L *flatus*, a blowing, a puff of wind). A crack is a fart, esp. a crack from the CHEEKS (buttocks). *Pet*: a crack, fart or scape (Cot). Even 'smite' puns on giving a *blow*, and producing a musical sound (ME).

Why this undercurrent to such a magnificent speech? Because Lear says he must take this insult from nature, to whom he never gave anything. But his children to whom he gave a 'kingdom' – why are they permitted to insult him in this way and why have the elements, the 'servile ministers', 'join'd' with them: ' 'tis foul!'

This use of 'join'd' develops into Goneril's being taken for a JOINT-STOOL (III.vi.54) or privy seat, when Lear, Kent and the Fool 'arraign' her, thus evoking the *rain* and thunder of the storm. It is the stool (obs., both a seat of justice and privy seat; see STATE, *1H4* for similar pun) whereon Goneril is permitted to SCAPE, i.e. fart at her father, and to scape or escape justice. 'False justicer, why hast thou let her 'scape?' (JUSTICE: the arse; a dung-heap).
See DISCHARGE.

Tiger A STRIPED/STRIPPED (castrated) animal; symbol for the homosexual, eunuch, or aggressive female. The chariot of the effeminate god Bacchus, 'a boy, pretty as a girl' (Ovid, *Metamorphoses*, Bk III) was drawn by docile-necked, harnessed tigers (Horace, *Odes*, Bk III, iii).

CE, III.i.95. Rejected by his wife, Antipholus E. is invited out by a merchant: 'Have patience, sir . . . . depart in patience,/ And let us to the Tiger all to dinner'. Since PATIENCE (said twice) or patiens is the passive male's role, the Tiger is a fit name for the inn.

Cor, V.iv.31. The frightened Sicinius asks if so short a time 'can alter the condition of a man?' ALTER is change sexually, assume another sexual role; and the condition, i.e. prerequisite of Coriolanus's manhood has been altered: 'there is no more mercy in him than there is milk in a male tiger'. No male animal has milk, but Menenius chose the tiger because it is doubly milkless, merciless: the *striped* tiger, *stripped* of cods, castrated, with no MILK (semen) – like the cow stripped (1610) of her milk. Coriolanus will show the 'poor city' – POOR (a catamite)/*puer* (boy) – what a merciless pederast he is, this male tiger, this *male mas* (L, unmanly male), when he buggers it. (He is 'a thing made for Alexander' – known for bisexuality and mockingly called 'Alisander' in *LLL*, V.ii.)

TN, V.i.65. Antonio was drawn to Illyria by the 'witchcraft' (WITCHCRAFT, L *ars magica*) of the 'boy' (BOY, catamite) Sebastian, 'pure for his love' (PURE, homosexual love). And now Sebastian's 'false cunning [CUNNING, arse]' rejects him. Orsino remembers Antonio as captain of a 'baubling vessel' that made 'grapple' with 'the most noble bottom' of Orsino's fleet; even the 'tongue of loss' cried honour on him. But the Officer reminds him that Antonio was banished because he did 'the Tiger board,/ When . . . Titus lost his leg'. Antonio's baubling vessel (bauble: penis – C; P) GRAPPLED and BOARDED (mounted sexually: see SHEEP, *TN*) *two bottoms*: (1) that of the Tiger (ship: 'bottom' – *MV*, I.i.42); and (2) that of Orsino's nephew or *regalo* (F), pun on RIGEL, a castrate. The TONGUE (penis) of *loss* leads to this pun on Titus, the castrate – with no 'leg' to boot. See PATIENCE, *RJ* for another nephew with no NOTE (prick; testicle).

Three masculine women are associated with tigers.

Mac, I.iii.7. A '*rump*-fed ronyon [the fundament, an invective that 'may be translated "arse", "prick" ' – TWR; runnion: the male organ – *OED*]' who had 'chestnuts [NUTS, testes] in her lap' that she would not share with the WITCHES (hermaphrodites) was married to the 'master o' the Tiger', whom the witches in retaliation will 'drain . . . dry [DRY, impotent] as hay'. This may be commentary on the barren Macbeth (SCEPTRE), married to and therefore master of his tiger, Lady Macbeth, who had wished herself unsexed. ('Men . . . Are masters to their females' – *CE*, II.i.24.)

TA, V.iii.195. Tamora – whose name may pun on TAME (castrate; see SEMIRAMIS, queen who did castrate males, and with whom Tamora is identified) plus *or* (1562, her., gold) – is the golden, striped tiger, 'that heinous [HEINOUS/ anus] tiger, Tamora', whose 'life was beast-like' (BEAST, sexual bestiality; LIKE, Gk *homoios*, *homo*-).

3H6, I.iv.137. The masculine Margaret (Index) is 'O tiger's heart wrapt in a woman's hide!' The 'h' in neither 'heart' nor 'hide' (art/heart/hart – K) is meant to be stressed. Margaret is wrapped (L *vulva*, wrapping) in a vulva, a woman'*s 'ide*, a woman's side (loin – *OED*); but she has the tiger's HEART/ 'art (L *ars*/ arse).

Tilt(h) Copulate. Tilth is husbandry, ploughing (coition – P). To tilt (like to fence, foin – P) is to JUST (coit – TWR). Middleton and Dekker, *The Roaring Girl*, III.iii: hoping to entrap his son with a lover, a father asks about 'The time of their tilting?'

MM, I.iv.44: 'Your brother and his lover have embraced . . . her plenteous womb/ Expresseth his full tilth and husbandry'.

IV.iii.17. To Mrs Overdone's brothel came 'Master Forthlight the tilter . . . all great doers [whore-mongers – C; P] in our trade [prostitution – C; P]'.

1H4, II.iii.95. Hotspur, off to war, tells his wife, 'I love thee not . . . this is no world . . . to tilt with lips'. See LIP.

Title/ tittle Orig. the same word. Chapman, *All Fools*, II.i: 'Every tittle/ Of your close amorous rites I understand' – tittle-rites and title-rights (to have a title is to have a right). *R3*, IV.iv.300: 'the doting title of a mother' – the dot on an 'i' is a tittle. Both words pun on penis: a 'prick' is a dot (tittle), a very small portion (tittle), a penis (*OED*).

LLL, iv.i.85. Armado, a Spaniard, is a 'king' (with title) and Jaquenetta is a 'beggar' (with tittle). Will she 'exchange for rags? robes; for tittles? titles; for thyself? me'. (1) Her tittle or small portion (1511) is a dowry, a dote; and her portion of virginity is, as we know, even smaller. Sp *parcía* is sl. for maidenhead (Rosensweig), and *porción* is portion. In Middleton and Rowley, *A Fair Quarrel*, V.i., the bride-to-be's dowry and chastity are in question: 'She has been tried. . . . She does not have that portion/ That a bride should have.' (2) Armado's title/ tittle is also a prick, a small portion.

TrC, II.iii.203. 'Things, small as nothing . . . He [Achilles] makes important' – things (genitals – C; P) small as nothing or tittles/ titles. Ajax should not 'assubjugate his merit/ As amply titled as Achilles is,/ By going to Achilles:/ That were to enlard his fat already pride'. Ulysses tells Ajax (his title or name a pun on *a jakes*, a privy – K) not to be *ass*ubjugated, made an ass of. He must not enlard (*lard*, fat; *lardasse*, 'a great pricke' – Cot) or make a greater prick of Achilles, already amply titled, whose pride (phallic prowess – F&H; C; P) is already 'fat'. Cf. III.iii.89: Achilles boasts, 'I do enjoy/ At ample point [penis – P; full points: erect phallus – C] all that I did possess'.

See ANNUAL, *H8*; RAISE, *AW*; LOAD, *H8*.

Token (1) Genitals, as in 'An old rybybe [ribibe, crone] . . . at the threshold comyin in,/ And fell so wyde open/ That one myght see her token' (John Skelton, in F&H 1529). (2) Plague spot (F&H). See EYES, *LLL*; LEPROSY, *AC*.

TGV, IV.iv.79. Proteus gives Julia (unrecognised in her masculine garb) a ring she had once given him, saying, 'She loved me well deliver'd it to me.' Julia: 'It seems you loved not her, to leave her token.' Julia reproaches him with betraying their past sexual intimacy. *Loved not* evokes her earlier phrase (II.vii.46), 'true-love knots' (KNOT: intertwine coitally; genitals – C; P). Julia had *deliver'd* her RING (pudendum – P) to him, a *token* he left. For substantiation of their intimacy, see IV.iv.165, when the disguised Julia says, 'Our youth got me to play the woman's part [PART, genitals]/ And I was trimm'd in Madam Julia's gown' – trimmed (sexual intercourse – P; deflowered – C) in her own GOWN (cunt).

MND, I.i.29. Lysander had 'interchanged love-tokens' with Hermia 'And stolen the impression of her fantasy'. This is another couple whose love, according to Egeus, had been consummated by their interchange of tokens: (1) STOLEN puns on made a stale or whore of; (2) 'press(ing)' meant in coitus (TWR; C; P); (3) FANTASY ('doon his fantasye' – TWR) is the sex-act.

Oth, V.ii.61. Ostensibly speaking of a handkerchief, Desdemona protests, 'I . . . never loved Cassio. . . . I never gave him token', unwittingly hitting on Othello's fear she had given away another token, her chastity.

Tomboy Strumpet and masculine girl (F&H). Effeminate boy.

Cym, I.vi.122. Iachimo tells Imogen her husband is disloyal to her 'With tomboys hired . . . with diseased ventures/ That play with all infirmities for gold . . . such boil'd [Folio sp. "boyl'd"] stuff'. *Boy*l'd stuff and Sh's only use of tom*boys*: Iachimo tried to infuriate Imogen with the ultimate in degradation: her husband's infidelity with diseased VENTURES (whores) was with young boys, boy-*stuff* (semen, whores – P; stuffed: fucked – C), SUCH (It *tale*) stuff, hired tomboys ('whyskyng and ramping abroade like a Tom boy' – Udall, *Ralph Roister Doister*, II.iv) or catamites. Or, if females, why this word compounded of two words both of which mean male (unless to indicate Posthumus uses them sexually as he would boys)?

Iachimo asks what man would leave Imogen's 'hand' and 'join gripes with hands/ Made hard with hourly falsehood . . . as/ With labour' – JOIN (coitally) gripes with HANDS (phallic symbols – K, here made *hard*; masturbation), the hired/ hard(?) hands of tomboys who play with all infirmities (in*firm* things and make them firm or hard) in their HOURLY (whoring) activities. Does 'gripes' (1601, spasmodic bowel pains) connote anal eroticism?

These puns are appropriate to Iachimo, one of Sh's prime examples of a freq. character in Eliz. lit., the ambisexual ITALIAN lover. See PRETTY for his similar taunting of her husband.

See RAMP.

Tongue Penis; clitoris. Lit. anything resembling the tongue in shape, position or use. Oldham, 'Upon the Author of a Play Call'd *Sodom*': 'Sure Nature made, or meant at least t'have don't,/ Thy Tongue a Clytoris, thy Mouth a cunt'.

MWW, I.iv.85. Dr Caius tries to quiet Mistress Quickly and to hear Simple: 'Peace-a your tongue. Speak-a your tale [penis – K; P].'

TSh, II.i.216:

Petruchio. Who knows not where a wasp does wear his sting?
  In his tail.
Katherina. In his tongue.
Petruchio. Whose tongue?
Katherina. Yours, if you talk of tails . . . .
Petruchio. What, with my tongue in your tail?

As in *MWW* above, the juxtaposition of tongue and tail. STING: penis.

TGV, II.iii.52:

Panthino. Where should I lose my tongue?
Launce. In thy tale.
Panthino. In thy tail!

Cym, II.iii.16, Cloten to musicians: 'Come on; tune: if you can penetrate her with your fingering, so; we'll try with tongue too.'

R2, II.i.149: 'all is said:/ His tongue is now a stringless instrument;/ Words, life and all, old Lancaster hath spent'. Gaunt's tongue is now a soundless instrument (penis – P): LIFE (penis) and ALL (penis) are spent (depleted of semen – *OED*; P). York says he is next 'that must be bankrupt so' (bankrupt: depleted of semen – P; no money in the purse: impotent – F&H).

This metaphor began at I.iii.245 when Gaunt's 'tongue' joined the King's in banishing his own son: in a conflict of interests 'my unwilling tongue/ Against my will [penis – C; P]' did himself 'wrong' (WRONG, a penis) – believing it politic, he unwillingly screwed himself.

Too/two See DUE.

Torch Penis. Fr *torche*: man's prick (F&H n.d.). See INCH, Jonson. Verge: penis; species of torch. L *pinus*: a pine; a torch (Vergil).

1H6, II.v.122. This scene puns on the torch and resinous pine (*pine*, man's 'pricke' – Cot), L *pinus*, of which torches were often made. *Torche*: pith of pine-tree (Cot). Mortimer says advancement to the throne is the cause he must 'pine' in prison (57); then we learn 'Here dies the dusky torch of Mortimer,/ Choked with ambition'. The point is not that Mortimer was choked (with ambition) but that his *torch* was choked (suffocated for lack of *air*) and died, so that Mortimer produced no *heir* to the throne. The thrust of the scene is who is the rightful heir, and Mortimer says, 'I no issue have' (94).

Tem, IV.i.97. Hymen, god of marriage (Gk *hymen*, virginal membrane), carried a torch: 'this man and maid,/ Whose vows are, that no bed-right shall be paid/ Till Hymen's torch be lighted'.

1H6, III.ii.26: 'Behold, this is the happy wedding torch/ That joineth Rouen unto her countrymen'. Pucelle's coital metaphor includes 'joineth' (JOIN, copulate) and 'countrymen' (cunt and coition – K; P). The happy wedding is really the rape of Rouen by those who enter disguised as bearers of 'sacks' of corn. 'Sack' (rape – *OED*; P) puns on *sac* (rights of jurisdiction – *OED*). As is said twice, they will be 'lords and rulers over Rouen ["Roan", Folio]' and over *ruin*: 'the towns defaced/ By wasting ruin . . . the pining malady of France' (iii.45) – the *torch*, the *pining* 'malady of France' (syphilis – C; P); the burning (syphilitic – *OED*) torch – consuming, raping France.

MV. How to provide Lorenzo with a 'torch-bearer' is mentioned three times in II.iv, thus fixing its significance in the play. And in vi.40 Lorenzo tells Jessica, 'you must be my torch-bearer'. Jessica: 'must I hold a candle to my shames?/ They . . . are too too light' – must she hold a candle (penis – TWR), wear a codpiece, to her SHAMES (L *pudenda*), hers already light (wanton – *OED*; P). Jessica is violating Jewish law, which specif. forbids masquerading as a member of the opposite sex (Deut. 22:5).

A pricket (or prick) is a candle-stick or torch-holder (torch-bearer). Jessica is the pricket or pricked. (*RJ*, I.iv.28: Mercutio tells Romeo, who twice asked to carry the 'torch' and be a 'candle-holder', to 'Prick love for pricking'.) Perhaps the audience snickered at a boy actor, playing a girl, who says he is TOO too light, light of TWO testes, castrated.

But the bawdiness carries an additional sordid implication that Jessica has bought Lorenzo, who sold himself to the highest bidder. *Emporter à la chandelle*, to bear away the candle, means to get an object because you offered the most, at an outcry or auction (Cot). Lorenzo still needed a torch-bearer ('we have two hours/ To *furnish* us' – iv.9) *until*, after reading Jessica's letter on 'What gold and jewels she is *furnish'd* with', he then concluded, '*Fair* [/ L *ferre*, bear] Jessica shall be my torch-bearer' (italics added). And Salanio and Solarino (more usually, Solanio and Salerio), these *two* who first mentioned 'torch-bearers', are also the two who report that Shylock, learning of Jessica's elopement, 'with *outcries raised* the duke' (viii.4; italics added). Lorenzo was bought at an outcry ('raised', too, is a bidding term) by Jessica who carried the candle (see BANK for a metaphor used by this money-mad young man).

Train Penis, testicles. *Train*: a great man's retinue; hinder part of a beast (Cot). Lit. tail of a bird. Also Fr syn. for the prick (F&H).

1H6, III.iii.7. Pucelle will deprive Talbot of his followers: 'Let frantic Talbot triumph . . . like a peacock sweep along his tail;/ We'll pull his plumes and take away his train'. Fig.

emasculation: let this proud pea*cock* display his tail (his sign of virility); she will deprive him of PLUMES (L *pennis*, feathers, dat. and abl. pl.) and train, ruin his tail (arse – C; P).

KL, I.iv.285. The Fool called Lear a 'shealed peascod' (219) – an empty *peas-cod* and *cod-piece*. Now Lear defensively says, 'My train are men of choice and rarest parts'. A man's attendants are his *train* and *suitte* (Cot); and *suites* / SWEETS are testicles (of a boar). Lear's train is made of men of (1) choice PARTS (genitals) – 'choose' is cull, and 'culls' are testes (Jonson in F&H); (2) rarest parts – RARE / rear parts, the *cul* ('arse . . . tayle' – Cot).

And in II.iv it is his train that his daughters diminish – his manhood they continually cut away. Kent: 'How chance the king comes with so small a train?' (64). Lear says Goneril 'hath abated me of half my train' (161) – one of his testicles. Regan will complete the process; for, though he says it is not in her 'To grudge my pleasures, to cut off my train . . . to scant my sizes', she suggests he cut his train in half again (251) and concludes, 'What need one?' By l.294 Regan will 'receive him gladly, / But not one follower' – no *suitte* or retinue, no *suites* or testicles; his SIZES (Fr *tailles*), the penises of himself and his followers, will be scanted (SCANTLING, a deformed monster). He is to be completely emasculated (see RAG; SHAKE).

See PROPORTION, *RJ*.

Traitor A trader: whore, bawd, brothel-customer (F&H; C; P; *OED*). Traitor: from L *tradere*, deliver treacherously. *Traistre*: traitor; a 'naughtie-packe' or whore; lewd fellow (Cot).

TrC, V.x.37: 'O traitors and bawds, how earnestly are you set a-work. . . . Good traders in the flesh'.

LLL, V.ii.604. Holofernes insists he is not Judas Iscariot but Judas 'ycliped [cleped or called] Maccabaeus'. And the lords, who *are* 'traitors' and guilty of treason (IV.iii.213) are parodied even as they mock:

Dumain. Judas Maccabaeus clipt is plain Judas.
Biron. A kissing traitor.

To 'clip' means to cut and to embrace. Hence, Judas Maccabaeus CLIPT is Judas CUT short or castrated. Judas clipt becomes PLAIN / plane, flat, smooth-docked, castrated Judas. To SHORTEN or *scortare* (F) puns on L *scortari*, associate with harlots. They shorten his name to Judas, the traitor who delivered Jesus with a kiss, who clipt or embraced him, who traded Jesus for 30 pieces of silver, who prostituted himself for silver. They shorten his name even further from 'Jud-as' to 'ass' and conclude 'poor Maccabaeus, how hath he been baited!' – (1) baited or mocked; (2) bated or shortened: castrated and prostituted – just like these emasculated lords, whom the ladies made asses of.

AYL, I.iii.74. The sexual implications of 'traitor' are heard in the Duke's accusation that Rosalind and her father were traitors; she was kept at court only for Celia's sake, 'Else had she with her father ranged along'. To *range* is to whore (F&H; as in *TSh*, III.i.91). Celia: 'if she be a traitor, / Why so am I; we still have slept together . . . like Juno's swans, / Still we went coupled and inseparable'. Rosalind, later GANYMEDE (Eliz. sl. for a homosexual), could not have been a traitor / trader or whore, says Celia, unless she too were one, since they slept together – were coupled (paired sexually, L *copula*, as in III.iii.45) like swans of Juno, protectress of marriage. Celia's description of their intimacy (see GANYMEDE; STRANGE) is another contribution to the bisexual ambience of the play.

See HORSE, *TrC*; PAINT, *Cym*.

Transform(ation) (1) Sexual mutilation. See MISUSE, *1H4*.

(2) Assumption of what is trad. considered the sexual role of the opposite sex. The same pun is made in Sh's one use of 'trans-shape' (DEFORMED; SWEET, *TGV*). Fielding, *Love in Several Masques*, I.ii: 'I see your women have gone through with the transformation and dress like us . . . I was frightened . . . just now by two girls in padusay coats, and breeches.' Told they were really two beaux (whose sexual ambivalence was a commonplace), Wisemore says, 'So much

the greater transformation, for they had, apparently more of the woman than the man about them.'

MV, II.vi.39. Jessica dressed as a boy: 'Cupid himself would blush/To see me thus transformed to a boy'.

CE, II.ii.197:

Dromio S. I am transformed, master, am I not?
Antipholus S. I think thou art in mind, and so am I. . . .

Luciana. If thou art changed to aught, 'tis to an ass.
Dromio S. 'Tis true; she rides me . . . .
'Tis so, I am an ass . . . .

Dromio has been emasculated. Both men feel they are (ART, arse) transformed in MIND (arse). 'Ride' is mount sexually (F&H; P; *chevaucher*: bestride a horse and swive a woman – Cot). Dromio is transformed: *he* is ridden by *her*; *he* is the ass/arse. (See WITCH, Wilmot.)

III.ii.151, Dromio: 'She had transform'd me to a curtal dog' – with a cut tail; of a person, mutilated, with esp. ref. to castration. (See DOG.)

AC, IV.ii.36. Antony tells his men, 'Scant not my cups' (21): '[I am] like a master,/Married to your good service, [and will] stay till death:/Tend me to-night two hours, I ask no more,/And the gods yield you for't!' Twice he says, 'Tend me tonight': 'tend' meant kindle, inflame; L *tentigo* is lecherousness from *tendare* (*tenda*, imp.), stretch out; and *tentigine* is a priapism (F), persistent penial erection. These are connotations Sh meant us to hear: (1) Antony *desires* them to inflame him, as he says he 'did desire you/To burn this night with torches [TORCH, penis]'; (2) he is 'married' to their GOOD 'service' (copular – P; prostitution – C; cf. *KL*, II.ii.21: the 'whoreson', 'pandar' Oswald, a 'bawd, in way of good service'); (3) he asks for TWO HOURS/*two whores*, no more. Scant not my CUPS (q.v.), Antony tells his wine-servers, cup-bearers, i.e. his GANYMEDES/catamites: a Priapus is a phallus and (1613) a drinking-cup shaped like one.

Enobarbus asks, 'What mean you, sir. . . ? Look, they weep;/And I, an ass, am onion-eyed: for shame,/Transform us not to women.' Antony had *meant*, Enobarbus said, 'To make his followers weep' (24) – not just to weep tears but to WEEP (whore), to transform them for SHAME (genitals – *OED*) into women. Now he tells his 'Servitors' that the gods will YIELD/geld them for their sexual tending. The implication of pederasty is present in Enobarbus's 'I, an ass' and Antony's response to Enobarbus: 'Ho, ho, ho!/Now the witch take me, if I meant it thus!' What does he mean by 'thus'? And what, at face value, is so ho, ho, ho – funny – about Enobarbus's remark? And why does he say let the WITCH (hermaphrodite or bisexual) take (coitally – F&H; C; P) him if he meant it *thus*? For more on Antony's ambisexuality, see ABOMINABLE; Index.

See PEAR, *MWW*.

Trash See RAG.

Tribute Castration or gelding; homosexual service. Geld: the tribute or tax paid to the crown by English landholders before the Conquest and continued under the Norman kings.

Cym, II.iv.13: 'He'll grant the tribute, send the arrearages' – Sh's only use of ar*rear*ages.

Tem, I.ii.113. Prospero describes the 'homage' (HOMAGE,/homosexual service), the 'most [MOST, buttocks; *la fin*: the end; the most – Cot] ignoble stooping' – the fine or end paid in the ignoble STOOPING (fornication) – the 'annual [ANNUAL/anal] tribute' that his brother, 'So dry [DRY: impotent; sodomitical] he was for sway', paid the King of Naples for his help in ousting Prospero. He paid tribute or geld, prostrated, fig. castrated, himself and may have served the King homosexually (see INCH).

2H4, III.ii.331. Falstaff sees 'the bottom' of Justice Shallow, who 'hath done nothing but prate to me of the wildness of his youth . . . feats he hath done about Turnbull Street; and every third word a lie, duer paid to the hearer than the Turk's tribute'. (1) Shallow did nothing but/butt PRAT(E) (buttocks); and all was LIES (buggery); (2) in II.ii.192 (and in *MWW*, v.v.3; *Ado*, v.iv.48; *WT*, IV.iv.28; *TrC*, v.i.60) the bull is Jove or Jupiter, who turned bull to woo Europa in sexual bestiality (and who also took young Ganymede for lover): feats like these Shallow boasted of doing on *Turn-bull* Street, a brothel street (cf. Nashe, *Pierce Penilesse*, in *Works*, vol. II, p. 217) – and every third WORD (whore) he boasted of, a lie; (3) TURKS (ambisexuals and castraters), whose tribute (geld – *OED*) was gelding the TWO (*due* – F) DUER PAID (Gk *paid*, the boy in a homosexual relationship) to the HEARER (a catamite); (4) Shallow the liar or *bugiard* (early 17th c., *CD*)/the *buggered* Shallow bottom.

Trot(h) (1) Trot, trat: whore, bawd (F&H; P). Dekker, Ford and Rowley, *The Witch of Edmonton*, IV.i: an old woman, a 'Witch', is called 'you old Trot', 'you hot-Whore'. Dekker, *The Comedy of Old Fortunatus*, v.i: a French doctor pronounces 'th' as 't' in 'by my trat . . . me lova musha musha merrymant: come, madam, letta me feel you' – 'by my troth' is a freq. bawdy reinforcement. 'Virytrate': Chaucer uses a medieval joke on L '*anus* = (1) old trot, but also (2) rectum' (TWR).

(2) Trattle, tret: rounded droppings of sheep, hare (*OED*). Trut: 'exclamation of contempt; Shit!' (F&H). *Tronzoli*: dung or truttles (F).

MWW, I.iv.64. Sh's French doctor also uses 't' for 'th': 'By my trot, I tarry too long'. And by his *traite* (prolonging of things – Cot) he does; for by tarrying he finds whom Mistress Quickly, housekeeper and bawd, hid in the closet; he discovers her *traite* (shift or trick – Cot), that she is playing go-between for someone else. See CUT: he uses 'troat' (a rutting bellow) for throat.

H5, III.vii.86, Dauphin: 'I will trot . . . my way shall be paved with English faces.' The Dauphin and his horse ('my mistress') will trot on English FACES/faeces or tret that the pavid(/paved) or fearful English, like sheep, will have dropped or shit in fear.

R3, III.vii.43. Buckingham failed to win the citizens over to Richard, to sell him, be his ORATOR (bawd). Richard: 'would they not speak?' – 'No, by my troth, my lord' (the last phrase in the Quartos but not the First Folio). Troth (truth) is ironic for his campaign of lies; but, by his trot, by playing the bawd, he had attempted to sell Richard to the populace (REPREHEND).

LLL, IV.iii.143. The Lords would renounce celibacy. For 'paradise' (see DICE) they would (1) 'break faith and troth' – which *ought* lead to loss, not gain, of paradise; (2) break faith and (go) trot with the princesses, to a different sort of paradise. They do, in fact, just that: go trot, disguised as RUSSIANS, lecherous horses (*roussiner*: to leap a mare – Cot).

See CHEVERIL, *H8*; LODGE, *H5*; HORSE, *Ado*; KNOT, *Oth*.

Trudge A whore or bawd. Trug: prostitute, catamite (*OED*: F&H). Dekker, *The Belman of London*, p. 144 ('The Sacking Law') : 'The *Whore-house*, which is called a Trugging-place'. Healey, *Discovery of the New World* (1620): 'Every other house keeps sale trugges or Ganymedes' (F&H, s.v. Trug). John Oldham, 'A Dissuasive against Poetry', from *A Satyr*: 'She must to Creswel's [a procuress] trudg to mend her Gains/And let her Tail to hire' (*Penguin Book of Restoration Verse*, p. 290).

See SHORE, *R3*; DOVE, *RJ*; AWAY, *MWW*.

True Buttocks, anus, pudendum. *Trou*: buttocks, anus (Cot); Fr syn. for 'cunt' (F&H, s.v. Monosyllable). *Truye*: a sow (Cot).

MND, v.i.111. The Prologue, delivered in defiance of punctuation, captures the flavour of the workers' play, the asses they will make of themselves: 'To show our simple skill,/That is the true beginning of our end.' To SHOW (exhibit something unnatural) their SKILL(L *ars*/arse) is the true *beginning* of their *end*. A slurred 'our' (it rhymed with 'progenitor' – K), sounded like 'are', making 'our simple' *arse-simple* skill.

LLL, I.i.313, Costard: 'I suffer for the truth, sir; for true it is, I was taken with Jaquenetta, and Jaquenetta is a true girl'. He was caught in intercourse with her, and many puns (DAMSEL; PREPOSTEROUS) indicate entrance was from the rear; three uses of 'true' indicate either pudendum or anus.

MWW, IV.ii.109: 'Hang him, dishonest varlet! we cannot misuse him enough. . . . We do not act that often jest and laugh; / 'Tis old, but true, Still swine eats all the draff.' Falstaff is a VARLET (male whore), whom the merry wives can't MISUSE (sexually debase) ENOUGH (Fr *assez* / ass). They JEST (Fr *rire*), are *rieurs* or laughers, who make asses or rear ends of people; they LAUGH (cause to rise phallicly), they tease but do not act (coit – P), commit adultery. Mrs Page condemns Falstaff and asserts their innocence, through an adage that is OLD (hoary / whory) and true, of *truye*, sows and swine, sensually degraded persons: it is the silent ones who eat the draff.

H5, III.vii.69:

Constable. I had as lief have my mistress a jade.
Dauphin. I tell thee, constable, my mistress wears his own hair.
Constable. I could make as true a boast . . . if I had a sow to my mistress.
Dauphin. 'le chien est retourné à son propre vomissement, et la truie lavée au bourbier': thou makest use of any thing.

The Dauphin had said his 'horse' was his 'mistress' (BEAST) but he is not a *jade*, worn-out horse or whore (F&H; P), venereally bald: he 'wears his own hair'. Sh's recurring contempt for wigs may be part of the contemporary jokes on merkins, i.e. counterfeit hair for the female pudendum (G; *W*; *CD*; P, s.v. Hair; ROOF, *Tim*): 'A health to all Ladyes that never used merkin' (F&H 1620). Wilmot, *Sodom*: Vertuoso is the merkin- and dildo-maker. Oldham, 'Upon the Author of a Play Call'd *Sodom*': 'Or wear some stinking merkin for a beard'.

In this context the self-evident, literal jest that, if the Constable had a sow (*truie*) for mistress, he could make *as true* a boast (since neither horse nor sow wears a wig) is obviously not adequate to the bawdy mood. Hence, we note: (1) the Dauphin's mistress wears *his own* (L *suus*) hair, so, if the Constable had a sow (L *sus*, swine) for mistress, he could make as *truie* a boast; (2) if the Constable had a sow, full-grown female pig (Gk *pyge*, the buttocks) for mistress, he could make as *trou* (buttocks) a boast; (3) cf. the 'rural vice of swine copulation' (P, p. 42; Gk *choiros*: sow, female genitals; a freq. pun, as in Arsitophanes, *The Archanians*, 777–815); (4) the Dauphin's retort from 2 Pet 2:22, 'the dog is turned to his own vomit again; and the sow that was washed to her wallowing in the mire', refers back to his filthy accusation that the breeches-less Constable would 'fall into foul bogs' – into the QUAGMIRE and BOGS (buttocks and whores) – or, as he now says, the Constable would make use (sexual employment – C; P) of ANY / Fr *âne* (ass) thing (genital – P).

See SHAPE, *AYL*; TRANSFORMATION, *CE*; SCREW, *TN*; ANNUAL, *Cor*; KEEN; TARTAR, *TN*; PURGATION, *LLL*; BESTOW, *2H4*.

Trull 1519, a low prostitute. *Trulla*: filthy slut, trull, close-stool pan; *trullare*: to fart or shit; *trullo*: a fart, a bum-hole, a chamber-pot (F). Butler, *Hudibras*, Pt I, c. ii, 365: 'He Trulla loved . . . A bold virago, stout and tall / As Joan of France or English Mall [Amazonian heroine of English ballad]'. A 'virago' is a man-like woman. Masculinity is a shared characteristic of trulls.

3H6, I.iv.114, York: 'How ill-beseeming is it in thy sex / To triumph, like an Amazonian trull'. ILL- (L *male*) beseeming Margaret is an Amazonian trull (see WOLF).

TA, II.iii.191. Tamora encourages her sons to rape Lavinia: 'my spleenful sons this trull deflour' (SPLEEN: semen). Lavinia: 'No grace [GRACE, vagina]? no womanhood? Ah, beastly creature!' (182) – BEASTLY CREATURE, whore who practises sexual bestiality. Each accuses the other of sexual deviation.

1H6, II.ii.28: 'the Dauphin and his trull . . . Like to a pair of loving turtle-doves'. The sexual distortions ('Pray God she prove not masculine ere long' – i.22) of Pucelle, i.e. courtesan (*OED*), for whom the Dauphin plans to 'rear' a statelier pyramid than that of 'Rhodope', Greek courtesan who married the King of Memphis, lead to their being LIKE (same sex) a PAIR of (turtle) DOVES (whores): cf. 'lascivious turtles' – *MWW*, II.i.83.

See ABOMINABLE, *AC*; VIRTUE, *WT*.

Trumpet 1. Symbol of virility. *Trompe*: trumpet, snout of an elephant (Cot). *Il n'a pas le fouet pour mener cette trompe*: 'he is too weake for such a wench' (Cot, s.v. *Trompe*, a top).

Ham, I.i.150: 'The cock [penis – TWR; P], that is the trumpet to the morn'.

H5, III.ii.116: 'the trumpet call us to the breach [female pudendum – P; also a pun on the *breech*, buttocks]'.

2. Buttocks and sound of its flatus (L *flatus*, a blowing). Aristophanes, *The Clouds*, 141–68: asked if 'a gnat buzzed through its proboscis or through its anus', Socrates answers that the air passed through 'the rump, which was distended like a trumpet' and it 'resounded sonorously'. – 'So the arse of a gnat is a trumpet.'

KJ, V.ii.117. Lewis emptily boasts of having the trump CARDS (q.v.)/cods or testes, and concludes, 'What lusty trumpet thus doth summon us?' But on his wedding-day the not-so-lusty boy had said, 'to arms!' (III.i.307), meaning military not amorous arms, and his disappointed wife had asked 'shall our feast be kept with . . . braying trumpets and . . . drums . . . ?' – the braying (*OED*) noise made by an ass and DRUMS (buttocks).

See CHEEKS, *LLL*; CHRONICLE, *TrC*.

Trunk Rump (Du *romp*, Ger *Rumpf*: trunk); covered by trunk-hose, trunk-breeches. 'Tree-trunk' (L *caudex*, *codex*) puns on *caudas*, tails; *cods*, scrotum. Nose–trunk–penis (P).

TA, II.iii.130. Chiron is a 'eunuch' if Lavinia die chaste. He and Demetrius drag her husband, whom they have killed, 'to some secret hole,/ And make his dead trunk pillow to our lust'. The conception is a necrophilous perversion, containing an ambiguity: (1) make his trunk the pillow on which they will sate their lust for his wife; (2) make (coitally – C; P) *his* dead trunk, rump and scrotum (cods: scrotum, a cushion) the pillow of their lust (CUSHION: buttocks, scrotum). This is a provocative word-cluster: encouraged by a mother whom they call 'Madam' (prostitute – *OED*), they drag the trunk to a secret (sexual – C; P) hole (pudendum – C; P; 'hol': anus – TWR). Perhaps Chiron's perversion included sodomising Lavinia (METAMORPHOSED) *and* her husband. In Greek myth Chiron was a CENTAUR, with the rump of a horse, symbol of sexual bestiality.

WT, III.iii.75. The Shepherd finds a deserted baby: 'This has been some stair-work, some trunk-work, some behind-door-work' – clandestine work (coitus – TWR, s.v. Werke; P).

Tim, IV.iii.229. Timon is now surrounded only by tree-trunks and animals, not pages or sycophants: 'will these moss'd trees . . . page thy heels . . . ? . . . Call the creatures/ Whose naked natures . . . whose bare unhoused trunks, To the . . . elements exposed,/ Answer mere nature; bid them flatter thee.' Creatures with *un-housed trunks* puns on no trunk-hose (HOSE; HOUSE); they whose naked trunks or rumps answer MERE (lecherous) NATURE (generative and excretory organs) are now his sole flatterers or CREATURES (whores). Moss'd tree trunks or *codices* are all he now knows of the mossy (1500, hairy, downy) cods and tails he left behind in Athens. UNHOUSED: (1) unhosed with codpiece or breeches; (2) without house/ HOSE (penis). Forest creatures, impotent to help him, replace the 'glib and slippery creatures' – the glib, lit. castrated, and SLIPPERY (androgynous) sycophants who earlier attended him. See POVERTY, *KL*, for another sexually exposed, 'houseless'/ hoseless impotent.

Turk Turks were reputed to be lechers, castraters, ambisexuals, sodomites. A common Eliz. view was that of Henry Maundrell, *Aleppo to Jerusalem*: 'Turks . . . know few other pleasures but such as are equally common both to Men and Beasts' (*CD*, s.v. Gross). Wycherley, *The Country Wife*, II.ii: 'a man can't come amongst virtuous women now but upon the same terms as men are admitted into the Great Turk's Seraglio'.

AW, II.iii.94. Lafeu says of the men who refused to marry Helena, 'I would send them to the Turk to make eunuchs of'.

Ado, III.iv.57. Love-sick Beatrice is ill for an 'H' (ill: ache/H), ill for *a nache*, i.e. the buttocks; for *an H* or *aitch*-bone, rump-bone – for Benedick's arse and/or Benedick, the ass/arse. This explains Margaret's mockery: 'Well, an you be not turned Turk'.

Oth, II.iii.170. Othello stops the sword-play with, 'Are we turn'd Turks, and to ourselves do that/ Which heaven hath forbid the Ottomites?/ For Christian shame, put by this barbarous brawl: / He that stirs next to carve for his own rage / Holds his soul light'. He forbids not merely the fighting but also the kind of fighting, the aberrant sexual indulgence. (1) For Christian *shame*, says Othello, who will (v.ii.211) refer to the 'act of shame' (coitus – P), put by the BARBAROUS (of the buttocks) brawl. The *barbarous* or pagan Turk also puns on the *barber* as a clipper – curtailer (Jonson in *OED*). (2) STIR means to arouse sexually, often to buggery; 'carve' meant circumcise and castrate; and 'rage' is sexual lust (TWR; P). (3) Iago says that, whereas they were a few minutes ago 'like bride and groom [certainly an erotic comparison] / Devesting them for bed', now they are 'Swords out, and tilting one at other's breast' – swords (C; P) or penises tilt at OTHER and BREAST, two puns on the arse or lap, the other two mounds. Othello forbids their sword-thrusting at each other's genitals – carving with intent to castrate, like the Turk, and TILTING (fencing; fornicating) with intent to sodomise (to goose), like the Turk. These tilting men hold their SOULS (arses) light, i.e. wantonly. (This is a possible foreshadowing of Cassio's fate – see TRASH. In the American Shakespeare Theatre Production, Washington, DC, September 1981, when Othello stabbed Iago in the final scene, he thrust his sword upward between Iago's legs as if to castrate, an impression the writhing Christopher Plummer continued to convey.) (4) Finally, Montano defends himself against Othello's anger by asking whether it is sinful to defend oneself 'When violence assails us?' – ASSAIL meant sexual assault (P) and it puns on anal eroticism.

See PHRYGIAN, *MWW*; TRIBUTE, *2H4*.

Turnip Rape: the common turnip (*OED*). See QUICK, *MWW*.

Tutor Older male in a homosexual relationship. Marston, *The Scourge of Villanie*, Satyre iii: 'Before some pedant Tutor in his bed / Should use my frie, like Phrigian Ganimede' – PHRYGIAN GANYMEDE (catamite).

LLL, IV.ii.77, Sir Nathaniel: 'their sons are well tutored by you, and their daughters profit very greatly under you: you are a good member of the commonwealth'. Holofernes replies, 'if their sons be ingenuous, they shall want no instruction; if their daughters be capable, I will put it to them'. (1) The daughters profit (physical joy of love – C; P) *under* him. He is a GOOD member ('privy member' – *OED*; *membro*: man's privy member – F) and will put it (coitally – P) to them (putours: fornicators, pimps – TWR; *OED*). (2) He will also put it to the sons (*putti*, boys – F). They shall be tutored well (a WELL, L *puteus*) by this *pute* (L, whore), this *good member* of the COMMONWEALTH (whoring community). Weever, *Epigrammes*, The Third Weeke, xvii: 'Many are beholding Lycus for thy pains, / Which with their sons and daughters thou hast taine. . . . the wenches prove so well you under: / If that but once to Learning's lore you win them . . . you can put learning in them.'

2H4, v.v.66. The final scene between Falstaff and Hal leaves little doubt about their relationship. Saying 'the young king is sick for me' (v.iii.142), Falstaff goes to the coronation: 'I will leer upon him as a' comes by' (v. 7) – LEER (amorous ogle, like the 'leer of invitation' he saw in Mrs Ford's eye – *MWW*, I.iii.50) and *lere*, impart learning (see Weever, above). There he stands 'stained with travel' and 'sweating with desire to see him'. He greets Hal, 'God save thee, my sweet boy!' and, despite rejection, continues, 'My king! my Jove! I speak to thee, my heart!' The tutor speaks (to) his 'eart / ART (L *ars*) learning. Hal is his SWEET (sexually intimate) BOY (catamite). Then, the Chief Justice asking if he has his 'wits? know what 'tis you speak?', he becomes more deferential: Hal is not his boy Ganymede (of which 'catamite' is a L corruption), but his Jove, supreme ruler of heaven and earth, Hal, the King.

But the King turns him away in a speech that starts out with 'I', 'me', 'my' and 'thou' but ends with the formal 'we', 'our' and 'you' – a quibble on 'tutor' and tutoyer (from the Fr 2nd pers. sg. pronoun *tu*, *toi* – *OED*: *W*), to treat as an intimate, address familiarly (*tutoyer*: 'to thou one' – Cot). Hal: 'When thou dost hear I am as I have been, / Approach me, and thou shalt be as thou wast, / The tutor and feeder of my riots; / Till then, I banish thee . . . As I have done the rest of my misleaders'. Not a word is idly chosen. (1) APPROACH / abroach or pierce the *butt* (of liquor), with coital implications. Thus Hal alludes to Falstaff's indiscreet ref. to Jove and his boy lover, Ganymede, his wine-server, cup-bearer. (2) *Riots* (debauchery and lust – *OED*; P) – what

Hal's father had complained of: 'riot and dishonour stain [sexually defile – C; P] the brow/ Of my young Harry' (*1H4*, I.i.85). And now Falstaff is *stained* with travel and *sweating* (from lechery and sexual desire – C; P) with desire. (3) His *tutor and feeder* (feed: supply sexually, 17th c. sl. for sexual intercourse. – P).

Falstaff is BANISHed (treated like excrement, *waste* matter, 'as thou wast').

See SLAVE, *TrC*; NAMELESS, *TGV*; STERN, *2H6*.

Twain See TWIN.

Twelve Height of a phallic erection, the penis of the recumbent man pointing straight up, like the hand of the clock at twelve or the shadow on a vertical sun-dial. Rabelais, Bk II, ch. 26 (1653 trs.): Eusthenes is ready for 'the whores': he was 'never so well winded up, as that my needle could mount to ten or eleven a clock till now, that I have it hard, stiffe and strong'. In many erotic scenes, the time is between twelve and one, erection and detumescence. For a variation, see Middleton, *Your Five Gallants*, I.i: Primero admits a maid can be close at ten, but 'Had you sworn but two years higher/ I would ne'er ha' believ'd you.' Frippery: 'Nay, I let twelve alone,/ For after twelve has struck, maids look for one.' See MIDNIGHT and NOON.

Ado, IV.i.85, Claudio: 'What man was he talk'd with you yesternight/ Out at your window betwixt twelve and one?/ Now if you are a maid, answer to this.' Hero answers, 'I talk'd with no man at that hour, my lord' – to which Don Pedro responds, 'Why, then are you no maiden.' Don Pedro's answer would seem a *non sequitur*, but Hero talked with 'no man', a pun on *gnomon* the projecting piece on the sun-dial, also known as the cock (penis – TWR; P). (For another pun on the *gnomone* (F) or 'knowman' of a dial, see FIX, *Oth*.) Therefore Hero is no maiden. Her father repeats the pun: 'Hath no man's dagger here a point for me?' (110). Is there not for him, too, a prick (lit. a dagger, point or penis) with a point (erection – C; P). Hero's chastity was allegedly lost betwixt *twelve* and *one*: when she swoons Beatrice asks, 'wherefore sink you *down*' and Don John says, 'Smother her spirits *up*' (italics added). Her father asks Fate not to remove its 'heavy hand! Death is the fairest cover for her shame'. He prefers the heavy hand of Death to the HEAVY (pregnant) HAND (penis – K) of twelve o'clock; prefers the cover of Death in a grave to the cover (lit. mount in breeding) of her SHAME (lit. genitals) in the sex-act.

We, too, question Hero's chastity (HEART). Don John says, '*smother* her spirits *up*' (italics added). In *H5*, IV.v.20, also with ref. to a pander by whom 'a fairest daughter is contaminated [whored]', Orleans says, 'smother up the English in our throngs [THRONG, fornication]'. Like that *contaminated*, *fairest* daughter, Hero, too, is called 'contaminated stale' (II.ii.25) and 'most fair' (IV.i.104), Hero, whose father wished the *fairest* cover of Death for her shame. Is there not a pun in s*mother*? Beatrice admits that for a 'twelvemonth' she had 'been her bedfellow', but *not* that one night. She says, 'My cousin is belied', pun on *belie* (to lie by the side of, sleep with – P). Was Hero slept with? And is she also *bellied* (*MND*, II.i.129: 'the sails conceive/ And grow big-bellied')? Is pregnancy the reason Hero fainted?

See GREEN, *H5*.

Twenty Numerical equiv. of a score. Cf. *Tim*, III.vi.86: 'Let no assembly of twenty be without a score of villains.' SCORE, lit. cut: pun on cunt; fornicate.

MV, III.iv.74. Portia, dressed as a man, will tell 'quaint lies' – will belie her QUAINT (cunt – TWR; F) with LIES (copulation, partic. buggery). She will tell 'twenty of these puny lies': PUNY/ punie, a bedbug – a bugger's lies, a SCORE of lies on her sexual exploits with women who died for her love.

See CAPER, *MV*; CROOK-BACK, *3H6*; GROAN; SCORE, *TGV*; SNATCH, *MM*.

Twin, twain (1) Testicle. Didymous: twin, twain, double, growing in pairs (Gk *didimos*, a testicle, twin). See MILK, Jonson's quote on masturbating the testicle duct, the 'epididimis'. Fr *les frères siamois*: Siamese twins (pop., testes – F&H, s.v. Cods, n.d.); cf. *Cym.* I.vi.15: 'twinn'd stones'.

(2) Homosexual love, the two partners alike as twins (see MUTUAL). Patrick White, *Flaws in the Glass* (New York: Viking Press, 1981) pp. 34–5, on his 'deviant sexuality': 'I did not question the darkness in my dichotomy, though already I had begun the inevitably painful search for the twin who might bring a softer light' (see ROUND for this idea in Plato).

H5, IV.i.251: 'O hard condition,/Twin-born with greatness . . . ! What infinite heart's-ease . . . private men enjoy! . . . what have kings, that privates have not too . . . ?' Henry talks of the *hard* condition (the same 'hard condition' of V.ii.303, glossed as erect phallus – C; P), twin-born, born of the testes: kings have nothing that private men have not TOO/TWO (testes; private and privates: genitals, *OED*; P). And private men enjoy more INFINITE (in*fin*ite, in the end) EASE (sexual intercourse and relief – TWR). See CLIP.

H8, IV.ii.58. Sh mocks Wolsey in Griffith's efforts to 'speak his good' after Katherine has spoken his bad qualities, among which is that he was 'ever double', 'ever ranking'. Griffith calls him a 'ripe' (RIPE, sexually rank) scholar, a 'good one', 16th c. syn. for whore and whoreson (GOOD): 'ever witness . . . Those twins of learning that he raised in you,/Ipswich and Oxford' – ever rank, ever double, ever WITNESS (L *testis*, also testicle) those twins he raised, the buggering he gave Katherine and the King – the moneys he diverted from such projects and *raised* for his own bank (a 'ripe' – *OED*), as his 'inventory' (III.ii) revealed.

The net effect of both speeches is the same, Katherine using DOUBLE ('in his words [WORD, whore] and meaning [MEANS, pandering]') and Griffith using WITNESS and 'twin'; and both meaning Wolsey had raised or risen through double-dealing and lewdness (see EXCELLENT).

See MUTUAL, *AC*; DOUBLE; CACKLE, *MV*.

Twist (1) The crotch (F&H). *Fourcheure*: 'that part of the bodie from whence the thighes doe part; (I, thinke we call it the Twist.)' (Cot).

(2) Masturbate. Chaucer, 'The Merchant's Tale', 761: signalling her 'queynte' (cunt) is his, May 'taketh hym by the hand, and harde hym twiste'. This age-old description of sexual acquiescence also meant to hold the penis in the hand for masturbation (TWR, s.vv. Twist, Hond). Masturbation is freq. linked to deception; *coglionare*: to play with one's stones; to deceive someone (F).

See FINE, *Ado*; OATH, *Cor*.

Two(fold) The two testicles (see DUE). 'Fold' means lap. Lap: female genitals (C; P); 'lappe': male flaps or folds of skin (TWR). See DEWLAP (vulva; testes).

See SWEET, *R2*; SCEPTRE, *Mac*.

Two hours Two whores (HOUR/Whore – K).

AYL, IV.i.180. Ganymede warns Orlando (170) of the inevitable 'neighbour's bed' in marriage (NEIGHBOUR, adulterer): Rosalind 'will do as I do'. For these *do-ers* (do: copulate – C; P), 'For these two hours, Rosalind, I will leave thee' (HOUR/whore was established II.vii.26). The pun encapsulates Orlando's dismay.

CE, II.ii.150. Adriana and Luciana invite Antipholus S. (mistaken for his twin, Adriana's husband) home and to bed, saying he would suffer were his wife 'licentious' as he and 'contaminate'. Antipholus: 'I know you not:/In Ephesus I am but two hours old'. He protests innocence, being only two hours OLD (hoary) in Ephesus: *they* are the only two whores he knows (MERMAID).

Ham, III.ii.135: 'within these two hours' – Hamlet's uncle and mother (see HOUR).

1H4, II.iii.39. Reading a letter from a lord who refuses him support, Hotspur fears the Lord will 'to the king and lay open' the rebellion – a sexually suggestive phrase representing lord and King as two political whores. Kate enters and he concludes his speech, 'I must leave you within these two hours.'

III.i.266. Hotspur believes the 'tripartite indentures' or planned division of land among these three rebels was drawn up to disadvantage him. As the scene ends he tells Kate, 'An the indentures be drawn, I'll away within these two hours', and Glendower adds, 'we'll but seal,/ And then to horse'. *Two hours* and *to horse* (HORSE/ whores – K): the two whores, Glendower and Mortimer, who took more than their share of land (BANK) and fail him on the battlefield, (1) seal the contract; (2) but / butt seal – SEAL, fuck or bugger Hotspur, the arse – Hotspur's 'bottom' ('To rob me of so rich a bottom' – 105).

U

Understand, undertake Coit, perh. as bottom man. Take: accept coitally (F&H; P); stand: have an erection (F&H; P). Undertake: 'woo (a woman) briskly' (P); take a woman beneath one for intercourse (C). 'Undertake' meant understand, 1510; puns on both are similar. Cf. a variation in Middleton, *Michaelmas Term*, III.i: Lethe's 'underput' is his 'courtesan, a backslider, a prostitution, or such a toy'.

MND, I.ix.92. *Bottom* offers to 'undertake' the PART of Pyramus.

TGV, II.v.25–31:

> *Speed.* What an ass art thou! I understand thee not.
> *Launce.* What a block art thou . . . ! My staff understands me.
> *Speed.* What thou sayest?
> *Launce.* Ay, and what I do, too . . . .
> *Speed.* It stands under thee, indeed.
> *Launce.* Why, stand-under and understand is all one.

His *staff*, or staff of life or love, the penis (F&H), understands what he says and stands under what he does INDEED/in *the* deed, i.e. in intercourse.

Cym, II.iii.80: 'I will make/One of her women lawyer to me, for/I yet not understand the case myself.' One of her women will lawyer/lower (K) to him, for he does not understand the *case*, either the legal one or the woman's (pudendum – K; P).

1H6, v.iii.117. Suffolk, sent to woo Margaret for Henry, wants her himself: 'I'll undertake to make thee Henry's queen . . If thou wilt condescend to be my –' and he quickly corrects himself, 'His love.' If she will condescend or lower (as in *Cym* above), he will *under-take* her (take her under) – undertake to make her Henry's QUEEN/quean and Suffolk's quean, both of which he does.

See OPPRESS, *TrC*.

Undone Made impotent or castrated; opposite of 'done' (do: copulate – C; P).

AW, III.ii.22. Bertram wedded but not bedded one who has 'recovered the king, and undone me'. Helen cured the King's FISTULA (impotence); he can now RECOVER (mount coitally again). But her husband is undone; him she renders impotent. See RAISE.

See KNOT, *AW*; CATERPILLAR, *1H4*.

Unkind(ness) Physically unnatural, against the usual course of nature: 'Such unlawfull lust, such unkinde desires' (Greene, in *OED*). Chaucer, 'The Parson's Tale', 575: 'dooth unkyndely synne, by which man or woman shedeth hire nature in manere or in that place ther as a child may nat be conceived' – *coitus interruptus* or masturbation (TWR, s.v. Nature). Cf UNNATURAL.

TA, v.iii.48. Titus's killing of his own daughter is 'unnatural and unkind'.

TN, III.iv.402: 'None can be call'd deform'd but the unkind'.

AW, II.v.35. Trying to understand the friction between Lafeu and Parolles (whom Lafeu admits he 'sinned against' and 'transgressed against'), Bertram asks, 'Is there any unkindness between my lord and you, monsieur?' and he concludes, 'It may be you have mistaken him, my lord' (MISTAKE: take the wrong way, sexually; anal sex – C).

See CROOKED, *R2*; BLUNT, *CE*.

Unmannered, unmannerly Not manly; unmanned. 'Unmannered' is used by Sh only for SLAVES and DOGS, i.e. pederasts.

TSh, IV.i.169: 'You heedless joltheads and unmanner'd slaves!' They are *heed*less jolt*heads* – less or minus their HEADS (*teste* – F), their testes or prepuces. They are castrated male SLAVES, like the eunuchs used as whores in Athenian brothels, or they are circumcised barbarians like the 'Turk' and 'circumcised dog' in *Oth*, V.ii.355.

R3, I.ii.39. The 'Unmanner'd dog' is a pederast (see BEGGAR).

MV, I.ii.54: '*unmannerly* sadness' parallels '*unmanly* melancholy' (*Tim*, IV.iii.203) and '*unmanly* grief' (*Ham*, I.ii.94). (Italics added.)

MWW, I.i.325. Slender is willing to marry Anne, but Evans questions, 'can you affection the 'oman? . . . precisely, can you carry your good will to the maid?' (234). Much about Slender makes everyone question his ability to carry his will (penis – C; P) to the maid; for example, his telling her, 'Truly, I will not go first; truly, la!'; 'I'll rather be unmannerly than troublesome. . . . la!'

See SWINE, *KJ*; DAINTY, *H8*.

Unnatural Used for sex-acts other than heterosexual copulation: homosexuality, masturbation, etc. Late in life, when Plato wrote the *Laws*, he condemned homosexuality: 'he calls it "unnatural", using an argument . . . it is not found in the animal world. . . . So it was that the emotive, question-begging phrase "unnatural vice" early took root in the Western world' (Wilkinson, p. 28). In the 16th c. 'unnatural' meant not in accordance with usual laws of nature; outraging moral standards. Peele, *The Old Wives' Tale*, 120: the wife of a smith tells three lost pages, 'One of you go lie with him'; and her husband exits with one: 'Come on, my lad, thou shalt take thy unnatural rest with me.'

R3, I.ii.60. Following Gloucester's exchange with the corpse-bearer, with its several puns on buggery (BEGGAR; WHITE-FRIARS), Anne reviles his 'heinous [HEINOUS/anus, anl] deeds'; his 'butcheries' (BUTCHER/bugger); his 'arm' [ARM, penis) that 'hath butchered'; and his never having dreamt on 'aught but[/butt] butcheries'. She tells him, 'Thy deed, inhuman and unnatural,/Provokes this deluge most unnatural'. The deed is murder; the deluge, 'blood' (said five times). But in this bizarrely erotic context, in which Richard proposes, and is accepted, over the coffin of the king whom he murdered (as he admittedly had murdered also her husband), *unnatural* deed (sex act – C; P) connotes (political) buggery; *unnatural* deluge, that Richard is to 'blush' for and God to 'revenge', the unnatural red rain of Gen 19:24: 'the Lord *rained* upon Sodom and Gomorrah *brimstone* and *fire*' (italics added).

KL, I.ii.81. Edmund opens the scene: 'Thou, nature, art my goddess; to thy law/My services are bound. . . . Well, then,/Legitimate Edgar . . . Edmund the base/Shall top the legitimate. . . . gods, stand up for bastards!' Asserting that his illegitimacy is the source of his problems, Edmund starts his speech by dedicating his (copular) services (C; P) to the goddess NATURE (generative organs – *OED*); and he concludes by asking the gods to *stand up* for, bestow the erect penis or give power to (F&H; P), bastards.

Edmund, the natural child (1586, bastard), will make all *un*natural, will turn the world upside down: the *base* will *top*. And he succeeds, for the deluded Gloucester concludes that his other, loving son Edgar is the 'Abhorred villain! Unnatural, detested, brutish villain! worse than brutish! . . . abominable villain!'

Though Gloucester had called Edmund his 'whoreson' (I.i), he now calls Edgar the ABHORred/whored one. Edmund said he would top (screw – *OED*; P) his brother; yet it is Edgar the father calls (1) unnatural, (2) ABOMINABLE (sodomitical), (3) DETESTED, which can only mean its pun, de*tested*, without testes (balls or virility), the strength Edmund is depriving him of – since, far from detesting him, Gloucester, a few lines later, confesses he 'tenderly and entirely loves him'. This continues the metaphor of testicles, since ENTIRE means uncastrated, and TENDERings are testicles: witnesses of his paternal and potent love. See WELL; and POVERTY for Edgar's impotence.

See GANYMEDE; HAGS.

Unstanched (1) Unchecked bloody flux; (2) unsated sexually. Lit. still bleeding; unsatisfied. Both meanings emerge in *3H6*, II.vi.83: 'with the issuing blood/ Stifle the villain whose unstanched thirst/ York and young Rutland could not satisfy'.

Tem, I.i.51. Sh's only other use of 'unstanched' also has both meanings: 'though the ship were no stronger than a nut-shell and as leaky as an unstanched wench'. The setting is a tempest (*cattivo tempo*: foul weather; monthly issues of a woman – F) and the ship, trad. a she and a bottom (*MV*, I.i.42) is like a wench (girl, specif. of loose morals – TWR; F&H; P); perh. like a sheep or courtesan, through a SHEEP/ SHIP pun as in *LLL*, II.i.220: 'Two hot sheeps, marry' – 'And wherefore not ships?' Oestrus, sexual heat (like the *hot* sheep), is a period characterised by a discharge of mucus and blood and a state of continual sexual readiness.

Cf. *KL*, III.vi.28. Bessy does not go over the bourn because 'Her boat hath a leak,/ And she must not speak/ Why she dare not come over to thee.' Bessy may be menstruating (MILK, *AW*); or she may be leaking from gonorrhoea, through a pun on 'bourn' and its alt. sp. *burn*, a brook *and* venereal infection (*OED*; P). (See HISS.)

Up and down (1) Sexual movements; including to frig (masturbate – F&H; *fregare*: 'to rub up and down' – F). Bring up, down, or off by hand (F&H, s.v. Hand, n.d.).

(2) Wander up and down like a whore or pimp. Alexander Radcliffe, 'Upon Mr Bennet, Procurer Extraordinary': 'Bennet the Bawd . . . Who was us'd to lead them in the dark,/ Like Beasts by Pairs into the Ark . . . Like Will'ith'wisp still up and down/ He led the Wives of *London* Town,/ To lodge with Squires of high renown.'

(3) *Pedigare*: to wander up and down; *pedicare*: to sodomise (F).

Tim, II.ii.120:

Servant. What is a whoremaster, fool?
Fool. . . . generally, in all shapes that man goes up and down in from fourscore to thirteen, this spirit walks in.

A whoremaster is a SPIRIT (a prick) that goes up and down in GENERAL (in the whore; on the whole/ hole: female pudendum – C; P; anus – TWR), in all SHAPES (genitals).

TSh, IV.iii.89: 'What, up and down, carved like an apple-tart?' Petruchio dismisses the gown Kate wants just as bawdily as he had the cap also intended for her (see VELVET). Since 'apple-squires' and 'apple-mongers' were pimps (F&H), the apple must be the whore they sell, the apple-tart (a tart or wanton).

The GOWN (cunt) is carved like an apple-tart's, i.e. cut like the CUT (vulva – C; K) of a whore (just as the cap had been compared to a diseased vulva).

See STING, *2H6*; DEFORMED, *Ado*; LOLL, *RJ*; BOOT, *1H4*; HAND, *Ado*.

Utter Thrust forth, shoot out, discharge. Pun on a seminal emission. L *uter*: animal skin used as a bag; connected with 'uterus' or womb. L *utor, uti*: to make use of, enjoy, be intimate with. Middleton, *A Chaste Maid in Cheapside*, V.iv: the bridegroom says, 'My joy wants utterance' and is told 'Utter all at night then brother.'

Ado, III.iii.108:

Conrade. I will owe thee an answer for that . . . now forward with thy tale.
Borachio. Stand thee close, then . . . I will, like a true drunkard, utter all to thee.

Having been insulted, Conrade owes Borachio an ANSWER (a prick, coital thrust). If Borachio is to *forward with* his tale (penis – K; P) of how he wooed Margaret and allegedly whored Hero, if he is to utter or discharge ALL (the penis) to him, then Conrade must stand CLOSE (lecherously). The Watch sees and hears and charges them with 'the most dangerous piece [PIECE: penis; whore] of lechery' (180). 'Borachio' means drunkard, a leather bottle (L *uter*) for wine.

See INWARD, *Ado*; GRACIOUS, *TGV*.

V

Variable, variety, vary Depart from some standard. Used with ref. to homosexuality, buggery; perhaps a ref. to the diversification, capability for variety, in the bisexual. Jonson, *Volpone*, I.ii: Nano tells Androgyno, a hermaphrodite: ' 'Cause here the delight of each sex thou canst vary!' Among some Eliz. poets intent on 'mocking homosexuality' (Keach, p. 126) is Middleton, *MicroCynicon*, Satyre v: 'As it is Sathan's usuall pollicie, / He left an issue of like quallitie; / The still memoriall if I aime aright, / Is a pale chequered Hermaphrodite [by which is meant also the homosexual – *OED*].' Chequered: variegated, diversified, broken into different colours. Perhaps a pun on buggery / *bigarré* (variegated, diversified, made of sundry colours – Cot).

H5, III.vii.35, Dauphin: 'the man hath no wit that cannot . . . vary deserved praise on my palfrey [a saddle horse, esp. a very small one for ladies; as distinguished from a war-horse]'. The MAN (L *homo*) who cannot vary the praise (or laud: 'I laud them, I praise them' – *1H4*, III.iii.215) *on* this horse that he calls 'my mistress' and that is the actual object of his sexual bestiality (Index), the man who cannot laud / LOAD (with semen) this horse, is inadequate sexually, without WIT (genitals).

AC, II.ii.241. For Enobarbus's puns on Cleopatra's disease and anal eroticism, see POOP and THRONE. Here we discuss her 'infinite variety' as including buggery. It was INFINITE / in*fin*ite, in the *fin*, end or buttocks (see ABOMINABLE). 'Aretino could have taught nothing to a reincarnated Cleopatra, nor Forberg have told her anything she had not known – and done' (P, s.v. Variety).

Enobarbus introduces her variety with his 'divers-colour'd [*bigarré*] fans':

> her own person,
> It beggar'd all description: she did lie
> In her pavilion . . .
> O'er-picturing that Venus where we see
> The fancy outwork nature; on each side her
> Stood pretty dimpled boys, like smiling Cupids,
> With divers-colour'd fans, whose wind did seem
> To glow the delicate cheeks which they did cool
> And what they undid did.

Two opening words evoke buggery: her person BEGGARED / buggered, and she did LIE (bugger). Cleopatra was more whore than Venus: she O'ER / whore pictured her, not a sentimentalised Venus, but the strumpet who had a 'wicked bastard' (*AYL*, IV.i.216); 'What Venus did with Mars' (*AC*, I.v.18); 'more intemperate in your blood / Than Venus' (*Ado*, IV.i.60).

On each side of her stood CUPIDS (panders), PRETTY / *prat*-y (prat-like) and smiling (SMILE, Fr *rire* / rear) Cupids (beautiful young boys – *OED*; the putti, nude children, of the 15th c.), young naked BOYS (catamites) with FANS (buttocks), q.v., of divers colour (*bigarré*; COLOUR / Fr *culier*, It *culare*: arse) – young buggering boys, whose wind seemed to COOL with one fan, but whose WIND (to 'wind' is to bottom) with the other FAN did *cul* or cule (buttocks – *OED*), undoing what they did: they dispelled one heat but made DELICATE (voluptuous, wanton) CHEEKS (buttocks) glow with another heat, ardour. As Enobarbus says, we see the FANCY (affection, partic. pederastic) outwork nature. Agrippa reacts, 'O, rare for Antony!' – RARE/rear (buttocks) for the delectation of the bisexual Antony (see Index).

This makes an interesting complement to a description in Horace, whose *Odes* Sh knew well (*LLL*, IV.ii.104; *TA*, IV.ii.22). See *Odes*, Bk I, no. xxxvii: Cleopatra 'with her squalid/Pack of diseased half-men – mad, wishful grandeur . . . But all her fleet burnt'. Footnotes say these are her 'eunuch slaves'.

See RAMP, *Cym*; TABLE, *Ham*; DAMSELL, *LLL*; ROUND. *AYL* ('dappled', also meaning varied in colour, is tied to buggery).

Varlet Harlot; pimp. Dekker, *The Honest Whore I*, III.iii: 'You shall not spurne my Punk [prostitute]', says Matheo – not 'Spurne my sweet Varlet!' John Skelton: 'The keeper of herlettes,/And captayne of verlettes' (*OED* 1550); Thomas Tusser: 'Such Lords ill example doth give, where verlets and drabs so may live' (*OED* 1573).

TrC, v.i.16. Thersites says that by 'Achilles' male varlet' he meant 'his masculine whore'. 'Nothing but lechery! all incontinent varlets!' (116)

iv.3. Thersites calls Diomedes a 'varlet' and 'Greekish whoremasterly villain'.

MM, II.i.174–99. Five times Elbow calls Pompey, the bawd, a 'varlet'.

2H4, v.iii.13:

Falstaff. This Davy serves you for good uses; he is your serving-man and your husband.
Shallow. A good varlet, a good varlet, a very good varlet. . . . a good varlet.

'Husband' means manager, sexual partner; 'use' is sexual intercourse (*OED*; P); 'serving' means coitally (*OED*; P); a SERVING-MAN is a lover; and GOOD is a descriptive for fornicators. Shallow later tells Bardolph (70) that Davy 'will stick by thee . . . he is true bred' – 16th c. phrase connoting whore (see COWARD, *1H4*). And Bardolph says, 'And I'll stick by him' – STICK: 16th c. euphemism for fuck.

See DITCH, *AC*.

Vary See VARIABLE.

Velvet (1) Vulva, in 17th c. use: 'much pricking between her fundament and vulva' (Rowse, p. 68). An 'obscure allusion to the clitoris' (P, s.v. Velvet and pile)

(2) THREE-PILE (rich velvet): VD. Patches of velvet: covered lanced chancres (C).

LLL, IV.iii.105: 'Love . . . Spied a blossom. . . . Through the velvet leaves the wind . . . can passage find;/That the lover . . . Wish himself the heaven's breath.' The leaf of a folding door is a valve (L *valva*), making *velvet leaves* a double pun on entrance into the vulva and vagina (a sheathing leaf-base that embraces the stem; also the female genital passage). PASSAGE: body orifice. See CHEEKS.

H5, I.ii.196: 'Others [bees], like soldiers, armed in their stings,/Make boot upon the summer's velvet buds,/Which pillage'. The phallic image of ARMED (with penises) soldiers with STINGS (pricks, penises) crushing buds under foot and making BOOT (i.e. booty) upon buds, connotes rape. In this metaphor of a bee-hive, the Archbishop has no female, not even a queen bee. Instead, there is the tent-royal of 'their emperor'. Even the buds may be male genitals, as in *WT*, IV.iv.94: 'we marry . . . And make conceive a bark of baser kind/By bud of nobler race': the bark (feminine) conceives by entry of bud (masculine) in the grafting-process, with allusion to human intercourse. If so, then velvet (from L. *villus*, shaggy hair) is man's pubic hair (*AYL*, II.i.50: 'velvet friends' are deer who abandoned a companion, velvet being the cover of the deer's antler, *horn*).

MM, I.ii.32. Lucio, who admits to the 'diseases' he 'purchased' in a brothel, is told: 'thou art piled, for a French velvet'. 'Piled' is infected with VD (C; P); and 'French velvet' is the THREE-PILE disease of the vulva of the French whore who communicated the disease (the 'malady of France' – *H5*, v.i.87).

TSh, IV.iii.65. Petruchio dismisses a cap brought Kate as bawdily as he had dismissed a

GOWN, cunt (UP AND DOWN): 'Why, this was moulded on a porringer; / A velvet dish: fie, fie! 'tis lewd and filthy'. Its shape indicates the cap is a pileus, a brimless felt hat (with piles).

Not only 'velvet' but 'dish' (woman – C; P), too, puns on the vulva and a whore: 'to cast away honesty upon a foul slut were to put good meat into an unclean dish' (*AYL*, III.iii.35).

The velvet dish or vulva is lewd and filthy – it is MOULDED (a womb; and diseased), has a furry mould-like growth. There may also be a pun on 'porringer' (dish for porridge) and porrigo, scalp disease (L *porrigo*, scurf).

Sh's contemporaries associated velvet caps with debauchery. Marston, *The Scourge of Villanie*, Satyre iii, 51–2: 'what cares he for faire Cynedian boyes? / Velvet cap'd Goates, duch Mares?' Jonson, *Bartholomew Fair*, IV.iii: 'poor common whores' can't compete with 'privy rich ones; your caps and hoods of velvet'.

AW, IV.v.100. The Clown tells Bertram's mother 'yonder's my lord your son with a patch of velvet on's face: whether there be a scar under't or no, the velvet knows; but 'tis a goodly patch of velvet: his left cheek is a cheek of two pile and a half, but his right cheek is worn bare'. Loss of hair was a venereal symptom; his left cheek has a pile (is infected) and his RIGHT (L *rectum*) CHEEK (buttock) is worn bare. A similar insult lies behind 'Patch-*breech* [buttocks]' (*Per*, II.i.17) and 'Thou scurvy patch!' (*Tem*, III.ii.71) (italics added).

See COPATAIN HAT, *TSh*.

Venice Eliz. byword for sexual immorality (C; Jonson, *Every Man in his Humour*, II.v.46). Day, *Humour out of Breath*, II.i: 'and you be not fitted in Venice, 'tis straunge, for 'tis counted the best Flesh-Shambles [brothel] in Italie'. Boccaccio, *Decameron*, p. 213: 'Venice, that welcomer of all wickedness'.

Oth, III.iii.202, Iago: 'I know our country disposition well; / In Venice they do let heaven see the pranks / They dare not show their husbands' (see NETHER).

Ado, I.i.274: 'Nay, if Cupid have not spent all his quiver in Venice'. Greene, *Greene's Never Too Late*: 'this great city of Venice is holden Loves Paradice'.

Venture See ADVENTURE.

Very (1) Pun on VARY (bisexuality). *LLL*, V.ii.487: 'it is vara fine', says Costard, who then switches an 'e' and 'a' again in 'to parfect one man'. Vairy, verre, verry: her., variegated.

(2) Of the arse. *Voirie*: where a town's dung and filth are unloaded; justice (Cot). *Assai* (It, mus.): adv., very.

Cym, V.iii.78: 'the veriest hind'.

IV.ii.107. Belarius recognises Cloten by 'the snatches in his voice. . . . I am absolute / 'Twas very Cloten.' Cloten is an androgynous 'ass' (I.ii.39; II.i.58) who 'turned up ace' (II.iii.3; ace / ass – K). Belarius hears SNATCHES (song fragments; female pudendum) in his VOICE / VICE, made of two jaws, a screw. He is therefore ABSOLUTE (of an ass / arse) this is very Cloten.

MND, IV.ii.12. 'Bottom's Dream . . . hath no bottom (i.221) and he will sing it in 'the latter end' of a play: 'he is a very paramour for a sweet voice' – perh. a very (*assai*) paramour for the same sweet VOICE / VICE as Cloten's (above). Cloten had a SNATCH (female pudendum) in his vice (jointure of the closed thighs) and Bottom's first name is Nick (female pudendum – C; K).

AYL, IV.i.68: 'Come, woo me . . . I am . . . like enough to consent. What would you say to me now, an I were your very very Rosalind?' She wants to CONSENT (give CON, cunt) – she is LIKE (homosexual) ENOUGH (Fr *assez*) to, ass enough – for she *is* both his very very Rosalind *and* his very very GANYMEDE (catamite).

See CREATURE, *CE*; ANY, *MWW*; SIEGE, *MM*; WAG, *WT*.

Vex Fart. *Vessare*: to vex, grieve; 'Also as Vesciare', to 'fiste or fizzle', i.e. fart (F). *Vesse*: a 'fyste' (Cot).

R2, II.i.3: 'Vex not yourself, nor strive not with your breath [L *flatus*]'.

KL, V.iii.313. After speaking of Cordelia's 'breath', Lear dies. Kent: 'Vex not his ghost: O, let him pass [PASS, emit a flatus]!' The many puns on farting (see THUNDER) ultimately, perh., comment on Lear's tragic flaw: vanity, arrogance and haughtiness, what Vergil called *flatus* (*Cassell's Latin Dictionary*).

See ENLARGEMENT, *1H4*.

Vice See VOICE.

Virtue Chastity in women (P); but, not surprisingly, the opposite for men: potency, virility (L *vir*, a man). *Vertue*: manhood, prowess (Cot).

Ado, II.i.127. Naughty Ursula, observant of Benedick's 'shape' (SHAPE, genitals) in III.i.98, here recognises the masked Antonio: 'can virtue hide itself? Go to . . . graces will appear, and there's an end.' GRACE (Gk *charis*) puns on horn (*keros*), the erect penis (C; P). Graces will (penis – C; P) appear/*a* PEAR (testes); masculine virtue cannot hide. She concludes (undoubtedly with a glance or gesture), 'and there's an end'.

MM, II.i.38. Thinking of Claudio's coming execution for having impregnated Mariana, Escalus says, 'Well, heaven forgive him! and forgive us all! / Some rise by sin, and some by virtue fall' (cf. Middleton, *Michaelmas Term*, I.ii: 'Women ne'er rise but when they fall'). Mariana's belly rises by her falling coitally in sin; and she and Claudio fall (by way of) his virtue.

WT, IV.iii.94. Autolycus describes a fellow (himself) who went 'about with troll-my-dames: I knew him once a servant of the prince: I cannot tell . . . for which of his virtues it was, but he was certainly whipped out of the court'. He went ABOUT/*a* (sexual) *bout* with 'troll-[roll round and round] my-dames'; and was banished for his virtues or sexual exploits, which included being a SERVANT (lover or pimp) of the Prince. He 'served Prince Florizel and . . . wore three-pile; but now I am out of service' (14). 'Serving' is prostitution (C) or intercourse (P); and THREE-PILE is VD. These are his 'virtues' – amended to 'vices' (VICE) by the Clown – for which he was whipped out of court and WHIPPED (castrated) out of COURT (fornication). See STRIP(E) for his loss of virtue, his castration; and MERCURY.

Visard, visor See MASK.

Voice/vice Voice/vice (K). Vice: penis, pudendum, fornication (C; P). Lit. a screw, grip; blemish.

Cym, II.iii.33. Cloten believes the music will 'penetrate' (said three times) Imogen; 'if it do not, it is a vice in her ears, which . . . the voice of unpaved [without stones, testicles] eunuch . . . can never amend'.

Cor, II.iii.1. The citizens recognise that Coriolanus may 'require our voices': 22 times they speak of his taking away their 'voices', symbol of their powers (their potency, screws or penises), and leaving them emasculated like the 'mules' (MULE, sterile hybrid) he calls them. (Charles Sedley, 'On a Cock at Rochester': 'Thou cursed Cock, with thy perpetual Noise, / May'st thou be Capon made, and lose thy Voice'.) The Third Citizen says he mocked them: 'now you have left your voices, / I have no further with you' (179). He will, says Brutus, leave 'them of no more voice / Than dogs [DOG, castrate]' (223).

III.iii.9. The Tribunes go to fight Coriolanus with 'a catalogue / Of all the voices that we have procured' – the people are procured as by procurers (bawds – *OED*; P); they are screwed by Tribunes and Senators alike, their voices taken from them. They are – a freq. sentiment of Sh's – both whores and whored.

H8, V.iii.176: 'The common voice, I see, is verified / Of thee, which says thus, "Do my Lord of Canterbury / A shrewd turn, and he is your friend for ever." ' This is not a sentimental statement, its political cynicism emerging even in 'shrewd', i.e. depraved, wicked – at best, cunning, artful; the meaning of clever or keen-witted (*OED*) is modern. The shrewd TURN refers back to the 'turn together' in the garden when the King gave Cranmer his ring; but even more pertinently to the original turn (in the bed – P) or sexual betrayal (C), Cranmer's assistance to Anne (and Katherine's cry, 'Turn me away' if guilty – II.iv.42). (In *AW*, III.v.71 another 'shrewd turn' turns out to be one in the bed.) So, unwittingly (?) the King expresses the view that the common (whore-like – C; P) vice, verified by the common voice, i.e. of the people, is true of Cranmer: namely, that, like the rest of mankind, he, too, could be had – for a shrewd turn.

See CACKLE, *MV*; SISTER, *MM*; DEVIL, *2H4*.

W

Wag Effeminate boy. *Zanzerare*: to ingle boys or wantonly play with them against nature; *zanzeri*: 'Ganimeds, Cinedos, Nigles, Wanton boies. Also knavish wags' (F) – a list comprised of young male homosexuals.

TGV, v.iv.86. Julia, disguised as a boy, is called a 'wag'.

Cym, III.iv.160. Imogen, disguising herself as a young man, is told to change 'fear . . . or, more truly,/Woman it pretty self – into a waggish courage'.

1H4, I.ii.18, 26, 50. Falstaff calls Hal a 'sweet wag' and a 'mad wag'.

WT, I.ii.66. Scene i had described the 'affection' (AFFECTION) and 'loves' of Leontes and Polixenes, who 'embraced, as it were, from the ends of opposed winds' (see HEAVEN). Now Hermione asks about their early days when they 'were boys . . . pretty lordings' (lording: a little lord, 'usu. contemptuous 1577' – *OED*) who thought, interjects Leontes, 'to be boy [BOY, catamite] eternal'. 'Was not my lord/The verier wag o' the two?' (see ETERNAL).

See ANGEL, *1H4*.

Wall Buttocks. Waulies (Robert Burns): buttocks. Dekker and Massinger, *The Virgin Martyr*, IV.i: 'make her thy whore . . . imagine thou assaultst a towne,/Weake wall, to't . . . beat but this downe . . . be witnesse to this battry'.

Luc, 464. Sh uses the same image: 'His hand, that yet remains upon her breast, – /Rude ram, to batter such an ivory wall! – /May feel her heart . . . rise up and fall . . . . This moves in him more rage . . . To make the breach and enter this sweet city.' The imagery evokes the rape to come: his HAND (phallus – K) on her BREAST (lap – P), with the suggestiveness of rising up and falling that MOVES him, too; he, the rude ram (symbol of lechery – C; P) that in his rage (carnal lust – TWR; P) will BATTER (rape) her wall and make (copulate – P) the breach (pudendum – P)/breech (buttocks). And so he enters the sweet city; the rape over, Tarquin has 'batter'd down her consecrated wall' (723).

H5. Sexual imagery conveys the violence of war. Prol.: Chorus describes the 'swelling scene': 'within the *girdle* of these *walls*/Are now confined *two* mighty monarchies,/Whose high up*reared* and *abutt*ing fronts/The perilous narrow ocean *parts as*under' (italics added). These puns on the buttocks anticipate similar metaphors in III, Prol., and the attack on France: 'the huge bottoms', 'the sternage' (STERN, posteriors), and Henry's first line in the Act: 'Once more unto the breach . . . Or close the wall up with our English dead.' In V.ii.349 the French king compares an unviolated city to a virgin: 'you see them perspectively, the cities turned into a maid; for they are all girdled with maiden walls that war hath never entered.'

Cym, II.i.68. Calling Imogen's 'wooer' Cloten 'this ass', a lord prays, 'The heavens hold firm/The walls of thy dear honour'. May her DEAR/deer (hind) honour (chastity – P) – the walls of her chaste behind – withstand that 'ass' of another sort.

MND, v.i. Wall has a 'hole', a 'cranny', and, it is said five times, a 'chink' (*fesso*: 'broken hole. Also a womans privy chinke' – F). Wall, guilty of 'parting' the lovers, is the buttocks and its PART (partition): Wall is, in fact, called 'partition', is played by Snout (*groin*, a snout – Cot), and exits on the line 'Thus have I, Wall, my part discharged so'. To DISCHARGE is to fart. (See LIP.) Cf. Rabelais, Bk II, ch. 15 (1653 trs.): Panurge recommends building walls with womens' 'sine quo nons, kallibristris, or contrapunctums' ('pleasure-twats' – Le Clercq; 'what-you-may-call-them' – Putnam), because they are cheaper than stones.

War Whore. Amorous struggle. Marston compares the two in *The Dutch Courtesan*, I.i: fearing cuckoldry, the married man approves of brothels, 'lest my house should be made one . . . married men love the stews, as Englishmen lov'd the Low Countries: wish war should be maintain'd there, lest it should come home to their own doors.'

Per, IV.vi.181. A delightful switch. Boult, 'door-keeper' in a whore-house, resists attempts to reform him: 'What would have have me do? go to the wars, would you?'

AC, IV.xii.15. 'Triple-turn'd whore! 'tis thou/ Hast sold me to this novice; and my heart/ Makes only wars on thee.' Antony, who only wars/ whores on Cleopatra, has (like a whore) been 'sold' to a 'young Roman boy [BOY, catamite]', Octavius.

2H4, III.ii.196. Bullcalf, not wanting to be 'pricked' for war, claims a 'disease': 'A whoreson cold, sir'; but Falstaff reassures him, 'Come, thou shalt go to the wars in a gown; we will have away thy cold': (1) they will have his cold AWAY (to a whore); (2) he can be pricked for war and still go to the 'wars' in a GOWN (cunt – K).

AW, II.iii.290, 295. Bertram deserts his unwanted wife: 'I'll to the Tuscan wars and never bed her.' (Plautus, *Casket Comedy*, 562: 'earn your own dowry in vile Tuscan fashion by selling yourself'; *Curculio*, 481: 'In the Tuscan Quarter are those worthies [men, *homines*] who sell themselves'.) Parolles encourages him: 'To the wars . . . to the wars!/ He wears his honour in a box unseen/ That hugs his kicky-wicky here at home,/ Spending his manly marrow in her arms . . . . to the war!'

See SISTER, *R2*; WHITE AND RED, *TSh*; JUST, *R3*; DOOR, *AC*; IDLE, *Cor*; FRANCE, *AW*; THRONG, *Ado*.

Ward (1) A defence against sexual penetration. Lit. a defensive position in fencing (*WT*, I.ii.33: 'He's beat from his best ward'). A ridge on a lock and the corresponding indentation in the key to prevent the key's entering the wrong lock (*Luc*, 302: 'The locks between her chamber and his will,/ Each one by him enforced retires his ward' – anticipating the entry of his will (penis – P) into her 'chamber'.

(2) Any orifice that can be penetrated sexually. Lit. a compartment (*Ham*, II.ii.252: 'in which there are many confines, wards and dungeons'). Broadbent, p. 73: 'thrust he ne'er so hard . . . Grisel lieth at her ward/ And gives and takes as blithe and free'.

MWW, II.ii.258, Ford: 'I could drive her then from the ward of her purity . . . her marriage-vow and . . . other [OTHER, the arse] her defences'.

2H4, III.ii.339. Shallow 'came ever in the rearward of the fashion' – a 'vague charge of monosexuality' (P), but really not so vague (see FASHION). Here we note he came in the *rear* ward, confine or compartment.

TrC, I.ii.282–92. Pandarus calls the Greeks 'Asses' and Achilles a 'porter . . . a camel' – they all carry on their *backs* (CAMEL: fornicator; bugger). As for Cressida, 'You are such a woman! one knows not at what ward you lie.' She answers that she LIES or relies 'Upon my back, to defend my belly' lest 'it swells past hiding'. To lie on one's back is (P) woman's coital position (*RJ*, I.iv.91; *TA*, IV.i.98), hence hardly a defence against penetration or conception. But Cressida *relies* on her back and, like the Greeks and Achilles, she carries on her back; that is the ward at which she LIES (buggers), to defend her belly (see DAMSEL, *LLL*).

LLL, IV.iii.279: 'if the streets were paved with thine eyes' – 'then . . . what upward lies/ The street should see as she walk'd overhead'. Paved with a different kind of stone (i.e. testicles), with EYES (ME, 'balls') or eye-balls, the street would see what up-ward lies.

Wardrobe Latrine. Garderobe: wardrobe; also, in wealthy homes, in the Middle Ages, a privy, 'corbelled out over water' (*OED*). Chaucer, 'The Prioress's Tale' (120): 'I seye that in a wardrobe they hym threwe,/ Where as thise Jewes purgen hir entraille.'

Tem, IV.i.222: 'look what a wardrobe here is for thee!' – 'Let it alone, thou fool; it is but trash.' The entering Trinculo had said (199), 'I do smell all horse-piss': (1) he himself reeks of it; (2) he scents it in the air. Then he spies the clothes-line. What hangs on it, Prospero had called (187) 'stale [urine] to catch these thieves', Trinculo calls a *wardrobe* and Caliban calls *but*/ butt *trash* (human excrement). Caliban continues punning on excreta: 'The dropsy [morbid accumulation of fluid] drown this fool!' Rabelais, Bk I, ch. 17 (1653 trs.), also jests on pissing and drowning: 'drawing out his mentul . . . he so bitterly all-to-bepist them, that he drowned two hundred'.

Warrant Used by a speaker alluding coarsely to fornication. Beaumont and Fletcher, *The Knight of the Burning Pestle*, I.ii: 'A whoreson tyrant . . . I warrant him.' Related to 'warren' (MLG *waren*, to warrant): place for breeding game; brothel.

2H4, II.ii.184: 'This Doll Tearsheet should be some road.' – 'I warrant you, as common as the way between Saint Alban's and London.' Road, way, common: whore (P).

Oth, II.iii.19. Desdemona is 'sport for Jove'; 'I'll warrant her, full of game'.

Tem, III.ii.112. Miranda 'will become thy bed, I warrant./ And bring thee forth brave brood.' *Brave brood*: Sh's comment (?) on Miranda's 'brave new world,/ that has such people in't!' – those 'confined' by Ariel and Prospero's 'potent' art (v.i.7,50).

MWW, II.i.76, Mrs Page: 'I warrant he [Falstaff] hath a thousand of these letters . . . . he cares not what he puts into the press, when he would put us two. I had rather . . . lie under Mount Pelion.' *Press* and *put*: introduce the male animal to the female (*OED*; P).

III.iii.174: Ford thinks he has caught Falstaff with his wife: 'Buck, buck, buck! . . . I warrant you, buck . . . . here be my keys . . . . I'll warrant we'll unkennel the fox. (*Locking the door*.)' Ford, the buck (cuckold – P), combines brothel and hunting language: locking doors and keeping KEYS was the pimp's function. *Chiavare*: to lock the door; to fuck (F).

TSh, III.ii.247: 'I warrant him, Petruchio is Kated.' 'Kate' (common name for a wanton – F&H; P; cf. Kate Keep-down, whore in *MM*) is repeated 12 times by Petruchio, over Katherina's remonstrances (II.i.183). See DAINTY.

See REST, *RJ*; THREE-PILE, *MM*.

Weather Wether (castrated ram, eunuch). 16th c. sp. 'wether', as in Montaigne, Bk I, ch. 12: 'bare to winde and wether'.

Cym, III.iii.64, Belarius's story: 'my body's mark'd/ With Roman swords . . . . Cymbeline loved me . . . then was I as a tree/ Whose boughs did bend with fruit; but in one night,/ A storm or robbery, call it what you will,/ Shook down my mellow hangings, nay, my leaves,/ And left me bare to weather' (cf. above: 'bare to . . . wether').

Cymbeline had loved Belarius, his body that swords (penises – C; P) had mark'd, i.e. pricked – his body the butt (archery) with a mark on it (*LLL*, IV.i.133: 'Let the mark have a prick in't'). But then his fruit, i.e. the seed and its envelope (in man, testes), the fruit on his boughs (Sc 1555, legs), were taken from him. He lost his mellow hangings (HANG: a 'well-hung' man has large testes). Belarius's boughs (L *rami*) were robbed, the ram was made a wether, left bare ('Stripped of flesh' and worthless – *OED*). He is a tree whose *leaves left* him. A 'leaf' means a fold: see TWO-FOLD (testes, male folds of skin – *TWR*). Belarius was castrated. False 'oaths [OATHS, testes]' of 'two villains' had prevailed. To revenge his own fruitless *boughs*, he stole Cymbeline's *two* sons who now 'bow' (84) in his cave. Cf. *MV*, IV.i.114: about to lose flesh, Antonio likens himself to a 'wether' and weak 'fruit' that drops to the ground.

See BANK, *1H4*; FEATHER, *LLL*.

Weep(ing) Whoring. Maudlin (weeping or lachrymose): from 'Magdalen', ptg. to Mary Magdalen, she 'which was a sinner' (Luke 7:37), represented by painters as having eyes red with weeping, and – in Western hagiology – a repentant harlot, elevated to saintship.

Tim, I.ii.67. Apemantus will never be so 'fond' as 'To trust . . . a harlot, for her weeping'.

WT, IV.IV.106: 'The marigold, that goes to bed wi' the sun/ And with him rises weeping'. She goes to bed with him; he rises (phallicaly); and she rises with him (perh. in pregnancy), whored and weeping. The marigold is Mary's plant, prob. with ref. to the Virgin Mary (*OED*), but here certainly no virgin and prob. an allusion to the other Mary, the weeping Mary Magdalen.

Oth, IV.ii.124:

Emilia. He call'd her whore; a beggar in his drink
 Could not have laid such terms upon his callat. . . .
Desdemona. . . . I am sure I am none such.
Iago. Do not weep, do not weep. . . .
Emilia. . . . To be call'd whore? would it not make one weep?

Othello in his drink ('maudlin drunk' – *OED* 1611) calls Desdemona whore and she weeps like Magdalen.

JC, III.ii.120. Sh's attitude toward Antony and toward the populace, shallow men whose love can be bought by anyone, like that of whores, emerges again. The citizens, one minute ago moved to the point where they wanted to crown Brutus in Caesar's stead, now are swayed by the new hero, Antony: 'Poor soul! his eyes are red as fire with weeping'. And the weeping Antony, with eyes red like Mary's (see above), tells them (174), 'If you have tears, prepare to shed them now . . . . O, now you weep' – and off they go to murder the man they had wanted to crown.

CE, III.ii.48. Antipholus S. believes that Luciana (who mistook him for his twin, her brother-in-law) is pimping for her sister: 'Your weeping sister is no wife of mine'.

See SPREAD, *Ham*.

Weight Ass/arse. Lyly, *Endymion*, I.iii: 'Then *as* (as you know) is a weight, and we . . . account you a weight.' L *as*: as a weight, a pound.

H8, III.ii.407:

Cromwell. Last, that the Lady Anne . . . .
Wolsey. There was the weight that pull'd me down . . . .
 In that one woman I have lost for ever.

The Lady ANNE/Fr *âne* (ass) – her ass/arse is the weight or *as* that ruined him.

TSh, II.i.206. After a series of puns on 'Asses' (see CATCH), Kate says she is '*as* heavy *as* my *weight* should be' (italics added).

See BOWELS, *1H4*; GANYMEDE.

Well Whore, pudenda, fornicate. Lit. that which receives or contains liquid. Well: L *puteus*, pun on (1) whores or 'puts' (F&H; *CD*), *putte* (F); (2) penis, Gk *poutsa*, *pouti*; (3) 'put': fornicate (F&H; P); breed (*OED*). In Nashe, *The Choice of Valentines*, a woman's lover fails to satisfy her: 'the well is dry that should refresh me . . . my little dildo shall supply . . . he'll refresh me well.' Marston, *The Dutch Courtesan*, I.ii: bawds 'live well and die well . . . they live in Clerkenwell, and die in Bridewell' – the London district frequented by whores, and the house of correction for whores, vagrants.

3H6, IV.i.7. Gloucester mocks Edward's 'well-chosen bride' – from Bridewell.

MWW, I.ii.6. The functions Mistress Quickly performs for Dr Caius, as Evans lists them, add up to the services of a bawd (DRY), so when he finishes Simple says, 'Well, sir' – neatly summing it up.

KL, I.ii.7. Edmund says his 'dimensions are as well compact' as Edgar's; in fact, bastards such as he have more quality, more manhood, than 'within a dull, stale, tired bed/Go to the creating a whole tribe of fops. . . . Well, then,/Legitimate Edgar'. Edgar is the product of a stale marriage-bed; and Edmund, bastard and 'whoreson' (i.24), is product of the bed of another kind of *stale*, a whore. Edmund's intention is to make legitimate Edgar look like a bastard in their father's eyes and then oust him as heir. A 'well' or pit is *puis*, *puits* (Cot); 'then' is *puis*: *well-then*-legitimate (a contradiction in terms) Edgar will look like the *whoreson*, *son* of a *stale* (marriage-bed). Edmund will show him up for a put (a gull), a *poutsa* or prick, one of the fops. See UNNATURAL for his success.

MM, II.i.111–37. Pompey Bum, bawd who deals in puts, discusses the goings-on in Mistress Overdone's brothel: 'Very well; you being then'; 'Why, very well; I telling you then'; 'Why, very well, then, –'; 'Why, very well'; 'Why, very well, then'. These incessant puns on puts, fornication, 'well' (*puits*, *puteus*), and 'then' (*puis*) exhausts Escalus, who calls him 'tedious fool'. See SUCH.

AW, II.i.6. Off to the Italian wars, a lord says, ' 'Tis our hope, sir,/ After well enter'd soldiers, to return/ And find your grace in health' – well enter'd, initiated in soldiery, well entered in Italian *putte*. These are the men who were 'sick/ For breathing and exploit' (BREATHE, fornicate). And, as they hope, on their return from 'higher Italy' (10) their king's GRACE (penis) is in health, well and higher, his FISTULA (impotence) cured.

See OLD, *2H4*; TUTOR, *LLL*; EPHESUS, *CE*; HEM, *2H4*; KNOT, *Oth*.

West(ern), westerly Buttocks. *Ponent*: the West; the arse (Cot). Postic: posteriors; *postica*: that part toward the West or behind us (F). Peele, *The Old Wives' Tale*, 750: 'He looks as though he crept out of the backside of the well, and speaks like a drum perished at the west end' – *backside*, DRUM (buttocks – TWR, s.v. Thakke), west *end*.

MM, IV.i.29. Angelo plans to seduce Isabella in a 'garden . . . whose *western* side is with a vineyard *back*'d' (italics added). The location is an erotic physiological map: on the western SIDE (loin) is a GARDEN (pudendum); he will make 'his opening with this bigger key [KEY, penis]'; there are 'a little door [DOOR, vulva]' and a 'gate' (GATE, anus); and this seduction will occur 'Upon the heavy middle of the night' (see MIDNIGHT and TWELVE, time of the full phallic erection, the 'heavy time' of the 'heavy hand [HAND, penis – K]').

AYL, IV.iii.79: 'West of this place [PLACE, pudendum], down in the neighbour bottom [rump].'

Per, IV.i.51. WIND, being flatulence, is also linked to the West. Dionyza tells Leonine to murder Marina: ' 'Tis but a blow' (2). Then, pretending solicitude, she tells Marina (36) she looks 'blasted' (blast: a blow; a disease of flatulence in sheep). Dionyza exits and Marina asks, 'Is this wind westerly that blows?' – unconsciously reflecting that Dionyza's concern for her is empty wind, hot air, a fart or butt-blow from the West – is, as Dionyza said, *but a blow* importing murder.

See STIR, *KJ*.

Whip (1) Castrate. *Fouetter*: whip (Cot); Fr *Frouettage*: whipping, castration (by ligature).

(2) For sadism. Oldham, 'Upon the Author of a Play Call'd *Sodom*': 'Whose *Muse* is impotent . . . 'T had need like Age, be whipt to *Lechery*'. Butler, 'A Quaker', in *Characters*, p. 199: 'some old extravagant Fornicators find a Lechery in being whipt'.

AC, II.v.65, Cleopatra (enraged by a messenger who said Antony had married): 'I'll spurn thine eyes/ Like balls before me . . . Thou shalt be whipp'd with wire, and stew'd in brine'. Wire is the ligature for tying off the EYES (testicles) like *balls* – her idea of fit punishment for the abhorrent sexual news.

III.xiii.88, 93, 99. Enobarbus warns a man who kissed Cleopatra's hand, 'You will be whipp'd.' Then the jealous Antony says, 'whip him . . . whip him . . . Till, like a boy, you see him cringe' (BOY: catamite, one who plays the woman). When he returns, castrated, Antony says, 'If that thy father live, let him repent/ Thou wast not made his daughter' (134).

150. Antony sends Caesar 'my enfranched bondman, whom/ He may at pleasure whip, or hang, or torture,/ As he shall like, to quit me'. *Quid pro quo*: at *pleasure* (the sexual spasm – P; F&H), as he shall *like* to revenge or QUIT/ coit Antony (to screw him).

2H6, II.i.137. Pizzles (*1H4*, II.iv.271) were penises of animals, used freq. for whips (*OED*; F&H). Gloucester: 'have you not beadles in your town, and things [penises – F&H; P] called whips?' He wanted them applied to a man who was pretending to be 'lame' (LAME, impotent) from a fall off a 'plum-tree' (PLUMS: testes; female pudenda). Told to 'leap [fornicate] me over this stool', the man had said 'master, I am not able to stand [have an erection – F&H; P] alone', so they whip him with a pizzle and he recovers and runs away.

Ado, V.i.84. The epithets all make one point: Antonio and Leonato are 'men', but Claudio is foppish, a 'milksop', a BOY (catamite), a *sir* (term of contempt) *boy*. 'He shall kill . . . men indeed . . . . Come . . . boy; come, sir boy . . . Sir boy, I'll whip you from your foining fence'.

Whipping will prevent Claudio's ability to thrust in both kinds of foining (fencing and copulating – F&H; P). As Claudio says (116), 'We had like to have had our two noses [penises – C; P] snapped off with two old men without teeth' – but with a whip!

See BOTCHER, *AW*; VIRTUE, *WT*; DARK, *AYL*.

Whistle (1) Symptom of syphilis, after the shepherd Syphilis, who, in a poem by Fracastoro (1530) suffered from the disease. 'Siffles' are whistles.

(2) A flatus, hiss of escaping air.

WT, IV.iv.805: 'An old sheep-whistling rogue, a ram-tender, to offer to have his daughter come into grace!' Autolycus compares the shepherd to Abraham, who asked by God to 'offer' his child, 'took the ram and offered him up for a burnt offering' (Gen 22:13–22). The shepherd offered his child (Perdita), not to come into *God*'s grace, but into grace, i.e. favour and a royal title. Like a pimp he sacrificed her, to acquire the grace of an *earthly* king, and the GRACE (penis) of *that* king's *son* (Florizel). He, diseased, whistling, siffling shepherd–pimp TENDERS (offers sexually) not a ram, but his daughter, a SHEEP (whore) for the burnt (venereally diseased – *OED*; P) offering.

2H4, III.ii.342. Shallow 'came ever in the rearward of the fashion, and sung those tunes to the overscutched huswives that he heard the carmen whistle' – came rearward (perhaps in sodomy – P) with the overscutched (Sh's only use of this word) or hard-beaten hussies ('scutch' is dress wool by beating it), the hard beaten woolly SHEEP (whores).

These carmen whistle. To carminate or expel wind from the bowels derives from L *carminare*, to card wool, hence to cleanse, purge. Shallow's tunes and *coming* in the *rearward* of the FASHION (Fr *taille*/tail) may also mean he farted. Like the Greeks (see FART), Sh associates farting and pederasty.

See THRONE, *AC*.

Whit, white See WIT.

White and red Colours associated with harlots, who in the 16th–17th c. were carted away 'on a cart with a striped red and white canopy, herself wearing a red and white striped harlot's cap' (Burford, *Queen of the Bawds*, p. 32). Dekker and Middleton, *The Honest Whore I*, II.i: the whore has 'two boxes, one with white, another red painting'. Dekker, *The Comedy of Old Fortunatus*, I.i: 'And on thy cheeks I'll mix such white and red,/That Jove shall turn away young Ganymede', says the 'painted strumpet' Fortune.

LLL, I ii.98. Moth says Samson's love had a 'green [GREEN, venery] wit'. Armado: 'My love is most immaculate white and red' – to which Moth returns, 'Most maculate thoughts, master, are masked under such colours.' Maculate (defiled, polluted) thoughts are masked (MASK, a whore) under those colours, i.e. the PAINT worn by whores.

TSh, IV.v.30. Petruchio addresses Vincentio as 'gentle mistress' and asks Kate, 'Hast thou beheld a fresher gentlewoman? Such war of white and red within her cheeks' – and the tamed Kate says, happy is the man whom the stars 'Allot thee for his lovely bed-fellow!' They never beheld a fresher (FRESH as 'your fresh whore' – *MM*, III.ii.61) gentlewoman than this bed-fellow, in whom is a WAR/whore of white and red.

See ROSE, *Per*.

White-Friars Locality that was the resort of libertines and rascals (*CD*), of rogues and debauchery (F&H, s.v. Alsatia). In Jonson, *Volpone*, IV.ii, a jealous wife meets her husband with another man, whom she takes to be a disguised girl or male homosexual whore: 'The gentleman . . . is . . . of our nation' – 'Ay, your White-friar's nation . . . a lewd harlot, a base fricatrice,/A female devil, in a male outside.' She had earlier vilified the same man as 'Your Sporus' (the castrated youth Nero married) and 'your hermaphrodite'. Marston, *The Scourge of Villanie*, Satyre iv: 'one more White-frier's queane. One drab more'.

R3, I.ii.227. After wooing Anne, Gloucester turns to the gentleman whom he had attacked as a pederast (BEGGAR): 'take up the corse'. When the man asks, 'Towards Chertsey, noble lord?', Gloucester answers, 'No, to White-Friars; there attend my coming.' Anne had already told the man, 'towards Chertsey with your holy load' (29) and Gloucester had also said, 'after I have solemnly interr'd/ At Chertsey monastery this noble king' (215). Gloucester's answer (which some call a slip of the pen or compositor's error) has to be accounted for. I suggest Sh was punning on a notorious locality of his day, Whitefriars, and that this is Richard's reproof for the stupid needlessness of a question to which the answer had already been twice given. He therefore tells the gentleman, no, take it to your usual haunt, White-Friar's, and there await my coming (coitally – F&H n.d.; C; P). Historically, Henry's corpse rested at *Black*friars, which abutted on the river, and from there it was conveyed to Chertsey (New Variorum edn, ed. Furness).

Willow Symbol of grief for unrequited love, lost chastity, or lechery. Sale: the willow; *sale*: sluttish, foul (Cot); *sale*: salt (F). *Salce*: a willow; salace, lecherous as a bitch (F).

Oth, IV.iii.49: 'Sing willow, willow, willow;/ Her salt tears fell from her'. Sh has only one Barbara/ BARBER (strumpet), this deserted girl whose fall from chastity is indicated in the puns on *willow* (slut) and *salt* (used of bitches in heat and salacious persons – *OED*). Desdemona's song reflects her having been linked to the word 'whore' eight times in the previous scene and echoes her own having been 'covered with a Barbary horse' (I.i.112), Othello, the Moor (person 'of mixed Berber and Arab race' – *OED*). Fiedler, p. 168, notes that 'Barbara' ('Barbarie', First Folio sp.) evokes a Barbary–Berber–barbarian cluster. Barbara's lover 'proved mad' like Desdemona's. Desdemona has 'much to do,/ But to go *hang my head all at one side*,/ And sing it [coit – C; P] like poor Barbara'. That strange phrase (italics added), suggesting to go awry or go wrong (which she and Emilia then turn their talk to) meant (17th c.) a sexually provocative gesture for either sex. Charles Sackville, 'A Song': Bess 'knows to soften her charms . . . how to lisp and to trip in her Pace;/ And with Head on one side, and a Languishing Eye' (*Penguin Book of Restoration Verse*, p. 138). Etherege, *The Man of Mode*, III.i: 'Now for a look and gestures that may persuade 'em I am saying all the passionate things imaginable –'; 'Your head a little more on one side, ease yourself on your left leg'.

Ham, IV.vii.167: 'There is a willow . . . shows his his hoar leaves'. The willow's hoar/ whore (K) leaves is only one of the puns in the Queen's speech, indicating her doubts about Ophelia's chastity and her own feeling of responsibility, her 'sick soul' and 'guilt': 'I will not speak with her' (V.1). She says Ophelia sang 'snatches [SNATCH, act of intercourse] of old [OLD, hoar/ whore] tunes [or "lauds" – 2nd Quarto]' till she was pulled from 'her melodious lay [the sex-act – TWR; P]/ To muddy death' (see SPREAD).

See STEAL, *Ado*.

Wind (1) A flatus. Jonson, *Sejanus*, I.i: a man asks the doctor which women have 'an indifferent stool [excrement] or break wind well'. Wind-mill: buttocks, as in 'She has no fortune but her mills; i.e. she has nothing but her **** and a*se' (in G).

(2) Coit. *Monter*: mount, as the male on the female; also as *monter une monstre*, wind a watch (Cot). 'Wind' is turn about, as in Marlowe, *Doctor Faustus*, I.viii: 'hast any mind to Nan Spit, our kitchen-maid, then turn her and wind her to thy own use as often as thou wilt'.

MND, II.i.129: 'to see the sails conceive/ And grow big-bellied with the wanton wind'.

IV.i.45: 'Sleep . . . I will wind thee in my arms . . . . the female ivy so/ Enrings the barky fingers of the elm', says Titania to *Bottom*. A common image: to en*ring* (vulva – F&H; P) the FINGER (penis). To wind around something (as a thread on a skein) is to *bottom*; cf. *1H4*, III.i.104: 'It shall not wind with such a deep intent,/ To rob me of so rich a bottom here'.

MV, I.i.154. Antonio reproves Bassanio, 'You know me well, and herein spend but time/ To wind about my love with circumstance'. Titania (above) used something round to wind around a Bottom; so does Bassanio use *circum-stance* to wind or bottom ABOUT (a sexual turn) Antonio's love. Antonio's ventures 'are not in one bottom trusted' (42) but depend on the 'wind' (18, 22).

1H4, V.i.52. Worcester: Henry is a usurper who was 'fed [amorously – C; P] by us' and 'used us' (coitally) as the 'gull [GULL, a buggerer], the cuckoo's bird,/ Useth the sparrow' (the cuckoo lays eggs in another's nest, the young ultimately destroying their foster-parents; *KL*, I.iv.235: 'The hedge-sparrow fed the cuckoo so long,/ That it had it head bit off by it young'). Henry 'did oppress our nest', 'enforced' them in 'violation of all faith'. He OPPRESSED (lit. forced), raped, violated them.

'What with the injuries of a wanton time . . . And the contrarious winds that held the king/ So long in his unlucky wars . . . You took occasion to be quickly woo'd'. Henry took advantage of the *wanton* times, of Richard's being *held* so *long in* his unlucky Irish WARS/ whores – in the CONTRARY winds, the cunts and their coital winds. He took the OCCASION (genitals) to be QUICKLY/ *a quick lay* wooed himself.

See THUNDER, *KL*; HISS, *RJ*; MUDDY, *AW*; VARY, *AC*; FLUTE, *AC*; PROVIDE, *TGV*; ANGEL, *1H4*.

Wine Semen. Wine: *vin*; *elles ont eu leur vin* means 'Those wenches have had it to a haire; viz. a full tast of the sap which they hold most savorie; (for the bestowing of wine being a principall courtesie in entertainments betweene man and man, it is fittest to expresse the other liquor [i.e. semen] which in courtesie a man giveth a woman' (Cot). Wilmot, in 'To a Lady in a Letter', parallels 'lusty' wine and semen: the lady's interest in men is 'that their Cods be full'; and, whereas '[I]/ Whole nights am taking in/ The lusty Juice of Grapes, take you/ The juice of lusty Men'.

Oth, II.i.256. When Iago says Desdemona, having tired of Othello, 'nature' (NATURE, the generative organs) has compelled her to a 'second choice' (a '*most pregnant* . . . position') and she has 'found him [Cassio] already', Roderigo demurs, 'she's full of *most blessed* condition' (italics added). Iago mocks, 'Blessed fig's-end! the wine she drinks is made of grapes; if she had been blessed, she would never have loved the Moor. Blessed pudding!'

Nothing in drinking the wine of grapes would prove chastity or its lack, but the three uses of 'blessed' ('bless' orig. meant to consecrate with blood) indicate Iago is contrasting the blessed wine that represents the blood of Christ in the Eucharist with the other wine that represents human BLOOD (semen). Desdemona, he says, has no blessed fig's *end* (*fica*: fig and vulva – F); nor a blessed PUDDING (fornication). Her *most pregnant* position is not a *most blessed* condition: she is not virgin, not chaste (Luke 1:42: 'Blessed art thou among women, and blessed is the fruit of thy womb'). The wine she drinks is from the Gk *oschos*, vine-branch, and from the *oscheon* (oscheo-), scrotum.

AYL, III.ii.211. Rosalind coaxes Celia to name whom she met: 'pour this concealed man out of thy mouth, as wine comes out of a narrow-mouthed bottle . . . take the cork out of thy mouth that I may drink thy tidings.' Celia: 'So you may put a man in your belly.' The conceit that drinking wine (semen) from a narrow-mouthed bottle will put a man into one's belly is clear. Rosalind will drink the *tid*ings (pun on L *vincire*, tie, and Fr *vins*, wines?).

Wings Genitals. *Penne*: privities of man; wings, feathers; pens, any written composition or poem (F). Pen: penis (C; P); L *pennis* (dat. and abl. pl.): wing. Cf. Nashe, *The Unfortunate Traveller*, p. 259: 'On either of his wings' the ostrich has a 'prick wherewith' to spur himself; hence the lover's devise is 'Aculeo alatus', winged with a spur. Son 78 has a sequence of 'verse', 'pen', 'feathers', 'wing': Sh's ignorance was advanced 'high' by the Muse of whom his verse is 'born' (and borne aloft). Inner lips of the vulva: the 'two . . . great wings within the lips of a womans Privities' (Cot, s.v. *landies*). See DEWLAP.

TGV, II.vii.11. Eager to see Proteus, Julia asks Lucetta to give '*Coun*sel . . . *ass*ist me/ And even in *kind* love I do *con*jure' (italics added). Give coun and con (cunt – P; K); KIND (sex – *OED*). What Lucetta gives is a 'round hose' and a 'codpiece' for her disguise. With 'Love's wings to fly', Julia says she will not weary. CONJURE: sexual congress.

MV, III.i.30: 'I, for my part, knew the tailor that made the wings she flew withal', says Salarino (Salerio), who made cynical use of 'Venus' pigeons' (II.vi.4). Perh. Salarino, for his PART (penis, arse), knew (carnally – *OED*; P) the *tailor* (C; P) Lorenzo, who made (knew sexually – C; P) Jessica's wings. Tailors (see FEEBLE, *2H4*) were traditionally (1) lecherous, as in Dekker and Webster, *Northward Ho*, II.1: 'Tailors will be saucy and lickerish'; and (2) inadequate men, as in Carlyle, *Sartor Resartus*, Bk III, ch. 11: 'Tailors are . . . not Men, but fractional Parts of a Man . . . Did not Queen Elizabeth, receiving a deputation of Eighteen Tailors, address them with a "Good morning, gentlemen both"? Did not the same virago boast . . . a Cavalry Regiment, whereof neither horse nor man could be injured; her Regiment . . . of Tailors on Mares?' (F&H, s.v. Tailor).

Since sails are wings, this is a sorry forecast for Jessica, likened to a 'scarfed bark' (II.vi.15) who 'puts' (fornicates – *OED*; F&H; P) forth, who sails forth (*saillir*: issue forth, leap as the male on the female – Cot) as she does with this partial man, Lorenzo, and returns with 'ragged sails' (see LEAN).

H5, IV.i.112: 'in his nakedness he appears but a man; and though his affections are higher mounted than ours, yet when they stoop, they stoop with the like wing'. Henry admits his humanity; his fears: when naked a king is a man like them, his affection higher mounted (coitally – *OED*; P) – with *high-borne* mates? – but using the same wing when his AFFECTIONS (sexual desires) STOOP (to coit). Mod. vulgarity says that seen on the toilet, on that throne, all men are alike.

R3, V.iii.106. Derby bids Richmond farewell: 'God gives us leisure for these rites of love! . . . be valiant and speed well!' Reacting to 'rites of love' and 'speed' (sexual potency – P; to arrive sexually – C), Richmond says he will nap now, 'Lest leaden slumber peise me down tomorrow,/ When I should mount with wings of victory'. SLUMBER, the eunuch, should not peise him *down* (the down of a quilt and of the first, *soft* feathers of a bird) when he should *mount* with *wings*, be valiant, virile, *speed* well.

See PURPOSE, *TGV*; PEGASUS.

Wit/whit/white Puns on each other and on genitals. Jonson, *The Alchemist*, II.iii: Mammon spies Dol Common (each part of her name means a mistress – F&H; P), a 'brave piece': 'Is she no way accessible? no means/ No trick to give a man a taste of her – wit – / Or so?' In archery, 15th c., the *white* or target was placed on a *butt* and was called the *prick* (*LLL*, IV.i.134: 'let the mark have a prick in it'). 'Prick', like a whit, is 'a minute particle' (*OED*). White/wight; wit/withe/with (K).

TSh, V.ii.186. Petruchio tells Lucentio, who married Bianca (white – F), 'I won the wager, though you hit the white'.

I.ii.175. Hortensio found 'A fine musician . . . So shall I no whit be behind in duty/ To fair Bianca'. Musical puns: with his FINE (mus., the end; buttocks) musician he will no whit be BEHIND a rival; in truth, he will *not* be a prick (musical note; penis) behind in duty (that which is owed: DEBT, marital duty) to fair (white) Bianca, will not be the prick on her white butt, for she rejects him: see NOTE, SPIT.

RJ, I.i.215. With ref. to hitting the 'mark' (vulva – C; P), Romeo says Rosaline will 'not be hit/ With Cupid's arrow; she hath Dian's wit' – the wit or chaste white mark of the goddess of moon and chastity cannot be hit with/ wit (K) the arrow ('the dribbling dart of love' – *MM*, I.iii.2).

II.iv.87. Romeo and Mercutio jest on another wit 'well served in to a sweet goose'; a 'wit of cheveril, that stretches from an inch narrow to an ell broad!' INCH (penis), CHEVERIL (penis): wit served in to a goose (whore – C; P).

TrC, II.i.85. Ajax has 'not so much wit – ' 'As will stop the eye of Helen's needle, for whom he comes to fight.' *Cul d'un esguille*: eye of a needle; *cul*: 'tayle' (Cot).

TA, IV.ii.53. The Nurse enters, hiding Tamora's illegitimate child, black like its father: 'O, tell me, did you see Aaron the Moor?' Aaron: 'Well, more or less, or ne'er a whit at all . . . what with Aaron now?' Puns on *more*/ Moor or *Less* (a whit, the smallest particle); what *with*/ wit (K) him; and the Moor's being black and *ne'er a whit*/ never white at all: this father of a black child was not white at ALL/ AWL, penis (his wit).

See OUT, *AYL*; GIFT, *Ham*; PRETTY, *Ado*; NEIGHBOUR, *AYL*; BLUNT, *CE*.

Witch(es), hag(s), sorcerer(s) Used interchangeably, as in *1H6*, III.ii.38: 'Pucelle [slut], that witch, that damned sorceress'; *MWW*, IV.ii.194: 'you witch, you hag, you baggage [whore –

OED; P]'. They are whores, bawds; hermaphrodites, ambisexuals, masculine women; castraters. Witches were probably possessed by Satan 'in anus and vagina at once' (Fiedler, p. 66). Richard Baxter: 'Ribalds, Buggerers, Sorcerers' (*OED* 1651). Procuring: a witch's sideline as in 'lewd dealings of witches and witchmongers' (C 1584). Wilmot, 'Satyr': 'Hard as the Arse of Mosely [a procuress] under which/The Coachman sweats, as ridden by a Witch' (*Penguin Book of Restoration Verse*, p. 250). See TROT, Dekker, Ford and Rowley.

Several puns are based on fabled beliefs that (1) Lapland was the home of witches (see EPHESUS, *CE*, for 'Lapland sorcerers' and lewdness); (2) witches scratched people, partic. as they lay asleep (Rowse, p. 86). 'Scratch' (F&H) and 'scrat' both mean a hermaphrodite and DEVIL. Cf. Heywood, *Lancashire Witches*, v: 'Then to work, to work my pretty Laplands;/ Pinch, here, scratch.'

RJ, I.iv.92. Queen Mab is 'the hag, when maids lie on their backs,/That presses them and learns them first to bear,/Making them women of good carriage'. *Deffleurer*: scratch; *defleurer*: deflower (Cot). Mab, hermaphroditic witch, scratches and deflowers; presses (in the sex-act – C; P) the maidens; is the first (the deflowerer) to learn them to bear (the weight of a man – C; P) a child. She makes them women of good carriage (during the sex-act and during pregnancy – C; P).

WT, II.iii.67. Leontes calls Paulina 'A mankind witch! Hence with her, out o' door:/A most intelligencing bawd!' A mankind and a *man-kind* witch; a MOST (buttocks) knowing (i.e. carnally) bawd. HENCE: whore; OUT o'door: Fr *hors* (whore).

Mac, I.iii.45: 'each at once her choppy finger laying/Upon her skinny lips: you should be women,/And yet your beards forbid me to interpret . . . so'. Witches, women with beards, hermaphrodites, laying FINGERS (penises) on their LIPS (vulvas): choppy/*choper* (to be faulty – Cot) or imperfectly developed penises of the hermaphrodite – faulty like 'chopping French' (*R2*, v.iii.124) and 'chop-logic' (*RJ*, III.v.150).

MWW, IV.ii.202. Evans: 'By yea and no, I think the 'oman is a witch indeed: I like not when a 'oman has a great peard; I spy a great peard under his muffler'. By *yea* and *no* is the hermaphroditic combination of opposites: Falstaff disguised as an OLD WOMAN (L *anus*), as 'Mother Prat [PRAT, buttocks]'. Ford says, 'I'll prat her . . . you witch, you hag, you baggage'. And the *peard* (said *twice*) that Evans spies is (1) Falstaff's *beard*; (2) his *paired* testicles, the 'dried pear [PEAR/pair, q.v.]' he himself mentions (v.103).

CE, I.ii.100: 'Soul-killing witches that deform the body' is usu. said to refer to an imperfection of the body characterising witches, a defect I suggest is their castration or hermaphroditism. Note what and how they deform: in III.ii.151, a 'diviner' would have 'transform'd [Dromio] to a curtal dog', curtailed or castrated him, so he 'ran from her as a witch'; in IV.iii, he compares the Courtezan (a 'sorceress' or 'witch') to devils who ask for, among other items, 'a pin,/A nut, a cherry stone' (genitals: PIN; NUT; CHERRY; stone or testicle – *OED*). In *Mac*, I.iii.ix, the witch who is 'like a rat without a tail' holds 'a pilot's thumb,/Wreck'd as homeward he did come'; and she goes off to wreak similar mischief on Macbeth and on his wife who asks spirits to 'unsex' her (v.42). See HAG, *KL* and SLEEP, *1H6* for a castrating 'hag' and 'witch'.

R3, III.iv.72. Gloucester: 'I am bewitch'd; behold mine arm/Is, like a blasted sapling, wither'd up:/And this is Edward's wife, that monstrous witch,/Consorted with that harlot strumpet Shore,/That by their witchcraft thus have marked me'.

He says ARM but his language evokes a penis: (1) the sfx. -blast: germ, seed; (2) his blasted sapling (SAP, semen). His short arm is the work of a MONSTROUS (bisexual) witch who CONSORTED (paired sexually) with another woman, the harlot strumpet SHORE, whore. By WITCHCRAFT they thus marked (Sh interchanges mark and prick), pricked him. His wither'd prick is the eventuation of the curse of Margaret (WORM), whom he had called 'wither'd [WITHER/wether, a castrate] hag' (I.iii.215). For another short arm, see ENGINEER, *TrC*.

See TRANSFORMATION, *AC*; ANGEL, *1H4*; WITCHCRAFT.

Witchcraft The craft (L *ars*, *artificium*) of the WITCH (hermaphrodite, homosexual, castrater). In the witchcraft era of the Middle Ages, 'women became the most frequent victims of heretical and magical rituals involving all manner of perverse sexual orgies' (West, p. 127).

1. Use of a dildo. Richard Burton, vol. x, p. 239: the dildo is an imitation of what 'the Latins called phallus and fascinum.' L *fascinum*: a spell, witchcraft; membrum virile.

Oth, I.iii.64. Brabantio said Desdemona was 'abused . . . corrupted/ By spells and medicines bought of mountebanks;/ For nature so preposterously to err . . . Sans witchcraft could not.' Earlier (i.172) he had asked if Roderigo had not read 'Of some such thing' as 'charms/ By which . . . maidhood/ May be abused [ABUSE: fuck, sodomised]'. He called Othello (ii.78) an 'abuser' and 'practiser/ Of arts inhibited'. Now he again uses 'abused', else NATURE (sex and excretory organs) would not err so PREPOSTEROUSly (of the posteriors; of buggery). He says this thing (penis – C; P), this SUCH (L *sic* / sick; It *tale* / tale) thing is a spell or witchcraft, a *fascinum*, that can be bought of mountebanks – like the DILDOS (q.v.) sold by the mountebank Autolycus in *WT*. Othello defends himself: 'I will a round unvarnish'd tale deliver/ Of . . . what drugs . . . charms . . . mighty magic' he used. His tale (penis – K; P) is not varnished (a display of reality lacking substance; a pretence), not a dildo made of glass, horn, leather, wax. But note it is ROUND (sodomitically inclined).

2. Impotence, castration. 'Ligature', lit. a binding or tying off, also meant an impotence induced by magic (*CD*), by witchcraft (*OED*). 3. Sodomy. Witchcraft: L *ars magica* / arse-magic(?).

CE, I.ii.101. Antipholus S. is repelled by EPHESUS, city of lust with 'Soul-killing witches that deform the body,/ Disguised cheaters, prating mountebanks,/ And many such-like liberties of sin'. It is a city of SUCH-LIKE (L and It *tale*), LIKE (Gk *homios*, *homo-*) liberty (sexual licence – C; P), of SUCH (*sic* / sick) liberty. SOUL-(buttocks) killing witches deform (castrate) the body. And prating (PRAT, buttocks) *mount*ebanks mount (coitally – *OED*; P) the BANKS (seats, buttocks). This pun on 'bank' (Fr *banc*, seat) is even more pronounced in *Oth* above, for there it is accompanied by another Fr word, *sans*. Hence, Antipholus goes to the CENTAUR (creature of sexual bestiality) inn to collect servant, money, and to leave.

See NORMAN, *Ham*; TIGER, *TN*; WITCHES, *R3*; GIFTS, *Ham*.

Withered Sexless. Whored, screwed or buggered, rendered impotent. Possibly *wether*ed, made a wether or castrate. Wilmot, 'The Imperfect Enjoyment': his 'dart of love' now 'languid lies . . . sapless, like a withered flower' (*Signet Classic Poets of the 17th c.*, p. 382). *Chizza*: old, withered; a strumpet, a trull (F).

AW, I.i.175: 'your old virginity, is like one of our French wither'd pears; it looks ill, it eats drily; marry, 'tis a wither'd pear'. See PEAR.

See CROWN, *AC*; CROOKED, *R2*; WITCH, *R3*; TENDER, *R3*; PEPPER, *1H4*; MISTAKE, *TSh*; ROSE, *R2*.

Witness Testicle. L *testis*: witness; testicle. Plautus, *Curculio*, 15–40: 'look out you don't lose your power to bear witness as a man' (*intestabilis*, one who lost power to bear witness in court; one who lost his manhood by the castration inflicted by an injured husband); 622–5: 'Can I call on you to testify?' – 'You can not' – 'Curse you. . . . May you live without testes yourself, then!' (Riley notes that by L *intestatus* or 'without witnesses' Plautus intends an indelicate allusion'.)

See HANG, *AYL*; TENDER, *R3*; ENTIRE, *TSh*; PEAR, *H5*; SEAL, *TrC*; TWIN, *H8*.

Wolf 1. Whore. L *lupa* and *louve* (Cot): she-wolf; whore. *Danse de loup*: lechery (Cot), as in *Oth*, III.iii.404: 'As salt as wolves in pride [sexual heat, esp. in female]'. 2. Werewolf. The 16th c. seriously believed in lycanthropy (Webster, *The Duchess of Malfi*). 3. Ravages of disease. Lupus (L, wolf): ulcerous skin condition, often of the nose (NAPLES, *3H6*).

3H6, I.iv.111, York: 'She-wolf of France, but worse than wolves of France . . . like an Amazonian trull . . . . thy face is, visard-like . . . abominable. . . . How couldst thou drain the life-blood of the child . . . ?' Brought from France to be Henry's queen, Margaret committed adultery with Suffolk; she is a French *louve*: she-wolf and whore. She is WORSE/ whores than wolves, worse than Lupa, wolf who suckled Remus and Romulus, symbol of the famous whore

Acca Laurentia. Margaret is an Amazon; Middleton, *A Mad World, My Masters*, III.iii: ' 'Tis an Amazonian time, you shall have women shortly tread their husbands' (the *male* treads in coitus). Margaret is a masculine TRULL (whore), ABOMINABLE (sodomitical, bestial). Isabella le Bel, wife of Edward II, also had the epithet 'She-wolf of France' (B) and, according to trad. she murdered the King by tearing out or burning with a hot iron his bowels (Thomas Gray, 'The Bard'). Margaret's face is VISARD- (a mask, prostitute – *OED*) like: a 'loup' was a half-mask (*loup*, wolf); and, like a werewolf, she drained the blood of his child. 4. Older lover in a pederastic relationship. Plato, *Phaedrus*: Socrates deplores 'yielding to a passionate love, which is as the desire of the wolf for the lamb' (Wilkinson, p. 26). In today's prison sl., a 'wolf' is a sexually dominant male (Rodgers).

Cor, II.i.8: 'Pray [/prey] you, who does the wolf love?' – 'The lamb.'

VA, 1097. For Adonis (whom Venus called 'the tender boy', 'more lovely than a man' – 32, 9), 'the wolf would leave his prey . . . the silly lamb'.

Tim, IV.iii.336. A cynical discussion of love and 'medlars', those who meddle (*OED*), fornicate (P): the fox eats the lamb, the horse is seized by the leopard, and 'if thou wert the ass . . . thou livedst but as breakfast to the wolf'. Apemantus's *ass* would be *but*/butt *as*/ass breakfast for the wolf. Apemantus says Athens is a COMMONWEALTH (brothel) of BEASTS (sexual bestiality). 'How has the ass broke the wall. . . ?': (1) how did he broke (pander – *Cham*) the WALL (his buttocks); (2) how did the ass/arse-hole for the *loup* make a *loop*-hole in the wall (*1H4*, IV.i.71: 'stop all sight-holes, every loop')?

See KINDLY, *Cor*.

Word 1. Whore(d)/hoard: *R2*, I.iii.253: 'hoard thy words'. See WORM, *R3*; SQUIRREL, *MND*.

2. Pudendum. *Mot*: word (Cot); *motte*: groin, pubes (Cot); mot: a wench (F&H; G). *Puttaneggiare*: to play the whore; go whoring; not keep one's word, as whores do (F).

Ham, II.ii.614: 'like a whore, unpack my heart with words'. Cf. his HORRID/whored 'speech'.

TrC, V.ii.98. Cressida equivocates about giving Diomedes a 'token': ' 'tis done, 'tis past: and yet it is not;/I will not keep my word.' Thersites: 'she could not publish more,/Unless she said "My mind is now turn'd whore." '

Oth, IV.ii.162 'I cannot say "whore":/It doth abhor [ABHOR/whore] me now I speak the word'.

1H4, II.iv.442: 'That thou art my son, I have partly thy mother's word, partly my own opinion'. Two PARTS (genitals) are evidence: her pubes and his OPINION (penis).

Tim, I.i.92. Painter and Poet stand in the hall of their patron, Timon (along with the Jeweller and Merchant), each with his latest PIECE (a whore) of work. The Painter's flattering portrait is 'a pretty mocking of the life. Here is a touch [sexual caress – C; P]'. The Poet, too, has shaped a man the 'world doth embrace and hug' (44); but when he slips none will accompany his 'declining foot [FOOT, fucking – P]'. Painter: ' 'Tis common [whore-like – *OED*; P]:/A thousand moral paintings . . . demonstrate these quick blows of Fortune's/More pregnantly than words.' PAINTINGs (panders) show the blows (screwings – C; P) of Fortune, in Eliz. lit. a strumpet – the QUICK (pregnant, sexual) blows, more pregnantly than do the poet's words, also whores, prostituted to their patron. See pornographic use of lewd paintings in Middleton, *Women Beware Women*, II.ii: the pimp shows an innocent 'naked pictures'.

Creative artists, though they show the world's depravity, are themselves no better than merchants. Apemantus: 'O you gods, what a number of men eat Timon' (ii.40), eat (screw – C; P) him, like ladies who 'eat lords; so they come by great bellies' (i.210). Among these whores are (1) the Painter, himself 'a filthy piece of work [fornication – C; P]'; (2) the Poet with his words, of whom Apemantus says, 'Thou liest' (222), who whores, LIES (buggers) and flatters Timon. Act V opens with these two whores off 'to tender [TENDER, offer sexually] our loves to him' in return for 'gold'.

III.v.26, Senator: 'Striving to make an ugly deed look fair:/Your words have took such pains as if they labour'd/To bring manslaughter into form'. To make an ugly deed (sex-act – TWR; P) fair/L *ferre* (to bear), Alcibiades's words (groin) took PAINS (laboured). But the deceitful words/whores took SUCH (L *sic*) pains and 'misbegot'.

See WORSE, *Ado*; TRIBUTE, *2H4*; BEAT, *AW*; ACCOMMODATE, *2H4*.

Worm Syphilis. *Tarolare*: to worm-eat; to grow to a cuntbotch, i.e. VD lesion (F). Lyly, *Midas*, V.ii: 'A pox of those saucy worms that eat men before they be dead.' OE *wyrm*: snake, creeping animal. Serpigo: syphilis, from L *serpere*, to creep (P). Worms: intestinal or skin disease.

RJ, III.i.111: 'I am peppered, I warrant, for this world. A plague o' both your houses!'; 'They have made worms' meat of me: I have it'. Mercutio calls down a retaliatory plague (L *lues*, plague), lues (a spreading disease, esp. syphilis – *OED*) on the houses that destroyed him by a plague o' (of) their houses, by the canker of their hatred. ('The worm, the canker, and the grief' – Byron, 'On his Thirty-sixth Birthday'.) The chancre of syphilis, symbol for 'The canker death' (II.iii.30). Mercutio is PEPPERED (syphilitic), he WARRANTS (expletive connoting a brothel). Their HOUSES (brothel – C; P) made worms' meat of him – food for the worms of syphilis and death. See POOP, *Per*, for a similar metaphor.

R3, I.iii.222: 'If heaven have any grievous plague in store' let it be hurled on Gloucester; and 'The worm of Conscience still begnaw thy soul!' says Margaret. She was French and knew *grivoise* means obscene. May a GRIEVOUS/*une grivoise* (a whore) plague, the obscene whore's plague or syphilis, the worm of *con*science (the cunt – P), be in *store* for him (in HOARD/whored; lit. a hidden store). May it eat away his SOUL/SOLE, bottom or arse (and it does: see WITCH). This is the same plague another woman, Volumnia (*Cor*, IV.ii.11), calls down on those tribunes her son had always called deceitful whores: 'the hoarded plague o' the gods/Requite your love!'

1H6, III.i.72: 'Civil dissension is a viperous worm/That gnaws the bowels of the commonwealth.' The social disease of civil dissension destroys society from within as the worm of syphilis eats away the bowels of the COMMONWEALTH (society of whores).

See RURAL, *AC*.

Worse Whores.

Per, IV.ii.42:

Bawd. Come, others sorts offend as well as we.
Pandar. As well as we! ay, and better too; we offend worse.

To offend: to sin against and cause to sin (biblical). The Pandar defensively asserts that (1) others offend *better* – that is, are *more offensive*; (2) others offend *better people*: those the Bawd and Pandar cause to sin are worse/whores and whore-mongers.

I, Gower, 27: 'And her to incest did provoke:/Bad child; worse father! to entice his own/To evil should be done by none'. (1) As enticer to EVIL (incest; sodomy), he is worse than the BAD/*bawdy* child; (2) as she is guilty of incest (L *incestum*, not chaste), he is a worse/whore's father.

Cym, V.v.217. Posthumus repents having said that his wife was a 'whore' (II.iv.128): 'it is I/That all the abhorred things o' the earth amend/By being worse than they'. He is worse, more a whore, than all the ABHORred/whored things of the earth.

KL, IV.ii.6. Goneril and Edmund (her paramour) are pointedly not met by her husband. Instead her STEWARD (pimp) Oswald greets them: 'I told him of the army that was landed;/He smiled at it: I told him you were coming;/His answer was "The worse".' The arrival of an invading army is only smiled at; the arrival of his wife and her paramour – the whores – is 'The worse.'

Ado, III.ii.113. Don John accuses Hero of being 'Leonato's Hero, your Hero, every man's Hero'. 'Disloyal?', Claudio asks. Don John: 'The word is too good to paint out her wickedness; I could say she were worse: think you of a worse title and I will fit her to it'. The word 'disloyal', even the WORD/whored, is too good for her. Think of a worse/whore's title (the title a whore would use, presumably more vulgar), and he can fit (be sexually apt – C; P) her to that, too. PAINT covers disease with cosmetics.

See WOLF, *3H6*; SOLE, *TGV*; Introduction, p. xii.

Wound The genitals (female pudendum – P). Copulate, Pun on 'prick': the penis; also 'to puncture; hence to wound (or hurt) with or as with a pointed instrument' (*OED*). Nashe, *The Choice of Valentines*: the dildo 'soon will tent a deep intrenched wound'.

PP, ix: ' ". . . See, in my thigh," quoth she, "here was the sore."/ She showed hers: he saw more wounds than one,/ And blushing fled'.

Cym, II.ii.14: 'ere he waken'd/ The chastity he wounded' – Lucrece's rape.

VA, 1063: 'Upon his hurt she looks so steadfastly/ That her sight dazzling makes the wound seem three'. Adonis's wound of THREE (male genitals): his hurt made by the boar, fig. Venus's rival, who, thinking 'to kiss' Adonis, killed him.

TGV, v.iv.71. Valentine tells Proteus, his 'common friend, that's without faith or love' that of all the harm he did 'The private wound is deepest.' 'Common' quibbles on whore-like (C; P), mutual, 1598 (MUTUAL, homosexual). See PRIVATE (genitals, where he made his deepest wound).

RJ, II.iii.50, Romeo: 'one hath wounded me/ That's by me wounded' and the remedy is 'holy [of the pudenda – P] marriage'.

Tim, III.v.66. Alcibiades pleads for one who fought well for Athens: he 'made plenteous wounds!' Second Senator: 'He has made too much plenty with 'em;/ He's a sworn rioter . . . in that beastly fury/ He has been known to commit outrages'. He wounded, pricked, too many. He did COMMIT (fornicate) out*rages* (sexual lust and action, TWR; P) in his BEASTLY (sodomitical) fury. He was a sworn rioter (copulator – P): he made too much PLENTY (L *copia*; Fr *assez*), too much coping or fornicating, too many asses. Alcibiades counters it is not his friend but the 'usuring [usury: prostitution – C; P] senate' ('usurers' men! bawds between gold and want!' – II.ii.61) who have fucked the public (see BANISH).

See BOLT, *MND*; H.

Wrinkle Wrinkles are *rides* (Cot); rides: coital acts (C; P). 'A wrinkle-bellied whore': one who has had a number of bastards (G). *Chizza*: old, wrimpled (wrinkled); a strumpet (F).

Tim, IV.iii.148. In a riding metaphor, Timon tells two whores: 'Whore still;/ Paint till a horse may mire upon your face:/ A pox of wrinkles'; 'mar men's spurring'. 'Whore still': HORSE/*whores till* they die. PAINT (q.v.) or wear fucus to cover their disease; and mar men's SPURring (pricking).

AC, I.v.29. Cleopatra hopes Antony thinks of her 'That am with Phoebus' amorous pinches black,/ And wrinkled deep in time'. Phoebus (whose 'fiery steeds' and 'burning car' 'scorch'd the earth' – *3H6*, II.vi.12) rides across the sky in what Antony calls 'Phoebus' car' (IV.viii.29). Cleopatra, 'whore' (III.vi.67) and HORSE, ridden and wrinkled by another lover, the hot sun-god with his PINCHES (pricks; coital acts).

Wrinkled *deep* connotes ruts: deep furrows in a road or deep marks on the skin; obs. deep wrinkles (*OED*). *Per*, IV.v.9: 'no more bawdy-houses' – 'I am out of the road of rutting for ever', connoting (1) the road with its ruts; and (2) the road (strumpet – C; P) with her ruts and wrinkles, rutting with customers. *Passo*: 'that hath . . . felt any passion. Also withered or sered with the heate of the Sunne. Used also for dry and full of wrinkles' (F).

See OLD, *AW*.

Wrong (1) To rape a woman, to impregnate out of marriage (P). To screw or ruin someone.

(2) The penis: rung/ wrong/ wrung (K), puns on 'rung', any stout rounded stick.

2H4, II.i.41, Mistress Quickly: 'unless a woman should be made an ass and a beast, to bear every knave's wrong'. The wrong or rounded stick with which asses are beaten and which women must bear is also the spoke of a wheel, attached to the nave/ knave.

See STIR, *Tim*; LUBBERLY, *MWW*; SUFFER, *CE*; PLAIN, *3H6*; TONGUE, *R2*.

Y

Yare Well equippped; sexually ready. Cf. its doublet, 'gear': genitals and lechery (F&H; P2).

AC, v.ii.286. The dying Cleopatra, readying herself to meet Antony in death, calls for her gear: her 'robe' (cunt, like the 'robe' in *H5*, III.iv.53 – P, s.v. Coun; K, s.v. Gown) and 'crown' (CROWN, vagina). 'Yare, yare, good Iras; quick . . . I see him rouse himself/ To praise my noble act . . . . husband, I come.' And she who is yare then uses the language that connotes a successful sexual act: Antony *rouses* himself for her act (coital act – P) and she *comes* (a sexual emission – P). It would be a pity to miss the fitting eroticism in the end of this pair of famous lovers, by saying 'Yare, yare' means nothing more than its synonym QUICK which immediately follows.

III.vii.39. Enobarbus warns Antony not to fight by sea, where he will be impotent: 'Your ships are not well-mann'd;/ Your mariners are muleters . . . . Their ships are yare; yours, heavy.' Antony's ships are meant to be thought of as bottoms, like those in *MV*, I.i.42: 'My ventures are not in one bottom trusted'. The mariners are muleters – hence what they drive, the ships, are MULES (emasculated males; lit. sterile hybrids). The ships are sterile bottoms; they are not WELL (the penis) *man*ned. Caesar's ships are yare, have the full complement of gear or potent genitals, are ready for lechery. Antony's ships are heavy, lack vivacity, are laden; Caesar's are yare ('reponsive to the helm' – *OED*).

These SHIPS/ SHEEP are whores: they will betray him. They are the 'quails' or harlots of whom the Soothsayer predicted (DICE) Caesar's would always beat Antony's (see PLANKS where Antony was given the same advice).

And so the battle ended in Antony's retreat, in which – as Enobarbus had predicted – Antony's 'manhood . . . Did violate so itself' (x.24).

See OCCASION, *MM*.

Year Arse, anus, anal. L *annus*: a year; annual or yearly. Ears/ years (K); EARS/ arse.

Ado, IV.ii.77:

Conrade. Away! you are an ass, you are an ass.
Dogberry. Dost thou not suspect my place? dost thou not suspect my years? O that he were here to write me down an ass!

Dogberry is *an* ass (*an*, *ans*: year, years; *âne*: ass – Cot). See AN/ ANNE for a similar pun. He wants his PLACE (1698, anus; pudendum), his *years* suspected (respected).

CE, IV.iv.30: 'I am an ass, indeed; you may prove it by my long ears. I have served him from the hour of my nativity to this instant'. Both the *long ears* (L *auritulus*, the long-eared one, i.e. the ass – from the fabulist Phaedrus) and implied *long years* (of service) signify Dromio E. is an ass. See EAR, *R3*; and DOG, *MWW*.

RJ, I.iii.72. Lady Capulet wants Juliet to marry: 'younger than you . . . ladies of esteem,/ Are made already mothers: by my count,/ I was your mother much upon these years/ That you are now a maid.' She swears by her count or cunt (C; Introduction, p. xi; K, p. 75) that ladies of esteem (*cas*: esteem; the genitals – Cot), including herself, were married and were much upon their years or asses, during these years that Juliet has been a maid. They were *made* (sexually – C; P), not a *maid*.

III.v.45. Juliet uses the same phrase when Romeo leaves: 'O, by this count I shall be much in years/ Ere I again behold my Romeo!' By 'much in years' (L *magnus annus*, a long time), she does *not* mean what her mother did. Sh is punning on the Annus Magnus, the Great year or Platonic year, after which all heavenly bodies [Romeo and she are both 'stars': I.ii.25; III.ii.22] were believed to return to their original positions (*OED*). She will then again behold and hold Romeo; but, till the Platonic year, these 'star-cross'd lovers' stay chaste. Cf. Weever, *Faunus and Melliflora, A Prophesie of this present yeare, 1600*: 'All spotless pure . . . began great Platoes yeare'. 'Platonic' connoted pure, asexual, as in Prior, 'Ode', st. 5: 'The heat with which thy Lover glows/ Will settle into cold Respect:/ A talking dull Platonic I shall turn,/ Learn to be Civil, when I cease to burn.' Like theirs, Sh's conceit reflects Eliz. interest in astronomy.

Yellow (1) Dung-colour: 'the colour of ordure as usually designated by the Greeks' (Oates, p. 1231). Aristophanes, *The Ecclesiazusae*, 299–338: Blepyrus 'squats' to 'take a crap' and is asked 'what's all that yellow about you?'

(2) Yellow hair designates effeminates. Robert Burton, p. 678: 'Synesius holds every effeminate fellow or adulterer is fair hair'd'. 'Long and soft hair . . . reddish or yellow in color "indicates . . . lack of virility, and effeminacy of mind" ' (TWR, s.v. Hair). Chaucer's Pardoner, a 'gelding', has yellow hair; Horace (*Odes*, Bk IV, no.iv) specifies 'Ganymede flava', the 'blond boy Ganymede' (Jove's catamite). Sir Andrew Aguecheek (*TN*, I.iii.108) has hair like 'flax'; Slender (*MWW*, I.iv.23) has a 'little wee face, with a little yellow beard' – the wee LITTLE (arse) *Slender*; Julia–Sebastian, girl–boy (*TGV*, IV.iv.194), has 'perfect yellow' hair (PERFECT: bot., bisexual); and *Bottom*, an ass (*MND*, I.ii.98), debates whether to 'discharge' his PART (division in the buttocks) in a 'perfect yellow' beard.

TSh, III.ii.54. Biondello says Petruchio's deplorable horse is 'rayed with the yellows', 'rayed' meaning berayed with filth and fouled with dung, as in IV.i.3, where it describes Grumio (see FIE, shit).

MND, V.i.339. Thisbe's moan over Pyramus's 'yellow cowslip [cow-dung – *OED*; see SLIP] cheeks' would amuse an audience that remembers that Titania also caressed those CHEEKS (q.v.), and then, too, they were Bottom's buttocks.

TN, II.v.219. The link between yellow and excrement may be why ' 'tis a colour she [Olivia] abhors'. She is 'addicted [L *addictus*, bound] to a melancholy'. MELANCHOLY/ colon trouble is, for obvious reasons, 'green and yellow' (IV.116) or 'sable-coloured' (*LLL*, I.i.233). Therefore the melancholic or constipated, the addicted or bound, lit. constipated, Olivia (olive: yellowish, brownish green) hates the sight of yellow. And therefore Maria's device tells Malvolio to wear 'yellow stockings'. And to SMILE (q.v.), Fr *rire*, pun on (1) *rire*/ rear; (2) smile/ smell; (3) the *bind*weed or Smilax (*OED* 1601, from Gk *smilax* or bindweed), with its small greenish–yellowish flowers. Her note says, 'let it appear in thy smiling; thy smiles become thee . . . . still smile'; and Malvolio says, 'I will smile' – no chance an audience will miss that word 'so unsuitable to her disposition'.

Malvolio says (III.iv.28) he is 'Not black in my mind, though yellow in my legs' – not melan-cholic (lit. black bile) in MIND (arse), nor melan-colic, black colon or bowel. On the contrary, he will appear loose-bowelled, fouled and yellow in his legs, stockings soiled and smiling/ smelling. 'I smell a device' is how Toby described Maria's plan (II.iii.176). 'I have't in my nose too', said Sir Andrew, adding they 'would make him an ass'. 'Ass, I doubt not', said Maria, whose purpose 'is, indeed, a horse of that colour' – that yellow COLOUR/ Fr *culier*, of the arse (see DRY). Toby said Maria's plan would make Malvolio 'run mad', have the runs or diarrhoea, 'run' in the ME sense of discharge matter, carry off a liquid (see TARTAR).

It was fabled that drinking the waters of the river Gallus in Phrygia made a man run mad. This river is associated with Gallus, the priest of Cybele, who emasculated himself, after which time all her priests or Galli were eunuchs. See EXCELLENT for the scene in which these jesters dance a *galli*ard.

Malvolio is locked up for a mad (infatuated – *OED*) man, infatuated with Olivia. And the Clown, who wanted to play 'Lord Pandarus of Phrygia' (III.i.58) – see PHRYGIA for orgiastic excesses – is he who later disguises himself as Malvolio's 'priest', Sir Topas: the topaz is characteristically yellow and (her., 1562) was the tincture 'or' (yellow, gold). Cf. Chaucer's

Tale of Sir Thopas': the hero is perh. named after the 'Topaze, the stone of chastity', a chastity Chaucer 'exploited . . . to make it seem downright effeminacy' (Donaldson edn, p. 935).

They emasculate Malvolio, make him an 'ass-head and . . . a gull!' (v.i.213), a GULL (yellow – *OED*), a dupe, and also a *Gallus* or eunuch – with his yellow stockings and his yellow legs (gall is a yellow or green digestive substance that passes into the intestines). 'Yond gull Malvolio is turned heathen' – a pagan (worshipper of Cybele). See MADONNA for the importance of this pun to the theme of the play.

The yellow thread of effeminacy runs through all these puns. It is an old one. *Cinedo*: a 'fish that is yellow all over. Also as Cinedulo'; *cinedulo*: 'a bardash, a sodomite' (F). The link continues to the present. Gilbert and Sullivan's opera *Patience*, mocking the Aesthetic Movement of the 1880s (and Oscar Wilde), contains a song on 'Greenery yallery Grosvenor Gallery'. And in the 1970s Scottish Young Liberals demanded an apology from a BBC *Nationwide* interviewer who asked a football-fan who had dyed his hair green and yellow (his team's colours) if he wasn't afraid people would think him a 'poof'.

Yield Rhymes with 'killed' (K): 'God 'ild you'. Puns on *yeld* (late OE *gielde*, *gelde*), barren; and *geld*: barren, sexually impotent (*OED*)

LLL, II.i.149: 'Aquitaine so gelded' and 'yield up Aquitaine' – pay the geld due the king or accept the gelding (maiming), yielding up of part of Aquitaine.

WT, IV.iv.623 and 701. Autolycus can easily 'geld a codpiece of a purse'; 'every . . . hanging, yields a careful man work'. In a man's codpiece were kept two kinds of purses: the money-bag, the scrotum (*OED*). The crowd at a hanging (and every HANGING, of male genitals) yields a *cut-purse* some geld and some gelding. See STRIPE for the same pun, previous scene.

See TRANSFORMATION, *AC*; SNATCH, *MM*; STRIPE, *MM*; TERMS, *Mac*; NOON, *KJ*.

Z

'Zounds/swounds God's wounds. Pun on (1) 'swounds' – faints ('she swounds to see them bleed' – *Ham*, v.ii.319); (2) SOUNDS – probes the bottom; (3) 'souns' – 'musical tone of the fart' (TWR). Fart: contemptible person (F&H).

RJ, III.i.52, Mercutio: 'Consort! what, dost thou make us minstrels? an thou make minstrels of us . . . here's my fiddle-stick; here's that shall make you dance. 'Zounds, consort!' Mercutio chooses to hear a sexual insult in Tybalt's saying he and Romeo CONSORT. *'Zounds consort*, he says: (1) sounds consort, i.e. make harmony; (2) souns or farts, such men, consort, i.e. mate, make sounds, probe bottoms – not he and Romeo. See FART for links to sounds and buggery. Here, says Mercutio, pointing to or extending something, is my fiddle-stick, masculine symbol. Marston, *Antonio and Mellida II*, III.ii: 'My mistress' eye doth oil my joints . . . O love, come on, untruss your points,/ My fiddlestick wants rozen.' Cf. *Ils accorderent tresbien leurs vielles ensemble*: 'They jumbled their fidles passing well together; (but this phrase hath a further (filthie) sence.)' (Cot).

And, if he and Romeo are MINSTRELS (effeminates), then here is the fiddle-stick: (1) the penis that will make Tybalt DANCE (the 'sex rite' – TWR), will prick or bugger him; (2) the sword that will make 'zounds or God's wounds – unlike Tybalt's sword, which (I.i.119) had merely made sounds, had 'cut the winds,/ Who nothing hurt withal hiss'd him in scorn' – the WINDS (farts), not hurt or wounded, had HISS'D (q.v.), farted at, him in scorn.

See SURETY, *TA*; THIGH, *2H4*.

Supplement

In addition to the new puns, the following entries include cross-referencing of old and new puns, amplifications and corrections (indicated by a preceding asterisk).

***Absolute**, *Oth* For 'Make the Moor love me' read 'Make the Moor . . . love me' (l. 1).

***Age(d)**, *Tem* See SINEW: cord of the scrotum; penis.

Air Gas generated in the stomach or bowels; a flatus.

Cym, I.ii.3. Cloten, the 'ass' (see DEBT), is told, 'you reek as a sacrifice [sacrifice–fise: fist or flatus – K]: where air comes out, air comes in: there's none abroad so wholesome [hole–w*hole*some: anal – K] as that you vent [of organs, to evacuate – *OED*]'.

Cor, IV.vi.130. To the citizens, always described as asses (see ROAR, ENOUGH, SMILE), Menenius says, 'You are they/That made the air unwholesome'.

V.vi.52. Coriolanus returns 'Splitting the air with noise [NOISE, a flatus]' – the culmination of the anal metaphors he used when banished from Rome (see DESPAIR, CHRONICLE).

See THRONE, *AC*, *TN*; BEGGAR, *TrC*.

***Altar** L *ara*: altar (*aras* is accusative pl.; *aris* is dat., abl. pl.); also pun on external pudenda (Adams, p. 87).

***Alter**, *MWW* See OTHERWISE: unchaste or aberrant sexual behaviour.

Ambition Excessively high aims that reveal one is an ass. It was proverbial that 'The higher an ape climbs, the more his hinder parts appear', that 'the filthe of the hyndere partis of an ape aperith more, whanne he stieth [ascends] an high' (Whiting, s.v. Ape). Jonson, *Volpone*, I.ii: 'Hood an ass with reverend purple,/So you can hide his two ambitious ears,/And he shall pass for a cathedral [of a chair, seat] doctor.' (It is inconceivable that Jonson did not also intend a pun on the *too ambitious* EARS/*arse* in rever*end* purple, who can p*ass*. . . .)

AW, I.i.101. 'The ambition in [her] love' makes Helen see herself as 'The hind [HIND, arse] that would be mated by the lion'.

JC, I.ii.324. 'Caesar's ambition shall be glanced at:/And *after* this let Caesar *seat* him *sure*;/For we will shake him, or worse days *end*ure' (italics added). Caesar's SEAT (position and buttocks) is in jeopardy: they mean to glance at, to graze – glances 'wound' (*TSh*, V.ii.137) and 'bruise' (*KL*, V.iii.148) – his ambition; to SHAKE ('fuck', in sense of debase, make impotent), un-seat him. Let Caesar seat him SURE/sewer – a whore; the pudendum, arse ('sweet sinke, sweet sure' – *TrC*, V.i.83; see POLE) – for they shall end his rule or themselves WORSE/whores' days *end*ure. For bawdy use of 'Sit sure', see Henke, s.v. Smock-grace.

III.ii.97. Antony: 'Ambition should be made of sterner stuff' (see STERN, the buttocks). Earlier (80) he had said, 'The evil [EVIL: crap, excrement] that men do lives *after* them' (italics added) and if Caesar 'was ambitious' it 'was a grievous fault' (GRIEVOUS: obscene, of whores; like the 'grievious fault' of feasting with harlots – *CE*, V.i); it was a whore's FAULT (arse; crack or flatus). As he pauses, waiting for his 'heart' (HEART/arse) to 'come *back*' (italics added), a Citizen says, 'If you consider rightly [RIGHT, L *rectum*] of the matter [MATTER: fecal or prostitution], Caesar has had a great wrong [WRONG: a fucking, a rape].'

Antony concludes, 'I have o'ershot myself' (155). A shot is a fart (see DISCHARGE; *petarrade*: 'Gunshot of farting' – Cot). We see that his speech is a whore's fart: O'ER/whore-shot.

Tem, v.i.75. Prospero addresses his 'unnatural' (UNNATURAL, pederastic) brother (see INCH, TRIBUTE) who '*enter*tain'd ambition,/*Expell*'d remorse and nature; who, with Sebastian,/Whose inward pinches therefore are most strong,/Would here have kill'd your king' (italics added). The link between Antonio's ambition and anal excreta becomes more blatant in Sebastian's MOST strong INWARD (the bowels) *pinches* or intestinal pains (as in 'pinched with the colic' – *Cor*, II.i.82; 'with . . . colic pinch'd' – *1H4*, III.i.29).

Mac, I.vii.27. Macbeth faces a 'deed' (14, 24) he cannot do, that will not be 'done when 'tis done'. The deed is murder, but *deed*, *do the deed* mean copulate (P; C), and 'Bellona's bridegroom' (I.ii.54) – so potent in war – is impotent in the face of this deed: he has 'no spur/To prick the sides of my intent, but only/Vaulting ambition, which o'erleaps itself/And falls on the other'. With no SPUR (penis), unable to 'prick' (see COMPUNCTIOUS), he cannot ride or 'leap' (both also meaning copulate – P; C) effectively. His vaulting ambition is the horse – really an ass – which, uncontrolled by him, therefore overleaps, aims too high, and falls on the other (side), but also on the OTHER (arse): on its own ass or on him.

See THROAT, *Oth*.

Amiable Amorous (obs. – *W*). Quips on being an able-*ami* (lover – Cot).

Ado, v.iv.48: Claudio: 'lusty Jove . . . would play the noble beast in love.' Benedick: 'Bull Jove, sir, had an amiable low. . . .' Claudio: 'For this I owe you: . . . .' Quibbles on the noble/no-bull Jove playing (sexually – P; C) a beast-in-love, a lover-bull or *ami*-ble, who had (1) an *ami*-bull low; (2) an *ami*-bellow; (3) an amiable O ('l' in 'low' silent). The O and eye are sexual circles (P, s.vv. O and Eye), whence the puns in Claudio's reply.

See ANY, *MWW*; CHEEKS, *MND*; ARISE, *KJ*.

***Any**, *MWW* See AMIABLE: quip on being an able lover.

Arch Fornicating (L *fornix*: brothel, orig. arch, vault). Fornicate (adj.): arched, arching over.

Cym, I.vi.33. Iachimo, intending to convince Imogen her husband revels in whorehouses and then to seduce her (see TOMBOY), opens his siege by describing the earth as a 'vaulted arch'. Vault: fornicate (P; C); vaulting-house: brothel (Henke).

H8, III.ii.102. Wolsey is angry on two scores: it is 'not w*hole*some [an anal pun – K, p. 117] . . . [Anne Bullen] should lie [LIE: fornicate, bugger] i' the bosom of' the king; and 'there is sprung up/*An* heretic, *an* arch *one*, Cranmer; *one*/Hath crawl'd into the favour of the king/*An*d is his oracle' (italics added). Perh. Cranmer is a bugger in both senses of the word (bugger: 'A heretic . . . a sodomite' – *OED*; these two terms were freq. linked: cf. Henke, s.v. Catzerie). AN/ANNE/Fr *âne* (ass) lies in the king's bosom (sexual part – P; C); and one (ane – *OED*) Cranmer crawled into his favour (sexual parts – P) and is his ORACLE (pubic–anal orifice). For Cranmer's treatment as a whore, pimp, one who can be bought, see VOICE.

MM, v.i.57. Isabella, who calls *Ang*elo 'an adulterous thief,/An hypocrite, a virgin-violator;/Is it not str*ange* and str*ange*' (41; italics added), concludes that he is 'an arch-villain'. The Duke says 'it is ten times strange'; and STRANGE (of fornication and pederasty) *is* used ten times in the scene – of *Angelo*, an 'angel' (III.ii.286; ANGEL, catamite) and THIEF (adulterer, bugger), an arch or fornicating villain.

Arise With a phallic erection (Henke), like 'rise' (P), RAISE and rouse (cf. VEIN, *H5*).

KJ, III.iv.27. Each phrase contributes to the eroticism of Constance's welcoming Death as a lover: 'O amiable, lovely death! . . . Arise forth from the couch of lasting night . . . And I will kiss thy detestable bones/And put my eyeballs in thy vaulty brows/And ring these fingers with thy household worms/And stop this gap of breath with fulsome dust. . . . Come, grin on me, and I will . . . buss thee as thy wife. Misery's love,/O come to me!'

She invites the AMIABLE (able lover), *love*ly death to arise forth (both the rising and forward phallic motion) from the couch (as verb: coit – P). She will kiss (embrace coitally) his detestable bones (DETESTED, without testes). And in the forward thrust of the embrace she will *put* (insert sexually – P; F&H) *my* (EYE)*balls* ('my'–'eye' elide) or testes (for she is, after all, played by a young male) into that hollow of his vault-y (ARCHED, vaulted; fornicate) BROWS (pubic mound), the brow that vaults (fornicates – P; C). The next image is one of RINGS put on FINGERS, old metaphor for copulation (Grose; F&H; P). And the gap of breath (the source of life) will be stopped with DUST (semen). Arise, come, grin (a risus/arise) on me.

Constance is in the French king's tent, speaking to him and the Dauphin. Perh. there are bilingual puns in her 'put' and 'breath with fulsome dust' (*poussière*: 'Thicke dust'; *pousser*: 'To push . . . to breath'; *poussée*: a putting – Cot); and maybe there is even a pun on those Fr equivalents and 'pussie' (used of a woman, 1583, and of her pudendum, 1664 – F&H). In her frenzy, her language is degenerating, for 'kiss' has become the more vulgar 'buss', as she concludes with her urgent, 'Come. . . . O, come to me!'

In her next speech, Constance again tries to stimulate death to arise, to take her: 'O, that my tongue were in the thunder's mouth!/Then with a passion I would shake the world;/And rouse from sleep that fell anatomy. . . .' Again her passion is sexually aggressive: her TONGUE (penis, clitoris) in thunder's MOUTH (genital orifice) would SHAKE the world sexually and *rouse* Death.

See Introduction, p. xiv, *MND*, *Cym*; HOPE, Son 29.

As Ass. Obs. form of 'ace', 'ass', 'ash'. Lyly, *Mother Bombie*, IV.ii: 'as for Riscio – !' – 'As for Dromio – !' – 'Asse for you all foure!'

Ham, v.ii.43. Hamlet mocks the style of 'statists' (see STATE, ass): 'As . . . As . . . As . . . And many such-like "As"es of great charge'.

See WEIGHT, *TSh*; TITLE, *TrC*; BEND, *TrC*.

Bed That upon or within which one rests: woman herself; her womb, vulva; or a male analogue.

R3, IV.i.54. Duchess: 'O my accursed womb, the bed of death!'

TGV, I.ii.114. Julia has so personified the torn love-letter that she jealously berates Lucetta for 'fingering' (FINGER, caress) the pieces (see COIL). She reads, '"love-wounded Proteus"./Poor wounded name! my bosom [sexual parts – P] as a bed/Shall lodge thee till thy wound be throughly heal'd': (1) her bosom will be the bed in which his torn name lodges till it heals, the pieces join; (2) it will be the bed in which she fantasies *he* LODGES (coitally) until *his* WOUND (said *three* times; see WOUND, *VA*), penis and testes, heals.

MV, v.i.228. When Bassanio says he gave the doctor (really Portia) his RING (sexual part), Portia retaliates, 'I'll not deny him any thing [vulva, penis – P; C] I have,/No, not my body nor my husband's bed:/Know him I shall . . . .' *Bed* would be anticlimactic after *body*, but for the equivalence of RING–thing–body–bed as sexual parts. She'll not deny herself ANY (ass) thing. No, him and her husband's bed she shall *know* carnally.

AW, v.iii.126. Bertram says a ring 'Wrapp'd' (L *vulva*: wrapper, uterus) in paper was thrown at him, and, if it can be proved 'This ring was ever' Helena's, then he 'husbanded her bed'. The King's reply, 'I am wrapp'd in dismal thinkings', confirms WRAP(T) as another link in this second play's concluding ring–bed chain of sexual equivoques.

See HOMAGE, *CE*; INCH, *Tem* ('*obed*ient . . . *bed*').

Bend, bent (1) Fornicate(d): lit. arched or bending over. Ger *gebogen*: bent, fornicate. Cf. the double pun in Marmion, *Hollands Leaguer* (early 1600s): a brothel lady tells the constable *'we have always been bent to Your Worship's will'* (Burford, *Queen of the Bawds*, p. 82).

(2) Copulate homosexually. Symbolic of the 'womanish', 'buggered' Persians is the figure on a Greek vase who says, 'I stand bent over', and 'suits his posture to his words' (Dover, p. 105). Bent: homosexual (Rodgers, p. 31). Martin Sherman's *Bent* (1979) is a play concerning homosexuals in Nazi Germany.

MM, III.i.144: 'Die, perish! Might but my bending down/Reprieve thee from thy fate, it should proceed.' So horrified is Isabella that her brother would sacrifice her chastity to save his life, that now she would not bend down even in prayer – let alone in fornication with Angelo – to gain him a reprieve.

2H6, II.i.167. Buckingham: 'A sort of naughty persons, lewdly bent,/*Under* the *coun*tenance and *con*federacy/Of Lady Eleanor . . . Dealing with witches and with *con*jurers'. Italics added for puns on Eleanor's CON/cunt. For this 'dealing' (doing sexual business with – C), see FACT.

TN, II.iv.38. Man should love a woman younger than himself, says the Duke, or his 'affection cannot hold [HOLD, coitally] the bent'.

RJ, II.ii.143: 'If that thy bent of love be honourable,/Thy purpose marriage . . . all my fortunes at thy foot I'll lay . . . .' Sexuality pours out of Juliet's phrases: *honourable* (chaste – C; honour/on her – P), PURPOSE (sexual intent), FOOT and *lay*.

2H4, II.iv.55. Falstaff: 'to serve bravely is . . . to come off the breach with his pike bent bravely' – in which the subject is amour, not warfare. The BREACH: the buttocks; the pike: the penis (P).

H5, III.i.16. Henry's speech is meant to incite the manhood of his soldiers: 'Once more unto the *breach* . . . . *Stiffen* the *sinews* . . . . *Hold hard* the breath and *bend up* every spirit/To his *full height*' (italics added). STIFFEN, SINEWS, HOLD and SPIRIT connote the erect, turgid penis.

AC, IV.xiv.73. Antony is ashamed of not following Cleopatra into death. He feels unmanly ('[I] lack/The courage of a woman'); hence his fears of the future are expressed in a metaphor of emasculation and a concentration of words connoting an arse (see ABSOLUTE for details). The 'exigent' (the *end* – *OED*) has come when he must 'see behind me/The inevitable prosecution of/Disgrace and horror'; and he asks that Eros *strike* him (as in sexual intercourse – P; C) with his sword and spare him from suffering DISGRACE (an illicit sexual act: dis-, loss of; GRACE, penis) BEHIND. Then Eros, too, will not have to 'see' Antony's lost manhood, his 'master . . . bending down/His corrigible neck, his face subdued/To penetrative shame, whilst the wheel'd seat/Of fortunate Caesar, drawn before him, branded/His baseness that ensued'. A second time (83) he asks Eros (Love) to penetrate him with his sword (penis – P): 'Draw [expose the sexual weapon – P], and come.' That act of love is preferable to the BUGGERY (q.v. for socio-political implications) of submission to Caesar. Antony pictures himself as *sub*dued to explicitly *penetrative* SHAME (castration), his NECK/nick, his FACE/fesse (buttock) *bending down*, the *seat* of Caesar drawn before him as a brand (stamp of infamy or ownership, and also a sword) of his ensuing baseness. Adulteresses were branded; but for males, such as Antony, common retribution was penetration 'behind' (see BROAD: raphanidosis – Richlin, p. 256). In Horace, Catullus, Martial, 'pedicatio, was regarded as a means of asserting one's rank or punishing a malefactor'; it and fellatio were 'threatened against or inflicted on adulterers' (Adams, p. 128). By l. 100 Antony sees himself as 'A bridegroom' who will 'run into 't [death and his own sword]/As to a lover's bed'; but he bungles it (ABSOLUTE).

TrC, I.iii.236. Sh's contempt for the Trojan War emerges early. Aeneas's praise is so fulsome that Agamemnon thinks he is being scornful or else the Trojans are 'ceremonious courtiers'. Aeneas answers, 'Courtiers as free, as debonair, unarm'd/As bending angels; that's their fame in peace . . . .' Unwittingly he tarnishes the Trojans as effeminates (BOLT, *TrC*), as COURTIERS (whores), as . . . as . . . AS/ass bending (L *angelus*, bend) ANGELS (Eliz. sl. for catamites; cf. Giroux, pp. 98–9). That's their fame in PEACE/PIECE (the genitals).

Son 143. As the 'housewife' (HOUSEWIFE, hussy) sets down her 'babe' and runs 'to catch' one of her 'feather'd creatures' (FEATHER, penis; to feather: of a cock, to tread coitally), a cock, 'the thing [penis – P; C] she would have stay, and as the 'neglected child . . . Cries to catch her whose busy care is bent/To follow that which flies before her face', so he, the poet, another 'babe', chases 'thee afar behind' (fair–far – K), *a fair* BEHIND. He chases his beloved, whose busy (BUSINESS, fornication) care (*care*: face – Cot; perh. whose busy FACE, buttocks) is *bent* on fornication; and he asks, 'if thou catch [CATCH sexually] thy hope [HOPE, penis], turn back to me . . . . So will I pray that thou mayst have thy will,/If thou turn back and my loud crying still.' He prays the beloved *will* catch the pursued CREATURE (a loose person), then have her Will (himself, a penis, sexual desire – P; C) and *turn back*, which (said twice) connotes return, and turn that fair behind back to him.

See BEGGAR, *Cor*; CAMEL, *Ham*; SCREW, *Mac*; SINEW, *H5*.

***Bite** For 'of Cockneys' read 'or Cockneys' (p. 25, l. 7); for 'buggery' read 'bugger' (l. 12).

***Blood**, *H5* For 'Voke-fellows' read 'Yoke-fellows' (l. 1).

***Board**, *TSh* May also pun on a 'crack' in BUT(T): in autumn/L *autem* (but). Cf. AS/ass.

***Bowels**, *1H4* See BURDEN (testicles = a 'weight').

***Boy** L *puer*: boy; in L lit. specif. a catamite (Richlin, pp. 34–44, 221–2).

Breach/breech As a break or gap, 'breach' puns on the fissures in the *breech* (buttocks) and can be read not only as female pudendum (C; P) but also as arse, anus. As Ross explains, 'Thou woldest make me kisse thyn olde breech!' (Chaucer, 'Pardoner's Tale') means his 'arse' and not his breeches; and 'I-blessed be thy breche, and every stoon!' ('Nun Priest's Tale') means the arse and its stones or testicles (TWR, s.v. Breech).

3H6, v.v.24. Queen Margaret to her son: 'Ah, that thy father had been so resolved!' Gloucester: 'That you might still have worn the petticoat,/And ne'er have stol'n the breech from Lancaster.' Had Henry had the RESOLUTION (testicles, 'balls') not to have disinherited his son, Margaret need not have been a warrior, not have usurped that breech meant in the 'Nun Priest's Tale' (above).

See FLEW, *TrC*, *1H6*; FAULT, *KJ*; BEND, *2H4*, *H5*.

Brow Mound over the pubes, as over the EYE (genitals). Lit. projection over a steep place.

RJ, I.iii.38, 52. The ever-bawdy Nurse says Juliet 'broke her brow:/And then my husband . . . A' was a merry [MERRY, wanton] man' said soon Juliet would fall, not forward, but backward, the broken (break: devirginate – P) brow leading him directly to the breaking of her virginity. The Nurse continues, 'it [Juliet] had upon its brow/A *bump* as big as a young *cock*erel's *stone*;/A parlous *knock*' – and again a jest about falling 'backward', when there would be another bump or KNOCK (coital act; genital) on another brow (italics added).

AC, I.iii.36. 'Eternity was in our lips and eyes,/Bliss in our brows' bent; none our parts so poor . . . .' Cleopatra extends her imaging from the sexually suggestive LIPS and EYES to all their PARTS (sexual). Hoping by evoking the intensity of their love to prevent his leaving, she surely intends the bliss (extreme sexual pleasure – P) in the brows' BENT (arching, fornicate) to suggest more than eyebrows to Antony.

Son 112.

Your love and pity doth the impression fill
Which vulgar scandal stamp'd upon my brow;
For what care I who calls me well or ill,
So you o'er-green my bad, my good allow?

An impression stamped on (press in, stamp on: verbs of sexual intercourse – P; C) by vulgar scandal, an 'impression' (made by the weight of a male during intercourse – Henke) that *love* and *pity* can 'fill' suggests a shamed pubic brow as well as a branded, forked forehead. This sense of pits or furrows other than those in the forehead, of the brow as projecting over a deeper gulf than an eyebrow protects, is strengthened by the image of the 'profound abysm' (9).

But nothing matters if the friend's love GREEN (q.v. for relation to love and copulation) over his 'bad'. With the sexuality implicit in this concentration of WELL and ILL (Booth, pp. 362–3), GOOD and BAD, I suggest a bad/bed pun, as in *Oth*, IV.iii.13, 22: 'commanded me to go to bed, / And bade me', and 'I have laid those sheets you bade me on the bed'; or in *AC*, II.v.55, 58: 'The good and bad together' – 'For what good turn?' – 'For the best turn in the bed.' It is also (the impression in) his *bed* (and his BED or pubic brow) that the poet wants covered by GREEN: Venus and love.

See FACE, *LLL*; GAIT, *LLL*; ARISE, *KJ*.

Burden Testicles, penis. 'Ful loude he soong, "Com hider, love, to me!" / This Somonour bar to hym a stif burdoun' (Chaucer, 'General Prologue'). Besides its musical meaning, the burdoun was a staff, and 'a stiff burdoun between these two possibly homosexual personages [the Summoner and the Pardoner] has an unmistakably libidinous sense' (TWR, s.v. Burdoun). Cf. *bourdon*, Rabelais (F&H, s.v. Prick). Latin writers, too, spoke of 'testicles' and 'the *mentula* [penis]' as 'a "weight" or "burden"' (Adams, p. 71). Man's coital weight (P; C).

WT, IV.iv.195. See DILDO (artificial penis), for the 'delicate burthens of dildos', more DELICATE (wanton) than nature's penises.

Son 23. An erotic comparison expresses the poet's difficulty in conveying his love. He is an 'actor' (act: coitus – C) who fails the demands on and of his 'part' (PART, penis). He compares himself to 'some fierce thing [sexual organ – P; C] replete with too much rage [sexual passion – *OED*; Booth, pp. 117, 246]'. The 'abundance' of his rage (it is *too* much: TOO/TWO, testicular) has weakened his 'own heart' (OWN and HEART can both pun on the arse). In his 'love's strength' he seems to 'decay / O'er-charged with burden of mine own love's might'. Overcharge means lay an excessive burden upon and also supply to excess. The sp. in Sh's text ('ore-charg'd') played on 'ore' ('O'er whom his very madness, like some ore / Among a mineral of metals base' – *Ham*, IV.i.25). The poet is o'er-*charged* (ready for sexual assault – C; P) with ore, meaning METAL/METTLE, strength and semen, love's *might* or potency that weights his *burden* (testes, penis) – a parallel to his *thing* filled with *passion*. He asks the lover to let his books plead for him 'M*ore* than that tongue [TONGUE, penis] that m*ore* hath m*ore* expressed' (italics added).

See CRUM (4); MULE, *Cor*; ROOF, *Tim*; HOPE, Son 29 (ref. to Son 97).

But(t) Freq. connotes the butt(ock).

1H6, V.iii.47. Smitten by Margaret's 'beauty' (Body – K), Suffolk's language is sexually charged: 'For I will touch thee but with reverent hands; / I kiss these fingers for eternal peace, / And lay them gently on thy tender side.' He will *touch*, *kiss* and *lay* – three verbs for the sexual embrace (P; C); will touch her butt with REVEREND (of the arse) hands, kiss his FINGERS for PEACE/PIECE, lay them GENTLY/genitally on her tender SIDE (loin). 'Thou art allotted to be ta'en by me', he continues: taken back to Henry by him, but now taken (possessed sexually – P; C) by him.

See ANY, *Tem*; BEHIND, *CE*; BARBER, *MND*; DRUM, *AW*; MARK, *LLL* and *MV*; PECULIAR, *Oth*; MUDDY, *AW*.

Cake, wafer-cake Harlot. *Zambella*: 'a fine harlot'; pl. *zambelle*: 'wafers or fine cakes' (F). Waferers were employed as go-betweens in intrigues (*CD*). Beaumont and Fletcher, *Woman Hater*, II.i: 'Those are the damnable Bawdes; 'twas no set meeting . . . for there was no wafer-woman with her . . . .' Chaucer, 'Pardoner's Tale', 17: 'bawdes, wafereres,/Whiche been the verray develes officeres/To kindle and blowe the fir of lecherye'.

TrC, I.i.15, 24. Pandarus says if Troilus wants Cressida, if he 'will have a cake', he must tarry 'the making of the cake, the heating of the oven and the baking'. Oven: womb (see POLE, Durfey quote); in today's sl. 'a bun in the oven' implies pregnancy. May also quibble on fuck her/*focare* (set on fire) and *focaccia* (cake – F).

CE, III.i.71. The wife of Antipholus E., thinking his twin to be her 'husband', retires with him, telling his servant to 'play the porter well' (PORTER: pimp and doorkeeper, who prevents interruption of prostitute and customer), and 'let none enter' (II.ii.213). Her real husband is thus refused entry, and his servant says, 'Your cake there is warm within; you stand here in the cold:/It would make a man mad as a buck to be so bought and sold.' The cheating meant by the last phrase emphasises the illicit intimacy indoors that is indeed making Antipholus 'horn-mad' and 'cuckold-mad' (as in II.i.57).

2H4, II.iv.159. Doll: '[Pistol] lives upon mouldy stewed prunes and dried cakes' – *upon* MOULDY (see *2H4*) prunes (brothel fare; diseased bawds) and dried (DRY, syphilitic) cakes or harlots. Cf. *prunes*: scrotum (F&H, s.v. Cods).

H5, II.iii.53. Pistol warns the Hostess (see CLOSE): 'Trust none;/For oaths [OATHS/OATS] are straws, men's faiths are wafer-cakes' – easily broken. But Pistol has in mind *faith* and the *wafer*, which meant specif. the Eucharist wafer, and puns on *waver* ('waver in my faith' – *MV*, IV.i.130) and *waiver*, abandon or outlaw a woman – esp. a waferer (bawd) such as the Hostess.

***Camel**, *Ham* See BEND: fornicate, bugger.

***Captain** For 'Fr *captain*' read 'Fr *capitan*' (l. 1).

Clap(per) (1) To coit (P). Jonson, Chapman and Marston, *Eastward Hoe*, III.ii: the pregnant Gertrude asks, 'Dost remember since thou and I clapped what-d'ye-call'ts in the garret?' See Introduction, p. xviii, footnote 21.

(2) Gonorrhoea (*OED*; F&H); *clapoir*: a venereal bubo in the groin (Cot).

WT, I.ii.104. Leontes is bitter, not sweetly sentimental, when he says, 'Three crabbed months had sour'd themselves to death,/Ere I could make thee open thy white hand/And clap thyself my love; then didst thou utter/"I am yours forever."' His wife had OPENed her HAND (genitals) and clapped him: struck the bargain and infected him forever. The repetition of *crabbed* in *sour'd*, which it means (*OED*; *TSh*, II.i.230), alerts us to the sour/sore pun (*H8*, IV.ii.15, 53: 'sorely tainted' Wolsey was 'Lofty [he *soared*] and sour'; cf. K, s.v. Soar–Sore). Thus, the three crabbed months were *sour'd to death* from the *sore*: used specif. as venereal sore (*CD*, s.vv. Sore and Venereal) or chancre, a venereal ulcer (see Donne citation in RING, *AW*; and the 'ulcerous sores' in *Tim*, IV.iii.39). Hermione's hand was *white*, an indication of death ('white death' – *AW*, II.iii.77) or symptom of disease (leucorrhoea – *OED* 1572; syphilis, see LEPROSY, *Tim*). Her hoary hand foreshadowed the moral disease of adultery that Leontes now espies in her.

H8, I.iii.18. The 'new proclamation/That's clapp'd upon the court-gate' alludes to the 'reformation' of the dissolute, clapped English 'gallants' who returned from France with 'lame' legs (LAME, impotent from VD) infected by French prostitutes; and among whom reign'd 'Death! . . . Their clothes are after such a pagan [prostitute – C; P] cut [CUT/cunt, gelding] too . . . .' They must amend or return, 'pack [PACK, whore] to their old playfellows'; ''Tis time to give 'em physic, their diseases/Are grown so catching.'

JC, I.ii.261. Casca doesn't know what the others mean by Caesar's 'falling sickness' (syphilis; see Introduction, p. xii), but he saw 'tag-rag' people 'clap him and hiss him, according as he pleased and displeased them'. A second (really primary) meaning condemns the amorality of this 'rabblement', this 'common [used of prostitutes – P; C] herd' who, swayed by base emotions, destroy good men and tyrants alike, with the indiscriminateness of whores who, pleased (sexually – P) still infect you with their clap, and, displeased, do so with their HISS (venereal wheeze).

MWW, II.iii.67. Host: 'He will clapper-claw thee tightly, bully.' Caius: 'Clapper-de-claw! vat is dat?' Being both French and a doctor, Caius has two reasons for hearing clapper as *clapoir*, a venereal sore; but a *clapoir de* (of) the claw or hand – that baffles him.

Coil Male genitals, possibly alluding to the penis coiled up in repose. Perh. also punning on L *coleus* (testicle); *couille* (penis, testicle – Cot; one of the four most freq. euphs in Fr fabliaux – TWR, p. 23); cule (*W*) and cul (*OED*), buttocks.

MND, III.ii.339. Hermia berates Helena for stealing the men's love: 'You, mistress, all this coil is 'long of you.' The fuss is because of Helena, and the jest lies in her being the cause of a *long* coil. Feeling threatened, the *longer*-legged Helena will *no longer* stay.

TGV, I.ii.99. Julia: 'This babble shall not henceforth trouble me. / Here is a coil with protestation!' – and she tears Proteus's letter, which she and Lucetta had naughtily handled and spoken of as if it were his genitals: they 'took [it] up' (incepted sexually – P; C), 'let [it] fall' (detumesce – C; P) and 'lie' (in sexual intercourse – P; C); it is 'too heavy' (TOO/TWO, testes), it has a BURDEN (testes). So, of course, Julia complained that Lucetta was 'fingering them [the "papers"] to anger me' (FINGER, caress amorously)!

The letter is a babble: 'a pricke, member, bable' (Cot, s.v. *Pine*). It is a coil with *protesta*tion: quibble on *Proteus*, his *testes*, maybe his 'pricke' – playing on It *testa*, head (prepuce – P; C). When 'babble' is glossed 'bauble', the old pun on the Fool's bauble (penis – P; C) comes into play. See BED for continuance of the banter.

Tim, I.ii.236. 'What a coil's here! Serving of becks and jutting-out of bums!' In his typical style, Apemantus anatomises these servile, ingratiating lords, as they curtsy low (tight trousers revealing their coils), serving up (copular service – P; C) themselves, their becks (bows; often as 'beck and binge', partic. servile bows – *OED*) and bums (buttocks) to Timon for favours.

***Conjunction** See also use of 'conjunct' in PLACE, *KL*.

***Copatain hat** For 'ldogers' read 'lodgers' (p. 58, l. 8).

Crum(b) Male genital. *Revenu* [recovered, swollen, puffed up again] *de queue* [tail, penis]: 'Whose taile is new growne (applicable to an old cokes, or callet, growne wanton on a sudden; or to any one which after a great weaknesse hath picked up his crummes, or is become lustie againe)' (Cot).

KL, I.iv.217. Another pun linking the Fool's conundrums equating money and potency, and the idea that Lear has given away both his purses – his money bags and his scrotum (a 'bag' – P; a 'purse' – *OED*). See RAGS, ASS.

> *Fool*. . . . now thou art an O without a figure: I am better than thou art now; I am a fool, thou art nothing . . . .
>
> He that keeps nor crust nor crum,
> Weary of all, shall want some.
>
> [*Pointing to Lear*] That's a shealed peascod.

(1) Lear is an empty peascod/codpiece (appendage worn in front of the penis, or the penis itself, as in III.ii.25): no peas/PIECE (genital) in the cod (scrotum – *OED*). To have no piece of money in the purse means to be impotent (F&H, s.v. Purse).

(2) 'Thou art [ART/arse]', said three times: the Fool insists that it is not he but Lear who is the arse.

(3) Crum (or crumb) was the soft inside of the bread, as opposed to the crust. Lear keeps neither, just as, in parallel metaphors, he *clove* his *crown* in the middle and gave away both PARTS (genitals; see ASS), and 'pared [his] wit o' both sides, and left nothing i' the middle: here comes one o' the parings [Goneril]' (207). Goneril and Regan are the *pair* who have

the power and money, symbolised by testicles. Lear's CROWN (genital) was *cloven* ('innuendo of vulva' – Henke); he pared – removed the SKIN (scrotum) of – his wit (WIT/WHITE, genitals) and left nothing (genital – P; C) in the middle.

Did 'crum . . . all' resonate as *crumenal*, a purse or pouch (*OED*), or as L *crumena* (a bag; by transf. money), 'perhaps for *scrumena, akin to scrotum, a bag' (*CD*, s.v. Crumen)? Be this as it may, in each case Lear had, as the Fool says, put down his own breeches and given his daughters the 'rod' (see ASS), had given away the codpiece *and* the soft cods inside, the 'meat' of the egg, the crust *and* the crum – and the *thing* that was in the middle.

(4) Then, weary of all (L *summa*, as in *3H6*, I.iii.48), Lear shall want some/sum (*2H4*, II.i: 'For what sum?' – 'It is more than for some, my lord; it is for all . . .'). Lear had got rid of 'all cares . . . Conferring them on younger strengths, while we/Unburthen'd crawl toward death' (I.i.42): weary of ALL (penis), he gave away the BURDEN (genitals) of power and is now an 'O', a no-thing, with no crum.

Curtail/curtal Render impotent, emasculate; lit. shorten the tail.

MWW, II.i.115. Ford: 'Well, I hope it be not so.' Pistol: 'Hope is a curtal dog in some affairs:/Sir John affects thy wife.' Pistol warns Ford that Falstaff affects (sexually desires; see AFFECTION) his wife, and that in some affairs (female pudenda – P; C) HOPE (potency) can be curtailed. He means Ford will be cuckolded; but it is the 'hope' with which Mrs Ford 'entertain[s]' (sexually – P) Falstaff (II.i.68) and the 'hope' she 'give[s]' him (sexually – P; III.iii.207) that gets curtailed, when the fairies intrude on his love-making (V.V.103) and 'Pinch him . . . Pinch him . . . Pinch him' (PINCH, render impotent).

See EAR, *Cym*; SHAPE and LAME, *R3*; TRANSFORM, *CE*.

Dare Conveys sexual giving. L *dare*, give: a 'racy' euph. for *futuo*, fuck (Martial, cited by Richlin, p. 53). Sh uses GIFT and 'give' (P; C) for the sexual gift; and he links 'give' and 'dare': '*Sex*tius Pompeius/Hath given the dare to Caesar' (*AC*, I.ii.191; italics added) – is 'fucking' him politically: 'much is breeding'.

Tem, III.i.77. Miranda: '[I] dare not offer/What I desire to give'. See Introduction, p. xiv.

Ham, I.i.84. Fortinbras was 'prick'd on . . . Dared to' the combat, both phrases conveying his virile aggressiveness (see METTLE).

MM, II.ii.91. Angelo: 'The law hath not been dead, though it hath slept:/Those many had not dared to do that evil,/If the first that did . . . Had answer'd for his deed: now 'tis awake,/Takes note of what is done . . . .' Angelo's obsession with 'that evil' of fornication is revealed in his use of one of its most common euphemisms, *do* (copulate – P; C), and similar-sounding words: dead, dared, do, did, deed, done. Cf. 'derring-do' (*OED*): daring to do (Chaucer, Spenser).

See SUBJECT, *MV*; DISGRACE, *RJ*.

***Despair** Also means sterility, impotence; see HOPE, *Cym* and *TGV*.

***Dewlap**, *Tem* See THROAT: arse, penis.

Disgrace Deprive of sexual function: dis-GRACE (penis or vulva). A reversal of or departure from sexual norms.

RJ, I.i.49. Samson: 'Nay ["let them take it"] as they dare. I will bite my thumb at them; which is a disgrace to them, if they bear it.' After much bawdy boasting, including 'My naked weapon is out' (39), Samson now makes a gesture whose sexual insult is repeated in his language. Let them *take it* (sexually – P; C) as they DARE (give it in copulation); it will be a disgrace of sexual submission if they *bear it* (the female role – C; P – as in I.iv.93, II.v.78).

Ado, IV.ii.57. Hero was accused (IV.i.66, 94) of being 'a common stale' who had 'vile encounters' (love-bouts – P; C), which were imputed to be sodomitical (see NAMELESS). As the First Watch said, they had meant 'to disgrace Hero [*her O*: pudendum – P]' before the *whole* ASSEMBLY (q.v.).

WT, I.ii.188. Leontes sees himself as one of the 'cuckolds'. 'Go, play, boy, play: thy mother plays, and I/Play too, but so disgraced a part . . . .' His unfaithful wife plays (sexually – P; C); and he plays, no longer the husband's role, but a dis-graced PART (sexual organ).

TN, III.i.25. Clown: 'But indeed words are very rascals since bonds disgraced them.' Viola: 'Thy reason, man?' Now that only bonds are binding, words are disgraced, impotent RASCALS, creatures without testes. In asking the *reason*, Viola continues the jest on their disgrace as an inability to *rise* (for the 'coarse joke' in reason–raising puns, see K, p. 139).

See BOY, *LLL*; BEND, *AC*; DOUBLET, *AYL*; PEACH, *2H4*; FLATTER, Son 33; HOPE, Son 29.

Dish A woman (P; C). More specif. her vagina, like the 'flesh' or 'ordinary dishes' the bawd Madam Horseleech sells in Dekker, *The Honest Whore II*, III.iii.

AC, II.vi.134. Antony 'will to his Egyptian dish again' – in which his *will* (penis – C; P) complements her *dish*. See EGYPTIAN.

Per, IV.vi.160. Marina, in the brothel, is mockingly called 'my dish of chastity'.

See VELVET, *TSh*; MEAT, *AYL*; PECULIAR, *Oth*.

*__Door__ Vagina, anus (Henke). Semi-open door: symbol for marital sex (Keuls, p. 373).

*__Doublet__, *AYL* See DISGRACE: reversal of sexual norms.

Droop Drop from sexual depletion or impotence, as in the complaint of 'One Writeing against his Prick', whose 'drooping head . . . lay Nodding on her wanton thigh' (*Penguin Book of Restoration Verse*, p. 184).

KJ, V.i.44. Ironically, it was 'Ascension day' when the king 'yielded up' his CROWN (power, genital potency; see NOON). But the Bastard urges him, in the name of his manhood, to fight: 'But wherefore do you droop? . . . Be great in act, as you have been in thought. . . . Be stirring . . . .' Drooping is contrasted with STIRring (copulation) and greatness in *act* (euph. for coitus – P; C). This resembles Lady Macbeth's challenge to Macbeth's manhood: 'art thou afeared/To be the same in thine act . . . As thou art in desire?' (*Mac*, I.vii.39). By the king's virile example, others too shall 'Grow great . . . and put on/The dauntless spirit of resolution' – *grow* great in act: put on (coitally – P; C) the SPIRIT (erect penis) of RESOLUTION (copulation).

1H6, II.v.12. Mortimer describes the end of life as ebbing potency: 'eyes, like lamps [LAMP, penis] whose wasting oil [OIL, semen] is spent [seminally exhausted – P; C] . . pithless arms [ARMS (penises) without pith or marrow (semen – P; Hulme, p. 128)], like to a wither'd [WITHERED, barren] vine/That droops his sapless [SAP, procreative juices] branches to the ground'.

R2, II.i.292. Northumberland says 'comfort' (love's solace – P; C) for their cause is near: 'well furnish'd [FURNISHED, sexually equipped]' nobles with '*tall* ships . . . men of war' mean 'to touch [caress erotically – P; C] our northern shore [the SHORE (pudendum) of England]'. Let's join them, he says, 'Imp out our drooping *count*ry's broken wing [WING, penis] . . . And make *high* majesty look like itself' (italics added). 'Imp' means to lengthen or enlarge something; in falconry, to engraft feathers (*OED*). He and the others – the tall SHIPS (knaves), the men of WAR (fornication) – will be the added FEATHERS (penises) to bring potency to drooping England, restore the country's (a *cunt* pun – P; C; K) strength.

See PINE, *2H6*.

*__Drum__, *AW* See BUT(T): buttock.

*__Dry__, *MWW* L humour often uses old women as 'madams, and (most significantly) as ex-wetnurses' who 'lead their grown-up charges astray' (Richlin, p. 68). Cf. the Nurse in *RJ*.

For 'Isa 56:3–51' read 'Isa 56:3–5' (l. 2).

Dust Semen. Genesis 28:14: 'thy seed shall be as the dust of the earth'. Cowley, 'All-over, Love', *The Mistress*: 'Hereafter if one *Dust* of Me/Mixt with another's *substance* be,/'Twill *Leaven* that whole *Lump* with Love of Thee.'

Ado, II.i.64. Beatrice will not be 'fitted [vaginally – P; C] with a husband' until 'God make men of some other metal [METAL, semen] than earth'. She refuses to be 'overmastered with a piece of valiant dust . . . make an account of her life to a clod of wayward marl [fertiliser – *OED*; *letame*: dung or marl – F]'. 'The primary notion [of "dust"] is that which rises or is blown in a cloud' (*OED*). Beatrice will not make (coitally – C; P) an ac*count*/cunt (C) of herself to a clod/cloud of dust, to the semen of a wayward fertiliser, such as Benedick is. See DISDAIN for another metaphor in which Benedick is described as fertiliser in both senses: dung and semen.

AC, III.vi.48. Underlying Caesar's anger that his sister's entry to Rome lacked ceremony is his real fury that Antony has 'given his empire/Up to a whore' (66). His complaint, therefore, emerges in sexual language symbolic of power, terms of potency and fertility: for Octavia's 'approach' (APPROACH, a sexual entry) 'the trees by the way/Should have *borne* men . . . *dust*/Should have *ascended* to the roof [ROOF, vagina] of heaven/*Raised* by your populous troops' (italics added). 'Love' should not have been 'left unshown'.

Egypt(ian) Same as 'gipsy' (*OED* 1514). Like it, implied a whore; Jonson, 'On Gipsy': 'Gipsy, new bawd, is turned physician . . . For what she gave, a whore; a bawd, she cures' (*Complete Poems*, p. 47).

AC, IV.xii.10. When used of Cleopatra, 'Egypt' freq. bespeaks her being Antony's whore. 'This foul Egyptian hath betrayed me . . . Triple-turn'd whore . . . O this false soul [SOUL/SOLE, arse] of Egypt! this grave charm . . . Like to a right [RIGHT, L *rectum*] gipsy, hath, at fast and loose,/Beguiled me . . . .' Puns on L *Pellaeus* (Egyptian), *pellicere* (to charm) and *pellax*, *-acis* (deceitful, seductive): Cleopatra, the Egyptian *pellice* (whore or concubine of a married man – F), who *charm*ed Antony to the *grave*.

See DISH, FAN and LEPROSY, *AC*.

Ell Lechery. A penis. Marlowe, *Doctor Faustus*, vi, Lechery: 'I am one that loves an inch of raw mutton better than an ell of fried stockfish, and the first letter of my name begins with L-echery.' Lucifer: 'Away, to h*ell*, to h*ell*' (italics added). Dekker, *Westward Hoe*, II.i: 'now her Husband has given her an inch, sheele take an ell, or a yard [penis – *OED*] at least'.

CE, III.ii.112. Jests on the 'kitchen wench' (see KITCHEN) are all bawdy: the *count*ries (cunt – C; P) in her, her 'buttocks', her 'hot breath . . . caracks' (CARACK/CRACK: vulva; a flatus) and *Nether*lands (buttocks – P).

Dromio S.: '[Her name is] Nell, sir; but her name and three quarters, that's an ell and three quarters, will not measure her from hip to hip.' The arithmetic is delightful. *A Nell* or *an ell* is a yard and one quarter. It and *three quarters* (cf. NAIL, *TSh*) equal two yards. So, not even two yards or penises would be enough to measure (with the 'penis' – Henke; fit erotically – P; as again in IV.iii: see EPHESUS) Nell's large arse.

1H4, III.iii.83. Falstaff had given away the 'shirts', the 'filthy' dowlas bought for him by the Hostess (whose first name is Nell: see *H5*, II.i). Hostess: 'Now as I am a true woman, holland of eight shillings an ell.' In the context of *filthy* holland (Holland/hole-land: genital area, but specif. 'anal area' – P; K, p. 117) – and perh. a pun on TRUE/*trou* (a hole, anus) – the price seems related to lechery, the filthy 'dowlas' (used only here by Sh) connoting filthy dolls (generic for harlots – F&H), specif. *Doll* Tear*sheet*, whose filthy sheets would have been made of coarse dowlas. See GRIEF, *RJ*, for allied puns.

See CHEVERIL, *RJ*; WIT, *RJ*.

***Evil**, *MM* Cf. Dekker, *The Honest Whore II*, III.i.6: Bellafront's vulva is called 'a waste piece of ground' that her husband 'stirs' in.

***Excellent**, *TN* See TO'T/toute (arse). Cinaedi were 'effeminate dancers who cut lewd capers at banquets' (Richlin, pp. 3, 92).

Exploit Sexual intercourse; like act and deed (P; C).

TrC, III.i.90. Hearing that Troilus wants to be excused for the evening, Paris asks, 'What exploit's in hand? where sups he to-night? . . . I'll lay my life, with my disposer Cressida.' His suspicions emerge from his use of *in* HAND, SUPS (consumes coitally) and *lay*.

See REST, *CE*; VEIN, *H5*.

Extremity The arse. Lit. the end (*OED*). Similar puns were made in Latin, where '*fines*, lit. "extremities, frontiers", = "genitalia"' (Adams, p. 90); see 'extremest' in OCCASION, *MV*.

MND, III.ii.3. Oberon wonders what Titania first saw when she awoke and 'which she must dote on in extremity'. It was, of course, *Bottom*, with his ass's head.

Tim, IV.iii.301. Apemantus's metaphor is based on coitally consuming or screwing someone; and, in today's sl., eating shit, being an arse-licker. 'The middle of humanity thou never knewest, but the extremity of both ends. . . . There's a medlar for thee, eat it.' Those whom Timon had known, the rich and the poor, had prostituted themselves to him: he had, fig., known (carnally) their arses. So Apemantus offers him a medlar, also called '*an open arse*' (P, s.v. Et Cetera; *Nesple*: 'A medlar, or Open-arse' – Cot); and he is to eat it – the same invective as Apemantus used in I.ii.210: '[ladies] eat [coitally – P; C] lords; so they come by great bellies'.

AYL, IV. iii.23. Rosalind: 'Come, come, you are a fool/And tun'd into the extremity of love.' Silvius, a fool, is the ass or butt of love.

Son 51:

Till I return, of posting is no need.
O, what excuse will my poor beast then find,
When swift extremity can seem but slow?
. . .
Then can no horse with my desire keep pace . . .

Riding a horse is a freq. metaphor for copulation. Using SEEM (unite sexually), Sh here juxtaposes two phrases, two arses: the *swift* extremity and the BUT(T)ock *slow* – for the (H)ORSE/arse cannot with the rider's desire keep (p)*ace* ('ass ['s] . . . pace' – *Ham*, v.i.64).

***Face**, *LLL* See BROW: the pubic mound.

***Fashion**, *Ado* See THIEF, *Ado*; MOUTH.

***Fault** Cf. fault/fart pun (Booth, p. 190).

***Fetch** To fetch mettle: to masturbate (Grose).

Flatter(y) (1) To pimp or prostitute. L *lenocinor*: to pursue the trade of a procurer, to flatter basely, to promote. (2) To flat (*flattir* – Cot; Old Norse *flatr*) for copulation. Tourneur, *The Revenger's Tragedy*, II.ii.30: Vendice describes his abilities in solicitation: 'I durst undertake . . . With half those words to flat a puritan's wife.'

Cor. Whether Coriolanus will 'flatter them [the people] for their love' (II.ii.26), be a 'harlot' for the consulship, is a question that runs through the play (see BEGGAR).

I.i.171. He tells the citizens, 'He that will give good words to thee will flatter/Beneath abhorring [ABHORRING/whoring].' In copulation, the one who is *beneath* the other is *flat*.

III.ii.92. Volumnia, who said 'a mother should not sell him an hour from her beholding' (I.iii.10; with the hour–whore pun – K), and who knows he 'hadst rather/Follow thine enemy in a fiery gulf/Than flatter him in a bower [bedroom – *OED*]', still sends him to sell himself, 'perform a part' – as Coriolanus says, 'To the market-place!'

v.vi.23. Aufidius says he 'raised' Coriolanus, who, 'being so heighten'd . . . water'd his new plants with dews of flattery,/Seducing so my friends; and, to this end/He bow'd his nature' – 'he sold the blood and labour/Of our great action'. Coriolanus se*duce*d with DUES (testicles) and DEWS (semen – Henke) of flattery, its dues or fees (gratification of lust – P; C). He bowed his NATURE (generative organs) to this *end* and *sold* the BLOOD (semen) and LABOUR (sexual exertion) of his and Aufidius's *action* (sexual activity – P; C). The political betrayal finds expression in a sexual metaphor or, more likely, was also sexual.

Oth, IV.i.133. Cassio says that Bianca, a 'customer' [prostitute – *OED*] is persuaded he will marry her 'out of her own love and flattery, not out of my promise [PROMISE, whoring]' – out of self-seduction, not his.

MWW, III.ii.7. 'O, you are a flattering boy: now I see you'll be a courtier' – being a flatterer, it follows logically he'll become a COURTIER (pimp).

R3, IV.iv.95. The political prostitution in the court (see JUSTICE), with its 'adulterate' lords (69), is encapsulated in Margaret's taunt to Elizabeth, 'Where be the bending peers that flatter thee . . . the thronging troops that follow'd thee?' BEND and THRONG: fornicate.

Son 33:

Full many a glorious morning have I seen
Flatter the mountain-tops with sovereign eye,
Kissing with golden face the meadows green,
. . . .
The region cloud hath mask'd him from me now.
  Yet him for this my love no whit disdaineth;
  Suns of the world may stain when heaven's sun staineth.

There is verbal tension between *flat*(ter) and mountain/mounting (K) tops: both 'mount' and 'top' mean get upon for copulation (*OED*; P). Morning had flattered (caressed – Booth, pp. 186, 481) by 'kissing' the GREEN (libidinous) meadows (MEADOW, prat or buttocks; perh. the 'pubic hair and anus' of a pathic, as in Persius's first satire, 39–41, says Richlin, p. 189). Kissing is coiting (P; C) and also one ball touching another in bowls when both are in motion (*OED*; *Cym*, II.i.2). The 'sovereign eye [ball]' or 'sun', and the 'world', both being balls in motion (like the 'searching eye of heaven' and 'terrestrial ball' in *R2*, III.ii.41), could by their kissing evoke other balls (testicles – P; C) and mutual male love-making (cf. SWEET, *TGV*). But 'Anon' the sun permitted 'basest clouds to ride/With ugly rack on his celestial face'. The baseness and ugliness of this riding (copulation – P; F&H), 'this disgrace' (DISGRACE, sexual transgression), suggest a pun on clouds/clods (anything base; a gross person – *W*; *CD*), which have the same root (*OED*) and are puns in *Ado* (see DUST). Heaven's sun 'staineth' (defiles sexually – P; C).

So, too, had the poet been shone on briefly, flattered, and betrayed, when man's son was 'mask'd' (MASK, a prostitute), prostituted, *stained*; but the poet's love di*sdain*ed him not.

Fry Spawn, simmer with passion. Roe, seed, offspring. The 'Fries or testicular parts of animals' (Robert Burton, p. 663); 'products of lambs' castration are called lamb's fries' (*OED*).

TrC, v.ii.57. Thersites: 'Fry, lechery, fry.'

AW, IV.iii.250. Parolles' reviling of two officers is unified by the identity of 'fry' and 'egg', as when Macduff's son is called 'you egg! Young fry of treachery!' (*Mac*, IV.ii.84): (1) Rousillon is a 'young count . . . a dangerous and lascivious boy, who is a whale to virginity and devours up all the fry it finds'. This count/cunt (C; K, p. 75) *devours* sexually (as in *Mac*, IV.iii.74) all the virgins, *all the fry* (male and female) he finds. (2) CAPTAIN (braggart and pimp) Dumain (see BOTCHER) is another who 'will steal, sir, an egg out of a cloister: for rapes and ravishments he parallels Nessus [a famed CENTAUR, symbol of sexual bestiality]'.

Dumain will steal an egg or fry from a cloister: a monastery or friary/friery. He will STEAL and 'rape' the young friars within, ravish their fries or testes, which enclose their fry or seed. Perhaps 'cloister', which also meant an enclosure (*OED*; *Mac*, III.ii.41), is a pun on the codpiece from which Dumain steals eggs, like the 'Codpiece Monestry' in which the 'Prick' is 'Confin'd' (Anon., *Penguin Book of Restoration Verse*, p. 184). Perhaps there is a cloister/clyster pun on the lover's clyster-pipe or penis, a *clysoir galant* (F&H, s.v. Prick), with its enclosed fry. These quibbles may help solve the old crux that the Arden edn 1969 calls the 'unexplained' cloister, tentatively noting 'clyster' as a plausible, but doubtful, meaning. Perh. in castigating both men as lascivious ravishers, Parolles (see MILK for his 'friar') reveals his own sexual bent, for the eavesdropping Rousillon five times calls him a 'cat' (whore; perh. catamite), a BOTH-SIDES rogue, a LINGUIST.

H8, V.iv.36. Porter calls the crowd at the christening of the royal baby, 'a fry of fornication' – perh. a comment on the timing of the event itself, the pre-nuptial relationship of Henry and Anne (see FLEW; QUEEN).

Gawds Gods.

TrC, III.iii.176. 'One touch of nature makes the whole world kin,/That all with one consent *praise new-born gawds*,/Though they are made and moulded of things past . . . Then marvel not . . . That all the Greeks *begin to worship* Ajax' (italics added).

MND, IV.i.172. Demetrius: 'my love to Hermia . . . seems . . . an idle gawd'. He no longer dotes on an idol, no longer dotes idly (IDLE, sexually wanton); now 'all the faith' he has 'Is only Helena' – whom, in the preceding scene, after the charm enlightened him, he had recognised as his 'goddess . . . divine'.

For a similar IDLE/idol pun, see *Tim*, IV.iii.27, where Timon says, 'No, gods, I am no idle votarist', meaning he did not worship his 'gold' as an idol (like the 'gods of gold' in Exodus 32:31).

Gentle/gently Genital. Also gentile, as in *MV*, IV.i.34 (K).

MND, IV.i.4, 44. Titania: 'I . . . kiss thy fair large ears, my gentle joy'. The large EARS/arse of hardly gentle Bottom (with his ass's head) is her genital joy (sexual pleasure – P; C). 'I will wind thee in my arms. . . . So doth the woodbine the sweet honeysuckle/Gently entwist; the female ivy so/Enrings the barky fingers of the elm.' She describes a genital embrace: the WINDING, ENTWISTING and enringing of fingers, freq. metaphor for copulation (Grose, s.v. Carvel's Ring). See CHEEKS.

148. Theseus finds the lovers lying side by side. 'Begin these wood-birds but to couple now? . . . How comes this gentle concord in the world . . .?' He is surprised by the coupling (sexual union, obs. – *W*; *OED*), the genital CONcord that now *comes* to these lovers.

TA, II.iii.66. 'gentle empress,/'Tis thought you have a goodly gift in horning'. Lavinia mocks the ferocious and hardly gentle Tamora for her *genital* em-press (in coitus – P; C), her GIFT (sexual) in cuckolding.

Oth, IV.i.204.

Iago. She's the worse for all this.
Othello. O, a thousand thousand times: and then, of so gentle a condition!
Iago. Ay, too gentle.

The exchange puns on Desdemona's gentle (yielding) genital *con*dition (CON/cunt) that made Othello a 'cuckold'; and the play on WORSE/whores anticipates her being called a 'whore' seven times in the next scene.

1H4, III.i.215. The ardent, PEEVISH (q.v.) Lady Mortimer of the 'self-willed harlotry', whose 'kisses' Mortimer understands, though little else, speaks to her father in Welsh and he translates: 'She bids you on the *wanton* rushes *lay* you down/And rest your gentle head upon her lap,/And she will sing the song that pleaseth you' (italics added). His genital HEAD (penis, testes) will REST (sexually poised) upon her lap (pudendum – P; C), and she will sing (make sexual advances – P; C) what pleaseth (sexually – P; C). My 'head upon your lap' is part of a bawdy conceit in *Ham*, III.ii.121 also.

Son 20. The poet tells the 'master-mistress of my passion' he has 'A woman's face . . . A woman's gentle heart, but not acquainted/With shifting change'. He has her gentle heart and genital HEART/arse, *but* – meaning 'except' and also, in apposition to 'heart', a BUTT(ock) – not ACQUAINTed (known sexually), and *not* a QUAINT/cunt, with shifting (shift: a woman's smock, a trick – *OED*; P; 'wenches?' – Henke) change. This picture of an *almost* feminine arse is repeated in his having been 'for a woman . . . first created' until 'prick'd . . . out for women's pleasure'. Cf. the genital heart in Middleton and Rowley, *No Wit Like a Woman's*, I.ii.295: 'I'll never leave the love of an open-hearted widow for a narrow-eyed maid again', where the pun on the maid's *narrow* eye–vulva (C, p. 13) is surely being countered by the experienced woman's more *open* heart–arse.

Son 96. 'Some say thy fault is youth, some wantonness;/Some say thy grace is youth and gentle sport . . . .' Genital sport is a balance to wantonness (sexual laxity – C; P) and accords with usual sexual gloss of 'sport' in the preceding sonnet (Son 95).

See CHEEKS, *MND*; DITCH, *AC*; THIEF, Son 40 and 48; SEAT, Son 41.

Glove (1) Any sheath (L *vagina*) for the penis: vagina. Condom or merkin (female private parts or false hair for them – F&H; *W*)? Lovelace's poem to 'Her muff' – that 'outward bliss' of 'furs' covering Lucasta's 'hidden muff' ('slang for pudendum' – Broadbent, p. 255) – is paralleled in his poem to 'Elinda's glove', another 'ermine cabinet' he kisses, for, 'though the lute's [pudendum's – F&H] too high for me', he is 'allowed to fiddle with the case'. Middleton and Rowley, *The Changeling*, I.i: De Flores recognises Beatrice's revulsion that he has picked up her 'glove' or, fig., 'thrust my fingers/Into her sockets here' (FINGER: 16th-c. pun on the penis).

(2) A whore. *Guagnastra*: 'a common whore' (F), from 'one who acts as a sheath' (F&H, s.v. Barrack-Hack); *guanto*: glove, mitten (F).

AW, V.iii.278. 'This woman's an easy [EASY, sexually compliant] glove, my lord; she goes off and on at pleasure'; she's a 'common customer' (287), a whore (*OED*; P).

WT, IV.iv.193. Autolycus sells 'songs for man or woman, of all sizes; no milliner can so fit [for sexual activity – P; C] his customers with gloves'. The songs (see DILDO, PIN) are artificial penises. Are the gloves woman's equivalent, merkins? White says, 'no one who reads the whole speech attentively, and who knows what articles some milliners even to this day traffic in, can fail to see that it contains allusions to matters more within the knowledge of city debauchees than of simple rustics' (vol. III, p. 404).

R2, V.iii.17. In a metaphor rampant with sexuality, the 'young wanton' Henry, all of whose time is spent with 'loose companions', mocked Percy's suggestion that he participate in the Oxford 'triumphs':

Percy. His answer was he would unto the stews,
And from the common'st creature pluck a glove,
And wear it as a favour; and with that
He would unhorse the lustiest challenger.
Bolingbroke. As dissolute as desperate . . . .

Several kinds of gloves are found in brothels: the whore's vagina, contraceptives, merkins. The last-mentioned are alluded to in *Tim* (see ROOF; Hulme, p. 117) and in *H5* (see TRUE). What kind of glove would Henry *pluck* (take sexually, as in another brothel – *Per*, IV.vi.46; see OPINION, *AC*) and *wear* (possess sexually, as in *Cym*, I.iv.96; *TSh*, III.ii.120) as a favour (sexual part or act – P; C)? Is 'dissolute' Henry to *unhorse* the 'lustiest' challenger riding (copulating – P; C) on (H)ORSE/arse/whore's back?

See PECULIAR, *Oth*.

Greek (1) Homosexual. Greek effeminacy was a recurrent theme in Latin lit. 'Sodomy;

this vice was customary in old times with . . . the Greeks' (Robert Burton, p. 651). (2) A 'pander or harlot' (Brewer's *Reader's Handbook*, s.v. Greek).

TrC, I.ii.118. Told Helen 'loves [Troilus] better than Paris', for whom she left her husband, Cressida said, 'Then she's a merry Greek indeed [INDEED: in coitus]'.

v.v.24. 'the strawy Greeks, ripe for his edge,/Fall down before him, like the mower's swath'. Blond, pale yellow (*OED*, s.v. Straw colour) Greeks *fall down* as in sexual submission (P; C; DOWN) RIPE (sexually ready) for Hector's edge (sexual appetite – P; C). This is Sh's only use of 'strawy'. Is it used here because STRAW is generic for worthless, and men of straw (*OED*) are sham men (as in Wycherley, *The Country Wife*, IV.iii, when Horner, alleged eunuch, complains to a husband, 'since I cannot be your journeyman by night, I will not be your drudge by day, to squire your wife about and be your man of straw, or scarecrow' to frighten away virile men from his 'forbidden fruit')? In this metaphor, is Nestor, who in this same speech bade Ajax 'arm for shame' and sent Achilles the body of his lover Patroclus, rebuking the strawy (pale YELLOW: of dung and effeminacy) Greek soldiers for being cowards and male whores (*paillasse à soldats*: a whore, lit. straw mattress for soldiers – F&H, s.v. Barrack-Hack) MOWED (sexually violated) by the 'appetite' (lust – P; sexual desire – Henke) of the 'thousand Hectors in the field'? (Cf. also *paille*: 'bed of straw . . . dung hill'; *pailleux*, *-euse*: 'Strawie . . . full of flaws' – Cot.)

Luc, 1384. Lucrece describes a 'painting' in which 'from the towers of Troy there would appear/The very eyes of men though loop-holes thrust,/Gazing upon the Greeks with little lust'. The apparently expected lustful gaze is, presumably, deadened by the 'lamentable' slaughter. This lust can only be sexual (not lust for further fighting), since that is its only meaning in its 22 other uses in the poem, and, indeed, in all the plays.

See MARK, *TrC*.

***Half (faced)**, *2H4* See MARK: a butt, a prick.

***Hateful**, *H5* See MOUTH: genital or anal orifice.

***Heart** See the quote from Middleton in GENTLE, Son 20.

Hearth Like HEART, a pun on the arse. For Sh's 'th'–'t' quibbles, see K, pp. 319–22.

Cor, IV.v.27. Coriolanus asks Aufidius's servants, who are trying to shoo him 'away', and whom he winds up pushing and beating away, 'Let me but stand; I will not hurt your hearth.' Let me BUT(T)/my butt stand, my arse remain; I won't hurt yours.

85. This time he addresses Aufidius, and the pun becomes clearer by the hearth/heart combination and the addition of EXTREMITY (arse): 'Now this extremity/Hath brought me to thy hearth . . . . Then if thou hast/A heart . . . .'

v.vi.31: 'he came unto my hearth'. For the contribution of this third and last use of 'hearth' to the picture of homoeroticism, see KNIFE.

Hedge A whoring locale. *Zambracca*: a common hedge-whore, strumpet (F). *Dict. Cant. Crew*: 'As common as the hedge or highway, said of a prostitute or Strumpet' (F&H, s.v. Hedge).

2H6, IV.ii.55. Part of the denigration of Cade's mother as a whore (see PACK) is that he was 'born, under a hedge, for his father had never a house but the cage'.

WT, IV.iii.5. Autolycus, who got his money 'with die and drab' – gaming and pimping – sings of 'The white sheet bleaching on the hedge' and says, 'My traffic is sheets . . . .' Hedge (*haye* – Cot) is part of his hay/heigh cluster of puns on copulation (see LARK) pertinent to his 'traffic' (sexual commerce – P; Henke) with bawds and adulterers and their sheets put out to bleach, stained (when the 'red blood reigns') by their use. See PUGGING TOOTH.

Hind(er) Of the behind or rump. Hind(er): posterior (*OED*).

LLL, I.ii.123. The 'obscene' event, of sexual entry from the rear (see PREPOSTEROUS), involved 'the rational hind Costard' and Jaquenetta – feminine form of *Jaques*, pun on a *jakes* or privy (K; P).

See BEHIND, *CE*; AMBITION, *AW*; DESPAIR, *R2* and *R3*; DEAR; HEART, *MND*; HISS, *RJ*; SCUM, *2H6*.

Hold Clasp sexually. 'Of a female animal: To retain the seed; to conceive. Also *to h. to* (the male). 1614' (*OED*). 'On the Happy Corydon and Phyllis': 'From talk they fell to sleeping,/Holding each other's hand/And something else but what I dare not name' (Broadbent, p. 421). For similar erotic holding, see HAND(LE).

RJ, I.v.118. Nurse: 'I nursed her daughter. . . . I tell you, he that can lay hold of her/Shall have the chinks.' One meaning of 'chinks' is money, but this woman's earthy language goes from her own intimate function of *nursing* to *laying hold* of Juliet's chink (*fesso*: 'Womans privy chinke' – F; chink-stopper: prick – F&H, n.d.; see WALL, *MND*).

Ham, V.i.182. The Clown says a corpse can last longer 'if he be not rotten before he die – as we have many pocky corses now-a-days, that will scarce hold the laying in'. Many 'whoreson' *corses* can't last the laying in the grave any more than they did the *laying in* coitally, in the COURSES (embraces) where they got the pox. The effect of whoring and disease on the ability to 'hold' sexually was a prevailing concern: Wilmot, in 'Satyr', mocks those 'who were . . . too rotten to consummate the Intrigue'; and Burford (*Queen of the Bawds*, p. 61) speaks of prostitutes who used 'alum and powders' or astringent 'wine or alcohol' in order 'to ensure that the gateway to pleasure was not too slippery'.

Tim, I.ii.159. First Lady: 'My lord, you take us [coitally – C; P] even at the best.' Apemantus: ''Faith, for the worst is filthy; and would not hold taking.'

TrC, II.i.122. Patroclus: 'No more words, Thersites; peace!' Thersites: 'I will hold my peace when Achilles' brach [bitch] bids me, shall I?' For the *double entendre* in a male's holding his PIECE (penis), see PEACE, *TN* and *TGV*.

See OLD, *2H4*; BEND, *H5*.

***Hood** The '*cucullus* ("hood" for the head; the "head" in this case is the *caput*, "glans")' is a term meaning the 'Foreskin' (Adams, p. 73).

Hope Connotes potency, fruitfulness: penis, testes. Tourneur, *Wild Goose Chase*, I.ii.47: Belleur complains of frustrated erections: 'When I am sometimes in my height of hope . . . my heart harden'd,/Some scornful jest . . . chops between me/And my desire.' Often opposed to 'despair' (ME dis-pair), hope ('spero' and 'sperato' – *2H4*), *has* the PAIR (testes, a mated couple).

TGV, III.i.246. Proteus: 'Time is the nurse and *breeder*. . . . Hope is a lover's staff [STAFF, penis] . . . manage [caress – P] it against *despairing* [sterile] thoughts' (italics added).

TA, II.i.119. Aaron tells Tamora's sons to 'rape' Lavinia (see HOME): 'This way, or not at all, stand you in hope.' To stand is to have a phallic erection (P; C).

KJ, V.ii.112. Lewis feels certain of the glory his 'ample [large, full] hope was promised', the victory his virile testicles ensured (see CARD). But PROMISE (a whore) plays false with him.

1H4, V.ii.69, 97. With the usual overlap of military and sexual language, the scene prepares us for the final confrontation of the two hopeful, virile youths who feel so ambivalently about each other: Henry, of whom Vernon says, 'England did never owe so sweet [SWEET, genital] a hope/So much misconstrued in his wantonness'; and Hotspur, who 'will embrace him with a soldier's arm': 'here draw I/A sword . . . . Now, Esperance! Percy! and set on.' With his *sword drawn* (sexual organ exposed, as a sword from a scabbard – P; C), with his *Esperance* (hope – Cot), *Per*-cy will set on (charge sexually – P) and *embrace* Henry with *arms* (a brace is a *pair* of arms).

Cym, I.i.137. Cymbeline: 'O disloyal thing,/That should'st repair my youth . . . .' He sees his daughter as an *O*, a *thing* (genitals – P; C) that should re-pair him with youth's vigour, re-*pere* (father – Cot) him with (grand)children. But Imogen is 'Past hope, and in despair' – a banished husband leaves her no *hope*, only dis-pair.

R3, IV.ii.60. Wanting 'to stop all hopes whose growth may damage me', Richard hires Tyrrell to murder 'two enemies', 'those bastards in the Tower'. Puns on L *specula* (little hope; watchtower) and the *two* little princes in the Tower, soon alluded to as testes (see TENDER): that is, England's future strength, potency, the *hopes* whose growth he fears.

Son 29:

When in disgrace with fortune and men's eyes,
I all alone beweep my outcast state,
And trouble deaf heav'n with my bootless cries,
And look upon myself and curse my fate,
Wishing me like to one more rich in hope,
Featured like him, like him with friends possessed,
Desiring this man's art, and that man's scope,
With what I most enjoy contented least;
Yet in these thoughts myself almost despising,
Haply I think on thee, and then my state,
Like to the lark at break of day arising,
From sullen earth, sings hymns at heaven's gate . . .

The poet's sense of sexual limitations and anxieties is implicit in his DIS-GRACE in men's *eyes* and BOOTless cr*ies*. He feels undesirable, inadequate. He looks *upon* himself and wishes what he saw were more impressive: that his *hope* were more rich, in the sense of increased virility, as in Son 97 ('The teeming [see TEEM] Autumn big with rich increase, / Bearing the wanton burthen [BURDEN: genitals, fruit] of the prime') or Son 135 ('So thou being rich in Will add to thy Will . . . to make thy large Will more'). He *desires* this man's ART/arse, that man's SCOPE (penis). Art and scope are paralleled by 'skill [SKILL, arse] and argument' in Son 100, where the sexual sense of 'argument' is the genitals (Booth, pp. 325, 196). With what he most enjoys (possesses sexually – P; C), he is least CONTENTED (satisfied sexually).

But when haply/happily the poet thinks *on* his friend (not looks *upon* himself), then his STATE (arse; L *status*, a standing; *stare*, *statum*: to stand; cf. *RJ*, III.iii.166: 'Here stands all your state') stands (an erection – P); it is like that 'arising' (ARISE phallicly) lark (see LARK, *Cym* for the sexual possibilities of the same metaphor). Then he *sings* (takes someone on sexually – P; no more bootless cries) hymns (like 'him' and 'him' – l. 6) at the gate of heaven – in which some might hear the GATE (sexual orifice) of HEAVEN (homosexual love).

See CURTAIL; BEND, Son 143; ORACLE, *Mac* and *WT* (V.iii); SCOPE, *RJ*.

Idolatry 'Adultery' (similar in sound) and 'fornication' were biblical terms for idolatry (*OED*). Jonson, *The Alchemist*, IV.i: when Mammon starts his seduction of the whore, *Dol* Common, Face says, 'O, we shall have most fierce i*dol*atry.' Dekker, *The Honest Whore I*, II.i: Hippolito's epithets for the 'whore' are 'harlot . . . courtesan . . . idol . . . whores'. *The Honest Whore II*, I.ii: hearing his daughter, 'a strumpet', is dead, Orlando says, 'the world has lost one of his [the 'devil's'] idols, no whoremonger will at midnight beat at the doors'.

TrC, II.ii.56. Discussing the 'value' and 'worth' of the adulterous Helen, Hector says, ''tis mad idolatry / To make the service greater than the god' – the sexual, as well as the religious, service (copular – P; C).

LLL, IV.iii.75. Biron: 'This is the liver-vein, which makes flesh a deity, / A green goose a goddess: pure, pure idolatry.' It is the liver (seat of passion) VEIN (penis) that makes flesh (generic for organs of generation – F&H; a prostitute – P) a deity; a green goose (whore – P; F&H) a goddess; PURE (of harlotry) idolatry/adultery, fornication.

***Impudent** Cf. '*impudicitia* (i.e. pathic behaviour)' (Adams, p. 163).

*__Inch__, *Tem* See BEND: fornicate, bugger; also AMBITION, Tem.

*__Index__ Cf. *verga*: the index of a dial; a man's yard [penis] (F).

*__Jest__ *Iocari* (jests) sometimes meant not 'verbal jests' but 'sexual acts' (Adams, p. 161).

*__Jet__ Cf. *fringuer*: 'To jet, or . . . to frig with the taile, in leachering' (Cot).

Kitchen(ed) Arse; feminine pudendum (F&H n.d.). Kitchen-stuff: garbage, specif. refuse fat; connoted whore, arse. Middleton, *A Trick to Catch the Old One*, III.iv: Audrey is called 'a queen, and a bawd' and a 'kitchen-stuff-drab' – both 'stuff' and 'drab' being a whore (P; C). Brome, *New Academy*, II: a man married a 'Chimney piece', 'a bold piece of Kitchen-stuffe' – puns on the chimney, sooty rectum (OUT, *AYL*) of this PIECE.

CE, v.i.415. Dromio S.: 'There is a fat friend at your master's house,/That kitchen'd [entertained – *OED*] me for you today at dinner:/She now shall be my sister, not my wife.' In light of her being FAT (arse, dung) and now being not his wife but his sister, her having 'kitchen'd' him – believing him to be his twin, to whom she was '*ass*ured' (italics added) and whose 'privy marks' (genitals) she knew (see MARK, *CE*) – suggests the entertainment she provided was specif. the kind provided by a wife, or by a SISTER, 16th-c. prostitute. This parodies the sexual intimacy bestowed on his master, Antipholus S., also mistaken for his twin (see CAKE).

2H4, II.iv.361. Bardolph's 'face is Lucifer's privy kitchen, where he doth nothing but roast malt-worms'. Does all this add up only to his face being red from drinking malt, or is not his FACE/*fesse* (buttocks) also Lucifer's privy (toilet) kitchen for nothing BUT(T) roast (L *assus*) worms? The DEVIL is freq. linked to anal imagery.

Cym, v.v.177. When Iachimo and his companions had praised their 'loves' for qualities incl. the 'hook of wiving', Posthumus outdid their superlatives *and* added his wife's chastity, making them feel their 'brags/Were crack'd [and CRACKS, pudenda] of kitchen trulls [prostitutes – *OED*]'; or they had been 'unspeaking sots' and merely CRACKED (farted) BRAGS (depraved sentiments) of kitchen trulls.

See NECK, *Cor*.

Knife Penis (TWR, s.v. Knyf).

RJ, II.iv.214. Nurse: 'O, there is a nobleman in town, one Paris, that would fain lay knife aboard . . . .'

Cor, v.vi.31. Aufidius: 'he *came* unto my hearth;/Presented to my knife his throat: I *took* him;/*Made* him joint-servant with me; gave him way/In all his own *desires* . . . *served* his designments/In mine own person. . . . He waged me with his countenance, as if I had been mercenary.' And for this behaviour, Aufidius concludes, 'my sinews shall be *stretch'd* upon him' (italics added to words of copulation – P; C).

Aufidius gives voice here to the homoerotic undercurrents of his relationship with Coriolanus: he came unto the warmth of my HEARTH (q.v.), heart and arse; and (as a soldier presents arms) PRESENTED (made a sexual gift of) his THROAT (sexual parts) to my knife. I made him JOINT (in coitus; a penis) SERVANT, lover. He waged me with his *count*enance (cunt) and then COUNTENANCE/continence (withdrawal and rejection) as if I had been a mercenary (perh. It *mercenario*, prostitute – F&H, s.v. Barrack-Hack). Therefore I will STRETCH (coitally) my SINEWS (penis) *upon* him, will fuck or destroy him.

Contrast this bitter retrospective *throat* and *knife* imagery – summed up by a co-Conspirator as 'your way his tale [tale/tail: penis – P; K] pronounced' (58) – to his ecstatic *throat* and phallic *sword* metaphor at the time of the event (IV.v.113): 'Let me twine/Mine arms about that body . . . here I clip [embrace – P]/The anvil of my sword [penis – P] and do contest/As hotly . . . with thy love/As ever . . . I did/Contend [struggle amorously – C; P] against thy valour. . . . I have nightly since/Dreamt of encounters [sexual bouts – C; P] 'twixt thyself and me:/We have been down together in my sleep,/Unbuckling helms, fisting each other's throat [THROAT, arse],/And waked half dead [seminally exhausted – P; C, s.v. Die] with nothing [NOTHING, fornicating]' – in another AS/ass hot contest.

Son 95: 'The hardest knife ill-used doth lose his edge' – a 'phallic proverb' (Booth, p. 96; see KEEN, *Ham*).

***Knot**, *Tim* See MOUTH: genital or anal orifice.

Labour Copulate (TWR). Chaucer, 'Merchant's Tale': on their wedding night, old January 'laboureth he till that the day gan dawe'; and his wife kept to her chamber for four days 'As usage is of wives for the beste,/For every labour som time moot han reste.' *Besongner*: 'to worke, labour . . .; also, to doe, or leacher with' (Cot). Sh freq. ties the labour of love-making to the resulting labour of birth.

Per, I.i.66. The riddle describes an incestuous relationship: 'I sought a husband, in which labour/I found that kindness [KINDNESS, the sex-act] in a father.'

TrC, IV.iv.40. Troilus laments the end of embraces, Cressida's departure that 'forcibly prevents/Our lock'd embrasures, strangles our dear vows/Even in the birth of our own labouring breath'.

See TOMBOY, *Cym*; LEATHER; FLATTERY, *Cor*.

Lark 1. Prostitute. Dekker, *The Honest Whore II*, v.ii.80, Lodovico: 'I told him his lark [Bellafront, the whore] whom he loved was a Bridewell [jail for bawds and whores] bird.' Seems to be one of the 'playhouse poultry', Jonson's term for prostitutes (*Bartholomew Fair*, II.v.). See the 'salacious nether-meanings' in two lists that include larks: the 'Good poultry' the procuress served in Marston, *The Dutch Courtesan*; and the 'mutton [loose woman – *OED*] . . . larkes' in Jonson, 'Inviting a Friend to Supper' (C, pp. 9–10). An aphrodisiac?

H8, II.iii.94. Among the jibes of the OLD LADY (q.v.), a bawd, concerning Anne's developing intimacy with the king is 'With your theme [THEME, genitals], I could/O'ermount the lark' – with Anne's talents the sky would be the limit; she could o'ermount (O'ER/whore; mount: copulate – *OED*; P) any lark.

WT, IV.iii.9. 'The lark, that tirra-lyra chants,/With heigh! with heigh! the thrush and the jay,/Are summer songs for me and my aunts,/While we lie tumbling in the hay.' The lark is linked to the thrush, used only this once by Sh, but elsewhere called a THROSTLE (turd, male effeminate); and with the jay (a wanton – C; a *putta*: 'a whore . . . Also a Jay' – F). These birds are songsters for Autolycus, a pimp who lives by 'die and drab [whore]' (27), and for his aunts (prostitutes, procuresses – *OED*), while they lie (copulate – P; C) tumbling (copulating – P; C) in the hay. Like music to Autolycus's ears is the lucrative copulation, the *tirelire* (a lark's song and a money-box – Cot), with heigh (a cry of pleasure)! The hay/heigh quibble (see HEDGE) elicits the sexual pun on 'hay' (*foin* – Cot) and 'foin' (to fence, to copulate – P; C); and on the hay or hai, a fencing-thrust that reaches home (*RJ*, II.iv.27). See PUGGING TOOTH.

2. Larking: 'Irrumation', i.e. fellatio (F&H); cf. 'to irrumate, bag-pipe, cunnilinge' (F&H, s.v. Gamaruche). To lark: to masturbate (F&H, s.v. Frig).

Cym, II.iii.21. 'Hark, hark! the lark at heaven's gate sings,/And Phoebus 'gins arise . . . .' This lyric, however lovely, is sung by the despicable Cloten, and perh. we ought not forget how he introduces it: he desires 'to give her [Imogen] music' because 'they say it will penetrate', and he tells the musicians, 'if you can penetrate her with your fingering [intimate caresses – P; C], so; we'll try with tongue too.' This lark sings (takes on sexually – P; C) at heaven's 'gate'; and the song addressed to Imogen, whom he is trying with tongue to have 'arise:/Arise, arise' (see Introduction, p. xiv, for details), is sung at her 'door' as at HEAVEN's 'gate' – at the DOOR and GATE (her vulva; and the penis, anus of the young male actor).

See THEME, *H5*; HOPE, Son 29.

***Leek**, *H5* See MOUTH: genital or anal orifice.

***Like** Donne, 'Sapho to Philaenis': 'Likenesse begets such strange selfe-flatterie,/That touching my selfe, all seems done to thee.'

Mark (1) Vulva (P; C). (2) Penis and buttocks. Lit. the target or butt, of which the *prick* is the centre. John Minsheu, *The Guide into Tongues* (1627 edn): 'a *Marke*, white or pricke to shoote at'. Sidney, *The Countess of Pembroke's Arcadia*, Bk I, chs 14, 15: disguised as a woman, Pyrocles says, 'she hath taken some other mark of me, that I am not a woman'.

MWW, IV.i.45. In a bawdy little Latin lesson (see HANG) on the 'cases [private parts – P; C] and the . . . genders', Sir Hugh tells *Will*iam: 'pray you, mark: *genitivo*, *hujus*' (alt. sp. *huius*). Quibbles on *you mark*: a genital hujus/huge/huius/Hugh's.

LLL, IV.i.133 (italics added):

Maria. A mark marvellous well shot, for they *both did hit it*.
Boyet. A mark! *O*, *mark but* that *mark*! A mark, says my lady!
Let the *mark* have a *prick* in't, to mete at . . . .

TrC, V.vi.27. Hector: 'Stand, stand, thou Greek; thou art a goodly mark.' The GREEK (q.v.) is the prick: a GOODly (coital) mark, told to *stand* (said of an erect penis – P; C), a pun Hector made earlier (BLOOD).

CE, III.ii.146. Dromio S.: '[she] told me what privy marks I had about me'. Privy: a latrine and as in 'privy part' (*OED*). ABOUT/a butt(ock).

MV, III.ii.82: 'no vice . . . *but ass*umes/Some *mark* of *virtue* on his outward *parts*:/How many cowards . . . wear yet upon their chins/The beards of Hercules . . .' (italics added). Bassanio's speech reflects on his circle, where the VICE (genitals)/VOICE of Portia in masculine guise (see QUAINT) did assume the *mark* of VIRTUE (masculine virility), a codpiece, on his–her outward PARTS (genitals); and COWARDS (effeminates), Antonio *et al.*, did wear beards (pubic hair, usu. female – P; Henke) of Hercules (q.v.) on their CHINS (penises). See CACKLE for details.

Oth, IV.i.88. Iago: 'I will make him tell the tale anew . . . when/He hath, and is again to cope your wife:/I say, but mark his gesture'. Iago's sexual innuendoes are meant to arouse Othello's jealousy: Cassio's tale/tail (penis – C; P), his prick; cope (copulate with – P; C); and the BUT(T) with the mark or prick in the centre.

Son 116. Love 'is an ever-fixed mark'. FIX: Fr *ficher*, 17th-c. euph. for *foutre* (fuck).

See STIGMATIC, *3H6*; APPROACH, *2H4*; HALF(FACED), *2H4*.

Metal/mettle Generative seed. Mettle ('Orig. a var. of Metal' – *OED*): semen (P; F&H). To fetch mettle: masturbate (Grose).

Ham, I.i.96. Fortinbras, 'prick'd on by a most emulate pride/Dared [Hamlet] to the combat' – his pride (sexual heat – *OED*; turgid penis – P; C) DAREd, *pricked* him on. And his son is likewise 'Of unimproved mettle hot and full'.

1H4, V.iv.24.

King. I saw him hold Lord Percy at the point
With lustier maintenance than I did look for
Of such an ungrown warrior.
Prince. O, this boy
Lends mettle to us all.

Lancaster uses the metal of his sword's point (head of penis – P) lustily – mettle from his LENDS/lendes (loins) invigorates ALL (the penis) of them.

KL, I.i.71. Regan: 'I am made/Of the self-same metal that my sister is . . . she names my very deed of love . . . .' The two elder daughters woo their father with insinuations of sexual, besides filial, love, their language evoking the *seed* that *made* them (common verb of copulation – P; C), the *deed of love* (specif. sexual intercourse – P; C). Contrast Cordelia's offering 'Nothing' (see LOVE, *KL*). She loves Lear as the child he 'begot', not as a surrogate wife: 'Why have my sisters husbands, if they say/They love you all [ALL: penis, vulva]?'

Mac, I.vii.73. 'Bring forth men–children only;/For thy undaunted mettle should compose/Nothing but males.' No *thing*: genital organ (P; C).

See CORINTHIAN, *1H4*; GRACE, *H5*; DUST, *Ado*.

***Minstrel** *Menone*: a minstrel; *Menon*: a gelded goat (Cot).

Mouth (1) Vulva: it has vaginal LIPS, kisses (coits – P) and eats (coitally – P; C); the 'mouth-thankless' (1500s, F&H). Nashe, 'The Choice of Valentines': a raised smock reveals a 'prettie riping wombe' and 'mouth . . . besett with uglie bryers resembling a duskie nett of wires'. See DOOR.

(2) Anus. 'Brother round-mouth speaks': 'he has let a fart' (Grose; F&H). Catullus likens 'the mouth to excretory orifices . . . used sexually' (Richlin, pp. 150–1). The personified *culus* (anus) is sometimes described as 'eating' the penis (Adams, p. 138).

(3) Tip of penis; creamstick (F&H). Updike (p. 152) describes 'Dale's prick' with its 'pink-mauve head . . . little lip or rounded eaves, the *corona glandis*' with 'nectar' in the 'slit'. In metaphors the penis is said to 'drink' and be 'fed' (Adams, p. 30).

Per, IV.ii.108: 'a Spaniard's mouth so watered, that he went to bed to [the] very description' of the new virgin in the brothel.

TGV, III.i.330. Launce's mistress has bad breath – 'is not to be kissed fasting, in respect of her breath'; *yet* 'She hath a sweet mouth' that 'makes amends for her sour breath'. These suggest two different mouths, the SWEET (genital) one that makes amends for the other's *sour* breath.

VA, 248. The sexual enticements Venus offers – 'a park . . . Feed where thou wilt . . . on my lips . . . lower, where the pleasant fountains lie. . . . Sweet bottom-grass . . . Round rising hillocks . . .' – are amply glossed; Adonis's parallel allurements, in the next two verses, are not:

At this Adonis smiles as in disdain,
That in each cheek appears a pretty dimple:
Love made those hollows, if himself were slain,
He might be buried in a tomb so simple;
  Foreknowing well, if there he came to lie,
  Why, there Love lived and there he could not die.

These lovely caves, these round enchanting pits,
Open'd their mouths to swallow Venus' liking.

If Love were buried in that 'tomb' (often a womb to Sh), there he would find eternal life and eternal love-making: for if he *came* (sexually – P; C) to *lie* there (in sexual intercourse), why, there he would not die (experience detumescence – C; P), but remain eternally the lively lover. That tomb is in Adonis's CHEEKS (buttocks); and the hollows, the PRETTY (of the *prat* or buttocks) dimples, *love*ly caves, and *round pits* (cf. 'Brother-round-mouth' above) are the male analogue of the female PIT, OPENED (sexually readied) to *swallow* her liking (amorousness – P), a possible pun on liking/licking (TWR, s.v. Likyng).

Son 81. The immortality of the beloved is repeated variously. 'Although in me each part will be forgotten': the poet's (pro)creative power, each PART (sexual organ) *will* (the one 'will' among seven uses of 'shall', serving to connote its nounal function: penis, sexual energy – P; C) soon be forgotten, but the 'memory' of the beloved shall survive for 'eyes not yet created'.

And tongues to be your being shall rehearse
When all the breathers of this world are dead;
  You still shall live – such virtue hath my pen –
  Where breath most breathes, even in the mouths of men.

When the present breathers, i.e. inspirers (L *inspiro*: to breath into, inspire) or homosexual lovers (see HEARER for this usage) are dead, there will be new tongues reciting the verse, new TONGUES (penises) and mouths breathing, making love: they will rehearse, replay the beloved's being (nature, essence – *OED* 1530). The poet's pen (penis – P) has such VIRTUE (virility, potency) that, wherever breath most BREATHES/breeds, whenever what he calls his 'gentle [GENTLE/genital] verse' is in men's mouths, the beloved shall be re-created.

See WINE, *AYL*; STIR, *KJ*; PAINS, *2H4*; LEEK, *H5*; HATEFUL, *H5*; OTHER, *Tem*; FASHION, *Ado*; KNOT, *Tim*.

Mow Sc word for copulation (Grose). 'I am not meat for his mowing' (F&H 1597).

H5, III.iii.13. King Henry: 'And the flesh'd soldier . . . In liberty of bloody hand shall range/With conscience wide as hell, mowing like grass/Your fresh-fair virgins and your flowering infants. . . . your pure maidens fall into the hand/Of hot and forcing violation . . . look to see/The blind and bloody soldier with foul hand/Defile the locks of your shrill-shrieking daughters . . . Your naked infants spitted upon pikes . . . .' Three parallel descriptions of sexual sadism, including an image of infant-*spitting* on pikes (penises – P; C) that mirrors the vile *mowing* of the flowering (flowers being the reproductive organs; virginity – TWR, s.v. Flour) infants. In each, the HAND is the penis. For 'Spitted' as sexual penetration, perh. sodomy, see Henke; and TAPER, *TA*.

See GREEK.

Nail Penis. Fr *clou*: lit. nail, syn. for the 'prick' (F&H). 'When as you do a Lady's work . . . Drive home your nayls to the very head, and do your work profoundly' (Henke, s.v. Nail, from a 1616 song). *Witts Recreations*: 'Venus tels [her husband] Vulcan, Mars [her lover] shall shooe her steed,/For he it is that hits the naile o' the head' (F&H 1654).

TSh, IV.iii.109. To mock the Tailor's 'monstrous arrogance', Petruchio belittles his 'yard' (penis – *OED*): 'Thou yard, three-quarters, half-yard, quarter, nail!' 'Nail' as a measure is one sixteenth of a yard or $2\frac{1}{4}$ inches (*W*; *OED*).

AW, II.ii.26. The Clown boasts of the potency of his wit (see PUDDING, ANSWER) that will 'serve fit [both words mean to accommodate sexually – P; C] to all questions'. It is 'As fit . . . as the nail to his hole' – a *hole* being the vulva (P; C) or anus (K, p. 117).

KL, II.iii.16. Edgar, who aims to 'preserve myself', compares himself to beggars who seek self-preservation by assuming unto themselves items symbolic of the penis, of potency, power: they 'Strike [verb of sadistic copulation – C; P] in their numb'd and mortified bare arms/Pins [PINS, penises], wooden pricks, nails, sprigs [*Verga*: a sprig; penis – F] of rosemary;/And with this horrible object . . . Enforce' charity. Their bare ARMS may connote penises, the weapons they bear to 'enforce' (rape – C; P) charity. His speech concludes on a note of lost identity and power: 'Edgar I nothing am', possibly a pun on NOTHING/noting or pricking – the pricking of Edgar, comparable to the pricking of the beggars.

Neck Vagina, anus. Often pronounced as 'nick' and used with the same sexual connotation of a slit or groove (K, s.v. Neck–Nick). Cf. the 'view that the stretching of the "neck" of the vagina by intercourse had a reflection in a swelling of the external neck'; hence occ. use of L *collum* (neck) for vagina (Adams, pp. 108–9).

H5, III.iv.35. 'le col' or 'neck', mispronounced as 'nick' and coupled to CHIN (q.v.), is an established bawdy pun.

TN, I.v.267. Olivia *inventories* her 'beauty' (beauty–body – K), 'labelled [L *labella*, little lips] to my will [sexual organ – P; C]: as, item, two lips [LIPS, vaginal] . . . item, one neck, one chin, and so forth'. These are the same puns as made in *H5* (above) – plus Olivia's 'and so forth' or *et cetera* (pudendum – P), her 'A womans &c' (Cot, s.v. *Con*; CON/cunt). Her repeated 'item' reminds us of Speed's uses of 'item' in his similarly bawdy '*cate*log of [Launce's sweetheart's] *con*dition' (*TGV*, III.i.304; italics added). As Kipling says, 'the Colonel's Lady an' Judy O'Grady/Are sisters under their skins'; perh. 'criticism has been overkind to Olivia' (Goddard, p. 301).

Cor, II.i.225. The throng come to view Coriolanus (see PUFF) is depicted in terms as vulgar as it is: 'the kitchen malkin pins/Her richest lockram 'bout her reechy neck,/Clambering the walls to eye him'. A KITCHEN malkin (slut; 1540, pudendum or pussie – F&H) when clambering (catching hold with hands and feet – *OED*; *W*) doesn't pin something about her *neck*, but does pin up her linen to cover from view her *nick*, more likely to be reechy, i.e. to reek (stink of anal odours – K, s.v. Sacrifice–Fise). Also *reechy* is her *rich*est lockram (Sh's only use of this word), *ram*mish (of a rank scent) from its nearness to her nick.
See BEND, *AC*.

***Office** According to Adams (p. 163), 'pathics were modishly called *officiosi*', from *officium* (duty, sexual services).

***Opinion**, *Cor* Coriolanus's metaphor grew out of Menenius's on body parts, ending with '*make* you ready your *stiff* bats' (165; italics added).

Oracle Seers and prophets were not necessarily respected 'either in or out of drama' (Hogan, p. 90). Beaumont and Fletcher, *The Prophetess*, I.iii, Maximinian: 'while she [Delphia, after the famed Delphi oracle] sits farting at us,/And blowing out her Prophecies at both ends'. Diocles: 'Dost thou think/So great a reverence . . . .' Maximinian: 'Sur-reverence, [Sir-REVERENCE, excrement] you would say.' As the gods' mouthpiece, and the 'holy of holies' (*W*, *OED*, s.v. Oracle), oracles are subject to the puns on MOUTH (pubic or anal orifice) and hole/holy (vulva, anus – P; K); perh. 'oracle' was heard as *ora* (L *orare*: to speak) + *cul* (bottom, anus – *OED*). Feminine pudendum (F&H, n.d.).
WT. Doubting his wife's honesty–chastity and her infant's legitimacy, Leontes sends to the oracle (mentioned 14 times) at Delphos. The freq. parallels between the oracle's *coun*sel and his wife's cunt (coun – P; CON – K) reflect his obsession.
II.i.185. For '*con*firmation' of the lovers' 'familiarity . . . *as* gross *as* [AS/ASS] ever touch'd [in coitus – P] *con*jecture', he sends to the 'oracle' for 'spiritual *coun*sel' (italics added).
V.ii. The story is resolved: a 'child', 'issue', 'delivery', 'passion', 'pregnant' – 'the oracle is [was] fulfilled' (24, 82).
V.iii.126. Since Leontes is 'content to look on . . . content to hear' and Hermione 'embraces him' and 'hangs about his neck', saying 'the oracle/Gave hope [HOPE, potency]', we assume that one *oracle* having been ful*filled*, another will soon be CONTENT (sexually satisfied).
Mac, III.i.9. Remembering the witches' prophecy that he 'should be the root and father/Of many kings', Banquo asks, 'May they not be my oracles as well' as Macbeth's 'And set me up [sexually – P; C] in hope [HOPE, potency]?' He the root (penis – P; C) and father, and they the female counterpart. And so they are; for in IV.i, from their 'cauldron' and 'mouths' (MOUTH, vulva), they produce 'potent' apparitions, 'Banquo's issue' or 'line'.
R3, II.ii.152. Characterised as a prostitute and pimp (ORATOR, PERFECT, REPREHEND, TROTH), Buckingham is here described by Gloucester as 'My other [OTHER, arse] self, my counsel's [COUNSEL, pimp] *con*sistory,/My oracle, my prophet!' (italics added).
See ARCH, *H8*.

***Orator(y)**, *AW* For the last word, 'whore', read 'pimp'.

***Other**, *Tem* See MOUTH: genital or anal orifice; also OTHERWISE.

Otherwise (1) Unchaste: freq. opposed to 'honest' (chaste – C; P). OTHER (arse) + WISE (q.v.). (2) Intimates *other-ways* ('-wise' and '-ways' are syns) of sexual practice: 'Women who behave like men, homosexuals who behave like women . . . embody the "other"', as in the phrase 'inexperienced girl, other place' (Richlin, pp. 16–17, 69–70). Cf. Henke, s.v. Places, other.
MWW, II.i.247. 'If I find her honest . . . if she be otherwise . . . .' See ALTER for details.

WT, II.i.134. Antigonus: 'If it prove/She's otherwise, I'll keep my stables where/I lodge my wife . . . .' If the queen be unchaste, his wife, too, is a whore; and the LODGE (brothel; lodgings: copulation – Henke) of his wife will be his stables, where he KEEPS (maintains a whore) his HORSE/whores.

Oth, II.i.124. Desdemona makes excuse for her quite broad banter with Iago: 'I am not merry; but I do beguile/The thing I am, by seeming otherwise.' She isn't really MERRY (sexually wanton), just SEEMING (behaving grossly) so.

Ado, IV.i.56. Denying he has 'known' her carnally, Claudio says he loved Hero as a brother loves a sister. Hero: 'And seem'd I ever otherwise to you?' Claudio: 'Out on thee! Seeming [SEEM, copulate]!' And he likens her to 'pamper'd animals/That rage in savage sensuality'.

TN, III.iv.252. Leaving the home of Olivia, who is infatuated with this boy–girl, Cesario–Viola is warned by Toby of an '*ass*ailant' (italics added; ASSAIL sexually), the unmanly Sir Andrew.

Viola: 'You mistake [MISTAKE, in buggery], sir . . . [I am] clear from any image of offence done to any man.' He–she has not *any* image (likeness) of OFFENCE (copulation; with ref. to buttocks) *done to* (coitally – P) ANY (arse) MAN (L *homo*). Toby: 'You'll find it otherwise, I *ass*ure you . . . . on, or strip your sword stark naked; for meddle [copulate – C] you must' (286; italics added).

H5, III.ii.136. Fluellen: 'if you take the matter otherwise than is meant . . . I shall think you do not use me . . . as in discretion you ought to use me'. In conjunction with *use* and *take* (verbs of sexual intercourse – P; C) the MATTER (penis, semen), *otherwise* is one more intimation of buggery in the exchanged insults between Macmorris ('By Chrish, la! tish ill done') and Fluellen, ending with Gower's fear they will MISTAKE (q.v.) each other.

See Introduction, p. xvi, *1H4*.

***Out**, *AW* 'Bite' was 16th-c. cant for money (F&H; P2).

***Passage** In L metaphors, 'passage' (*meatus*) can refer to vagina and anus (Adams, p. 89).

***Patient** Cf. the 'homosexual *patientia*' (Adams, pp. 163, 189–90).

***Peach**, *2H4* The puns in COLOUR, DISGRACE, FACE, NOTE, PAIR and h*ast* stress Poins's arse.

Peculiar (1) Of the private parts. L *peculiaris*: of private property. Plautus, *Pseudolus*, 1182: 'My own private property' – 'Something private right about your thighs, no doubt.' '*Peculium* (lit. "private property") = "penis" tends to occur in puns' (Adams, pp. 43, 251). Rabelais, too, used *peculium* for prick (F&H). (2) Lit. strange, odd, queer; hence puns on pederastic.

MM, I.ii.91. The OFFENCE (q.v.) was 'Groping for trouts in a peculiar river'.

Oth, I.i.60. Iago: 'In following him, I follow *but* myself . . . not I for love and duty,/*But* seeming so, for my peculiar *end* . . .' (italics added). Iago follows Othello – he SEEMS so (behaves obscenely) – to serve BUT(T) his own 'peculiar end' or arse: he is one of the knaves whom, in this same speech, he calls their 'master's ass' (see ANCIENT).

III.iii.79. Desdemona impishly tells Othello he is doing not her but himself a favour: ''Tis as I should entreat you wear your gloves,/Or feed on nourishing dishes, or keep you warm,/Or sue to you to do a peculiar profit/To your own person'. Each phrase conveys a wife's sexual services: wear GLOVES (pudendum); feed (gratify sexually – P; C) on DISHES (vulvas) for the peculiar profit (sexual reward – P; C) to his own person/purse (K), his scrotum (*OED*, s.v. Purse).

TrC, II.iii.175. Ulysses says that Achilles 'But carries on the stream of his dispose/Without observance or respect of any,/In will peculiar and in self-admission'. The *stream* of his dispose sounds like a seminal flow, from his *will* (lust, penis – P; C) *peculiar*, like the seminal 'pale streams' in Son 33 (Pequigney, p. 108); and it and 'self-admission' (self-emission?) may carry overtones of masturbation, like 'self-willed' in Son 6 (Booth, p. 143) and 'self-mettle' in *H8* (see ANGER; SEAM *TrC*).

Peevish Lit. perverse; used by Sh for sexual behaviour that was considered unnatural.
AYL, III.v.110. Rosalind–Ganymede is 'but a peevish boy [BOY, catamite]'. See SISTER.
Per, IV.vi.20, 130. Marina is a 'peevish baggage' who defends her 'peevish chastity'.
1H4, III.i.198, and *RJ*, IV.ii.14. Two fathers accuse their daughters of 'A peevish self-will'd harlotry'. Glendower is scolding Lady Mortimer for 'desperate', uncontrollable harlot-like ardour (see GENTLE). Lord Capulet, who had similarly attacked Juliet in the previous act (see GRAZE, GREEN SICKNESS), may also be implying that Juliet, in obstinately refusing marriage, is gratifying herself in *self*-will (sexual desire – P; C) or masturbation (as 'self-willed' has a 'bawdy potential' for in Son 6 – Booth, p. 142).
MWW, I.iv.14. Mistress Quickly calls John Rugby 'something peevish that way', an allusion to his customary farting and loose bowels (Fr *pet*: a fart; pet: a fit of peevishness; see PRAYER) and probably to his pederasty ('associations of feces or loose bowels with anal intercourse' – Richlin, p. 169; see FART), esp. since her phrase 'that way' may connote sodomy (see ITALY and RING, *Cym*, I.iv).
Oth, II.iii.185. For the sexually perverse nature of the fighting, instigated by Iago, who perversely says he 'cannot speak/Any beginning to this peevish odds', see TURK, prototype of 'ambisexual lubricity' (C).
See MASK *JC*; THROAT, *1H6*; Introduction, p. xv, *TN*.

Pick To coit; lit. to prick. *Cym*, II.ii.41: 'pick'd the lock' (took her chastity – P). Picking-meat: a whore, esp. her vagina (Henke).
2H4, II.iv.399: 'Now comes in the sweetest morsel of the night, and we must hence, and leave it unpicked.' The SWEETest (sexually intimate) morsel (woman as a dish to be tasted – P; C) was about to *come in* (coitally – C; P) when Peto called Falstaff away from the tavern. However, the scene ends with a blubbering Doll hurried to 'come to my master'; 'run, good Doll: come. . . . Yea, will you come, Doll?'
1H4, III.iii.113. There seem also to be bawdy implications in Falstaff's assertion he had his 'pocket picked: this house is turned bawdy-house; they pick pockets', else why the insistent repetition (61, 70, 94, 176, 190)? The humour prob. lies in the picking of the money pocket and the POCKET as codpiece and scrotum. Loss of money and potency were intimately linked (F&H, s.v. Purse): see YIELD, *WT*.

Pine Penis. *Pine*: man's 'pricke, member' (Cot). L *pinus*: pine.
2H6, II.iii.45. The king took away Gloucester's 'staff' (23; STAFF, penis), politically emasculated him. Queen: '[He] bears so shrewd a maim; two [TWO, testes] pulls at once;/His lady banish'd, and a limb lopp'd off./This staff . . . let it stand . . . in Henry's hand.' Suffolk: 'Thus droops [DROOP, be impotent] this lofty pine and hangs his sprays:/Thus Eleanor's pride dies in her youngest days.' His wife's pride (sexual desire – *OED*) and craving for power are no more to be satisfied. The staff now stands (a phallic erection – P; C) back in Henry's HAND.
AC, IV.xii.23. Antony: 'O sun, thy uprise shall I see no more. . . . this pine is bark'd,/That overtopp'd them all.' No more *uprise*: Antony, ruler and lover who over-*topped* (copulated – P; C). is now stripped of potency, barked.
See TORCH, *1H6*.

***Pink** A small boat; cant for a loose woman (Halliwell).

***Plain**, *3H6* Cf. MM, II.iv.141: 'Plainly *conceive* I love you' (italics added).

Pocket Scrotum; codpiece. 'I have a poket for the nonys,/therine ben tweyne precyous stonys': a 'clear' allusion to scrotum and testes (Ross, s.v. Purse). Same as a 'poke' (*OED*; *poche*: pocket, poke – Cot), which is a pun on the codpiece in *AYL*, II.vii.20 (K).

See LEEK, *H5*; PICK, *1H4*.

Pole Penis. Durfey, 'The Jolly Trades-men', *Wit and Mirth*: a baker sings, 'I have as fine a Wrigling-Pole/As any is in all this town Sir;/But if my Oven be over-hot,/I dare not thrust it in Sir.'

2H6, I.iii.53. The Queen complains to Suffolk of amorous dissatisfaction with Henry: 'I tell thee, Pole, when . . . Thou ran'st a tilt [TILT, sexual bout] in honour of my love . . . I thought King Henry had resembled thee/In courage, courtship, and proportion [PROPORTION, penis]/But all his mind is bent to holiness . . . .' Suffolk advises her to 'be patient' (PATIENT: submissive, like the 'homosexual *patientia*' – Adams, p. 163) with Henry, BENT (in sexual perversion) to *hol*iness; for, unlike her husband, ' so will I/In England work your grace's full content'. He, *Will*iam Pole, *will* (penis – P; C) work (copulate – P; TWR, s.v. Werke) her GRACE (vulva) to its *full* CONTENT (sexual satisfaction).

IV.i.70.

Captain. . . . Strike off his head.
Suffolk. Thou darest not, for thy own.
Captain. Yes, Pole.
Suffolk. Pole!
Captain. Pool! Sir Pool! lord!
Ay, kennel, puddle, sink . . . .

The Captain – as befits their past intimate relationship (see CUP) – wants the *Pole*'s HEAD (testes, prepuce), his *poll*, cut off, wants him emasculated and calls him *pool*, puddle and sink, the last two being common terms for a whore or a vagina (Henke; SURE, *TrC*; Robert Burton, p. 779, where the whore calls herself 'a puddle . . . a sink').

See CROWN, *AC*; BEGGAR, *R3* (for the contempt implicit in 'lord').

***Poor** Pun on L *puer*, boy; specif. the BOY (see above) in a pederastic relationship.

***Preposterous**, *LLL* See HIND, *LLL*.

***Privily** For 'east' read 'ease' (p. 204, l. 8).

***Puff**, *Cor* Cf. 'Pooff', imitation of the 'noise of a fart' (Henke).

Pugging tooth Penis; a taste for sex. *Puga*: man's prick; a dildo (F). Pug: prostitute (*OED*; F&H). L *puga*: a rump.

WT, IV.iii.7. Autolycus sings of 'the doxy [loose wench] over the dale' when 'comes in the sweet o' the year' (see PICK, *2H4*, for the sexual meaning of this phrase). In this context, 'The white sheet bleaching on the hedge . . . Doth set my pugging tooth on edge' means that the *puga* or prick of Autolycus (seller of DILDOS, *puga*s) is on edge (sexual appetite, with ref. to erect penis – P; C) by what sheets and HEDGES (q.v.) bring to his mind; he has a pugging tooth for that 'sweet'. 'Clean linen' connoted sheets and the bed as a sexual playground (Henke, s.v. Linen, clean).

Reverend, reverence Descriptive for an ass/arse. See K, pp. 324–6, for examples of the loss of 'the medial *v*' in such words as 'never' (ne'er, nere, neare). By the same process, *re(v)erend* becomes a *rear-end* pun. Beaumont and Fletcher, *The Prophetess*, I.iii, Jester: 'Can you be such an Ass, my reverend Master . . . .' – 'I am not the first Ass, Sir,/Has born good office, and perform'd it reverendly.' Cf. AMBITION, Jonson citation. Sir reverence:

excrement and to shit (F&H; Grose, s.v. Reverence); see ORACLE, Beaumont and Fletcher citation.

MWW, III.i.52. Page identifies the 'most [MOST, of buttocks] reverend gentleman' as 'Master Doctor Caius, the renowned French physician'. See CAIUS (arse) and PHYSICIAN (arse) for what an ass this FRENCHman is.

R3, III.vii.61. Richard is 'with two right [RIGHT, L *rectum*] reverend fathers', and nothing can 'draw him from his holy [holy/hole: anus – K; TWR] exercise'.

See FIE, *RJ* and *TGV*; CREATURE, *CE*; BUT, *1H6*.

*__Ring__, *AW* Cf. the venereal 'disease' of Monsieur Veroles (*Per*, IV.ii.115).

*__Same__ Androgynous; cf. SCRUBBED for illustration.

Scope (1) A mark for aiming at (*OED*: 'marked scope', Spenser); hence, like MARK, a sexual target: vulva, penis, arse. (2) When scope is preceded by a word ending in 's', one hears it as (s)*cope* (copulate – P; C). Cf. It *scopare*: to sweep, sl. 'to fuck'.

Tim, V.iv.5. Alcibiades rages at the Senators of the 'lascivious town' who 'fill'd the time/With all licentious measure, making your wills/The scope of justice'. He describes their misrule in sexual terms: they filled (impregnated – *OED*), screwed away the time with their ALL (penis) licentious measure (copulation – P; F&H; Henke). He juxtaposes *their wills* (penises and sexual desires – P; C) to *justice's scope* (genitals and desires); their making (a sexual achievement – P; C) their wills the scope/thi*s cope* or rape of JUSTICE, itself a whore and an arse.

RJ, I.ii.18. Capulet does not want Juliet 'marred' by too early marriage and motherhood:

The earth hath swallow'd all my hopes but she,
She is the hopeful lady of my earth;
But woo her, gentle Paris, get her heart,
My will to her consent is but a part;
An she agree, within her scope of choice,
Lies my consent and fair according voice.

Earth, said twice, is both tomb and womb (as in II.iii.9). His HOPES (potency) gone, no other children alive, it is now *within* the scope (womb) of Juliet, the HOPEful (fruitful) lady, that his hope for perpetuation of their line lies; hence the anxiety in his extensive punning identification of their sexuality: his will (penis – P; C) is but a PART (genital) of her CONSENT; within her *scope* lies (in sexual intercourse – P; C) his CONSENT and VOICE (genitals). So, woo her GENTLE/genital Paris (L *pars*, part); get her HEART.

JC, IV.iii.108. A metaphor of mutual sexual submission conveys a political reconciliation. Cassius offers his 'dagger' to Brutus and bares his 'naked breast' so Brutus can 'take' his 'heart' – plunge the dagger (phallic symbol) into his BREAST and take (sexually – P; C) his HEART/arse. Brutus forgives: 'Be angry when you will, it shall have scope' – Cassius can be ANGRY (sexually enflamed) when he *will* (sexual ardour; penis – P; C). 'It' (penis – Henke; sexual intercourse – P), his ANGER, shall have scope in Brutus, who has 'love enough to bear with' him (the feminine role and position in intercourse – C; P).

Son 52. The poet finds the silver lining to abstinences, postponements of sexual satisfaction: they avoid 'blunting the fine point of seldom pleasure' (4), the sexual innuendo in which is clear. 'Blessed are you whose worthiness gives scope,/Being had to triumph, being lacked to hope.' Blessed is the beloved whose worthiness, being had (sexually possessed – P), gives scope, the sexual achievement, in which to triumph. But also blessed is the absent beloved, whose worthiness, being lacked, gives (s)cope, i.e. a covering – like the 'chest' and the 'wardrobe' – to HOPE (potency), provides the separation necessary to avoid satiety and 'To make some special instant special blest,/By new unfolding his imprison'd pride' (sexual ardour – *OED*; insurgent penis – P; C). Cf. 'unfold the passion of my love' (*TN*, I.iv.24).

Son 103:

Alack, what poverty my Muse brings forth,
That having such a scope to show her pride,
The argument all bare is of more worth
Than when it hath my added praise beside!
. . .
And more, much more, than in my verse can sit
Your own glass shows you when you look in it.

The conceit is one of creation, in which nature wins out over art. The Muse, despite having such a scope (womb) to *bring forth* her pride (ME, flower – *OED*) or progeny, i.e. the poet's verse, can produce nothing as worthy as the beloved's bare *argument* (genitals – Booth, pp. 332, 196) can bare (display, show)/bear (bring forth, give birth to) (K). Cf. Son 79, in which the beloved's 'lovely argument/Deserves the travail [labour in birth or copulation – Henke] of a worthier pen [penis – P]'. There is a second pun in scope/Gr *skopein* (to look at, see). It operates in the parallel between the muse's 'scope to show' its creation and what the beloved's 'glass [GLASS, genital organ] shows' – and perh. what 'appears' (6) in the poet's 'verse', which reflects and is also a glass (a verre – Chaucer), since it must be differentiated from the beloved's *own* glass.

Does the more-than-can *sit* in the poet's verse activate the idea of *ass* in the 'p*ass*' (PASS; italics added) to which his verses tend (11), and in the 'face' (FACE/*fesse*, buttocks) seen in the beloved's OWN (arse) gl*ass*? This pun on 'face' was a well-known contemporary one; cf. Ober, p. 246, on the relationship of Rochester (John Wilmot) 'with a French youth bearing the callipygeous name of Baptiste de Belle Fasse (cf. *fesse*)'.

See HOPE, Son 29; THEME, Son 105.

***Screw** Perh. 'copulate' (Henke). Cf. Jonson, *Volpone*, v.xii.88: 'my substance [large penis – Henke] shall not glue you [copulate – Henke],/Nor screw you into a family'.

Seam/seem (1) Copulate; semen. *Seme*: seed; kind, generation (F). Puns on *sew* a seam, join together (L *copulare*) and *sow* seed or semen. Dekker, *The Shoemaker's Holiday*, III.i: 'For yarking [stitching] and seaming let me alone, an I come to't', says Firk, who barely rewords the boast in IV.ii, when he scoffs at what Ralph can 'do for' a girl: 'thou might'st have sent her to me . . . I would have yarked and firked [fucked – C; P]' her.

(2) Behave obscenely. Seamy: obscene, filthy. A seam was a definite amount 'of hay or manure' (*OED*), 'seam of dung' (*CD*). Seam is grease, fig. any body exudation, such as semen or coital sweat, when seen as gross. Nashe, *Pierce Pennilesse*: 'Dame Niggardize . . . sate barrelling up the droppings of her nose . . . to sayme wool withall' (*CD*, s.v. Seam).

Oth, IV.ii.146. Emilia: 'Some such squire he was/That turn'd your wit the seamy side without,/And made you to suspect me with the Moor.' The some SUCH (sick) SQUIRE (pimp) was Iago himself; it was he who turned his seamy SIDE (loin) WIT-out, reversed reality and suspected her of seeming, sexual deception.

Ham, III.iv.92: 'Nay, but to live/In the rank sweat of an enseamed bed,/Stew'd in corruption . . . making love/Over the nasty sty, – ' Her bed is permeated by the obscene seam (specif. *hog*'s lard, 1530) of bestial love-making over the na*sty pig*-sty; and she lives *stewed* in *corruption*, like the 'corruption [that did] boil . . . Till it o'er run the stew [brothel]' (BOIL, *MM*).

I.ii.76. For Hamlet the death of his father and remarriage of his mother are one ('the funeral baked meats/Did coldly furnish forth the marriage tables').

Hamlet. Ay, madam, it is common.
Queen. If it be,
Why seems it so particular with thee?
Hamlet. Seems, madam! nay, it is; I know not 'seems'.

Distinguishing between 'common' and 'particular', the queen, unfortunately, links them with the phrase 'seems . . . so [sew/sow]'; thus all three (common: as in prostitution – C; P; PARTICULAR: a whore) achieve their bawdy potential and trigger Hamlet's anxieties about the death of his father and remarriage of his mother (the second 'madam' connoting a prostitute – *OED*). As for him, *he* knows (carnally) not 'seems'.

134. 'How weary, stale, flat and unprofitable, / Seem to me all the uses [sexual employment – *OED*; P] of this world! [So Hamlet does know "seems" – is, in fact, obsessed by it.] . . . 'tis an unweeded garden, / That grows to seed; things rank and gross in nature / Possess it merely' (see MERELY for details). Hamlet's first soliloquy (revealing the concerns he only hinted at in court) is devoted not to the death of his father but remarriage of his mother. The *uses* of the world *seem* – are fornication merely – *stale* (play on n. harlot – C). The world is a GARDEN or womb, grown to seed or *semen*. *Rank* things *possess* it (sexually – P), this womb and that of his mother, who is possessed in the 'rank sweat' (from coital exertion – P; C) of her enseamed bed (and BED, genitals).

TrC, II.iii.195. Ulysses calls Achilles 'the proud [sensually excited; "swelling" – *OED*] lord / That bastes his arrogance with his own seam' – the terminology of cooking (to baste with seam) puns on his basting his arrogance (or pride: sexual heat – *OED*; insurgent penis – P; C) with his own *seme* (seed). Ulysses repeats the metaphor (205), saying they should not 'enlard his fat already pride' (cf. Henke, s.v. Lard: increase supply of semen) or give him more power (see TITLE). To baste was to moisten meat with fat and also to beat soundly (*OED*). The picture is basically one of Achilles' self-gratification, his masturbation; in modern sl., Achilles is beating his own meat. See PECULIAR for a similar metaphor.

Son 138. 'O, love's best habit is in seeming trust' works two ways. Just as 'lie(s)' (2, 13, 14) is to be understood as both deception and sexual intercourse, so *seeming* puns on feigning and engaging in sexual intercourse. Love's best *habit* (custom or use, i.e. sexual intercourse – P) in seeming, that is in love-making, is to trust. Just as a habit or dress has seams that hold it together, so the habit of love is trust/trussed, fastened, held together by (1) seams or love-making; (2) seems or illusions, 'lies'.

Son 102: 'My love is strengthen'd, though more weak in seeming . . . .' His love is stronger *though* less frequently or ardently expressed (see below, where a less damaging 'because' implies that the limitation is by choice). It is not as when 'Our love was new, and then but in the spring / When I was wont to greet it with my lays'. It is not as when love and he were young, both 'spring' and 'lays' connoting the vigour of youthful sexual activity. Now, like Philomel, who 'stops his pipe [penis – P; TWR, s.v. Baggepipe] in growth of riper days', he too does 'sometime hold my tongue [TONGUE, penis], / Because I would not dull you with my song [singing: copulating – P; C]'. Cf. SCOPE, Son 52, for a similar metaphor. [Note: 'his' pipe, for it is the 'cock nightingale' that sings – Variorum edn.]

See OTHERWISE, *Oth* and *Ado*; PECULIAR, *Oth*; EXTREMITY, Son 51.

Seat The posteriors (*OED*). *Assis*: seated (Cot). L *sedes*: seat, anus (Adams, p. 115). Marlowe, *Tamburlaine, the Great*, I.i.97: upon swearing 'by this my royal seat', Mycetes is jeered: 'You may do well to kiss it then.'

Son 41:

Those pretty wrongs that liberty commits,
When I am sometime absent from thy heart,
Thy beauty and thy years full well befits,
For still temptation follows where thou art.
Gentle thou art and therefore to be won,
Beauteous thou art, therefore to be assailed;
And when a woman woos, what woman's son
Will sourly leave her till he have prevailed?
Ay me! but yet thou mightst my seat forbear . . . .

Those PRETTY/prat-y (of the buttocks) sexual WRONGS committed when I am absent full well befit (overtones of a full WELL: genital) thy beauty/body (K) and thy YEARS/arse (thy *y*ears sounds like thy EARS/arse). You are GENTLE/genital and beauteous and therefore to be ASSAILed sexually (L *asellus*: a little ass). Yet you might forbear my seat – yours, that belongs to me. Perh. a pun on beauteous/beauty-ass is also implied, as in *LLL*, v.ii.41: 'beaute*ous as* ink; a good conclusion [CONCLUSION: end, buttocks]' (italics added).

See ABSOLUTE, *Oth*; BANK; BARBARIAN, *H5*; ALTAR, *1H4*; AMBITION, *JC*.

***Shadow** Cf. Marston, *The Malcontent*, I.ii: 'Ganymede . . . Shadow of a woman [male homosexual – Henke] . . . smooth-chinn'd catamite'.

***Share**, *MND* The metaphor suggests heraldic double coats belonging to *man* and *wife* as *one person* (Globe edn, p. 1335).

Shrine Female pudendum. Lit. a box, case or niche for sacred images.

2H6, II.i.92. The LAME (impotent) Simpcox (see PLUM) went to St Alban's 'holy shrine' because he had been called 'A hundred times and oftener, in my sleep,/By good Saint Alban; who said, "Simpcox, come,/Come, offer at my shrine, and I will help thee."' His wife says, 'and many time and oft/Myself have heard a voice to call him so'. One strongly suspects it was she imploring the sleeping Simp*cox* to *come* to her holy/hole (K; P) shrine for his cure.

Cym, v.v.168. Iachimo and his friends praised their 'loves' for 'beauty that made *barren* the *swell'd* boast/Of him that best could speak, for feature, *laming*/The shrine of Venus' (italics added). Cf. the Temple of Venus (pudendum – F&H).

Sinew Cord of the scrotum; penis. Job 40:17: 'his strength is in his loins . . . the sinews of his stones are wrapped together'. Ovid, *Amores* (trs. Marlowe), Bk III, Elegy vii: explaining his impotence the lover says, 'It mocked me, hung down the head and sunk. . . . Why might not then my sinews be enchanted?' *Nervo*: a sinew or nerve; a 'mans yard' (F). *Nerf*: sinew; *nerf de cerf*: 'A stags pizzle' (Cot).

Tem, IV.i.260. Prospero charged Ariel to render his enemies impotent: 'shorten up their sinews' (see AGE).

JC, I.ii.108. Once a man 'With lusty sinews', Caesar is now like a 'sick [SICK, effeminate] girl'.

H5, III.i.7. With the usual mix of manliness in war and sex, Henry urges, 'Once more unto the breach . . . . Stiffen [STIFF, erect] the sinews, summon up the blood . . . bend up every spirit/To his full height.' *Up* with the BLOOD (semen); bend *up* the SPIRIT (erect penis) to *full* height.

See TAME, *TGV*; KNIFE, *Cor*.

***Smooth** According to Richlin (p. 258), 'smooth or depilated skin' typified Roman effeminates.

***Spirit** Booth notes its use for 'penis erectus' and semen (p. 442).

***Squirrel** For 'among the trees' read 'among the nut trees' (l. 3).

Staff Penis. Rabelais, Bk I, ch. xi (1653 trs.): her 'fiddle-diddle, her staff of love'.

See UNDERSTAND, *TGV*; DISPERSE, *R2*; PINE, *2H6*.

***Stir**, *KJ* See MOUTH: genital or anal orifice.

***Stoop** Suggests 'sexual submission' (Henke).

***Strange(r)** See ARCH, *MM*, for further illustration.

***Subject**, *MV* See DARE: give sexually.

Sup(per) Consume coitally; fornication. Supperless to bed: without copulation (Henke).
2H4, II.i.172, 177. Hostess: 'I hope you'll come to supper. . . . Will you have Doll Tearsheet meet you at supper?' Falstaff: 'No more words; let's have her.' He will *have* her (carnally – P; C) as the MEAT (whore's flesh) when they MEET (coitally) for supper.
Oth, IV.ii.239. Iago: '[Cassio] sups tonight with a harlotry . . . '
V.i.117. Iago: 'This is the fruit of whoring. . . . Go know of Cassio where he supp'd tonight.'
RJ, II.iv.135. Benvolio: '[The nurse] will indite him to some supper.' Mercutio: 'A bawd, a bawd, a bawd! So ho!'
See EXPLOIT, *TrC*; FRANK, *2H4*.

***Table** Cf. 'Tables' in *2H4*, II.iv.290: a pun on pimp and whore (Hulme, p. 137).

***Tame**, *TGV* See SINEW: cord of the scrotum.

Theme (Exercise on) copulation and the genitals. Booth (p. 196) gives examples of '*argument* meaning "subject" or "theme"' and shows that the 'obscene potential of argument' is male and female sex-organs.
RJ, I.iii.64: 'Marry, that "marry" is the very theme/I came to talk of.'
TrC, IV.v.30:

Menelaus. I had good argument for kissing once.
Patroclus. But that's no argument for kissing now;
For thus popp'd Paris in his hardiment,
And parted thus you and your argument.
Ulysses. O deadly gall, and theme of all our scorns!

Menelaus once had his own and Helen's GOOD argument for kissing (copulation – F&H). But then Paris popped (thrust, protruded – *W*; *CD*) in his hardiment/argument (similar in sound) and with his *hard*iment he parted Menelaus from his argument: Helen and her genitals. This is the *theme* of all their scorns (SCORN/SCORE: fornicate). As Thersites had said, 'all the argument is cuckold and a whore' (II.iii.78).
H5, III.vii.36. The Dauphin's palfrey, a gelding (see PEGASUS), has the 'neigh' (NEIGH, a horse's call to mate) of a monarch, a 'countenance' (COUNTENANCE, cunt – Henke) that enforces HOMAGE, (homo)sexual submission: 'Nay, the man hath no wit that cannot, from the rising of the lark to the lodging of the lamb, vary deserved praise on my palfrey; it is a theme as fluent as the sea: turn the sands into eloquent tongues, and my horse is argument for them all: 'tis a subject for a sovereign to reason on, and for a sovereign's sovereign to ride on . . . .'
'Theme', 'argument' and 'subject' are again equated; and, in the context of a scene dealing with sexual bestiality (ABSOLUTE, BEAST, PARTICULAR), the quick succession of the following words inevitably activates the bawdy potential of each: *Nay*/NEIGH; the MAN (L *homo*) who has no WIT (the genitals of either sex); the *rising* (see ARISE) of the LARK (a whore: fellator, masturbator) and *lodging* (copulation – Henke; LODGE: pudendum – Henke; brothel) of the *lamb* (young mutton or whore, catamite – Henke); and VARY (q.v. for the implied buggery in this speech).
And the Dauphin's palfrey is a theme; his HORSE/arse is an argument. It is a SUBJECT (a female or a pathic) on which to reason or have an erection (reason–raising: rising of the phallus – K); it is a subject for a sovereign and a sovereign's sovereign or coin (coin–quoin:

penis – K) to ride on (copulate – P; C), to ride/write on, for 'my horse is my mistress'. And his theme is a horse/arse and copulation.

Son 105:

Let not my love be called idolatry,
Nor my beloved as an idol show
. . . .
Fair, kind, and true, is all my argument,
Fair, kind, and true, varying to other words;
And in this change is my invention spent –
Three themes in one, which wondrous scope affords.
  Fair, kind, and true, have often lived alone,
  Which three, till now, never kept seat in one.

The poet's love is not IDOLATRY/adultery (mere fornication); nor his beloved an idol/IDLE (wanton, lustful) SHOW (q.v.). The argument or theme of his verse is still 'constant' (6), to 'constancy confined' (7). It is not, like the 'idle theme' of *MND*, v.i.434, a story of false loves and doting in 'idolatry/Upon' an 'inconstant man' (I.i.110).

The VARYING is not 'difference' but homosexual devotion (cf. the meaning of ALTER, the unexpressed syn. elicited by the 'idol', as on an *altar*). And it is in this 'change', this 'varying' that his invention (in + L *venire*, to come) is spent. Invention (which Booth, p. 332, notes has a 'vaguely bawdy cast' in Son 103) puns on his coming-in or copulation that is 'spent' (discharged seminally – P; C)

So THREE (penis and testes) *themes* (genitals) in *one* affords (again the idea of spending) *won*drous scope (SCOPE: (1) genitals; (2) cope: copulation). It is a wondrou*s* (*s*)cope or bargain and exchange; see BOOT for playing 'three to one'. And these THREE are now for the first time kept in one SEAT (arse) to which he is constant. (Note the three words starting with CON/cunt, and the five uses of KIND: 'Gender; sex – 1590' – *OED*.)

See LARK, *H8*.

Thief Perpetrator of illicit sexual acts. L *furtum* (theft) 'indicates illicit sexual intercourse, such as adultery' (Adams, pp. 167–8). Thievery was linked to sodomy (Richlin, pp. 120–2, 138, 151): in the *Carmina Priapea* the god Priapus rapes thieves, usu. as a punishment but occ. for their pleasure; and Catullus describes the thief 'with a hungrier ass'. Ger *Fiesel*: thief-protector of brothels (F&H, s.v. Area-Sneak). Brome, *New Academy*, II: 'That Thief has sold her into some Bawdihouse.'

MND, III.ii.283. Hermia: 'you juggler [fornicator – P; C]! . . You thief of love!'

MWW, II.i.126. Pistol warns Ford of 'The horn [of cuckoldry]. . . . Take heed . . . for thieves do foot by night . . . .' He alludes to Falstaff's intention to FOOT/Fr *foutre*, fornicate with Ford's wife, whose love-letter from him had been signed 'Thine own true knight/By day or night'.

Ado, III.iii.134. Watch: 'I know that Deformed; a' has been a vile thief this seven year; a' goes up and down [UP AND DOWN: to pimp; to sodomise] like a gentleman . . . .' The simple-minded watch none the less summed up the sexual villainy being disclosed. See DEFORMED for details.

Son 48:

Thou best of dearest, and mine only care,
Art left the prey of every vulgar thief,
Thee have I not lock'd up in any chest,
Save where thou art not, though I feel thou art,
Within the gentle closure of my breast,
From whence at pleasure thou mayst come and part,
  And even thence thou wilt be stol'n, I fear,
  For truth proves thievish for a prize so dear.

Prey of every *vulgar* thief, the beloved is not *locked up* (for sexual innuendoes, see Booth, p. 211) in ANY/Fr *âne* (ass) *chest* (can mean buttocks; see APPLAUSE), except the one that has *feel*ing: the GENTLE/genital *closure* (CLOSE, lustful embrace) of the poet's BREAST, arse (bosom: genital parts – P), from whence the beloved may, at *pleasure* (sexual – P) *come* and *part* – perh. *come 'n* (in) PART (a sexual part, the buttocks division) – and even thence be STOLEN (prostituted). For so dear a *prize* (object of love; innuendo of copulation and pudendum – Henke), even truth proves thievish. In the succession of puns on the arse – incl. three uses of 'art' (ART/arse) plus 'p*art*', as well as 'dearest' and 'dear' (DEAR/deer: hind, arse) – the arse may simply connote the object of desire, be a catch-all phrase for the buttocks *and* genitals (cf. today's 'wanting a piece of ass'), or suggest a 'thievish' approach from the rear.

Son 40. 'Take all my loves, my love, yea take them all', the poet tells the 'gentle thief', the 'lascivious grace'. The two vocatives are phrases balanced by inversion: the GENTLE/genital *thief*, the *lascivious* GRACE (genitals), is forgiven his 'robbery'.

See ARCH, *MM*; RING, *Cym*; STIR, *AYL*; GOUT, *Tim*; GOOD, *Per*; HEINOUS, *1H4*, VEIN, Son 99.

***Thigh** On male 'intercrural' sex, cf. Keuls, pp. 41, 284, 287; Dover, pp. 195, 197.

Throat As the *guttur*, windpipe, any devouring agency, 'throat' puns on the body's gutters, pipes, devouring orifices. Cf. the puns on penis, vagina and rectum in L *gurgulio* and *guttur*, windpipe and throat (Adams, pp. 33, 108, 115).

1H6, II.iv.79:

Plantagenet. . . . I scorn thee [Somerset] and thy fashion, peevish boy.
Suffolk. Turn not thy scorns this way, Plantagenet.
Plantagenet. Proud Pole, I will, and scorn both him and thee.
Suffolk. I'll turn my part thereof into thy throat.
Somerset. Away, away, good William de la Pole!

Plantagenet threatens to SCORN/SCORE (fornicate) or fuck the FASHION (penis, arse) of the PEEVISH (sexually perverse) BOY (homosexual lad), and also the proud ('Sensually excited; "swelling"' – *OED*) POLE (q.v.), penis. Will (penis – P; C) -iam of the Pole retorts that he will turn (perform sexually – P; C) his PART (penis) – of the scorn/scoring – in the other's throat, in fellatio or buggery.

Oth, III.iv.13. Clown: 'I know not where he lodges [LODGE, a brothel], and for me to . . . say he lies here or he lies there, were to lie in mine own throat.' He speaks of Cassio, who lies with and to Bianca (170–200); and were the Clown to lie in his OWN (arse) throat he would make a LIAR, a bugiard (bugger), of himself. Cf. Jonson, *Every Man in his Humour*, II.iv: 'the lie . . . is as ominous a fruit as the fico' (a gesture meaning 'Fuck you!' or 'Up your ass!' – Henke, s.v. Fico). In many plays this pun is the heart of the accusation that another lies in his throat.

III.iii.355. Othello: 'And, O you mortal engines, whose rude throats/The immortal Jove's dread clamours counterfeit,/Farewell! Othello's occupation's gone!' Immortal Jove's clamours are the roar of thunder, a sound the mortal, meaning deadly, cannon of war counterfeit. However, the ROAR (sound of farting) of THUNDER (Jove's farting), from the *rude* or anal throats of the mortal, meaning human, engine (a person used as a tool, arch.) is also a counterfeit of Jove's clamour. And Othello has said farewell to his 'occupation', to 'wars/That make ambition virtue' (350) – AMBITION, an ass's aims and activities, here mocked as farts.

See BEGGAR and KNIFE, *Cor*; CATERPILLAR, *1H4*; DEWLAP, *Tem*.

***Throne**, *TN* and *AC* See AIR: gas expelled from the anus.

*__Thunder__, *KL* For 'Goneril' read 'Regan' (l. 13).

*__Title__, *TrC* See SEAM, *TrC*; also AS/ass.

To't The bowels; their expulsion of wind. A tout(e): arse (TWR; F&H). A horn's toot–to't (K). To (go) to it sexually (P, s.v. To't).

Oth, III.i.16. The Clown relays Othello's rejection of Cassio's serenade as 'noise' (NOISE, a fart) from a 'wind-instrument' (anus: see SAKE, *Oth*): 'If you have any music that may not be heard, to't again'; otherwise 'vanish into air' – meaning the musicians' tune and AIR (breaking wind).

Cor, V.iii.124. Volumina weeps to see her son 'tearing/His country's bowels out. . . . thou shalt no sooner/March to assault thy country than to tread –/Trust to't, thou shalt not – on thy mother's womb/That brought thee to this world.' Imploring Coriolanus not to ravish Rome, she stresses their physical bond and pulls out all stops. You will, she says, no sooner march to *as*sault (ASSAIL sexually – P; Henke) your *country* (its cunt, pudendum – C; P; K) – Trust *to't*, your bowels (seat of feeling), that you won't – than *to t*read (mount sexually – P) on your mother's womb (in today's sl., be a mother-fucker). Cf. *KJ*, V.ii.152: 'bloody Neroes, ripping up the womb/Of your dear mother England'; and the 1588 commonplace: 'he that will not sticke to rippe up the wombe, and to teare out . . . the bowels of his owne mother' (Arden edn, 1965).

See FACE, *KL*; SMILE, *Cor*; EXCELLENT, *TN*; GRACE, *H5*.

*__Trot(h)__ Cf. *MM*, III.ii.52: hailed as 'Trot', Pompey the bawd replies, 'Troth, sir . . . .'

*__Tutor__ On schoolmasters as pederasts, see Richlin, p. 223.

*__Twins__ Gk pun on the testicles (Adams, p. 68; Richlin, p. 235).

Vain/vein Penis (not infreq. '*vena* = "penis"' – Adams, p. 35). Horace, 'The Women': 'When with base lust, the arrant vein must swell,/Go to a fancy house, and you'll do well' (Godolphin, p. 287).

TrC, II.iii.210. Nestor: 'O, this is well; he rubs the vein of him.' Ulysses verbally masturbates Ajax into believing he is the 'better man'. His 'vain-glory' (III.iii.260) is aroused. If glossed as 'mood', there is the awkwardness in rubbing a mood, and the play's only other 'rub' is clearly a fricative caress (CLOSE). The erotic use of 'swell' (I.ii.294) is heard again in 'is *well*'.

MM, II.ii.70. Isabella: 'I would to heaven I had your potency . . . .' Lucio: 'Ay, touch him; there's the vein.' She touches (caresses sexually – P; C) his male vein, a vain pride in 'potency'; and he *is* sexually stirred, unconsciously twice (79, 105) telling her to be *cont*ent (CONTENT, sexually satisfied) and twice to *come* tomorrow.

H5, I.ii.119. With the familiar overlapping of martial and erotic imagery, Ely urges Henry to be like his ancestors, whose 'blood and courage . . . Runs in your veins'; he is 'Ripe for exploits'. Their BLOOD (semen) runs in his veins; he is RIPE (sexually mature) for EXPLOITS (copulation). Exeter seconds the appeal with a phallic 'rouse yourself' – exhortations comically repeated in Pistol's 'my manly heart doth yearn [pun on phallic erection, as in *MWW*, III.v.41; see Hulme, pp. 125, 139]. . . . Nym, rouse thy vaunting veins: Boy, bristle thy courage up' (II.iii.2).

Luc, 427. Lucrece's body 'Unto a greater uproar tempts [Tarquin's] veins;/And they . . . Swell in their pride . . . . Anon his beating heart . . . Gives the hot charge [a sexual assault – P; C] and bids them do their liking.'

Son 99:

> The forward violet thus did I chide:
> Sweet thief . . .
>
> The purple pride

Which on thy soft cheek for complexion dwells
In my love's veins thou hast too grossly dyed.

The poet chides the *forward* violet ('In bad sense': bold, immodest – *OED*); as in *TSh*, III.i.1: the Fiddler who *grows* 'too forward'! has not this SWEET (sexually intimate) THIEF (adulterer; perh. bugger) of purple *pride* (sexual heat – *OED*; phallic swelling – P; C) also too grossly (obscenely – *OED*; P) died (in sexual consummation – P; C) in the beloved's veins? (Syntactical difficulties do not obscure the basic sense of the metaphor.)

***Wings** See the 'winged phallus' of the ancients (Keuls, p. 78; Fig. 6).

Wise Sexually experienced, with negative overtones. Fielding, *Tom Jones*, Bk 14, ch. 6: 'Miss Nancy hath had a mind to be as wise as her mother . . . [she] sat down to dinner before grace was said; and so there is a child coming for the Foundling-Hospital.'

AYL, IV.i.162. Rosalind details (see OUT) the ways a woman finds to be unfaithful: 'the wiser, the waywarder' – more experienced, more '-wise', more '-ways'.

1H4, II.iii.110. A departing Percy teases his wife: 'I know you wise, but yet no farther wise/Than Harry Percy's wife; *con*stant you are,/But yet a woman; and for secrecy,/No lady closer [CLOSE, in lechery]. . . And so far will I trust thee, *gentle* Kate.' Lady Percy: 'How! so far?' Percy: 'Not an inch [INCH, penis] further.' (italics added to words stressing the subject of his teasing: her CON/cunt; GENTLE/genital). The puns make their movements clear, the close distances each is measuring from the other.

See OTHERWISE; ENOUGH, *MND*.

***Witch** See SINEW for erectile failure attributed to witchcraft.

***Wolf**, *Tim* The 'medlar' was also known as 'an open arse' (Cot, s.v. Nesple).

Wrap(t) Womb or vulva. L *vulva*: 'wrapper, uterus' (*OED*).

See BED, *AW*; TIGER, *3H6*.

Bibliography

Primary Sources

Anon., *The Merry Devil of Edmonton*, in *Five Elizabethan Comedies*, ed. A. K. McIlwraith (London: Oxford Univ. Press, 1945).

——, *The Woman Taken in Adultery*, in *The York Cycle of Mystery Plays, A Shorter Version of the Ancient Cycle*, ed. J. S. Purvis (London: SPCK, 1951).

Aristophanes, *Comedies*, trs. with notes by William James Hickie (London: George Bell, 1910) 2 vols.

——, plays in individual vols, trs. Benjamin Bickley Rogers (London: George Bell, 1902–11).

Beaumont, Francis, and Fletcher, John, *Dramatic Works*, general ed. Fredson Bowers (Cambridge: Cambridge Univ. Press, 1966).

Boccaccio, Giovanni, *The Decameron*, trs. Richard Aldington (Garden City, NY: Doubleday, 1949).

——, *Forty-Six Lives from Boccaccio's De Claris Mulieribus*, trs. Henry Parker, Lord Morley, and ed. Herbert G. Wright (London: Oxford Univ. Press, 1970).

Broadbent, John: see *Signet Classic Poets of the 17th Century*.

Brome, Richard, *The Dramatic Works of Richard Brome* (London: John Pearson, 1873) vol. 2.

Brooke, Arthur, *Brooke's 'Romeus and Juliet' being the Original of Shakespeare's 'Romeo and Juliet'*, ed. J. J. Munro (New York: Duffield; and London: Chatto & Windus, 1908).

Burton, Richard F. (trs.), *The Book of the Thousand Nights and a Night* (Benares: Kamashastra Society, 1885).

Burton, Robert, *The Anatomy of Melancholy* (New York: Tudor Publishing, 1941).

Butler, Samuel, *Hudibras*, ed. John Wilders (Oxford: Clarendon Press, 1967).

——, *Characters*, ed. Charles W. Daves (Cleveland, Ohio: Case Western Reserve Univ. Press, 1970).

Chapman, George, *All Fools; The Gentleman Usher*, ed. Thomas Marc Parrot (Boston, Mass: D. C. Heath, 1907).

——, *The Widow's Tears*, ed. Ethel M. Smeak (Lincoln, Nebr.: Univ. of Nebraska Press, 1966).

Chaucer, Geoffrey, *Works*, 2nd edn. ed. F. N. Robinson (Boston, Mass.: Houghton Mifflin, 1957).

——, *Complete Works*, ed. W. W. Skeat (Oxford: Clarendon Press, 1894).

——, *Poetry*, ed. E. T. Donaldson (New York: Ronald Press, 1958).

Coffey, Charles, *The Devil to Pay, in A Collection of Farces*, vol. f, ed. Elizabeth Inchbald (London: Longman, Hurst, Rees, Orme and Brown, 1815).

The Complete Greek Drama, ed. W. J. Oates and E. O'Neil (New York: Random House, 1938).

Congreve, William, *Love for Love*, in *Three Restoration Comedies*, ed. Gãmini Salgãdo (Harmondsworth, Middx: Penguin, 1978).

Cotton, Charles, *Poems*, ed. John Beresford (London: Richard Cobden-Sanderson, 1923).

Cowley, Abraham, *Poems* (London: Cambridge Univ. Press, 1905).

Davenant, Sir William, *Dramatic Works* (Edinburgh: W. Paterson, 1872–4).

Day, John, *Humour out of Breath*, in *Nero & Other Plays* (London: T. Fisher Unwin, 1888).

Dekker, Thomas, *'The Guls Hornbook' and 'The Belman of London in Two Parts'* (also including *Lanthorne and Candle-light*) (London: J. M. Dent, 1921).

——, *Works*, ed. Fredson Bowers (Cambridge: Cambridge Univ. Press, 1953).

Deloney, Thomas, *Jack of Newbury*, in *Elizabethan Fiction*, ed. Robert Ashley and Edwin M. Moseley (New York: Holt, Rinehart and Winston, 1965).

Donne, John, *Complete Poetry and Selected Prose*, ed. John Hayward (London: Nonesuch Press, 1949).

Dryden, John, *Poems*, ed. James Kinsley (Oxford: Clarendon Press, 1958), 4 vols.

Durfey, Thomas, *Wit and Mirth: or Pills to Purge Melancholy*, introduction by Cyrus L. Day (New York: Folklore Library, 1959).

——, *Madam Fickle*, in *Two Comedies by Thomas Durfey: 'Madam Fickle' and 'A Fond Husband'*, ed. Jack A. Vaughan (London: Associated Univ. Presses, 1976).

Etherege, Sir George, *Dramatic Works*, ed. H. F. B. Brett-Smith (Oxford: Basil Blackwell, 1927).

——, *The Man of Mode* in *Three Restoration Comedies*, ed. Gãmini Salgãdo (Harmondsworth, Middx: Penguin, 1978).

Fielding, Henry, *Tom Jones*, ed. R. P. C. Mutter (Baltimore: Penguin, 1973).

——, *Jonathan Wild* (New York: New American Library, 1962).

——, *Joseph Andrews* (New York: Holt, Rinehart and Winston, 1948).

——, *'Joseph Andrews' and 'Shamela'* (London: Oxford Univ. Press, 1970).

Fletcher, John, and Shakespeare, William, *The Two Noble Kinsmen*, ed. G. R. Proudfoot (Lincoln, Nebr.: Univ. of Nebraska Press, 1970).

Ford, John, *Works*, ed. William Gifford and the Revd Alexander Dyce (London: Lawrence and Bullen, 1855).

Gay, John, *Poetical Works* (Boston, Mass.: Little, Brown, 1854).

Greene, Robert, *Friar Bacon and Friar Bungay*, in *Five Elizabethan Comedies*, ed. A. K. McIlwraith (London: Oxford Univ. Press, 1945).

Halliwell, J. C., *A Dictionary of Archaic and Provincial Words* (London: J. R. Smith, 1850).

Henry VIII, 'Pastime with Good Company', in *Poetry of the English Renaissance*, ed. J. W. Hebel and H. H. Hudson (New York: F. S. Crofts, 1932).

Herrick, Robert, *Poetical Works*, ed. F. W. Moorman (Oxford: Clarendon Press, 1915).

Heywood, Thomas, *Dramatic Works* (London: John Pearson, 1874).

Horace, *Odes*, trs. James Michie (Baltimore: Penguin, 1978).

Jonson, Ben, *Dramatic Works*, ed. C. H. Herford and Percy Simpson (Oxford: Clarendon Press, 1925).

——, *Volpone*, in *Eight Famous Elizabethan Plays*, introduced by Esther Cloudman Dunn (New York: Random House, 1950).

——, *The Complete Poems* (New Haven, Conn.: Yale Univ. Press, 1982).

Langland, William, *Piers the Ploughman* (Baltimore: Penguin, 1966).

Lyly, John, *Complete Works*, ed. R. Warwick Bond (Oxford: Clarendon Press, 1967).

——, *Galathea' and 'Midas'*, ed. Anne Begor Lancashire (Lincoln, Nebr.: Univ. of Nebraska Press, 1969).

Marlowe, Christopher, *The Tragedy of Doctor Faustus*, ed. Louis B. Wright and Virginia A. LaMar (New York: Simon & Schuster, 1959).

——, *Plays* (London: J. M. Dent, 1909).

Marston, John, *Works*, ed. A. H. Bullen (London: John C. Nimmo, 1887).

Massinger, Philip, *Plays and Poems*, ed. Philip Edwards and Colin Gibson (Oxford: Clarendon Press, 1976).

Middleton, Thomas, *Works*, ed. A. H. Bullen (London: John C. Nimmo, 1885).

Montaigne, Michel de, *The Essayes of Michael Lord of Montaigne*, done into English by John Florio (London: Grant Richards, 1908).

Nashe, Thomas, *The Unfortunate Traveller*, in *Elizabethan Fiction*, ed. Robert Ashley and Edwin M. Mosely (New York: Holt, Rinehart and Winston, 1965).
——, *Selected Works*, ed. Stanley Wells (London: Edward Arnold, 1964).
——, *Works*, ed. from the original texts by R. B. McKerrow, repr. from original edn and ed. F. P. Wilson (Oxford: Basil Blackwell, 1958), 5 vols.
Oates and O'Neil: see *The Complete Greek Drama*.
Oldham, John, see *Penguin Book of Restoration Verse*.
Otway, Thomas, *Venice Preserved*, ed. Malcolm Kelsall (Lincoln, Nebr.: Univ. of Nebraska Press, 1969).
Ovid, *Metamorphoses*, trs. Mary M. Innes (Baltimore: Penguin, 1980).
Peele, George, *The Old Wives' Tale*, in *The Chief Elizabethan Dramatists*, ed. William Allan Neilson (Boston, Mass.: Houghton Mifflin, 1911).
Penguin Book of Restoration Verse, ed. Harold Love (Baltimore: Penguin, 1968).
Plato, *Great Dialogues*, trs. W. H. D. Rouse (New York: New American Library, 1958).
——, *Dialogues*, trs. B. Jowett and ed. Irwin Edman (Oxford: Clarendon Press, 1928).
Plautus, with an English trs. by Paul Nixon (London: Heinemann, 1937), 5 vols.
——, in *The Complete Roman Drama*, ed. George E. Duckworth (New York: Random House, 1942), 2 vols.
——, literally trs. into English prose, ed. Henry Thomas Riley (London: Bohn, 1852), 2 vols.
Plutarch, *Lives, The Translation called Dryden's*, corrected and rev. Arthur Hugh Clough (Boston, Mass.: Little, Brown, 1909), 5 vols.
Pope, Alexander, *Epistles to Several Persons (Moral Essays)*, ed. F. W. Bateson (London: Methuen, 1951).
Rabelais, Francis, *The Lives, Heroic Deeds and Sayings of Gargantua and his Son Pantagruel*, trs. Sir Thomas Urquhart and Peter Le Motteux, 1653–94 (London: Chatto and Windus, 1928). See also Nock and Wilson edn of this trs., which includes *Pantagruelian Prognostication* (New York: Harcourt, Brace, 1931).
——, *The Portable Rabelais*, ed. Samuel Putnam (New York: Viking Press, 1946).
——, *Complete Works*, trs. Jacques LeClercq (New York: Random House, 1944).
——, *Works*, trs. Sir Thomas Urquhart and Peter Le Motteux, with the notes of Duchat, Ozell and others, introduction and revision by Alfred Wallis (London: Gibbings, 1901), 5 vols.
Scott, Sir Walter, *The Fortunes of Nigel* (New York: A. L. Burt, 1822).
Shakespeare, William, *Complete Works*, Globe edn, with complete notes of *The Temple Shakespeare* by Israel Gollancz, ed. William George Clark and William Aldis Wright (New York: Frederick A. Stokes, 1911).
——, *A New Variorum Edition of Shakespeare*, ed. Horace Howard Furness (Philadelphia: Lippincott, 1871–).
——, *The Arden Shakespeare*, general eds Harold F. Brooks and Harold Jenkins (London: Methuen, 1951–).
——, *Works: The Plays*, ed. Richard Grant White from the Folio of 1623 (Boston, Mass.: Little, Brown, 1892).
——, *Sixteen Plays*, ed. George Lyman Kittredge (Boston, Mass.: Ginn, 1964).
——, plays in individual vols, ed. William J. Rolfe (New York: Harper, 1898).
——, *Hamlet* (text plus critical essays), ed. Cyrus Hoy (New York: W. W. Norton, 1963).
——, *King Henry the Fifth,* New Hudson edn, introduction and notes by Henry Norman Hudson (Boston, Mass.: Ginn, 1881).
——, *The Merry Wives of Windsor*, Folger Library edn, ed. Louis B. Wright and Virginia A. LaMar (New York: Washington Square Press, 1964).
Shirley, James, *Dramatic Works and Poems*, ed. William Gifford and the Revd Alexander Dyce (London: J. Murray, 1833).
Sidney, Sir Philip, *The Countess of Pembroke's Arcadia*, ed. Albert Feuillerat (Cambridge: Cambridge Univ. Press, 1969).

Signet Classic Poets of the 17th Century, vol. II, ed. John Broadbent (London: New English Library, 1974).
Smollett, Tobias, *Humphrey Clinker* (London: J. M. Dent, 1968).
——, *Peregrine Pickle* (Oxford: Basil Blackwell, 1925), 4 vols.
Spenser, Edmund, Works, *A Variorum Edition*, ed. Edwin Greenlaw *et al.* (Baltimore: Johns Hopkins Univ. Press, 1932).
Sterne, Lawrence, *Tristram Shandy* (London: William Collins, 1955).
Swift, Jonathan, *Polite Conversation*, ed. Eric Partridge (New York: Oxford Univ. Press, 1963).
——, *Gulliver's Travels*, ed. Harold Williams (London: Oxford Univ. Press, 1926).
Tourneur, Cyril, *Plays and Poems*, ed. John Churton (London: Chatto and Windus, 1878).
Udall, Nicholas, *Ralph Roister Doister in Five Pre-Shakespearean Comedies*, ed. Frederick S. Boas (London: Oxford Univ. Press, 1958).
Vergil, *Aeneid*, trs. H. Rushton Fairclough (Cambridge, Mass.: Harvard Univ. Press; and London: Heinemann, 1947).
Webster, John, *The White Devil*, ed. John Russell Brown (Cambridge, Mass.: Harvard Univ. Press, 1960).
Weever, John, *Epigrammes in the Oldest Cut and Newest Fashion*, ed. R. B. McKerrow (London: Sidgwick & Jackson, 1911).
——, *Faunus and Flora*, ed. A. Davenport (Liverpool: Univ. Press of Liverpool, 1948).
——, *The Whipping of the Satyre* in *The Whipper Pamphlets*, ed. A. Davenport (Liverpool: Univ. Press of Liverpool, 1951).
Wilmot, John, 2nd Earl of Rochester, *Complete Poems*, ed. David M. Vieth (New Haven, Conn.: Yale Univ. Press, 1968).
Wycherley, William, *The Country Wife*, in *Three Restoration Comedies*, ed. Gãmini Salgãdo (Harmondsworth, Middx: Penguin, 1978).

REFERENCE WORKS

Adams, J. N., *The Latin Sexual Vocabulary* (Baltimore: Johns Hopkins Univ. Press, 1982).
Booth, Stephen, *Shakespeare's Sonnets* (New Haven, Conn.: Yale Univ. Press, 1977).
Brewer, E. Cobham, *Dictionary of Phrase and Fable*, new rev. edn (Philadelphia: Lippincott, n.d.).
——, *The Reader's Handbrook* (Philadelphia: Lippincott, 1894).
Burford, E. J., *'Orrible Synne* (London: Calder & Boyars, 1977).
——, *Queen of the Bawds* (London: Spearman, 1973).
Chute, Marchette, *Shakespeare of London* (New York: E. P. Dutton, 1949).
Colman, E. A. M., *The Dramatic Use of Bawdy in Shakespeare* (London: Longman, 1974).
Cotgrave, Randle, *A Dictionarie of the French and English Tongues* (Columbia, SC: Univ. of South Carolina Press, 1950).
Dover, K. J., *Greek Homosexuality* (New York: Random House, 1980).
Empson, William, *Seven Types of Ambiguity* (New York: New Directions, 1966).
Farmer, J. S., and Henley, W. E., *Slang and its Analogues* (New York: Arno Press, 1970).
Fiedler, Leslie, A., *The Stranger in Shakespeare* (New York: Stein & Day, 1973).
Florio, Giovanni, *A Worlde of Words, or Dictionarie in Italian and English* (Ann Arbor, Mich.: Univ. of Michigan, Univ. Microfilms, n. d.).
Giroux, Robert, *The Book Known as Q: A Consideration of Shakespeare's Sonnets* (New York: Atheneum, 1982).
Goddard, Harold C., *The Meaning of Shakespeare* (Chicago: Univ. of Chicago Press, 1963).
Godolphin, Francis R. B. (ed.), *The Latin Poets* (New York: Random House, 1949).
Grebanier, B., *The Heart of Hamlet* (New York: Crowell, 1960).
Grose, Francis, *Dictionary of the Vulgar Tongue* (Northfield, III.: Digest Books, 1971).

Harrison, G. B., *Shakespeare at Work: 1592–1603* (Ann Arbor: Mich.: Univ. of Michigan Press, 1963).
Henke, James T., *Courtesans and Cuckolds: A Glossary of Renaissance Dramatic Bawdy (Exclusive of Shakespeare)* (New York and London: Garland, 1979).
Henn, T. R., *The Living Image: Shakespearean Essays* (London: Methuen, 1972).
Hogan, James C., *A Commentary on the Complete Greek Tragedies* (Chicago and London: Univ. of Chicago Press, 1984).
Hoy: see Primary Sources, under Shakespeare, *Hamlet*.
Hulme, Hilda M., *Explorations in Shakespeare's Language* (London: Longman, 1962).
Johnson, Samuel, *Dictionary of the English Language* (New York: Arno Press, 1979).
Keach, William, *Elizabethan Erotic Narratives* (New Brunswick: NJ: Rutgers Univ. Press, 1972).
Keuls, Eva C., *Reign of the Phallus: Sexual Politics in Ancient Athens* (New York: Harper and Row, 1985).
Kökeritz, Helge, *Shakespeare's Pronunciation* (New Haven, Conn.: Yale Univ. Press, 1953).
Kott, Jan, *Shakespeare our Contemporary* (New York: Anchor Books, 1966).
Leitner, M. J., and Lanen, J. R., *Dictionary of French and English Slang* (New York: Crown Publishers, 1965).
A New Dictionary of the Terms Ancient and Modern of the Canting Crew, in its Several Tribes, of Gypsies, Beggers, Thieves, Cheats, etc. . . . (various edns, from c. 1690; repr. London: Smith, Kay, 1899).
Norton, Rictor, *The Homosexual Literary Tradition* (New York: Revisionist Press, 1974).
Ober, William B., *Boswell's Clap and Other Essays* (Carbondale: South Illinois Univ. Press, 1979).
Onions, C. T., *Shakespeare Glossary* (London: Oxford Univ. Press, 1929).
Partridge, Eric, *A Dictionary of Slang and Unconventional English* (London: Routledge & Kegan Paul, 1966).
——, *Shakespeare's Bawdy*, rev. and enlarged edn (London: Routledge & Kegan Paul, 1968).
Pequigney, Joseph, *Such is my Love: A Study of Shakespeare's Sonnets* (Chicago: Univ. of Chicago Press, 1985).
Richlin, Amy, *The Garden of Priapus: Sexuality and Aggression in Roman Humor* (New Haven, Conn.: Yale Univ. Press, 1983).
Rodgers, Bruce, *The Queen's Vernacular* (San Francisco: Straight Arrow Books, 1972).
Rosensweig, Jay B., *Calo: Gutter Spanish* (New York: E. P. Dutton, 1973).
Ross, Thomas W., *Chaucer's Bawdy* (New York: E. P. Dutton, 1972).
Rowse, A. L., *Sex and Society in Shakespeare's Age* (London: Scribner, 1974).
Saccio, Peter, *Shakespeare's English Kings* (London: Oxford Univ. Press, 1977).
Updike, John, *Roger's Version* (New York: Knopf, 1986).
West, D. J., *Homosexuality Re-examined* (London: Gerald Duckworth, 1977).
Whiting, Bartlett Jere and Helen Wescott, *Proverbs, Sentences, and Proverbial Phrases: From English Writings Mainly before 1500* (Cambridge, Mass.: Harvard Univ. Press, 1968).
Wilkinson, L. P., 'Classical Approaches: IV. Homosexuality', *Encounter*, vol. LI, no. 9 (Sept 1978) pp. 20–31.
Young, Robert, *Analytical Concordance to the Bible* (Grand Rapids, Mich.: William Eerdmans, 1979).

Index to Characters

This index is a comprehensive list of the words in the Dictionary that appertain to a particular character and play. It is made up of words that Shakespeare used for a wide variety of puns and that, seen together, may provide clues to an understanding of the play or character in ways not usually explored: for example, in *All's Well that Ends Well* the whoring, effeminacy and castration of Parolles tell us more about Bertram's weaknesses; in *As You Like It*, as the title itself may have been intended to communicate, a feeling of bisexuality pervades the whole play: in *Coriolanus*, the ambivalence in the military relationship of Marcus and Aufidius is mirrored in their sexual relationship; in the *Henry IV* plays, Falstaff and his corrupt little world with its sexual offences and its betrayals mirror the court world, in which the sexual corruption expresses the political decay and results in a diminished stature for all; in *Richard III*, a sexual deformity is symbolic of the court's; in *The Merchant of Venice*, there is no one – neither Antonio and the other slave-owners, nor even the women – who through some deception is not buying his pound of flesh.

Each word is listed under the character(s) it sheds light on: the speaker, the one addressed or the one spoken about. The reader may find that a sophisticated pun becomes clearer when read together with a simpler one that conveys a similar meaning. Thus, in *King Lear*, the emasculation of Lear, implied in CARD, becomes more of a certainty when CARD is studied in the context of a list that also includes RAGS, SCANT and TRAIN. I hope that, through these clusters and those listed under the individual words, the reader will derive his own insights not touched on in the Dictionary.

The new puns discussed in the Supplement are italicised.

Hotspur (Percy)	Creature, *Glove*
King Richard	Age, Camel, Caterpillar, Crooked, Finger, Heinous, Order, Pernicious, Puny, Rose
Mowbray	Tame
Prince Henry	Creature, *Glove*
Queen	Despair, Sister, Soul
Worcester	Disperse
York	Groan, Joint, Sister, Tongue, Vex

King Richard III

Anne	Angel, Hedgehog, Key, Unnatural
Buckingham	Disperse, *Oracle*, Orator, Part, Perfect, Reprehend, Troth
Clarence	Frank, Shore
Edward	Beast, Caper, Just, Loll, Servant, Shore
Elizabeth	All, Despair, Ear, *Flattery*, Justice, Tender, Witch
Grey	Knot
Hastings	Open, Tender
King Richard	All, Angel, Beggar, Bob, Caper, Deformed, Direction, Disperse, Dog, Ear, Frank, Hedgehog, *Hope*, Knock, Lane, Loll, *Oracle*, Part, Paul's, Perfect, Rags, *Reverend*, Shape, Swine, Tender, Unnatural, White-Friars, Witch, Worm
Margaret	*Flattery*, Justice, Rags, Witch, Worm
Norfolk	Direction, Knock
Ratcliff	Knot, Throng
Richmond	Bob, Plenty, Swine, Wings

Love's Labour's Lost

Armado	Barbarous, Dainty, Feather, Foot, Graze, Green, Heart, Homo, Inward, Melancholy, Ministrel, Paint, Porter, Preposterous, Purgation, Subdue, Title, White and red
Biron	Boy, Breast, Copper, Cupid, Dance, Eyes, Face, Field, Gait, German, Hose, *Idolatry*, Intent, Love, Pitch, Progress, Russian, Season, Sick, Skill, Taffeta, Terms, Traitor
Boyet	Bowler, *Mark*, Peace, Sheep
Costard	Damsel, Graze, *Hinder*, Matter, Pin, Preposterous, Purgation, Threshold, True
Dumain and Longaville	Boy, Breast, Cheek, Eyes, Paint, Russian, Traitor, Velvet, Ward
Holofernes	Barbarous, Elder, Hang, Ignorant, Traitor, Tutor
Jaquenetta	Beggar, Damsel, Graze, *Hinder*, Matter, Preposterous, Title, True
King	Dice, Field, Inward, Mind, Minstrelsy, Russian, Troth, Yield
Moth	Green, Heart, Love, Porter, Pretty, Three, White and red
Nathaniel	Part, Tutor
Princess	Feather, Intent, Mind, Peace
Rosaline	Dance, Eyes, Face, German, Love, Pitch, Rest, Season, Skill

Macbeth

Banquo	Delicate, Glass, Malice, *Oracle*, Sceptre

The Merry Wives of Windsor

A Midsummer Night's Dream

Much Ado about Nothing